# A Contemporary Introduction to Sociology

D1531038

# A Contemporary Introduction to Sociology

**Paradigm Publishers**

Boulder • London

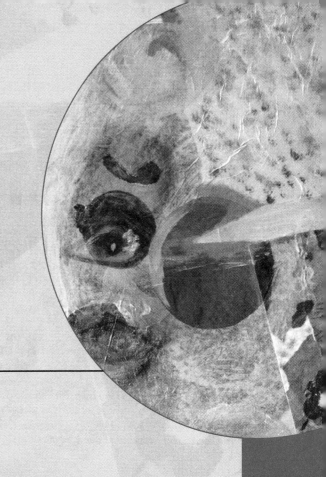

# Culture and Society in Transition

## Jeffrey C. Alexander
## Kenneth Thompson

WITH THE ASSISTANCE OF

Lisa McCormick

Tanya Goodman

Taly Noam

Jesse Einhorn

Inge Brooke Schmidt

Jason Mast

In Margaret Thompson's *Globes*, on the cover and interior of this book, geometric forms of ill-defined and fragmented spheres with ambiguous surfaces are suggestive of themes of globalization and social fragmentation. They also visually resonate with the title of Jeffrey Alexander's major work, *The Civic Sphere*. The use of painterly, abstract techniques, layering, and spatial confusion all encourage the viewer to reflect on ideas of social/visual reality, spectatorship, and representation.

Photo credits for chapter openers: page 2: Reuters/Corbis; page 28: Bloomimage/Corbis; page 62: Photograph © Jonathan Hyman 2001 (Muralist: Rocco Manno); page 90: Roger Ressmeyer/Corbis; page 120: Sean Justice/Corbis; page 166: Henry Diltz/Corbis; page 204: AP Photo/Steven Liow; page 238: Shaul Schwarz/Corbis; page 268: istockphoto; page 298: John Nakata/Corbis; page 330: Clay McLachlan/Reuters/Corbis; page 364: Sven Hagolani/zefa/Corbis; page 394: istockphoto; page 426: istockphoto; page 456: Alaa Badarneh/epa/Corbis; page 484: Steve Raymer/Corbis; page 510: istockphoto; page 554: AP Photo/Pat Roque

Published in the United States by Paradigm Publishers,
3360 Mitchell Lane Suite E, Boulder, CO 80301 USA.

Paradigm Publishers is the trade name of Birkenkamp & Company, LLC,
Dean Birkenkamp, President and Publisher.

Library of Congress Cataloging-in-Publication Data is available.
ISBN 978-1-59451-270-4

Printed and bound in the United States of America on acid-free paper
that meets the standards of the American National Standard for
Permanence of Paper for Printed Library Materials.

DESIGNED AND TYPESET BY JANE RAESE
Figures and tables rendered by Sagecraft, Inc.

08 09 10 11 12 / 5 4 3 2 1

# contents in brief

# contents

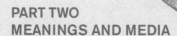

viii CONTENTS

# boxes, tables, and figures

## BOXES

### media moments

### theory

# preface

We decided to write this new introduction to sociology because we wanted to provide a fresh and contemporary approach. We wanted to make the culture of society a central focus, to put changes such as those in sexuality and gender up front, and to relate sociological explanations to the stories that the media spin everyday in every technological way.

This is a new kind of textbook, one that takes its historical moorings from the changes you are experiencing *now*. We take the "contemporary" in our title seriously. Other introductory textbooks place their description of present-day society in a familiar but by now old-fashioned historical framework—the transition from traditional to modern societies. We don't think this contrast is useful anymore. It fails to highlight what is really interesting and important, and also sometimes dangerous, about contemporary trends in social life.

To highlight trends in *contemporary* society, we make a contrast between modern and postmodern aspects of social life. It has been centuries since Western peoples lived in a traditional social order. What is most significant today is the contrast between the way we live today and the previous period of post-traditional life. It is our strong conviction that the first period of modernity, which stretched from the Renaissance to the middle of the twentieth century, differed in basic respects from contemporary life. Indeed, it differed in so many respects that it is useful to think of it as a different historical time. Emotionally, culturally, and institutionally the time in which we live now is not the same. For example, in many societies, though difficult and often dangerously hard labor remains, mental work is becoming vastly more important than physical labor. This development makes education central to mobility and productivity and puts advanced research and education at the forefront of the institutional order of society.

New forms of media have penetrated every nook and cranny of contemporary societies, allowing new forms of freedom and yet also new forms of control. Gender has been revolutionized, and the economic and cultural citizenship of women is transforming love, marriage, family, and reproduction in ways that would have been incomprehensible and unacceptable in earlier modern times. Social integration is also dramatically changing. The earlier modern ideal was homogeneity and assimilation. Today, everybody is talking about "difference." The goal is diversity, and the buzz is about multicultural society.

These are examples of the kinds of changes we trace in every chapter of our book. Every topic is treated inside a framework that highlights historical change. These developments have not happened all at once; postmodernity is not a revolution in that sense. They have occurred gradually inside of modern society, at different tempos throughout the course of the twentieth century. Only toward the end of that century did these discrete changes coalesce to create what many social scientists have begun to consider a new social form.

In the chapters that follow, we will document these changes and put them into a perspective that highlights how different contemporary society is when compared with earlier times. Do you agree with us? Well, after studying this book, that is something you will certainly be in a position to decide!

## Theme and Organization of the Book

This new textbook is about an extraordinary social transformation—the combustible leap from modern to postmodern life. As mentioned, for many years, introductory sociology texts have focused on the important transition from traditional to modern societies. We cover that transition and show how the modern has been overtaken by the postmodern. We consider this phenomenon the most contemporary and most exciting aspect of our societies as they are emerging today—as well as the most disturbing. Students implicitly know this, but they need a framework in which to understand it. The transition from the modern to the postmodern world is the central framework for our text.

Even though our theme is new, the book is organized in such a way as to fit in with conventional introductory courses. It is also easy to adapt to courses of different length or taught in a different order. The sequence of the chapters taken as a whole has a certain logic. The book begins by laying out some of the basic building blocks of sociology, in terms of key concepts and explanations of how the sociological perspective developed over time. Most of the basic concepts, theories, and approaches are introduced in the context of discussing actual social developments and topical issues. We also try to help the reader to reflect on

how sociology itself has always been affected by time and place, including the late modern or postmodern period.

The book can be used selectively to fit time constraints. It can be seen as falling naturally into two halves, the first of which may be thought of in three informal parts.

The first section of Chapter 1, "What Is Sociology," spells out our fresh approach, emphasizing what is distinctive about sociology and why it is relevant for understanding contemporary social changes. **Chapter 1** shows how sociology offers a particular way of thinking and speaking about social phenomena, telling **sociological stories** and introducing some key concepts. **Chapter 2** explains and demonstrates the basic **methods** used in sociological research and analysis.

The next two chapters show how and why cultural factors are central to our sociological understanding of contemporary developments. **Chapter 3** discusses the various components of **culture** and how they affect our perception and performance in social situations. **Chapter 4** examines the pervasive influence of **media and communications.**

The next group of chapters covers some of the most intimate and personal aspects of life, which affect our sense of identity. **Chapter 5** examines the processes of **socialization** at different periods in the **life cycle. Chapter 6** is concerned with one of the most fundamental human activities, **sexuality.** In **Chapter 7** we look at those social arrangements most closely associated with socialization and the regulation of sexuality, **marriage and the family.**

The second half of the book provides comprehensive coverage of the various ways in which social life is structured and organized, and gives prominence to the cultural dimensions of those structures and institutions.

Four chapters are devoted to forms of inequality and their impact on identities. **Chapter 8** introduces the main concepts and theories of **inequality,** giving particular attention to wealth, power, status, and other resources. In **Chapter 9** we focus on the very basic division of **gender** and the inequalities to which it gives rise. Another set of inequalities attach to **race and ethnicity**–the subject of **Chapter 10**. In **Chapter 11** we trace out some of the most extreme forms of social regulation that relate to these inequalities–the ways in which society defines and deals with **crime and deviance**.

The next part of the book is where we examine some of the main social institutions that give meaning and organization to areas of social activity. **Chapter 12** deals with **work and the economy** and their changing forms, especially in a period of increasing knowledge-based industry and globalization. Changing economic demands are only one of the sets of competing pressures for change in **education**, the subject of **Chapter 13**. **Health and medicine**, the topic of **Chapter 14**, might seem to be one of the institutions most shaped by scientific knowledge and modern organization, but it also reflects cultural differences, such as those between groups, nations, and periods. Just as alternative New Age medical ideas are gaining media attention, so too New Age religion is one of the competing contemporary forms of **religion** discussed in **Chapter 15**. A common theme in all of these chapters is that developments in contemporary institutions can be portrayed in many different ways; to analyze them we need the most subtle tools, drawing on the latest thinking in the arts and sciences as well as those deriving from classical sociology.

The last part rounds off the book with three chapters devoted to examining the global changes that may determine the future of the planet. **Chapter 16** looks at demographic and environmental developments, including the rapid expansion of **urban population** areas and the pressure on resources. In **Chapter 17** we enter the realm of **politics**, discussing the competing ideologies and political processes both inside and outside the official sphere of government. Finally, **Chapter 18** examines theories and processes of **social change**, ranging from gradual social evolution to social rev-

olution, and asks whether the future will be determined by technological and other global forces or by **collective action and social movements** that marshal cultural resources to defend or create desired identities and social structures.

Whether the sequence of chapters is followed or altered to fit course requirements, the main themes and structuring principles hold together throughout. Each chapter begins with an example of a contemporary issue, usually in the form of a media story, and argues for the superiority of a sociological interpretation over a purely individualist view ("An individual or social story?"). There is constant emphasis on the need for attention to cultural factors in sociological analysis, especially in view of the pervasiveness of media representations in contemporary society. It is partly this "mediatization" of contemporary social life that persuades us to refer to it as "postmodern," in order to highlight the change from the earlier modern period in which the study of sociology arose. We hope the reader will appreciate this as a positive attempt to develop a fresh introduction to sociology that reflects the latest developments in the discipline and in contemporary thought more generally.

## Features of This Innovative New Text

We have tried to combine the best traditional, pedagogically helpful elements with some new aspects that are difficult to single out, and yet that deserve highlighting.

First, the book **does not patronize students by talking down** to them. It invites them to get involved in ongoing debates in contemporary sociology.

Although the book is **informed by the latest in research and theory**, it focuses on real social issues and the ways in which sociology can help to understand them. Even the **"Theory" and "Data" boxes** are easily accessible to students.

The book frames contemporary social problems less as individual issues and more as symptoms and products of postmodernity. Each chapter opens with a section that poses a central sociological question: *An individual or social story?* Beyond answering that central question, the book extends the social analysis into the postmodern realm.

The book gives greater prominence to the fruits of the **cultural turn** in sociology—the greater appreciation of the ways in which meanings are constructed and transmitted, especially through new media and popular culture, in which students are thoroughly enmeshed, which are highlighted in **"Media Moment" boxes.**

Along with the social and cultural themes, this book emphasizes **politics** in the major substantive part concluding the text.

Although the main focus is on the United States, this book is situated within a **global perspective,** reflecting the reality of globalization and its effects on different peoples and cultures around the world as well as within the United States.

In addition,

- ✓ the text is **clearly—some say eloquently—written** with crisp definitions of key terms and contemporary examples.
- ✓ a **running glossary** provides students with explanations and examples of key terms.
- ✓ numerous **figures, tables, and photos** have been added for their diversity and relevance.
- ✓ **theme boxes** cover issues of high sociological concern: Media Moments, Theory, and Data.
- ✓ chapter opening outlines, chapter conclusions, exercises, study questions, and further reading round out the **complement of pedagogy.**
- ✓ an **Instructor's Manual** with **test questions** is electronically available to professors for examination and free upon adoption.

We would not have been able to complete this book without the creative, expert, and dedicated assistance of our student researchers. We have acknowledged them on the title page. We also acknowledge the indispensable work of Nadine Casey, senior administrative assistant to the Yale Center for Cultural Sociology, who has coordinated every phase of this manuscript's preparation. We would also like to thank manuscript reviewers for their valuable suggestions: Laura Edles, Ron Jacobs, Gabriel Acevedo, Eric Magnuson, and Paul Colomy. Finally, we are indebted to those colleagues who offered advice on trends in their areas of specialism, including Viktor Gecas, Lynn Smith-Lovin, Steve Seidman, Michele Lamont, Judith Lorber, Jeylan Mortimer, Mike Shanahan, Arne Kalleberg, Francisco Ramirez, Michael Schudson, Bryan Turner, Karin Knorr Cetina, and David Snow.

## About the Authors

We'd like to share our backgrounds to give you an insight into how we came to write this special text.

### Jeffrey C. Alexander

I came to sociology during the late 1960s. During those times of great social conflict and cultural and political change, I felt an urgent need to figure things out. Why was everything in flux, I wondered. What was the "system," and how does it work? Gender relations were shifting rapidly. Racism seemed pervasive, as well as radical efforts to fight against it. American foreign policy was going ballistic. The generation gap was becoming cavernous. Sociology gave me a way of figuring out why all this was happening, and what we might do in response.

So during my years as an undergraduate at Harvard, I began with the most contemporary sociology, but during my graduate school days at Berkeley I went back to the classics, studying and reinterpreting the founding theorists of our discipline—Marx, Weber, Durkheim, and Parsons. Perhaps because of my experience in the cultural revolutions and radical politics of the 1960s, I was particularly interested in shifting social meanings and subjectivities. As I read more anthropology and philosophy after leaving Berkeley for my first teaching position at UCLA, I began to feel strongly that scholars of contemporary societies should find a way to remain sensitive to "traditional" concerns of meaning, culture, religion, and values. At the same time, I was fascinated by the new culture industries—movies, television, and advertising—that were playing an increasingly important role in what seemed like a new social phase, a postmodern society.

As I developed new sociological theories about culture and politics, I continued to be deeply concerned with the ongoing crises of American and world societies, worried by Watergate in the 1970s, engaged in protests against South African apartheid and efforts to end the arms race in the 1980s, and transfixed by the dismantling of communism in the 1990s.

It was toward the end of the millennium, as I was moving from the West Coast to New Haven, that Ken Thompson and I decided the time had come to write a new, truly contemporary introduction to sociology. Close friends and colleagues, we had worked together through decades of extraordinary social change, creating an international network of theoretical researchers inside the International Sociological Association.

We dedicated ourselves to this challenge: We would try to create a new framework for making sense of it all. If we succeed, then we'll give the young people of today the same opportunity for sociological clarification that we once had ourselves. Because, if you stop to think about it, the problems of today are not all that different, are they?!

## Kenneth Thompson

I first chose to study sociology as my undergraduate major after having worked as a journalist and completed military service. In light of those experiences it seemed the most relevant field for making sense of my experience of the world. I was also influenced by my first exposure to the subject at the introductory sociology lectures of brilliant German refugee scholar Norbert Elias. In his hands, sociology took in all knowledge from history to psychoanalysis, from UN health statistics to cultural innovations such as the introduction of the fork as an eating utensil. The ambitious view of sociology as "Queen of the Sciences" dates back to Auguste Comte, the French scholar who gave the discipline its name and who was the subject of one of my first books. Elias's colleague and fellow refugee Ilya Neustadt introduced me to the study of Comte and the other theorists who influenced me, including Max Weber and Emile Durkheim. My doctoral thesis at Oxford University was a mainly Weberian analysis of religious organization, although my later works drew more on Durkheim and other French sociologists. My research interests have progressed from religion to other institutions and organizations, including more recently the media and episodes of "moral panic." Perhaps because I came into education as a mature student, I have always had an interest in making academic knowledge accessible to people from different backgrounds. Consequently, I have worked in a variety of educational institutions, beginning as a tutor at Oxford University, followed by appointments at Rutgers, Smith College, UCLA, Yale, and the British Open University, where multimedia teaching included making BBC television and radio programs. My appreciation of international trends in sociology has been strengthened by holding offices in the International Sociological Association, where I first began collaborating with Jeffrey Alexander more than twenty years ago.

We hope that both professors and students will enjoy this text as much as we have enjoyed collaborating on it.

*Jeffrey C. Alexander and*
*Kenneth Thompson*

# A Contemporary Introduction to Sociology

# PART ONE

# What Is Sociology?

# chapter 1

# Sociological Stories and Key Concepts

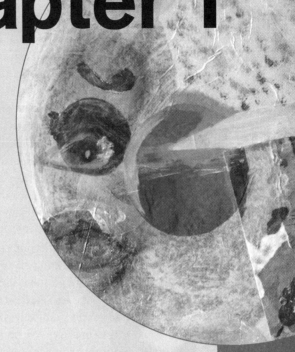

## THE INDIVIDUAL AND THE SOCIAL

Sociology is the science (*-ology*) of society (*socio-*). This may sound either scary or pretentious. It could be scary if you think a scientific study of **society** must be all about experiments and mathematics. On the other hand, it might seem pretentious if sociology is claiming to be the only way of understanding a society with which we are already familiar. Neither is true. We would like you to think of **sociology** as offering particular kinds of commentaries or stories (though they're not the only ones available to us). As the sociologist Zygmunt Bauman puts it: "Sociology is an extended commentary on the experiences of daily life, an interpretation which feeds on other interpretations and is in turn fed into them" (Bauman 1990: 231).

As individuals we all have personal stories to tell that are unique to us. They are based on our experiences and by telling them to ourselves, and others, we give meaning to our lives. We hope that the more we think about those experiences and discuss them with others, the more we will understand them. Sociology can help us to make sense of our experiences by taking our accounts of them and comparing them with others. It can tell us how they make sense as part of a larger story—a story about groups of individuals sharing similar experiences and perhaps constituting a significant social trend. This sociological perspective is now part of our contemporary worldview and is something we encounter every day—for example, in newspaper stories and broadcast news. We may take it for

When we decipher media stories, we all become sociologists. (iStockphoto)

granted and not stop to consider how the sociological perspective works in constructing the stories. One of the most important reasons for studying sociology at the beginning of the twenty-first century is to develop a better understanding of how we gain our knowledge of society, and perhaps gain a better understanding of ourselves as well.

Although we tend to think of ourselves as unique and special, in control of our own actions, we also know that we share many characteristics with others and that we are subject to similar social pressures. The mass media are constantly presenting us with stories that make us think about these similarities and differences, and their causes. In a sense, we are all sociologists now, because we practice these skills of interpretation, comparison, and looking for causes. Normally, however, it is only when the story grabs our attention that we are motivated to do this thinking in a really serious way, perhaps because it involves people with whom we can identify.

Take the story of the Columbine High School massacre in Littleton, Colorado, where, on April 20, 1999, two teenage students, members of the self-styled "Trenchcoat Mafia," shot dead thirteen people before turning the guns on themselves. It is a story that shocked almost everyone, but it was of particular concern to students and their parents, who could readily imagine themselves in a similar

**Society** A population distinguished by shared norms, values, institutions, and culture. Societies are often defined by geographic, regional, or national boundaries.

**Sociology** The science of society. The sociologist studies how everyday, individual stories and relationships relate to the larger, collective stories of social groups, social systems, and societies.

situation. Many explanations were offered by the media. Some emphasized how deviant or different the killers were from "normal" students. Other commentators stressed the pressures on individuals to conform and to be like other students, especially successful students. Essayist Roger Rosenblatt in *Time* magazine (May 3, 1999) focused on cultural differences, particularly the boys' choice of clothing, noting that "[i]n an odd way, I think much can be explained by the trench coats, not because they are long and black and what the kids call gothic, but because they look alike, they conceal differences." He argued that people who are attracted to groups, such as clans and cults, seek to lose their individuality by dressing the same as the others in that group. In sociological terms, he was saying that these students were choosing to adopt the group identity of a subculture. (While **culture** refers to the symbolic and learned aspects of human society, which are socially rather than biologically transmitted, **subculture** refers to the symbols and lifestyles of a subgroup in society, often one that deviates from the "normal," more general culture of the larger society.)

The cover-story reporter for *Newsweek* (May 3, 1999), on the other hand, talked about forceful social pressures to conform to the majority, quoting students at Littleton who explained why the two killers looked "shifty" in school photographs: "They'd walk with their heads down, because if they looked up they'd get thrown into lockers and get called a 'fag.'" In other words, in addition to the official (formal) social structure of the school, there were unofficial (informal) structures and processes, which exercised constraint. (**Social structures** are the patterns of organization that constrain human behavior.)

The *Denver Rocky Mountain News* commentator covering the same story (April 21, 1999) rejected such cultural or social structural explanations, preferring a *reductionist* explanation (i.e., one that reduces a social phenomenon to a matter

Columbine was one of the most important sociological stories of the 1990s. The killers, Eric Harris and Dylan Klebold, were caught on film by the high school cafeteria video camera. (Wikipedia)

of individual psychology)—claiming that these were psychologically unbalanced individuals simply imitating other individuals: "Surely part of the answer is a relatively simple phenomenon: unbalanced, resentful kids imitating the highly publicized actions of other unbalanced kids." It dismissed the other explanations: "The influence of violent entertainment, for example, or too easy access to guns suffer[s] from the weakness of having predated the recent trend of gun-toting students invading their schools."

**Culture** The symbolic and learned aspects of human society. Culture is not biological but, instead, is transmitted and shared via social interaction.

**Subculture** The symbols and lifestyles of a subgroup in society, one that deviates from the "normal," more general (dominant) culture of a society.

**Social structures** Patterns of organization that constrain human behavior. These can be formal (such as school or government) or informal (such as peer pressure or trends).

However, this rejection of more complicated sociological explanations, and the reduction of the level of explanation to individuals simply imitating each other, is something that sociology has always resisted. Good sociological explanations often entail constructing accounts, or stories, that involve a combination of social structural and cultural factors, and trying to calculate their respective contributions.

The mass media may offer sociological or other forms of explanation without making clear the concepts and principles on which they are based. As a knowledgeable consumer of the mass media, you are already familiar with these and have a certain amount of sociological skill, perhaps without knowing it! By studying a sociology course and reading this book you are building on that existing stock of knowledge and refining that skill.

Of course, there is more to daily life than puzzling over social problems in the media and thinking about what their stories have to do with us. As noted earlier, in everyday life we tend to think of ourselves as unique individuals. This means that we think, we feel, we act on the basis of our taken-for-granted conviction that our selves are separate from society. We are aware, of course, that there is a vast world outside of this self. We often talk about the world getting us down, the sacrifices it demands, our triumphs over it. From our subjective perspective as individuals, this outside world presents itself to us as resources, as objects, as other persons, as organizations. We see these as positive or negative, as sources of pleasure or pain, as things that can help us to realize our goals (no matter how vaguely sensed or defined), to express our feelings, and to satisfy or reduce the pressures we feel from our moral obligations to ideals. Sometimes, of course, we are aware that we're not really alone, that we share goals, experiences, emotional expressions, and feelings of obligation with others such as friends, fellow workers, students, or family. More often, however, we do not feel we share them, and we do not feel particularly connected.

This is only natural. In the second-to-second, day-to-day sequence of our everyday lives, we are alone. It is our energy that makes things happen, and it is our responsibility, and our problem, if they do not. This may mean that, insofar as we have a perspective on everyday life, it is likely to be that of individualism. (*Individualism* is the name given to the philosophical view that sees society only as a collection of unique individuals, each with his or her own special qualities. All are responsible for their own actions, and their success and happiness are regarded as their individual achievements.)

Sociology offers a very different story to describe what is going on. From the sociological perspective, we do not see society as if it were composed simply of separate individuals, certainly not in the old-fashioned "rugged individual" sense so beloved by whose who uphold traditional American ideals. Believing that we are radically separated from others is an illusion, and sometimes a dangerous one. Indeed, according to this approach, there is no clear break between the outside world and our individual inner selves. To varying degrees we are constrained and determined in our actions by the social circumstances in which we live. Even when we think for ourselves, we do so with a language and a culture that have been given to us, the rules of which we are scarcely able to discern. However, we do not have to accept a totally deterministic view, as if individuals were parts of a big social machine. Although social structures may constrain and regulate our behavior in various ways, social life is also enabling. It provides us with the cultural resources for thinking and communication, and the social resources for cooperation and organization. Furthermore, human beings have the creative capacity to imagine the outcomes of their future actions, to choose among different strategies, and to reflect on their actions—what sociologists call *agency* or *purposive action*. Given this capacity, we should not think of structure and agency as opposites but, rather, should focus on the interplay between structural constraint and agents' creative autonomy.

Within this broad sociological perspective there are many ways of giving accounts of, or telling stories about, social behavior. Sociologists sometimes speak about the society as a whole, about "our **values**" and "our way of life." At other times they focus on the parts. There are many ways in which the social whole has been broken down. For instance, sociologists may give accounts of institutions (e.g., kinship, the law, and religion) as well as their concrete organizations (e.g., schools, families, police, and churches). And, in turn, they can describe these institutions and organizations in terms of their constituent parts, such as the **norms** (or rules) that prescribe correct behavior, the **status** (or position) that people occupy, and the **roles** they are expected to play. Some institutions, such as the family and education, have a special responsibility for preparing people to take on roles and statuses in the wider society (a process known as *socialization*), although all **institutions** involve at least some socialization into their specific roles, statuses, and norms.

Roles and institutions are two of the key building blocks in the sociological conception of social structure. Roles are the expectations associated with social positions, such as those of teacher and student. And we can think of institutions as bundles of roles that are formed within a broader culture. Institutions ensure that particular actions are regularly and continuously repeated. When they aren't repeated in expected ways—when actors don't conform to the role expectations of families, schools, or workplaces—institutions typically try to sanction them, formally or informally. Culture, roles, and institutions are at the core of social structure.

It is important to keep in mind that, however much social structures and cultural factors seem to constrain and determine behavior, it is individuals who act—even when they act as the agents of insti-

**Values**  Shared ideas of what is good/bad, desirable/undesirable, or sacred/profane in a society.

**Norms**  Rules that prescribe correct behavior. In some cases, rules are made official (e.g., as laws). In others, they remain unofficial but commonly understood (e.g., when the Pledge of Allegiance is recited in the United States, people are expected to stand).

**Status**  A position in social relations (e.g., mother, father, teacher, president). Status is normatively regulated; it is assumed that when a person occupies a particular status, he or she will behave in particular ways.

**Roles**  Bundles of socially defined attributes and expectations associated with social statuses or positions (again, e.g., mother, father, teacher, president).

**Institutions**  Patterned sets of linked social practices, such as education, marriage, or the family, that are informed by broader culture, are regularly and continuously repeated, are sanctioned and maintained by social norms, and have a major significance for the social structure.

tutions and organizations. Accordingly, when considering an incident like the Columbine High School massacre, we, as sociologists, would examine the various factors that might have influenced the course of events, paying special attention to the perceptions and accounts of the individuals who were involved. We would not claim that the outcome was totally socially determined, as if the individuals in question were bound to perceive and act in that particular way. However, we *are* interested in examining accounts of the troubling incident to see what they might have to tell us about wider social trends and problems.

## THE SOCIOLOGICAL IMAGINATION

In his book *The Sociological Imagination* (1959), sociologist C. Wright Mills describes some of the conditions of modern life that make the cultivation of a **sociological imagination** important for all of us. He observes that, nowadays, people often feel that their private lives are a series of traps and that they cannot overcome their troubles. And, in a sense, they are correct in this feeling, because underlying their private troubles are large-scale changes in society. Unless people develop a sociological imagination, they cannot accurately define the troubles they experience in terms of historical changes and the workings of the institutions of society. In other words, they lack the quality of mind necessary for grasping the interplay of individual and society, of biography and history, of self and world. Mills explains the way the sociological imagination works by distinguishing between what he calls "personal troubles" and "public issues." He says that "troubles" are "personal" in the sense that they occur within the character of the individual and his or her social environment (*milieu*); in other words, **troubles** are a private matter, having to do with the self. **Issues,** however, are public matters, transcending one's self and one's immediate social milieu—they are institutional in nature, and often involve crises in institutional arrangements:

> *Troubles* occur within the character of the individual and within the range of his [*sic*] immediate relations with others: they have to do with his self

and with those limited areas of social life of which he is directly and personally aware. . . .

*Issues* have to do with matters that transcend these local environments of the individual and the range of his inner life. They have to do with the organization of many such milieux into the institutions of an historical society as a whole, with the ways in which various milieux overlap and interpenetrate to form the larger structure of social and historical life. (Mills 1959: 8)

The distinction between private troubles and public issues can be illustrated by looking at the problem of family breakdown and divorce in America. This is often experienced as a private trouble by parents and their children—something that is personal to them and is accompanied by arguments about who is to blame. But if we compare divorce rates in various developed countries we might begin to see this as more of a public issue. As early as 1970, the United States had double the international average rate of divorce (33 percent compared with 15 percent). And by the end of the century, approximately 51 of every 100 marriages ended in divorce in the United States, compared with 14 in Greece and 12 in Italy (OECD 2002: Table GE5.1). Now, if the U.S. figure were as low as that of Greece or Italy, we might argue that the divorces in question were probably the result of the personal biographies ("troubles") of the individuals involved (one spouse or the other had misbehaved, one was neurotic, they just didn't get along). But with such relatively high figures in one country it would be absurd to conclude that all these cases were merely the result of individual/psychological troubles. Accordingly, we need to ask questions about the institution of marriage and the family in that particular society, and about the factors that might be causing the problems that make this a social issue rather than just a personal trouble. Perhaps it is the result of structural factors, such as easy divorce processes and women's greater financial independence compared with

**Sociological imagination** As theorized by C. Wright Mills, the ability to understand not only what is happening in one's own immediate experience but also what is happening in the world and to imagine how one's experience fits into the larger world experience.

**Troubles** Personal problems, private matters having to do with the self. An individual's unemployment is an example of a trouble.

**Issues** Problems extending beyond the individual and local environment. These are institutional in nature and often involve crises in institutional arrangement. The high unemployment rate across the United States is an example of an issue.

Divorce rates have skyrocketed in the United States. Today one out of two marriages between a man and a woman end in divorce. (iStockphoto)

previous eras. Or maybe it is due more to changes in culture, to different standards and expectations concerning relationships, or to perceptions of divorce as normal rather than deviant. Indeed, U.S. culture offers more and more images and models of relationships, including sexual relationships, from which we can supposedly choose. As we emphasize frequently in this book, sociology is increasingly having to turn its attention to one of the defining features of contemporary society—the enormous variety of cultural images and models that are communicated through the media and that affect our perceptions of ourselves and the social world around us.

Perhaps the greatest benefit the sociological imagination can offer to students, including troubled ones like those at Columbine High School, is to teach ways of understanding how "personal troubles" may in fact be "public issues." An individual student who comes to understand that his or her feelings of alienation, boredom, and lack of respect and status are shared by a significant number of other students may begin to ask questions about the structure and culture of the educational institution. These questions, in turn, can lead to constructive strategies for changing the institution. Using the sociological imagination to distinguish between personal troubles and private issues—

and, when justified, learning to translate personal troubles into public issues—empowers us to work to change the conditions that give rise to so much anguish. It is in this sense that the craft of sociology is self-enlightening and liberating.

Another example of the liberating effect of translating personal troubles into public issues is the women's movement, which developed in the 1960s and 1970s. It was only when women began to talk about what they thought of as their personal troubles of frustration and lack of fulfillment that they realized these translated into public issues concerning political power and institutions such as the economy with its inequalities of pay and career opportunities for women. Feminist sociologists have opened up areas for investigation previously overlooked, ranging from childbirth to housework, in addition to demonstrating that topics like date rape and domestic violence against women are not "private matters" but "public issues" concerning the ways men exert power over women.

Although the sociological imagination can assist us in seeing the difference between personal troubles and public issues, the problems that interest the sociologist are not necessarily limited to the everyday understanding of "problems." Sociologist Peter Berger has pointed out the difference between the sociological perspective and this common view, noting that people tend to refer to something as a **social problem** when it does not work out the way it is "officially" supposed to. They then expect the sociologist to study the "problem" as they have defined it and perhaps even to come up with a "solution" that will take care of the matter to their own satisfaction. It is important to understand that a sociological problem is something

**Social problem**  A situation that contradicts or violates social norms and values. Widespread drug abuse and racism are examples of social problems.

quite different from a "social problem" in this sense. For example, it would be sociologically naive to focus on crime as a "problem" simply in terms of the way law enforcement agencies define it, or on divorce solely on the grounds laid down by those who see it as a moral problem. As Berger puts it: "The sociological problem is not so much why things 'go wrong' from the viewpoint of the authorities and the management of the social scene, but how the whole system works in the first place, what are its presuppositions and by what means is it held together. The fundamental problem is not crime but the law, not divorce but marriage, not racial discrimination but racially defined stratification, not revolution but government" (Berger 1963: 49–50).

So, asking sociological questions means being interested in looking some distance beyond the officially defined or commonly accepted accounts of actions and institutions. It means being aware that there may be different levels of meaning, some of which are hidden from our everyday consciousness. The sociological perspective is frequently concerned with seeing through the facades of social structures and debunking official interpretations. This *debunking* motif is one of four dimensions of the sociological consciousness described by Berger. The other three are unrespectability, relativizing, and cosmopolitanism.

The *unrespectability* motif of sociology, prominent in some American sociology (particularly the so-called Chicago School's studies of the urban ghetto in the 1920s and 1930s), involves a fascination with the unrespectable view of society. Berger points out that, although it is possible to distinguish between respectable and unrespectable sectors in all Western societies, "American respectability has a particularly pervasive quality about it" (Berger 1963: 56). He suggests this may be due to lingering effects of the Puritan way of life and also to the predominant role played by the bourgeoisie (middle class) in shaping American culture. In contrast to the official respectable America represented symbolically by the Chamber of Commerce, churches, schools, and other centers of civic ritual, there is an America that has other symbols and speaks another language: "It is the language of the poolroom and the poker game, of bars, brothels and army barracks. . . . The 'other America' that speaks this language can be found wherever people are excluded, or exclude themselves, from the world of middle-class propriety" (Berger 1963: 56). However, it is not confined to minorities or marginal groups; even middle-class "nice people" may drop into or out of unrespectable and respectable cultures in various situations. For example, the student killers in the Columbine High School massacre were described as being completely different characters at school compared with how they were known at home—members of the Trenchcoat Mafia at school and yet sons of respectable middle-class families.

The *relativizing* motif refers to the capacity, typical of the modern mind, but especially developed in sociology, to see how identities and perspectives vary depending on the situation or context. This is sometimes contrasted with so-called traditional societies, which assigned definite and permanent identities to their members, and where it was more difficult to imagine adopting different perspectives. In modern societies, identity is more fluid and fragmented, more uncertain and in flux. Geographical and social mobility means we encounter numerous ways of looking at the world. Through the mass media we are exposed to other cultures and perspectives, which implies, at least potentially, the awareness that one's own culture, including its basic values, is relative in space and time.

Finally, there is the *cosmopolitanism* motif. The turbulent urban centers of modern times have tended to develop a cosmopolitan consciousness, a knowledge of a variety of lifestyles and perspectives, and a certain sense of detachment from them. This mentality was described in a classic sociological essay, *The Metropolis and Mental Life* (1903) by the German scholar Georg Simmel. Whereas Simmel emphasized some of the negative aspects of the cosmopolitan mind, such as its de-tached and calculative characteristics, Berger con-trasts it with narrow parochialism and says that the sociological perspective is a "broad, open, emanci-pated vista on human life" and that sociologists, at their best, are people "with a taste for other lands, inwardly open to the measureless richness of hu-man possibilities, eager for new horizons and worlds of human meaning" (Berger 1963: 67).

In *A Contemporary Introduction to Sociology,* it is this liberating vision of the sociological perspec-tive that we will bring to our examination of the various dimensions of today's rapidly changing so-ciety. In doing so, however, we will not hesitate to draw on the accumulated wisdom of the great soci-ologists of the past, who sought to do the same in their own time. We will be standing on the shoul-ders of giants, so that we might see further. But we also must be prepared to ask whether the ways in which sociology's "founding fathers" posed their sociological questions about the transition from traditional to modern society are the most relevant for understanding today's changing society. Per-haps we need a change of focus, new concepts to describe the social forms that we see emerging today.

## SOCIETY TODAY: SO WHAT'S NEW?

Sociology came into being as an effort to under-stand and diagnose what lay behind the personal troubles and social issues that accompanied the massive changes associated with modernity. Modernity, in the sense used by sociologists, is not the same as its popular meaning of being up to date or contemporary. It refers to a historical period, to the culmination of the set of historical processes—economic, political, social, and cultural—that brought about the end of the traditional social or-der and replaced it with new and more dynamic forms. These include the rise of the nation-state and such political arrangements as parties, public life, and democracies; economic capitalism, based

> **Modernity**  In sociology, a term referring to the set of histori-cal processes that transformed the traditional order. Early soci-ologists (e.g., Karl Marx, Max Weber, George Simmel, and Emile Durkheim) set out to understand the social upheaval and disruption caused by these processes, which include the rise of the nation-state, economic capitalism, bureaucratization, ur-banization, and secularization.

on the systematic pursuit of profit and the promo-tion of industrialization; new forms of social orga-nization, such as the modern bureaucracy based on salaried employment and recruitment on merit; urbanization, with large cities populated by recent migrants from rural areas or other nations who had suffered a loss of old community ties; and the un-dermining of religious belief by secular culture, es-pecially science and technology.

Those who first laid the foundations of sociol-ogy believed that modernity automatically meant social progress. If the study of society were based on rigorous methods equivalent to those in the natural sciences, the findings could be used to en-sure that further progress would follow in the fu-ture. However, the generation of sociologists who established sociology as an academic discipline in the universities toward the end of the nineteenth century (e.g., Emile Durkheim in France, Max We-ber in Germany, Robert Park at the University of Chicago) could see that modernity brought with it many problems. Sociologists in the twentieth cen-tury focused on these problems: the politics of the nation-state, class inequalities and conflicts, the rigidities of bureaucratic organization, the prob-lems of the inner city, the decline of religion, and the search for a new moral consensus.

The issues that face sociology at the beginning of the twenty-first century do not exclude such questions. The ideas we develop in this book will certainly draw on the concepts and theories that sociologists have developed before. But there are good grounds for thinking that, as this new cen-tury begins, new questions are beginning to be

Premodern societies, known as feudal societies, were based on serf labor for wealthy landowners. (Bettmann/Corbis)

posed. These require new concepts and theories, or at least a revision of older ones. Before we go on to look at some of these new developments, it might be useful if you thought about your own experience of these changes. (See Exercise 1 at the end of the chapter.)

Sociologists have their own lists of significant changes, some of which are specific to particular social institutions, such as the family, economy, politics, education, religion, health and medicine, and the media. Many of these specific changes feature in later chapters. Other changes are more general, and these are the ones that pose the greatest challenge to the sociological imagination as it seeks to translate private troubles into public issues today. There is an anecdote about the American writer Gertrude Stein. As she lay dying, she asked, "What is the answer?" When no answer came, she laughed and asked: "In that case what is the question?" (See Exercise 2.)

It is the new questions that we must get right if we are to understand contemporary societies. The world's most highly developed societies are in the midst of a profound transition, one that affects less developed societies as well. Classical sociologists at the end of the nineteenth century, as well as the mid-twentieth-century creators of modern sociol-

ogy, developed their models during a phase of social development that differed significantly from our own (see Table 1.1). Let's consider the main concerns of those sociologists of modernity, and then turn to some of the key issues that have begun to come into focus today.

## The Sociology of Modernity

### Economic Life

From the early nineteenth century to the middle of the twentieth, it seemed to many of the most acute social observers that industrial capitalism had turned earlier and more traditional societies upside down. Sociologists focused on the often disastrous consequences of this great transformation—specifically, on the growing inequality between economic classes as well as the physically demanding and often degrading quality of work.

### Social Organization

The shifting economic order was not by any means the only development that caught the attention of the early sociologists of modernity. They were struck by the centralizing tendencies of social organization more broadly conceived. They traced the movement of population from scattered rural settlements to urban centers and saw the future as demanding ever larger cities. They observed what they believed to be an irreversible movement away from arbitrary and personal forms of authority in "traditional" societies—rule by a king or local "strongman"—to impersonal control based on bureaucratic rules.

### Integration

Alongside their preoccupations with the material inequalities of industrialism and the centralization of social organization, classical and modern sociologists were deeply concerned with reintegrating a social order they viewed as increasingly stratified and divided. Some believed that greater inclusion could be achieved through progressive and incre-

**TABLE 1.1  Characteristics of Premodern, Modern, and Postmodern Societies**

| Premodern | Modern | Postmodern |
|---|---|---|
| Feudalism; agricultural economy | Industrial capitalism; urbanization; material inequality | Postindustrial economy based on services and information |
| Arbitrary, personal forms of authority | Pressure for centralization and bureaucratization (impersonal authority) | Decentralized organization |
| Shared moral universe based on religion | Problem of integration | Cultural turn<br>• dominance of mass media and popular culture<br>• displacement of production by consumption<br>• recognition of language, symbols, and meaning in sociological stories |
| Superstition; tradition | Rationalization | Derationalization |
| Rigid gender roles | Gender relations unchallenged | New social movements, multiculturalism, and difference |
| Local, ascribed identity | Public versus private life | Socialization, identity, and life cycle redefined |
|  | Occidentalism versus Orientalism (implied superiority of the West); narrative of progress and evolution | Globalization; new forms of inequality |

mental reforms; others imagined that a revolutionary transformation would introduce socialism and communism. What reformers and radical sociologists shared, however, was the vision of social integration as allowing greater unity, a vision of equality that depended on increasing uniformity among people from different groups—economic, religious, ethnic, and racial.

### Culture

The classical and modern sociologists contrasted their own societies with an earlier social order they called "traditional," "feudal," or simply "premodern." It was because they worked with this contrast in mind that they were particularly likely to see the major trend in culture as that of increasing rationality: thinking based on formal rules or calculations of efficiency rather than on tradition or emotion. Above all, they emphasized the central importance of science and the declining significance of religion. For better or worse, they believed, culture was becoming rationalized, abstract, and subjected to organized control.

### Gender and Socialization

As we can see so clearly from the perspective of the present, one of the most remarkable characteristics of both classical and modern sociological stories

The economic life of modern societies was characterized by mass production and a large manual labor class. The Ford automobile plant, with its Model T, was a leader in this industrial movement. (AP Photo/Ford Motor Company)

was that they took gender arrangements for granted. As women confronted the wrenching economic, political, and cultural transformations of their time, the fact that their opportunities for public accomplishment were highly restricted failed almost completely to arouse sociological interest. If the position of women inside and outside the home was noticed at all, it was seen as the result of nature. Family and child-rearing arrangements were explained in the same manner. Is there perhaps a connection between these stories and the fact that almost all of the classical and modern sociologists were men?

### Public Versus Private

With only a few exceptions, these classical and modern sociologists paid little attention to emo-

tion, love, friendship, recreation, and entertainment. Once again, we must look to the nature of these earlier forms of modern societies to find out why. In the transition from more traditional social orders, a stiff barrier had been erected between the private and the public spheres. (This, too, relates to the fact that the sociologists were men, whose concern was the public sphere, whereas the private sphere was more the concern of women.) The efficiency and distinctiveness of modern institutions seemed to depend upon the "rational" control of emotions and the construction of associations on universal, abstract, and universal principles. Identities that were less universal and more particularistic, structures of feeling that were more expressive and spontaneous, the pursuit of pleasure in recreation and entertainment—these were understood to be private issues. As such, they were rarely the subject of classical or modern sociological texts.

### Occidentalism Versus Orientalism

These sociological accounts were presented as part of a larger story about the distinctiveness of Western (occidental) societies as compared to non-Western (oriental) ones. Rationalization, centralization, industrialization, and the public-private split were described in evolutionary terms, as a movement of progress from East to West. They were seen as "advances" that defined the superiority of modern societies and the deficiencies of more traditional ones. This historical narrative suggested that non-Western civilizations did not possess the social capacity for modernization. Whether harshly or sympathetically, classical and modern sociologists told stories about the backwardness of societies outside the West. Could this have anything to do with colonialism as opposed to intrinsic capacities, with the political, economic, and cultural dominance of the European colonial powers as well as America's later "neo-colonial" expansion?

## Beyond the Sociology of Modernity

As we enter a new century and a new millennium, we cannot help but notice how the cultural and structural facts emphasized by the sociology of modernity have been dramatically transformed. Once taken for granted as the basic foundations of any posttraditional social order, such facts have themselves fundamentally changed. These transformations have stimulated contemporary sociologists to construct new theoretical and empirical stories, accounts that raise as many questions as they answer.

### Postindustrial Economies

By the end of the twentieth century it had become evident that technological growth had transformed the nature of economic production, at least in the most advanced economies. Because so much less time is now required to produce material goods, the workforce devoted to manufacturing—to blue-collar jobs—has dramatically declined. In its place, economic activity increasingly concentrates on nonmaterial goods. As the service economy has displaced manufacturing, the nature of work has changed. Many sociologists see this in terms of progress; they believe that education and flexibility are more important today than in the past, and that workers in service-oriented societies have much more autonomy than those in industrial societies. Other sociologists tell more depressing stories about the "deskilling of labor"—what were once the worker's skills are now programmed into the computerized machine. All agree that, in the most developed societies, the class structure is more differentiated and less homogeneous and that the overall level of material well-being has vastly increased.

### Decentralized Organization

In a postindustrial economy, information and communication are more important than the en-

Postmodern, or postindustrial, society is dominated by service industries in which large corporations employ millions. The cubicle has become a ubiquitous workplace configuration. (iStockphoto)

Malls have become "cities in miniature," where people gather in their leisure hours. Not only are they economic centers of communities but often social hubs. (iStockphoto)

ergy supplied by muscle and coal. As information becomes digitalized and communication almost instantaneous, transportation of goods, services, and people is also transformed. These economic changes have undercut the pressure for centralization. Residential patterns have changed from urban to suburban and then to ex-urban, blurring the divisions between city, suburb, and country. Shopping malls have become cities in miniature. Home-based work has become possible, contributing to the shifting balance between public and private life. Yet, while sociologists agree that these changes are occurring, they tell different stories about their effects. Some see increased opportunities for cooperation, local control, and community; others find increasing fragmentation and privatization and the creation of more artificial forms of social order. Still others have suggested that organization in general is becoming less hierarchical and bureaucratic. The contemporary sociological story about bureaucracies is much more skeptical about their efficiency. It documents vast slippage between what managers at the top of the hierarchy say happens and what the organization's working practices really are. Whether this slippage is a sign of growing irrationality or healthy decentralization is a point of heated debate.

## The Cultural Turn

The term *cultural turn* refers to two developments: the increasing importance of cultural industries and of knowledge more generally in the economy, and the increasing attention being given to cultural factors (such as language, symbols, and meanings) in sociological explanations.

The postindustrial organization of contemporary economies has allowed an increasingly substantial segment of social time and energy to be devoted to cultural activity. Some sociologists, in fact, have said that we live in an age characterized by "postscarcity" and "postmaterial" values—that is, in which people have less need to worry about finding the necessities of life and so can concentrate on more intellectual, emotional, or spiritual matters. In service economies, culture itself has become a gigantic industry. Popular culture, once peripheral to prestige and power, now takes center stage as the new common language spoken by people, no matter how high or low their position in society. Consumption has displaced production as the dominating experience of economic life. Increasingly large amounts of disposable income are spent on travel, entertainment, clothing, restaurants, and recreation. Knowledge itself has become an industry. For these social-economic as well as technological reasons, the mass media have become central to contemporary societies, providing not only much more immediate access to information but also more immediate forms of pleasures. The example of people watching public entertainment at home with friends and family crystallizes the manner in which the once-rigid division between public and private life has eroded. Private pleasures have become public pursuits.

It is not difficult to see how such a deep and pervasive cultural transformation of contemporary society has generated conflicting sociological stories. Everyday life is indeed now less constricted by material shortages, but has it increased in quality or become more satisfying? Has the growth of knowledge facilitated moral or artistic growth? Do we have more wisdom, or just more information?

The other important aspect of the *cultural turn* is that people, including sociologists, are increasingly aware of the ways in which language shapes our experiences, our descriptions of them, and the meanings we give to them. The sociologists of the future will be much more alive to questions of language than were even the best of the classical sociologists.

### Derationalization

Despite the extraordinary progress of contemporary science, there is now less confidence that science will displace religious and other nonscientific modes of thought. People are quite likely to be critical of the authority and effects of science, pointing to the risks its applications sometimes present to human life and the environment. New Age beliefs, religious "fundamentalism," and nationalism are just a few of the examples that have led sociologists to talk about a "return of the sacred."

### New Social Movements

In earlier periods, the prototypical protest was the movement of impoverished workers against the industrial system. As that earlier social order has receded, other kinds of protest movements have become more visible and more powerful, and altogether new kinds of protests have emerged. Perhaps the most visible and most successful has been the modern women's movement. Although earlier feminist protests had gained some political and social rights, they had not envisioned a fundamental shift in gender relations. Since the 1960s, precisely this has been the aim of the contemporary feminist movement, and its success has had far-reaching effects on economic arrangements, lifestyles, socialization patterns, and the public-private divide. "The personal has become political," as in controversies about women's right to control their own bodies, such as terminating a

Derationalization is evident among American "New Agers," who borrow spiritual practices such as yoga from the East. (iStockphoto)

pregnancy. This issue, in turn, raises questions about the balance between individual rights and social rights and obligations.

The American civil rights movement, organized by African-American leaders and energized by African-American masses, preceded the contemporary women's movement and partly inspired it. It created the model for the growing racial and ethnic protests against exclusion that, with feminism, have marked the contemporary period. Other forms of social protest, such as environmentalism and gay rights, have emerged only in the contemporary period itself. In identifying and explaining these new social movements, most sociologists have presented them as stories of emancipation and liberation. There are some influential commentators, however, who employ these movements in a story of antiprogress. One old-fashioned radical story sees the new movements as diversions from the struggle for economic equality, whereas in a more conservative narrative these movements are described as destroying the solidarity that glued earlier societies together.

### Multiculturalism and Difference

Interacting with the forces that are undermining centralization and softening the public-private boundary, this new emphasis on race, gender, and sexuality has had the effect of introducing a new framework for social integration. Whereas modern societies in an earlier phase prided themselves on achieving color-blind unity, contemporary societies boast about their diversity and their ability to give positive recognition to difference. The idea of the melting pot, in which outgroups are assimilated into a larger national identity, has given way to a multicultural model of incorporation. Minority groups have become increasingly concerned with preserving their distinctive cultures, not in order to isolate themselves from contemporary society but, rather, to enter it in a different way and to gain recognition and respect. Because there are many possible group identities, there are constant struggles over "identity politics." Questions have been raised about whether these struggles could result in social fragmentation.

### Socialization, Identity, and the Life Cycle

The changes we have identified are producing dramatic shifts in marriage, child-rearing, and individual development. As women have moved beyond

Celebrating diversity marks a radical departure from the demand for homogeneity. It is a new approach to integration. (iStockphoto)

their traditional domestic roles, their financial dependence on the marriage bond has decreased. One consequence is that women now marry at a much later age, delay having children, more often decide to have children outside marriage, and, with increasing frequency, decide not to have children at all. Divorce has become more widely accepted and is now the statistical norm. In the context of dual-career couples and less stable relationships, the socialization of children has assumed a new and sometimes bewildering range of forms, from private and public daycare centers and after-school programs to much more clearly defined roles for grandparents and professional babysitters.

The growing demands for highly educated labor have extended schooling and created new life cycle stages between childhood and full adulthood, including what has recently been called "emerging adulthood," the twenty-something period when persons try on different careers and relationships without settling down. The service economy has shifted its production and marketing to these new life cycle stages, when there is more disposable income and less imperative to save for the future. The life cycle has also been stretched at the other end. With increasing wealth and leisure, the scientific transformation of medical care, and lifestyles emphasizing fitness and recreation, people are living longer and healthier lives. This trend has opened the way for new forms of human relationship, new markets for entertainment and marketing, and new challenges for socialization and care.

The expanding life cycle, increased education, new forms of consumption, the instability of marriage, and new lifestyles focused on gender, race, ethnicity, and sexuality—all these changes have created a new emphasis on "identity" as central to contemporary life. Individuals today have more scope than in earlier modern societies to define themselves and their destinies. From weight-control programs and personal trainers to psychotherapies, from talk radio and reality TV to twelve-step programs for reforming everything from love to addiction, there has been an explosion of knowledge and industries devoted to improving and recasting identity. These processes of identity change and the creation of multiple identities raise questions about the stability and unity of the self. We see some of these questions raised when people talk about a "split personality" or dispute a politician's ability to be "all things to all people."

### Inequalities

Although modern citizens are formally equal and have certain basic entitlements, new forms of inequality have emerged. As once-marginalized ethnic groups have made use of new opportunities and the more successful members have moved out of the ghettos, they have left behind a new kind of isolated and highly vulnerable "*underclass.*" (As we will see in Chapter 10, this term is questionable, which is why some sociologists prefer *ghetto poor.*) Also, as women are more frequently compelled to raise children on their own, single-parent families have become a growing source of poverty, and the percentage of children living in poverty is on the rise. The postindustrial economy has had an uneven impact, producing more affluence for some but more instability and poverty for others. Even at the height of the Silicon Valley technology boom in 1999, the *San Jose Mercury News* (February 12, 1999) reported increasing poverty in the most affluent area of California, Santa Clara County. Quoting data from the U.S. Census Bureau, it specified that about 13 percent of Santa Clara County's children were impoverished. That amounts to more than 55,000 kids—or nearly one of every eight youngsters. (By comparison, 9 percent of county residents of *all* ages were living in poverty.) The problem was that the supply of relatively well-paying manufacturing jobs had dwindled, forcing many mothers and fathers to seek less lucrative wages in service-related jobs. In short, when marriages came under pressure, leading to single-parent households, child poverty in-

Becoming a parent is a major shift in a person's life cycle. (iStockphoto)

creased. Children generally have higher rates of poverty than the population as a whole because poor families tend to have more children and are more likely to have only one adult present. Also, new parents tend to be young with little work experience, and thus earn relatively low salaries.

### Globalization

The stories told by classical and modern sociologists implicitly identified "society" with the framework of the nation-state. For many contemporary sociologists, this identification seems out of date. For example, multinational business corporations are just that—*multi*national. They may have originated in a particular country, but many of them now operate out of several countries and have global connections, making it difficult for any national government to regulate and control them. Communication networks, including the Internet as well as mass media programs (ranging from CNN news and television sitcoms to movies like *Titanic* and the *Star Wars* epics), break down national boundaries. Electronic transfers of money around the world amount to more than a trillion dollars being turned over each day on global currency markets.

According to the more optimistic sociological accounts, this is all part of modern progress, of becoming "one world." A more skeptical story is presented by sociologists who see nothing very new in all this—who point to a similar emphasis on international free trade during the nineteenth century, along with trade in currencies. Or, they may say, if the scenario is new in scale, that it is still a case of richer states dominating poorer ones, either in the form of American economic and cultural imperialism or through the establishment of regional arrangements such as the European Union (EU) and the North American Free Trade Agreement (NAFTA). Some of these developments may be increasing inequalities in the world. According to the *Human Development Report 2005,* for instance, the world's richest 500 individuals have a combined income greater than that of the poorest 416 million. And the *World Development Report 2005* revealed that the 2.5 billion people living on less than $2 a day—40 percent of the world's population—account for 5 percent of global income. The richest 10 percent, almost all of whom live in high-income countries, account for 54 percent. Similarly, people in the advanced economies are increasingly "information rich" compared with their "information poor" neighbors in the global village. For example, although the Internet made possible e-mail communications among many people in the 1990s, most of those communications were confined to the United States and parts of Europe.

**Globalization** A social phenomenon characterized by the growing number of interconnections across the world. Rather than studying society in terms of various nation-states, sociologists today are concerned with multinational and global problems. Whether globalization is a new phenomenon marking "modern progress" toward becoming "one world," or simply a new (or even disguised) form of American imperialism, continues to be debated.

Even relations between economically powerful nation-states are not equal—and, rather than requiring a new concept such as **globalization,** some sociologists prefer to use older terms such as *nationalism, imperialism,* or just plain *international competition.* Certainly some sociologists outside the United States have favored these ways of telling the story. They believe *globalization* is a term that disguises inequalities in economic or cultural relations between their own country and the United States. A good example is France's efforts to resist global free trade in cultural products, out of the fear that its culture is in danger of being swamped by Hollywood movies. In 1998, French movies accounted for only 27 percent of tickets sold in France, whereas during the same year (to cite just one example) the Hollywood blockbuster *Titanic* alone accounted for 21 million of the total 170 million tickets sold. Defending its national cultural industry, the government insisted that French productions account for 40 percent of films shown on television. This may seem reasonable at first glance, but might we also feel entitled to ask whether such nation-centered thinking is practical or even desirable in an increasingly globalized world? For example, at the same time as this new national policy was unfolding in the French movie industry, a former French prime minister and two other former ministers were put on trial during a scandal over HIV-tainted blood. These French officials, it was revealed, had for months delayed national blood tests for the HIV/AIDS virus because only a U.S.-made testing device had been available. They waited to require the national test until a French-designed test emerged that could compete commercially with the American product. As it happened, both stories were published on the same day in the *New York Times* (February 10, 1999).

Clearly, the new concept of globalization raises as many questions as it answers. It seems to direct us to important new developments, but it may have to be complemented by other concepts such as *power geometry,* which refers to the unequal distribution of power in different parts of the world, and *world system,* which is consistent with the idea of a single global system but distinguishes between the regions at the core and those on the periphery.

## HOW DO WE UNDERSTAND TODAY'S SOCIAL WORLD?

We have indicated some of the key themes of classical and modern sociology and also some of the new developments that raise fresh questions. Surely, you might be saying, we can now get on with finding some answers! We are about to do so, but we first need to set the scene. Specifically, we need to briefly examine some venerable philosophical debates, for our responses to them will inform all the empirical discussions that follow.

### Determinism Versus Free Will

Earlier we noted that, although social structures and cultural factors seem to constrain and determine behavior, it is individuals who act—even when they act as the "agents" of institutions and organization. This may seem obvious, but we need to see where sociologists stand on this issue before we can judge the adequacy of their empirical explanations. Some theorists have given compelling accounts of the forceful determinism of society and its various parts. In the middle of the nineteenth century, the revolutionary social thinker and socialist Karl Marx dramatically insisted that "it is not consciousness that determines society, but society that determines consciousness." Some fifty years later, Emile Durkheim, the French founder of modern scientific sociology, described social facts as "things" that are "objective" and "constraining" and against which individuals have little power.

Other equally influential sociologists have been appalled by such deterministic story lines. They have argued against them by creating accounts that center on the freedom of the individual. George Herbert Mead, at the University of Chicago, who exerted extraordinary influence over early American sociology, insisted that the ever creative self is at the basis of institutions. Mead conceded that inside every self there is a "me" that represents established values and attitudes, but he insisted that the self also contains an "I," which is an active, spontaneous source of creative, anticonforming activity. Erving Goffman, one of the leading American sociologists of the twentieth century, took Mead's ideas much further. He told a theoretical story that centered on the self and its ingenuity. Just because people espouse accepted social values, Goffman said, they don't necessarily believe in them. He likened people to actors for whom, as Shakespeare put it, "the whole world's a stage." Social actors present selves that can be maximally convincing to others, hiding true feelings that might get in the way.

Over the centuries, philosophers and sociologists alike have spilled a lot of ink arguing first one side of this debate and then the other. However, there is no need for us to choose a side. Very often the heat of the debate could be attributed to the fact that what was being put forward was not just a sociological theory but also a moral and emotional account. For example, the actions of students who join a subgroup that deliberately breaks school rules may be explained as the result of too much pressure in the educational system to get good grades (social determinism). Or it may be interpreted as a creative act of rebellion by individual students (free will). A full and convincing account needs to give due weight to both sides.

### Structure Versus Culture

If the first dispute is about the nature of society's effects, the second one is about what exactly society is and what affects the inside of it.

Many of the greatest sociologists have made "structure" central to the stories they tell about institutions, processes, and groups. As they see it, social structure is analogous to a material or biological thing—it is a concrete, stubborn fact, located outside the individual self. Structure could be a factory or a labor market, offering financial incentives and threatening financial punishments to compel people to work. Structure could also be something less obviously material; it could be a "role" in the family or church. When sociologists describe family and religious roles as structures—"father" and "priest," for example—they focus on how performance in these roles is compelled from outside. They might point to the importance of positive and negative psychological reinforcements, such as love, anger, prestige, and ridicule, in compelling persons to become good fathers and priests.

Such structural accounts do not have to stress determinism. Just because a social element is described as a stubborn fact external to the person acting, it doesn't have to be thought of as producing automatic conformity. Indeed, theories can emphasize an individual's free will and his or her resistance to structural pressure, as in the emancipatory stories told by women, ethnic and religious minorities, and underprivileged classes. For example, some feminist sociologists have written about women's attempts to take back control of their own bodies in pregnancy and childbirth. They describe such efforts as a struggle against state governments and even doctors and husbands who use legal sanctions to force women to change their behavior—to alter their diets (stop drinking alcohol during pregnancy), modify their daily activity (be confined to a hospital throughout the last weeks of pregnancy), or undergo caesarian section—to protect the rights of the fetus (Martin 1989).

The structural approach is not the only way to account for society and its effects. A very different kind of story can be told—a story about culture rather than structure. In this account, it is values and beliefs that are central to society. From the sociological perspective, of course, values and beliefs are collective. They go beyond the wishes or ideals of a particular individual; they exist before her

birth, and they will continue to exist after her death. Yet, while collective, culture is not objective. It is subjective. It is inside the mind of the individual, part of her, not outside of her. It has to do with her ways of thinking and feeling. Structure gains its effect through coercion or bargaining; culture gains its effect through persuasion and conviction. Sociologists who emphasize cultural factors are likely to focus on such topics as emotion, morality, consciousness, and belief. They need not do so, however, in a deterministic way. Culture not only constrains but enables. Creating resistance and independence, it gives us a sense of who we are, of individual worth. American individualism is a case in point. In the United States, liberty is not so much a natural fact as a cultural value. There is a great collective national story here that creates and sustains individualism, sometimes for better and sometimes for worse.

Some sociological perspectives have given more emphasis to structure; others, to culture. But to truly understand contemporary societies, we must make a renewed attempt to bring the two sides together. In this book, we will draw on concepts and insights from different perspectives as and when we need them. Structures are very much at work in every institution, group, and social process. Yet, at the same time, it is difficult to see how structures can ever really work by themselves, how they can be separated from the meanings that people attach to them. Social structures do not work like structures in the natural world. They are not mechanistic forces like gravity. What we think of as structures are, in fact, nothing more than congealed sets of beliefs that assume an objective form. As they become external rather than internal, they develop into organizations that control resources, such as money and power, that can compel people to act no matter what they believe.

In order to provide a convincing analysis of social issues, such as the increase in violent incidents in schools involving students using guns against fellow students and teachers, we have found it necessary to focus on both structural factors and cultural factors. On the one hand, it is obviously relevant to look at school structures at the microlevel and explore how they relate to wider social structures, such as the American educational institution, as well as at related structures such as the family, the economy (including the gun industry), politics, and the community. On the other hand, as we have mentioned, it is also important to take into account both the meanings that people attach to those structures and the various cultures and subcultures that supply values and symbols. None of these factors inevitably determines an individual's actions. There is always an element of choice and decisionmaking; individuals are the product of culture, too.

## CONCLUSION

The post-tragedy conversation in the box titled "The Virginia Tech Murders" reminds us how sociological stories circulate as the mass media ask "why." It also demonstrates, in spite of itself, how careful we must be to avoid easy answers. We have seen that the sociological imagination is interested in showing how individuals' private troubles may be connected with public issues. In the chapters that follow, we will clarify this relationship by providing sociological explanations. One temptation sociologists are anxious to resist is the rush to offer readymade answers and solutions—the kind of slick, often plausible prescriptions that promise cures for all social problems, and that we find in books filling the shelves in airport shops. They range from "How to Get Rich" to "How to Solve America's Problems." They vary in quality, often mixing secondhand scientific ideas and a sprinkling of statistical "facts" with a lot of anecdotes, all of which are supposed to be explained by an all-purpose, big idea. There is usually nothing wrong with the idea itself. The problem is that it gets inflated to cover situations beyond the scope

of its modest beginnings. A recent example is the term *social capital,* which was initially used to refer to the types of close family and community relations that potentially benefit adolescents' educational attainment (Coleman and Hoffer 1987). But this term has since been unwisely extended to refer, very broadly, to interpersonal and social trustworthiness, the alleged deterioration of which is then blamed for all kinds of social ills (Putnam 1995a, 1995b, 2000). In the end, it has seemed to cover just about everything and thus no longer lends itself to testable propositions.

As the American sociologist Robert Nisbet pointed out, sociology needs both the imaginative ideas of the artist and the rigor of the scientist. The ideas of a sociologist such as Emile Durkheim may be dependent upon thought processes like those of the artist, "but none of them would have survived in sociology or become fruitful for others were it not for criteria and modes of communication that differ from those of art." In particular, Nisbet mentions the need for sociologists to present their ideas in ways that others can test against the same kind of evidence. "No one asks a Picasso to verify one of his visions by repeating the process; and conversely, we properly give short shrift to ideas in science that no one but the author can find supported by experience" (Nisbet 1962: 156–157).

Yet, although sociologists are keen to establish the facts, they also appreciate that there are no facts without theories to interpret them. Facts do not speak for themselves. For example, in her study *The Time Bind* (1997), Arlie Hochschild found that statistics showed few people were taking advantage of new family-friendly employment policies allowing shorter hours, part-time work, parental leave, or flexible time. Rather than accept the conventional political explanation blaming economic pressure or organizational coercion, Hochschild drew on feminist theories about family and work in order to develop possible interpretations of the facts. She then tested these against

## media moments

### The Virginia Tech Murders

The need to both distinguish between and inter-twine the sociological and individual levels of explanation was put into bold relief in the days after the Virginia Tech murders in Blacksburg, Virginia, on April 16, 2007. On that tragic day, Cho Seung-Hui gunned down thirty-two of his fellow students, wounded many others, terrorized the campus, and triggered an anxious national conversation. Seung-Hui had come with his family to the United States as a child—just one of the tens of thousands of people who immigrate legally to this country each year. From a sociological perspective, he seems to have assimilated rapidly, majoring in English literature when he entered college ten years later. The same degree of integration did not occur in psychological terms. He remained an isolated loner, suffered severe mental problems, and felt persecuted by society.

When Seung-Hui engaged in his murderous mayhem, he transformed his private problems into public issues—"public" in the sense that the killings deeply affected hundreds of other people and abruptly engaged the legal order, but also by virtue of the cultural anxiety that followed in their wake. "You have vandalized my heart, raped my soul, and torched my conscience," Seung-Hui declared in one of the videos he mailed to NBC shortly before the suicide that ended his murder spree. "Thanks to you, I die like Jesus Christ to in-spire generations of the weak and the defenseless people." In these declarations, the young man was blaming society for his problems. And in the national discussion that followed, while nobody endorsed his heroic frame, there was wide agreement that Cho Seung-Hui's actions could not be understood outside their social context. Whether that context absolved him of personal responsibility is, of course, another story.

In this horrific crime and its aftermath, we find the fundamental elements of postmodernity.

1. *The media.* Sociologically inflected stories reverberate throughout the print, visual, and digital media. "What Made Him Do It?" *Newsweek* asked; "Why They Kill" the *Los Angeles Times* proposed. The killer took videos of himself and, in sending the package to a national television company, ensured its wide distribution after his death. Some cultural critics suggested that Seung-Hui had modeled the murders upon a grisly South Korean movie that appeared in 1996.
2. *Postindustrialism.* The setting for Seung-Hui's crime was not a village or a crowded city but a vast and sprawling educational institution—one specifically dedicated to training the scientists and engineers needed for postindustrial economies.
3. *Organization.* This institution—Virginia Tech—is a decentralized and fragmented organization, not a top-down bureaucracy. Although information about Seung-Hui's troubles had emerged from several sources over three years' time, it was never coordinated centrally and remained unavailable to concerned students and teachers. And, in any case, administrative and police authorities had limited options owing to strong protections for individual privacy.

**Postmodernity**  In sociology, a term referring to contemporary developments in historical, social, and economic processes. Unlike modernity, postmodernity is characterized by postindustrial economies, decentralized organization, the cultural turn, derationalization, multiculturalism, life cycle changes, new inequalities, and globalization.

4. *The self*. Questions have arisen as to whether Seung-Hui should be viewed not just as a lonely and pathologically disturbed individual but as a self whose care was a public responsibility. Was his rampage an effect of the antidepressant medication he was taking? Were Virginia Tech's mental health facilities adequate in terms of their diagnosis and support?

5. *Globalization*. More than 2 million ethnic Koreans had emigrated to the United States by the time the Virginia Tech murders occurred. Through television reports, newspapers, and websites, South Koreans back home closely monitored these events, worrying about possible international repercussions.

6. *Multiculturalism*. *New York Times* reporter Jennifer Steinhauer noted that "across the nation, Koreans have braced for harassment in the wake of the Monday shooting rampage," given "what many Koreans interviewed perceive to be ominous portraits of their culture" (2007: A19). One individual she interviewed, a Korean-American anthropology professor at UCLA, observed that "calling Cho Seung-Hui a South Korean native, as if he arrived yesterday, doesn't make sense to me" and that "characterizing the young man as a loner and antisocial fits the stereotype about Asian-American men, when in fact this person seems like a psycho." Steinhauer further noted that, according to the National Institute of Mental Health, "Asian-Americans are much less likely to seek care for mental health problems than other groups" (2007: A19).

Yet, even as Americans acknowledged these sociological factors, debate raged via blogs, radio waves, and editorial pages about whether, and how much, individual responsibility remained. In

The massacre at Virginia Tech echoed that at Columbine in many ways, but also highlighted important sociological differences. (Corbis)

the *New York Times,* liberal columnist Bob Herbert ridiculed the notion that "the periodic eruption of murderous violence ... was all so inexplicable" (2007: A27). Herbert put the blame squarely on social facts. Sounding very much like an academic sociologist, he insisted that there were "remarkable consistencies" among the "patterns of murderous violence ... wherever the individual atrocities may have occurred." He cited young men's anxieties about women and homosexuals and described how, according to American culture, feelings of shame can be balanced by violence. He also mentioned the fact that, in the United States, 200 million firearms are in private hands. On the same day, in the same place, conservative *New York Times* columnist David Brooks, while acknowledging that such a social focus is "important knowledge," warned that "it's had the effect of reducing the scope of the human self," of likening the individual to "a cork bobbing on the currents of giant forces." The danger, he added, is that "the scope for individual choice has been reduced, and with it so has the scope for morality" (Brooks 2007: A27).

people's testimonies as to the meanings they attached to time at home and at work. She found that for many middle-class people, work and home were changing places. Home was becoming more of a hassle. In her previous book, *The Second Shift* (1989), Hochschild had documented that, even as women were working more paid hours, they continued to receive relatively little help from their husbands at home. One of their responses has been to gradually abandon the home battle, shifting the emotional center of their lives to their work.

In the chapters that follow, we will trace the pathways of contemporary societies by presenting the newest empirical research. At the same time, we will be arranging the myriad of new social facts into theories—some big, some small. We want you to take away from *A Contemporary Introduction to Sociology* not only a bunch of new empirical facts but also new ways of thinking.

# EXERCISES

## Exercise 1

If you made a list of the most significant new developments in society during your lifetime, ranked in order of importance, what would it look like? (*New developments* could refer to anything of social significance: technologies, consumption, education, work, family life, attitudes toward the opposite sex or people from other ethnic groups, entertainment, politics, etc.) Jot down a few entries and then compare your list with that of your friends or classmates, if they have completed one.

It would also be interesting to ask your parents or grandparents to do the same and, again, to compare your list with theirs.

Of course, everybody's list will be different in some respects, but the similarities could provide

useful clues as to what we think are the most important social changes. The comparison with parents and grandparents could also tell us something about social changes in different historical periods. For example, changes in your own lifetime might include the rapid spread of access to information and communication via the Internet and the World Wide Web. Your parents may note that more than half of all the marriages that originated in their generation now end in divorce, whereas the latter was in the minority when they were children. And your grandparents may have a long list of the changes that have taken place since they grew up in the period after World War II, such as differences in the way children relate to their parents, changes in attitudes toward sexuality, a more ethnically mixed population, and so on.

## Exercise 2

Think about the possible links between private troubles and public issues in terms of problems affecting your own family, neighborhood, or town. Can you see how concerns that seem to arise in the private lives of individuals might be part of a bigger picture that includes changes in social structures and cultures? Are these troubles and issues different from those that might have been experienced by people living a hundred years ago?

# STUDY QUESTIONS

1. How does the sociological perspective challenge individualism?

2. What is the difference between personal troubles and public issues? Can you think of an example that falls into both categories?

3. Briefly describe Berger's four dimensions of sociological consciousness.

4. What do sociologists mean by *modernity* and *postmodernity?*

5. What is determinism? Describe sociological arguments against this position, and explain why both sides have been heatedly debated in the field.

6. What is the difference between structural and cultural approaches? Is either deterministic?

# FURTHER READING

Alexander, Jeffrey, C. 1995. *Fin de Siècle Social Theory.* London/New York: Verso.

Berger, Peter. 1963. *Invitation to Sociology: A Humanist Perspective.* New York: Doubleday. Reprinted in 1966.

Lash, Scott. 1990. *Sociology of Postmodernism.* London/New York: Routledge.

Loseke, Donileen, and Joel Best, eds. 2003. *Social Problems: Constructionist Readings.* New York: Aldin Transaction.

Mills, C. Wright. 1959. *The Sociological Imagination.* New York: Oxford University Press.

Newman, Katherine S., with Cybelle Fox, David Harding, Jal Mehta, and Wendy Roth. 2004. *Rampage: The Social Roots of School Shootings.* New York: Basic Books.

Ritzer, George, and Douglas J. Goodman. 2004. *Modern Sociological Theory.* New York: McGraw-Hill.

# chapter 2

# Sociological Methods

Once, it was thought that sociological research could be undertaken and understood only by an elite. In the nineteenth century the elite was composed of "armchair scholars," who attempted to explain the whole course of social development on the basis of information that they could find in the library. Auguste Comte, the reputed founder of sociology, even stopped reading after some years and practiced what he called "mental hygiene," which meant avoiding being "contaminated" by other people's writings. Needless to say, this is not a procedure that we recommend to sociology students who have exams to pass! After all, Comte had been a brilliant student and had read extremely widely before writing his major works. Karl Marx, another scholar whose work left a lasting mark on sociology, spent most of his time in the British Library in London, where he not only read books but also studied the statistics being gathered by government factory inspectors and local health officers. Herbert Spencer, also based in London, whose social evolutionary sociology had a major impact in America, was reputed to have done most of his reading in the Athenaeum, a gentlemen's club.

In the twentieth century, sociological research became a professional occupation and was directed by a new elite of trained scholars and researchers, based in universities and research centers. Exhaustive graduate training leading to a Ph.D. became the minimum entry requirement to this elite. The research model was that of the expensively funded natural sciences.

Interviews are one of the most important sociological tools. (iStockphoto)

One of the distinguishing features of the postmodern culture of the twenty-first century is that sociological thinking and research have spread through all levels of society. In a sense, then, sociology has been diversified and democratized, because all sorts of people undertake research and almost everyone is exposed to it. This is particularly true of the various kinds of sociological knowledge and research disseminated by the mass media. Society itself has become a kind of **text** into which diverse meanings are woven (see box titled "Society as Text").

How do you react to this kind of media research? Would you be inclined to regard it as scientifically sound and its findings valid, or do you find yourself asking critical questions about the methods the producers used? Bear in mind that, nowadays, television producers often have some knowledge of sociological research methods and findings, perhaps as a result of taking a sociology course or reading sociology books. They may even claim to be carrying out sociological studies, as in the case of renowned director Michael Apted, who, not content with merely making an entertaining documentary, claims in his television series *Married in America* to provide the basis of "a sociological study about what the institution of marriage

**Text** Anything, whether written or nonwritten, that is capable of carrying or conveying meaning. Society itself is a text, made up of multiple texts about social nature, social relationships, social processes, and so on.

**Sample** A portion of a population selected to be the subjects of a particular research project. In most cases a sample is expected to be a microcosm of the whole population in some respect, such that the findings are generalizable.

**theory**

## Society as Text: Documents, Artifacts, and Social Practices

Contrary to popular belief, sociological enquiry does not necessarily involve a large survey, a questionnaire and a researcher with more degrees than a thermometer! All of us are perfectly capable of engaged sociological thought—at any time, in any place. Constantly surrounded as we are by a ready supply of documents, artifacts, and social practices the sociologist can always find a rich and plentiful resource for his or her sociological imagination. ... C. Wright Mills' classic statement on the "sociological imagination" continues to provide a useful vantage point from which the changing nature of society and the social can be approached. Informed by a historical sense of change, a cross-cultural or anthropological understanding of difference, and a critical questioning stance to the nature and forms of contemporary society, the sociological imagination helps us to see and understand social processes—no matter how seemingly matter-of-fact or mundane. Moreover, it can help us to relate "personal troubles of milieu" to those wider "public issues" involving changing social structures. When directed at documents, artefacts and social practices the sociological imagination takes us into fascinating, often uncharted, territory, prompting new ways of seeing and even new departures for further sociological inquiry. ...

A narrow view of documents as written texts may blind us to the rich and increasingly plentiful, nonwritten texts that are produced, circulated and consumed in society. If a "text" is understood to be anything, written or nonwritten, that is capable of sustaining or being invested with meaning, clearly society itself becomes a "text" composed of a multitude of texts, promising to reveal much about its characteristic social nature, changing social relations and processes. ...

However, the meanings sustained by these "texts" do not simply reside within the texts themselves, but must be actively interpreted by the "reader." This, as we have seen, may well involve a consideration of the text's origins, purposes and its subsequent uses. The conditions under which it has been produced, circulated and consumed can all influence our interpretation, as can our own value position and interests.

*Source:* Cottle (1997).

means in America today" (see box titled "For Richer, for Poorer, and for a Documentary"). We will examine that claim in the next section, when we discuss basic research issues concerning **samples** and **interviews.** But, first, we need to consider this example of a mass-media documentary as part of a wider postmodern phenomenon of **infotainment.**

The mass media are constantly engaged in the systematic gathering and dissemination of information. Postmodern culture does not lack information; indeed, it may suffer from information overload. The mass media are part of our everyday

**Interview** A method of research whereby subjects are asked questions. Interviews can be formal, involving a set list of questions and topics to address, or informal, resembling a conversation or dialogue.

**Infotainment** A genre of mass media prevalent in postmodern society that provides research results, information, and knowledge in the form of an entertaining media product. Mass media documentaries are a good example of infotainment, inasmuch as they strive to be informative about a particular subject but also to entertain.

## media moments

### For Richer, for Poorer, and for a Documentary

When a couple named Chuck and Carol describe their impending marriage as "a miracle moment," they aren't kidding. In their 30s, they met at an Alcoholics Anonymous meeting. Between them they've had five previous marriages and five children. He has many tattoos and a prison record, for raping a woman with whom he'd had a relationship. They could barely scrape together the money they needed for a formal wedding, but that's what they wanted, white gown and all.

Michael Apted's documentary "Married in America" records their prenuptial concerns and their wedding, complete with the image of Chuck and Carol zooming off into their future on a motorcycle, with her dress's lacy train trailing behind. But Mr. Apted recognizes that miracle moments are indeed moments, and he plans to catch up with Chuck and Carol in a couple of years, to see how they're doing. They are among nine couples interviewed for Phase 1 of this smart and sensitive project, which begins tonight on A&E and concludes on Thursday.

This kind of real-life story has become familiar on television; TLC even has a regular daytime real-

ity program called "A Wedding Story." But Mr. Apted has a bigger ambition: to use the marital (or miracle) moment as the basis for a sociological study about what the institution of marriage means in America today. So he and his producers selected the couples demographically as well as telegenically. They include Mexican-Americans from California, Southerners, partners who are gay, mixed race and mixed religion, with varying levels of wealth and education.

In one sense, then, this three-hour film is a prologue, and Mr. Apted's gently leading questions serve two purposes: to convey some sense of character but also to establish a benchmark for future answers and behavior. When he asks, for example, if fidelity is important, you know that some of the affirmative answers will later prove to be lies.

You sense that the competitive young man who says he doesn't mind if his wife-to-be out-earns him may change his mind. You wonder how things will turn out for the couple already in counseling because they can't decide whether the children they don't yet have should be brought up Jewish or Catholic.

The questions go beyond the basics of "Where did you meet?" to address long-term concerns

lives, and we depend on them for much of our understanding of what goes on in the world. Compared with earlier generations, we are fortunate in having the mass media to bring the world into our living rooms. The problem is, we may tend to assume that what they bring is a fair reflection of that world, and that they observe the same rigorous standards as those of social science research. This is not to suggest that the mass media should be regarded suspiciously as inclined to be biased or

sloppy. Rather, it is a matter of raising questions about the differences between mass media procedures and reports, on the one hand, and those of social science, on the other. You can probably think of some of these differences for yourself, but here are some suggestions.

Because they are competing for attention with other media outlets, the mass media must give the "customers" what they want, or at least what can be afforded, bearing in mind that the media must like: Which partner is more ambitious? Who tends to take charge? The portraits become windows into the diversity of American life, which can seem so hopeful and accepting but also so strange and trashy. One couple celebrates with a Mexican feast in Baja California; another dances the hora at Walt Disney World, wearing Mickey Mouse ears.

Mr. Apted has had a successful career as a feature-film director, in a wide range that includes "Coal Miner's Daughter" and a James Bond picture, "The World Is Not Enough." But he began in television documentary; in 1964 he had the job of finding 14 British children for a film called "7 Up," which was intended as a study of the class system in England. Subsequently Mr. Apted revisited those children every seven years, most recently in 1999 with "42 Up." That marathon documentary series proved to be as transformative, lovely and absorbing as a fine novel.

Who knows if "Married in America" will resonate like that over time? In this documentary-saturated world it's far more difficult to capture the public imagination and hold it.

But these three hours deftly convey the optimism and poignancy—and sometimes foolishness—of people willing to gamble on marriage.

None of the couples are completely naïve: too many divorced parents in the background and other complications. For some, reality bites much too quickly: one couple from Lower Manhattan, honeymooning in Mexico, were in the air flying home when the World Trade Center was attacked.

Yet most of the couples seem willing—some astonishingly so—to overlook obvious gaps and questions. What will happen to Amber and Scott, the Southerners, who married three months after they met at a football game? They decide to figure out whether she'll take his name or hyphenate when they get their wedding license; they haven't discussed where they'd like to live but seem to have very different ideas about it.

Betty and Reggie met as children and have dated for years, so they are well aware of the raised eyebrows they inspire because she is white and he is black. Yet the interracial aspect seems almost incidental to them. They are more concerned about keeping their weight down and whether Reggie will abandon accounting, his career, for stand-up comedy, his dream. But then this film is about dreaming. The accounting will come later.

*Source:* Salamon (2002).

make a profit or at least balance their budget. So, unlike academic research, media coverage of a topic is partly determined by the criterion of what will attract or entertain consumers.

The information must be readily available and be presented in such a way that the consumers of the media can understand it. This places heavy demands on the information-gathering capacities of the media as well as on those who interpret and present the information (usually journalists). Frequently, journalists will call in experts, sociological researchers among them, to help them—but in the end it is the journalist who has to take the responsibility. Unlike professional social scientists, journalists do not have to qualify in research methods! They may present the results of social science research, but they are less likely to discuss and evaluate the methods used.

Limitations of time (deadlines) and space (column inches or program length) add to the pressures affecting what information is collected and how it is presented. The book-length research monograph does not have an equivalent in the mass media. In addition, the values and priorities of the media may not be the same as those they are reporting on, sometimes leading to unconscious bias even when fairness is intended. Journalism often depends on finding an "angle" that shapes the story. The angle may draw on various implicit theories or hypotheses, but not necessarily in a rigorous or testing way that would meet the standards expected in social science research. The angle is often more like a hunch or a slant.

The criteria for verifying whether media research results are valid are not spelled out or formally agreed upon. This contrasts with sociological research, in which such issues are constantly debated and there is a shared knowledge about the kinds of criteria that should be used in evaluating research methods—even in cases where specific disagreements have occurred.

These are just a few of the points that come to mind when considering the differences between media reports and sociology research reports. But there are also positive similarities. Both the journalist and the sociologist are interested in accurately describing and plausibly explaining some social phenomenon that they judge to be significant. And both professions are committed to certain values and standards, such as accuracy and fairness in the pursuit of truth. They may even use the same or similar sets of data, such as government statistics, surveys of attitudes and opinions based on questionnaires or in-depth interviews, and observations of people's behavior.

The key differences are in the natures of the two institutions—the media and the scientific community. The latter has been developing as an institution over several centuries and sociology has accepted its rules, while insisting on the distinctive character of its human subject matter. The mass media, by contrast, are a relatively new institution. Although small-circulation and short-lived newspapers began to appear in the seventeenth century, mass-circulation newspapers date from the nineteenth century. The electronic mass media—film, television, and radio—developed in the postmodern period, which started around the mid-twentieth century. They were not around during the time of the classical sociologists—namely, Emile Durkheim and Max Weber. Even the sociologists of the immediate post–World War II era tended to regard just a few newspapers, such as the *New York Times* and the *Washington Post*, as the only serious mass media of information. The way in which television has developed since then has not reassured sociologists about the seriousness of the medium as a reliable means of gathering data and presenting findings, for some of the reasons that we mentioned above. And yet, television is tremendously active and influential in providing the general public with versions of sociological knowledge that cannot be ignored (see box titled "Conceptualizing and Investigating the Viewing Culture").

The postmodern dilemma about knowledge is that there is so much of it, and in such a variety of forms, that it is difficult to sift through and evaluate. This is why an understanding of the basics of social scientific research and analysis is vital. The task is complicated by the fact that sociologists themselves are engaged in lively debates about the validity of different types of research and analysis. Feminists have objected that some well-established methods of research and analysis are undertaken from a masculine position that neglects women's perspective and experience. Similar arguments have been made by gays and lesbians, and other groups, such as nonwhites and nonwesterners. The question of "relativism" then becomes unavoidable. Is all knowledge, including "scientific knowledge," only relatively valid, its validity restricted by the fact that it derives from a limited perspective? And if this is so, are all perspectives or standpoints equally valid? Before trying to answer these questions, we will look at some of the basic terms used in various types of sociological research and analysis.

**data**

## Conceptualizing and Investigating the Viewing Culture: Research Strategy and Methods

Generally speaking, conceptualizing television use involves reconstructing the practical ways in which people who watch television situate themselves with the medium on a day-in, day-out basis. Contrary to appearances, television use is a multifaceted activity, one that is much more complicated than it seems. Assessing its meaning for people and the significance it carries in their lives involves nothing short of the analytical reconstruction of it as a distinctive kind of culture. I have referred to this elsewhere as the "viewing culture."

My strategy of empirical research, beginning in 1987, was to reconstruct people's social experience with television across the different, yet interrelated phases of the viewing culture: the turn to television, interaction with television imagery, and leaving television and fitting it back into daily life. I used a variety of methods to do this. The bulk of my empirical documentation came from 60 two-hour interviews with wage and salaried workers. I also spent considerable time watching television with people (participant observation), and in addition, I asked a smaller number of people to fill out viewer diaries.

In carrying out my field research and in conducting depth interviews, it was my intention from the very start to account for the social relations that were a part of people's television use. Virtually all research perspectives acknowledge (even if they don't focus on it) that what people do with one another can mediate the power of television in important ways, in some cases amplifying it and in other cases deflecting and qualifying it. I documented the social interactions and the group life that often shaped what happened in the home, but I also focused on capturing individual thoughts and feelings that emerged both when people watched with others and when they were alone. A good deal of the mindful encounters that people have with objects in their world, such as with television and with other people, can be socially constituted, without it ever having to find outer expression, either in words or actions. ...

Approximately 25 of the 60 people that I interviewed did not typically separate their turn to television from their turn to other activities. Instead, they said that they turned to television and other activities at the same time. This way of watching television represented one of the most significant, and unanticipated, findings that emerged from my research. I have come to refer to this particular use of television as viewing while simultaneously participating in other activities, or more simply, simultaneous viewing. ...

As a quite common viewing practice, simultaneous viewing is also indicative of our entry, as a society, into a new historical era, one marked increasingly by the corporate production of goods, ideas, and imagery of all kinds—not just television imagery. ... As I see it, this is not simply another cycle or stage of modern dilemmas regarding individual identity and community formation. It is, instead, a distinctly postmodern condition. This proliferation of image-worlds generates disjunctures, a time and space of split-off experiences, in which continuity doesn't occur, meanings don't add up to anything, people no longer construct a developmental course to things, and unified experience is no longer a given.

*Source:* Lembo (1997: 203–233).

## SOME KEY RESEARCH TERMS

What does it mean to select a sample of a population? In support of Michael Apted's claim to be undertaking sociological research, a commentator on *Married in America* states that Apted and his producers "selected the couples demographically as well as telegenically." In other words, he tried to cover a representative sample of the American population. A sample is a small number of individuals drawn from a larger population. A **representative sample** (also called a *stratified sample*) is one that aims to provide an accurate representation of the different sections that make up the population, distinguished by attributes such as race, religion, income, location, education, and sexual preference. (This contrasts with a **random sample,** which is selected purely statistically—as when, say, every tenth person in the population is chosen for

---

**Representative sample** (or *stratified sample*)  A sample that accurately represents the various attributes (e.g., race, religion, income, age, gender) found in the whole population.

**Random sample**  A sample that is selected purely statistically. For example, a random sample might include every tenth person in a population, or every hundredth person.

**Snowball sample**  A sample created through a process whereby the researcher asks the first few interviewees for the names of other individuals who might fit the study, then asks those individuals for names, and so on. The problem with snowball samples is that they may be heavily skewed toward particular demographics, because people tend to know and recommend others like themselves.

**Survey**  A method of research whereby information is gathered from a sample of a population about a specific list of variables and questions.

**Opinion poll**  A type of sociological survey in which the members of a population sample are asked about their attitudes and beliefs on a wide range of issues. An example is the General Social Survey (GSS), which asks a nationwide random sample of at least 1,500 respondents to address issues such as capital punishment, family statistics, and religiosity.

---

a sample.) In fact, Apted's sample might more accurately be termed a *purposive sample*, on the grounds that he selected people on the basis that they were likely to be relevant to the subject he was studying. The drawback of such a sample is that it reflects the prior judgments of the researcher-producer, which may be open to question, especially as another criterion of selection was that the participants should be "telegenic." Presumably, boringly "average" people were not selected because they were not sufficiently interesting or attractive. Another intention was to do follow-up interviews with the couples after a certain period of time, and this resembles the kind of sample referred to as a *panel sample,* whereby the same group of people is studied at intervals in order to record any changes. Sometimes, for convenience, a researcher may use a **snowball sample,** which involves asking the first few interviewees for the names of other people who might fit the criteria of the study. This is probably the most problematic type of sample, because it depends so much on the recommendations of a small number of people, who, in turn, are likely to recommend people like themselves.

Modern **survey** techniques rely on random sampling, making it possible for social scientists to use relatively small samples to arrive at generalizations about an entire population. For example, election polls using a sample of 1,500 to 2,000 respondents may be used to predict the distribution of votes in a presidential election. Such surveys are used not just for election polling but for many other sociological and governmental data-gathering purposes as well. For example, the U.S. Census Bureau's Current Population Survey (CPS) uses sample surveys to provide monthly estimates of marriages, divorces, births, deaths, poverty, employment and unemployment, and many other social indicators.

**Opinion polls** are another form of sociological survey that is widely used by governmental and other agencies. One of the best known of these is the General Social Survey (GSS) conducted by

## United States Census 2000

**U.S. Department of Commerce • Bureau of the Census**

This is the official form for all the people at this address. It is quick and easy, and your answers are protected by law. Complete the Census and help your community get what it needs — today and in the future!

## Start Here
*Please use a black or blue pen.*

**1. How many people were living or staying in this house, apartment, or mobile home on April 1, 2000?**

Number of people

**INCLUDE** in this number:
- foster children, roomers, or housemates
- people staying here on April 1, 2000 who have no other permanent place to stay
- people living here most of the time while working, even if they have another place to live

**DO NOT INCLUDE** in this number:
- college students living away while attending college
- people in a correctional facility, nursing home, or mental hospital on April 1, 2000
- Armed Forces personnel living somewhere else
- people who live or stay at another place most of the time

**2. Is this house, apartment, or mobile home —** *Mark* ☒ *ONE box.*
- ☐ Owned by you or someone in this household with a mortgage or loan?
- ☐ Owned by you or someone in this household free and clear (without a mortgage or loan)?
- ☐ Rented for cash rent?
- ☐ Occupied without payment of cash rent?

**3.** Please answer the following questions for each person living in this house, apartment, or mobile home. Start with the name of one of the people living here who owns, is buying, or rents this house, apartment, or mobile home. If there is no such person, start with any adult living or staying here. We will refer to this person as Person 1.

**What is this person's name?** *Print name below.*

Last Name

First Name                                    MI

**4. What is Person 1's telephone number?** *We may call this person if we don't understand an answer.*

Area Code + Number

**5. What is Person 1's sex?** *Mark* ☒ *ONE box.*
- ☐ Male    ☐ Female

**6. What is Person 1's age and what is Person 1's date of birth?**

Age on April 1, 2000

*Print numbers in boxes*

Month    Day    Year of birth

➡ **NOTE:  Please answer BOTH Questions 7 and 8.**

**7. Is Person 1 Spanish/Hispanic/Latino?** *Mark* ☒ *the "No" box if not Spanish/Hispanic/Latino.*
- ☐ **No,** not Spanish/Hispanic/Latino
- ☐ Yes, Mexican, Mexican Am., Chicano
- ☐ Yes, other Spanish/Hispanic/Latino — *Print group.* ↗
- ☐ Yes, Puerto Rican
- ☐ Yes, Cuban

**8. What is Person 1's race?** *Mark* ☒ *one or more races* to indicate what this person considers himself/herself to be.
- ☐ White
- ☐ Black, African Am., or Negro
- ☐ American Indian or Alaska Native — *Print name of enrolled or principal tribe.* ↗

- ☐ Asian Indian
- ☐ Chinese
- ☐ Filipino
- ☐ Other Asian — *Print race.* ↗
- ☐ Japanese
- ☐ Korean
- ☐ Vietnamese
- ☐ Native Hawaiian
- ☐ Guamanian or Chamorro
- ☐ Samoan
- ☐ Other Pacific Islander — *Print race.* ↗

- ☐ Some other race — *Print race.* ↗

➡ **If more people live here, continue with Person 2.**

OMB No. 0607-0856: Approval Expires 12/31/2000

Form **D-61A**

The U.S. Census, taken every ten years, gathers crucial data that sociologists use to analyze American society. (U.S. Census Bureau) the National Opinion Research Center (NORC). Using a nationwide random sample of at least 1,500 respondents, the GSS is able to generalize about the whole American adult population's opinions on a wide range of selected issues.

## CONCEPTS AND THEORIES

In some respects, media documentaries and sociological research are similar in their resemblance to detective work. Sometimes there are brilliant insights; at other times it seems to be more a matter of sifting through evidence to find clues and then meeting with failure or success in finding a solution. The aim in all three contexts is to get at the truth or the facts about something that is a puzzle. What constitutes the puzzle for sociologists is different from that which presents itself to the television producer or the detective. The detective has to solve a crime, whereas the sociologist has to solve a puzzle about society. The detective's object of study—a crime—is defined by the law and how the police and the legal system interpret the law in each case. The sociologist's puzzle is defined by his or her application of sociological concepts and theories. The television producer may seem to be investigating the same puzzle as the sociologist, such as what factors are affecting people's decisions about marriage? The difference is that the television producer—in this case, Michael Apted—need not be explicit about concepts and theories (although these may be implicit in the way he chooses to angle the program). The sociologist is not permitted such license.

Concepts and theories are important for the sociological researcher because they make it possible to pose relevant questions about social phenomena in ways that indicate clearly what would constitute an adequate answer. A **concept** is a mental construct that represents some aspect of the world in simplified form. It may also be a category or classification, such as social class, race, or gender. People can then be classified in these terms—for example, as upper-class, middle-class, or lower-class; black or white; male or female.

A **variable** is a concept whose value changes from case to case. This changing value is demonstrated by an indicator. According to Weberian theory (deriving from the sociologist Max Weber), for example, income is the key indicator for deciding the variable of class. A researcher would be interested in discovering whether two variables seem to change their values in tandem, as this might mean there is a relation between them—a **correlation**. However, a correlation does not mean that one variable is the cause of the other's change. During summer, there appears to be both a rise in ice cream sales and a rise in sports participation. This is a correlation. It would be erroneous, obviously, to assume any causal relation. Ice cream eating does not cause sports participation, or (usually!) vice versa. It may be the operation of a third variable—hot weather—that explains the correlation, in the sense of specifying a cause. In developing causal explanations, it is customary to distinguish between an independent variable and a dependent variable. An **independent variable** is a factor that causes change in another variable—namely, the **dependent variable.**

**Concept**  A mental construct that represents some part of the world in a simplified form. A concept might also be a category or classification, such as race, gender, or social class.

**Variable**  A concept whose value changes from case to case. The changing value is noted by an indicator. For example, income might be an indicator of the variable *class*.

**Correlation**  A term that refers to the relationship between two variables whose values change together. It is important to note, however, that correlation does not imply causation. For example, in wintertime, people tend to wear scarves and car accidents tend to occur more often. Increased scarf wearing and increased car accidents are correlated, but this does not mean that wearing a scarf causes car accidents.

Concepts and variables, and the causal processes they lay out, are linked together to make up a theory. A **social theory** is an organizing framework of concepts, based on empirical evidence, that explains why society, or some aspect of society, works as it does. Facts do not speak for themselves. We need a theory to guide us in gathering, ordering, and interpreting facts. An **explanatory theory** contains one or more hypotheses about cause and effect, proposing that a specified independent variable is the cause of an effect on a dependent variable. (A *hypothesis* is a conjecture that relates two or more concepts.) A famous example in sociology is Durkheim's theory of social integration, according to which he posited that for every society there is an optimum level of social integration. From this he made deductions about the probable occurrence of various social problems, such as suicide, when social integration is weakened. In particular, he deduced that a decrease in social integration (independent variable) would cause an increase in the suicide rate (dependent variable) (Durkheim 1897). Using this theory, Durkheim went on to test more specific hypotheses. Protestants would have higher rates of suicide than Catholics, he hypothesized, because Protestantism is more individualist and produces less forceful social integration. (Jews ranked even higher than Catholics on social integration and had lower suicide rates.) Durkheim tested his theory of suicide by making statistical samples of suicides and then testing them, in turn, by seeing if there were correlations with other variables. His results seemed to validate the theory, as regions or countries with higher numbers of Protestants than Catholics did have higher rates of suicide.

Durkheim's study, *Suicide*, provides one of the earliest examples in sociology of the use of *secondary data*—information collected for another purpose often, as in this case, by governments. Its chief advantage is that it can provide the sociologist with extensive statistical or other information that is not readily available or would be costly and time-consuming to gather. The disadvantage is that it is usually collected for some other purpose than that envisaged by the sociologist, and so it may have to be adapted or reinterpreted. In the case of suicide statistics, Durkheim had to bring together data from different government sources and different dates. He was also conscious that societies differed in their attitudes to suicide and that this might have affected the figures. Despite these problems, he decided that the figures were sufficiently reliable to make it worth advancing conclusions (e.g., "Thus, everywhere, without exception, Protestants show far more suicides than the followers of other confessions") on the basis of data such as those shown in Table 2.1.

Because Durkheim believed that sociological explanation (like exploration in the natural sciences) should be based on externally observable factors, he rejected explanations in terms of individuals' internal motives and purposes. He sought to formulate his explanations solely in terms of externally observable rates of covariation of variables. So, variations in the recorded rates of suicide corresponded to variations in the rate of social integration between religious denominations: Protestant doctrines and practices encouraged individual

**Independent variable** A variable that causes change in another factor. In our wintertime example, weather can be considered an independent variable, since ice, snow, and cold temperatures cause people to wear scarves and can increase car accidents.

**Dependent variable** A variable that changes as a result of independent variables. In our wintertime example, scarf wearing and car accidents are the dependent variables.

**Social theory** A framework based on empirical evidence that is used to organize concepts, and that explains why society or some aspect of society functions as it does.

**Explanatory theory** A theory that has one or more causal hypotheses suggesting that a particular independent variable causes a particular effect on the dependent variable.

**TABLE 2.1  Suicides in Different Countries per Million Persons of Each Faith**

|  |  | Protestants | Catholics | Jews |
|---|---|---|---|---|
| Austria | (1852–59) | 79.5 | 51.3 | 20.7 |
| Prussia | (1849–55) | 159.9 | 49.6 | 46.4 |
| Prussia | (1869–72) | 187 | 69 | 96 |
| Prussia | (1890) | 240 | 100 | 180 |
| Baden | (1852–62) | 139 | 117 | 87 |
| Baden | (1870–74) | 171 | 136.7 | 124 |
| Baden | (1878–88) | 242 | 170 | 210 |
| Bavaria | (1844–56) | 135.4 | 49.1 | 105.9 |
| Bavaria | (1884–91) | 224 | 94 | 193 |
| Württemberg | (1846–60) | 113.5 | 77.9 | 65.6 |
| Württemberg | (1873–76) | 190 | 120 | 60 |
| Württemberg | (1881–90) | 170 | 119 | 142 |

*Source:* Adapted from Durkheim (1951 [1897], 154).

responsibility, whereas Catholicism offered absolution for sins through the ministration of the priest. Jews, in Durkheim's day, were supported by the close-knit bonds of the ghetto and, hypothetically as a result of this high level of social integration, had the lowest rates of suicide.

Sociologists following the example of Max Weber and his **interpretive sociology** have taken a different approach to explanation, insisting that sociological explanations should try to interpret

**Interpretive sociology** A form of sociology that bases its approach to the task of sociological explanation on the assumption that social actions can be fully understood only by interpreting the motives and meanings that guide individuals' actions.

the motives and meanings that lie behind the actions of individuals. In the context of explaining suicide, J. Jacobs (1970) examined suicide notes in order to find the reasoning used by would-be suicides in overcoming the moral prohibitions against suicide found in each of the three religions. Like Weber, Jacobs believed it is possible to reconstruct typical processes of reasoning that make it possible to put forward general explanations (as opposed to those specific to an individual). After studying the reasoning in a sample of suicide notes, Jacobs pointed to differences among the religious groups in their moral evaluation of suicide.

Comparing the beliefs taught by Christianity to Judaism, he argued on the basis of his evidence about motives that Christianity promises rewards in the hereafter whereas Judaism does not, and that Christians represent their deaths as "going to heaven" whereas Jews do not. Jacobs suggested that what encourages potential Christian suicides is their ability to convince themselves of ending an intolerable life on earth and obtaining a better one in the beyond. On these grounds, Jews will have a lower suicide rate than Christians, whether Catholic or Protestant. Protestantism is more rationalistic than Catholicism and stresses the ability of the individual to work out his or her own balance sheet of salvation. Catholicism lays greater stress on the supremacy of dogma. Therefore, Protestants will find it easier to construct a justification of their suicide than will Catholics, who are more constrained by the dogmatic prohibition of suicide.

Jacobs thus arrived at an explanation of the same observed differences in religious suicide rates that Durkheim found. However, it is a very different form of explanation. Jacobs constructed schemes of motives for suicide that could be shown to typify the different religious groups and, in this sense, arrived at causes for suicide that were intelligible for being "understandable." In contrast, Durkheim's explanation was deliberately free of any terms that would ascribe purposes or motives to the individual.

Both explanations could be considered correct, since they both predict the effect of the religious factor in the same way. So, the choice between the explanations depends on what the researcher considers to be an "adequate" explanation. Those who, like Durkheim, believe sociology should follow the model of explanation favored by the natural sciences do not emphasize the distinctive nature of human action—the role played by cultural meanings and emotional motives. Others, like Jacobs, following Weber's lead, would insist on explanations that link remote causes (such as social integration) and effects (suicide rates), whereby the necessary link is provided by an understandable scheme of motives. They would argue that Durkheim's explanation can be made "intelligible" only by the addition of certain assumptions about how individuals react to different levels of social integra-

tion. In other words, if one added a subsidiary theory containing hypotheses such as "a subject's experience of low social integration produces subjective feelings of purposelessness," these individual suicides could be explained. However, Durkheim did not think that sociology could use concepts relating to individual purposes or inner feelings. In this respect, he was attempting to follow the *hypothetical-deductive model* of natural science.

Science aims to establish certain laws based on predictable and reliable theories about causal relationships between dependent and independent variables. And, indeed, Durkheim believed that his theory of social integration would provide such laws in sociology. But critics have objected on two counts. The first is that sociological theories are far below the level of precision achieved in natural science. Durkheim's theory of social integration is said to suffer from this lack of precision. It is difficult, for example, to be precise about what is meant by *social integration*—the bonds between individuals that constitute social integration are not objective and visible but rather vague and indistinct. The other, more radical criticism is the one we have been discussing: The natural science form of explanation is said to be inappropriate for sociological explanations of human actions. Two reasons are given for this. Human actors (unlike the "objects" of physics) follow rules in deciding on and carrying out their actions, rather than responding mechanically to scientific laws. Order and regularity in social life stem from the sharing of common beliefs, values, and purposes among individuals in society. Behavior becomes understandable only when we find out *why* certain actions are being performed. If we see a roomful of students frantically writing in bluebooks, we may explain their behavior by finding out that they are taking a sociology exam. Their actions are intelligible to us, and thus explained, when we come to know the purpose behind what they are doing. Conversely, a researcher who does not share, or cannot readily imagine, a culture in common with those she is studying may be unable to understand the purpose of actions she observes. Australian aborigines' ritual of killing and eating a totemic animal puzzled anthropologists until they were able to learn the aborigines' own reasons why their ritual was performed. (Interestingly, Durkheim used the same kind of anthropological data in his last great book, *The Elementary Forms of Religious Life* [1912], suggesting that he was more flexible about models of sociological explanation than was evident either in *Suicide* [1897] or in his earlier book, *The Rules of Sociological Method* [1895]— both of which insisted, as we have seen, on examining social facts as "things," from the outside.) What is true of exotic tribal people is true in a less dramatic way of street gangs; they, too, have their own cultures, and these need to be understood by the academic researcher before he or she can comprehend and explain their actions.

Thus far, we have contrasted two forms of sociological explanation as extremes. In actual research, however, since a sociologist may well use aspects of both forms, the opposition between ways of explaining social patterns is not always so stark. Still, the two poles of the hypothetical-deductive model—sometimes referred to as a *covering-law explanation*, on the one hand, and as the *interpretive approach* or *explanation-by-understanding method*, on the other—are real and have consequences for the choice of methods adopted by the researcher. Explanation by understanding requires evidence of meaning—the purposes and motives of individuals and groups—and so usually requires methods such as participant observation (joining in with those being studied) or documentary research (written documents, such as files, government reports, and personal diaries; and visual documents, such as photographs or films). Covering-law explanations ideally prefer to use quantified concepts of observable behavior (such as divorce rates) in which the element of motive or purpose is lost, owing to the emphasis placed on the need for precise models and hypotheses.

Quantification is one way of looking for precision. Careful qualitative research can also be "precise," but it is harder to put qualitative hypotheses in a form that can be rigorously replicated—namely, in the form of tests that the covering-law model of explanation requires. The use of interviewers to administer questionnaire surveys of attitudes and opinions, perhaps supplemented by observation of actual behavior, is one way in which researchers have tried to bridge the gap between quantification and qualitative understanding of motives and meanings.

In short, opinions differ among sociologists as to what is an adequate explanation. The covering-law model requires theories with precisely stated hypotheses and explanations that take the form of validly deducing a conclusion. A good or well-grounded theory is one that has withstood determined attempts to falsify one or more of its hypotheses. And, indeed, application of the covering-law model in sociology is often held back by the weakness of sociological theories (imprecise hypotheses) that are difficult to test. Alternatively, the explanation-by-understanding model is a scheme of explanation in which the purposive nature of human action is recognized, with the result that culture and meaning become necessary parts of the sociological theory in question. This purposive nature of action requires a scheme of explanation that makes human action intelligible. Each of the two forms of explanation has its preferred research methods.

As noted earlier, sociologists often use a combination of approaches and methods. Most researchers are reconciled to the fact that sociological theories cannot be as precise and quantifiable as natural science theories and thus tend to be rather tentative and "sensitizing"—composed of hypotheses suggesting what connections may exist between variables and where to look for possible relations of cause and effect. At some point, then, such theories are likely to depend on assumptions about the typical motives and meanings of those involved in the action being described or explained. This is one unavoidable reason for the relativism of sociological theory. To understand *motive*, we must be thoroughly enmeshed in our own time, or at least believe ourselves to be.

## METHODOLOGY AND METHODS

There is a wide range of research methods available to sociologists. Why some methods are chosen rather than others, and what the different methods are intended to do, is the subject of methodology (literally: the study of methods). The methodological reasons for choosing a particular research method (or combination of methods) may reflect a preference for either the natural science model of explanation or the interpretive approach. If it is the former, then there will be a desire to employ methods that produce **quantitative** data (i.e., in the form of numbers or statistics). If the preference is for the interpretive approach, then the inclination will be to use methods that produce **qualitative** data (i.e., in the form of words).

In principle, methods are simply technical tools for getting a job done. But, in practice, methodological reasons may lie behind the choice of a particular method or set of methods for a research project:

In a sense, methods are a-theoretical and a-methodological (meaning, independent from methodology). Interviews, for instance, like observation, experiments, content analysis, etc., can be used in any methodology type, and serve any chosen research purpose. The same methods can be used in the context of different methodologies, and the same methodology can employ different methods. ...

Nevertheless, although methods are in general a-methodological, their content structure and process are dictated by an underlying methodology. Although interviews, for instance, can be

used in a qualitative and a quantitative methodology, the former employs an unstructured, open or in-depth interview, while the latter normally opts for a standardized interview. In a similar vein, participant observation is used in qualitative studies while structured observation is employed in quantitative studies. (Sarantakos 1993: 33)

Quantitative data in the form of statistics are useful because they allow researchers to consider trends over time. Statistics have also become the common currency for making public comparisons between groups. For example, we could compare church attendance rates for various income groups. If there seemed to be a correlation, such as "the lower the income, the higher the church attendance," we might hypothesize that the two variables are linked in some way. But remember, the fact that there is a correlation between two variables does not necessarily mean that one has caused the other. There may be another variable that intervenes (an intervening variable). For example, it could be a difference in ethnic origin that has led to the correlation between church attendance and income, with poor Mexican-American Catholics ranking higher on church attendance but lower on income, compared with white Anglo-Saxon Protestants. (In fact, the links between income and church attendance vary considerably, because there are, indeed, many intervening variables, including not only ethnicity but such other

**Quantitative** Referring to research that relies on numerical or statistical data for calculating findings. Quantitative research is typically used in cases where one is trying to apply a natural science model of explanation, as opposed to an interpretive model.

**Qualitative** Relating to research that is typically used in cases where one is taking an interpretive approach. The data are often textual; examples include interview transcripts and ethnographic field notes.

cultural factors as differences between religious denominations.) Sociologists who prefer a qualitative methodology are likely to want to emphasize the importance of getting at the motives and meanings that lie behind people's actions. In our example of the correlation between church attendance and income or ethnicity, they would concentrate on posing probing questions about what church attendance means to people from a particular income or ethnic group.

The availability of computers has made it possible to manipulate large bodies of statistical data very quickly, making it relatively easy for sociologists to obtain findings from social surveys with large samples. In addition, computers can be used for reanalysis of data, so that sociologists years from now can reuse data that had been collected earlier. They also enable sociologists to make large-scale comparisons between groups; consider, for instance, the cross-national comparisons that yield statistics on health, education, poverty, and so on that are compiled by the United Nations and its agencies.

Despite these advantages, quantitative methods have some drawbacks as well. In the case of *descriptive statistics* (numbers that communicate characteristics of a population, such as income, marital status, race, or ethnic background), the disadvantage may be that they do not go into sufficient detail and so gloss over significant differences. For example, the U.S. Bureau of Justice uses "racial" categories, such as "whites, blacks, American Indians, and Asians," in tables of statistics on "Violent Victimization and Race." But there are various ethnic groups included within the very broad category "Asians" (e.g., Chinese, Indian, and Japanese), and the possibility that these ethnicities are associated with very different

cultures may be highly significant with respect to violence and crime. Another sort of problem emerges when quantitative sociologists wish to use *secondary statistics* (statistics first collected earlier for another purpose). The fact that someone else collected them for a different purpose may mean that they are not suitable for reuse without adaptation, and the process of adaptation may distort the findings.

The **census** is a specific form of social survey, using questions designed to gather information that will provide a description of a whole population (see box titled "Social Survey Methods"). There are other types of survey research, too, as we will see in subsequent chapters dealing with topics that have attracted academic researchers using surveys. However, the two main types are the interviewer-administered questionnaire and the self-administered questionnaire. Whichever type is used, the basic characteristics of the survey method are as follows:

1. The survey method requires that a sample of respondents reply to a number of fixed questions under comparable conditions.
2. The survey must be administered by an interviewer who completes a form for each respondent by asking him or her the survey questions; alternatively, a form on which the questions are printed is sent to each respondent for self-completion.
3. The respondents in the survey represent a defined population. If all the members of a population are interviewed or fill in a self-completion form, then a *census* (i.e., a 100 percent sample survey) has been taken. If only a fraction of the population is covered, then a *sample survey* has been conducted.
4. A sample survey should be representative of its population. If it is, then we can generalize results from the sample to the population.
5. By using the same questions for a sample of respondents, we can make comparisons of individuals within the sample.

**Census** A type of social survey in which the questions are designed to gather information that is descriptive of an entire population.

**data**

## Social Survey Methods

*The most famous and extensive form of social survey is the national census, such as that carried out by the U.S. Census Bureau, described below.*

Fact-finding is one of America's oldest activities. In the early 1600s, a census was taken in Virginia, and people were counted in nearly all of the British colonies that later became the United States.

Following independence, there was an almost immediate need for a census of the entire nation. The first census was taken in 1790, under the responsibility of Secretary of State Thomas Jefferson. That census, taken by U.S. marshals on horseback, counted 3.9 million inhabitants.

As America grew, the nation's interests grew more complex. The country needed *statistics* to help people understand what was happening and to plan for growth, and the content of the decennial census changed accordingly. In 1810, the census was expanded to obtain information on the manufacturing, quantity and value of products. In 1840, the census added questions on fisheries. And, in 1850, the census collected data on issues such as taxation, churches, pauperism and crime.

Over the decades, censuses spread to new states and areas under U.S. sovereignty or jurisdiction. There were so many inquiries and so many new geographic entities in the census of 1880 that it took almost a full decade to tabulate and publish the results. This led to the first use of tabulating machines in the 1890 census, which counted nearly 63 million people. These punch-card machines, invented by former Census Bureau employee Herman Hollerith, evolved into computers when Hollerith founded what was to become the IBM Corp. Throughout its existence, the Census Bureau has played a pioneering role in the use of technology to fulfill its role as "America's Fact Finder."

As America grew, changes in the economy became more frequent and far-reaching. Since government officials and businesses had to adjust their plans as these changes occurred, they needed more frequent reports on them. To meet these needs, the Census Bureau became a permanent institution by an act of Congress in 1902.

Today, in addition to taking a census of the population every 10 years, the Census Bureau conducts censuses of economic activity and state and local governments every five years. And *every year,* the Census Bureau conducts more than 100 other surveys.

The sole purpose of the censuses and surveys is to collect general statistical information from individuals and establishments in order to compile statistics. The confidentiality of replies is important. By law, no one—neither the census-takers nor any other Census Bureau employee—is permitted to reveal information that could identify any person, household or business.

The Census Bureau employs nearly 12,000 people. The workforce expands dramatically when the census is taken every 10 years. About 860,000 temporary workers were hired for Census 2000.

The Census Bureau is headed by a director, who is appointed by the President with the advice and consent of the U.S. Senate. Headquartered just outside Washington in Suitland, Md., the Census Bureau has 12 regional offices, in Atlanta, Boston, Charlotte, Chicago, Dallas, Denver, Detroit, Kansas City, Los Angeles, New York, Philadelphia and Seattle, and a processing center in Jeffersonville, Ind. Call centers are located in Hagerstown, Md., and Tucson, Ariz. A computer facility is housed at Bowie, Md.

*Source:* U.S. Census Bureau (2003).

The advantages of the social survey method are that it allows information from large samples to be collected quickly and relatively cheaply, and it allows comparisons among individuals because answers to questions are comparable. The main disadvantage, compared with participant observation, is that it may be superficial in measuring sensitive or difficult aspects of behavior. A researcher can minimize this oversimplification of replies by testing questions on a small part of the sample beforehand, using a less structured and more conversational method of interview in which replies are probed more deeply than is possible in the full-scale survey in the main sample. Well-conducted surveys often utilize a number of *"pilot" interviews* before the main questionnaire is finalized.

All surveys are structured to some extent, even though the more open and conversational forms of interviewing are sometimes referred to as "unstructured." In the category of highly structured methods of asking questions, the two main ones—the *self-administered questionnaire* and the *interview schedule*—have many points in common. Note, however, that the interviewer-administered questionnaire allows for more control over the interview situation than does the self-administered questionnaire, which is either sent by mail or administered to a group such as workers in an office or factory.

The interviewer (or a *coder* working after the event) should be able to organize the responses to any question into a set of mutually exclusive and exhaustive categories, such as "Yes," "No," and "Don't know." A less simple categorization of responses—named after its inventor, Rensis Likert—involves coding into one of five or seven categories. Typical Likert categories are as follows:

Strongly agree
Agree
Neither agree nor disagree
Disagree
Strongly disagree

(with a particular statement).

This is a fivefold Likert categorization. (Sevenfold categorizations, by contrast, list three categories on either side of the neutral category of "Neither agree nor disagree.") The language used for these categories either invites agreement with a given statement or asks for responses to a question that the interviewer then has to code into a specific category. An example using a fivefold Likert scale can be found in this statement from a study of Americans' views of the police as a public service: "How would you rate the overall quality of police services in your neighbourhood? Remember, we mean the two or three blocks around your home. Are they outstanding, good, adequate, inadequate, or very poor?" (paraphrasing Zeller and Carmines 1980).

## Questionnaire Surveys

A popular quantitative method (or research instrument) is the questionnaire survey, which is often composed of closed questions that allow only a limited number of possible responses. Often these responses are written on the questionnaire itself, where a space or box is allocated for a tick or cross. Another kind of closed question elicits attitudes of people by providing them with a set of scales ranging from "strongly agree" to "strongly disagree" or some other set. For example, a survey of people's attitudes toward their neighborhood might ask a closed question such as "Which answer best sums up your feelings about the number of shops in your neighborhood?"

Too few
About right
Too many
Don't know

Alternatively, questions may be more open-ended, and these are capable of producing data that are more qualitative. Here the respondents are provided with spaces in which they can construct their own answers. For example: "How do you feel about the shopping facilities in your neighborhood?" Although open-ended questions are more difficult to code—and thus to quantify and analyze statistically—than closed questions, they offer more scope for individuals' expression of real opinions and attitudes. The criticism of closed questions is that they impose a limited set of options, and that these are the products of the mind of the researcher rather than of the respondent. The meanings of the possible responses may vary among respondents, and so what appears to be a block of like-minded people may in reality be no such thing.

Open-ended questions are aimed at avoiding these problems by allowing respondents to speak for themselves. However, the problem with such questions is that they make it difficult to compare answers, because these can be so varied in their expression. The researcher is left with a great deal of work to do in trying to categorize the answers. Sometimes this may be done through content analysis, whereby a computer program picks out certain words or phrases that are taken to represent a certain attitude or position on an issue. (This method can also be used in research on documents, such as newspaper articles.)

Written questionnaires are the easiest to administer to a large sample (especially if they can be mailed out), and they usually feature closed questions. The completed questionnaires can then be fed directly into the computer, which quickly produces quantitative data. Face-to-face interviews are more time-consuming, but they offer the advantage of raising the response rate (securing an adequate response rate to written questionnaires is more difficult). The interview schedule (design of questions) may be structured or semistructured. A *structured interview* is one consisting of questions that allow the interviewer little scope for varying the way the questions are presented or followed up. A *semistructured interview* allows the interviewer more scope in these respects. The semistructured interview schedule initially provides a brief guide as to what should be asked (perhaps also including some closed questions of a factual

sort, such as those concerning biographical facts—name, age, education, occupation, etc.) and then lists broad subject headings for further questioning. An in-depth interview is one in which the interviewer can encourage the interviewee to talk at length in answer to "prompt questions."

## Observation

Observation of behavior is a sociological research method that can take various forms. Experiments are a favored form for quantitative research because they are the epitome of research methods in the natural sciences, allowing the researcher to control the situation—holding some variables constant in order to study the effects of change in one variable. However, experiments are difficult to set up in sociological research and so are less frequently used than other methods, although they have been attempted in research on social psychological factors, such as group behavior and social interaction in a small-scale, laboratory-like setting. Observation of real-life groups may be more feasible, but these situations are harder to control than experimental situations.

Researchers may be nonparticipant observers, perhaps observing from a distance or hidden from view, so as not to disturb the normal functioning of the group. This is necessary in order to avoid the "Hawthorne effect," which occurred when Elton Mayo (1933) and Fritz Jules Roesthlisburger and William J. Dickson (1939) undertook a **field research** experiment at the Hawthorne factory of

> **Field research** Research that is based on the observation of behavior rather than on the use of existing quantitative data. Field researchers select a location and a field site and then spend time observing. They may be participant observers who engage directly in the activities of their field site, or they may remain at a distance. Field research raises important issues regarding consent and research ethics. Ethnography is an example of field research.

the General Electric Company in Chicago. The intention was to study the effect of certain variables on group performance, including physical changes in the work situation, such as the lighting. However, productivity seemed to go up in response to *all* changes, not just one or two. Eventually it became clear that the workers were reacting to the fact that they knew they were being observed, and this seemed to increase their group morale.

In participant observation the researcher has a choice regarding the degree to which he or she gets involved in the activities of those being observed, and also whether the subjects of the research are informed that they are being studied. A good example of partial involvement is Ned Polsky's (1967) study of poolroom hustlers. Using the methods of direct observation, informal talks, and participant observation during the poolroom activities, Polsky was sufficiently involved to be able to further his research objectives, but without becoming engaged in other aspects of the hustlers' lives (especially the illegal ones). In contrast, William Foote Whyte, during his study of an Italian-American street gang in Chicago, *Street Corner Society* (1943), lived in a house with the group and joined in on most of their activities. Both studies are examples of ethnographic fieldwork. *Ethnography*, broadly defined as the study of a way of life, was originally associated with anthropology and the analysis of small-scale societies. It was developed in sociology for the purpose of studying deviant groups, such as gangs—a topic of particular interest to the Chicago School of Sociology during the 1930s. (For more discussion, refer to Chapter 11, on crime and deviance.) Another early example of an ethnographic study in Chicago is Paul Cressey's *The Taxi-Dance Hall* (1932), which investigated the "taxi-dance" halls where attractive young women were paid by male partners for each dance. Cressey described the taxi-dance hall as a distinct "cultural world," comprising not just lonely immigrant men but also the sons of some of Chicago's most respectable families: "For those who attend the taxi-dance hall, even irregularly, it is a distinct world, with its own ways of acting, talking, and thinking. It has its own vocabulary, its own activities and interests, its own conception of what is significant in life, and—to a certain extent—its own scheme of life" (Cressey 1932: 31).

Polsky, who did his graduate training in the Sociology Department at the University of Chicago, described his ethnographic method as an effort to "present hustlers and hustling on their own terms" rather than from a "social problems" focus. In other words, he deliberately reversed the usual perspective: Instead of spotlighting the problems the hustlers posed for society, he approached the study from the perspective of the hustlers themselves: "In so far as I treat social problems, they are not the problems posed by the hustler but for him; not the difficulties he creates for others, but the difficulties that others create for him as he pursues his career" (Polsky 1971: 32–33). Polsky admitted that "the disadvantage for the scientifically minded reader is that the underlying sociological framework may be obscured." However, he explained that his framework was the same as that of one of his Chicago teachers, Everett Hughes, who had studied more legitimate work occupations with the same ethnographic approach. Although Polsky attempted to adopt the perspective of his subjects, there were sociological questions regarding them that he was seeking to answer: (1) How was the hustler's work situation structured? (2) What was the career pattern of the hustler? (3) How was the hustler's work situation affected by changes in the larger society? (See box titled "Field Research.")

## Ethnographic Research

The central characteristic of ethnographic research is that it asserts that all social action has meaning for those involved in it. If we want to understand others' behavior (regardless of our own view of it), then we must examine it from their per-

## Field Research

Successful field research depends on the investigator's trained abilities to look at people, listen to them, think and feel with them, talk with them rather than at them. It does not depend fundamentally on some impersonal apparatus, such as a camera or tape recorder or questionnaire, that is interposed between the investigator and the investigated. Robert E. Park's concern that the sociologist become first of all a good reporter meant not that the sociologist rely on gadgets to see, hear, talk, and remember for him; quite the contrary, it asked the sociologist to train such human capacities in himself to their utmost and use them to their utmost in direct observation of people he wants to learn something about. But the problem for many a sociologist today—the result of curricula containing as much scientism as science—is that these capacities, far from being trained in him, have been trained out of him. He "knows" that Park-style sociology produced merely "reportage" (this is less than a half-truth at best) and insists that the real way for him to learn about people is to place one or more screens between him and them. He can't see people any more, except through punchcards and one-way mirrors. He can't talk with people anymore, only "survey" them. Often he can't even talk about *people* any more, only about "data." Direct field study of social life, when he is forced to think about it at all, is something he fondly labels "soft" sociology, as distinguished from his own confrontation of social reality at several removes, which in his mysterious semantics is "hard" sociology.

Colleagues in older disciplines have begun to give up such scientism—for example, psychologists studying child development have lately come out of the laboratory in droves to look at the child in his natural habitat—and when sociology has finished anxiously proving it is scientific it too will abandon scientism. ...

Although I have insisted that in studying criminals you mustn't be a "spy," mustn't pretend to be "one of them," it is equally important that you don't stick out like a sore thumb in the criminal's natural environment. You must blend in with the human scenery so that you don't chill the scene. One consequence is that often you must modify your usual dress as well as your usual speech. In other words, you must walk a tightrope between "openness" on the one hand and "disguise" on the other, whose balancing point is determined anew in each investigation.

*Source:* Polsky (1967: 119–120, 128).

spective—we must try to get inside their heads. As Colin Robson (1993: 148) describes it: "[Ethnography] seeks to provide a written description of the implicit rules and traditions of a group. An ethnographer, through involvement with the group, tries to work out these rules. The intention is to provide a rich, or 'thick,' description which interprets the experiences of people in the group from their own perspective."

Ethnographic research is both expensive and time-consuming. It is labor-intensive and can take months or even years to complete. Critics maintain that it produces "soft" data that are less reliable than the "hard" data produced by quantitative methods, since there is no way of checking the data and conclusions through replication. For example, it may well be that researchers like Polsky become overinvolved with the group being studied, such that some of the necessary researcher detachment is lost. However, the advantage is that ethnography and participant observation can produce rich data, especially for understanding the meanings and informal rules that shape a culture and motivate the actions of those who share it.

## The Ethnographic Case Study and Participant Observation

A classic example of the ethnographic method is Donald Roy's study of a work group in an American machine shop (1952). Roy was investigating a well-known problem in the sociology of work and organizations—namely, the effect of different systems of payment on workers' productivity. Piecework payment, whereby a worker's pay is bigger the more he or she produces, appears to be rational on the assumption that workers wish to maximize their earnings. However, experience shows that workers in the same job tend to have outputs that are very similar to one another—and that these outputs are generally less than expected by management. Why is this so, given that one would expect to see considerable differences among individual workers in the quantity of work each produced, according to their various skills or the amount of money they need to earn? Roy became an operative in the machine shop in order to find out how and why workers control the outputs of their group. His role as researcher was unknown to both management and workers; to all appearances, he was simply another worker.

Roy's method involved participant observation inasmuch as he fully shared the experience and work of the group he had joined. Every day he kept a diary of the conversations he had with fellow workers. Some jobs had piece-rates that workers thought to be unfair, and the "rule" here was to underproduce so as to force the rate-fixers into retiming the task. Other jobs had very easy piecework norms, which the workers "protected" by producing a comfortable amount, but not too much. The workers shared the belief that the easy rates would be retimed by management if the fact of their "easyness" became known. Roy noted that new recruits were guided by their fellow workers on how to perform, and that a new worker's failure to pick up on the hints and suggestions of the "old hands" led to harassment and even ostracism. Eventually, nearly all the workers conformed to the group's own rules of factory life.

It was only by fully immersing himself in the group, and sharing its ways of thinking and speaking, that the participant observer, Roy, was able to understand these subtle processes of group control. A survey would not have yielded such knowledge.

A major advantage of the ethnographic method is that it is *naturalistic*. It involves the study of individuals and groups in their natural settings, specifically with regard to how behaviors and meanings depend on interaction with others and how statements taken from their contexts can be distorted and lead to bias. It is thus a good method for investigating covert behaviors and meanings, but it is not limited to these. Any given social group is full of spontaneous activity, which, in turn, reflects a structure and culture that are difficult to capture through a formal method of questioning. Since the actual performance of members in a group is what defines social positions and shared culture, questioning a respondent in isolation can easily miss the group nature of social behavior. And, indeed, since individuals are often inarticulate when asked to reflect on the full meaning of their actions, an observer inferring meanings by understanding the context (through participation in the group's "life") is in a better position to get an account of the group's collective purpose than is a researcher who is limited to "artificial" interviews or the use of a questionnaire.

The most obvious disadvantages of the ethnographic method, as suggested earlier, are that it is laborious and time-consuming. To do the job effectively, the researcher must gain acceptance by the group. If he or she is keeping the research role secret for fear of biasing the results, then two roles have to be performed—the normal group role as well as that of the researcher. A naturalistic method of study requires that a group's activities be followed throughout the whole of their cycle. The observer is observing and recording as things happen in real time. He or she cannot short-circuit natural processes. For example, if Roy had asked individual members of the group "Why do you limit output?" or "How do you get new workers to toe the line on how much they produce?" he would perhaps have been met with suspicion or incomprehension (especially if members were not conscious that they were deliberately limiting production). In short, group rules are informal, not formal; they are embedded in concrete behavior and must be inferred from actual performances rather than from what group members say they do.

Another problem has to do with *representativeness* (or *typicality*). If limitations of resources and time mean that only one group can be studied, how do we know that this particular group is typical of all such groups in a complex society? There is a limit, therefore, on the capacity for *generalization* from an ethnographic study.

Two further problems concern *reliability* and *replication*. The reliability of the observer's analysis depends on his or her personal abilities in techniques of observation and recording data. Selection of significant actions or comments has to be made by the researcher, who, if not careful, may miss or discard potentially significant data. Reliability in science normally means that another observer using the same methods on the same group would obtain the same results. But ethnography does not involve fixed procedures that can be written down and followed exactly by another observer. Indeed, it is much more elastic and flexible than the above rule of reliability allows. The observer is necessarily unique in terms of his or her own behavior (and how it affects respondents),

what he or she selects for recording, and how it is interpreted. The replication of an ethnographic study in order to check the original author's findings is thus very difficult (Roy 1952).

## Life Histories and Personal Narratives

Personal narratives, as collected and used by social scientists, are stories that provide accounts of lives and events as told by or from the perspective of the narrator—usually the person(s) being studied. To call a personal narrative a story is not to call it a fiction, although, like any other sociological data, it is "constructed"—put together from a particular perspective. Figuring out what it is constructed *for* is one of the tasks of sociological analysis. In particular, the sociologist may be trying to understand the emotions and intentions of the author of the narrative, as well as taking account of the social context in which the narrative was constructed—for example, the hopes and fears of moving from a European farm to an American inner-city ghetto, as experienced by many Polish immigrants at the beginning of the twentieth century. This was the challenge taken up by the best-known and earliest use of personal narratives in American sociology: *The Polish Peasant in Europe and America*, by W. I. Thomas and Florian Znaniecki (1927).

Personal narratives come in a wide variety of forms, including autobiographies, oral histories, and life history interviews. Various types of per-

**Personal narrative** A type of qualitative data in which an account of life events is given from the perspective of a narrator, usually the individual being studied. The term *narrative* connotes not fiction but, rather, a story that is socially constructed and put together. Personal narratives can come in many forms, including autobiography, oral history, and life history interviews.

sonal writing may also have a narrative dimension: biographies, diaries, personal journals, correspondence, even obituaries. These personal writings are forms of data that historians are familiar with, and sociologists have learned a great deal from the research practices of historians about how to analyze such documents. Oral histories and life history interviews, which are similar to the interview forms of research that sociologists customarily undertake, demonstrate the contribution that can be made by recording the words of people who are not accustomed to writing down their experiences. In addition, they can reveal how the lives and perceptions of individuals relate to social networks and institutions over a period of social change.

A good example is provided by the oral histories brought together by Brigid O'Farrell and Joyce Kornbluh in *Rocking the Boat: Union*

The life histories of Polish immigrants constituted one of the most well-known studies of personal narratives in early twentieth-century sociology. (Bettmann/Corbis)

*Women's Voices, 1915–1975* (1996). They tell us about the individual lives of women trade-union activists and the organizational forms, social networks, and historical changes that were witnessed throughout six decades of American history. Unlike questionnaire surveys, a study based on oral histories is likely to have a relatively small number of contributors; in this case, volunteer interviewers collected life stories from eighty-seven female trade-union activists. Although it is difficult to draw generalizations from such small numbers, tentative conclusions are possible. For example, *Rocking the Boat* shows how workers' involvement in educational programs figured into the development of social activism in this period. Many of the early women activists, especially those from immigrant and less-educated backgrounds, were taught, encouraged in their activism, and formed solid networks through their participation in the "school for union organizers established in 1914 by the Women's Trade Union League, the Bryn Mawr Summer School for Women Workers, and government-sponsored programs established in the mid-1930s under the New Deal" (O'Farrell and Kornbluh 1996: 7) as well as in schools within their own unions. Another interesting conclusion reached in this study is that the inclusion of "union feminists" in definitions of feminism has the potential to bring about change in contemporary perceptions of feminism. Specifically, the authors argue that referring to women who seek economic justice and occupational advancement as a "group," rather than discussing them individually in terms of upward mobility, creates a more inclusive definition of feminist activism. The suggestion here is that too much of the theorizing about feminism is based solely on the experiences of academic women. Collecting the life stories of those who do not normally publish their ideas can raise important questions about how feminism is conceptualized and what effect it has on sociological theory. Indeed, one of the best tests of sociological research, whatever the method employed, is to

Oral histories of these industrial working girls who attended summer school at Bryn Mawr in the early 1900s taught sociologists about turn-of-the-century feminist activism. (Bettmann/Corbis)

see whether it leads to modifications in sociological theory.

## POSTMODERNISM, RELATIVISM, AND RESEARCH METHODS

In the nineteenth century, Auguste Comte expressed the belief that sociology would develop research methods enabling it to discover laws of social behavior, following the example of the natural sciences. This view, which has been termed **positivism,** often lies behind the preference for quantitative research methods. In the twentieth century, positivism was countered by sociologists, such as Max Weber, who emphasized the need for "interpretive" analyses using qualitative methods that would facilitate an understanding of the cultural meanings that motivated social actions. Many ethnographic studies follow this approach, as do studies that focus on interpreting the content of documents (including not just written accounts but also visual documents such as television programs and photographs) and oral histories. What these interpretive approaches have in common is an appreciation of the "standpoint" of the actors

**Positivism** An approach to research that follows the example of the natural sciences in that it assumes sociology will employ methods that enable it to discover laws of social behavior. Positivists are often inclined toward the use of quantitative data and methods.

themselves. The researcher should not elevate herself above those she is studying and impose her own meanings on them. Instead, she should seek to put herself in their place and understand the situation from their standpoint.

Comte's hope that sociology could discover laws of social behavior and promulgate them with authority in a scientific "grand narrative" is no longer on the agenda for most sociologists. Sociologist Zygmunt Bauman (1987) suggests that sociologists should now see themselves more as "interpreters" than as "legislators" (Bauman 1987). He argues that, whereas earlier sociologists believed they were developing a science that would hand down judgments of what is true, based on laws, their successors today should be content with reconstructing and analyzing the varieties of discourse that exist in the many different cultures of postmodernity.

Feminist sociologists contributed to this discussion by arguing that ways of seeing and describing social phenomena are relative to the particular standpoint of the investigator—and, in so doing, they identified with the perspective known as **relativism**. Beginning in the 1960s, many feminist sociologists have argued that positivist methodology and quantitative methods favor a male perspective, and that an interpretive methodology and qualitative methods are better suited to the feminist perspective. Canadian sociologist Dorothy Smith, in particular, suggests that the notion of a feminist "standpoint" is the only valid position from which to undertake research

that is respectful of women's experience. For her, research in itself begins with everyday life and routines. She recommends what she calls "institutional ethnography" as the core of a feminist methodology. Such an ethnography uses methods based on in-depth interviewing of selected samples of women, attention to the details of what women say, and forms of analysis dedicated to reproducing these details as "faithfully" as possible (Smith 1988). Feminists also reject Max Weber's idea that sociological research should be "value free." Specifically, they see their research as a means of furthering women's emancipation from a male-dominated (patriarchal) society, not as a scientifically neutral activity.

However, not all female sociologists accept the argument that qualitative methods are more suited to feminist research. Ann Oakley (1988) has argued that quantitative methods, too, can serve the ends of emancipatory research. She points out that historical innovations in quantitative methods, such as the social survey, were made primarily by people, including women, who sought policy-relevant knowledge as ammunition for social reform. For example, activists such as Jane Addams in America and Harriet Martineau in Britain carried out social investigations that served the reformist cause by revealing the extent of poverty and inequality in the nineteenth century (McDonald 1993). Feminist social reformers have also advocated the need for statistics to demonstrate the conditions of women's lives. In 1875 the astronomer Maria Mitchell urged the collection of statistics to describe the inadequate opportunities for women scientists in the United States. And in the campaign against women's exclusion from higher education, statistics were used to disprove the masculinist medical notion that education damaged women's health (Reinharz 1992). Oakley further argues that the tendency of some feminist sociologists to polarize quantitative and qualitative methods, identifying the former as masculine and the latter as feminine, risks playing into the hands

**Relativism** An approach to research that counters positivism by asserting that a particular social behavior may be understood differently if viewed from different perspectives or in different social contexts. In other words, the interpretation of a behavior may vary depending on the perspective or setting. Relativists tend to prefer an interpretive approach to sociology and to rely on qualitative data.

of those who use gender differences as a means of discriminating against women. It is a short step from accepting that men and women are bound to think differently, on the one hand, to saying that men are essentially rational and women are emotional, on the other. According to Oakley, this is exactly the kind of discriminatory thinking that feminism aims to dispel.

Oakley is clearly not convinced by the arguments of feminists who believe that qualitative methods are more in tune with women's experience and feminist values than quantitative methods. Sometimes, the way we judge an issue like this depends on the purpose at hand, which may lead us to find one type of study more insightful and useful than another. Many women (but perhaps also men) have found that ethnographic studies help them to see their own experiences in a new light; they also feel ethically comfortable with the procedures used in such studies. Others, engaged in a struggle against inequalities, may find that quantitative methods better suit their purpose.

Sociological research of the future, some argue, should move beyond collecting and analyzing data, whether in the lab or the field; it should involve discovering new methods based on partnering in different ways with the subjects of research themselves. (iStockphoto)

## RESEARCH IN THE FUTURE

In a special symposium titled "Charting Futures for Sociology" and published at the beginning of the new millennium, the official review journal of the American Sociological Association, *Contemporary Sociology*, invited the Australian sociologist R. W. Connell to write the opening article. Connell (2000) began by noting that it was not preordained that sociology should come into existence in the way that it did, and goes on to say that its continued existence cannot be guaranteed unless it draws on new sources of experience and discovers new standpoints. After all, there are many competing sources of knowledge about society, including those of the mass media. The question Connell poses is whether there is a future for sociology if it is confined to being a "reformist science"—helping government and other institutions

to carry on their activities more efficiently by providing expertise in carrying out surveys and making field observations in the form of small-scale ethnographies—and, indeed, whether it might have a more challenging future. You may well react to this criticism by asking what's wrong, after all, with being reformist and useful. Fair enough. But it's important to note that Connell is being true to the more ambitious project envisaged by early sociologists. His fear is that sociology will become nothing more than a "salvage ethnography" of marginalized lifestyles, which he disparagingly describes as similar to the old ethnographies of "nuts, sluts, and perverts" and to the science of "losers"—the poor, the chronically sick, the disturbed, the violent, the linguistically challenged, the illiterate (including the computer illiterate), and the unemployed. None of these functions, in Connell's view, matches the comprehensive scope and critical edge of the earlier sociological tradition. To escape such marginalization, he argues, sociological research must be "reconstituted as a democratic science," which entails stepping outside the confines of the Western academic world and entering into partnerships with new participants in research.

Where are these new partnerships to be found? Among those Connell mentions as possible partners are activists in various spheres of society— community activists, social reformers, educators, and mass media professionals. The idea is that, in a knowledge-based society, knowledge is an important tool of power and social control, and so it is crucial to spread access to that tool, especially to those who are disadvantaged. In some cases, it's simply a matter of using research to reveal the facts about inequalities; in others, a community might be given the tools to reveal processes that have been obscured by ideology. Connell has in mind dominant discourses through which society classifies things as binary opposites (e.g., "rational/ emotional," "modern/traditional," "normal/deviant") and then relegates the second term in each of those pairs to an inferior position. He calls, instead, for a kind of research that "deconstructs" such binary opposites. For example, in responding to feminist and gay-lesbian movements, some sociologists have engaged with the ways in which issues of sexuality and sexual difference destabilize and de-essentialize such categories as "woman," "heterosexual," and "homosexual." Such stereotyping is not confined to marginal groups. Indeed, Jeffrey Alexander and Philip Smith (1993) have shown how binary thinking pervades public discourse about economic crisis, political scandal, election fraud, and war. Their "deconstructive" analysis of texts, including media texts such as television programs, is a fairly recent development in sociological research. But when allied with a commitment to a radical vision of the future of sociology, as in Connell's case, it can be particularly forceful and productive. Connell proposes this approach as an alternative to what he sees as the dominant tendency at present, whereby sociological information is to be collected and used for commercial purposes and to the advantage of the powerful.

## CONCLUSION

Understanding the advantages and disadvantages of these methodologies is particularly important in postmodern societies, where people are increasingly being inundated with research findings. Postmodern citizens must learn to become intelligent and knowledgeable consumers so that they can evaluate how data are presented and distorted by the various media. Data are presented either narratively or diagrammatically every day in newspapers, magazines, and advertisements as well as on television and the Internet. That's why you are probably familiar with some or all of the following: official reports, tables, graphs, bar charts, and pie charts. The type of data and the intentions of the producers and disseminators often determine the method of representation. Graphs, bar charts, and pie charts can give readers or viewers a powerful picture of the data, whereas tables provide figures, usually in the form of percentages. But unless they are read carefully and critically, these data forms can be offputting or even misleading. It is important to read any notes explaining the presentation, such as why a particular period or measure was chosen. And be alert for spotting any omissions of information that might be relevant to forming an accurate judgment.

Narratives, whether written, spoken, or in pictures, are also capable of being misleading. The more attractive and entertaining the presentation, the easier it is to sit back and passively consume what is offered rather than reading or listening critically. Indeed, what makes good television is not necessarily the same as what makes good sociology. In his *7 Up* television series on class cultures in Britain, Michael Apted offered some fascinating insights into various class cultures, but his presentation was also hugely entertaining be-

## media moments

# Monster Hype

Contemporary discussions about social issues, especially within education, almost always involve statistics. Numbers have become an essential element in policy rhetoric, a form of evidence needed to persuade others. Statistics let us claim that we can measure the size of our problems and the effectiveness of our solutions.

Yet even as we rely on numbers, we are bedeviled by innumeracy, the mathematical equivalent of illiteracy. Too often, we fail to think critically about the statistics we encounter, to ask even the most basic questions. This is important, because accepting numbers uncritically may cause us to badly misunderstand our problems. There are few better examples of this failing than some of the recent figures regarding school violence.

The March 5, 2001, shooting spree at Santana High School in Santee, California, which left 2 dead and 13 injured, revived concerns over the seeming escalation of school violence and its potential links to the age-old schoolyard tradition of bullying. School shootings first became a serious issue in the wake of a series of tragic incidents, the most famous being Dylan Klebold and Eric Harris's April 1999 rampage at Columbine High School, in Littleton, Colorado, during which they murdered 12 students and a teacher before turning their weapons on themselves. Of particular interest was that nearly every shooting was accompanied by reports that the teenagers involved were marginalized in some way; the Santee shooter especially appears to have been a victim of bullying....

This is how contemporary Americans create new social problems. Typically, the process involves a three-part recipe:

1. Illustrate the problem with an awful example (e.g., the mass murder at Columbine High School).
2. Give the problem a name ("school shootings").
3. Use statistics to suggest the problem's size and importance.

Statistics play a crucial role in this process, because we tend to assume that numbers are factual—that somebody has counted something, that the problem has been measured and therefore is as big as the claims suggest. Coupled with dramatic, headline-grabbing incidents, they have created the impression that both school violence and bullying are on the rise. This may make for compelling television, but the oversaturated media coverage can portray a few isolated incidents as a national trend. Take CBS anchor Dan Rather's post-Santee warning: "School shootings in this country have become an epidemic." Such claims have become commonplace among journalists who haven't thought carefully enough about the evidence. The statistics on violence and bullying that are trucked out by pundits and activists often exaggerate or distort the case. The result is that the public and policymakers tend to overreact as they look for solutions to problems that appear to be out of control. A closer look at the statistics, however, reveals a more complicated and hopeful picture.

### A Phantom Epidemic

... A good deal of evidence indicates that school violence has actually been declining in recent years. When researchers at the National School Safety Center (NSSC) combed media reports from the school years 1992–93 to 2000–01,

*continues*

## media moments

### Monster Hype, *continued*

they identified 321 violent deaths at school. However, not all of these incidents involved student-on-student violence: they included, for example, 16 accidental deaths and 56 suicides, as well as incidents involving nonstudents, such as a teacher killed by her estranged husband, who then shot himself, and a nonstudent killed on a school playground during the weekend. Even if we include all 321 deaths, the average fell from 48 violent deaths per year during the school years 1992–93 through 1996–97 to 32 per year from 1997–98 to 2000–01. If accidental deaths and suicides are eliminated from the data, the decline remains: from an average of 31 deaths per year in the earlier period to 24 per year in the later one. Moreover, the later period includes all of the heavily publicized cases mentioned above. And the later figure may be further inflated by the likelihood that the media were more apt to report school shootings after the topic vaulted to public attention. ...

This decline is consistent with the evidence suggesting that crime rates were declining nationwide. During the 1990s, the overall crime rate fell, as did the rates of major violent crimes such as homicide, robbery, and aggravated assault. The crime rate, which is the Federal Bureau of Investigation's tally of crimes reported to the police, is only one of two national measures of criminal activity. The second, less familiar measure is the rate of victimization reported in the National Crime Victimization Survey. Researchers with the victimization survey interview a large national sample and ask respondents whether they or anyone in their households have been victims of crime. This survey showed instances of criminal victimization falling during the 1990s. Moreover, reports of teenagers being victimized by violent crimes at school dropped. The data also showed that instances of victimization were less common at school than elsewhere; in other words, teenagers were safer at school.

The federal Centers for Disease Control and Prevention's Youth Risk Behavior Survey also found steadily declining percentages of high-school students who reported fighting or carrying weapons on school property during the 1990s. It is also important to recognize that the risks of school violence are extremely low. For every million children who attend school, there is less than one violent school-related death per year. Moreover, only about 1 percent of children killed by violence are hurt at school, despite the large amount of time they spend there.

None of these data are especially hard to come by; all of them were readily available—and the trends they showed were apparent—before, during, and after the various school-shooting incidents that became subjects of extensive news coverage. All of this evidence flatly contradicted the claims that there was a wave, trend, or epidemic of school violence. In other words, the wave of school shootings was a phantom—that is, a nonexistent trend. What accounts for this misperception? Why did the press and the public assume that school shootings were increasing?

In large part, media coverage promoted this distorted view of the problem. The Columbine killings in particular became a huge story. Columbine involved many victims, and the story unfolded over hours. Because the crime occurred in the suburbs of a major city, there were plenty of reporters nearby, and they had time to arrive on the scene for live coverage. The result was dramatic video footage that would be replayed many times. Furthermore, Columbine was a bastion of suburban privilege; it challenged stereotypes about inner-city violence. It was a story made for television.

The Columbine coverage also reflected recent media transformations. Most Americans now have access to cable or satellite television systems; they are no longer limited to receiving broadcasts from a handful of local stations. Most viewers now can choose among several all-news or public-affairs channels. Those channels need constantly to fill the time with content. In the aftermath of the Columbine shootings, broadcasters like CNN, Fox News, and MSNBC devoted hours, not just to reporting the story and commentary about the violence, but also to live coverage of many funeral and memorial services. Columbine remained a major story for days, and during that period, politicians, activists, and commentators used it as evidence to justify their calls for a wide range of measures, including tougher gun laws, restrictions on adolescents' access to violent popular culture, and so on.

The Columbine killings were a terrible event, but we are accustomed to thinking about such incidents as instances—that is, as examples of some larger problem. The extraordinary level of media coverage reinforced the interpretation that these killings must have had some larger significance. It also gave people the sense that school shootings must be a large and growing problem, regardless of what the available statistics actually showed.

Perceptions that school violence is a national crisis have clearly affected educational policy. Resources have been directed toward purchasing and operating metal detectors, stationing police officers in schools, and enhancing other security measures, restrictions that many schools expanded in the aftermath of the September 11 terrorist attacks. ... These are not necessarily bad choices, but they may have been based in part on inaccurate perceptions of the nature and level of school violence.

*Source:* Best (2002).

cause of the personalities of the people he chose to focus on. His series *Married in America*, which we discussed at the beginning of this chapter, promised similar qualities. This kind of journalism is often derided as "infotainment" because it does not submit to the rigors of critical theoretical and empirical evaluation of the kind required in professional sociology. For example, the series never specifies what sociological theories of marriage Apted is using, if any. Also unclear is how he drew up his sample of couples. Were they selected more for their "telegenic" qualities than for their representativeness? And could such a small sample of couples really be said to be representative of marriages in America? These are just two of the questions a sociological researcher would be expected to answer.

The early sociologists had limited information on which to base their theories and subject them to testing. Today, by contrast, we are in danger of falling prey to an overload of information of diverse sorts. The presentation of information by the mass media reflects the postmodern experience of onrushing impressions, disorientation, fragmentation, and passive cynicism. Television documentaries and news programs epitomize these tendencies. Critics have pointed to the "fragmented narrative and highly segmented form" of television news and its focus on "personality" rather than on issues and performance, and to the "singularly abrupt and jumpy" style of television dramas with their quick cuts from one scene to another, and one character to another, such that no one talks long enough to express anything complex (Bellah et al. 1997: 280; Gitlin 1983). Often supposedly informational programs present the viewer with so much visual and linguistic information, and at such a frenetic pace, that the result is stimulation without registration (Brough-Williams 1996: 24). The dominance of entertainment criteria in television may mean that the pleasure of the viewer has become paramount, making exposition of complex issues the enemy of programming. Indeed, what appears to have been rejected is the sustained and disciplined marshaling of "arguments, hypotheses, discussions, reasons, refutations or any of the traditional instruments of reasoned discourse" (Postman 1987: 151–152).

In an earlier period of sociology, these issues were of little relevance to the discussion of research methodology and analysis. In the postmodern culture, they cannot be ignored. It is unlikely that the general public will ever be required to carry out its own sociological research, except at the fairly basic level of finding and sorting existing information. But knowledge of sociological methods of research and analysis is essential in developing the ability to be critical consumers of information and thus responsible citizens.

## EXERCISES

### Exercise 1

Write an outline detailing a sociological research project that you would like to undertake in your hometown. Then, explain which methods you would adopt, giving reasons why they are appropriate.

### Exercise 2

It has been suggested that, in the postmodern culture in which we live, much of our knowledge is mediated by television. Think of a television documentary or news program that you viewed recently. How much attention did you give to the broadcast? (Recall Ron Lembo's findings about television viewing, which are summarized in the box titled "Conceptualizing and Investigating the Viewing Culture: Research Strategy and Methods.") Do you have a clear recollection of the main conclusions you reached while watching the program? How would you go about verifying those conclusions if you could undertake further research?

## STUDY QUESTIONS

1. In what ways can society be regarded as a "text"?

2. What differences are there between the procedures involved in constructing a television documentary and the procedures used in social science research?

3. One notable difference between television documentaries and much social science research has to do with how they are received by their "audiences." Discuss this difference in audience reception in terms of the combination of methods employed in Lembo's research.

4. Why might some groups want to emphasize that all knowledge, including scientific knowledge, is only relatively valid?

5. List the different types of samples that may be used in social science research.

6. What is the difference between an independent variable and a dependent variable?

7. Distinguish between the two forms of sociological explanation of suicide offered, respectively, by Durkheim and Jacobs.

8. Outline the different methods of gathering quantitative versus qualitative data, and list some of their advantages and disadvantages.

9. The postmodern culture has been described as "mediatized"—meaning that much of the knowledge and information that we accumulate has been constructed and transmitted by the mass media. Sometimes the process seems to spiral out of control and people are panicked into believing that a threatening social trend is advancing upon them, when in fact a more critical analysis of statistics would counter this belief. How does Joel Best illustrate this point with regard to school violence?

## FURTHER READING

Alvesson, Mats. 2002. *Postmodernism and Social Research*. Buckingham, U.K./Philadelphia: Open University Press.

Bellah, Robert N., R. Madsen, W. M. Sullivan, A. Swidler, and S. M. Tipton. 1997. *Habits of the Heart*. Berkeley: University of California Press.

Best, Joel. 2001. *Damned Lies and Statistics*. Berkeley/Los Angeles: University of California Press.

Denzin, N., and Y. Lincoln, eds. 2000. *Handbook of Qualitative Research*, 2nd ed. Thousand Oaks, CA: Sage.

Fonow, Margaret, and Judith A. Cook. 1991. *Beyond Methodology: Feminist Scholarship as Lived Research*. Bloomington: Indiana University Press.

Jacobs, J. 1970. "The Use of Religion in Constructing the Moral Justification of Suicide." In *Deviance and Respectability: The Social Construction of Moral Meanings,* edited by J. D. Douglas. New York: Basic Books, 229–250.

Oakley, Ann. 1988. "Gender, Methodology, and People's Ways of Knowing: Some Problems with Feminism and the Paradigm Debate in Social Science." *Sociology* 32, no. 4: 707–731.

Polsky, Ned. 1967. *Hustlers, Beats, and Others*. Chicago: Aldine.

Postman, Neil. 1987. *Amusing Ourselves to Death: Public Discourse in the Age of Show Business*. London: Methuen.

Roy, Donald. 1952. "Quota Restriction and Goldbricking in a Machine Shop." *American Journal of Sociology* 57: 427–442.

Smith, Dorothy. 1988. *The Everyday World as Problematic: A Feminist Sociology*, Milton Keynes, U.K.: Open University Press.

Sudman, S., and N. Bradburn. 2004. *Asking Questions: A Practical Guide to Questionnaire Design*. San Francisco: Jossey-Bass.

# PART TWO
# Meanings and Media

# chapter 3

# Cultural Structures

We live our lives and navigate our way through the social world as "individuals." We deal with other people as "individuals" (whether friends, enemies, colleagues, bosses, or subordinates), and it is as "individuals" that we try to make our own sense of what we experience. However, sociologists do not see individuals as free actors, who have the power to do whatever they like. Sociologists do not deny the power of individuals to determine their own fate (to an extent, at least), but they are more concerned about the social and cultural parameters within which individuals live.

In this chapter, we examine one particular kind of parameter that shapes and limits our very perception of reality: *culture.* In its broadest sense, culture refers to the entire way of life of a people or group; however, as we will shortly see, culture can also be defined in a narrower way as the specific systems of meaning that we use to weigh and consider our social world.

Consider, for instance, fashion. Each and every one of us gets up in the morning and decides what to wear and how to look. We have a wide range of options, depending on our particular personality and situation—whether we're going to work, church, or the beach; whether we are 10 or 80 years old, a surfer, or a punk rocker. And even within a specific situation there is a wide range of choice. At the beach, for example, do we wear a thong bikini or a one-piece bathing suit? Further, what we wear or how we look is not just a personal issue. It depends mightily on social and cultural factors as well. Our very notion as to what looks good and what does not, or what looks like us and what does not, exists within very narrow and specific cultural, social, and historical parameters.

Standards of beauty, notions as to what is beautiful and what is not, vary significantly not only between societies but also over time. In Georgian England it was quite popular for women to wear their hair as high as they could possibly manage. Natural hair was built up over horsehair and wool-padded frames, then supplemented by vast amounts of false hair, resulting in a hairdo as tall as 30 inches. This was about half the height of the average female of the day. Hair was worn so high that the chin was halfway between the top of the head and the feet. It took hours to dress the hair so high, and women expected the style to last for a minimum of a week, preferably longer. Since hygiene was poor, lice in the hair and persistent headaches caused by the dragging weight became acceptable facts of life. Women slept in chairs so as to not disrupt their hairdo. Frequently they would have difficulty getting through doors and riding in carriages. Most people today would consider such hairstyles not just odd but disgusting. More generally, many would consider it both odd and disgusting that women should physically alter or reshape their bodies—and suffer significant physical pain—in the pursuit of beauty.

Until about a hundred years ago a small dainty foot was considered essential to a Chinese woman's eligibility for marriage. The desire to make the foot smaller in the name of beauty was strong enough that the Chinese actually mutilated female feet for nearly 1,000 years. The procedure they used, called foot-binding, introduced an organically grown heel that caused the woman to hobble when she walked; the inability to walk was viewed as increasing the woman's desirability as a love object. Foot-binding entailed tremendous distortion.

A practice common in ancient Mayan society (1200 B.C.–900 A.D.) was "head flattening," whereby protuberances such as the nose, ears, and forehead were flattened to conform to the cultural beauty ideal. Newborn infants' heads were positioned between two wooden boards, creating a mousetrap-like cradle, and held in place with bindings. The soft skull slowly molded to the cultural ideal of flatness. Only after a few years were the boards permanently removed.

In the Western world, the outlines of women's bodies have historically been controlled by corsetry and petticoat constructions. Today's "figure faults" are "corrected" by cosmetic surgery, im-

**FIGURE 3.1 Cosmetic Procedures Performed, by Gender, 2005**

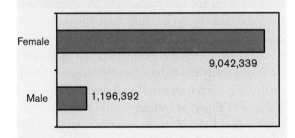

*Note:* Totals include all surgical and minimally invasive procedures.

*Source:* American Society of Plastic Surgeons (2005).

**FIGURE 3.2 Top Five Female Cosmetic Surgical Procedures, 2005**

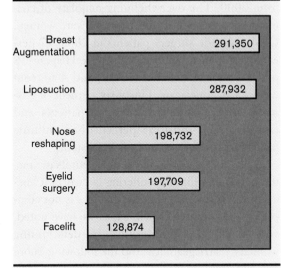

*Source:* American Society of Plastic Surgeons (2005).

**FIGURE 3.3 Top Five Male Cosmetic Surgical Procedures, 2005**

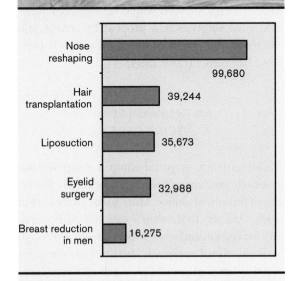

*Source:* American Society of Plastic Surgeons (2005).

plants, liposuction, bone remolding, and radical dieting. Plastic surgery was originally developed thousands of years ago in India for treating injuries and birth defects. Then just over a century ago, in 1885, when local anesthetics were invented, surgeons began performing various cosmetic operations.

In 1901 the first face-lift was performed by Eugene Hollander of Berlin. The wealthy liked face-lifts. A face-lift meant they could actually buy some youth, even though their body cells were aging.

In the 1920s some women endured breast reductions so they could wear the flat boyish fashions of that era. But by the 1930s the breast in all its glory was back in fashion. The fuller the bosom, the better. Expensive surgical enlargement was often done for such people as actresses, but not talked about much.

Nowadays, even people with ordinary incomes view breast enlargement as their "right"—as a way to satisfy emotional and fashionable needs. Older teenage girls particularly favor breast implants. Liposuction, tummy tucks, nose jobs, lip manipulation, and implants for fuller breasts have all become popular in women's search for the ideal silhouette.

More than 10 million cosmetic surgery procedures were performed in 2005, an increase of 11 percent from the previous year and of 38 percent from 2000. The overwhelming majority of cosmetic surgery patients (88 percent) were women. Of all cosmetic surgery patients in 2005, 77 percent were Caucasian, 9 percent were Hispanic, 8 percent were African American, and 4 percent were Asian American. Thirty-six percent of cosmetic surgery patients were repeat patients, and more than one-third (38 percent) had multiple procedures performed in a single session.

As in other societies and at other points in time, the perception that the suffering is "worth it" because it will lead to better life chances is not completely unwarranted. In China, as we have noted, very small feet were critical in determining women's marriageability. And the following, more contemporary example is just one of many: Cindy Jackson, a former factory worker from Fremont, Ohio, and self-proclaimed "world champion" of cosmetic surgery—she has had more than twenty operations and spent over $55,000 to turn herself into a "living doll"—maintains that her life completely changed after her surgeries. Attractive, wealthy men who never would have glanced at her before her surgeries now proposed marriage, and she received a variety of other job offers that she never had before (Lord 1994).

## AN INDIVIDUAL OR A SOCIAL STORY?

Sociologists are skeptical about the supposition that such insistent self-reshaping is simply the result of individual choice. More social factors are at work. One way to develop a sociological explanation for fashion and standards of beauty is through an institutional approach. *Institutions* are organized spheres of social life—such as the government, big business, and the courts—that exercise power and distribute resources, and in so doing exert direct control over individual behavior. Although **institutional explanations** are concerned with the question of normative conformity, advocates of them see this conformity as being forced from the outside. As a result, their attention is focused on the sources of money and social power. Thus, if we are taking an institutional approach, we might study the fashion/beauty industry. Obviously, big corporations like Armani, Gap, and Tommy Hilfiger, as well as small businesses like manicurists, hairstylists, and plastic surgeons, benefit tremendously from the popular belief that we need to continuously reshape our physical bodies to look good. The very idea that clothes go out of fashion, or that we must buy new clothes every "season," is quite useful if you are a capitalist entrepreneur in the business of making and selling clothes.

So too, one might argue that the very idea of fashion and beauty ideals is a symptom of patriarchy. *Patriarchy* refers to a form of social organization in which males dominate females. The patriarchal explanation is clearly relevant in the case of Chinese foot-binding, as women were literally crippled in order to ensure not only their appeal to but also their dependence on men. But one could also argue that the current emphasis on body sculpting benefits the male members of our society. As wealthy and powerful men "trade up," divorcing their older wives for younger "eye candy," even upper-class women feel compelled to look young in order to maintain their social position and their "man."

Yet this very reference to patriarchy shows the limits of a purely institutional approach. There are many systems of meaning behind and within fashion and beauty ideals. For instance, beauty ideals are not only highly genderized but highly racialized as well. Western European features are idealized to such an extent that we can call the preoccupation with "Barbie" a white beauty ideal. And look at how effectively the famous pop singer Michael Jackson once titillated the American population with his dramatic changes from "black" to "white" features—though of course he fervently denied he'd had plastic surgery.

Institutions are not, however, the only kind of social force that directs the patterns of social life. There is also the level of culture. *Culture* refers to the subjective meanings that individuals attach to events. An implication of **cultural explanations** is that power and material resources do not exist apart from meaning. Cultural explanations differ from institutional explanations in that they emphasize the established frameworks of meaning that shape and mark the boundaries for individual actions, thoughts, and feelings. In cultural explanations, the external force of money and power is not seen as exclusively significant, but as interacting with internal structures of meaning.

It is culture that tells us what to do and how to act. It is culture that enables us to identify events and people as being of a particular type—for example, as being beautiful. It is culture that enables us to forge our own place in the world. But culture is transmitted to us so subtly from the very beginning of our lives—through parents, friends, siblings, mass media, schools, and everyday interactions with strangers—that we don't even notice it. We cannot really "see" culture happening. Most of the time, we experience culture as if it were simply our own volition, our own very personal taste. Indeed, we may be conscious of the particular characteristics of our culture only when we see behavior that does not follow it, such as when traveling abroad. Yet, for all its invisibility, and its implicit rather than explicit power, culture exerts an incredible force.

In the early 2000s, as the American military occupation of Iraq unfolded, the inability of American soldiers to understand Iraqi culture put them at increasing risk. Because it was impossible for the mass of soldiers to learn Arabic, analyzing spoken or written speech for cultural clues was out. The only possibility was to interpret body gestures. Yet the meaning of such physical signals was invisible to the untrained eye. Pentagon officials

asked Dr. Hannes Vilhjalmsson, of the University of Southern California, to help them out. According to Vilhjalmsson, "in Western countries, we control our body language more," whereas "in Arabic culture, it is important [that] you show how open you are." In order "to show sincerity you have to put more effort into your gestures," he explained. Moreover, as pointed out in a BBC News article, the reserved body language of American culture could "be interpreted as having something to hide" and thus of "potentially escalating a tense situation" (Rincon 2006). Another cultural difference concerns physical proximity. American military personnel need to understand that, in Iraq, "people can approach each other more closely than one normally might in the West," so American troops "should not automatically interpret close proximity in an exchange as a threat."

In the context of beauty ideals, a cultural approach would emphasize that for as long as there have been human societies, men and women have found interesting ways to mark and adorn their bodies, whether by piercings, tattoos, or even clothing. Such symbols can indicate not just a person's unique identity but also his or her tribe or nationality, particular place in the world, gender, and class. Of course, in the postmodern, global, capitalist world of today, those systems of meaning are heavily marketed as never before in history. Still, the point for cultural sociologists is that fashion is a powerful symbolic system. Unless we understand this symbolic dimension, we cannot

**Institutional explanations** Explanations that focus on the way institutions (e.g., government, the law, patriarchy) act externally—as sources of social power—to influence social behavior.

**Cultural explanations** Explanations that consider the way internal systems of meaning influence and dictate social behavior. Rather than emphasizing the power and material resources of institutions, cultural explanations emphasize symbols that shape and limit our individual actions, thoughts, and feelings.

**TABLE 3.1  Components of Culture**

| Concept | Definition | Example |
|---|---|---|
| Symbol | Something that stands for something else | Flag, cross |
| Symbolic system | System or pattern of symbols | Language, fashion |
| Social code | System or pattern of meanings that undergird specific situations | Stopping at red lights |
| Norms | Written or unwritten rules that govern specific situations | Take off shoes when you enter the house |
| Values | Ideals and anti-ideals | Individualism<br>Socialism |
| Attitudes | Statements people make about their values and beliefs | Prochoice<br>Anti–affirmative action |
| Subculture | Culture within a culture | "Punks," surfers, gangs, sociology professors |

explain why men and women in both capitalist and noncapitalist societies seem willing to endure great pain in order to follow beauty and fashion trends and ideals.

In this chapter, we explore the cultural dimension of society. We discuss several basic components of culture—symbols, symbolic systems, social codes, norms, values, attitudes, and subcultures (see Table 3.1)—as well as the particular systems of meaning at the heart of U.S. culture, both today and earlier in our history.

### THINKING SOCIOLOGICALLY ABOUT CULTURE

Culture is one of sociology's most important—but also most complicated—concepts. In order to get a handle on what culture is and how it works, many sociologists break culture down into the specific parts or components listed earlier. But, while we need to break culture down into its parts, so as better to understand it, this is not how we experience it. We are born into and feel it without knowing it's there.

### Symbols, Codes, Categories, and Classifications

Among the basic components of culture are symbols. In his classic article "Religion as a Cultural System," Clifford Geertz (1973: 91) defined **symbol** as "any object, act, event, quality or relation which serves as a vehicle for a conception—the conception is the symbol's 'meaning.'" In other words, a symbol is something that stands for something else. The dollar sign ($) and the Christian cross (†), for example, are important symbols; more than just crosshatches or curves and lines, they carry significant meaning or symbolic weight.

Symbols are organized into two categories: the sacred and the profane (see Chapter 15 on religion). The *sacred* consists of the emotionally charged symbols of good that are set off from the everyday world. As we will see later in this chapter, the American flag is a potent, emotionally charged symbol that "stands for" the United States. The sacrality of the flag is evident in the special rules we have about caring for and disposing of the flag. In the aftermath of September 11, 2001 (hereafter "9/11"), many Americans were upset that the flag was now being flown every which way as well as all night long without illumination. For these folks, such casual everyday display and care were offensive and violated the flag's sacred character.

The *profane* comprises the emotionally charged symbols of bad and evil. In the religious realm, Satan is the most obvious symbol of the profane. In the secular world, stomping on the American flag or flying it at night without a light shining on it is considered profane. During the Vietnam War, protestors engaged in flag burning, which conservatives wanted lawmakers to designate as a criminal offense.

Another important category of symbols is not emotionally charged. This is the realm of the mundane or the routine. A pencil or ruler is (normally) considered an everyday object with little symbolic value, neither sacred nor profane. In contrast to sacred symbols, such as the American flag, there are no rules or laws about how pencils and rulers should be disposed of: We don't have to put away our rulers at night if a light isn't shining on them, and people are unlikely to become upset if we break a pencil during math class!

But whether related to the sacred, profane, or mundane (like the pencil), the meaning of things rarely comes from properties inherent in the things themselves. Rather, symbols gain their meaning from the society in which they are a part, as well as from their relationship to other symbols. For instance, there is no reason that the United States *has* to be represented by a flag with thirteen stripes and fifty stars. Even though this flag symbolizes the original thirteen colonies and the fifty states, theoretically there are lots of different ways the United States could be represented visually. Similarly, there is no inherent reason that a red

traffic light has to mean "stop" and a green one has to mean "go." We could just as well use other colors to mean these same things.

In this latter example, it is not the actual color but the relationship between symbols that is most important: That red means "stop" would not make sense or be useful without the corresponding notions—the related symbolization—that green means "go" and yellow means "proceed with caution." Put another way, the meaning of symbols is relative and relational, not objective. The relations form **symbolic systems.** Cultural sociologists are particularly intrigued by the challenge of figuring out what the symbolic systems in a society are and how they work. Their research explores the systems of meaning that undergird our every thought and action (see Alexander 2003).

One of the most important of all symbolic systems is language. We can't communicate or even think without a language. We are always inside its symbolic order, yet most of the time we are barely aware that we are even speaking it. The exception is in a foreign country where the language is not our own. When we don't know the language others are speaking—that's when we can learn just how important this symbolic system really is.

We share not just language without being aware of doing so but many other social codes as well. **Social codes** provide the hidden "scripts" for every social activity. It's as if society puts thousands

---

**Symbol** Something that stands for something else—for example, a flag, a dollar sign, or a cross. Symbols are often organized into two categories: the sacred and the profane. The sacred consists of emotionally charged symbols of good that are set off from the everyday world, whereas the profane comprises emotionally charged symbols of bad or evil. Symbols can also be categorized as mundane—that is, as emotionally uncharged, everyday, and routine.

**Symbolic system** A system or pattern of symbols—for example, language or fashion.

**Social code** A system or pattern of meanings that undergird specific situations. For example, a young child can eat spaghetti with her hands at a restaurant, but for an adult to do so at a business dinner would be considered inappropriate and unprofessional.

of prearranged texts inside the heads of its members. The texts have directions like "stop," when driving a car and encountering a red traffic light symbol, and "shake her hand," when introduced to someone. What's so amazing about these hidden scripts is that they are widely shared. Some are shared by all members of a group or society. Every car driver, in every country of the world, knows what to do upon seeing a red traffic light. Other codes vary between groups and societies. There are thousands of language groups in the world and, within them, different dialectics and ways of speaking. A nation like the United States can certainly be said to share a single culture, and we'll see later in this chapter how cultural sociologists have teased out its meanings. But it is equally the case that inside the United States there are widely different cultures, and that these are often opposed. Anybody who, in the last few years, has watched the election returns after an American presidential vote

This map of "conservative" and "liberal" states from the 2004 election showed how evenly divided Americans' values are. (credit to come)

knows that there are "red" and "blue" states: the rock-hard Republican regions and the committed liberal and Democratic ones. Sociologists, in fact, have described the United States as fractured by "culture wars" between religious fundamentalists and conservatives, on the one side, and secular cosmopolitans, on the other (Hunter 1991).

Fashion is a powerful symbolic code. When we see teenagers with a Mohawk hairstyle or a man in an Armani suit, we understand their appearance using specific systems of meaning. This is why many of us think long and hard about what to wear each day. It is not that we are all fashion moguls; it is just that we don't want to be misinterpreted as to who we are; we want our clothes and hair and body image to match our "identity." To convey the meaning that we want to convey—that we are this type of person and not that type—we need to have a feel for society's invisible symbolic codes of fashion.

This brings us to another major component of culture: **classifications** (also referred to as categories). Unfamiliar events and objects can be given some kind of meaning if they can be classified and filed with events and objects that are familiar, and either similar or different. Thus, there are classifications as to what is food (beef) and what is not (dogs); what is appropriate to wear at the office (a dress suit) and what is not (a bathing suit); what is appropriate sexual behavior and what is not. In just going about our day, we rely on a whole host of classificatory schemes. We use these codes to make our way through both routine and unfamiliar situations. We are not born with these understandings; rather, we learn them as members of specific social groups. In some societies (e.g., India), beef is not classified as human food; in others (e.g., Thailand), dogs are edible. And, of course, these schemes are always changing. Even in the United States, the appropriateness of beef is under question, and vegetarianism is on the rise. So is formal attire in offices, where "casual Fridays" are increasingly common. And the wheres, whys, and wherefores of appropriate sex seem to be in continuous flux. None of this means that codes and classifications no longer exist. Every activity is subject to classification. People want their actions to be appropriate to the relevant standard, whatever that might be, whether conforming or rebelling, conservative or bohemian.

> **Classifications** Groupings of events and objects that are familiar, similar, or different. By classifying unfamiliar objects or events with familiar objects or events, we are able to give meaning to the unfamiliar ones.

## Norms and Values

In its classical and modern phases, sociologists tended to conceptualize the cultural dimension of society not so much in terms of symbolic and social codes as in terms of norms and values. These concepts are still quite prevalent and they remain useful today.

*Norms* are the written or unwritten rules that govern specific situations. The purpose or function of norms is to regulate and control behavior in precise ways. For instance, in many Asian societies it is "normative" to take off your shoes before entering someone's home. It is considered gross to wear shoes in the house. In the contemporary United States it is normative to give a gift if you are invited to a wedding. It is usually considered rude not to follow this "rule," even though it is nowhere written down. Within the university, it is normative for students to take their seats as soon as they enter the classroom. It would be considered odd if students just stood there, waiting for the professor to come in and greet them before they sat down. In these and many other ways, norms guide our everyday actions and behavior.

### People Behaving Badly

Following are three examples from Tim Phillips and Philip Smith's (2003: 94–99) study of "everyday incivility." This term refers to norm-breaking behavior that is bad enough to provoke a negative response but not serious enough to be illegal.

> Everybody felt very uncomfortable and we didn't know what to do, it was just terrible. ... The inci-

dent shocked me and I just felt sick for days about that boy that urinated on the train.

> I no longer go to the movies even though I can get in for $5 because of the persistent talking by elderly people. ... I am absolutely totally fed up with people treating it like their own lounge room.

> I've been in a situation where somebody has left their mobile phone on in the middle of a christening and um, decided to actually take the call.

Smith and Phillips conducted a focus-group study in order to learn more about the experience of incivility. Let's begin with rude behaviors that the focus-group participants experienced, which are listed in Table 3.2.

What kind of uncivil behavior have you had to endure lately? How do you react when you en-

The way we dress, especially in the workplace, often reflects how we subscribe to the cultural norms around us. (iStockphoto)

### TABLE 3.2 Commonly Reported Verbal and Physical Incivilities: Frequency Distribution

| Physical Incivilities | (%)<br>(76) | (N)<br>(223) |
|---|---|---|
| Road rage; aggressive and selfish driving | 15 | 45 |
| Pushing and shoving | 8 | 24 |
| Queue jumping (cutting in line) | 6 | 19 |
| Spitting | 4 | 12 |
| Littering | 4 | 11 |
| People walking into you/inconsiderate use of footpath | 4 | 11 |
| Aggressive or inconsiderate use of shopping trolley (cart) | 3 | 8 |
| Inappropriate or inconsiderate use of seats on public transport | 2 | 6 |
| Smoking | 2 | 6 |
| Bad parenting | 2 | 5 |
| Begging | 2 | 5 |
| Dirty looks | 2 | 5 |
| Other physical incivilities | 22 | 66 |
| **Verbal Incivilities** | **(24)** | **(71)** |
| Inappropriate language (swearing, sexual remarks) | 10 | 28 |
| Verbal aggression | 4 | 12 |
| Inappropriate use of mobile phones | 3 | 8 |
| Ignoring or challenging complaints | 2 | 7 |
| Other verbal incivilities | 5 | 16 |
| **Total** | **100** | **294** |

*Note:* Incivilities with fewer than five mentions (N = 16 for verbal incivilities; N = 66 for physical incivilities) were classified as "other."

*Source:* Adapted from Phillips and Smith (2003).

counter rude behavior? Do you do anything about it, or do you try to pretend nothing happened? Smith and Phillips were also interested in reactions to uncivil incidents, depending on whether the person was directly involved or only witnessed the norm-breaking. As you would expect, people are more likely to react to uncivil acts if they feel personally violated.

Their most surprising finding concerned what kinds of people perform rude acts (see Table 3.3). The perpetrators most frequently mentioned by focus-group participants as they recounted the in-

civilities they'd experienced were "people in general," a vague and abstract category that does not target any particular gender, age, or racial group. But the next category on the list was truly unexpected: middle-aged adults. So much for the negative stereotypes targeting male minority teenagers!

Some norms are codified into actual laws. For instance, it is not only normative to stop at a red traffic light but illegal not to do so. **Laws** are written norms that prescribe and proscribe specific sets of behaviors under threat of punishment. But even in the case of norms that are not laws, there are in-

**TABLE 3.3 Commonly Reported Perpetrators of Incivilities: Frequency Distribution**

|  | (%) | (N) |
|---|---|---|
| People in general | 42 | 96 |
| Middle-aged adults | 32 | 51 (men = 32, women = 11) |
| Children and teenagers | 13 | 32 (men = 12, women = 0) |
| Older adults | 10 | 22 (men = 2, women = 4) |
| Young adults | 5 | 13 (men = 4, women = 2) |
| Ethnic people | 5 | 11 |
| Other reported perpetrators | 3 | 6 |
| **Total** | **100** | **231** |

*Note:* Perpetrators with less than five mentions (N = 6) were classified as "other." Of this group, four perpetrators were identified as drug pushers/drug users.

*Source:* Adapted from Phillips and Smith (2003).

formal punishments for failing to follow them. If you cut someone off in traffic, the other driver might give you a dirty look or "flip you off," whether or not there is a police officer on hand to give you a ticket. Similarly, if you wear inappropriate attire to the office, you might end up on the receiving end of some long, hard stares. So, even if we don't believe in a norm, most of us will attend to it simply because it's easier than subjecting ourselves to formal and informal sanctions. Following norms also enables us to go about our day without rethinking our every move. Indeed, we live our lives so conditioned by norms and social codes that we don't even realize we are following them. It is not an easy task to account for all of the norms we follow in just going about our day (see Exercise 1).

*Values* are more generalized than norms. They provide the frameworks for ideals and anti-ideals within which norms make sense. Not walking on the grass makes sense to us only if we share the value of respecting private property. Norms against speeding make sense only if we maintain the broader value of respecting human life and being courteous to other human beings. And sodomy laws regulating sexual practices between two con-

senting adults make sense only if we believe that "that kind" of sex is morally wrong, that homosexuality violates sacred values.

## Cultural Change in the United States

In 1951, sociologist Robin Williams published a book called *American Society*. Revised and reprinted several times over, it became established as one of the most influential sociological studies of the United States. Investigating various dimensions of the U.S. social system, its most enduring contribution was cultural analysis. Williams set out to uncover this country's core values. He found that American culture was composed of a series of distinctive, sometimes interrelated, and often conflicting values. It is fascinating to look back at this cultural list from the perspective of our own time.

**Laws** Written norms that prescribe or proscribe specific sets of behaviors under threat of punishment.

### Core American Values in the 1950s

*Achievement and success.* Citing the American myth of the "self-made man," Williams found that Americans valued achievement above all else. They defined achievement as mastery in the physical sense, focusing particularly on success in occupational terms.

*Activity.* Americans were competitive rather than contemplative, always seeking out new challenges.

*Science and secular rationality.* Americans valued scientific knowledge over other kinds such as aesthetic or spiritual knowledge. Scientific knowledge allowed control, calculation, and predictability.

*Individualism and freedom.* Americans believed in the "cult of the individual." They asserted the intrinsic worthiness of the self above that of any collectivity or group. Being free from control was valued more than cooperation directed toward some greater good, for such cooperation implied submitting to authority.

*Progress.* Americans were optimistic. They ignored the darker sides of history and believed in the human and social perfectibility of the common person. For every problem, Americans believed, there is a solution that can be found.

*Moral orientation.* Americans wanted to think of themselves and their society in moral terms. They liked to apply notions about right and wrong, good and bad, moral and immoral to persons and events.

*Humanitarianism.* Despite their emphasis on worldly success and active achievement, Americans valued what Williams calls "disinterested concern and helpfulness." They praised people who were motivated by personal kindness and who provided aid and comfort to those in distress.

*Racism and in-group superiority.* Alongside the democratic dimensions of American culture, Williams discovered a chauvinistic sense of superiority and exclusivity. There was, he wrote, an "ascription of value and privilege to individuals on the basis of race or particularistic group membership." Owing to this cultural tendency, prestige in American society was often distributed not according to what individuals actually do but "according to birth in a particular ethnic group, social class, or related category." (adapted from Williams 1951: 439)

Many of you would probably agree with the assertion that most of the values Williams identified seem every bit as powerful today as they were in the 1950s. Others will no doubt argue that many of those earlier values seem almost to have disappeared. The core culture of a society changes more slowly than less important values, and often much more gradually than do organizations and institutions. But there is certainly no such thing as a permanent culture that goes "naturally" with a given group or a nation. As Williams (1951: 440) himself noted, "it must be always kept in mind that those themes, values and systems of belief do not operate as single and separate units but are in continually shifting and recombining configurations."

The segregation laws in the American South, known as "Jim Crow" laws, were an extreme example of U.S. commitment to in-group superiority. (Library of Congress)

Antiwar protestors at Berkeley in 1969 formed a counterculture of their own. (Bettmann/Corbis)

### The Radical 1960s

In fact, in the years after Williams came up with his list of core values, American society underwent many changes. The turbulent 1960s were dominated by antiestablishment fashions, a massive and compelling struggle for civil rights, and an unprecedented peace movement demanding an end to the war in Vietnam. In actuality, the so-called radical 1960s spanned the decade from the mid-1960s through the mid-1970s. (Note that terms such as *1960s*, *1970s*, and *1980s* are not so much chronological as generational, indicating overlapping trends that do not begin and end on a particular date.) During the course of that decade, sociologists found that nationalism and patriotism were in dramatic decline, symbols of material comfort and worldly success were becoming much less attractive, scientific rationality was often being questioned, and traditional ideas of progress were being treated more skeptically than ever before. The 1960s are now remembered as a time when countercultures and deviant subcultures proliferated. **Countercultures,** such as those associated with "flower power" (urging advocates to "make love not war") and drug use ("turn on, tune in, drop out"), promoted values and behavior that

**Counterculture**  A term referring to values and behaviors that go against those of mainstream society. (Compare with **Culture** and **Subculture** in Chapter 1.)

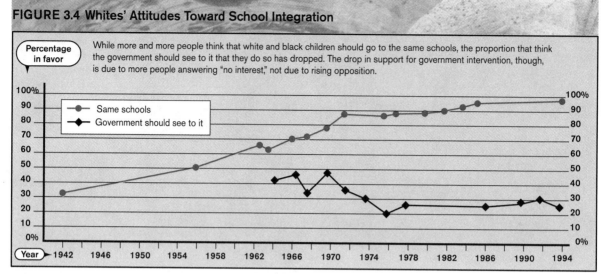

FIGURE 3.4 Whites' Attitudes Toward School Integration

While more and more people think that white and black children should go to the same schools, the proportion that think the government should see to it that they do so has dropped. The drop in support for government intervention, though, is due to more people answering "no interest," not due to rising opposition.

Percentage in favor

- Same schools
- Government should see to it

Year → 1942 1946 1950 1954 1958 1962 1966 1970 1974 1978 1982 1986 1990 1994

*Sources:* Frey, Abresch, and Yeasting (2001), with data drawn from Schuman and Steeh (1996).

went against those of "straight" or mainstream society.

Subcultures of the 1960s, such as that of the hippies, represented the lifestyle of groups that set themselves apart from the majority culture. During the same period, fundamental attitudes toward racial or ethnic differences—including racial prejudice itself—underwent a drastic change (see Figure 3.3).

### The Conservative Backlash

Yet, even as this decade entered American mythology, the national culture continued to change. It's as if there were a pendulum in which society swings back and forth between periods of intense public involvement and periods of withdrawal into private life, when enthusiasm and energy for politics have become exhausted (Hirschman 1982). In America during the late 1970s and 1980s, increasingly powerful backlash sentiments developed against the 1960s scripts about the possibilities, and desirability, of radical change. During this later period, the core values of American society swung markedly toward the more conservative side. Americans twice elected Ronald Reagan president; sexual experimentation declined and religiosity revived; familial and social authority became more respected once again. As a result of these shifts, egalitarian social reform programs were eliminated, taxes were cut, and the United States put more money into military preparation and forcefully reengaged its anticommunist sentiments in the Cold War.

Sociologists of culture tried to document and understand these changes in the national psyche. Among them, in the early 1980s, were Robert Bellah and his colleagues, who conducted a series of interviews and published their findings in *Habits of the Heart*—a book that sold tens of thousands of copies and left an indelible intellectual mark on the era. They discovered that there had been another drastic shift away from the core American values that Williams (1951) had originally laid out. Their findings convinced them that materialist values had now displaced moralizing ones. Concern with worldly and occupational success seemed to have pushed other kinds of values to the backburner. Individualism and self-interest had apparently replaced the humanistic, disinterested concern with the society as a whole.

Bellah and his colleagues were alarmed by these findings. They warned that such a radical turning away from moral and collective commitments could undermine the very idea of value commitment as such. If Americans were interested only in themselves, how could culture and society continue to exist?

As the new millennium dawned, sociologists continued to ponder how the contending values of individualism and social responsibility could be reconciled. Yet, with the cataclysmic shock to the national psyche administered on 9/11, it became very clear that, even in such a huge, heterogeneous, and postmodern consumer society as the United States, feelings of emotional solidarity still exist. Stories, symbols, and codes still supply the resources for collective identity. These emotional and cultural structures supply reserves to draw upon in times of crisis.

### American Values and Symbols Post-9/11

On September 11, 2001, Al-Qaeda terrorists flew passenger planes into the Twin Towers in New York City and the Pentagon in Washington, D.C. The minutely planned attacks killed thousands, and the conflagration in New York and its nightmarish aftermath were watched in real time by hundreds of millions of people on their TVs.

The reaction to the events of 9/11 demonstrated that American culture still had strong reserves of collective values and symbols. Most readily apparent was the intense praise for the heroic, public-spirited actions of the rescue workers. In Williams's (1951) terms, the firefighters' humanitarianism stood in stark contrast to the excesses of individualism and selfishness that were so evident in the financial scandals at Enron and elsewhere. Americans responded to these sacred heroes by "matching" their selflessness with their own. The American Red Cross (2002: 2) quickly raised $1 billion for the families of victims of 9/11, and firefighters across the nation collected millions of dollars for the families of their lost comrades. Never before in American history had so much money

been raised in so short a time. *Firefighter* became an iconic and revered symbol. Money could be raised simply by holding up a firefighters' boot at football games and grocery stores. New York City firefighter t-shirts became the fashion rage.

The tragic events of 9/11 had the unintended effect of reinvigorating America's core symbols. A cross was erected on the site of the destroyed World Trade Center (WTC), constructed out of broken girders. Hundreds of other symbolic items were hung on the fencing, including flowers, T-shirts, pictures, and flags from other countries covered in personal messages to the victims of the attack. It was the American flag that became one of the most enduring symbols of 9/11. A simple American flag had been raised by three firefighters over the still-smoldering ruins of the WTC. The image of this flag, which had come from a luxury yacht moored near the site, was captured by a news photographer and subsequently reproduced and imitated around the world. This image evoked comparisons to the famous picture of the American flag being raised at Iwo Jima during World War II. In fact, the photographer might have had the famous Iwo Jima photograph in mind when he composed his own picture fifty years later, for he selected a shot whereby the flag was in exactly the same, not fully erect position. So the image of the American flag took on significance and meaning in the aftermath of 9/11 not only because of that tragedy but because it evoked other sacred collective memories as well. The martyrs and heroes of 9/11 became linked to the national martyrs and heroes of what has been called "the last good war." World War II had also been a time of suffering and loss that inspired tremendous outpourings of selflessness and national solidarity. The suffering and selflessness had been redeemed with a historic victory. (On 9/11, see Calhoun 2002; on cultural symbols and war, see Fussell 1975.)

The flag that the New York firefighters hoisted at the site of the World Trade Center then "traveled a very patriotic route, going from Yankee Stadium on September 23 (where it was signed by Mayor

This bronze statue by J. Seward Johnson was found in the rubble after 9/11. People adorned it with mementos, which the artist then recast in bronze exactly as they were placed. (Shutterpoint/Anthony Borzone)

Rudolph W. Giuliani and Governor George E. Pataki) to the Middle East (where it spent several months flying on ships involved in the war in Afghanistan) to [New York's] City Hall (where it was signed by Mayor Michael R. Bloomberg and honored in a solemn ceremony on April 1). It was then returned to its original owners, Shirley B. Dreifus and her husband, Spiros E. Kopelakis (who owned the yacht from which the three firefighters plucked the flag). But there was one problem: 'This isn't our flag,' Mrs. Dreifus said. 'It's too big'" (quoted in Chen 2002: B3). The flag initially hoisted by the New York firefighters had somehow disappeared, and a larger flag was substituted without anyone noticing. It was this larger flag that actually made its pilgrimage across the world.

That this traveling icon of American values was not the actual 9/11 flag shows how images and symbols take on a reality of their own. This story of the "wrong" flag making its pilgrimage across the

United States also reveals the power of mediated images in postmodern society. As further discussed in Chapter 4, on media and communication, the representations of what we believe to be reality are, in fact, carefully constructed images. Photographers, filmmakers, journalists, and editors shape what they present to us—for maximum effect. They are able to achieve performative power and to tell us their story only if they can attract and hold our attention (see Alexander, Giesen, and Mast 2006). Given this construction, then, the images that attract and fix our gaze are never simply reflections of an underlying, unmediated social reality, even when they claim to be the real thing.

## Culture Is Not "Civilization"

We have seen how culture is woven into every part of our everyday lives, providing symbolic codes, norms, and values for every action, every social crisis, every institution. From this cultural perspective, we can understand how moments of crisis like 9/11 become occasions when these taken-for-granted cultural elements are called up. The invisible now becomes visible, and culture is reinvigorated, clarified, reworked, and/or reaffirmed.

However, culture has not always been conceived in this way. During the eighteenth and nineteenth centuries, it was discussed much more narrowly. Culture was identified with the beliefs and practices of the social elite—specifically, with its artistic and intellectual achievements—and was thereby equated with "civilization." This understanding of culture was elitist and ethnocentric. Behind it lay the idea that only the practices of Western Europe's social elite were subtle, ethical, and cultivated. Even today, it is not unusual to find culture being equated with the study of the great achievements of Mozart, Picasso, Tolstoy, and the ancient Greek and Renaissance masters.

The German philosopher Johann Gottfried von Herder (1744–1803) was among the first to criticize the notion that European culture was superior to the artistic and intellectual products of other civilizations. Herder argued that "the very thought of a superior European culture is a blatant insult to the majesty of nature" (quoted in Mukerji and Schudson 1991: 2). Rejecting the exclusive identification of culture with civilization, he spoke of "cultures" rather than a single high culture. He set out, with other pioneering spirits, to study folk cultures: the symbols, values, narratives, and expressions of ordinary people. It is this anti-elitist understanding that informs sociological thinking about culture today.

## POSTMODERNITY, GLOBALIZATION, AND THE CULTURAL TURN

Especially in our postmodern society, this anti-elitist approach to culture seems the obvious way to go. Our contact with nature and even our relations with one another are increasingly filtered through symbolic mechanisms produced by ever-attentive service industries as well as by the new armies of educated experts and New Age gurus. As further discussed in Chapter 4, the airwaves and Internet circuits overflow with information about how we should be leading our lives. We know what we know not so much through direct, personal experience as through the media and their pundits. For instance, we are aware of the "evil deeds" of Saddam Hussein not because we have been to Iraq and witnessed his crimes, nor because we have met victims from his cruelly repressive and violent political campaigns. Rather, we know about his crimes because we have heard news reports on television and the radio, have read about them on the Internet and in newspapers, and, perhaps, have seen Saddam immortalized in feature-length cartoons like *South Park.*

Stuart Hall explains the centrality of culture in contemporary society this way: "Culture creeps into every nook and cranny of contemporary social life, creating a proliferation of secondary environments, mediating everything. It is present in the disembodied voices and images which address us from the screens on our local petrol station. It is a key element in the way in which the domestic environment is harnessed, through consumption, to worldwide trends and fashions. It is brought home to us through the sports and fan magazines" (quoted in Thompson 1997: 215).

Globalization increases interconnections across the world. It involves both international movement of peoples between countries and global mass communications that bring the world into our living rooms. Yet, though we learn more about people and places far from our homes, *what* we learn about them is intensely mediated. Via the mass media, we feel that we "know" all about the nations and peoples of the Middle East, despite their being so far removed from our own personal experience. In just the same way, foreigners come to "know" all about the United States through Hollywood television shows and films.

One of the most important consequences of such intense postmodern mediation is that fact and fiction do not seem as neatly separated as they were in earlier, modern societies. *South Park* cartoon images of Saddam Hussein as Satan's lover mesh quite nicely with news reports documenting the reality of Hussein's actual crimes. And shown throughout the world are American TV shows like *Beverly Hills 90210, Friends, Will and Grace, The OC,* and *Desperate Housewives*, which, though clearly fictional, are often taken as genuine reflections of American superficiality, individualism, and materialism.

The recent proliferation of reality television has further confused fact and fiction. Television audiences around the world can now see what life is "really" like for every social stratum in American society—from the underclass on *Cops* to the suburban youth on MTV's *Real World* and the celebrities on *The Osbournes, Newlyweds,* or *Cribs.* Although these shows are not filmed in a studio on a carefully designed set, they are often highly scripted by teams of writers, and technical crews devote hours to careful and creative editing to achieve the effect of immediacy and spontaneity. The values of materialism and individualism figure as prominently in reality television as they do in the more traditional sitcom and drama genres, but they are especially pronounced in the competition format where participants are gradually eliminated through a series of trials. The prize in these competitions is usually a large sum of money (*Survivor, Big Brother*), but it can include something in addition to money as well, such as a career (*American Idol, America's Next Top Model*) or a spouse (*Joe Millionaire, The Bachelorette*).

The extraordinary centrality of globally projected symbols in postmodern society is also reflected in the changing conceptual framework of sociology. As we noted in Chapter 1, social theorists have recently taken a "cultural turn," the result of which is a greater appreciation of the symbolic as compared with the purely institutional aspects of social life. This new sociological understanding has borrowed ideas and methods from the humanities, from disciplines such as English and film studies. And concepts such as social drama, performance, discourse, code, and narrative are more and more frequently finding their way into the pages of hard-headed sociological books and journals. The roles such concepts play in the sociological analysis of contemporary society will be highlighted throughout the chapters that follow, especially chapters 4–7, Chapter 15, and Chapter 16.

## ARE CULTURES WHOLES OR PARTS?

With the recent "cultural turn," sociologists now emphasize that while symbols must be shared to constitute a culture, they certainly do not have to be shared by every single member of a social group. Cultures do not have to be, and usually are not, integrated wholes. In fact, they are often divided and conflicted. Sets of cultural **beliefs** can be at war with each other inside the same society. Often fragmented and hierarchical, culture is affected by the same kinds of divisions as the supposedly noncultural aspects of societies.

Nowhere is this point more readily apparent than in the so-called culture wars, which involve volatile social and political debates on issues of race (affirmative action), religion, and morality (school prayer, capital punishment, abortion). These "wars" are cultural in that they pit core American values—the same ones identified by Williams (1951)—against one another.

Consider, for instance, the controversial issue of abortion. One side calls itself, significantly, "prochoice" and emphasizes freedom and individualism in Williams's terms. Prochoice advocates view the fundamental issue as one of women's rights. They maintain that women have the right to legal abortion—that it is a basic choice, central to women's autonomy and freedom. They see questions about the viability of the fetus—"when life begins"—either as a fact to be established by science or as a private, moral, or religious issue to be decided by the woman alone.

How do proabortion groups achieve their aims? For them, doing so is more than a matter of organizational efficiency and political opportunity. They must also gain public sympathy by framing their objectives in a manner that resonates with the core values of society. In a recent article, Myra Marx Ferree (2003) compared the cultural frames used by organizations that are prochoice versus neutral in Germany and the United States. Her analysis of public discourse about abortion based on newspaper articles over a twenty-four-year period demonstrated both gender and national differences.

Autonomy is a core value in both countries, but it is expressed quite differently in each case. In Germany, the right to choose tends to be gendered. Both men and women make arguments that point to a *woman*'s right to self-determination. In the United States, however, the value of autonomy is more often expressed in gender-neutral language, and the arguments revolve around abstract ideas of *individual* rights (see Figure 3.4).

Moreover, in contrast to the United States, a core value in German society is the state's responsibility to protect its citizens. Figure 3.5 shows how arguments stressing protection figured more prominently in the German abortion debate, even among those who were prochoice.

The other side, which evocatively calls itself "prolife," emphasizes a moral orientation in Williams's terms. It takes a clear right and wrong approach, viewing abortion as morally wrong—indeed, as tantamount to murder. Prolife advocates classify the fetus as a person and maintain that it is well within the duty of the law to proscribe this "homicide" just as it criminalizes other sorts of immoral behavior.

This debate does not reflect a difference in individual opinion or attitude. Rather, it rests upon

One of the most divisive issues in the United States and around the world is whether women should have the right to terminate pregnancies. (courtesy of Melanie Stafford)

conflicts between symbolic codes and narratives, between freedom on the one side and moral distinctions separating right from wrong on the other. Yet, paradoxically, it is precisely the moral sincerity of their opponents that neither side can question. The right to life and the right to be free are, indeed, equally compelling moral postulates. But to prochoice groups the contention that the fetus is a person, such that killing it is murder, seems outrageously biased (not to mention factually inaccurate)—just as the contention that women should control their own reproduction seems immoral if, as prolifers believe, it can result in the murder of a tiny human being. It is because of the *cultural*

**Belief** A statement that attempts to describe some aspect of collective reality—for example, "God exists" or "The Earth is round." The validity of our beliefs is not as important as the way in which they shape our day-to-day experience. In other words, regardless of whether it is true or false that, say, God exists or the Earth is round, certain assumptions underlying our social interactions and relationships are based on these beliefs.

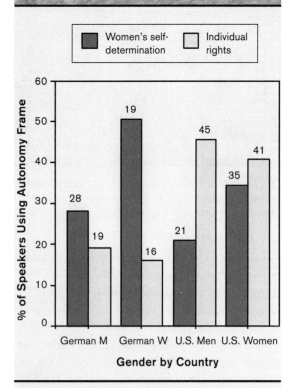

FIGURE 3.5 Percentage of Speakers Who Include Any Pro–Abortion Rights Claim in the Women's Self-Determination and Individualism Frames, by Country and Gender

*Note:* The weighted *N* of cases is 368 for German men, 403 for German women, 964 for U.S. men, and 731 for U.S. women, with 160 cases where no gender is given excluded along with all speakers who are either antiabortion overall in their framing in an article or neutral but speaking for an antiabortion party or organization.

*Source:* Ferree (2003).

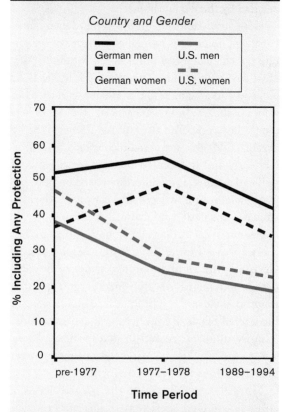

FIGURE 3.6 Inclusion of Protection Frames Among Prochoice and Neutral Men and Women Speakers, by Country and Time Period

*Note:* Weighted *N* of cases by period for each group: German men, 147, 52, 170; German women, 63, 74, 266; U.S. men, 194, 354, 416; U.S. women, 85, 257, 389. In all periods speakers who are on balance antiabortion in an article or neutral and representing an antiabortion party or organization are omitted.

*Source:* Ferree (2003).

status of this conflict that compromise on abortion is so difficult to achieve. That cultural values are relative becomes clear when we look at the abortion debate in a comparative way.

In heterogeneous and postmodern societies, there is a wide variety of classificatory schemes to choose from. Is it that different people have divergent social experiences—or that the "facts" of geography, age, economic status, gender, religion, race, and ethnicity are mediated through such different classificatory schemes? A teenager with a Mohawk hairstyle might be viewed by a classmate as simply a kid who likes punk music. The parents of the same teenager, by contrast, might view his hairstyle as a sign of rebellion, anger, or even suicidal "angst." Each response calls upon an established culture classification—one relating to music, the other to attitude and age. Inside the cultural code that the classmate uses to frame "Mohawk," the hairstyle is a relatively mundane routine symbol. But in the classificatory scheme that the parents call up, it has a more threatening and profane connotation.

## Cultures and Subcultures

By *subculture* we mean a culture within a culture. In some cases, subcultures subvert dominant values; in others, they extend them in a radical way. Adult "Satanists" and teenage "Goths" subvert mainstream moral codes. Emphasizing the negative, the eerie, and the dark, their demeanor and clothing display sadness and their ritual activities celebrate evil. "Survivalists," by contrast, do not so much subvert the moral code of American individualism as push it to the extreme—they emphasize autonomy to the exclusion of everything else. In cases where a subculture becomes closed off to contact and influence, totally isolating its members from outsiders, sociologists usually consider the group a cult. Because of this isolation, cults can be dangerous to their members—and, on rare occasions, to the broader society as well. But most subcultures are not cults (though they may be cultish). We all participate in subcultures, and our lives are enriched by them. Surfers, poets, and intellectuals can be said to have subcultures, as do basketball players and garage bands, aerobic instructors, Internet hackers, corporate bankers, househusbands, and housewives.

The very notion that groups and organizations can be subcultures casts them in a different light. That is, instead of considering just the specific goals and material interests that group members pursue, and the power hierarchy that regulates them, we can also think of groups and organizations as symbolic orders. As sociologists, we want to decipher the distinctive meaning systems that organize commitment, the group rituals that sus-

Surfers have their own distinct subculture, which includes language, fashion, behaviors, and lifestyle. (iStockphoto)

tain them, and how these beliefs might decline over time.

## "Attitudes" Versus "Behavior"

A dynamic symbolic conceptualization of culture also helps explain what some thinkers see as an alarming gap between beliefs and practices (see box titled "Employer Hypocrisy"). Skeptics about cultural influence will sometimes ask: If values are so important, then why do individual and institutional actions so often contradict them? It is important to understand, however, that while culture establishes patterns and ideals, it does not define the specific ways in which these symbolic patterns are established in the world. There is necessarily some distance between the systems of symbols

## data

### Employer Hypocrisy

Researchers often use surveys to gauge people's attitudes toward specific social groups. For example, surveys have shown that white Americans' attitudes toward blacks have become increasingly positive (or decreasingly negative) in recent decades. We might assume that people's actions reflect the attitudes measured by these surveys. But do surveys really give us an accurate picture of how people behave?

Devah Pager and Lincoln Quillian (2005) addressed this enduring question by comparing 350 employers' actual hiring behaviors to their self-reported attitudes toward hiring ex-offenders. These attitudes were initially recorded by means of a survey. Next, to measure the employers' behaviors, the authors used an "experimental audit" method in which matched pairs of young men were sent to apply for entry-level jobs. The pairs consisted of either two black men or two white men, and one of each pair was assigned a fictional criminal record. The authors then tallied the number of callbacks each applicant received. The same employers were later asked how likely they would be to hire hypotheti-

cal applicants with profiles matching those who had actually applied during the audit study.

Pager and Quillian found that the attitudes expressed in the survey did not match up with the behaviors exhibited during the audit study. A statistically significant number of employers reported a much greater willingness to hire an ex-offender than they showed when actually presented with one. Specifically, those who had expressed positive attitudes toward hiring ex-offenders were only slightly more likely to call them back than were employers who expressed negative attitudes. In addition, although the survey results revealed no difference in the employers' preferences for hiring whites versus blacks, discrimination appeared in the auditing situation: The employers called back white applicants more than three times as often as they called back black applicants, despite having expressed positive attitudes toward hiring blacks during the survey. These results cast doubt on the link between surveyed attitudes and actual behaviors. People often say one thing but do another.

*Source:* Armato et al. (2006).

that constitute culture, on the one hand, and concrete social behaviors, on the other. This "distance" is what makes social life creative and unpredictable. It is a good thing that cultural patterns and concrete **behavior** are not exactly the same thing.

**Attitudes** refer to the statements people make about their values and beliefs. Attitudes are hearable and recordable verbal accounts; but they are not actions. In public opinion surveys of attitudes, researchers typically ask simple and direct ques-

tions aimed at eliciting clear and unequivocal responses. These are aggregated statistically to demonstrate the variations in attitudes among different social groups. The strength of attitudinal research is that it lends itself to quantification in the form of statistics, as we see in opinion polls. The numbers show what proportion of the sample of the population surveyed share an attitude or opinion.

The fact that people claim to have a certain attitude or opinion does not necessarily mean that they will act in accordance with it. Even when they are restricted by the options of a particular cultural order, people still have a wide variety of classificatory schemes to draw from. What they evoke verbally, moreover, is often sensitive to their immediate context. They are providing a reasonable "account" of themselves to another party, rather than offering an accurate or sincere reflection of their beliefs. Even these accounts, however, refer to some widely accepted cultural code. (See Harold Garfinkel's description of "accounts" in his pathbreaking book *Studies in Ethnomethodology*, 1967.)

In the context of being interviewed by public opinion pollsters, most contemporary white Americans will say that they believe that racial discrimination is wrong. Yet, in the context of organizational life, they may act in discriminatory ways—for example, by excluding a black employee from an important business or social occasion. This distinction does not make symbols, values, and classificatory schemes any less real. It demonstrates, instead, the plurality of culture and the complexity of institutional life.

Inconsistent behavior may be a reflection of internal cultural schisms. People's values tend to be manifest, or public ("Racial discrimination is wrong"), whereas their symbolic schemes tend to be latent, or private ("I just felt more 'comfortable' with John Smith in the interview process"). However, inconsistency might simply be the result of cultural plurality. For example, Americans believe in democratic values that support conflictual challenges to authority and, at the same time, they believe in organizational values that emphasize deference to authority and cooperation. Which value is evoked depends on where you are acting at a particular time—in the boardroom, the marketplace, or in the public world of politics. Take the statement "I thought it would be 'awkward' for our client if our black associate attended the power lunch and I didn't want to do anything that might upset the deal." Is this an expression of racism that contradicts the value pattern of equality? Or is it an acknowledgment of context, a pragmatic if less than heroic response to the knowledge that racism continues to exist?

## Class, Culture, and Genre

One of the most important ways that social perception and experience are categorized in the contemporary United States is by **socioeconomic class.** As we will see further in Chapter 18, on social change, the United States is simultaneously one of the wealthiest nations on earth and a country with tremendous socioeconomic stratification, or hierarchical layering. In that chapter, we will analyze the institutional as well as cultural aspects of economic stratification in more detail. Here, however, we are concerned with the ways that sharp differences in economic status allow vastly different ways of life, social codes, and classificatory schemes. Language, dress, music, and speech can all vary significantly by socioeconomic class.

As long as societies have been stratified, there have been highly visible differences in the expressive forms produced and consumed by elites versus people from less privileged classes. Only the

**Behavior** Anything we do. Our behaviors may be consistent with our attitudes, as when an antiwar activist attends a protest against a war. Or they might be inconsistent with our attitudes, as when someone says that recycling is the best way to save the environment but never recycles.

**Attitudes** The statements that people make about their values and beliefs.

**Socioeconomic class** One of the most common classifications in society, closely tied to occupation and income. Members of different social classes are often seen as occupying different positions in a social hierarchy, and as having unequal access to resources, opportunities, and power. From a cultural perspective, however, socioeconomic class is most relevant in the context of understanding various ways of life, social codes, and classificatory schemes.

elites have had the leisure time to devote themselves to certain kinds of cultural activities, as well as the money to acquire the training and education that the more difficult and demanding arts often require. It is certainly not the case that people outside the elite are less interested in artistic expression. They simply have less time to devote themselves to learning about producing and consuming it. For this reason, popular or folk culture is less self-conscious and more accessible than elite culture. Passed down from one generation to the next rather than created by specially trained artists, popular culture typically places less emphasis on originality.

Some of the most important studies of the relationship between culture and class have been done by the French sociologist Pierre Bourdieu. In his highly acclaimed book *Distinction* (1984), Bourdieu argued that people of higher social status were more likely to equate artistic achievement with abstraction, whereas those of lower social status were more likely to prefer art that is representational and realistic. Having discovered that men and women in the lower strata of French society prefer photography to painting, he reasoned that this was so because photography is more realistic and its production and appreciation require little formal training.

Bourdieu's team of researchers showed photographs to people from different classes. They found that lower-class people rarely made an aesthetic response. Rather, they viewed each photograph as a window, and expressed interest in the information this frame contained. Here is a typical response from a manual worker in Paris, commenting on a photograph of an old woman's hands: "Oh, she's got terribly deformed hands! … The old girl must've worked hard. Looks like she's got arthritis. She's definitely crippled, unless she's … got her hand bent like that. Not like a duchess's hands or even a typist's! … I really feel sorry seeing that poor old woman's hands, they're all knotted, you might say."

People from higher classes reacted differently to this photo. They understood it aesthetically, as a work of art, not just as a picture about reality. Here's a comment from a highly educated Parisian engineer: "I find this a very beautiful photograph. It's the very symbol of toil. It puts me in mind of Flaubert's old servant-woman. … That woman's gesture, at once very humble. … It's terrible that work and poverty are so deforming" (quoted in Bourdieu 1984: 44–45).

Yet, though we must certainly recognize that forms of cultural expression vary with class, we cannot accept the high- versus low-culture distinction without serious qualifications. There is a danger of implicitly equating high culture with civilization, which, as we have seen, was a mistake commonly made in the late eighteenth and nineteenth centuries. In this old-fashioned view, elites are credited with having culture whereas popular artistic practices are not seen as cultural at all. In the research that we just reported, for example, Bourdieu does not hesitate to speak of "the culturally most deprived" (1984: 44–45).

Today, most sociologists reject the notion that elite culture is a better or higher form of culture than folk or popular culture. Indeed, in his book *Highbrow, Lowbrow: The Emergence of Cultural Hierarchy in the U.S.* (1988), historian Lawrence Levine demonstrates just how silly, as well as corrosive, such cultural snobbery can be. Levine points out that for a good part of the nineteenth century, upper-, middle-, and working-class Americans consumed what today would be considered high culture—Shakespearean dramas, Mozart operas, Dickens and Twain novels, Longfellow and Lowell poems. Things changed after industrial capitalism created new and less stable class relations, and immigration to the United States from outside Northwestern Europe increased. Only then did members of the old American upper class begin stridently insisting on the great distinction between their own cultural sensibilities and those of the newcomers.

In the late 1850s, for example, the Boston magazine *Atlantic Monthly* declared that Italians "have by no manner of means reached so high a degree of development in the arts of musical composition as the Germans have" and dismissed Italian operas, such as those by Puccini, as "merely a few singers lifted up on the cheapest platform of an opera" (quoted in Levine 1988: 220). And in the early twentieth century, as black Americans began to make their way into the centers of American cultural life, the New Orleans *Times-Picayune* described jazz, a distinctively African-American art form, as an "atrocity in polite society." Judging "its musical value is nil," the white Southern newspaper declared that "we should make it a point of civic honor to suppress it" (quoted in Levine 1988: 221).

In fact, throughout the course of the twentieth century, virtually every new form of artistic expression was initially declared lacking in cultural refinement. In 1913, the *Nation* magazine asserted that movies were "not a very high art." Their growing popularity was said to reveal "the common predilection of the popular taste for the lurid and the fantastic"; as compared with literature or painting, cinema supposedly required "no thought and little attention" (quoted in Levine 1988: 232). Similarly disparaging and elitist remarks greeted the emergence of television and rock-and-roll music fifty years later.

It was actually from efforts to protect the privilege and culture of established elites that the very terms *highbrow* and *lowbrow* emerged in the late nineteenth century. In those days, a pseudoscience called phrenology promoted the bizarre notion that the size and shape of people's skulls revealed their intelligence and moral character. Because apes had smaller foreheads and more protruding brows, they were described as lowbrow. Soon, the same terminology came to be applied to lower-class social groups—such as blacks, Asians, Jews, and Italians—who were judged, according to elite standards, as more animal-like and less than fully human. White Christian Northern Europeans were believed to have the largest foreheads and the least protruding brows. Only such a highbrow race, it was believed, could produce and appreciate sophisticated culture.

Today, sociologists reject these biased and racist approaches to culture. Rather than ranking groups according to whether they "have culture" or not, contemporary thinkers maintain that every group and every action has a cultural dimension. Similarly, contemporary specialists in aesthetic judgment, such as postmodern art and literary critics, no longer assume that "elite" culture has higher artistic value than "popular" culture. Isn't rock-and-roll as much an aesthetic achievement as symphonic music? Doesn't good rock music—or blues, folk, gospel, or rap—also require creativity and many years of training? Isn't it also evaluated according to demanding aesthetic criteria? There are good and bad rock songs just as there are good and bad operas and paintings. All art forms demand great skill and craft, even if some require less formal education to practice.

## Genres

Today the concept of cultural **genres** has increasingly displaced notions of high and low culture. Commercial art is one genre, or form, of art; framed oil paintings (whether by Matisse or an unknown contemporary artist) are another. Both genres have their geniuses, their conformists, and their charlatans. The same is true for jazz, rock, musical comedy, evening sitcoms, and even the afternoon soaps. Each of these genres represents a distinctive

**Genre** A distinctive form of cultural expression that aims to create symbols that engage, entertain, and sensitize. Commercial art, framed oil paintings, jazz, musical comedy, and evening sitcoms are examples of genres.

and challenging form of cultural expression; each aims to create symbols that engage, entertain, and sensitize.

Once we accept the notion that culture is a dimension of every human group, it is no surprise to find that every group develops at least some distinctive symbols of its own. Gary Alan Fine (1987: 126) calls these symbols "idiocultures" to emphasize that they are distinctive, or idiosyncratic: "An idioculture consists of particular examples of behavior or communication that have symbolic meaning and significance for members of a group. Although the list is not exhaustive, phenomena classifiable as idioculture include nicknames, jokes, insults, beliefs, rules of conduct, clothing styles, songs, narratives, gestures, and recurrent fantasies." In one of his studies, Fine (1987) found that every team of Little League baseball players, along with their coaches and parents, has an idioculture all its own, over and beyond the culture of Little League baseball as such. In another, Fine (1997) studied the subculture of a somewhat more exotic group: hobbyists who dedicate their free time to mushroom gathering! In 1993 the North American Mycological Association recorded some 1,800 members, and in the same year the seventy-seven state and local mycological clubs in the United States and Canada had an estimated membership of 10,000. Fine discovered that mushrooming is not just about "the thrill of discovery, identification, and (on occasion) consumption of natural objects." Indeed, mushrooms are symbols that gain meaning inside a subculture that energetically divides the sacred from the profane: "Mushroomers accept the boundary between 'good' nature and 'rough' civilization. Boundaries must prevent the contamination of the former by the latter. Being in the woods is a magical time. When the mood is broken, a sharp malaise is evident. On one occasion, foraging in a deep woods, we stumbled across a clearing where houses were to be built. Our leader commented sarcastically, 'I think we're back in the real world'" (Fine 1997: 71–77).

## CONCLUSION

Classical and modern sociologists understood that culture was central to social life, but they tied their understandings of cultural patterns too closely to institutional interests and organizational and psychological strains. For example, they spoke about modern culture as if it simply reflected the political and economic constraints and interactional and intellectual rigors of secular, industrial, and bureaucratic societies. This "sociology *of* culture" approach was reductionistic, and it rendered culture relatively unimportant compared to heavy-duty institutions. Why should culture be studied, in fact, if it is merely a reflection of something else? In postmodern societies, when institutions and interactions are so conspicuously saturated by mass-mediated symbols, it has become more clear that cultural patterns have a power that is (relatively) independent of institutional contexts. Having made the "cultural turn," sociologists are now borrowing concepts from the humanities, especially from studies of literature and film, to analyze social life. With these tools in hand, they have investigated the "textuality" of the environments of action within which we live and work today.

# EXERCISES

## Exercise 1

From the time you wake up in the morning until you go to sleep at night, your activities are guided by norms, values, symbols, and classificatory schemes. In this exercise, you are asked to write down all the norms, values, and social codes that you follow from the time you first wake up in the morning until the time of your first class. Be as precise and thorough as possible in describing each norm, value, and social code. Also indicate what happens if you do not follow these norms and codes. You might even experiment by engaging in a "breaching experiment" with your family and friends; but please, no illegal behavior!

## Exercise 2

Describe your present hairstyle and apparel in terms of the specific symbolic and social codes they reflect. What statement about yourself and your identity do your clothes and hairstyle make? Is it possible that other people might suggest different interpretations of your clothes and hairstyle?

## STUDY QUESTIONS

1. Describe the two standard social explanations offered for fashion and social standards of beauty. Then describe the cultural explanation of fashion. How does it differ from the first two?

2. What are the three categories of symbols? Which categories are emotionally charged, and why?

3. Does the meaning of a symbol come from the properties of the thing to which it refers?

4. What are norms? And why do we tend to conform to them in everyday life, even though not all norms are codified into laws?

5. How are norms related to values?

6. What do sociologists mean when they use the term *subculture*? How does this concept facilitate the study of groups and organizations?

7. In the eighteenth and nineteenth centuries, the term *culture* was used to describe "the best of what has been thought and said" in Western European society; it was also equated with *civilization*. Why do contemporary sociologists reject this definition? What alternative definition of *culture* do they propose?

## FURTHER READING

### Fashion and Beauty

Barthes, Roland. 1990. *The Fashion System*. Berkeley: University of California Press.

Crane, Diana. 2000. *Fashion and Its Social Agendas: Class, Gender, and Identity in Clothing*. Chicago: University of Chicago Press.

Davis, Kathy. 2003. *Dubious Equalities and Embodied Difference: Cultural Studies on Cosmetic Surgery (Explorations in Bioethics and the Medical Humanities)*. Lanham, MD: Rowman & Littlefield.

Gimlin, Debra. 2000. "Cosmetic Surgery: Beauty as Commodity." *Qualitative Sociology* 23, no. 1: 77–98.

### American Culture

Bellah, Robert N., Richard Madsen, William M. Sullivan, Ann Swidler, and Steven M. Tipton. 1985. *Habits of the Heart: Individualism and Commitment in American Life*. Berkeley: University of California Press.

Hunter, James Davison. 1991. *Culture Wars: The Struggle to Define America*. New York: Basic Books.

Williams, Robin. 1951. *American Society: A Sociological Interpretation*. New York: Knopf.

# chapter 4

# Media and Communication

The **mass media** constitute one of the most important and controversial institutions of postmodern society. In fact, their saturation of the culture of everyday life is one of the reasons for calling it "postmodern society," as we will explain. The life of the individual is increasingly spent consuming images on television, film, and computer screens. The media are indeed everywhere, but there are controversies about just how much influence—for good or bad—they have over us. As an example of the pessimistic view, there are critics who claim that many Americans are becoming "couch potatoes," mindlessly watching hour after hour of "dumbed down" television programs and violent movies, which, in turn, lead some individuals to act in mindless or violent ways. We are in danger of "amusing ourselves to death," as the title of one book put it (Postman 1985). Another, somewhat more optimistic view is represented by those who believe we are entering a new "information age" (Castells 1996, 1997, 1998) in which media developments, such as the Internet and cable and satellite television, have the potential to empower individuals and strengthen grassroots democracy.

Another example of the pessimistic view is provided by an article in *Rolling Stone* magazine, under the title "A Boy's Life," suggesting that the multiple-victim school shootings in the 1990s were perpetrated by individuals who had been exposed to violent images in the media. Indeed, a considerable body of anecdotal evidence supports the belief that movies like *Natural Born Killers* have influenced a number of young killers—including Barry Loukaitis, the youth described in "A Boy's Life." Loukaitis had told a friend, for example, that it would be "cool" to go on a murder

Are Americans becoming "couch potatoes"? Studies have shown that exposure to many hours of television per day negatively affects children and adults. (iStockphoto)

spree like the one in Oliver Stone's movie (Sullivan 1998: 46–53).

One of the first of the multiple-victim school shootings by white teenagers in rural communities or small towns that have so wounded the national psyche in the past two and a half years took place in February 1996, in the farm town of Moses Lake, Washington. The killer was a fourteen-year-old honor student named Barry Loukaitis who strode into math class one day and shot two students, then fired a bullet into his teacher's back. "Sure beats algebra, doesn't it?" Barry asked as he stood over a boy who was choking to death on his own blood.

Like nearly every one of the young killers who came after him, Loukaitis was a depressed boy of above-average intelligence, who suffered an inferiority complex and was enthralled by violent images from film or television. ... Suicide rates

**Mass media** An umbrella term referring to the variety of technical devices and processes through which mass communication takes place. These devices and processes are used to transmit organized messages designed to reach a large number of people.

among young Americans have increased steadily for forty years, leveling off recently at their all-time high. The National Institute of Mental Health says that more than 1.5 million Americans under the age of fifteen are seriously depressed (Sullivan 1998: 46–53).

## AN INDIVIDUAL OR A SOCIAL STORY?

What are we to make of this kind of media report? Part of a long article presenting a string of stories about teenagers who committed violent acts, it offers explanations in terms of their psychological state at the time. It refers to a single external causal factor—television and film images of violence—that might have affected each individual's mental state or led him to imitate actions he had seen on screen. Bear in mind, however, that the sociologist Émile Durkheim, in his classic study *Suicide* (1897), demonstrated the inadequacy of explanations based on the presumed mental states of individuals or psychological mechanisms such as imitation. If there was a social trend, he said, then there had to be a social explanation. Furthermore, as anecdotal evidence about individuals is notoriously unreliable, a psychiatrist would need to thoroughly examine other types of evidence before he or she could be sure that exposure to the media was really the cause of an individual act of teenage violence. To be fair, the *Rolling Stone* report did make references to general statistical evidence, some of which was drawn from newspaper articles at the time of the murders. In particular, the report "trotted out the now familiar numbers: the 8,000 onscreen murders that the average American child will witness before finishing elementary school; the 106 deaths in *Rambo 3* and the 264 in *Die Hard 2*, et cetera" (Sullivan 1998: 51–52). However, it then went on to further its claim, quoting a former U.S. Army ranger and psychology professor at West Point, Dave Grossman, who stated that "television is a greater factor in this increased de-

gree of violence in our society than all other factors combined." He added, "And that includes broken homes and abuse and neglect and all those sorts of things."

Not surprisingly, sociologists and media experts hotly contested these sweeping claims. One critic described the *Rolling Stone* article as "drive-by journalism" and pointed out that "Nielsen surveys show kids today watch only about half as much TV as kids did in the '70s. And if TV's the cause, why is the murder rate 14 times higher among black teens than among white teens?" (Males 1999). In other words, there might be other important causal factors involved. Clearly, as we will be emphasizing in this chapter, the links between individuals and the media cannot be understood in isolation from the web of cultural and social factors in which they are enmeshed. In particular, researchers need to examine the institutional factors involved in media production as well as the social and cultural practices of media consumption.

The same kinds of questions about social constraint and individual action that are raised in the context of violence also arise in debates about politics and the media. The questions are often posed as alternatives: Are developments in the media empowering individuals and increasing choice? Or are they dumbing down and indoctrinating people with ideologically biased views?

As individuals we tend to think of the media as offering us the choice of various sorts of entertainment and pleasure. But if we think more in terms of our social roles, such as that of citizen, we see that the media are vitally important to the democratic processes that bind the diverse interests of individuals and groups into a united nation. Can these two functions be reconciled? Or are the mass media in postmodern society increasingly mixing entertainment with information (a conglomeration known as "infotainment") in what they offer consumers? Some critics—especially those influenced by a conflict theory, such as Marxism, and advocating what is called a political-economy approach—maintain that there is noth-

Violence in the media is a major concern for those who believe it may influence actual social behavior. Here, a protestor of President George W. Bush's visit to East Germany compares him to "Rambo." (AP Photo/Fabian Bimmer)

ing new here, and that the mass media are just part of the capitalist economy. Others, following a more cultural approach, argue that there are important cultural factors that can lead to different outcomes in the production and consumption of mass-media products. We will examine both sets of arguments in this chapter, but first, let us consider the importance of the media as illustrated by their coverage of an event—the terrorist attacks of September 11, 2001—that not only highlights this importance but also potentially offers evidence in support of both approaches. In particular, the upcoming section demonstrates how central the media are in a postmodern culture where our gaze is constantly engaged by the rapidly changing screens of MTV-like images that seem to offer information. But this

information makes sense only when we bring background information to bear to decipher their meanings.

## THE IMPORTANCE OF THE MASS MEDIA

For much of its history, sociology regarded the media and popular culture as relatively unimportant subjects. The "Founding Fathers" of sociology, at the end of the nineteenth century and the beginning of the twentieth, at least had the excuse that the mass media were little developed and mainly consisted of newspapers and books. And in the middle years of the twentieth century, many sociologists thought there were more important topics to focus on than the media and popular culture, which they regarded as mainly trivializing entertainment. Some conservatives worried about the threat to morals purportedly posed by the media, particularly with regard to sexual or violent content, and were concerned about popular culture lowering cultural standards. Among liberals and socialists on the Left, there was concern about mass culture indoctrinating the working class with conservative ideology that supported the interests of the capitalist class. Radical sociologists accepted Marx's statement that "[t]he ideas of the ruling class are in every epoch the ruling ideas: i.e. the class, which is the ruling material force of society, is at the same time its ruling intellectual force" (Marx and Engels 1844–1846: 64). The neo-Marxist social theorists Max Horkheimer and Theodor Adorno (1947), who formed the Frankfurt School in Germany before World War II, drew on their experience of the effectiveness of Nazi propaganda and, then, of American mass entertainment to criticize the ideology of the **culture industry.** According to these theorists, the culture industry plays a major role in the reproduction of capitalism, producing a mass society of passive consumers without any critical faculties. It was only in the late 1960s that Marxist sociologists began to adopt a more cultural approach, moving toward the position whereby culture is regarded not as completely determined by the economic structure but as having at least a relative autonomy. They took up the ideas of the Italian Marxist Antonio Gramsci (1971), who maintained that there was a constant struggle between groups or classes for ideological "hegemony"—that is, intellectual and moral leadership.

Most sociologists in the post–World War II era agreed with C. Wright Mills (1959) that the main aim of the sociological imagination was to enable individuals to see the connections between their personal troubles and public issues of social structure. But, like him, they had relatively little to say about media culture itself. Mills's main examples were concerned with the personal troubles caused by social structural factors, such as the economy, war, the family, and the urban metropolis. Only after the "cultural turn" in sociology did it become clear that the media are what most often act as the bridge between the troubles experienced in people's private lives and public issues of social and cultural change. As we have already seen, for the social sciences this turn to culture was due in part to the growing economic power and social presence of the culture industries—and indeed, new methods of cultural analysis and theory began to develop. We will look at how these methods have affected the sociology of the mass media; but keep in mind the broader point, which is that the mass media are now central to the working of society and, thus, to its study.

The problem is that, because the mass media have become so pervasive in postmodern society, we may not realize the extent to which they are responsible for the symbolic construction of our shared reality. The **cultural products** of the mass media are the invisible sea within which all of us swim. Perhaps it takes a disaster to reveal their power and how much we depend on them. Terrible and exceptional events do sometimes serve sociologists in much the same way that extreme events in the natural world provide experimental data that natural scientists can use to reveal the inner workings of nature's phenomena. Recall from Chapter 3 how the tragic events that transpired on 9/11 not only laid bare the basic elements in cultural life but also disturbed the normal routines of

**Culture industry** Organizations with an interest (economic or otherwise) in having their products reach the widest possible market, an aim they achieve through use of the mass media.

**Cultural products** Information and knowledge that are produced and communicated by the mass media (i.e., through news articles, television shows, books, and advertising).

## media moments

### On the Air: TV Shifts Back to Entertainment Coverage

Unlike newspapers, which in times of crisis exist primarily to gather and report the news, TV has always performed multiple functions, some of them contradictory. As [we saw in the days after 9/11], television has served as an information source, but also as a site where nearly unedited footage of the attacks was broadcast. TV, usually so careful not to offend or frighten, needed to present the offensive crimes that had been committed against America, and those images were, of necessity, scary and disturbing.

TV is also a natural comforter in a way the print medium is not: Televised images of calm anchors and broadcasters, and the immediate way TV imposes a structure, a narrative, on anything that occurs in the world, are elements of order, and people find order in chaotic times a reassurance.

As with any major event, TV describes an arc of activity: The indescribable occurs, we absorb it, and TV eventually finds a way to fit that experience into its process. Thus, over the past few days, the terrorist attacks still dominate all the major channels, but the business of television is also beginning to proceed. Entertainment programming is slowly moving back onto various networks.

*Source:* Tucker (2001).

the mass media, revealing a great deal about their character. An article in *Entertainment Weekly*, one week after the event, reflected on the ways in which television operated during the crisis and how these differed from its normal functions (see box titled "On the Air"). It also exposed some important differences between television and newspapers.

What does the coverage of 9/11 tell us about the media and their construction of social reality? And what does this analysis, in turn, tell us about the dynamics of both media production and consumption?

First, normal television programming was suspended and TV channels that usually competed with one another found it necessary to share their news footage in order to provide live coverage of such an important event in the real world. What this tells us about the commercial organization of media production is that they are usually less cooperative and more partial in what they communi-

cate: They see themselves and their rivals as competitors in a market, with the primary aim of making a profit. During the 9/11 crisis, however, this competitive and profit-oriented approach was temporarily suspended in favor of giving priority to performing a public service. As a rule, this public service orientation is largely confined to the relatively small Public Broadcasting System (PBS), which exists alongside the private system. Although PBS receives some federal backing, it is much smaller than its equivalents in some other societies.

A second aspect of media production in the wake of 9/11 was that the small number of large conglomerate organizations, which own much of the media, were able to use their resources and outlets to reach mass audiences. This entailed suspending entertainment programs and giving pride of place to news from the most prestigious network—in this case, CBS. In short, media ownership is concentrated in a few large corporations,

Media coverage of the 9/11 terrorist attacks on the World Trade Center and the Pentagon was a prime example of the "24/7 news cycle." (AP Photo/Moshe Busuker)

and this is useful for reaching mass audiences. In an emergency situation, such an arrangement makes it easier to construct a shared national consciousness and identity. However, in normal times, entertainment programs and entertainment values dominate the mass media.

Third, the various types of media, such as television and newspapers, have some similarities in terms of the functions they serve, but also some differences. As it turns out, despite the normal predominance of television's entertainment function, this medium is shown to be able to serve more functions than newspapers in times of crisis. Newspapers specialize in gathering and reporting news, and then reflecting on its significance, whereas television not only provides information but also can provide immediate, minimally edited images of what is happening, even though they may be fright-

ening. Such images contrast with normal fare, which is usually carefully constructed to suit the mass audience. Clearly, the strength of television is its capacity to transmit powerful images, but because of its mass audience such images are usually edited (or censored) to avoid giving offense. This illustrates why television in particular is subject to media regulation by government agencies like the U.S. Federal Communications Commission.

Fourth, given television's capacity for constructing and producing programs that have popular appeal, TV can provide "natural" comfort in a way that the print medium cannot. This is achieved through powerfully "realistic" images of calm anchors and broadcasters—familiar personalities of a particular type, such as the friendly but authoritative male anchor and the pleasant and reassuringly attractive female. Indeed, TV imposes a structure, or narrative form, on news that might otherwise seem meaningless and chaotic. Newspaper journalists' stories also tend to follow a conventional narrative structure, but minus the aesthetic power of the moving image they often seem much less realistic and compelling. This is ironic when we consider that television news, as noted below, depends for its "natural" look on all sorts of contrived techniques, from camera angles and makeup to editing.

Fifth, television and newspapers differ technologically in their modes of transmission, which affects their reception. Newspapers are still, to a large extent, physically transported (even those that have been electronically printed) and, as such, can be read by people on the move—whether in the office or on a plane or train. Television, by contrast, usually has a fixed location in the home and is a part of everyday, familiar routines. Consequently, it gradually absorbs exceptional events into its normal routines. This includes, in the post–September 11 example, resumption of entertainment alongside the news and even within the news. Because viewing is usually embedded in the private sphere of the home, TV offers reassuring familiarity. Thus it has a paradoxically privileged position as a public presence. Yet it is precisely this routinized quality that leads to the varying amounts of attention that viewers give to television. For instance, some viewers may be watching a program while engaged in other activities such as preparing a meal, eating, or even writing a school essay. (We further examine this issue of reception—that is, of how people use television—in a later section, "Reception of Culture.")

## KEEPING INFORMED: U.S. PUBLIC NEWS HABITS

How do you keep up with the news? When asked about news use on a typical day, most Americans (60 percent) said they watched TV news. Forty-two percent said they read a newspaper, while 40 percent said they listened to the radio. As you can see in Table 4.1, there are some interesting gender and age differences hiding within these aggregated statistics. For example, the rate of watching television news is identical for men and women and similar in terms of magazine-reading, but there is a more noticeable difference between them when it comes to reading the paper or listening to radio news. Another interesting trend can be seen in the age breakdown of radio listening. The group consuming the most radio news is between the ages of 30 and 65. Why is this the case? Might it have something to do with the amount of time spent in the car commuting to work and picking up children from their after-school activities? Can you see any other trends in media use related to age?

Table 4.2 shows the statistical breakdown of people who go online to get news three or more days a week. While the trend for nearly all categories is a steady increase in online news use, significant age and education differences persist. Even more interesting are the figures comparing racial and ethnic groups. The gap between blacks and whites has decreased significantly since 2000,

**SURVEY QUESTIONS:** Did you get a chance to read a daily newspaper yesterday, or not? Did you watch the news or a news program on television yesterday, or not?

Thinking about yesterday, did you spend any time reading magazines? About how much time, if any, did you spend listening to any news on the radio yesterday, or didn't you happen to listen to the news on the radio yesterday?

and in 2004 the proportion of Hispanics (32 percent) was higher than that for Americans in general (29 percent). How might these results be explained? In thinking about this question, you might also want to refer to Table 4.4 (somewhat later in the chapter), which charts the overall demographics of Internet users.

While a national crisis like 9/11 might seem to have brought out the best in American media, making them central to the national reconstruction of collective identity, it also exposed them to powerful critical scrutiny. In the wake of the media coverage, at a *Newsworld* international conference of television executives in Barcelona, Spain, one television reporter attacked the media's decision to repeatedly project images of the attack. He called this technique sensationalistic, even "pornographic." He was also disturbed by the media's decision to project these images as background to interviews and as promotions for upcoming news specials, to which evocative background music was frequently added (Wells 2001). This concern was shared by a group of American communications experts who issued a stinging "Call for Responsible Journalism." They explained that, as scholars in the field of communications, they were deeply troubled by the tone and substance of the news coverage of the September 11 terrorist attacks. Of greatest concern to them were the use of

**SURVEY QUESTIONS:** How frequently do you go online to get news? Would you say every day, three to five days per week, one or two days per week, once every few weeks, or less often?

## TABLE 4.1  Daily Media Consumption

| | Newspaper | | | Television | | | Magazine | | | Radio | | |
|---|---|---|---|---|---|---|---|---|---|---|---|---|
| | Yes % | No % | DK % | Yes % | No % | DK % | Yes % | No % | DK % | Yes % | No % | DK % |
| Total | 42 | 58 | *=100 | 60 | 40 | *=100 | 25 | 75 | *=100 | 40 | 59 | *=100 |
| Male | 47 | 53 | * | 60 | 40 | * | 23 | 77 | * | 45 | 55 | * |
| Female | 37 | 63 | * | 60 | 40 | * | 26 | 74 | * | 37 | 63 | * |
| 18–29 | 23 | 77 | 0 | 44 | 55 | 1 | 26 | 74 | * | 28 | 71 | 1 |
| 30–49 | 39 | 61 | * | 58 | 42 | * | 24 | 76 | 0 | 47 | 53 | * |
| 50–64 | 52 | 48 | * | 67 | 33 | * | 23 | 77 | 0 | 47 | 53 | * |
| 65+ | 60 | 40 | * | 74 | 25 | 1 | 27 | 73 | * | 33 | 67 | * |

*Note:* Results for this survey are based on telephone interviews conducted under the direction of Princeton Survey Research Associates International among a nationwide sample of 3,000 adults, 18 years of age or older, during the period April 19– May 12, 2004.

*Source:* Pew Research Center for the People and Press (2004).

## TABLE 4.2  Going Online for News

| | 2000 % | 2002 % | 2004 % |
|---|---|---|---|
| All | 23 | 25 | 29 |
| Men | 28 | 30 | 33 |
| Women | 18 | 20 | 25 |
| White | 23 | 26 | 29 |
| Black | 16 | 15 | 25 |
| Hispanic | 21 | 22 | 32 |
| 18–29 | 30 | 31 | 36 |
| 30–49 | 26 | 29 | 36 |
| 50–49 | 19 | 24 | 28 |
| 65+ | 8 | 7 | 8 |
| College Graduate | 40 | 44 | 50 |
| Some College | 29 | 29 | 35 |
| High School Grad | 13 | 16 | 18 |
| Less than High School | 8 | 7 | 8 |

*Note:* Results for this survey are based on telephone interviews conducted under the direction of Princeton Survey Research Associates International among a nationwide sample of 3,000 adults, 18 years of age or older, during the period April 19– May 12, 2004.

*Source:* Pew Research Center for the People and Press (2004).

the "war" metaphor to describe the attack and potential responses to it as well as the reliance on current and former government and military officials to interpret events. After having researched and documented the historical development of the media system in the United States and other countries worldwide, they concluded that fewer corporations now control more sources of news and information than ever before. They also pointed out that corporate pressures for increased profits may have resulted in newsroom cutbacks and reduced investigative capacities, leaving journalists ill-equipped to report comprehensively on events as complex and significant as the terrorist attacks of 9/11. Yet, despite the difficult conditions confronting contemporary journalism, these concerned scholars believe that individual producers, editors, and reporters could have drawn on the best traditions of journalism to serve the public interest in this time of international crisis. They appealed to journalists to adopt the following practices and policies immediately:

- ✓ Expand and balance the range of information sources beyond current and former military and government officials to include domestic and foreign academics, think tank analysts and civic leaders.
- ✓ Seek diverse and contrasting perspectives, including ethnic and gender diversity that will broaden and deepen discussions regarding potential courses of action in response to this tragedy.
- ✓ Incorporate historical, cultural, and religious dimensions into interviews and reports whenever possible, rather than treating them as discrete topics isolated from routine reporting.
- ✓ Expose audiences to the research, practices, and guidance of the large body of scholars and practitioners of peace studies.
- ✓ Select language and images that most dispassionately and accurately describe events and conditions; avoid routinely adopting the terms

and interpretations of officials into breaking and continuing news portrayals.

- ✓ Limit the repetition of extreme images of destruction, violence, pain, and suffering, and balance them with routine examples of cooperation, reconstruction, and reconciliation.
- ✓ Reassign employees to non-editorial responsibilities if they have conflicts of interest with current policy discussions. This would include former employment in key government agencies and family relationships to high-ranking government officials. (Available online at http://la.indymedia.org/news/2001/10/11703.php)

These various responses to media coverage of a dramatic event echo some of the questions that have featured in the political-economy and cultural approaches to media sociology. On the one hand, those who analyze the mass media through a political-economy lens see issues of consolidation, ownership, and politics as the most significant factors shaping the media. For example, reflecting on the deregulation in the media, one critic (Stern 1999: 5) asked whether "the production and consumption of mass media are simply … operating in the service of a system that favors the interests of the rich." As evidence, he cited "the successful pressure by large media corporations on the Federal Government to abolish regulations that restricted their accumulation of ownership of radio stations." Indeed, since deregulation began accelerating, "some half of U.S. stations had been sold by 2000, and a few giants, owning hundreds of stations, had come to dominate the market" (quoted in Nichols and McChesney 2000: 31). Even the central trade publication of mass entertainment, *Variety,* responded to this development with alarm. Observing that "a huge wave of consolidation has turned music stations into cash cows that focus on narrow playlists aimed at squeezing the most revenue from the richest demographics," it warned that "in this era of megamergers, there has never been a greater need for a little diversity on the dial" (quoted in Nichols and McChesney 2000: 31).

Certainly economic factors play a role in media coverage; but do cultural factors, such as the values of media professionals and those of different audiences, have important effects that are not accounted for by economics? A cultural-sociological approach reveals symbolic and normative constraints on both media production and media consumption, such as the professional values of journalists, the types of narrative structure in media contents ("texts"), and differences between audiences in terms of the ways they consume media products. Recall our earlier discussion of *Rolling Stone*'s story about multiple-victim school shootings: The article exemplified the overreporting of violent crimes in relation to their actual incidence, which in turn reflected the news values of journalists and media organizations; it used the typical narrative structure of reporting such an event, which involved presenting it as a personalized "human interest" story with vivid profiles of individuals; and it was written to appeal to the typical readers of that magazine, who are mainly young people.

Before examining this contrast between economic and cultural approaches more closely, we need to know something about the history of the modern mass media and the issues that they have generated.

## THE MASS MEDIA: CONCEPTS AND HISTORY

*Mass media* is an umbrella term that refers to the variety of technological devices and processes through which mass communication takes place. The mass media use technology to transmit organized messages that are designed to reach large numbers of people. The potential for mass communication emerged with the printing press and expanded with technological developments that

In the early nineteenth century, "penny" newspapers were the equivalent of today's tabloids. (Library of Congress)

transformed the media and its capacities: the telegraph and telephone, the phonograph and radio, film and television, the computer and the Internet. The mass reproduction of cultural items and their transmission to mass audiences gave rise to culture industries, involving organizations eager to supply their products to the biggest possible market. In the modern era, small-scale production for elite or local audiences evolved into mass production for mass audiences. This trend was particularly evident in the case of newspapers, which began to gain a wide readership only in 1835 with the appearance of "penny newspapers," such as the *New York Herald,* whose news values favored human-interest stories about crime, suicides, fires, entertainment, and the exotic. The more elite "six-penny newspapers" accused their upstart rivals of

Staged media events, such as presidential debates, have taken place throughout the history of newspapers, radio, television, and the Internet. Here is the famous debate between Nixon and Kennedy in 1960, which many believe influenced enough voters to put Kennedy in the White House. (AP Photo)

sensationalism, but the *New York Herald* claimed it was living up to its pledge "to record facts, on every public and proper subject, stripped of verbiage and coloring" (Shi 1995: 95).

A list of key dates in the history of mass media is bound to be selective, leaving out some developments that might be considered equally important, depending on the criteria used. Nevertheless, we offer such a list in Table 4.3, which includes as significant dates not just those involving technological progress but also those relating to organizational developments such as the formation of certain production companies in publishing, radio, film, and television. For example, though not included on our list, the way Bill Gates developed Microsoft

arguably has had a massive effect on the use of computers. This was certainly the belief of the U.S. trade regulators who took Microsoft to court for allegedly pursuing monopolistic, anticompetition policies. Another set of important dates we might have included are those marking developments in the content or format of media products. For example, the "fireside chats" on radio, introduced by President Franklin D. Roosevelt in 1930, and the live confrontations between Richard Nixon and John F. Kennedy in their 1960 televised debates were important not just as political events but also as media developments. Along these lines, we also want to note the development of popular entertainment programs, such as soap

## TABLE 4.3 Some Key Dates in the History of Mass Media

| | |
|---|---|
| 1451 | The method of printing using moving type is invented by Johannes Gutenberg in Mainz, Germany. |
| 1650 | The first daily newspaper, *Einkommenden Zeitungen,* is published in Leipzig, Germany. |
| 1689 | Increase Mather publishes *Present State of New England Affairs,* followed in the next year by Benjamin Harris's *Publick Occurrences Both Foreign and Domestick;* both are one-issue papers. |
| 1704 | John Campbell publishes the *Boston Newsletter,* the first U.S. newspaper not to be a one-issue failure. |
| 1783 | The *Pennsylvania Evening Post,* America's first daily newspaper, is published. |
| 1820 | The first black paper in the United States, *Freedom's Journal,* is established, followed in 1828 by Chief Sequoia's publication of the *Cherokee Phoenix.* |
| 1833 | The first mass-circulation paper in America, the *New York Sun,* concentrating on stories of sex and violence, is published by Benjamin Day. The *New York Herald,* a 1-cent popular paper. follows in 1835, with specific pages dedicated to sport and finance. |
| 1844 | The first press telegram, from a Congress reporter in Washington, D.C., to the editor of the *Baltimore Patriot,* is transmitted by Morse Telegraph. |
| 1872 | The first illustrated daily newspaper, the *New York Daily Graphic,* is issued. |
| 1877 | Thomas Edison Bell patents the phonograph, the first sound recording system. |
| 1880 | The radiophone, devised by Alexander Graham Bell and Charles Sumner Tainter, successfully transmits speech between the top of Franklin School in Washington, D.C., and Bell's laboratory on 14th Street. |
| 1885 | Louis Aimé Augustin Le Prince, French-born but living in the United States, projects the first moving pictures—in this instance, onto a wall at the Institute for the Deaf in New York. |
| 1895 | Brothers Auguste and Louis Lumière project the first-ever film onto a screen in Paris, marking the birth of cinema. |
| 1906 | The first radio broadcast is aired from a radio station in Brant Rock, Massachusetts. |
| 1909 | The U.S. National Board of Censorship of Motion Pictures is established. |
| 1910 | Scotsman James Logie Baird creates the first television pictures. |
| 1927 | *The Jazz Singer,* starring Al Jolson, is the first talking movie. |
| 1944 | The automatic digital computer, invented by the American Howard Aiken, is followed in the next year by the electronic computer invented by J. Prosper Eckert and John W. Mauchley. |
| 1945 | The first television sets go on sale in the United States. |
| 1948 | Both 33- and 45-rpm records appear. |
| 1956 | Packet-switching technology, a precursor to the Internet, is developed by the U.S. Department of Defense Advanced Research Projects Agency. |
| 1960 | Paperback sales surpass trade hardcover sales for the first time. |
| 1967 | The Corporation for Public Broadcasting is formed. |
| 1972 | The Home Box Office is founded. |
| 1980 | Ted Turner's Cable News Network (CNN), the first twenty-four-hour news network, goes on the air. |
| 1985 | The first National Science Foundation Network, a backbone network linking supercomputer centers in the United States, is created. A year later, the second NSFNET forms the basis for the worldwide Internet. |
| 1992 | The first commercial Internet service providers are established in the United States. |

operas and talk shows on radio and television, that have been the subject of vigorous debate between sociologists.

Sociologists who adopt a political-economy approach tend to focus on technological and organizational developments, although they may also give some attention to the political character of media content, especially its ideological effects. In contrast, cultural sociologists are particularly interested in the form and content of mass-media "texts" (not just written but also visual) and the ways in which these are interpreted and used.

The political-economy approach to the kinds of programs made possible by early radio and television mass broadcasting, such as soap operas, was to regard them as advertising vehicles for selling goods like soap powders to housewives—as the term *soap opera* implies. Critics maintained that the soap operas also served an ideological function in promoting "bourgeois" family values, which, in turn, prevented the kind of critical thinking that might call for radical change and pose a threat to the capitalist system.

Cultural theorists were more inclined to study such programs in terms of their content—whether artistic, moral, or emotional. Conservative cultural critics complained that their appeal to the lowest common denominator of popular taste lowered cultural standards, whereas feminist sociologists, who study how women viewers and listeners actually interpret soap operas, have sometimes presented a more positive view (Brown 1994).

In sum, the political-economy approach emphasizes the structures and processes involved in the production of culture: the ownership of media organizations, the drive to make profits, the pressure to gain and keep a mass audience, the opposition of private owners to government regulation or to radical change that might threaten profits. Because this approach privileges production, it assumes that **consumption** of the media's cultural products is a secondary matter. For a long time, audiences were viewed solely as passive recipients of whatever radio, film, and television projected. In contrast, cultural sociology not only sees media audiences as active interpreters of the meanings of media messages but also pays much more attention to the normative commitments that constrain media **production.**

## The Creation of Cultural Products: Structural and Cultural Approaches

How are information and knowledge produced and communicated by the mass media? Some people see television, radio, and newspapers simply as neutral means through which individuals give and receive information. If this is indeed the case, the only relevant question is whether the interests of all individuals are equally served by the media or, conversely, whether inequality distorts the free flow of information. In fact, studies from a political-economy standpoint emphasize that, although most people in industrialized societies have gained access to a growing variety of means of communication, significant inequalities remain. For example, although computer access has grown rapidly in the United States—such that, as of August 2000, 51 percent of all households had one or

**Consumption** A term referring to the ways in which an audience takes in and interacts with a cultural product. For a long time, consumption was viewed as secondary to production, such that audiences were considered merely passive recipients of what the media projected. Cultural sociology, however, sees media audiences as active interpreters of the meanings of media messages.

**Production** A term referring to the ways in which cultural products are created and transmitted. When considering the production of a cultural product, we have to look at not only the product itself, such as a television show or news story, but also structural factors such as the ownership of media organizations, pressure to gain and keep an audience, and the opposition of private owners to government regulation.

more computers and 77 percent of white non-Hispanic children lived in homes with a computer—only 43 percent of African-American children and 37 percent of Hispanic children have such access (U.S. Census Bureau 2001). The same stratification of access applies to the Internet, as Table 4.4 makes clear—despite the encouraging trends we saw earlier in Table 4.2.

Even greater inequalities can be found in the areas of ownership and control of media production: "Two dozen or so firms control the overwhelming percentage of movies, TV shows, cable systems, cable channels, TV stations, radio stations, books, magazines, newspapers, billboards, music, and TV networks that constitute the media culture that occupies one-half of the average American's life. It is an extraordinary degree of economic and social power located in very few hands" (Nichols and McChesney 2000: 29). Furthermore, although globalization has increased the number of international communications networks throughout the world, media production capabilities in industrialized countries are much more developed than those in nonindustrialized countries.

At the opening of the twenty-first century, the U.S. media system was dominated by fewer than ten transnational conglomerates: Disney, AOL–Time Warner, News Corporation, Viacom, Seagram (Universal), Sony, Liberty (AT&T), Bertelsmann, and General Electric (NBC). Estimates of their revenues ranged from $8 billion to $30 billion per year (Nichols and McChesney 2000). These conglomerates comprise one of the largest sectors of the U.S. economy, and their products dominate popular culture. Their influence throughout the world is so great that many countries accuse America of **cultural imperialism**—that is, of swamping local societies with American popular culture, ranging from Hollywood films and popular music to Nike trainers and Levi jeans (Schiller 1969).

Another important determinant in the creation of cultural products is advertising. In the United States, radio and television have been dependent

## TABLE 4.4  The Unevenly Wired Nation: Demographics of U.S. Internet Users

| | % Who Go Online |
|---|---|
| Women | 61 |
| Men | 66 |
| **Age** | |
| 18–29 | 78 |
| 30–49 | 74 |
| 50–64 | 60 |
| 65+ | 25 |
| **Race/ethnicity** | |
| White, Non-Hispanic | 67 |
| Black, Non-Hispanic | 43 |
| Hispanic | 59 |
| **Community type** | |
| Urban | 62 |
| Suburban | 68 |
| Rural | 56 |
| **Household income** | |
| Less than $30,000/yr | 44 |
| $30,000–$50,000 | 69 |
| $50,000–$75,000 | 81 |
| More than $75,000 | 89 |
| **Educational attainment** | |
| Less than High School | 32 |
| High School | 52 |
| Some College | 75 |
| College + | 88 |

Note: N = 2,200 adults 18 and older. Margin of error is ± 2% for results based on the full sample.

Source: Pew Internet and American Life Project (2004).

**Cultural imperialism**  A term that refers to the ways in which societies throughout the world have become swamped with aspects of American popular culture, such as Hollywood films, television shows, and popular music.

## FIGURE 4.1  The Unevenly Wired Globe

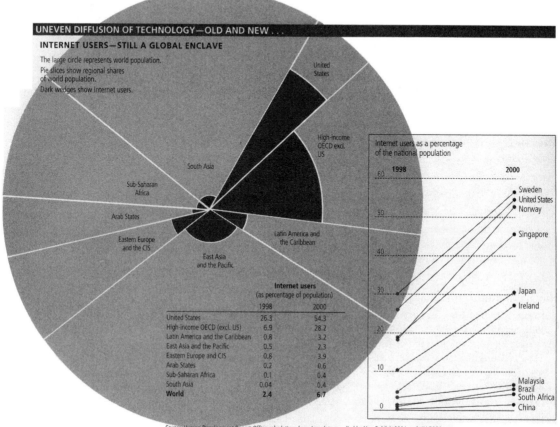

**UNEVEN DIFFUSION OF TECHNOLOGY—OLD AND NEW . . .**

INTERNET USERS—STILL A GLOBAL ENCLAVE

The large circle represents world population.
Pie slices show regional shares
of world population.
Dark wedges show Internet users.

United States

High-income
OECD excl.
US

South Asia

Sub-Saharan
Africa

Arab States

Eastern Europe
and the CIS

Latin America and
the Caribbean

East Asia
and the Pacific

Internet users as a percentage
of the national population

**Internet users**
(as percentage of population)

| | 1998 | 2000 |
|---|---|---|
| United States | 26.3 | 54.3 |
| High-income OECD (excl. US) | 6.9 | 28.2 |
| Latin America and the Caribbean | 0.8 | 3.2 |
| East Asia and the Pacific | 0.5 | 2.3 |
| Eastern Europe and CIS | 0.8 | 3.9 |
| Arab States | 0.2 | 0.6 |
| Sub-Saharan Africa | 0.1 | 0.4 |
| South Asia | 0.04 | 0.4 |
| **World** | **2.4** | **6.7** |

1998    2000

Sweden
United States
Norway

Singapore

Japan
Ireland

Malaysia
Brazil
South Africa
China

*Source:* Human Development Report Office calculations based on data supplied by Nua Publish 2001 and UN 2001c.

### The digital divide within countries

**The divide narrows—but ever so slowly**

More than three-quarters
of Internet users live in high-income
OECD countries, which contain 14%
of the world's people

High-income
OECD

**World population**

14%

**Internet user population**

High-income OECD 88% in 1998

79% in 2000

*Source:* Human Development Report Office
calculations based on data supplied by Nua
Publish 2001 and UN 2001c.

Though data are limited on the demography of Internet users, Internet use is clearly concentrated. In most countries Internet users are predominantly:

• *Urban and located in certain regions.* In China the 15 least connected provinces, with 600 million people, have only 4 million Internet users—while Shanghai and Beijing, with 27 million people, have 5 million users. In the Dominican Republic 80% of Internet users live in the capital, Santo Domingo. And in Thailand 90% live in urban areas, which contain only 21% of the country's population. Among India's 1.4 million Internet connections, more than 1.3 million are in the five states of Delhi, Karnataka, Maharashtra, Tamil Nadu and Mumbai.

• *Better educated and wealthier.* In Bulgaria the poorest 65% of the population accounts for only 29% of Internet users. In Chile 89% of Internet users

have had tertiary education, in Sri Lanka 65%, and in China 70%.

• *Young.* Everywhere, younger people are more apt to be online. In Australia 18–24-year-olds are five times more likely to be Internet users than those above 55. In Chile 74% of users are under 35; in China that share is 84%. Other countries follow the same pattern.

• *Male.* Men make up 86% of users in Ethiopia, 83% in Senegal, 70% in China, 67% in France and 62% in Latin America.

Some of these disparities are easing. For example, the gender gap seems to be narrowing rapidly—as in Thailand, where the share of female users jumped from 35% in 1999 to 49% in 2000, or in the United States, where women made up 38% of users in 1996 but 51% in 2000. In Brazil, where Internet use has increased rapidly, women account for 47% of users.

*Source:* UNDP, Country Offices 2001; Nanthikesan 2001.

on advertising revenues since their earliest days, and some types of programming have been developed specifically for the purpose of targeting groups of consumers, as our earlier example of soap operas reveals. However, with the media's even greater dependence on advertising over the last decade, a fierce debate has been unleashed. Journalists and other defenders of the media resent the suggestion that, simply because they rely on advertising for a large share of their income, their editorial independence has been undermined. If autonomy between the two exists (and the present authors believe it does), it is based on the independent power of journalism, both as a profession and as a representative of civil culture. We will discuss these factors below. But meanwhile, it's important to acknowledge the enormous increase in advertising in the media that occurred over the last decade of the twentieth century. By 1999 the four major TV networks were providing nearly sixteen minutes per hour of commercials during prime time, a substantial increase from a decade earlier (Teinowitz 1999). Not content with traditional advertising, media firms were reported to be working on "virtual ads," whereby a marketer's product could be seamlessly inserted into actual programs, so that viewers would be unable to avoid the commercials through zapping (Ross 1999). Another growth area for revenues in television involves the selling of merchandise that is shown on its programs (Donaton 1999; Ross 1999). These developments have led John Nichols and Robert McChesney to conclude that "[i]n sum, the entire U.S. media experience increasingly resembles an infomercial" (2000: 32).

The search for profits from advertising products in the media has been particularly directed to the increasingly lucrative youth and children's market. In 2000, it was estimated that girls between the ages of 7 and 14 spent $24 billion per year and influenced parental decisions worth another $66 billion. The influence of such advertising on children was demonstrated by a particularly revealing empirical study. When 8-year-olds were shown two pictures of identical shoes, one with the Nike logo and the other with the Kmart logo, they liked both equally. But the response of 12-year-olds was "Kmart, are you kidding me?" (Edgecliffe-Johnson 1999: 16).

But there are also other important questions to ask about the creation of cultural products—questions that lead away from this focus on ownership and funding. These concern the actual creation process itself—the way it is "manufactured," as some critics would say (e.g., Fishman 1980). In terms of the news media, this process has clearly become a lot more artful, with participants displaying increasing sophistication in the skills of presentation. As organizations ranging from school boards to governments and social movements have become more aware of the power of the media, public relations have become vastly more important. Staff are now trained to present themselves and their messages in the most persuasive and entertaining way through the mass media of communication. At the same time, audiences are becoming more knowledgeable and harder to please (or deceive), so more effort and money are being spent on image construction—and not just by advertisers and politicians.

This new self-consciousness about image constructions does not mesh well with the classical ideas about democracy that often inspire journalists themselves, who see themselves as providing an undistorted and unbiased message. The pioneering broadcast reporter Edward R. Murrow once famously insisted that journalism "must hold a mirror behind the nation and the world" and that "the mirror must have no curves and must be held with a steady hand" (quoted in MacDonald 1979: 310). Although this idealistic ambition continues to inspire journalists today, from the sociological perspective—whether structural or cultural—such autonomy and transparency are not possible. Media sociologists see media news as the product of a complex social process, and they examine how this product actually contributes in a powerful way to the creation of the very social phenomena upon which they report. Although this emphasis on the social construction of the news might offend journalists, it does not imply that they falsify the news. It simply draws attention to the social processes that shape the ways in which the news is presented.

Cultural studies of the production of news date back to the **gatekeeper studies** of the 1950s, when David Manning White (1950) studied a wire editor at a small American newspaper. For one week, "Mr. Gates" (as White called him) made available to the researcher every piece of wired copy that came his way—both those he rejected and those he selected to print. Then, for every story he turned down, he listed his reasons for rejection. Some of the reasons were not very illuminating—"not enough space." Others were technical or professional—"dull writing." Still others were explicitly political—"propaganda" or "He's too Red." These last criteria greatly influenced White's interpretation of gatekeeping, and that of the sociologists who followed him, even though political reasons for rejection accounted for just 18 out of 423 cases. A subsequent study of 16 wire editors in Wisconsin, by Walter Gieber, came to the conclusion that what influenced the selection of stories was not political values but organizational production factors (Gieber 1964).

It wasn't until the 1970s that the sociology of media production really began to take off. Previously, studies of the media had been hung up on questions about the psychological effects on individuals of exposure to the media. Among the favorites were: Do the mass media manipulate people on behalf of advertisers and politicians? Are the mass media a bad influence, catering to the lowest common denominator of taste, and promoting low culture at the expense of high culture, soap operas like *Days of Our Lives* rather than Shakespearean plays? (See the discussion of highbrow and lowbrow culture in Chapter 3.) But, while such questions raise legitimate concerns about the artistic and moral effects of the mass media, they are difficult to answer directly through sociological research.

It was only when sociologists began to turn their attention to other questions, from the 1970s onward, that the sociology of mass media began to make real progress. Influenced by the gatekeeper studies, scholars began to look seriously at mass media as **cultural texts** produced by real people in real organizations under real constraints. These people and organizations have specific cultures that enter into the production process. And it is these cultural commitments, after all, that enable them to create cultural products.

Every cultural product can be analyzed as a text, including photographs and music. But an even better example is to think about how newspaper stories function in this manner, precisely because news is typically taken in exactly the opposite way—as factual information. Textual analysis is concerned with analyzing the language of a product, with interpreting the patterns of meaning that make up its cultural structure or code. From this perspective, then, a news story does not simply reflect the factual reality of a news event. Indeed, it works less as a science than as a kind of realistic "literature"—constructing a codified definition of what *should* figure as that event's reality. Each newspaper has its own preferred way of addressing its readers—its characteristic "mode of address" or style of expression. In order to make sense of events for its readers, a newspaper thus

**Gatekeeper studies**  Studies performed during the 1950s in which researchers considered the factors that determine which stories get produced in the mass media.

**Cultural text**  Any cultural product (e.g., a photograph, musical selection, or television program) that can be read and analyzed as one would analyze a written text—that is, in terms of the language or patterns of meaning that make up its cultural structure or code.

frames a story within a familiar "map of meaning" about the social world. As British sociologist Stuart Hall put it:

> The social identification, classification and contextualisation of news events in terms of these background frames of reference is the fundamental process by which the media make the world they report on intelligible to readers and viewers. This process of "making an event intelligible" is a social process—constituted by a number of specific journalistic practices, which embody (often only implicitly) crucial assumptions about what society is and how it works. One such background assumption is the consensual nature of society: the process of signification—giving social meanings to events—both assumes and helps to construct society as a "consensus." We exist as members of one society because—it is assumed—we share a common stock of knowledge with our fellow men [and women]; we have access to the same "maps of meaning." Not only are we able to manipulate these "maps of meaning" to understand events, but we have fundamental interests, values and concerns in common, which these maps embody or reflect. (Hall et al. 1978: 54–55)

This meaning-making function is perhaps most apparent when it is breached. In crisis situations like 9/11, there is often a short period of incomprehension during which the media struggle to fit the event into existing maps of meaning. As a foreign journalist, Charlotte Raven, reflected one week after September 11: "It [America] was taken unawares last Tuesday and part of the trauma of that event was the shock of being forced to listen to a message that it hadn't had time to translate. The subsequent roar of anger was, amongst other things, the sound of the U.S. struggling to regain the right to control its own narrative" (quoted in the *Guardian* newspaper, September 18, 2001); see also box titled "The Struggle to Make Sense of September 11, 2001").

The civil rights movement was the first large social movement to be covered on television; here reporters interview Martin Luther King, Jr., on a civil rights march in Selma, Alabama. (Bettmann/Corbis)

The fact that journalism helps society regain a sense of identity in times of crisis points up its cultural role in more general terms. Journalism makes new events continuously comprehensible in terms of culture's existing codes and narrative. It does so by causing events to seem either to conform to normative expectations or to violate them. The aim of news is to make meaning, not simply to provide information. This cultural role is not necessarily stabilizing, however, as exemplified by journalism's role in the American civil rights movement.

The civil rights movement in the American South was one of the most radical struggles of the twentieth century. It was led, of course, by Martin Luther King and fueled by the skill and courage of tens of thousands of other Southern African-Americans. But these demonstrations could not, by themselves, have triggered the sympathy, indignation, and later social reforms that the civil rights movement achieved. An essential additional factor was the arrival of younger journalists from liberal

## The Struggle to Make Sense of September 11, 2001

### Reading Headlines from Across the United States as Dramatic Texts

**Using history to make sense of the present:**

"A New Day of Infamy," *Boston Globe*, September 12, 2001

"Second Pearl Harbor," *News-Gazette*, September 11, 2001, Extra

**Expressing confusion:**

"Chaos," *Democrat & Chronicle*, Rochester, NY, September 11, 2001, Extra

"Unthinkable," *Arizona Daily Star*, September 11, 2001

"Beyond Belief," *Quad City Times*, September 11, 2001, Extra

"Horror!" *Los Angeles Daily News*, September 12, 2001

"Nightmare," *Abilene Reporter-News*, September 12, 2001

"Who Would Do This?" *Oakland Press*, September 12, 2001

**Terrorism or war? Who are the victims of the attacks? New York and the Pentagon, or the entire nation?**

"Terrorists Attack New York, Pentagon," *Los Angeles Times*, September 12, 2001

"Terrorists Attack U.S.," *Las Vegas Sun*, September 11, 2001, Home

"Terror Strikes Home," *Lee's Summit Journal*, September 12, 2001

"'Evil Acts,'" *Miami Herald*, September 12, 2001

"War at Home," *Dallas Morning News*, September 12, 2001

"Act of War," *Hartford Courant*, September 12, 2001

**Tragedy that should be mourned, or attack that should be avenged?**

"American Tragedy," *Diamondback*, September 12, 2001

"Nation in Anguish," *San Diego Union-Tribune*, September 12, 2001

"A Nation Mourns," *Eastern Echo*, September 12, 2001

"America's Darkest Day," *Richmond Times-Dispatch*, September 12, 2001

"Assault on America," *Wichita Eagle*, September 12, 2001

"U.S. Attacked," *New York Times*, September 12, 2001

"Outrage," *Atlanta Constitution*, September 12, 2001

*Source:* www.september11news.com.

Northern newspapers—journalists who were citizens, not just professionals. They carried inside of themselves the egalitarian values of American democracy, and whether northerners or southerners by birth, they did not accept the system of racial domination that had compromised these values in the Southern states. As the executive editor of the *Chicago Daily News* emphasized at the time, reporters could be no more "unbiased" than other American citizens, for "the racial crisis is an issue that no American of this generation can push off into a corner and say with accuracy that it has no personal connection with him." Attacking the "pose of impartiality," the editor insisted that "any decision to disseminate or not to disseminate news is in itself a partisan act." The managing editor of the *St. Louis Post Dispatch* testified that, in comparison with most of their Southern counterparts, Northern journalists tried "harder … to determine the needs, the desires, and the hopes of the Negro community." A journalist from the *New York Times* declared that "everyone is emotionally involved" and suggested that the symbolic classification of stories—"the way the news is worded"—had a critical effect on political events. Most Northern journalists had taken sides in the great struggle for civil rights even before they arrived in the South. In fact, it had been their emotional and moral values that compelled them to get involved. Another *New York Times* reporter, born and raised in the South, confessed that "for reasons that I never have been able to understand but never thought of as remarkable, I grew up with an intense dislike for segregation." It was this sense of emotional revulsion, not simply his professional ethics or ambition, that made him "desperate to go south and help cover what clearly was going to be the biggest story of my time." Thirty years later, at the close of a long and distinguished career, he confessed: "I was and am … biased in favor of the Movement. More than that, I was and remain completely taken by it. I still believe it is the most important event in American history since Independence." (All of the quota-

tions in this paragraph were taken from Alexander 2006: ch. 12.)

Is the meaning produced by news journalism tied not only to the broader national culture but also to a more specifically media culture? Many media sociologists believe that it is, and that this journalistic culture has narratives and codes of its own. Michael Schudson has shown how such a culture can be traced to the professional values and criteria shared by American journalists:

The news … is produced by people who operate, often unwittingly, within a cultural system, a reservoir of stored cultural meanings and patterns of discourse. It is organized by conventions of sourcing—who is a legitimate source or speaker or conveyer of information to a journalist. It lives by unspoken preconceptions about the audience—less a matter of who the audience actually may be than a projection by journalists of their own social worlds. News as a form of culture incorporates assumptions about what matters, what makes sense, what time and place we live in, what range of considerations we should take seriously. A news story is supposed to answer the questions "who," "what," "when," "where," and "why" about its subject, but understanding news as culture requires asking of news writing what categories of people count as "who," what kinds of things pass for "facts" or "whats," what geography and sense of time are inscribed as "where" and "when," and what counts as an explanation of "why." (1995: 14)

It has been argued that the culture of journalism favors certain types of answers to questions about why events have occurred. For most news, the primary type of explanation has to do with motives. And for professional journalists, Schudson explains, "acts have agents, agents have intentions, intentions explain acts" (1995: 14). In the context of coverage of politics, for example, the agent is usually taken to be a politician or candidate, and the motive is assumed to be political power or advantage. It is only when this type of explanation fails to shed light on an act or event that journalists look beyond motives to causes—broader social or institutional forces. Furthermore, although there seems to be an unspoken convention permitting reporters to ascribe motives on their own authority, if they refer to "causes" they must find "experts" or "pundits" to make the case (Carey 1986). Returning again to our example of the *Rolling Stone* article on the multiple-victim school shootings of the 1990s, note that journalist Randall Sullivan dismisses both the explanation of liberals that the availability of guns was the main cause of the deaths and the contention of conservatives that guns are not the problem but the solution. The liberal and conservative politicians, according to Sullivan, were simply motivated by their different interests with regard to gun control. He then quotes experts, such as psychologist Dave Grossman, to support his own explanation, which concerns exposure of individuals to violent images in film and television.

Journalism, then, is hardly a mirror of reality. The very fact that it follows conventions in constructing stories lends support to a cultural understanding of media production.

## Reception of Culture

Although the ways in which media content is produced constitute an important topic, it is equally important to look at the reception of that content, or how it is used by audiences. The most influential studies in the past generation were those performed by scholars who examined television entertainment. Earlier American mass communications researchers had tended to adopt a view of the mass media as "injecting" ideas into masses of individuals, as with a hypodermic syringe. Gradually, however, a different approach emerged after World War II, one known as "uses and gratifica-

tions studies" (Katz and Lazarsfeld 1955). This work attended to the many ways people use the media rather than assuming that the media overwhelmed people. Audiences choose which medium to attend to, and they use it for different purposes. Sometimes it is taken seriously and sometimes it's sheer entertainment; sometimes the media content is given close attention; at other times it's an empty but reassuring time-filler, a kind of audiovisual wallpaper. For example, movies can be occasions for dating or for just hanging out. Radio often provides company for the lonely or distraction for shopping or commuting drivers. And television, according to one recent study, is an ever-present companion for many children; as many as two-thirds of the total population studied (65 percent) live in homes where the TV is left on at least half the time or more, even if no one is watching, and one-third (36 percent) live in homes where the TV is on "always" or "most of the time" (Kaiser Family Foundation and the Children's Digital Media 2003).

Media consumers are not passive, even though many people who watch a lot of TV laughingly refer to themselves as "couch potatoes." Media researchers have emphasized the capacity of ordinary people to put their own interpretations on what they receive from the media, describing them as "active viewers" (Fiske 1989). These new audience studies have been energized by a rising feminist perspective in media studies. They reject academia's contempt for female-oriented genres such as soap operas and romance novels. Indeed, feminist critics have sought to rescue these genres and, especially, their fans. An influential example is Ien Ang's study of female viewers of the extraordinarily influential 1970–1980s drama *Dallas* (Ang 1985). Ang found that many women recognized the patriarchal ideology of the program, but could still enjoy it by interpreting it in their own ironic way.

Another stimulus for new audience studies has come from a new understanding of the multivoiced character of texts, what literary theorists call "polysemy." British cultural studies have been especially influential in following this lead, which, in turn, has involved them in a debate with orthodox Marxism. In the 1970s and 1980s, under the leadership of Stuart Hall, members of the "Birmingham school" of cultural studies challenged overly rigid notions of cultural domination. They found, instead, that mass-mediated culture is actually a very contested terrain. It is the ground on which various groups struggle to define popular understandings of the world. Hall's essay "Encoding/Decoding" (1980) provided a theoretical framework for explaining how the mass media's projection of meaning is never automatic. The sender of a message must first "encode" it, and the receivers must "decode" it. They will do so not necessarily according to the sender's intentions but in terms of the frameworks of interpretation and background information that they, as an audience, bring to the message. In short, the effect of a message cannot be read from the message itself but, rather, must be determined by looking at what audiences make of it. Audiences, of course, are not free to take up just any meaning at all. Indeed, Hall (1980) believes that there is a "dominant" or "hegemonic" way to decode the text. Yet, there is also a "negotiated" form of decoding as well as an "oppositional" decoding that runs against the dominant reading.

The most influential empirical study that followed from this understanding was David Morley's *The Nationwide Audience* (1980). Morley examined various group readings of two episodes of *BBC News,* the British Broadcasting Corporation's popular newsmagazine program. His results revealed that different people interpreted the show in different ways. These interpretations were not random but, rather, were affected by social location. Morley had initially focused on differences in interpretation between groups according to class or occupation. However, recent reanalysis suggests that his data are more readily understood when race, gender, and age differences are examined. For

example, working-class persons who read the program in a "dominant" mode tended to be white and male, whereas those who read it in an "oppositional" mode tended to be black and female. Younger persons were more likely than older people to accept a dominant or negotiated rather than an oppositional reading (Kim 1999).

In America, the most notable contribution to audience research came from a sociologically minded literary scholar, Janice Radway (1984). In an effort to comprehend the passions of women who read romance novels, Radway used sociological survey and interview methods to get at how romance readers understand the novels they read. Radway recognized that romance novels are highly commercial and formulaic, but she argued that, although the reading of them was patterned, it was also done in a personal way. The content of these popular novels was not feminist but, rather, offered a dominant message urging women to accept as natural the hierarchies of customary gender relations. What Radway discovered, however, was that women use the act of reading itself to carve out private time in the face of demanding husbands and children. The books thus represent "escapist" literature in a double sense: They not only make room for fantasy as a response to oppressive conditions but also provide time off from the actual demands of women's everyday lives.

The new "active audience" approach might seem to support a kind of radical and anti-authoritarian political stance. For example, according to

**Reception** The way in which mass-media content is received or used by audiences, including such factors as what the audiences selectively choose to attend to and the purposes for which the media are consumed. For example, the media are a source of serious information for some and a source of sheer entertainment for others. Sometimes audiences think carefully about what they are receiving; at other times media content is just background noise.

researcher John Fiske (1989) and social theorist Michel de Certeau (1984), everyday life is a site full of resources with which ordinary people can engage in tactics of resistance to the powerful who control the media. However, recent empirical studies of people's actual usage of television in their everyday lives present a more complicated picture. They suggest neither populism nor conformity. Sociologist Ron Lembo (1997) found large variations in the amount of attention that viewers give to media. After studying the viewing habits of a sample of sixty working people with the intention of finding out how much attention, or **mindfulness,** they paid to television as part of their everyday activities, he proposed the following "continuum of mindfulness":

- ✓ *Habitual*, the least mindful way of approaching activities, whereby people orient themselves to media in an unthinking way.
- ✓ *Escapist*, a slightly more mindful approach, whereby people have some awareness of a desire to be freed—mentally, emotionally, physically, or socially—from their situation.
- ✓ *Playful*, whereby people are not only getting away from what they were previously doing or feeling but also turning toward something else in a creative frame of mind.
- ✓ *Reflective*, the most mindful state, whereby people monitor and evaluate their thoughts and feelings, trying to anticipate what difference it would make if they chose another activity, and generally trying to be conscious of how media viewing might fit into the context of their free-time activities. (adapted from Lembo 1997)

**Mindfulness** A theoretical concept introduced by Ron Lembo describing the amount of attention individuals paid to television as part of their everyday activities. Along the "continuum of mindfulness," as he called it, are four approaches: habitual, escapist, playful, and reflective.

Lembo's study led him to distinguish between periods in the day when viewers were more attentive and reflective in their viewing (often later in the evening, when they were watching films or dramas) and periods when they were simultaneously carrying out other routine everyday activities while the television was on (early evening, while watching news, soaps, sports, and game shows). The men and women he studied varied in terms of the balance they struck between selective-attentive viewing and simultaneous viewing. However, a substantial number at one end of the continuum were identified as doing all their viewing while simultaneously engaging in other activities. Lembo concluded that simultaneous viewing was indicative of an emerging trend in which people could disengage from the powerful discourses of television. The social and political implication of this trend, if substantiated, is that television may be less powerful than has sometimes been argued, either as a tool of dominant groups or as a resource for popular resistance.

A related study performed in 2004 yielded the following findings:

**Media Multitasking**

- ✓ People who regularly or occasionally watch TV and read the newspaper at the same time: 74.2 percent
- ✓ People who regularly or occasionally watch TV while going online: 66.2 percent
- ✓ Regarding simultaneous online users: TV viewing is down 8.8 percent among 18- to 24-year-olds and down 12.2 percent among 25- to 34-year-olds—in both cases, in favor of video games.
- ✓ What people do as they wait for downloads from the Internet: listen to the radio (52.1 percent), watch TV (61.8 percent), read the newspaper (20.2 percent) (adapted from BIGresearch 2004)

Media consumers today often multitask, watching television or the Internet at the same time they read a newspaper or magazine, talk on their cell phones, and sometimes also listen to the radio! (iStockphoto)

## The Media and Postmodernity

Lembo's findings raise another concern as well—namely, that the seemingly innocuous everyday practice of simultaneous TV viewing may support a tendency toward "disengaged sociality"—seeing others as fragmentary images or objects, as if they were being observed from a distance. Critics believe that such distancing is a disturbing pathology of postmodern life. They claim that, in modern society, communal relations in the home socialized individuals to play roles and take on identities in sustained face-to-face interaction. But in the image-based society of postmodernity, they argue, people see others and themselves merely in terms of fleeting images. One critic in particular, French Marxist sociologist Guy Debord (1994), has denounced postmodern mass-mediated life as producing "society of the spectacle." He connects this condition not just to media effects but, more broadly, to the tendency of capitalism to turn everything into a commodity, into objects that can be bought and sold. This tendency is most obvious in the messages that television ads send to viewers, but Debord finds it increasingly typical of all television.

Debord's Marxist emphasis on political effects and commodification is not the only way to tell a critical story about the postmodern prominence of the media. According to sociologist Jean Baudrillard, the pivotal role of mass media has transformed modern society into postmodern society. He describes society as resembling a hall of mirrors, in which people possess only "simulacra," reflections of reflections. Rather than presenting us with a mirror-like reflection of reality—with truth—the mass media impart merely their own manufactured images. Baudrillard went so far as to write a book titled *The Gulf War Did Not Take Place* (1995). His point was that the only knowledge the public had concerning the conflict between America and Iraq, after the latter's invasion of Kuwait in 1990, came from media reports and television images that depended heavily on U.S. military sources. And there was no way, at least for the ordinary viewer, of checking the extent to which these television images and other inputs corresponded to any reality. Similar criticisms have been made in connection with the more recent mass-mediated wars in Afghanistan and Iraq.

Are these critics right? If the media are not informational but culturally mediated, in terms of both production and reception, does this mean that we live in a society of spectacle and shadowy simulacra? As noted earlier, in the aftermath of 9/11 there were complaints that media coverage had taken on a sensationalistic and even "pornographic" character. Whether or not we agree with such harsh indictments, it certainly was the case that in order to imaginatively convey the meaning of 9/11 the media resorted to plotting and editing techniques usually reserved for fictional programs such as soaps, dramas, and talk shows. New York mayor Giuliani and the emergency workers were portrayed as heroes in a traumatic drama, their sacred qualities contrasted with the "cowardly" qualities of the "evil" terrorists and governments who sheltered them. And throughout this post-trauma coverage, just as in daytime talk shows, ordinary people from the "audience" of citizens were continually being interviewed, asked to give their views and to become "actors" in the show.

Daytime talk shows, such as those pioneered in the 1970s by Phil Donahue and, later, by Oprah Winfrey and Jerry Springer, have been described by Wayne Munson as marking the transition from modern to postmodern culture:

> The term "talk show" combines two communicative paradigms, and like the term itself, the "talk show" fuses and seems to reconcile two different, even contradictory, rhetorics. It links conversation, the interpersonal—the premodern oral tradition—with the mass-mediated spectacle born of modernity. It becomes, among other things, a recuperative practice reconciling technology and commodification with community, mass culture with the individual and the local, production with consumption. In so doing, the mythic American past of the participatory town meeting and the interpersonal "handshake" politics of speech and presence meet the imagined "present" of technological simulation, reproduction, and commodification. The talk show's rampant inclusions make it a postmodern phenomenon. (1993: 6–7)

There are various types of talk shows, including phone-in programs on the radio and the "news/ talk magazine" on television. Examples of the latter are *Today* and *Good Morning America,* which combine rotations of lifestyle segments with reported news, service-oriented features such as consumer advice and film reviews, and celebrity interviews. More personality oriented is the celebrity talk or chat show—sometimes called "talk/variety"—among whose familiar hosts are Arsenio Hall, Conan O'Brien, Jay Leno, and David Letterman. "Talk-service" is the name given to the kind of talk show that involves a lot of audience participation, as in the programs moderated by Donahue and Oprah as well as their more recent counterparts such as Ricki Lake, Montel Williams, and Jerry Springer. This type of talk show is regarded as the best example of postmodern culture because it is an example of what John Fiske, in his *Understanding Popular Culture* (1989), calls "producerly texts"—commercial products that lend themselves to an audience's own production of popular culture by bringing into the public sphere aspects of everyday life that are normally confined to the private sphere. Participants make confessions on topics ranging from sexual deviance to cheating on partners, and outrageous audience reactions break with the norms of conventional public behavior in ways that resemble the public carnivals in traditional societies. While such shows keep faith with the modern idea of searching for "authentic selfhood," they are postmodern in that they turn this search into playful entertainment and explode the idea that there is a single authentic self or route to self-fulfillment and progress.

While media developments like the talk show are easy to criticize, it has also been suggested that they play a positive role by turning into visible public issues certain personal troubles, such as problems experienced by heterosexual or homosexual couples and other issues normally confined to the private sphere (Gamson 1998).

Another area of media development that has contributed to the transition from modern to postmodern culture is the Internet. With its ability to compress space and time, making possible almost instantaneous communication across vast distances, the Internet creates networks of virtual communities that transcend national boundaries. As a result, some social theorists (e.g., Castells

**Network society** The idea that, in postmodern culture, a new kind of social system has emerged that has neither national borders nor centers. New media, such as the Internet, enable this social system to function by providing widespread access and immediate communication.

2000) have begun to speak about the **network society,** a new kind of social system that has neither national borders nor centers. In modern society, one-way media messages were broadcast to mass audiences through a limited number of channels. The new media, by contrast, are much more flexible. They can narrowcast messages to specific segments of audiences and respond to their specific moods. And through a single digitized box, individuals can access hundreds of channels as well as a variety of media forms, from network and cable TV to radio and VCR, the iPod, personal communication devices, the Internet, and blogs. With these latter forms, consumers can be independent of central distributors, arrange their own messages, and talk back to more central and organized media sources. The rise of such an interactive audience suggests that everyday life now includes an increasing element of "virtual reality," along whose paths each of us surfs each day.

Can the Internet's virtual communities bring back a postmodern equivalent of the old New England town meeting or the hubbub of eighteenth-century British coffee shops? This is the question facing critical theorists such as Jürgen Habermas (1989), who bemoan the loss of such face-to-face community sites and believe it has undermined democracy. Other questions also need to be asked at this juncture: Does the Internet provide the long-sought-after community-at-a-distance that might be needed if modern (and postmodern) democracies are to survive? Or will the spread of globalized networks be monopolized by states and corporations, or fragmented and polarized by extremist political and religious sects? For that matter, will the Internet become merely a purveyor of "infotainment" and spectacles?

## CONCLUSION

These are some of the outstanding issues that face us as the media saturation of everyday life trans-forms modern society in a postmodern direction. The work of sociologists is vital for developing public understanding of the media's role in the social construction of reality. Whether exposure to violent media images led Barry Loukaitis to kill his fellow students is not something that sociologists can establish. But we can develop a sociological analysis of the combined factors involved in the production and consumption of media images—an analysis that will also facilitate our understanding of the links between the private troubles of the individual and public issues.

In short, the relationship between the public sphere of democratic politics and the private sphere of pleasures, problems, and self-understandings can be clarified only if we develop a sociological understanding of the role of the media in postmodern society.

# EXERCISES

## Exercise 1

Find an advertisement in a magazine or newspaper that you read regularly. Bearing in mind the functions of the print medium and the target audience of this particular publication, analyze the advertisement using Hall's concepts of "encoding" and "decoding." What do you think is the ad's intended message? Can you suggest an "oppositional" reading of this message?

## Exercise 2

Take a minute to make a list of the ways you use the Internet. For example: Do you look up information about your favorite music and download songs? Do you use online news services (mainstream or independent) to find out about current events? Do you shop online? Do you receive newsletters from groups or organizations with which you are affiliated? Do you keep in touch with friends and family who are far away? Now consider, based on your actual experience, whether and to what degree the Internet resembles television as the latter has been described in this chapter. In other words, is the Internet a purveyor of "infotainment" and spectacle, a vehicle for informing yourself and for challenging the powerful, a vehicle for commercials and consumption, a tool for the wealthy to promote their interests, or a way of talking back to centralized power? Do you think the Internet can change society for the better, or is it merely contributing to Lembo's "disengaged sociality"?

6. How does the textual analysis of newspaper stories challenge the ideal of the media as reflecting an undistorted picture of reality?

7. Briefly describe the four points along Lembo's "continuum of mindfulness."

8. What does Lembo believe are the possible implications of the growing trend toward watching television while simultaneously engaging in other activities?

9. Why are talk shows—especially talk-service shows—considered to exemplify postmodern culture? What elements of premodern, modern, and postmodern society do they combine?

## STUDY QUESTIONS

1. What did the media coverage of the September 11 disaster reveal about the normal organization of television media?

2. How do television and newspapers differ in terms of their function, production, and reception? How did coverage of the September 11 disaster transform television's function?

3. Explain the difference between the terms *mass media* and *culture industry*.

4. If you were to study the production of mass media from a political-economy approach, what kind of questions or concerns would guide your research? Does this approach emphasize production or consumption of mass media?

5. From a cultural-sociological perspective, how would you study media production and media consumption?

## FURTHER READING

*Television and News Media*

Bourdieu, Pierre. 1998. *On Television*. New York: New Press.

Fiske, John. 1987. *Television Culture*. New York: Routledge.

Gitlin, Todd. 1985. *Inside Prime Time*. New York: Pantheon.

Schudson, Michael. 2003. *Sociology of the News*. New York: W. W. Norton.

*Popular Culture*

Adorno, Theodor W. 2001. *The Culture Industry: Selected Essays on Mass Culture*. London/New York: Routledge.

Fiske, John. 1989 *Understanding Popular Culture*. Boston: Unwin Hyman.

*Internet*

Castells, Manuel. 1996. *The Rise of the Network Society*. Cambridge/Oxford: Blackwell.

Holmes, David, ed. 1998. *Virtual Politics: Identity and Community in Cyberspace (Politics and Culture)*. London/Thousand Oaks, CA: Sage.

Poster, Mark. 2001. *What's the Matter with the Internet?* Minneapolis: University of Minnesota Press.

Smith, Marc A., and Peter Kollock, eds. 1998. *Communities in Cyberspace*. New York: Routledge.

Wellman, Barry, and Caroline Haythornthwaite. 2002. *The Internet in Everyday Life (The Information Age)*. Malden, MA: Blackwell.

# PART THREE

# Personal Worlds and Identity

# chapter 5

# Socialization and the Life Cycle

On November 6, 1939, the director of a home for children with mental disabilities in Pennsylvania recorded his observations about one of his most obdurate cases (see the box titled "Anna, a Child with Disabilities").

Lack of speech and concentration, of course, is normal for an infant. The problem here was that Anna was 7 years old! Five months later, a child development specialist conducted tests revealing that Anna had the mentality of a 19-month-old and the social maturity of a 2-year-old. After that time, despite the care and attention of experts, Anna was scarcely able to develop much further. When she was 9, she could bounce and catch a ball and follow directions in groups. Her eating habits were normal. She was toilet-trained, and she could dress herself. What she could not do was speak or act in an independent, self-motivated way. She could call attendants by name, but she could not form complete sentences to express her desires or needs. One year later, a final report on Anna's condition indicated that she had still not progressed beyond the psychosocial development of a 2-year-old.

## AN INDIVIDUAL OR
## A SOCIAL STORY?

This heart-wrenching story is not simply a historical tale. Thousands more much like it could be told about the suffering of "feral" children today. (For further information on this topic, consult http://www.feralchildren.com.) Each of these stories can, of course, be viewed as the account of one individual's terrible fate. Anna had the bad luck to be born at the wrong time, in the wrong place, to the wrong people. If only her mother had not lived on a farm, if only her grandfather had been kinder, if only she'd had a father who could have helped her mother out.

Yet Anna's story can also be read as a sociological parable, for it reveals not only what was lacking in Anna's unfortunate life as an individual but also what was lacking in her society. Institutionally, there was no safety net of child support services for Anna's parents, who couldn't afford private help and who, for one reason or another, were unable to be good parents on their own. There were cultural factors at work as well. It's obvious that patriarchal authority—the social and symbolic power of men to make women do what they want—played a disastrous role. So did the old-fashioned sense of cultural shame attached to children born outside of marriage.

But these historically specific institutional and cultural deficits took their toll only because of another kind of social failure, the absence of socialization—a failure that continues to create the conditions facing feral children today. **Socialization** refers to the simultaneously cultural and psychological process that brings an unformed person into society. Babies are biologically complete, but

This feral child was raised by wolves in India until the age of 12. The study of feral children helps sociologists determine which human behaviors come from "nature" or "nurture." (Archive Photos/Getty Images)

**theory**

## Anna, a Child with Disabilities?

Anna walks about aimlessly, makes periodic rhythmic motions of her hands, and, at intervals, makes guttural and sucking noises. She regards her hands as if she had seen them for the first time. It was impossible to hold her attention for more than a few seconds at a time—not because of distraction due to external stimuli but because of her inability to concentrate. She ignored the task in hand to gaze vacantly about the room. Speech is entirely lacking. Numerous unsuccessful attempts have been made with her in the hope of developing initial sounds. I do not believe that this failure is due to negativism or deafness but that she is not sufficiently developed to accept speech. ...

Anna could follow directions, string beads, identify a few colors, build with blocks, and differentiate between attractive and unattractive pictures. She had a good sense of rhythm and loved a doll. She talked mainly in phrases. ... She walked well and could run fairly well, though clumsily.

One month later, Anna died. She was ten and a half. Her death was related to severe malnutrition from the difficulties of her earlier life.

Anna had first come to the attention of health officials because visitors and neighbors to her Pennsylvania home had expressed increasing concern about her upbringing, in fact about whether she was receiving any upbringing at all. Anna had been born illegitimately to a mother without the means to support herself, a woman whose father strongly disapproved of his daughter's "indiscretion." For months after her birth, Anna was shifted around to one place after another, first to the family farm, then to the home of one of her mother's friends, then to an adoption agency, which reported that at the age of only three weeks she was already "in very bad shape." Perhaps for this reason, the agency could not place her, and after eight weeks Anna's mother was asked to take her back. Soon after the hapless mother gave Anna away to another couple, a social worker found the unwanted child and pleaded with the grandfather to allow Anna's mother to bring the child back home. He refused. Anna spent three weeks in another agency, and four months in a private foster home, which she was eventually taken out of because her grandfather would not pay.

At six months old, Anna was returned to the "home" where her mother lived with her grandfather. Because her mother was afraid to incur the grandfather's wrath, she was reluctant to bring Anna downstairs and kept the child in an attic-like room on the second floor. A sturdy farm woman, Anna's mother spent from early morning to nightfall doing chores on the grandfather's farm. Anna was left without any human attention, receiving only enough care to keep her barely alive. Her clothing, bedding, and body were rarely cleaned. She was barely spoken to or asked to respond in turn. She received no instruction of any kind. She was seldom even moved from one position to another. When Anna was discovered by health authorities at nearly six years of age, she could neither walk nor talk, much less demonstrate the range of behaviors that indicate intelligence or comprehension.

*Source:* Davis (2001: 129–137).

**Socialization** The process by which individuals are incorporated into society, internalizing its codes, narratives, values, and symbols. This process begins at birth and usually takes place first in the family.

they are not psychologically whole; they do not have selves. It takes social interaction, and the culture that directs it, to allow a **self** to develop.

Socialization takes place on two fronts. There are the family's actions, both overt and unconscious, which surround the child and provide the cultural knowledge that she internalizes from the first days of her life. And there are the child's own internal developmental processes, what is called self-development. This refers to changes in the child's subjectivity that result from her exposure to her family's actions—changes that are both cognitive and emotional.

Anna grew up in the physical but not the social sense. She had no caretakers; she was neither nurtured nor instructed by society. Without society, there cannot be a self, and that is exactly what Anna lacked. She had the biological capacity for development, and in her short life her physical capacities continued to unfold. Psychologically, however, she was severely handicapped. The reason was that she had been socially deprived.

The self is a social thing. Its capacities for speech, decisionmaking, and planning, even for feeling and desiring, develop only through interaction. This interaction—first with mother, father, and siblings; later with peers, teachers, co-workers, and media-conveyed information—brings us into society. It ensures that we will share basic cultural traits with others, that we will be roughly similar to—and familiar with—the other members of our society. At the same time, paradoxically, socialization ensures that we will become unique, autonomous individuals. If socialization works properly, in other words, we become simultaneously social and individual, the same and different.

## THE PARADOX OF SOCIALIZATION

In the current chapter we explore this paradox. What is this strange thing called socialization? It brings us into society and allows us to internalize the codes, narratives, values, and symbols that already exist, thereby ensuring the continuity of our societies over time. Yet, especially in postmodern society, learning to be "like us" means, at the same time, learning how to be unique.

While socialization is made possible because of biological givens, sorting out the differing proportions of inborn (biological) as compared with environmental (social) contributions to the self is notoriously difficult—as the Minnesota Twin Family Study made clear (see Figure 5.1 and Table 5.1). Scientists do concur, however, that these must be seen as *dispositional* tendencies rather than as destinies: "The heritability of psychological function does not imply the genetic determinism of human behavior" (Rose 1995: 648, quoted in McGue and Bouchard 1998). Another interpretation of the Minnesota Twin findings is that, at best, "biology" explains only about half of our "personality." Identical twins reared apart were just about as different as they were similar. The question then becomes, how do we explain the rest of the equation, the half of our personality that is *not* determined at birth?

Taking the biological person and making her into a social person has meant different things at different times in history. Today, it means giving people the ability to act freely within broad social and cultural parameters. It means providing them, through social and cultural institutions, with the psychological capacity and cultural skills to structure and restructure their own subjective boundaries, to be flexible, and even to play with the culture transmitted to them at birth.

**Self** Our sense of who we are in relation to ourselves, others, and society. The self is a social thing; its capacities for speech, decisionmaking, planning, feeling, and desiring develop through social interaction. In sociology, the self is often understood as dual, or in tension with social forces. That is to say, the individual has a sense of him- or herself as an autonomous individual with desires and capacities for action, but the self is at the same time limited by society's norms, values, and regulations.

## FIGURE 5.1 Nature or Nurture: Sources of Variation in Personality

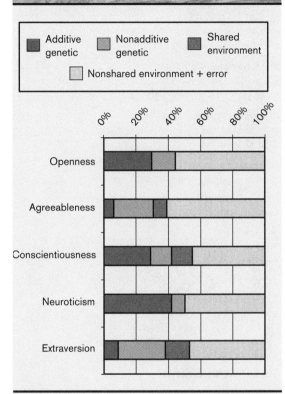

*Note:* The Minnesota Twin Family Study, which began in 1983, is a birth record–based registry that documented some 8,000 pairs of twins born in Minnesota between 1936 and 1955 plus some 1,200 pairs of male twins born 1971–1981. This means that the registry comprises about 80 percent of the approximately 10,400 surviving intact pairs born in Minnesota from 1936 through 1955, about 8,400 pairs in all. The study discovered five broad "super factors," biological traits that these identical twins seemed to exhibit from birth–extraversion, neuroticism, conscientiousness, agreeableness, and openness.

*Source:* Bouchard (1994).

In classical and modern sociology, socialization was conceptualized in a more one-sided way—as bringing social values to the individual, without bringing the individual to social values. In other words, socialization aimed at absorbing the bio-logical person into the all-encompassing society. Durkheim, for example, began one of his lectures in *Moral Education* in the following way: "Having determined the several elements of morality, we are about to inquire how they can be built into, or developed in, the child" (Durkheim 1925: 129).

This sociological understanding pretty much reflected the distinctive qualities of nineteenth- and twentieth-century society. In these earlier periods, the vaunted individuality of modern life was severely undercut by the rigid demands of industrial production and bureaucratic efficiency, and by the homogenizing thrust of modernist culture. Not only were class, ethnic, racial, and gender roles strictly defined and confining, but the age frames within which individuals were allowed to behave were narrow and rigid. In recent decades, these restrictions have begun to break down. Postindustrial society, the globalization of information, the rise of informal modes of organization, the new reality and culture of racial, religious, and gender diversity—all of these changes have demanded from the social self more creativity and independence. As a result, contemporary roles are much more responsive to individual definition. Age sequencing is less lockstep, less confined. It is hardly surprising, then, that postmodern socialization has come to be understood very differently than were modern and traditional forms. In postmodern society, as the individual self becomes socialized, the social self also becomes individualized.

## THE "SELF" IN HISTORY

Not surprisingly, it has only been in this recent period that we've come to understand the self, and socialization, in a historical way. We now see not just that the self is social but also that the very existence of a "self" is relative to historical time. Clifford Geertz put this understanding well: "The Western conception of the person as a bounded, unique, more or less integrated motivational and cognitive universe, a dynamic center of awareness,

TABLE 5.1  The Five Main Determinants of Personality

| Extraversion | (Introversion) |
|---|---|
| Is outgoing, decisive, persuasive, and enjoys leadership roles | Is retiring, reserved, withdrawn, and does not enjoy being the center of attention |
| **Neuroticism** Is emotionally unstable, nervous, irritable, and prone to worry | **(Emotional Stability)** Quickly gets over upsetting experiences, stable, and not prone to worries and fears |
| **Conscientiousness** Is planful, organized, responsible, practical, and dependable | **(Authoritarianism)** Is impulsive, careless, irresponsible, and cannot be depended on |
| **Agreeableness** Is sympathetic, warm, kind, good-natured, and will not take advantage of others | **(Aggression)** Is quarrelsome, aggressive, unfriendly, cold, and vindictive |
| **Openness** Is insightful, curious, original, imaginative, and open to novel experiences and stimuli | **(Narrowness)** Has narrow interests, is unintelligent, unreflective, and shallow |

*Note:* The percentage of variance is explained by genetic and environmental influences on personality traits in the Minnesota study of twins reared apart.

*Source:* Bouchard (1994).

emotion, judgment, and action organized into a distinctive whole and set contrastively both against other such wholes and against its social and natural background is … a rather peculiar idea within the context of the world's culture" (1983: 59).

As the most influential American anthropologist of the last half-century, Geertz places these insights into the self in comparative terms—as a difference between East and West. But they can also be seen as distinguishing between certain historical phases of social development. In traditional societies, selves were bound to tribe, class, religion, and physical location in a seamless, undifferentiated way. The purpose of socialization in such societies was to reproduce the existing culture so that the parameters of social structure could be maintained. Rather than making the self unique, the point was to make people as identical to others as possible.

## Before the Self

In these traditional societies, as well as in earlier modern ones, the aim of socialization was to bring neophytes into the "we." In contemporary societies, we understand the self as an "I" that not only shares broad social understandings but also carries on an internal conversation, an internal dialogue separated from the demands, instructions, and seductions of the outside world.

In earlier societies, such an "I" was either non-existent or much less fully developed. When it began to emerge is a matter of both historical research and informed but still speculative debate. In *The Origin of Consciousness in the Breakdown of the Bicameral Mind* (1976), Julian Jaynes drew from his study of Homer's great epoch stories, the *Iliad* and the *Odyssey,* to advance the intriguing argument that the ancient Greeks did not possess a subjectivity, self, or consciousness as we understand these and experience them today: "The characters from the *Iliad* do not sit down and think out what to do. They have no conscious minds such as we say we have, and certainly no introspections" (1976: 72).

In Homer's books, there is no word that translates into our modern notion of *mind*. Thoughts and feelings are portrayed as free-floating and disembodied, as happening to people for reasons unrelated to their subjective decisions and desires. Gods tell people what to do; they inhabit bodies and direct intentions, with the result that Homer's human beings take little responsibility for their actions. Rather than confronting themselves, Homer's heroes typically blame the gods for the consequences of their acts. Only in the *Odyssey,* the book that followed the *Iliad* both in plot and in real historical time, do Homer's characters begin to show signs of having an inner life. The concept of a *change of mind* is introduced, and Odysseus, the book's moody, boastful, courageous yet still insecure hero, slowly develops a sense of self-awareness.

## Toward the Modern Self

If Jaynes is right about this shift in selfhood emerging in the transition from *Iliad* to *Odyssey,* there must have been some pretty significant social changes at work during that time. In fact, already by the eighth century B.C., the period when Homer is thought to have composed his epochs, Greece had become a center of international trade and commerce. It had also become a land of immigrants and a military power that had begun a long involvement in the affairs of other lands. With urbanization, democratization, and the emergence of a secular intellectual life, such changes eventually led, in the fifth and fourth centuries B.C., to the emergence of city-states, such as Athens. It was in these highly developed city-states that Greek civilization laid the foundation for modern life. And only in this later period did the self as we understand it emerge. In fact, one of the Western world's most famous parables of selfhood dates to this time. Plato told the story of the great Athenian philosopher, Socrates, having been threatened with death because he refused to give up his nonconforming beliefs. Socrates ultimately accepted death because he felt he could not betray his individual integrity, and because he believed that his example of individual autonomy would be healthy for Athenian democracy.

As the first person to remain "true to himself"—at least in the recorded history of the West—the story of Socrates demonstrates that the self now had its own moral life, separated from society. With such a notion of the self, there emerged the division between "higher" and "lower" elements of the person. Instead of giving in to sexual, aggressive, or even simply unthinking and conformist behavior, human beings began to wrestle with the internal conflicts that were generated by their moral and reasoning faculties. During the Renaissance, the French philosopher René Descartes (1596–1650) placed this independent, knowing, and knowable subject at the center of the social world. He began his famous *Meditations* (1641) with the proclamation, "I think, therefore I am." Descartes started what came to be called the philosophy of consciousness, but his work can also be treated as indicating not only a philosophical but an empirical, psychological, and ultimately sociological shift:

> [It was] the prototypical declaration of the modern self, established as a fully separate, self-defining entity, for whom its own rational self-awareness was absolutely primary—doubting everything except itself, setting itself in opposition not only to traditional authorities but to the world, as a subject against object, as a thinking, observing, measuring, manipulating being, fully distinct from an objective God and an external nature. (Tarnas 1991: 180)

When Hamlet contemplated suicide, in the famous tragedy that William Shakespeare wrote some forty years before Descartes' declaration, the young Danish prince memorably proclaimed, "To be or not to be, that is the question." Hamlet had a choice. The self did not exist automatically; its being had to be justified. The issues that Hamlet was worried about—guilt, revenge, love, and duty—could be concerns of literature only after the social conditions for an autonomous self had been developed.

In between the high points of self and social development reached in Greek civilization and the European Renaissance (when Descartes and Shakespeare wrote) Western society sank into the Middle Ages. Rather than evolving, Europe underwent devolution. Social structure became less complex; secular intellectual life rapidly declined; institutions such as law, which had the capacity to extend urban and political life, virtually disappeared. There were corresponding changes in socialization, and the ability to sustain an autonomous sense declined. At the end of the Middle Ages, as Norbert Elias (1994 [1932]) explained in his classical account of the modernizing movement that came out of this period, Europeans were exposed to a "civilizing process" that placed new constraints on individual instincts and emotional impulses. Elias used etiquette manuals to gain access to a record of these subtle shifts in socialization and emotional life. To contemporary ears, the instructions in these manuals may seem bizarre—a dissonance that underlines how different socialization was in those earlier days.

> "Those who stand up and snort disgustingly over the dishes like swine belong with other farmyard beasts."

> "To snort like a salmon, gobble like a badger, and complain while eating—these three things are quite improper."

> "A man who clears his throat when he eats and one who blows his nose in the tablecloth are both ill-bred."

> "Do not scrape your throat with your bare hand while eating."

> "Do not slobber with your drink, for this is a shameful habit."

> "Avoid cleaning your teeth with a knife at table."

> "It is not decent to poke your fingers into your ears or eyes, as some people do, or to pick you nose while eating. These three habits are bad."

> "Before you sit down, make sure your seat has not been fouled."

> "Do not touch yourself under your clothes with your bare hands." (Elias 1932: 69–71, 105, 106)

These manuals reflected a new insistence on interpersonal manners: "The change in behavior at table," Elias suggests, "is part of a very extensive transformation of human feelings and attitudes" (1932: 116). They were a response to demands by this more complex early-modern society for a deeper internalization of normative constraints, marking "the beginning of the mode of observation that will at a later stage be termed 'psychological'" (1932: 78). "What was lacking in [the medieval] world," Elias (1932: 69) further observed, "was the invisible wall of affects which seems now to rise between the human body and another, repelling and separating, the wall which is [so] perceptible today." Today "people see things with more differentiation, i.e., with a stronger restraint on their emotions" (1932: 71). In early-modern society, as such manuals make abundantly clear, these new self-restraints were forced upon adults—whether upper-class peers or lower-class "inferiors." As modernization gathered more speed, the restraints became imposed by the family—a phenomenon known as *primary socialization:*

> Stricter control of impulses and emotions is first imposed by those of high social rank on their social inferiors or, at most, their social equals. It is only comparatively late … that the family becomes the only—or, more exactly, the primary and

dominant—institution with the function of installing drive control. Only then does the social dependence of the child on its parents become particularly important as a leverage for the socially required regulation and molding of impulses and emotions. (Elias 1932: 137)

As a result of such historically produced changes in the socializing process, there eventually emerged a self that could sustain modern democracy. Indeed, the anti-authoritarian, consent-based system of democracy rests upon the deeply rooted belief that the self is autonomous and internally integrated. Only the presumption of such autonomy allows us to think of the human as possessing "inalienable rights" that can be protected only by a democratic form of government. This, of course, is what Thomas Jefferson meant by the words he wrote in *The Declaration of Independence,* which initiated the American Revolution in 1776. While Jefferson and the other Founding Fathers believed such rights to be "self-evident" and natural, they were, in fact, very much enmeshed in a historically specific, relatively recent, socially constructed sense of the independent self.

## Toward the Postmodern Self

By the middle of the twentieth century, this modernist self was already beginning to change. The notion of the autonomously directed self began to give way to demands for less rigid, more flexible identities and for more responsiveness to rapidly shifting social environments. In the transition from modern to postmodern society, cultural ideas, information, and traditions changed quickly. With the development of advanced communication technologies, words and symbols leaped across formerly rigid boundaries, demanding instant familiarity with unfamiliar and foreign ideas. The rapidity of migration, the displacement of assimilation, the promotion of difference and multiculturalism—these patterns, too, exposed people to

much more variation in their environments and demanded steep increases in individual sensitivity and responsiveness. Vertical as well as horizontal mobility accelerates, and at every stratification level people engage in far more frequent interactions with people they do not know and initially may not understand.

## Measuring Changes in Selfhood

In 1964, Manford Kuhn developed the "Twenty Statements Test" in which participants are asked to list twenty responses to the question "Who am I?" Researchers interpret these answers to sort participants into four categories, developed by McPartland, Cumming, and Garretson (1961):

1. Physical: statements that identify the self as a physical being (e.g., I am six feet tall).
2. Social: reference social role, status, institutional membership (e.g., I am a student).
3. Reflective: the self is described as a situation-free agent; statements include preferences, interests, aspirations, activities, and psychological attributes (e.g., I enjoy sports).
4. Oceanic/Global: statements that are irrelevant to social action and do not convey personal attributes (e.g., I am at one with nature).

Researchers have been using this test on university undergraduates since the 1950s to compare the self-conceptualization of different groups and determine the influence of a changing sociocultural environment on conceptions of the self. As Table 5.2 shows, it has become increasingly rare for students to describe themselves according to their social relations, preferring instead to describe their selves according to their attributes. Does this demonstrate effective socialization into a society that values individualism? Is this a legacy of the "me" generation or a product of postmodern society? Or could it be that college students tend to answer this way because institutions of higher

**TABLE 5.2 Comparative Data on TST Self-Responses Across Five Decades**

| Year | N | A Physical (%) | B Social (%) | C Reflective (%) | D Oceanic (%) |
|---|---|---|---|---|---|
| | | | **Mode of Response** | | |
| 1957(a) | 1,653 | 2.0 | 51.0 | 31.0 | 16.0 |
| 1969(b) | 400 | * | * | 68.0 | * |
| 1976–79(c) | 1,125 | 4.0 | 16.0 | 68.0 | 12.0 |
| 1981(d) | 484 | 0.0 | 11.0 | 88.0 | 1.0 |
| 1988(e) | 333 | 0.6 | 12.2 | 85.2 | 2.0 |
| 2001 | 324 | 0.0 | 8.4 | 91.3 | 0.3 |

Notes: (a) Hartley (1968), (b) Zurcher (1977), (c) Snow and Phillips (1982), (d) Roscoe and Peterson (1983), (e) Babbit and Burbach (1990).

*Zurcher reported percentages for only the C category.

*Source:* Grace and Cramer (2002).

education encourage students to examine and evaluate their attributes and aspirations?

Some social observers have lamented these changes, criticizing the newly emerging, postmodern self as inferior to its modern predecessor. David Reisman, in his mid-century best seller *The Lonely Crowd* (1950), asserted that history has provided three types of personality profiles: the tradition-directed, the inner-directed, and the other-directed. He associated the inner-directed person with classic American individualism and believed it was essential for democracy. And he decried the other-directed self he saw as emerging in the America of his day. In particular, he described other-directed people as torn between having to maintain a constant identity and needing to keep up with the times, which demanded new and continuous adjustments. "The other-directed person," Reisman complained, "is, in a sense, at home everywhere and nowhere, capable of a superficial intimacy with and response to everyone" (1950: 26).

Other social observers have taken a decidedly different view. Anthony Giddens (1991), for example, links the more socially responsive contemporary self to the decline in traditional sources of moral authority and the rise of a globalized system of rapidly changing cultural information. In such a world, the self must be open and responsive to the diagnoses and suggestions of experts in every area of personal life, from marriage and child-rearing to eating and dressing, and even to thinking and feeling. These demands for responsiveness, Giddens finds, may well generate existential anxiety, but they also create reflexivity and human empowerment. As the sense of absolute individual autonomy recedes, there is a corresponding shift away from the "emancipatory politics" of the modern era to the "life politics" of our own time. During the industrial phase of society and the early phases of modern democracies, social movements focused on inequality and redistribution. But in the postindustrial society of "emotion work" (see section later in chapter) and the postmodern world of multiculturalism, these classical social movements have tended to be displaced by cultural movements that focus on identity, meaning, and self-actualization.

## FIGURE 5.2 Historical Stages of the Self

Premodern Self ⟶ Modern Self ⟶ Postmodern Self
Jaynes's bicameral mind: no self, consciousness,
or subjectivity in the *Iliad*; these only begin to emerge
in the *Odyssey*.
    Socrates refuses to betray individual integrity.
        Descartes' *Meditations*
        Shakespeare's *Hamlet*
            Elias's "civilizing process"
                Declaration of Independence:
                emergence of autonomous, integrated self
                possessing inalienable rights
                    Reisman's "lonely crowd"
                        Giddens's reflexive self, "life politics"
                          Gergen's "saturated self"
                            Lifton's "protean self"

In a complementary examination of the psychological effects of recent social changes, social psychologist Kenneth Gergen speaks of the new "saturated self." Concomitant with the decreasing sense of an irreducible core self, he says, is the "acquisition of multiple and disparate potentials for human beings": "There is no individual essence to which one remains true or committed. One's identity is continuously emergent, re-formed, and redirected as one moves through the sea of ever-changing relationships. In the case of 'Who am I?' it is a teeming world of provisional possibilities" (Gergen 1991: 139).

Robert Lifton (1993), a psychoanalyst, talks in much the same way about the emergence of the "protean self." As compared to the autonomous and self-referential self of modernity, this more contemporary protean self willingly accepts and engages changes in identity, forming and reforming value orientations and ways of organizing life. There is more fragmentation but also, as fluidity and change are embraced, more possibility of maintaining continuity. And because of this new "multiplicity of varied, even antithetical images

and ideas that are held at any one time by the self," Lifton believes, the contemporary self has a much wider repertoire for meeting her constantly shifting social environment. (See Figure 5.2 for a summary of the historical stages of the self.)

## CREATING THE SELF

Now that we have some sense of the historical context of the self, let's examine in more detail how it is created. Socialization occurs to varying degrees throughout our life. Studies have traditionally focused on moments and situations that generate radical changes in psychological and social perspectives, and these situations occur much more often in early life because younger people are less formed than older ones. But socialization is also an experience for persons who already possess relatively coherent personalities. Adult socialization occurs whenever people enter into situations that reshape in fundamental ways their sense of self, their outlook, and, eventually, their everyday engagements with the world. Reforming alcoholics, religious converts, mentally ill and criminally institutionalized individuals, even college students going through "rush" to gain membership in a fraternity or sorority—all are experiencing socialization, sometimes voluntarily, sometimes not.

## Culture and Social Structure

In forming and reforming the self, whether that of an adult or a child, socialization relies on both culture and social structure. Simple language learning guarantees internalization of a wide swath of society's culture. To speak a language fully means to understand such complex and important social facts as time and place, and to know what it means to be a member of different groups, from the family to the neighborhood, peer group, nation, and world. Learning to speak involves not just learning grammar, syntax, and vocabulary. It also involves learning to think about social relations and self and to make sense of the world.

These cultural lessons are not transmitted formally. Most socialization occurs via informal practices and latent messages. These are transmitted at family get-togethers, during Little League games and cooking lessons with Mom or Dad, and in visits to a friend's house, a restaurant, or a pharmacy or store. Through these intimate and spontaneous experiences, young people are exposed to the narratives, values, and codes that structure social life. They learn—take into themselves—lessons about what it means to be successful and what, to the contrary, tempts failure; lessons about good and evil, morality and immorality; lessons about what

is socially possible, what is realistic, and what is unrealistic and, in social terms, simply not possible at all.

As this notion of possible and impossible suggests, the cultural messages transmitted via socialization carry the heavy limits of social structure inside of themselves. Rank and hierarchy, race and gender, sexuality and its boundaries: One's initial place in society, learned from family, friends, and schools, is transmitted to every child.

These structural referents of culture, imparted to every child through socialization, give a reality to the emerging self. In "white-collar" families, the parents do mental work in the postindustrial sectors that process information and require advanced education. Indeed, studies show that the socialization white-collar parents impart to their children reflects this work experience; the values emphasized in such socialization include curiosity, creativity, flexibility, and independence. By contrast, in "blue-collar" families, where parents work in hierarchical, routinized, and physically demanding environments, the parents stress discipline and obedience to authority; they want their children to learn mechanical skills and punctuality (Kohn and Schooler 1983). As society becomes postindustrial, the percentage of blue-collar workers drastically declines, and the self and socialization change accordingly.

Culture is a powerful influence on the development of the self. It is within a sociocultural system that we develop our understanding of what it means to be a person and learn how to enact this in everyday life. This is the context in which Hazel Rose Markus and her colleagues (1997) developed the concept of selfways. As they explain:

> Cultural and social groups in every historical period are associated with characteristic patterns of sociocultural participation or, more specifically, with characteristic ways of being a person in the world—what we will call here *selfways*. ... These culturally constructed patterns, including ways of

**Selfways** As defined by Hazel Rose Markus and her colleagues, the characteristic cultural ideas and values associated with particular social and cultural groups in the world. These emerge from living one's life in particular sociocultural contexts.

thinking, feeling, wanting, and doing, arise from living one's life in particular sociocultural contexts [which are] structured according to certain meanings, practices, and institutions. ... Selfways include key cultural ideas and values, including understandings of what a person is, as well as senses of how to be a "good," "appropriate," or "moral" person. (Markus et al. 1997: 16)

Like many other researchers, Markus and her associates have been interested in comparing selfhood in American and Japanese societies because these are archetypal examples of Western and Eastern cultures with equally advanced postindustrial economies. Figure 5.3 outlines the basic elements of the "independent" self of Western society and the "interdependent" self of Eastern society. While this schema might strike you as an oversimplification or stereotype of Western and Eastern cultures, empirical studies would suggest they are on to something. Researchers who have tried to import traditional methods of measuring selfhood, such as the interview format and the Twenty Statements Test, are often met with confusion in Asian contexts; their methods, based on a Western definition of selfhood, assume certain ways of thinking and acting. Should we expect that Japanese pathways to the self will change as this rapidly developing "Eastern" nation enters ever more firmly into postmodern ways of life? Are the interdependent selfways associated with socialization in Japanese society shared by other Asian countries? And are Western socialization and selfhood themselves subject to change, such that—in the context of globalization—the autonomous self that is so deeply entrenched in Western society will eventually come to be expressed in more interdependent ways? These are questions that, no doubt, will direct future social-psychological research in our increasingly globalized world.

Culture and social structure create the *content* of socialization. But what about the *process*? In the pages that follow, we look at process in terms of two dimensions. First, we examine the **agents of socialization**—the influences from the social environment that transform the child from a gurgling infant, who is human only in the biological sense, into a competent social person. Second, we explore the internal changes that these agents induce in the child's subjectivity.

## PRIMARY SOCIALIZATION: THE FAMILY

One thing about socialization hasn't changed over time: The family is still what marks its beginning and plays the most important role. Apart from a few biological givens and genetic propensities, in social terms children pretty much come into the world as blank slates. Uncritical and sponge-like, they lack any frame of reference for evaluating what comes at them from their environment. That's why family socialization is termed "primary." It provides the first and most formative experience of self-formation. At the beginning of their lives, young children take in everything around them, without much sifting and winnowing.

### Parents

Within every family—regardless of the civilization or historical period in question, and however *family* is defined—there is a small subset of older adults who assume primary socializing responsibility. (See also Chapter 7, on marriage and the family.) These older adults may be grandparents, uncles and aunts, even longtime family friends.

**Agents of socialization**  The influences from the social environment that transform a child from an unaware infant into a competent social person. Agents of socialization might include the family, parents, school, or peer groups.

# FIGURE 5.3 Cross-Cultural Studies of the Self

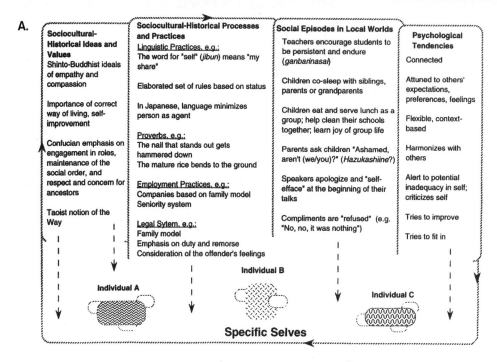

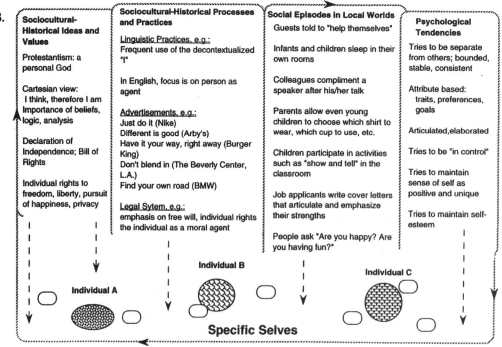

*Source:* Adapted from Markus et al. (1997).

Typically, however, the older family members who become the primary socializers are the parents, the adults biologically involved in procreation. Yet, while being a parent is biological in nature, acting out the parental role is something that has to be learned. In fact, during "child-rearing," both children and parents are socialized. Biological parents must learn new roles; as they confront their care-taking responsibilities, they develop new values and priorities and new conceptions of themselves. They become "fathers" and "mothers."

Parents influence the development of their children through the support they offer and the control they exert (Peterson and Rollins 1987: 471). *Support*—which entails warmth, affection, nurturance, and acceptance—is communicated through the physical and symbolic gestures that parents make to demonstrate that they value the child's actions and the child's self. Such support triggers the identification of children with parents. It is because parents support their children that children consider their parents the most "significant others" in their lives. And it is because parents are so significant that young children are responsive to their wishes.

This responsiveness sets the stage for the second dimension of parenting, which is *control*. Parents not only support their children but make continuous efforts to shape and structure their environments and their actions. Control certainly involves the exercise of power, but power does not necessarily have to be applied in a threatening way. Control can be exercised either inductively or coercively. If it is inductive, control is positive. The child experiences discipline as closely connected to the parents' love. Such control is described as inductive because it is presented as growing naturally out of the pragmatic requirements of the situation, not from some arbitrary rule or personal parental whim. The parents justify such discipline on rational grounds, offering an explanation that points to the consequences of the child's actions and their own. This rational, inductive approach

makes "role-taking" more likely, for it allows the child to more easily understand the parents' expectations and to imaginatively assume some elements of the parental role. Role-taking allows internalization. It is at the heart of socialization.

Coercion represents another dimension through which parental control is exercised. Always present to one degree or another, it can become the dominant mode of control. In the coercive approach to control, power is simply asserted, not explained. When this happens too often, parental power appears arbitrary, irrational, and unconnected to clear expectations. Feeling rejected rather than connected, children respond by placing a lower value on their developing self. They also are much less likely to identify with their parents. When parents exercise control via coercion rather than induction, their children are more likely to develop values and expectations that significantly differ from their own.

Socialization is most effective when supportive parenting is combined with inductive control. For example, this combination is the best predictor of a child's academic achievement. The least effective approach to parenting is one that combines low levels of emotional support with coercive control. Drawing on numerous observations and statistical studies, Gary Peterson and Boyd Rollins (1987) have constructed a diagram that shows the different ways in which the two dimensions of parental socialization interact (see Figure 5.4).

Despite their centrality, however, control and support are not the only variables that determine whether parental socialization is a success. The extent to which parents are involved in their children's lives crosscuts these dimensions. A father may be coercive, but he may also be highly involved in his child's life. In this case, the exercise of coercive control would not undermine the child's self-esteem to nearly the same degree as would occur in the absence of such involvement. The performance expectations that parents exert are yet another factor. Supportive and inductive

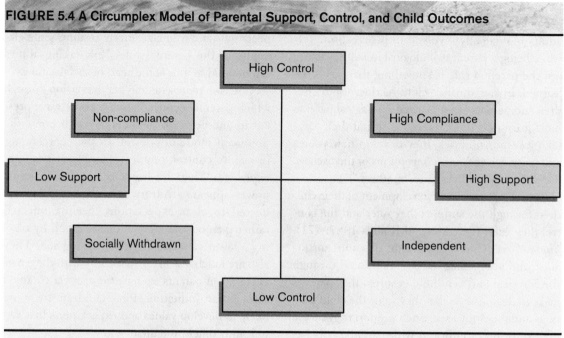

**FIGURE 5.4 A Circumplex Model of Parental Support, Control, and Child Outcomes**

*Source:* Peterson and Rollins (1987).

parents may undermine the socialization process by having low expectations for their children's behavior—emotionally, morally, or academically. Finally, there is the simple but all-important matter of what kinds of people the parents are. What are their qualities as human beings? Are they confident and self-respecting people? Are they able to exercise patience and tolerance? Can they demonstrate honesty, integrity, and competence? The sociological dimensions of parental socialization are always filtered through such unpredictable, individual traits.

## Siblings

Parents are the most influential socializing agents in the family, but brothers and sisters—siblings—also have important roles (Peterson and Rollins 1987: 483–484). The sheer number of siblings has a clear and measurable effect, inasmuch as the size of a family affects the ability of parents to exercise support and control. With greater numbers of children, order becomes more difficult to maintain, frustration increases, and parents become less likely to offer emotionally supportive forms of control. In larger families, parents spend less time with each child. As a result, they are less likely to offer inductive, rational explanations, and they turn more often to coercive forms of control. This situation, in turn, undermines the possibility that strong identification will develop between child and parents. Role-taking is less likely, and external conformity becomes more important than the growth of a self-confident, individuated self.

The time spacing between children—child density—can mitigate or intensify the effects of family size. Wider spacing means that parents can use their time more effectively, leading to less frustration, more relaxed discipline, greater use of reasoning, and a higher degree of emotional support. Birth order also plays a role in sibling socialization. Although the effects of this factor are more difficult to assess, it is known that firstborns, compared to lastborns, tend to get more attention and verbal stimulation, yet they are also subjected to much less relaxed parenting and stricter disciplinary demands.

## Birth Order

In *Born to Rebel* (1996), Frank Sulloway explores the sibling factor in family socialization, focusing on birth order in particular. He shows that, at least in modern societies, the very strength of socialization can sometimes also be a handicap as far as creativity is concerned.

With a primary emphasis on the modern period, Sulloway developed a list of thousands of individuals who were responsible for initiating significant social innovations, including political revolutionaries, scientific creators, musical geniuses, intellectual radicals, economic entrepreneurs, and inventors of every kind.

This book is inspired by a perplexing puzzle. Why do some people have the genius to reject the conventional wisdom of their day and to revolutionize the way we think? Copernicus, Newton, and Darwin are just three of the bold visionaries who have radically transformed our understanding of the world. [Moreover,] no matter how radical the idea, and no matter how fierce the opposition, some people [and not others] have quickly recognized the brilliance of the innovation and come to its defense. (1996: xi)

In trying to interpret this data set regarding modern history's bold visionaries, Sulloway began with the theoretical premise that the nature of the self holds the key. Specifically, the adult's relation to inherited values is determined by his psycho-logical orientation and social proclivities. The innovator has to be comfortable with his culture, and with himself, but he must also have a critical distance from both and the motivation to change. While age has often been considered crucial in this respect, Sulloway found that it had little effect:

Age has sometimes been suggested as a relevant factor, but this influence cannot explain why parents have sometimes championed new ideas and why their own offspring have sometimes opposed the same innovation. The great naturalist Étienne Geoffroy Saint-Hilaire believed in evolution a quarter of a century before Darwin announced his theory of natural selection. Yet Étienne's son Isidore, who was also a naturalist, opposed these heterodox ideas. In the political domain, Benjamin Franklin's eldest son, William, opposed the American Revolution and was expelled from the country as a Loyalist. Many further examples could be given to show that age is surprisingly independent of revolutionary proclivities. (1996: xii)

Arguing that the nature of socialization is much more critical than age, Sulloway conducted a series of statistical tests to determine the relative effects of different dimensions of socialization. He discovered that birth order explains much more than any other variable—more than parental style, more than gender, more than religion or family wealth, more even than family size and the time spacing between siblings. Sure, being first in line for parental attention tightens identification, ensures value transmission, and heightens the chances for social success. But these benefits become decided disadvantages where creativity and social innovation are concerned: "It is natural for firstborns to identify more strongly with power and authority. They arrive first within the family and employ their superior size and strength to defend their special status. Relative to their younger siblings, firstborns are more assertive, socially dominant, ambitious, jealous of their status, and defensive" (Sulloway 1996: xiv).

Indeed, it is because of these qualities that first-born children get the lion's share of parent attention and energy. To survive and prosper, second-borns must be more creative. They must find for themselves a special niche, developing skills that set them apart and allow them to divert attention away from their older brother or sister. A sense of injustice may also be involved. Laterborn children are likely to perceive parental favoritism. If unassuaged, this sense of being wronged can undermine identification and respect for authority. Once established by socialization, these patterns continue into adulthood and determine the individual's relationship to society: "As underdogs within the family system, younger siblings are inclined to question the status quo and in some cases to develop a 'revolutionary personality.' In the name of revolution, laterborns have repeatedly challenged the time-honored assumptions of their day. From their ranks have come the bold explorers, the iconoclasts, and the heretics of history" (Sulloway 1996: xiv).

## Gender

Let's step outside of this examination of the structure and process of socialization to consider, for a moment, the nature of the values transmitted and the nature of the self that can emerge. Nothing provides better evidence for the power of socialization as a mediator between self and society than

Basic socialization takes place on a daily basis in families, even when parents are not intentionally teaching their children. (iStockphoto)

the pressure that parents exert on their children to adopt gender-appropriate behavior. Through socialization, parents transmit both the culture of gender relations and the unequal social structure that informs it. Referring to gender-oriented parental pressure, feminist social psychologist Margaret Anderson puts the matter of **gender** succinctly: "First, it gives us a definition of ourselves. Second, it defines the external world and our place within it. Third, it provides our definition of others and our relationships with them" (2005).

In one study of gender socialization, parents were asked to describe their male and female babies twenty-four hours after birth, when no objective differences other than genitalia were evident. The parents of female babies described their children as smaller, softer, and less attentive than did the parents of boys. Fathers were even more influ-

> **Gender** A term that refers to cultural ideas, norms, and values that construct images and expectations of females and males, particularly in terms of behavior and appearance. Unlike sex, which is limited to biological distinctions between males and females, gender is socially and culturally constructed and understood.

Stereotypical gendered roles are learned at a young age; for example, boys are expected to play outside and be active in sports, whereas girls are thought to enjoy quiet, artistic activities inside. (iStockphoto)

enced by gender than mothers, showing a greater inclination to describe their sons as stronger, more alert, bigger, and better coordinated, and their daughters as weak, delicate, and inattentive—all within twenty-four hours of birth! (Rubin, Provenzono, and Luria 1974). Other sociological investigations have revealed how such similarly preconceived notions lead parents to create entirely different environments for their children. Compared to girls' rooms, those of boys tend to contain toys of greater variation—ranging from educational and military toys to those relating to sports, animals, and machines. Boys' toys, moreover, are designed to encourage improvisation and flexibility, what Harriet Rheingold and Kaye Cook (1975) call "competency-eliciting potential." Boys are also more encouraged by their parents to go outside and play.

Gender socialization, in other words, starts right at birth, if not before the actual delivery. If parents learn the child's sex prior to birth, they set about preparing an environment that is heavily gendered, not only in terms of toys but also furnishings, clothing, and color schemes. And the gender of the newborn is frequently the first thing friends and relatives inquire about. Why is this? Because they want to know how to interact with the child, what to say, what kind of physical gestures to make, and how to describe the child to others. If the crying baby is male, he is said to have strong lungs, to be assertive and active. If the crying baby is female, she is described as tired or as wanting her mother. The baby boy is said to have a strong grasp on the parent's probing finger; the baby girl is said to have a gentle touch.

Parents use the baby's sex to interpret and differentiate among physical features and emotional actions that are, in reality, indistinguishable from one another. In this manner the unformed infant learns what gender to become, and how. Parents expect each gender to react differently to different kinds of attention, support, and discipline, but it's the expectations themselves that produce the baby's responses. For example, as numerous studies (e.g., Peterson and Rollins 1987: 485) have demonstrated, female infants receive more attention, stimulation, vocalization, and smiles from mothers. Male infants, by contrast, receive much more complex responses from their fathers, more visual and physical stimulation, and more encouragement for exaggerated body movements. Female infants are in general given more emotional support and subjected to more inductive, less coercive control. Boys receive less support, higher levels of punishment, and more coercion (see box titled "Becoming Male"). Is it surprising, then, that girls identify more with their parents and are more cooperative, less assertive, and less independent? Because identification is more attenuated in boys, they are less responsive to their parents as well as more independent and assertive.

## theory

### Becoming Male

Our parents gently and sometimes not so gently push us into a predetermined course. First they provide clothing designated appropriate to our masculine status. Even as infants our clothing displays sexual significance, and our parents are extremely careful that we never are clothed in either dresses or ruffles. ... Generally plain, often simple, and usually sturdy, our clothing is designed to take the greater "rough and tumble" that they know boys are going to give it. ...

Our parents' concern is always present. If during a supermarket expedition even a stranger mistakes our sexual identity, this agitates our parents, challenging their sacred responsibility to maintain the reality-ordering structure of the sex worlds. Such mistaken identification forces them to rethink their activities in proper sex typing, their deep obligation to make certain that their offspring is receiving the right start in life.

They will either ascribe the mistake to the stupidity of the stranger or immediately foreswear some particular piece of clothing. ... We also learn something about our world vis-à-vis that of those strange female creatures who coinhabit our space. We learn that we can get dirtier, play rougher, speak louder, act more crudely, wander farther from home, stay away longer, and talk back more. We see that girls live in a world foreign to ours. Theirs is quieter, neater, daintier, and in general more subdued. Sometimes our worlds touch, but then only momentarily. ... They cannot really enter our world, and we certainly do not want to become part of theirs, with its greater restrictions and fewer challenges. ...

Seldom do we think about being masculine. Usually we are just being. ... We know there are two worlds, and we are grateful for the one we are in.

*Source:* Henslin (1991: 124–127).

---

Yet in contemporary, postmodern society, such radical divisions between the genders are thought of as anything but natural. As social scientific research and feminist social narratives have proliferated, researchers have become increasingly critical of the construction of gender difference. They have repeatedly found gendered socialization to be detrimental not only to girls but to boys as well. Most obviously, of course, it contributes to gender inequality by creating personality differences that facilitate the subordination of women to men (Chodorow 1978). Equally important, if less obvious, is the fact that gender socialization narrows the range of male experience, intensifies performance demands, and restricts emotions and needs in ways that lead many adult males to feel isolated and inadequate.

What can be done? With girls, parents need to be more demanding, in order to facilitate independence and achievement. If girls receive too much emotional support, they become less inclined to tackle obstacles on their own. If they receive less emotional support, but still are controlled in inductive rather than coercive ways, they achieve higher academic results. Boys, by contrast, should be socialized with higher levels of nurturance and intimacy. Strong emotional support and positive, noncoercive control not only enhance the "affiliative qualities" of boys but actually motivate them to higher levels of academic achievement.

Games and playtime are two of the informal practices through which children are socialized. Parents, siblings, and even other children can teach a child about gender roles indirectly by en-

## media moments

### Liberating Barbie?

*Teen Talk Barbie* proved to be the final straw. People who were already upset at Barbie's anorexic figure and her way of turning play into superficial consumerism couldn't believe their ears when Barbie's electric voice box giggled: "Math is hard!" "I love shopping!" "Will we ever have enough clothes?"

### Snigglers to the Rescue

In 1989 the Barbie Liberation Organization was formed. Taking advantage of similarities in the voice hardware of *Teen Talk Barbie* and the *Talking Duke G.I. Joe* doll, er, "action figure," they absconded with several hundred of each and performed a stereotype-change operation on the lot.

The surgery was no simple matter—circuit boards had to be trimmed, a capacitor moved, and a switch re-engineered. The press made it sound like an easy pop-and-switch operation, but this took some research and dedication.

The BLO returned the altered dolls to the toy store shelves, who then resold them to children who had to invent scenarios for Barbies who yelled "Vengeance is mine!" and G.I. Joes who daydreamed "Let's plan our dream wedding!" Cleverly placed "call your local TV news" stickers on the back ensured that the media would have genuine recipients to interview as soon as the news broke.

One BLO member counted up the many benefits of their program: "The storekeepers make money twice, we stimulate the economy—the consumer gets a better product—and our message gets heard."

*Sources:* Laline and Leibovich (1997); Sniggle.net.

couraging certain kinds of play with certain kinds of toys. As the pink aisle in any toy store will demonstrate, toys are often manufactured with such roles in mind. While many toys are gender-neutral, some of the most popular toys have been criticized for their exaggerated and problematic portrayal of gender roles. As demonstrated in the box titled "Liberating Barbie?" the not-so-innocent gender socialization embedded in children's toys is best described through the activism it has inspired.

## SECONDARY SOCIALIZATION

Within the traditional societies that spanned most of human history, people spent not only their early years but their entire life inside what was, in effect, a kind of very large family. In such societies, tasks were divided up and distributed in prearranged, "time immemorial" ways that had almost nothing to do with individual abilities. Sex and age determined what kinds of activities people performed: whether they stayed at home and prepared meals, whether they hunted and fished, whether they cared for the old and injured, whether they made clothes, cleaned animal skins, or tended the fire.

In these earlier and more simple societies, the self was pulled tightly to already existing culture and social structure. What individuals wanted to do, and what their immediate society wanted them to do, were more or less one and the same. Society required conformity rather than autonomy. The self was neither individuated nor independent. In such a situation, the socialization that was provided in the family was socialization enough. No further training was required.

Over the course of thousands of years, at different rates in different regions of the globe, human societies gradually became more complex. One way of thinking about complexity is to say that new kinds of social institutions became differentiated from the family. The community became less personal and more extended, eventually developing into villages and cities. Economic considerations became much more clearly separated from considerations of family, age, and gender. Crafts emerged that required special skills and training, and markets began to connect traders who had no personal knowledge of one another. Large enterprises that depended on economic talents alone eventually came to the fore, bringing together people of different religions, races, and classes. Leadership ceased to be a matter for community "elders," the ruling group defined by gender and age. States formed, political competition developed, bureaucracy and legal rules emerged.

As these extrafamilial institutions developed, the overlap of family and society broke down. What happened in the family remained important, but it became increasingly distant from other institutions in the same society. As a result, much less about a person's life was determined by birth, early childhood, and primary socialization—and much more depended on what happened later. **Secondary socialization experiences,** such as peer groups, schools, and the media, were more directed toward fostering individuation than primary socialization.

It is fair to say that in modern and postmodern societies, secondary socialization experiences, such as peer groups, schools, and the media, *compete* with, rather than simply complement, familial values and ways of life. In contrast to primary socialization, with its mutually reinforcing effects on family and community, secondary socialization via peer groups, schools, and media provides a wide variety of experiences for children—experiences that articulate and complement but also contradict the teachings of the family. It is perhaps in reaction against such distinctive possibilities that home-schooling has been burgeoning in the United States in recent decades. Home-schooling parents seek to ensure that what children learn in school more closely coheres with what is taught at home. Given the basic structures of modern and postmodern societies, however, home-schooling is unlikely to shield and protect children from bad influences. As societies become more complex, secondary socialization—and this very much includes schooling outside the home—is necessary and inevitable if young people are going to succeed in finding positions within these societies. The separation from the home environment is, in fact, integral to the formation of individual autonomy.

## Schools

Although the most obvious purpose of schools is "education," socialization is one of its primary tasks. Compared with the family, schools focus less on emotional and ethical concerns than on developing cognitive capacities and instilling social interaction skills. Schools are also more competitive, more impersonal, and more stratified. Whereas families tend to provide a warm and enveloping ethos, schools tend to hand out rewards based on results. In ranking students by effectiveness, schools transmit capacities and prepare youth for the rigors of adult economic life.

Especially in the early grades, impersonal discipline and responsiveness to authority are central. In "Learning the Student Role," Harry Gracey noted that kindergarten "teachers expended most

**Secondary socialization experiences** While institutions, such as the family, are crucial in early socialization, secondary socialization experiences often foster individuation and challenge primary socialization. For example, peer groups, schools, and the media often compete with, rather than complement, familial values and ways of life learned in early socialization.

of their efforts ... in training the children to follow the routines which [the] teachers had created."

The children were, in a very real sense, drilled in tasks and activities created by the teachers. ... The structure is established by the very rigid and tightly controlled sets of rituals and routines through which the children are put during the day. There is first the rigid "locating procedure" in which the children are asked to find themselves in terms of the month, date, day of the week, and the number in the class who are present and absent. This puts them solidly in the real world as defined by adults. ... Spontaneous interests or observations from the children are never developed by the teacher. ... Her schedule just does not allow room for developing such unplanned events. (1991: 379, 388)

This is not to say that schools are valueless entities. Quite the contrary: Competition and performance are themselves values, and schools teach other social values, too—though often in an implicit rather than explicit way. Indeed, a central value embraced by American educational institutions is *individualism*. The emphasis on individual performance in American schools contrasts significantly with the approach taken by other countries, such as Japan, where the goals of the group are considered more important than individual interest. Whereas an American teacher might categorize students according to their ability to perform math problems (i.e., into remedial, average, and accelerated groups), in Japan the entire class works on the same problems together, ensuring that everyone maintains the class's pace of learning such that slower students avoid becoming discouraged.

## Peer Groups

One of the most important things children learn in school is how to get along with others. As the child's school career develops, the child begins spending significant amounts of time with her peers, removed from direct adult supervision. For many home-schooling parents it is not what the *teachers* are teaching but what the students are learning from other students that compels them to want to teach their kids at home.

By interacting with playmates in organized play groups and schools, children engage in the first in a series of **peer groups** in which childhood knowledge and practices are gradually transformed into the knowledge and skills necessary to participate in the adult world (Corsaro and Rizzo [1988: 881]).

Of course, it is not that members of peer groups consciously set out to socialize each other. Rather, children form groups so they can accomplish something together or just because they want to hang out and have a good time. Inadvertently, however, peers do socialize one another, simply through their interactions. They do so in distinctive ways.

Peer groups are voluntary associations, not established institutions. They give children a freedom of choice in deciding whom they want to associate with. Peers start out as status equals. Because their interaction is relatively egalitarian, the status distinctions that emerge are based on recognition, negotiation, and achievement. The peer arena allows for cultural exploration. Children are exposed to beliefs different from those held by family members, and they develop different lines of action.

Gary Alan Fine studied the peer-group life of Little League boys and reported the results in his book, *With the Boys: Little League Baseball and*

**Peer groups** Voluntary organizations and associations of children, such as school groups or play groups. These groups are instrumental in early socialization in that they provide an arena in which children not only learn from one another how to interact with others but also engage in cultural exploration—especially in situations where they are exposed to beliefs that compete with those of their families.

*Preadolescent Culture* (1987). In the background of Fine's discussion is his understanding of what the present authors refer to as the postmodern demands for complexity and an increasingly responsive self: "During preadolescence the child finds himself or herself in several different social worlds, which require different sets of appropriate behavior. The popular and socially integrated preadolescent is not the one who behaves consistently but the one who has mastered techniques of impression management to present himself or herself through flexible role performances" (Fine 1987: 104).

Peer groups can contribute to these new self requirements because of their independence from the structure and hierarchy of the family. As Fine points out, "Friends feel free to discuss all subjects of mutual interest with each other, including, of course, many subjects that are not fit topics for conversation with adults. Preadolescents typically 'take seriously' the comments of their peers. ... Taken together, these comments shape the moral perspectives of preadolescents" (1987: 79).

The Little Leaguers and their parents appear to be focusing above all on learning to play ball, but Fine observes that value transmission is, in fact, the main focus of this father-son recreation activity: "Little League baseball is an arena in which the moral basis of behavior is brought to bear on individuals by legitimated arbiters of the social order" (1987: 78). For their part, coaches "attempt to construct an approved social identity for the preadolescent," and they thoroughly intend to "teach their preadolescent boys to see the world from their perspective" (1987: 78). Yet, Fine insists, "the fact that messages are transmitted doesn't mean they will be acquired in quite the way they have been taught" (1987: 2).

Under the surface of parental control there is conflict between the cultural imperatives of the peer group and the goals of adult socialization. Once again, individuation and complexity emerge as the critical referents:

Whereas adults focus on hustle, teamwork, sportsmanship, and winning and losing, the preadolescent transforms these concerns. Adults are trying to get the preadolescent to play properly and through this to be a good citizen and person. Preadolescents are more concerned with their self-presentation, which involves related forms of propriety. Although preadolescents use the themes of adults, more significant is the "moral theme" of behaving properly. This includes (1) the display of appropriate emotions—being tough or fearful when the situation calls for it; (2) controlling one's aggression, fears, and tears (a transformation of sportsmanship); (3) publicly displaying a desire to win (hustle); and (4) not breaking the bond of unity (teamwork) among preadolescents. (Fine 1987: 79)

## The Media

As societies become more postmodern, the media become an increasingly important source of socialization. In 1949, just 9 percent of American households had a TV. In 1995, 95 percent had television, more than two-thirds had cable, and over three-quarters had VCRs. Today, surveys show, people average about two and a half hours of television watching per day, and in children's lives television competes with time that might otherwise be devoted to schoolwork or to interacting with parents and friends.

Things sure have changed since the 1950s. Today, more American families have a subscription to the Internet than to a daily newspaper (Woodward 2000: 4), and televisions, DVDs, and other media have migrated from the living room into the bedroom. The average American kid can now have a multimedia experience in the privacy of his or her own room (see Figure 5.5) and watching TV has become a solitary activity, especially for older kids (see Table 5.3).

On average, American kids are exposed to

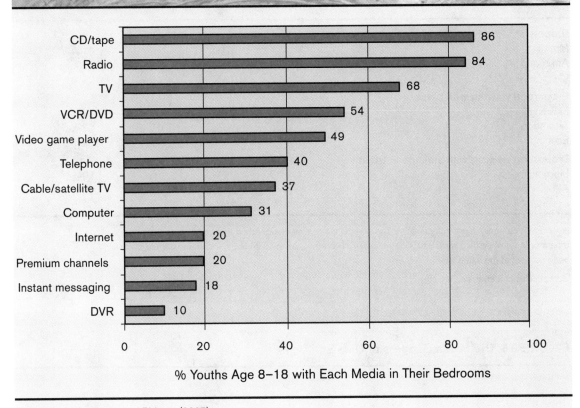

**FIGURE 5.5 Growing Up in the Digital Age: Media in the Young Person's Bedroom, United States, 2004**

% Youths Age 8–18 with Each Media in Their Bedrooms

| Media | % |
|---|---|
| CD/tape | 86 |
| Radio | 84 |
| TV | 68 |
| VCR/DVD | 54 |
| Video game player | 49 |
| Telephone | 40 |
| Cable/satellite TV | 37 |
| Computer | 31 |
| Internet | 20 |
| Premium channels | 20 |
| Instant messaging | 18 |
| DVR | 10 |

*Source:* Roberts, Foehr, and Rideout (2005).

seven and a half hours of media content a day (Roberts and Fuhr 2004: 326). This estimate takes into account media multitasking, such as listening to music, instant messaging, and reading a magazine at the same time. But which form of media claims the majority of kids' time? In Figure 5.6, you can compare the "media budgets" of boys and girls from the ages of 8 to 18. These pie charts show how time is distributed across all the various forms of media. As you can see, both boys and girls spend the most time with television, which claims about 40 percent of their media budgets. Boys and girls also spend about the same amount of time with computers, reading, and other screen

media, such as movies and videos. The only significant gender difference pertains to the time spent with video games and audio media. How would you explain this difference? How much does it have to do with the content of these media forms? Do you think this difference is more a cause or a result of gender socialization?

Despite the fact that their manifest purpose is to entertain and often to advertise commercial products, media such as television undoubtedly also provide people with specific cultural knowledge. We learn the language and values of our culture simply by being surrounded by those who speak and practice them, and today's world is indeed a

**TABLE 5.3  Context of Television Viewing by Part of Day and Age (in percentages)**

|  | 2–7 years | 8–18 years |
|---|---|---|
| **Proportion viewing mainly alone** | | |
| Morning | 30% | 41% |
| Afternoon | 25% | 42% |
| Evening | 10% | 35% |
| **Proportion viewing with parents** | | |
| Morning | 21% | 8% |
| Afternoon | 15% | 13% |
| Evening | 30% | 24% |
| **Proportion viewing with siblings or friends** | | |
| Morning | 25% | 19% |
| Afternoon | 22% | 26% |
| Evening | 25% | 32% |

*Note:* Each category is not independent. The questionnaire was designed so that children could indicate all others present while they were watching television. Therefore, parents, siblings, and friends could all have been present at the same time.

*Source:* Roberts et al. (2004: 78).

**FIGURE 5.6  The Media Budgets of Girls and Boys**

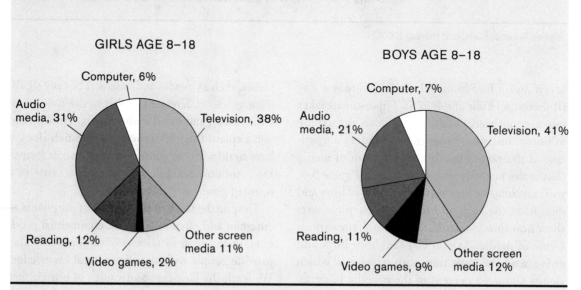

*Note:* "Other screen media" includes video recordings of TV programs, commercial videos, and movies in theatres. "Reading" includes all print media, such as magazines, newspapers, and books not required for school.

*Source:* Adapted from Roberts and Foehr (2004).

mediated one. But now that television is a new socializing agent—with the Internet emerging as next in line—what values it transmits are subject to scholarly as well as public dispute (see Thompson 1997). Early critics (e.g., Bronfenbrenner 1970) claimed that television produced passivity because it substituted for direct action. Others (e.g., Bandura 1979) have blamed it for exposing children to violence and crime. These are simplistic criticisms. They betray an old-fashioned insensitivity to the complexities of symbolic life. Television shows, after all, are fantasy-driven cultural narratives—not straightforward purveyors of information and values. When viewers, even very young ones, enter symbolically into such media, they engage in complex, active, and selective processes of interpretation. They project themselves into the plot and imagine themselves in the role of every character. In doing so they learn to get outside of their own particular experience and lives.

Most viewers do not uncritically absorb the negativity they see on the TV screen. Nevertheless, the cumulative, relatively *unconscious* effects of the media on individuals should not be underestimated. Although people rarely simply act out what they see on television, watching hour after hour of commercial television and movies inevitably cultivates specific worldviews, images, and ideas (Edles 2002: 68).

## LIFE STAGES AND THE LIFE CYCLE

Thus far we have seen that parents, siblings, schools, peers, and the media are all important agents of socialization. We learn what is right and wrong, and how to act and how not to act, via informal practices and latent messages transmitted at the breakfast table, at Little League games, at friends' houses, at school, on television, on the Internet, and in the movies.

Yet, socialization is not simply the process of taking outside things in, of internalizing social values. As our earlier discussions of historical variations of selfhood suggest, the self can be thought of as a kind of motor of its own. It has its own internal structure and shows a clear developmental path. It depends on outside stimulation and connectedness, but as it develops it becomes a powerful, active selector mechanism in its own right.

In postmodern society each of our lives depends not only on primary and secondary socialization but also on our ability to maneuver independently, to be self-motivated and responsive to the variety of influences pressuring us in multiple directions. To move from our position in the family to our position in society we now have to undergo a series of transitions. Individual life experience becomes stretched and elongated. This social process has given rise to the idea that there

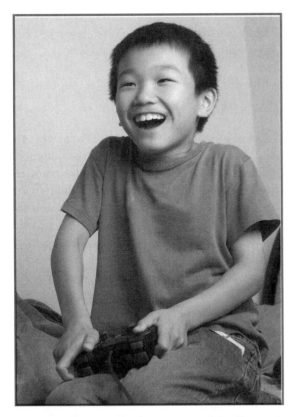

Postmodern children are increasingly "socialized" not only by their families, peer groups, and educational environments but also by computer games and media they play and watch in isolation. (iStockphoto)

is a life "cycle." According to this notion, a person's life is less a straight shot than a series of distinctive open-ended stages that have to be negotiated one at a time. Each new and clearly distinguished stage of life marks out a new set of social roles, and each new role set has to be learned and worked through. Since more learning is required, socialization becomes stretched over a longer period of time, and a more independent and differentiated self has time to emerge.

Conflicting values and information mark life cycle transitions with tensions and challenges. It has become harder to grow up. Being young is now more difficult and middle age more complex. Even getting old has become a new life transition that demands learning and negotiation. For a full appreciation of this postmodern situation, some historical perspective is necessary.

## Separating Childhood from Adulthood

In his path-breaking historical study *Centuries of Childhood* (1962), Philippe Ariès demonstrates that in medieval society the distinctive period of life called childhood simply did not exist: "As soon as the child could live without the constant solicitude of his mother, his nanny, or his cradle-rocker, he belonged to adult society" (Ariès 1962: 128).

Ariès is not saying that children were entirely absent from medieval society; obviously very young people who could not perform the tasks of adults existed during this period. Rather, what he means is that there was no distinctive cultural identity that defined and separated this biological and psychological period as a unique phase of life. In medieval art, for example, little children were depicted as waist-high grown-ups with mature musculature, clothing, and facial expressions. In pictures of the Madonna and Child from the Byzantine period, in the eleventh and twelfth centuries, the baby Jesus appears as a little adult. Only later, in Gothic and Renaissance Europe, did the

Christ child come to be portrayed as a real baby, looking innocent and trusting, kissing and hugging his mother, playing typical children's games. And only after that, in the sixteenth and seventeenth centuries, did European society symbolically represent childhood and fully distinguish it from adulthood. "A new concept of childhood had appeared," Ariès noted, "in which the child, on account of his sweetness, simplicity and drollery, became a source of amusement and relaxation for the adult" (Ariès 1962: 129). This shift was indicated by the provision, for the first time, of special children's clothing, which Ariès describes as "a special costume which marked him out from the adults" (1962: 129). With growing social complexity, a protected period of the life cycle came to be defined, leading to the emergence of distinctive, child-oriented associations and institutions. Increasingly, children did not do adult work. They played with peers, and they went to school.

## Childhood Is Not Global

We must bear in mind, however, that in many parts of the world today, these special conditions of modern, let alone postmodern, life have not arrived. Around the globe, millions of children are leading very hard lives that bear little resemblance to the protected stage of "childhood" that Ariès described. The International Labour Organization (ILO) estimates that in 2000 there were some 211 million children ages 5 to 14 working in the world, 73 million of whom were less than 10 years old. As shown in Table 5.4, the majority of the world's working children are found in Asia (127.3 million), followed by Africa (48.0 million), Latin America and the Caribbean (17.4 million), and the Middle East and North Africa (13.4 million). While Asia had the largest number of child workers, the highest proportion of working children relative to nonworking children was found in sub-Saharan Africa.

"Childhood" is a relative term; some children rarely experience child-play, as they work from an early age, like these boys working in a sweatshop in Afghanistan. (Paula Bronstein/Getty Images)

**TABLE 5.4  Regional Estimates of Economically Active Children Ages 5–14 in 2000**

| Region | Number of Children (in millions) | Work Ratio (%) |
|---|---|---|
| Developed economies | 2.5 | 2 |
| Transition economies | 2.4 | 4 |
| Asia and the Pacific | 127.3 | 19 |
| Latin America and Caribbean | 17.4 | 16 |
| Sub-Saharan Africa | 48.0 | 29 |
| Middle East and North Africa | 13.4 | 15 |
| **Totals** | **211.0** | **18** |

Source: ILO (2000).

During the same year, moreover, an estimated 171 million children ages 5–17 worked in hazardous situations or conditions—a stunning 55 percent of whom were very young child laborers (i.e., those under 12). Among all of these children, about one-half of the working boys were working in hazardous situations as compared with a little more than two in five working girls. In addition, about 8.4 million children were involved in other illegal and/or immoral forms of child labor as defined by the ILO (Convention 182, Art. 3). This latter category includes trafficking (which affected 1.2 million children), forced and bonded labor (5.7 million), armed conflict (0.3 million), prostitution and pornography (1.8 million), and illicit activities (0.6 million).

## New Life Stages and Emotional Challenges

Life course analysis is a new specialty in sociology. It devotes itself to studying how individuals and groups navigate the increasingly distinctive and separate phases of the life span. There are now a number of different pathways through these age stations. They differ in terms of time spent during this or that phase and even in which order the different stations of aging—education, work, family, children—are taken. In postmodern society, aging is no longer an automatic unfolding process but a socially structured trajectory that allows people unprecedented opportunities for choices, some of which are tragic mistakes! Continuing through the trajectory of the life course trajectory, in other words, is an individual accomplishment, for better and for worse (Shanahan, Macmillan 2008).

In premodern and modern societies, trajectories were relatively fixed and predictable, and individuals could plan accordingly—although, of course, these plans often were interrupted by biological events such as disease and social events such as famine and war. The major transitions to adulthood involved leaving school, getting a job, and becoming married. Leaving adulthood was marked by retirement from work, the sickness or death of a spouse, and the onset of old age. Throughout most of the nineteenth and twentieth centuries, marriage plans and job decisions were finalized early in life, coinciding with either puberty or the completion of education. Throughout the first two-thirds of the twentieth century, retirement was conceived as coinciding with changes in biological life.

However, amidst the fluidity and flux of postmodern culture and social structure, the coherent sequencing of life cycle stages has broken down. Trajectories are now less predictable, and the qualities required for successful life cycle passage have changed.

With the elongation of socialization, for example, the life transitions of marriage and parenthood are put off in time. Rather than fixed, they have become variable. The more youthful and postmodern the cohort, the less likely he or she is to marry or to have children. (We will discuss this topic further in Chapter 6, on sexuality.) When people do bear children, moreover, the percentage of their life course devoted to this once all-consuming activity is dramatically lower than in earlier times. In 1830, Canadian women spent 90 percent of their lives rearing children. In 1950, they spent only 40 percent, and today this percentage is much lower still (George 1993: 367). Underlying this shift are the increased demands of secondary socialization, on the one hand, and changes in gender roles, on the other (again, see Chapter 6 for more details). An equally sharp decline has occurred in fertility

**Life course** A term that, instead of describing life as a linear biological path from birth to death, refers to the role of historical, social, and cultural contexts in shaping an individual or group's life trajectory.

rates, brought about not only by scientific advances in controlling pregnancy but also by the much more independent status of women.

Postmodern sociologist Alberto Melucci articulated this growing independence of the socially formed self and the role-requiring society in a particularly acute way. "It is impossible," he wrote, "to draw a rigid distinction between the individual aspects of identity on the one hand, and its relational social aspects on the other."

As we pass through the various stages of our life, we develop a capacity to resolve the problems posed by the environment and become increasingly independent in constituting our relationships. ... Learning does not end with adolescence: as we pass through the various stages of life that follow it, we continue to question and reformulate our identities. It is above all in situations of crisis that our identity and its weaknesses are revealed—as for instance when we are subjected to contradictory expectations, or when we lose our traditional bonds of belonging, when we join a new system of norms. (Melucci 1996: 30)

### Life Cycle or Obstacle Course?
### Suicide and Self-Harm

The most extreme response to the anxiety of moving through stages of the life cycle is to take one's own life. The common wisdom on suicide is based on two assumptions. The first is that suicide is primarily a crisis of adolescence. But as you can see in Figure 5.7, this assumption is false. In the United States, and indeed in the majority of countries (Lester 2003), the highest rate of suicide is among the elderly. How can this age distribution of suicides be accounted for? What might explain the decrease in the suicide rate between the ages of 45 and 74? Why might the transition to late adulthood (the "golden years" after the age of 75) be

**FIGURE 5.7 Deaths from Suicide, United States, 2002**

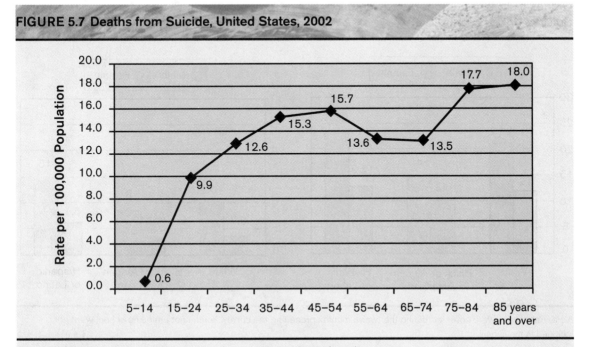

*Source:* U.S. Census Bureau, Statistical Abstract of the United States (2002).

more difficult than retirement (which typically happens between the ages of 65 and 75)? What social sources of the self are likely to come under threat in the final stages of life?

The second assumption about suicide is that it is more of a problem among men than among women. In addition, cultural notions of masculinity that encourage high-risk behaviors and autonomy are believed to make men more susceptible to stress-related diseases, violence, and suicide. This pattern is certainly reflected in the death rates from suicide. In 2003, the suicide rate among males between the ages of 15 and 19 (11.6 per 100,000) was four times that of females in the same age group (2.7 per 100,000). For people 85 and older, the difference was even more dramatic: The suicide rate among males (47.8 per 100,000) was fourteen times higher than that of females (3.3 per 100,000) (NCHS 2004: Table 46).

A closer look at the statistics reveals yet another gender difference. While completed suicide is more common among males, suicidal ideation and attempts are far more common among females. As Figures 5.8 and 5.9 demonstrate, young American women of high school age are much more likely than their male cohorts to consider and attempt suicide, no matter what their race or ethnicity. This paradoxical pattern has also been found in Canada, Western Europe, Australia, and New Zealand. But it is not universal. In some Asian countries, such as Singapore, the rates of suicide attempts and completion are the same for men and women. And in China, the majority of suicides are committed by women (Gould et al. 2003).

Not all youth who are overwhelmed by anxiety resort to suicide. A growing trend among young men and women is to engage in self-injury, such as cutting or carving the skin, self-poisoning, bruis-

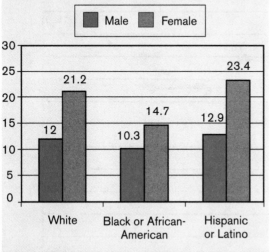

**FIGURE 5.8 Percentage of Students Grades 9–12 Who Seriously Considered Suicide, United States, 2003**

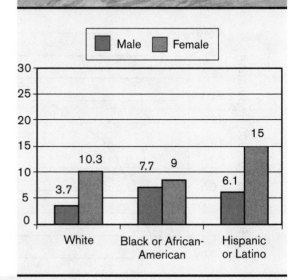

**FIGURE 5.9 Percentage of Students Grades 9–12 Who Attempted Suicide, United States, 2003**

*Note:* Responses were collected during the twelve months preceding the survey. Youths not attending school were not included in the survey.

*Source:* NCHS (2003).

ing, and breaking bones. In the U.K., teens are more likely than any other age group to wind up in the emergency ward as a result of deliberate self-harm (Rodham et al. 2005). But the practice is even more widespread than these figures suggest: Only a fraction of the youth who self-harm actually wind up in the hospital. In a recent survey of more than 6,000 students in forty-one schools across England, researchers found that only 12.6 percent of self-harm episodes resulted in emergency medical treatment. They also concluded that gender was a significant factor. As you can see in Figure 5.10, considerably more young women than young men reported self-harm in the previous year (Hawton et al. 2006).

### The New In-Between Stages

If childhood was the creation of the early-modern society that followed the Middle Ages, it was nineteenth-century industrialization that created adolescence—at least for the more secure and affluent middle class. The technological and administrative demands of that new stage of modernity triggered the growth of formal mass schooling. For increasing segments of the population, this meant staying out of the workforce, and remaining unmarried, long past the onset of puberty—the biological shift that earlier had marked the end of childhood and the beginning of adulthood. Adolescence represented a new stage in the development of the self, between childhood dependency and adult independence. Adolescence is a period of growth, self-exploration, and experimentation with new tastes and behaviors; but its other side is instability, emotional mood swings, and anxiety-filled uncertainties.

As societies became more complex in the twentieth century, demands for handling new knowledge and for individual autonomy increased. The life cycle expanded accordingly, leading to the identification of new postadolescent **life stages.** As with adolescence, these new stages of life both widened opportunities and expanded anxieties. Well before the mid-century period, psychologist Charlotte Buhler (1935) had already identified a new "preparatory stage" of self-development—one that she described as an institutionalized period of

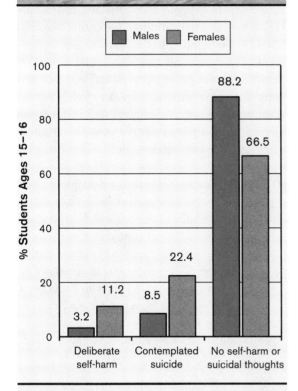

**FIGURE 5.10 Prevalence of Deliberate Self-Harm and Suicidal Thoughts, England, 2000–2001**

*Note:* Responses were collected during the twelve months preceding the survey.

*Source:* Hawton et al. (2002).

**Life stages** Various points of transition and experience throughout the life course. For example, adolescence and retirement are two life stages. They entail not only biological stages of development, such as adolescence, but also key social stages, such as marriage or retirement.

unsettledness before adulthood. It was precisely at the mid-century mark that Erik Erikson, in his acclaimed *Childhood and Society* (1950), introduced the notion of "identity crisis" to describe the psychological correlate of what he termed a new stage of "prolonged adolescence." In particular, he noted that young people in their later teenage years seemed to be granted a kind of psychological moratorium, or time out, "during which the young adult through free role experimentation may find a niche in some section of his society" (Erikson 1968: 156). Sociologically, the challenge was to find a job, a marriage partner, or a career. Emotionally, the challenge was to overcome the sense of emotional diffusion and to forge a coherent new self that was independent of parents and peers.

In the second half of the twentieth century, the transitional period between adolescence and adulthood came more clearly into focus, becoming a major topic for psychological research. Kenneth Keniston's research on alienated youth—whether aimlessly uncommitted (Keniston 1965) or politically radical (Keniston 1968)—led him to posit the existence of a new postmodern stage of "youth, which follows the resolution of what are usually called 'adolescent' problems."

> The basic contours of the individual's fundamental outlook on the world have usually been arrived at. He has effectively emancipated himself from his emotional dependency upon his family. He has come to terms with his own sexuality ... [and] by and large knows what kind of person he is. ... *Yet such men and women are unwilling to move directly into adulthood.* Although many doors are open to them, they lack the will to enter any of them, fearing that once inside they will be trapped or robbed of their freedom to change and be themselves. ... The fluidity of the postmodern style and the flux of the modern world are thus closely connected. The postmodern emphasis on process involves a simultaneous identification with, and effort to deal with, historical change. On the one hand, postmodern youth floats with the tide, remains open to

the changing world, is alterable and malleable. ... On the other hand, each variant of the postmodern style involves an effort to find an anchor in the cross-tides of modern history. (Keniston 1968: 268, 276–277, italics added)

Thirty years later, when Jeffrey Jensen Arnett introduced the concept of "emerging adulthood," the period of sociological timeout and emotional uncertainty identified by Erikson and Keniston grew longer still. As the subtitle of Arnett's book *Emerging Adulthood* (2004) asserts, it was now "the winding road from the late teens through the twenties." Arnett's research demonstrates that in the contemporary societies of postmodern times, there is an increasing likelihood that people do not regard themselves as adults until they have entered their 30s. He explains this "new and historically unprecedented period of the life course" (Arnett 2004: 4) by pointing to the increasing postponement of marriage and parenthood and to heavier demands for lengthier technical training. But perhaps "the most important reason of all," he suggests, is a "less tangible" cultural shift, "a profound change in how young people view the meaning and value of becoming an adult."

> What is different now that young people are freer than they were in the past to use the intervening years between the end of secondary school and entry into marriage and parenthood, to explore a wide range of different possible future paths? Young people of the past were constricted in a variety of ways, from gender roles to economics, which prevent them from using their late teens and twenties for exploration. In contrast, today's emerging adults have unprecedented freedom. (Arnett 2004: 7)

During the 1970s and 1980s, Daniel Levinson developed the first research-based theory of adult life cycle stages. In "early adulthood," which lasts from the late teens to the mid-40s, the challenge is "establishing a niche in society, raising a family, and, as the era ends, reaching a more 'senior' position in the adult world" (Levinson 1990: 40). This can be a time of rich satisfaction but also one of "crushing stresses," for, as Levinson notes, "we incur heavy financial obligations when our earning power is still relatively low" and "we must make crucial choices regarding marriage, family, work, and lifestyle before we have the maturity or life experience to choose wisely" (1990). It is owing to these stresses, on the one hand, and to the consequences of having made these basic commitments, on the other, that a new period called the "midlife transition" has emerged, roughly spanning the ages of 40 to 45. Levinson finds that "the character of living always changes appreciably between early and middle adulthood," and that if people do not make big changes in themselves and their social roles, their "lives become increasingly trivial or stagnant" (1990). While such a transition can be filled with positive feelings associated with growth, it can also be a time of great stress—hence Levinson's notion of "midlife crisis" (Levinson et al. 1978), which quickly became useful for explaining the ruptures and readjustments of later adult life. Only when the midlife crisis is resolved, Levinson and his colleagues argued, can the third era of adulthood begin—the years of "middle adulthood" between 40 and 65. During this time our biological capacities, though at lower levels than in earlier years, remain more than sufficient for an energetic life. The psychological challenge is to become less involved with our own careers and families and more concerned with mentoring the younger generation and creating institutions to pass on to them.

While Levinson and his colleagues found that "late adulthood" begins after 65, research since that time suggests that the major milestones that once so clearly demarcated the onset of old age are in the process of disappearing (Gunsteren 1991, cited in George 1993: 366). Or perhaps it is more accurate to say that they are being transformed and differentiated in a manner that parallels the period between childhood and early adulthood. Older persons today are not only more likely to remain

Seniors no longer take to the "rocking chair on the porch"; increasingly they do everything younger generations do, such as keeping physically fit. (iStockphoto)

"youthful" in their physical appearance and sexual lives but also much less likely to retire from work. When they do retire, moreover, they are much less likely to give up the other kinds of commitments that shaped their working lives, whether related to sports, travel, love, or sex. In a study of public and private institutional arrangements that shape retirement decisions in seven different nations, Kohli and his colleagues found that, both across and within these societies, chronological age no longer functions as the basis for exit from the labor force (cited in George 1993: 365).

In fact, the heterogeneity of contemporary societies increasingly challenges the idea that there is any such thing as a structured and predictable life course. Gundsteren has written, for example, about the "deinstitutionalization" of trajectories (cited in George 1993: 365). In an effort to study these changes, Ronald Rindfuss and his colleagues (1987) developed longitudinal data for the high school class of 1972. They recorded data for such critical life course decisions as work, education, homemaking, and military service. Variation in trajectories was so high that for the 6,700 men in the sample, researchers recorded 1,100 different sequences; and for the 7,000 women, 1,800 different sequences. Even the simple two-stage sequence of moving from education to work applied to only slightly more than half the men in the sample and to fewer than half the women.

### The Longer Road to Adulthood

In the 1950s, adulthood was defined through family roles. For women, becoming an adult meant getting married and having children. For men, it meant having the financial means to support a family. Since then, the conception of adulthood has changed. As Figure 5.11 makes clear, marriage and parenthood are no longer considered prerequisites for adulthood. The more important benchmarks today are completion of education, financial independence, and full-time employment. More than 95 percent of General Social Surveys (GSS) respondents considered these the critical milestones. (For further discussion of the changing meanings and trends in marriage and child-bearing, see Chapter 7 on marriage and the family.)

The transition to adulthood is also taking longer to accomplish. If we define adulthood according to the traditional benchmarks—leaving home, finishing education, achieving financial in-

**SURVEY QUESTION:** People differ in their ideas about what it takes for a young person to become an adult these days. How important is it for them to be ... financially independent from their parents/guardians?

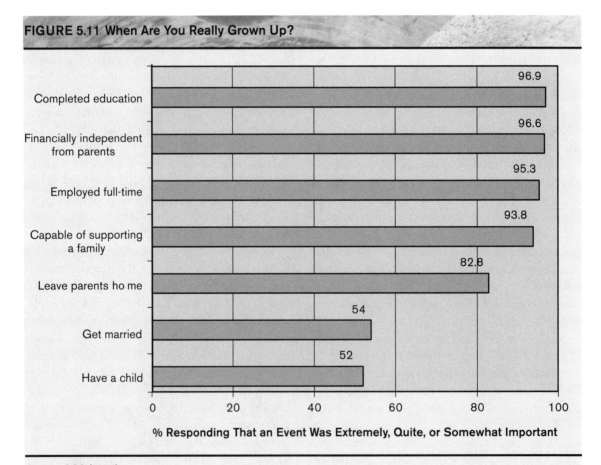

**FIGURE 5.11  When Are You Really Grown Up?**

% Responding That an Event Was Extremely, Quite, or Somewhat Important

- Completed education — 96.9
- Financially independent from parents — 96.6
- Employed full-time — 95.3
- Capable of supporting a family — 93.8
- Leave parents ho me — 82.8
- Get married — 54
- Have a child — 52

*Source:* GSS (2006).

dependence, getting married, and having children—far fewer men and women are achieving this transition by the age of 30 than was the case forty years ago. Figures 5.12 and 5.13 show a comparison of how many young adults have accomplished all five milestones by the ages of 20 and 30 (men) and 20, 25, and 30 (women) in 1960 versus 2000. As you can see, there has been a remarkable decrease in the percentage of men and women who satisfy the traditional definition of adulthood. In 1960, 65 percent of men and 77 percent of women had made a complete transition to adulthood by age 30. But in the year 2000, this could be said of only 31 percent of men and 46 percent of women. You might also notice a gender difference. Women's consistent "outperformance" of men on this measure was due in part to the fact that they tended to start families at a younger age than men. Because it was unusual for women to combine work and motherhood in the 1960s, full-time

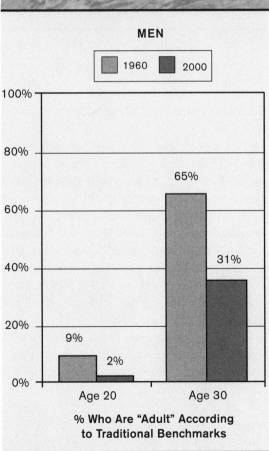

FIGURE 5.12 Proportion of Men Who Have Completed the Transition to Adulthood, United States, Selected Years

MEN

□ 1960   ■ 2000

% Who Are "Adult" According to Traditional Benchmarks

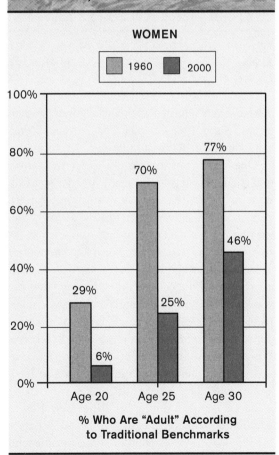

FIGURE 5.13 Proportion of Women Who Have Completed the Transition to Adulthood, United States, Selected Years

WOMEN

□ 1960   ■ 2000

% Who Are "Adult" According to Traditional Benchmarks

*Source:* Furstenberg et al. (2004).

FIGURE 5.14 Proportion of Young Adults Receiving Financial Assistance, United States

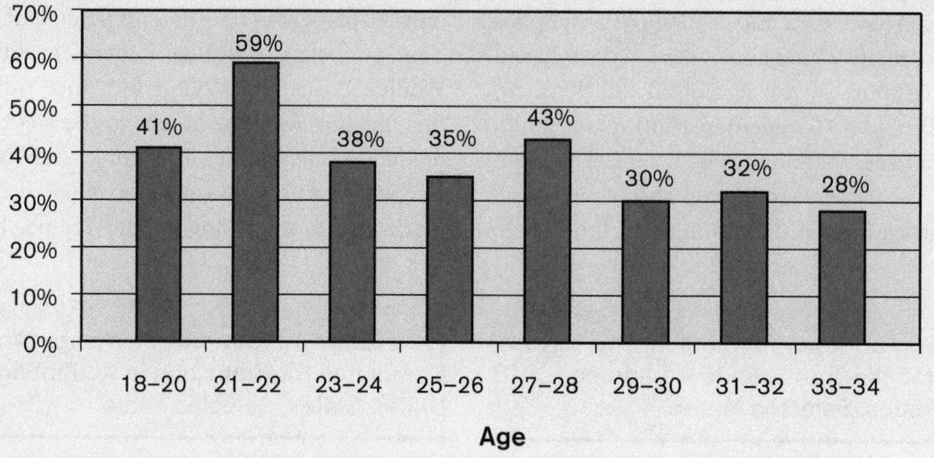

*Note:* These data are based on the 1988 Panel Study of Income Dynamics, special supplement on Time and Money Transfers.
*Sources:* Furstenberg et al. (2004); Schoeni and Ross (2005).

mothers were counted as financially independent in both years. (See Chapter 7 for further discussion of mothers in the labor force.)

One factor contributing to the delayed transition to adulthood is the difficulty of securing a full-time job with adequate pay to support a family. Because it is now necessary to have a college degree to attain a decent standard of living, an increasing proportion of young men and women are pursuing postsecondary education. More Americans are attending college today compared to forty years ago, but it is also taking them longer to complete their degrees. As a result, financial independence has become increasingly difficult to achieve. It is now common for parents to provide financial assistance to their young adult children. Indeed, an estimated 23 percent of the total cost of having a child is incurred during his or her transition to adulthood (Schoeni and Ross 2005: 405). Figure 5.14 shows the proportion of young people who live independently from their parents but still receive financial assistance.

## Caring for the Self: Psychotherapy

The emotional demands of new life cycle transitions and the physical challenges of expanding the length of active living have placed great strains on the modern and postmodern self. These stresses have paradoxically made it more difficult for people to maintain the psychological and biological autonomy that the expanded life course facilitates and demands. In response there has emerged, first in modern and then in postmodern society, an intense concern for what Michel Foucault (2005a) called "care for the self."

Psychotherapy is a practice that did not exist before Sigmund Freud created it in the first years of the twentieth century. It became an increasingly central institution as the century progressed and now takes many different forms—from old-fashioned individual and group "talking" therapies, to marriage and trauma counseling, to twelve-step programs for addictions that range from alcohol and sex abuse to overeating and heedless consumerism that creates mind-boggling credit-card debt.

Psychoanalysis made its initial public appearance on the first day of the twentieth century, when Sigmund Freud published *The Interpretation of Dreams* (1900). Insisting on the subjective origins of action and institutions, Freud suggested that moderns should stop asking "Why do bad things happen to me?" and instead ask "What have I done to create these bad things?" Internal psychical process, he argued, creates the *sense* of exterior compulsion. This process moves from the subjective to the objective—the "projection" of attitudes onto others that are in reality one's own. According to Freud, projection creates the seeming immobility and externality of modern life.

This is where the psychotherapeutic care for the self comes in. In the practice of therapy, patient and therapist must assume that the self alone is responsible for the actor's social world.

This presupposition triggers the basic questions of psychotherapy. The first question is "Who am I?" The attempt to answer it has led millions of persons away from modernity's seemingly rational sensibility and realistic obligations. To find out "who am I" is to leap into the inner and invisible world of illogic, subjectivity, and fragmented experience. By participating in therapy and reading Freud, modern persons discovered that they are guided less by discipline and common sense than by desires and deceptions, fears and infantile illusions. They learned that modern people are rarely fully grown up, that they remain childlike in an adult world, hoping to maintain dependence as much as autonomy.

The second question in the psychotherapeutic care for the self is "How did I become this way?" The answer is that people become themselves as a result of what later Freudians called their "object relations." These are not the external objects of the material world—the "real" objects encountered by modern and rational human beings. They are, rather, the *human* objects encountered by vulnera-

ble and half-formed children, at a time when they are not able to distinguish fantasy from reality. Such objects cannot be understood rationally and dealt with effectively, in a modern and pragmatic way. Instead, one encounters such objects emotionally: They are "cathected" and internalized, which means they are brought from outside and placed inside one's self. From early childhood on, the actor is formed by these internalized objects; their actual relations become dynamics inside the self.

Counter to the claims of modernist thought, Freud insisted that, even for adults, the most important object relations are not outside but inside. It is to the reconstruction of these objects that psychotherapy is directed. The therapeutic goal is to develop a more real and independent self. By talking about the object relations that have been internalized in our early lives, and the often irrational and destructive anxiety they inspire, we might be able to prevent the compulsive repetition of painful behavior.

Prolonged therapy can allow patients to rearrange these internal objects. Only after this inner transformation, therapists believe, can more fulfilling relationships be formed with the external world. The practice of psychotherapy is not about the alteration of time and space. Such modern operations are suspended. Objects are explored not through distant and neutral study but through free associations and inner experience. Nothing "happens" in psychotherapy. There is only insight.

Every sophisticated Western person in the twentieth century professed to know something regarding these Freudian "truths" about caring for the self. They deeply influenced intellectual as well as artistic life, from the social sciences to painting and poetry, from novels to film. As a practical philosophy, Freudianism created a new form of self-care undertaken by tens of millions of people. Just as being in therapy became a common experience in everyday life, being a therapist became a widely accepted career. Associated with therapy today are schools and disciplines, examinations and licenses, salaries, insurance companies, conferences and professional hierarchies—all the trappings of professional life. Also today, at the beginning of the twenty-first century, depression, anxiety, and eating disorders are considered major illnesses. At any one time, some 25 percent of elite American college students are taking selective serotonin reuptake inhibitor (SSRI) medication, even as the queues for publicly insured "talking" therapy are being extended and private practices are filling up.

On November 30, 2005, bold headlines in the *Guardian,* a leading British newspaper, announced: "Therapy for all who need it on the NHS [National Health Service]. A network of the counseling centres for the depressed and anxious. Could the government be about to take mental health seriously?" The report's opening lines illustrate the institutional centrality of psychoanalytic theory and practice at the beginning of the new century:

> Lying across the path of productive happiness, goes the theory, stands mental illness, the common afflictions of depression and anxiety. Our society may be more affluent than ever before, but never has it been less at ease with itself. In the next few weeks, the government is expected to announce plans aimed at transforming the mental well-being of millions of people across Britain. The Department of Health is expected to back recommendations … advocating the widespread introduction of psychological treatments—the so-called talking therapies—in the NHS for the estimated 5 million people in Britain with non-acute mental health conditions. (O'Hara 2005: 1)

The *Guardian* story goes on to report about plans for recruiting 10,000 new NHS therapists and creating a network of 250 independent therapy treatment centers as "a ringing endorsement of what some critics dismiss as a 'therapy culture,'" which the newspaper defines as "the notion that individual and societal ills can be solved through talking things through with a counselor" (O'Hara 2005: 1).

As mentioned earlier, therapy culture has indeed become much less Freudian in the process of adapting itself to various institutional domains in postmodern life. For example, in the United States short-term and emotionally oriented "employment counseling" is now provided by major companies and public institutions. Churches supply "pastoral care," and there is a movement called Christian therapy. Twelve-step programs, which originated with Alcoholics Anonymous, have been developed for every form of addiction from eating to sex to spending money. And remedies for ruinous childhoods and inner pain are provided on call-in radio programs and in therapy-like encounters organized on TV by talk-show hosts.

In all of these different manifestations, however, the philosophy of therapeutic care remains pretty much the same: The instruction is to turn away from external things and authorities and to move toward the inner self, with the goal of "taking on board" the irrational and regressive impulses and beliefs that threaten the self's independence. In short, therapy is about providing an experience of private life, of protecting it from the intrusions of the public sphere, of nurturing the self so that it can experience fuller and more balanced emotions and become healthy enough to manage the transitions and complexities of postmodern life—while being able to maintain objectivity and control and to sustain love and friendship. In postmodern society, it has become apparent that such care of the self cannot be provided by the community or state. This new form of social subjectivity must be nurtured in private, in a space that allows individuals to experience themselves and others in a relationship of dialogue and respect.

## Caring for the Self: Body and Soul

The new focus on self-management is by no means restricted to psychotherapy, even in its nontraditional forms. It can also be seen in the explosive and unexpected new culture of the body and its physical form. Gyms were once tawdry and out-of-the-way places reserved for boxers and professional bodybuilders. Now fitness is a major industry, personal training a new career, the caring for the muscles, bones, and heart a vibrant and conspicuous new arena for learning new forms of culture and interaction. Health and wellness have emerged as adjacent new domains. Vitamins, organic food, heart symbols on restaurant menus, health sections in daily newspapers, the professional status of nutritionists—all signal new forms of self-caring. So does the emergence of "wellness centers"—medical establishments that aim not at curing the sick, but at increasing the vitality of normal and healthy people.

This new postmodern caring for the self also extends to the "soul." In *The Easternization of the West* (2007), Colin Campbell notes that the last three decades have witnessed a vast borrowing of mystical techniques from non-Western civilization that offer Western people new pathways for emotional and spiritual well-being. In part, this borrowing manifests itself in the rising practice of Eastern religions such as Buddhism and Hinduism. And perhaps even more significantly, it has taken a secular form in the practices and beliefs of the "New Age." Massage has become widespread as both a therapy and a profession. Day and vacation spas have become prevalent forms of leisure. Relaxation techniques, from meditation and yoga to "mindfulness" training, have become not only familiar topics of discussion and practice but commodities and businesses themselves. Psychologists associated with these New Age practices suggest that their popularity points to possibilities for new and "higher stages" of psychic life (Alexander et al. 1989; Alexander et al. 1990). What in earlier societies were forms of feeling, thinking, and believing available only to a few exceptional people—gurus, wise men, artists, and saints—are now becoming available to all. With New Age con-

Many people concerned with physical fitness hire personal trainers to facilitate their self-care. (iStockphoto)

sciousness, the modernist emphasis on cognitive and moral rationality, as well as on emotional self-restraint, are becoming less central.

## EMOTION WORK IN POSTMODERN LIFE

Socialization produces not only a social but a psychological self, one with emotional capacities for interaction. We have learned in this chapter how in postmodern societies these demands for interaction have changed. One way to describe this change, from a psychological point of view, is to say that the subjective and the objective "environments" of action have grown farther apart. In this situation, interaction becomes more challenging. As individual actors, we cannot close the gap that has opened up between culture and social structure, but we can learn how to manage it.

Because socialization has been radically transformed, the postmodern self has the *capacity* to manage complex emotions, to refer to multiple and simultaneous cultural frameworks, and to project a convincing relation to the ambiguities of social structure. One way to describe this capacity is to say that the socialized inner self develops a "working" self to handle the complexities of interaction, or a series of working selves. The self becomes a matter for presentation, not something fixed and static.

Modern social thinkers were not particularly sensitive to the need for such emotion management. They viewed emotions as feelings that affect action from the outside, as impulses that express themselves *through* individuals. Biological scientists such as Charles Darwin, the father of evolution, defined emotions in an instinctual, organic way. Psychological scientists such as Freud, the founder of psychoanalysis, viewed feelings as variable impulses deposited in the unconscious by early family experiences.

Sociological theorists saw emotional impulses as imposed by social structures. Because Marx portrayed individual personalities as by-products of efforts to "reproduce" labor power, he viewed emotions—in capitalist society—as little more than externally manipulated things. Durkheim conceived of emotions as channeled by cultural symbols; people, he believed, achieved health if their feelings could find cathartic release in collective rituals. While Parsons was much more sensitive to the foundational role of emotions in social action and social structure, he was interested in how they were shaped within social roles. Socialization, then, referred to internalization of the normative guidelines of social roles, ensuring that adults would externalize their emotions in predictable and coherent ways.

If emotions and the interactions they inform are understood in such a manner—as merely the products of "society"—they do not seem a worthy object for sociological study. Until quite recently, in fact, the field that we now call the "sociology of emotions" did not exist.

A sign that postmodernity would change this neglect could already be seen several decades ago, when Daniel Bell published *The Coming of Post-Industrial Society* (1974). Bell described how the growth of the economic service sector ensures that "communication" and "encounter"—rather than brute physical strength and mechanical coordination—define the "central working relationship" of economic life: "The fact that individuals now talk to other individuals, rather than interact with a machine, is the fundamental fact about work in the postindustrial society" (Bell 1974). It is this kind of economic shift, along with the other sorts of (noneconomic) changes we are tracing throughout this book, that makes emotions central to contemporary society.

In Arlie Hochschild's sociological theory of emotional performance, discussed in *The Managed Heart* (1983), the author acknowledges that there *is* a "biologically given sense" to emotions. She insists, however, that people *act* in relation to these sensations: "People actively *manage* feelings in order to make their personalities fit for public contact work." In other words, we don't simply feel emotions; we act upon them. "That is why," according to Hochschild, "emotion work is *work*" (1983: 219–220, italics added).

In the complex uncertainty that marks postmodern life, individuals must work to put cultural scripts into action. The scripts are not automatic or prescribed. For Hochschild, these cultural scripts are **feeling rules.** Feeling rules direct how we want to try to feel, and how we want others to interpret our feelings. Feeling rules also take work. "People sometimes talk as much about their *efforts* to feel," Hochschild writes, "as they do about *having* feelings" (1983: 38, italics added). In short,

**Feeling rules** As theorized by Arlie Hochschild, cultural scripts that direct how we want to feel and how we want others to interpret our feelings. "Feeling rules" are significant in that they mark how, in the uncertainty of postmodern life, we must work to manage our emotions, as well as to be interpreted and understood by one another.

emotion work is the effort that people expend to deal with feeling rules in ever-changing social situations. We need to monitor our feelings, to continually modify and adjust them.

In postmodern societies, there is an ever-present possibility for ruptures among situations, feeling rules, and actual feelings. These can be prevented—situation, rule, and feeling can be made to cohere—through emotion management. By appropriately managing our emotions, we can develop the kinds of subtle and complex emotional performances that postmodernity demands. We may say that we have "the right to feel angry" but might, at the same time, work hard not to express this feeling. Or when somebody we know dies, we might remark that his death "should have hit me harder." Other people often tell us how we should or shouldn't feel. "You shouldn't feel so guilty," they remark. They make suggestions about the modulation of our emotions, about their intensity, direction, and duration: "Why don't you relax and calm down?" "I should think you'd be relieved, not upset." "It's been a year now, and it's time to stop moping about." We also make suggestions to ourselves: "I psyched myself up"—"I tried hard not to feel disappointed"—"I forced myself to have a good time"—"I tried to feel grateful"—"I killed the hope I had burning inside me" (Hochschild 1983: 39).

Hochschild conceptualizes two fundamentally different approaches to managing feelings. "In surface acting," she writes, "we deceive others about what we really feel, but we do not deceive ourselves." Instead, we are "disguising what we feel" and "pretending to feel what we do not." Hochschild suggests that diplomats and actors do surface acting best, and that "very small children do it worst (it is part of their charm)" (1983: 33). In what Hochschild calls "deep acting," by contrast, we deceive ourselves as much as we deceive others. This makes performance particularly easy because pretending to feel something becomes unnecessary.

In postmodern societies, deep acting has become a particularly valuable skill. The prominence of white-collar over blue-collar work, the significance of the service and entertainment industries, the centrality of the mass media—all this makes emotion work central. In her ethnography of the Delta Airlines flight attendant school, Hochschild observed how deep acting becomes integral to economic life:

At Delta, the techniques of deep acting are joined to the principles of social engineering. Can a flight attendant suppress her anger at a passenger who insults her? Delta Airlines can teach her how—if she is qualified for the job by a demonstrably friendly disposition to start with. She may have lost for a while the sense of what she would have felt had she not been trying so hard to feel something else. By taking over the levers of feeling production, by pretending deeply, she alters herself. ... Sincerity is taken seriously, and there was widespread criticism of attendants who did not act "from the heart." For example: "I worked with one flight attendant who put on a fake voice. On the plane she raised her voice about four octaves and put a lot of sugar and spice into it (gives a falsetto imitation of 'more coffee for you, sir?'). I watched the passengers wince. ... They're tired of that empty pretty young face." (1983: 33, 108)

## CONCLUSION

As we have seen in this chapter, socialization is vital for human development. The human "self" cannot emerge without social interaction, as the horrific story of Anna reveals. The most important social learning is done in the early years of life, and parents are usually the primary agents of this socialization. They exert their influence using support and control. However, as society becomes first modern and then postmodern, extrafamilial institutions, such as peers, schools, and the media, play an ever-increasing role. "Growing up" and taking our place in society is, today, a complex process of elongated socialization. So, too, the stages of the life course are more complicated than in previous eras; hence the notion of the life cycle emerges. In earlier, modern societies, the transitions into and out of adult roles were dictated by biological capacities. These changes were clearly understood and forcefully demarcated, and they did not involve a great deal of self-reconstruction. The transitions of contemporary adult life, by contrast, are both more demanding and more diffuse. They are triggered by the requirement for various kinds of creativity; by the completion of life tasks, such as parenting, that in earlier eras occupied much larger parts of adult life; and by the extension of physical and emotional capacity into older age. New forms of caring for the self have emerged to deal with the stresses and strains of the independent self as it seeks to navigate through life stages. The idea of emotional performance has also emerged as a new and vital task for the self in postmodern life.

# EXERCISES

## Exercise 1

In many respects, you've been socialized into becoming a college student. Officially, you might have gained this status as soon as you received your acceptance letter, but you probably did not "feel" like a college student until well into the semester when you figured out what this really meant in practice. In other words, taking on the role of college student involved adopting new values and priorities, and developing a new conception of the self. What events, practices, or rituals helped you make this transition to college student "selfhood"? In this new status, are you treated differently by your family and old friends? Do you act

differently? Have different feelings? How does the structure of your social environment, as organized by the university, facilitate and enforce this new identity?

## Exercise 2

As we saw in the last chapter, the media are becoming increasingly important agents of socialization. Young children spend a considerable amount of time watching television, using the computer, and playing video games. Is this trend necessarily a bad thing? Can television be an effective teacher of cultural lessons?

## Exercise 3

For advertising to be effective, it has to draw on the values and codes that structure society while remaining sensitive to cultural change. Over the next week, take note of all the advertisements you run across on every kind of media (television, Internet, print). Do these draw on the modern conception of the self as unique, autonomous, and independent? Or do they appeal to the postmodern sense of self, offering the means to help you change, improve, or evolve the self?

# STUDY QUESTIONS

1. What is socialization, and in what sense is it paradoxical?

2. How did classical and modern sociology conceive of socialization, and in what ways did this conception reflect modern social life? How does postmodern society challenge this conception?

3. What is Julian Jaynes's provocative argument about selfhood in ancient Greek society?

4. Why did the concept of the autonomous self disappear during the Middle Ages?

5. What role did the "civilizing process" play in the modernization of European society?

6. Why do some social observers believe that the postmodern self is an improvement on its modern counterpart while others believe it is a degradation of its predecessor?

7. When children are socialized, how are most cultural lessons learned? What is the content of these cultural lessons? What is the "social" dimension of culture imparted to children in socialization?

8. According to Gary Peterson and Boyd Rollins, what is the best style of parenting? What qualities does it combine, and why are these effective? What is coercive control, and what are the consequences of a parenting style that overuses it?

9. When does gender socialization begin in a child's life? How do parents contribute to the "gendering" of the child?

**FURTHER READING**

Ashmore, Richard D., and Lee Jussim, eds. 1997. *Self and Identity: Fundamental Issues.* New York: Oxford University Press.

Bargh, John A., Katelyn Y. A. McKenna, and Grainne M. Fitzsimons. 2002. "Can You See the Real Me? Activation and Expression of the 'True Self' on the Internet." *Journal of Social Issues* 58, no. 1: 33–48.

Corsaro, William A. 1997. *The Sociology of Childhood.* Thousand Oaks, CA: Pine Forge.

Elliott, Anthony. 2001. *Concepts of Self.* Cambridge, U.K.: Polity.

Gould, Madelyn S., Ted Greenberg, Drew M. Veltin, and David Shaffer. 2003. "Youth Suicide Risk and Preventive Interventions: A Review of the Past 10 Years." *Journal of the American Academy of Child and Adolescent Psychiatry* 42, no. 4: 386–405.

Gubrium, Jaber, and James A. Holstein. 2000. *The Self We Live By: Narrative Identity in a Post-Modern World.* New York: Oxford University Press.

Lester, David. 2003. "Adolescent Suicide from an International Perspective." *American Behavioral Scientist* 46, no. 9: 1157–1170.

Rodham, Karen, Keith Hawton, and Emma Evans. 2005. "Deliberate Self-Harm in Adolescents: The Importance of Gender." *Psychiatric Times* 22, no. 1 (January). Available online at http://www.psychiatrictimes.com.

Thorne, Barrie. 1993. *Gender Play: Girls and Boys in School.* New Brunswick, NJ: Rutgers University Press.

# chapter 6

# Sexuality

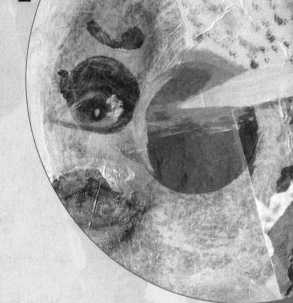

## media moments

### America Rallies to Teenage Gay Icon

A year ago, Corey Johnson, 18, revealed to team-mates at Masconomet High, near Boston, that he was gay, an act of bravery given the reputa-tion of football jocks for being the most boorish and bigoted of all schoolboys. They did not beat him up. Instead they sang him the gay anthem "YMCA" on the team bus and finished the sea-son with seven wins and four defeats. Since Johnson's story became public earlier this year he has become the country's latest gay icon, a hero in a tale of youthful tolerance. ...

Johnson has been approached for a profile in *Vanity Fair* (he declined: not enough teenage readers who might benefit from his experience) and is one of the hottest "gets" on the talk show circuit. Such has been the media interest that he is being advised by Kevin Costner's publicity agent.

Johnson says he is no hero and that in reveal-ing himself as the only openly gay pupil in a school of 1,200 he was just telling the truth. He hopes his example will encourage others of his age to feel safe in revealing themselves, too. "People at my school would have said this was impossible—for the captain of the football team to come out and have it be an accepting environ-ment," he told *School Sports*, the magazine that first published his story. "Just by telling the truth, I've been able to help people because they see

The gay pride movement has become increasingly vocal and publicly visible since the 1970s, chal-lenging heterosexuals to examine their values about love and hate. (Ian Barrett, Reuters/Corbis)

that somebody can live their life without hiding things about an integral part of who they are."

The lack of shock at Johnson's declaration, says the magazine's editor Jonathan Segal, sug-gests discrimination even in sports at school is fading. "The more Corey Johnsons that come out the more readily prejudices will dissipate."

*Source:* Helmore (2000).

"Here's how far we've come in the last five years," says *Will & Grace*'s co-creator David Kohan. "The question networks used to ask was whether their shows had too many episodes with gay plotlines in them. Today, they ask whether they have too many gay shows."

"Television is a pretty accurate reflection of society as whole," believes *Will & Grace*'s other co-creator, 34-year-old Max Mutchnick. "Gay stereo-types on TV today would be like black stereotypes. Nobody would buy it" ("Is Your TV Set Gay?" 2000: 24).

## media moments

### That's Not a Scarecrow: A Brutal Assault in Wyoming

Matthew Shepard was not openly gay. He was just himself. If people asked and he felt comfortable in their presence, he'd say, "I'm gay." There was no flaunting it. After all, he was a freshman at the University of Wyoming in the Cowboy State, a campus where real men were supposed to love football and all-night parties. ...

Last Tuesday night, at the Fireside Lounge, a campus watering hole where he was a favorite regular, Shepard, 21, was enough at ease to strike up a conversation with two tall, muscular men, Russell Henderson, 21, and Aaron McKinney, 22, both high school dropouts. In fact, Shepard was comfortable enough to get into a pickup truck with them at about midnight. According to the police in Laramie, Wyoming, the pair had apparently led him to believe that they too were gay.

But all pretense vanished as the journey got under way. Police say the three were barely a half-mile on Grand Avenue, Laramie's main street, when McKinney abruptly pulled over and, apparently taking turns with Henderson, began pounding Shepard on the head with a .357 Magnum revolver. The pair then drove about a mile east of town and, on Snowy Mountain View Road, they dragged Shepard out of the car. "They tied him to a post," says police commander Dave O'Malley, and as he begged for his life, they "beat him and beat him" ... The back of his head bashed to the brain stem, his face cut, his limbs scorched with burn marks, Shepard hung spread-eagled on a

Antihomosexual protestors attended the funeral of Matthew Shepard after he was beaten and left for dead in a brutal hate crime in Wyoming in 1998. (Gary Caskey/Reuters)

rough-hewn deer fence through a night of near freezing temperatures, unconscious and losing more and more blood.

On the evening of the next day, 18 hours after he was abandoned, two bicyclists saw him. At first, they thought they were looking at a scarecrow. On seeing his nephew's near lifeless body hooked up to a respirator, Robert Eaton told a reporter, "It's like something you might see in war."

The comparison was apt. The brutal assault came at a time when the U.S. is buzzing with a dissonant debate over sexual orientation. It is a controversy fueled by reports of increased violence against homosexuals and a new campaign by religious conservatives touting the power of faith to overcome what they proclaim to be a sinful sensuality.

*Source:* Chua-Eoan (1998).

"Five years ago, when *Entertainment Weekly* published its first issue devoted to gay entertainment, Ellen [Degeneres] was still heterosexual, ... [and] gay men never kissed on prime time. ... What a difference a half decade makes. ... A sitcom about a gay man is now one of the biggest hits on TV. And, audiences are more accepting of gay entertainment than ever before" ("Hollywood's Gay Power Surge" 2000: 23).

## AN INDIVIDUAL OR A SOCIAL STORY?

When we read news stories like these about newly public expressions of gay sexuality and the sometimes welcoming, sometimes terrible responses, we participate symbolically in the great social drama about sexuality that is unfolding in postmodern society. This drama is presented in the form of stories that are animated by the personal qualities of its protagonists—their courage and their fears, their knavery and their virtue, their tolerance and their prejudice.

> New stories emerge when there are new people to listen to and understand them through interpretive communities. The new stories about gender, sexuality, and the body that have been told since the 1960s have been possible because of the emergence of new movements and communities that both give rise to and circulate and rewrite these stories. The most common narratives are stories which tell of discrimination, prejudice and empowerment, stories which tell of coming out as lesbian and gay or as a strong, independent woman, stories of victimization and survival, stories of difference and of similarity, stories of identity and stories of relationships. ... They pose questions about who should control our bodies, the limits of the body, the burden of custom and the state. They are stories which spring up from everyday life, but in turn place new demands on the wider community. (Weeks 1998: 47)

Implicit in these stories is the idea that sexuality is a matter of individual choice, that the actions and attitudes taken toward it are matters that individuals control. We talk to one another about being "grown up" about sexuality, suggesting that it's time to stop being childish, impulsive, and self-indulgent in our reactions. We talk about being truthful or falling for illusions, as if each person has the power within him- or herself to see sexuality as it really is.

These contemporary stories are permeated by what we have called, throughout *A Contemporary Introduction to Sociology*, the language of naturalism. In this cultural idiom, sexuality is presented as something presocial, or biological. The actions that people don't "like" are often spoken about as forms that are unnatural, requiring social control. Conservatives view homosexuality as unnatural, and that nature calls for supporting heterosexuality. Liberals, by contrast, present homosexuality as natural and criticism of it as repressive.

We will learn in the present chapter that this is not the most productive way to think about sex. It is antisociological. Sexuality is a thoroughly social thing. Religions have always had a strong interest in controlling sexuality, in stipulating what are moral and immoral practices in the eyes of God, and in punishing those who deviate from sexual purity. But secular states have also shown an abiding interest in sex, trying to control and direct it through their laws and public policies. In the course of modern history, democratic and authoritarian governments alike have encouraged large families; have distributed birth control and invested in advertisements urging safe sex; have banned movies and erotic materials; have attached binding guarantees to marriage vows and made divorce virtually impossible, or made it easy and "no fault"; and have sometimes prevented, at other times enabled, homosexuals to marry or to raise children.

Society has made its pressure felt much more informally as well. Sexual orientations and practices are subtly but powerfully regulated through popular language. American slang still calls men who engage in frequent sexual encounters with women "studs," while labeling women who openly solicit sex with men "sluts." Heterosexual encounters are still called "normal" and "healthy" and homosexual ones are still too frequently characterized as abnormal and deviant. Male homosexuals—as the tragic case of Matthew Shepard demonstrates—are still sometimes tagged as "perverts" and "fags"; and female homosexuals, as "dykes."

By the fourth grade, children, especially boys, have begun to use homophobic labels—"fag," "faggot," "queer"—as terms of insult, especially for marginal boys. They draw upon sexual allusions (often not fully understood, except for their negative and contaminating import) to reaffirm male hierarchies and patterns of exclusion. As "fag" talk increases, relaxed and cuddling patterns of touch decrease among boys. Kindergarten and first-grade boys touch one another frequently and with ease, with arms around shoulders, hugs, and holding hands. By fifth grade, touch among boys becomes more constrained, gradually shifting to mock violence and the use of poking, shoving, and ritual gestures like "give five" (flat hand slaps) to express bonding. The tough surface of boys' friendships is no longer the gentle touching of girls in friendship. (Thorne and Luria 1986: 182)

Attitudes toward sexuality are always in flux. They vary as institutions and cultures change. In the television series *I Love Lucy*, the networks forbade mention of the word *pregnant* during Little Ricky's gestation period in 1952–1953. The first double marital bed appeared on American television only in 1964, on *Bewitched*. And in 1965, Barbara Eden was forbidden by NBC to show her belly button in *I Dream of Jeannie*. Today, in stark contrast, there is seminudity and open sexual flirtation even on family-oriented shows. Nonmarital sex is the rule. Young female stars play hookers. Not only lesbians but male homosexuals star on TV. *Seinfeld*, the most popular sitcom of the 1990s, featured an episode that focused on masturbation.

It is almost a sure bet that, as a college student reading this textbook, you view this shift in the presentation of sex as a process of naturalization. The reason is that you and most other Americans still think of sex as something physical, as a matter of biology. It is because of this supposed connection between sex and nature that people can speak about society in terms of repressing, tolerating, encouraging, or liberating "it."

## NATURALISM VERSUS CONSTRUCTIVISM

For a long time, sociological thinking was also informed by the equation *sex = biology = natural*. In recent decades, however, this perspective has radically changed. Scholars have begun to ask whether the social dimension of sexuality runs much deeper than the matter of whether, and how, it is controlled. Perhaps sex is not only regulated but actually created by society. Obviously, sex is a powerfully physical act, and has strong, chemically generated feelings attached to it. But even its physical form may be socially determined and the emotional feelings involved may be the product of socialization and culture:

We are now very conscious that the idea of sexuality as a separate continent of either experience or knowledge is itself an historical invention, with traceable conditions of existence. It is a contingent, culturally specific, often unstable linkage of related, but separable, elements: bodily potentials, desires, practices, concepts and beliefs, identities, institutional forms. It is highly gendered, but notoriously malleable. … [It is] marked by variations shaped by culturally and materially defined differences: class, age, ethnicity, nationality, geography. The erotic is neither a thing in itself, nor predominantly (if at all) a natural phenomenon, neither something that can be detached from the body, nor cut off from the mind. (Weeks 1998: 35)

In fact, despite its indispensable evolutionary connection to the reproduction of the species, there is little that is simply natural about the psychological and social expression of sexuality. It is social through and through, and it changes shape in different societies and at different times. In Western Christianity, which is based on the dualities of flesh/spirit and mind/body, sex involves moral conflict and is a continual source of anguish. In Islamic cultures, by contrast, there is often an interweaving of religion and sexuality, and sacred texts themselves may contain lyrical views of physical love. In contemporary Western societies, males are circumcised, a practice some other civilizations view with horror. On the other hand, some Islamic societies practice female circumcision, which Westerners term "female genital mutilation" because it removes the clitoris, a major source of female sexual stimulation. One hundred million women worldwide have been circumcised—sometimes voluntarily, sometimes not.

Female circumcision often involves infibulation, whereby the vagina is sewn up in a manner that prevents all sexual activity (Crossette 1998). In the United States, by contrast, pharmaceutical companies are beginning to market drugs to women that increase the blood flow to female genitalia. The aim is to allow women to overcome what has recently been labeled as SAD—sexual arousal disorder (Hitt 2000).

Homosexual relationships between adult men and adolescent males have been condoned in many societies, particularly among classes where marriage and regular access to young women have been denied. This has been true not only of simple tribal societies such as the Kiman of Melanesia,

**Essentialism** An approach based on the idea that there is an "inner truth" that exists apart from the individual observer or participant. A naturalist perspective of sexuality can be characterized as essentialist in that it considers sexuality a biological "given" that is dictated by the body through genetics, hormones, and brain structures.

where homosexuality was thoroughly institutionalized (Schlegel and Barry 1991: 124–125), but among the ancient Greeks and the Ottoman Turks as well (Greenberg 1988).

As one sociological observer put it, each culture makes "who restrictions" and "how restrictions" about sex (Plummer 1984). The "who" concerns the gender of the partners, and their age, kin, caste, class, race, and number. The "how" defines the body parts that are brought into play, the positions of intercourse, how things are touched, and when.

## BEYOND ESSENTIALISM

As developed societies have moved from modern to postmodern, the sociological analysis of sexuality has taken a cultural turn. From the cultural perspective (see Chapter 3), it is not only the "who" and "how" of sex that get decided but also the "what." According to the earlier, naturalistic perspective of modernism, sex is a "biological imperative located in the genitals" (Weeks 1986). It was viewed as spontaneous, as an overpowering force, as the basis of our passions and feelings. And people believed that it was through sex that they experienced their real selves. As the French historian and philosopher Michel Foucault (1978) once put it, sex was thought to be the truth of our being.

With this modernist language of naturalism there developed the rigid distinction between normal and abnormal. The former was reserved for heterosexuality; the latter, for homosexuality. The binary distinction between the genders was taken as invariant. There existed a hierarchy of normalcy from heterogenital love to perversions. True sex had one true meaning.

With the cultural turn in postmodern societies, it has become evident that sexuality is a language, not a biological fact. As Plummer put it, "[N]othing is sexual, but naming makes it so" (in Weeks 1986: 25). Society is therefore inside of sex, not just outside of it. Theorists refer to the naturalism that marked modernist approaches to sexuality as **essentialism,** based on its view of sex as having an essence, an unchanging inherent quality.

The prevailing wisdom in the United States is that there are really just two kinds of people: straight (heterosexual) and gay (homosexual). It is very common for people to believe that distinct differences exist between these categories, and that it is possible to figure out the category to which a person "really" belongs. Many are convinced that, gay or straight, we have an inborn desire that cannot change. But research into sexual behavior has challenged this essentialist view by demonstrating that there is no inherent connection among homosexual acts, desire, and identity. Consider, for example, the controversial data that Edward Laumann and his colleagues collected from a small sample of people who reported same-gender sexuality in their 1994 study. As you can see in Figure 6.1, many more people experience homosexual desire or display homosexual behavior than those who claim a homosexual identity. Another problem for essentialism is the difference between female and male homosexuality. As Figure 6.2 makes clear, it is more common for women to experience same-sex desire, but more men than women claim a homosexual identity. If homosexuality is an unchanging and undeniable essence, what are we to make of these data?

In regard to sex, essentialism created a "fictional unity" (Weeks 1986: 15) among social things that, in point of fact, were not inherently connected. Essentialism links together gender identities, bodily needs, reproductive capacities, and notions of autonomy and dependence by defining male and female, hetero- and homosexual, in what are actually historically restricted ways. Other cultures, including those at other times and in other places, have intertwined these elements differently. Essentialism is highly ideological, for it justifies as natural only a very restricted set of sexual practices. Ways of making and thinking about sex that are outside this narrow

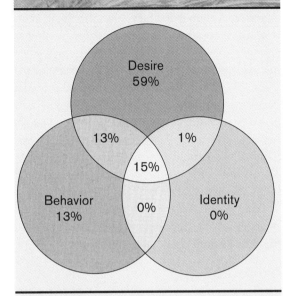

**FIGURE 6.1 Female Homosexual Desire, Identity, and Behavior**

*Source:* Laumann et al. (1994: 300).

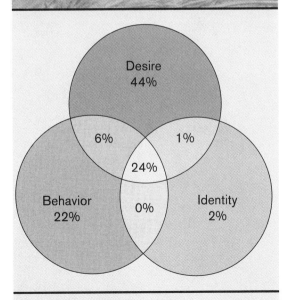

**FIGURE 6.2 Male Homosexual Desire, Identity, and Behavior**

*Source:* Laumann et al. (1994: 301).

set are labeled as unnatural, unjust, even danger-ous. Essentialism substitutes biology for history and society. This makes particular social arrange-ments seem eternal and inevitable, though in actu-ality they are the products of specific power arrangements and specific cultural meanings. Male lust and sexual aggression are viewed sympatheti-cally; "forward" expressions of female sexual desire are most definitely not. Female sexual reti-cence is encouraged as consistent with women's inner nature, rather than seen as the result of gen-dered social structure, socialization, and culture. Sexual violence by men against women is regretted but, until very recently, typically left unpunished.

This essentialist position is famously captured by the (probably apocryphal) remark attributed to Sigmund Freud that "anatomy is destiny." The great Viennese founder of psychoanalysis did more than any other modern intellectual figure to cement the essentialist understanding of sexuality, even as he created a framework that formed a bridge to later, more constructivist perspectives. (See the further discussion under "Freudianism" later in this chapter as well as under "Caring for the Self: Body and Soul" in the previous chapter.) Less than a century later, Michel Foucault, the French founder of postmodern philosophy, cre-ated the framework for a radically different, con-structivist approach.

## SEXUALITY BEFORE MODERNITY

The originality of Foucault's extraordinarily influ-ential *History of Sexuality* (1978, 1979, 1985) de-rived from his ability to investigate the past, and thus implicitly to theorize the present, without modernist preconceptions, and without wearing the blinders of his own time. Foucault professed to be "agnostic" about the question of sexuality. It was not that he didn't believe in its importance: This would be analogous to an "atheistic" posi-tion. Rather, it meant that Foucault had given up entirely on the idea that any particular sexual con-ception or practice is natural, or right. To separate himself entirely from naturalism, Foucault rejected the notion that sex was biological. He viewed it in-stead as a kind of exterior, physical envelope for a sociocultural fact. Rather than seeing the social as repressing or facilitating a natural or presocial sex-uality, he believed that the social production of sexuality is brought about by the very discourses that ostensibly describe it. Sexuality is also pro-duced by the institutional arrangements—laws and institutions like families—that societies create in order to allow this purportedly natural sexual un-derstanding to be expressed and controlled. A ho-mosexual himself, Foucault looked beyond the

Gender-bending is a postmodern form of challenging essential-ism. Although cross-dressing has been accepted in some cultures for centuries, transgendered and intersexed people are emerging as a social movement only recently in mainstream U.S. culture. (iStockphoto)

confinements and restrictions of the modernist package. He did so by looking back to the pre-modern era in a new way.

## Ancient Greece: Cultivating the Self

Classical Greek society is seen as the cradle of modern Western civilization, yet the sexual practices in this earlier time differed strikingly from modern ones. Specifically, male homosexual relations were prized above all others, publicly engaged in by the most prestigious, wealthy, and respected members of Greek society. This highly valued sexual relationship, moreover, was different from romantic erotic love in the modern sense.

Foucault wanted to find out how this could be so. What he discovered was that, in Greek society, sex itself was not highly charged. It represented simply a pleasurable act. The Greek word for it was *aphrodisia*. In modern society, this term has become associated with sexual pleasure completely distanced from affection and connection, but it captures only one of the implications of its meaning in Greek. Foucault found that, for Greeks, sexual pleasure was situated in an "agonistic field of forces difficult to control" (Foucault 1985: 250). What he meant by this statement is that, at least for Greek men, the specific social implications of sexual pleasure were up for grabs. What mattered most of all to the male members of the polis was the "art of self conduct." Learning to cultivate the self allowed a person to achieve an ethical life. This capability of styling and shaping one's conduct reflected an aesthetic ideal of beauty and proportion rather than a moral goal concerned with right and wrong: "Beauty for its own enjoyment, due to perfect dominion that each individual exercised over himself" (Foucault 1985: 91). **Self-cultivation**, whether tied to hetero- or homosexual love, involved moderation in the pur-

suit of pleasure and equilibrium in the exercise of authority: "The ruler publicly exhibited a mastery and a restraint that spread to everyone," displaying a "careful supervision of the soul and the body." Sexuality, like every other physical passion in Greek society—from wrestling to oratory as well as track and field contests—demanded "careful supervision of the soul and the body." In each of these activities, the issue was not the specific nature of the action but, rather, how it was performed, for an "individual fulfilled himself as an ethical subject by shaping a precisely measured conduct that was plainly visible to all and deserving to be long remembered" (Foucault 1985: 91).

In the public sphere of Greek society, men were dominant not only politically but also intellectually, and male beauty, both in face and body, was prized above all. It is hardly surprising, in such a context, that the highest plane of ethical self-styling became male homosexual love, especially between older, well-established men and younger, adolescent boys. However, the fact that such relationships were not stigmatized does not necessarily mean that Greeks viewed them as entirely unproblematic. Homosexual love relationships were criticized to the degree that they violated the cultural ideal of ethical self-conduct. What worried Greeks was the asymmetry between the male lovers. Their ethical ideal of self-mastery raised concern for the younger partner's relation to the older partner: "It was not good (especially in the eyes of public opinion) for a boy to behave 'pas-

**Self-cultivation** An important concept in ancient Greece, requiring moderation in the pursuit of pleasure. An ethical life meant fashioning one's self according to aesthetic ideals of beauty and proportion; moral preoccupations were focused on questions of excess, overindulgence, and passivity. Self-cultivation was important to all forms of physical passion, including wrestling, oratory, and sex.

sively,' to let himself be manipulated and dominated, to yield without resistance" (Foucault 1985: 211). Such anxieties seem remarkably like the ones that would later preoccupy modern critics of male domination over women in asymmetrical heterosexual relationships.

## Christianity: Moralizing Heterosexual Sex

In the course of Christianity's battle with Greek and Roman "paganism," sex came to be constructed in a radically different way. Cultural ideals shifted from cultivation of the self to cultivation of God. Correspondingly, there was a movement away from aesthetic issues of beauty to moral concerns of righteousness and sin. Self-mastery became criticized as egocentric and indulgent. Divining God's will, and sacrificing for the sake of it, became critical.

Following ancient Judaism, Christians believed that God had created woman not only to serve man but to complete him. In this context, the marital relationship became the major field for displaying the Christian approach to the "art of the self." Aphrodisia remained important—but inside of heterosexual marriage, not outside of it. And the moral significance of sex changed: Boys as potential sex partners became "ethically inaccessible" (Foucault 1985), the ideal of reciprocity assumed a heterosexual frame, and marriage monopolized physical pleasure.

Within the context of the moralization of marriage, this restriction of sex to marriage constituted a major source of inhibition and restriction. It is important to note, however, that such regulation was not unique to the West. It was promoted by all of the world's "high" religions, not only Judaism and Christianity but also Buddhism, Hinduism, Confucianism, and Islam. When Max Weber spoke about "the tension of religion and sex," he

was referring to this broad interest in ascetic regulation: "The prophetic religions, as well as the priest-controlled life orders, have, almost without significant exception, regulated sexual intercourse in favor of marriage" (Weber 1958: 344). Sexuality left the public world to take up residence in the hidden world of private life. When it was pursued outside of marriage, it became a source of potential shame. As a sin, sexual deviance became the object of religious confession. These restrictions laid the basis for modernity, first in the West and subsequently in the other civilizations formed by the high religions.

## MODERN SEXUALITY

According to historians of sexuality influenced by Foucault, Christianity did not promote negative feelings about sexuality itself but, rather, produced inhibitions about pursuing sexual pleasure outside of heterosexual marriage: "Within the confines of the marriage bed, sexuality and sexual pleasure were ... seen as good things. Sex was not simply for procreation or to avoid fornication but was good in itself to the degree that it gave pleasure and comfort to both husband and wife" (Leites 1986: 12).

Indeed, there was a bawdiness and physicality about heterosexual relations in medieval Christian Europe, both inside and outside of marriage, that characterized the behavior of learned Christian monks as much as it did peasant celebrations and social life in the emerging urban areas. Only by the end of the first millennium did celibacy—abstinence from all sexual relations—become an ideal for the Christian religious elite. Yet enthusiastic expressions of heterosexual interest continued to be encouraged and sustained in Western societies until the Protestant Reformation in the late sixteenth and seventeenth centuries, which in critical respects marked the cultural onset of modern life.

## Puritan Asceticism

We can deduce from Shakespeare's ribald comedies, for example, that pre-Reformation Elizabethan England positively brimmed over with sexual enthusiasms. It was the Puritan extension of the Reformation that changed all this. As transmitted in texts about the dangers of excess and loss of control, as well as by black-coated censors of pleasure, Puritanism changed the sexual tenor of England and symbolized the great shifts in sexuality that characterized modern life.

In the eyes of its leading proponents, the social and cultural revolutions of modernity seemed to demand extraordinary sexual control and asceticism, and even abstinence. In his famous essay *The Protestant Ethic and the Spirit of Capitalism* (1904), Max Weber, one of the classical founders of sociology, illuminated the critical role that the Protestant Reformation played in making modernity possible. Against the authoritarian hierarchies of medieval Catholicism, Martin Luther championed the ability of individuals to lead a godly life on their own, thus making them individually responsible for their religious fates. As Weber put it, the Reformation broke down the walls separating the monasteries, which housed the religious elites, from everyday life. Yet the effect of this transformation was not liberation, Weber cautioned, but rather the broadening and deepening of regulation and control. The irony was that in modern societies, every man became a monk!

## State-Building and Sexuality

This expanding religious regulation of sexuality during the early-modern period was reinforced by political and economic developments. As the nation-state was formed in the sixteenth and seventeenth centuries, the biopolitics of population—the health and reproductive capacities of a nation's citizenry—became vital for power politics. Sexuality was confronted by political pressures, by demands for regulation and control in service to the nation. Just as new forms of bureaucratic organization emerged to create social discipline, so the physical body and its pleasures became subject to rational manipulation and control. One sociological student of this historical process has written about the **desexualization** of the public sphere that the modernization process demanded: "In the course of the civilizing process, the sexual drive is subject to ever stricter control and transformation. The development of social constraint is matched by individual restraint in these matters. Pressure is placed on adults to privatize all their impulses, there is a conspiracy of silence when children are present. ... The monogamous marriage takes on the form of a social institution" (Burrell 1984: 103).

## Work and Patriarchy

This desexualization can be vividly seen in the area of work. Capitalist economic forms demanded that actors behave in impersonal, efficient, and highly controlled ways. Spontaneous and public expressions of sexuality were definitely not compatible with this emerging new form of wage labor.

With the advent of industrialization in the nineteenth century, these general economic prohibitions became more strongly tied to patriarchy, the maintenance of male control over women. In the absence of contemporary reproductive technologies, it was in a man's interest, and within the

**Desexualization** The effort to control, transform, and limit sexual desires, actions, and behaviors in the modern public sphere. Desexualization is a historical process and, as such, varies according to time, place, and culture.

scope of his almost unlimited private power, to control his wife's reproductive capacities. Before anything like child labor laws existed, children were an important part of the workforce, contributing to a family's earning power and economic survival. Men sought to control the child-bearing capacities of their wives, for their own and their family's benefit. They also sought to inhibit sexual access to their daughters. Young women remained much more "marriageable" as virgins, and the "marrying off" of a man's daughters was viewed as a form of economic success. Conversely, unmarried daughters constituted an economic burden, for as spinsters they were compelled to live with their parents throughout their adult years.

## POLLUTING NONPROCREATIVE SEX

The desexualizing of the public sphere, as well as the moralizing of sex and its restriction to marriage and heterosexuality, contributed to the construction of a strict division between "normal" and "abnormal" sexuality. Virtually every kind of nonprocreative sexual activity was proscribed. Oral sex, for example, was discouraged even within

 **theory**

## America Keeps Onan in the Closet

The anti-masturbation wave began with a Swiss doctor, S.A.D. Tissot, and his wildly popular pamphlet, published in 1741, called "Onanism, or a Treatise on the Disorders of Masturbation." Dr. Tissot proclaimed that the action drained the body of vital fluids, causing wasting illnesses like tuberculosis. Too much sexual excitement, and masturbation in particular, he said, causes neuroses and could damage the nervous system.

"Onanism," reprinted dozens of times and translated into all of the major European languages, sounded the first alarm in what was to become a wave of dire warnings that masturbation was not only immoral but also dangerous. Benjamin Rush, a signer of the Declaration of Independence and a physician keen on bleeding and purging patients, wrote that masturbation caused poor eyesight, epilepsy, memory loss and tuberculosis. Doctors argued that masturba-

tors were easy to spot because they looked sickly and repugnant.

In the nineteenth century industrious entrepreneurs produced and peddled cures. J. H. Kellogg invented corn flakes and Sylvester Graham, the graham cracker. Both wrote best-selling books detailing the terrible ills that befell masturbators. In his 1886 book, *Plain Facts for Young and Old Embracing the Natural History and Hygiene of Organic Life*, Mr. Kellogg informed parents that there were no fewer than 39 signs of masturbation, including acne, bashfulness, boldness, nail biting, use of tobacco and bed wetting. He advised parents to bandage their child's genitals, to enclose them in a case or, simply, to tie the child's hands. He also suggested circumcising boys without an anesthetic. For girls (by now at risk), the cure was a carbolic acid on the clitoris. And yes, corn flakes eaten daily would prevent masturbation.

*Source:* Kolada 1994: E5.

marriage itself. In the 1920s, American marriage manuals recommended it only as an extraordinary display of expressive intimacy and emotional closeness between spouses, not as a regular part of the relationship (Michael et al. 1994: 142–143). Masturbation was subjected to an even harsher fate. Long condemned as sinful by Judaism and Christianity, with modernity it became interpreted as abnormal and unhealthy (see box titled "America Keeps Onan in the Closet").

Homosexuality became subject to equally severe public approbation. In previous eras, religion had criticized homosexual practices, condemning sodomy as sinful. But in modernity, the emerging vocabulary of natural science was employed to stigmatize homosexuals themselves, framing them as an abnormal class of "inverts" or "perverts" and marking them as a kind of separate species. A new group of pseudoscientists emerged—sexologists—who studied homosexuality as a disease carried by

an inferior race. In their eyes, this race constituted a danger to the health and reproduction of the species.

## SEXUALIZING NONWHITE RACES

In constructing the simplistic distinction between normal and abnormal sexuality, modernizing societies projected their fears outside of themselves, linking such "perversions" to a separated, deviant, morally polluted race. This process of sexual projection and pollution was, in fact, part and parcel of the European colonial expansion. During their conquest of the Americas, Europeans encountered native peoples among whom nudity was common and premarital sex, polygamy, and even cross-dressing were much more widely accepted. Being neither modern nor Judeo-Christian, Native Americans did not link sex with morality, on the one hand, or with sin and shame, on the other. It is

*Left:* Like other women of color, African-American women are stereotyped as more sexually available than white women. (iStockphoto)

*Below:* Women of Asian heritage are often stereotyped as the exotic "other" by white culture, which views them as sexual objects. (iStockphoto)

hardly surprising that, for the European missionaries who first encountered them, these Indians became the paradigm of sexual abnormality, revealing "impurity and immorality, even gross sensuality and unnatural vice" (Irvine 1995: 58).

When Europe expanded into Africa, fears of abnormal sexuality were similarly transformed into condemnation of a nonwhite race. In 1730, one European observed that "at some places the Negroes have been suspected of bestiality" with apes and monkeys. Africans were said to be too "ignorant" and "stupid" to "guide or control lust," and they were criticized by white Europeans for "the boldness and affection they are known under some circumstances to express to our females" (Winthrop Jordan, quoted in Irvine 1995: 56).

This projection of the normal/abnormal sexual divide during European expansion laid the basis for the centuries-long portrayal of minority groups' sexuality as bestial, lewd, and depraved. The English described the Irish as being apelike savages, as pursuing animalistic gratifications. The Americans described the Chinese as lustful and depraved. Christian men considered Jewish women to be particularly easy in their sexuality. And during the Reconstruction period after the American Civil War, whites described blacks as sexually lascivious and uncontrollable, their women as lustful, their men as predators. These perceptions fueled lynchings to protect "white womanhood."

**Victorian love**  The approach to sexual relations that characterized the Victoran era. Victorian society was particularly strict in its construction and regulation of such relations, requiring that all sexual behaviors take place within the confines of marriage. Marriage was meant to control the sex instinct. This regulation, however, was not entirely successful; an extensive sexual underground emerged, red-light districts were located in nearly every major city, and there is little evidence that Victorian campaigns against masturbation and fornication were actually effective.

## UNDERGROUND SEXUAL PRACTICES

The narrow construction of sexuality during modernity established rigid norms and broad prohibitions that were continuously violated in the actual practices of sex. Indeed, the obsessive effort to keep sexuality private, and to minimize its expression in every possible respect, had the effect not of suppressing an interest in sexuality but of turning sex into an obsession. Excluded from the public sphere, sexuality went underground. In thinking about sex and modernity, then, we would be inaccurate in saying that "abnormal" practices were banished. In fact, they were widely practiced. But they were also kept as far away as possible from the public eye. In *The Other Victorians* (1966), Steven Marcus describes the illicit subterranean sex literature that flowed in great torrents among the supposedly upright and puritanical Victorian men of the late nineteenth century (see box titled "The 1859 Rough Guide to Manhattan Brothels"). Prostitution was widely practiced and homosexuality common among both elites and working classes. Indeed, behind the patriarchal pretenses of **Victorian love,** men indulged in every sort of sexual practice that they denied for women. Despite the public cult of the virginal woman, sexual harassment was common in modern societies, rape much more widespread than commonly believed, and less violent forms of forced male-to-female sex widely practiced.

The mutual attraction that Victorians described as love was basically a spiritual, mental and moral one. … Ideally, love was to be the basis of marriage. Such a marriage was not intended to be chaste. Sex was too powerful a force to be denied. Under the proper conditions, sex was a beneficent power, potentially invigorating and uplifting. Marriage was the legitimate sphere of sex. Marriage functioned as a sphere of control over the sex instinct. It desensualized sex. … [But] the Victorian

## The 1859 Rough Guide to Manhattan Brothels

Her furniture is of the most costly, and the decorations and upholstering will vie with any we have seen. Her lady boarders are courteous, pretty and accommodating. The hostess is a lady of pleasing manners, sociable, and well understands the art of entertaining visitors. The wines are the best the market affords, selected from the best brands, and cannot be surpassed. In fact, she seeks nothing but the pleasure of her visitors. We know of no better house to recommend strangers and others to, than this.

Mrs. Everett
No. 158 Laurens St.

This is a quiet, safe and respectable house, and altogether on the assignation order, and conducted on true Southern principles. She accommodates a few charming and beautiful lady boarders, who are from the sunny South, and equal to any of this class in the city. The proprietress strictly superintends the operations of her household, which is always in perfect order. The beautiful señoritas are quite accomplished, sociable and agreeable, and pattern after the much admired landlady. Gentlemen visitors from the South and West are confidently recommended to this pleasant, quiet and safe abode. The Landlady possesses all the charming mannerisms which so highly characterize that soothing clime. The very best wines constantly kept on hand, and selected from the best brands the market affords.

Miss Clara Cordon
No. 119 Mercer St.

We cannot too highly recommend this house, the lady herself is a perfect venus: beautiful, entertaining and supremely seductive. Her aids-de-camp are really charming and irresistible, and altogether honest and honorable. Miss G. is a great belle, and her mansion is patronized by Southern merchants and planters principally. She is highly accomplished, skillful, and prudent and sees her visitors are well entertained. Good Wines of the most elaborate brands, constantly on hand: and in all, a finer resort cannot be found in the city.

Miss Thompson
No. 75 Mercer St.

This lady keeps one of the largest and most magnificently furnished mansions in the central part of the city. She has spared no expense in fitting up this establishment—which is furnished and decorated in the most suberb style. The hostess is a great favorite, and always happy to see her friends and visitors. She accommodates a number of handsome lady boarders, who are agreeable and accomplished. We recommend visitors and others to give them a call, and partake of the good things of this life.

Miss Mary Temple
No. 122 Green St.

*Source:* A Free Loveyer (1859: 8–9).

sexual regime was not entirely successful. The sexual impulse that was to be controlled and sublimated into companionship, career, or domesticity found an outlet outside marriage. A vast sexual underground emerged that centered around an elaborate system of prostitution and pornography. In virtually every major city there appeared red light districts. On the eve of the Civil War, men could purchase guides telling them the addresses and relevant details of the available brothels. One such guide listed over one hundred houses of prostitution in New York City. Further, the campaigns against masturbation and fornication that figured prominently in the Victorian century suggest that the efforts to restrict eroticism to marriage and spiritually transfigure it were less effective in practice than in theory. (Seidman 1991: 60–61)

## The Counterculture of Eroticism

The effort exerted by modernity to moralize, discipline, privatize, and minimize sexuality had an unintended consequence that proved eventually to have profound social importance. It created the formally proscribed but mysteriously magnetic sphere of eroticism, a kind of countercultural, oppositional zone in the area of sex. In the **erotic sphere,** sex is valued as an end in itself—not as something purely physical but as something purely romantic, a highly stylized, intensely idealized pleasure disconnected from morality. In the zone of eroticism, sexuality is separated from the

**Erotic sphere** The zone in which sex is pure, transcendent, and valued as an end in itself, and whose existence undermines modernity's efforts to restrict sexuality to the private institution of marriage and challenges the impersonal, ascetic ethic on which modernity is based. The erotic sphere contrasts with the public sphere, in which sex is highly regulated and often labeled as "profane."

institutions and normative regulations of modernity's official public life but also of its culturally acceptable private life. In both of these spheres, modernity not only regulated but minimized and denigrated sexuality as a potentially dangerous and diverting experience. With eroticism, by contrast, sex is purified and transcendent. Defined as the modern source of sacred experience, eroticism also has the effect of valorizing the nonprocreative sexual practices that modernity condemned.

## Max Weber on Eroticism Versus Modernity

Max Weber is often thought of as the classical sociologist who illuminated the rational and ascetic bases of modernity, as epitomized in the bureaucratic demands for impersonal discipline and control. In his conclusion to *The Protestant Ethic and the Spirit of Capitalism* (1904), Weber called such demands the **iron cage** of modernity. Less widely known is the fact that Weber was especially sensitive to the sexual costs of such demands for impersonal control, and that in exploring these costs he developed a sociological theory of the special position of eroticism in modern societies.

Weber wrote that the "tension" between sex and modernity had created a "nonroutinized sphere" of "consciously cultivated" sexuality. Anticipating postmodern **constructivism,** he emphasized that the eroticization of sex could not be understood as the physical expression of desire in the presocial, natural sense. To the contrary, he wrote, "the extraordinary quality of eroticism has consisted precisely in a gradual turning away from the naïve naturalism of sex" (Weber 1958: 344). In fact, it is modernity's very destruction of the naturalism of traditional life that creates eroticism. "The estrangement of life-value from that which is merely naturally given," Weber asserted, gives "further enhancement [to] the special position of eroticism" (1958: 344).

Despite its constructed character, however, the effect of eroticism is to counterpose the "natural" and "unregulated" to the "artificial" cultural restrictions of modernity. Equating sex with "the most sublime," eroticism presents itself to moderns as "a gate into the most irrational and thereby real kernel of life, as compared with the mechanisms of rationalization" (Weber 1958: 345). Eroticism opposes the impersonal, regulatory nature of modern culture. It does so by placing "a tremendous value emphasis on the specific sensation of an inner-worldly salvation from rationalization" and on "a joyous triumph over rationality" (Weber 1958: 346). Because of this value emphasis—the "culture" of eroticism—there emerges a fundamental "tension between the erotic sphere and rational everyday life," for in a highly rationalized society "sexual life … gains the character of the only and the ineradicable connection with animality" (Weber 1958: 347).

Eroticism produces a contradiction within modernity itself: It is inevitable that "this sphere [would collide] with the unavoidably ascetic trait of the vocational specialist type of man" (Weber 1958: 346). By producing eroticism, modernity threatens its own strenuous effort to restrict sexuality to the privacy, regulation, and routines of marriage. For, according to the culture of eroticism, "extramarital sexual life, which had been removed from everyday affairs, could appear as the only tie which still linked man with the natural fountain of all life."

Modernity was premised on the prohibition of nonprocreative sex. According to the culture of eroticism, however, sexual fulfillment is available only in sexual practices outside of marriage. Weber described modernity as based on the triumph of religious asceticism over mysticism. And he described eroticism as creating a kind of "mystical" emphasis that contradicted the ascetic, impersonal, and generalized ethic upon which modernity was based:

**Iron cage** A concept used by Max Weber to describe modernity. Weber argued that as modernity becomes more rational, with increasing bureaucracy and emphasis on discipline and control, it takes on the characteristics of an "iron cage" that distances and prevents individuals from manifesting their passions and callings.

**Constructivism** A perspective that assumes that day-to-day phenomena are socially created, regulated, and defined. For example, a constructivist perspective of sex would assert that while sex is a physical act tied to chemically based feelings, it is also a social relationship that is marked by cultural and material differences (i.e., class, age, race, nationality, and gender). Constructivism contrasts with naturalism, which assumes that day-to-day phenomena are biological and inherent to human beings.

The erotic relation seems to offer the unsurpassable peak of the fulfillment of the request for love in the direct fusion of the souls of one to the other. This boundless giving of oneself is as radical as possible in its opposition to all functionality, rationality, and generality. It is displayed here as the unique meaning which one creature in his irrationality has for another, and only for this specific other. However, from the point of view of eroticism, this meaning, and with it the value content of the relation itself, rests upon the possibility of a communion which is felt as a complete unification, as a fading of the "thou." It is so overpowering that it is interpreted "symbolically": as a sacrament. The lover realizes himself to be rooted in the kernel of the truly living, which is eternally inaccessible to any rational endeavor. He knows himself to be freed from the cold skeleton hands of rational orders, just as completely as from the banality of everyday routine. This consciousness of the lover rests upon the ineffaceability and inexhaustibleness of his own experience. The experience is by no means communicable and in this respect it is equivalent to the "having" of the mystic. (Weber 1958: 347)

## SEXUALITY IN THE POSTMODERN TRANSITION

The structures that regulate sexuality, and the cultural norms that describe it, have been foundational for modern life. They continue to exert a powerful influence even in the most highly developed, post-industrial, and postmodern societies. Criticism about sex that is nonprocreative abounds. There are public controversies about masturbation, about prostitution, about the virtues of sexual abstinence as a way of fighting against the spread of sexually related disease. Homosexuality remains highly controversial. It is prohibited from being openly expressed in the American military, and those who practice it cannot be married in the vast majority of American states (see Figure 6.3).

The "erotic complex" continues to play an underground and oppositional role. Forbidden talk emerges everywhere, but it remains transgressive, and although urban sex zones make underground sexual practices public, they are still segregated. In an ethnography of the British newspaper industry, for example, a feminist sociologist made the following observations: "The social currency of the [all-male] composing room is women and women-objectifying talk, from sexual expletives and innuendo through to narrations of exploits and fantasies. The wall is graced with four-colour litho 'tits and bums.' Even the computer is used to

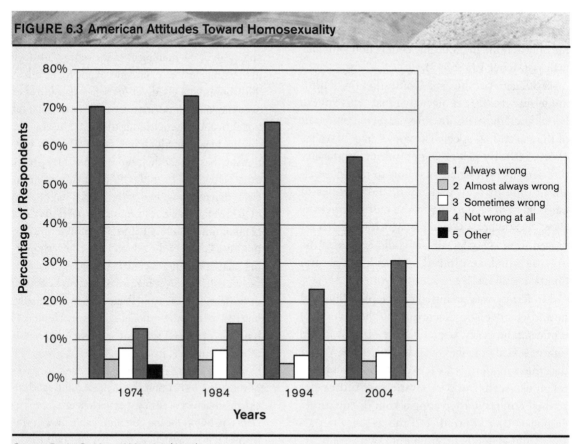

**FIGURE 6.3 American Attitudes Toward Homosexuality**

Legend:
1 Always wrong
2 Almost always wrong
3 Sometimes wrong
4 Not wrong at all
5 Other

*Source:* Davis, Smith, and Marsden (2005).

produce life-sized print-outs of naked women" (Cockburn 1983: 134).

Sexploitation is big business. Strip clubs and movies have transformed eroticism into a profit-making, often pornographic commodity (Hearn and Parkin 1987: 49). Sexual services from prostitution to massage therapies are advertised in widely available (if still underground) papers and on Internet sites read by millions. As you can see in Table 6.1, the rates at which men and women engage in sexual fantasy and use pornography are markedly different. How would a naturalist explain these disparities? How would a social constructionist explain them?

Patriarchy continues to distort sexual experience. The most ambitious recent sociological study of American sexuality suggests that "the problem of coerced sex and sexual abuse is particularly troubling since it seems so often to happen under the auspices of affectionate or friendly relations" (Laumann et al. 1994: 547). Four percent of American women reported that their first experience with intercourse was forced, and 25 percent reported that, while unforced, the sex had been unwanted. Twenty-two percent of American women have been forced to have sex sometime during their lives (Laumann et al. 1994: 547).

Yet, despite these continuities with modernity, it seems obvious that the most basic structures and cultures of sexuality have begun to change dramatically. There are clear signs that a very different, postmodern understanding of sexuality is emerging. These changes parallel, and interrelate with, the other transformations that we have described as triggered by the shift away from modern society.

In the second half of the twentieth century, the tight constraints that regulated sexuality—that minimized it, moralized it, and sought to contain it within the private sphere—began to unravel. What happened was that the erotic sphere, the counter-

**TABLE 6.1  A Taste for the Erotic: Gender Differences in Sexual Fantasy and Porn Preference**

| Thinking About Sex | Men (%) | Women (%) |
|---|---|---|
| "Every day" or "several times a day" | 54 | 19 |
| "A few times a month" to "a few times a week" | 43 | 67 |
| "Less than once a month" or "never" | 4 | 14 |
| Use of Autoerotic Material: Any porn | 41 | 16 |
| X-rated moves or videos | 23 | 11 |
| Club with nude dancers | 22 | 4 |
| Books or magazines | 16 | 4 |
| Vibrators or dildos | 2 | 2 |
| Other sex toys | 1 | 2 |
| Sex phone numbers | 1 | 0 |

Source: Adapted from Laumann et al. (1994: 135).

culture that emerged in opposition to the sexual strictures of modernity, moved from the periphery into the center of public life. As Zygmunt Bauman noted, sex became much more free-floating. It is now less hardwired, less rigid in its social sequencing, and much less subject to moral stigmatization.

The late modern or postmodern rendition of eroticism appears unprecedented—a genuine breakthrough and novelty. It enters alliance with neither sexual [physical] reproduction nor love, claiming independence from both neighbors and flatly refusing all responsibility for the impact it may make on their fate; it proudly and boldly proclaims itself to be its only, and sufficient, reason and purpose. ... "Desire does not desire satisfaction. To the contrary, desire desires desire." When (seldom, and in a whisper) voiced before, such claims were classified as the heresy of libertinism and exiled to the Devil's Island of sexual disorder and perversion. Now the self-sufficiency of eroticism, the freedom to seek sexual delights for their own sake, has risen to the level of a cultural norm. ... Nowadays, eroticism has acquired substance it was never before able to carry on its own shoulders, but also an unheard-of lightness and volatility. Being an eroticism "with no strings attached," untied, unbridled, let loose—the postmodern eroticism is free to enter and leave any association of convenience. ... Postmodern eroticism is free-floating; it can enter chemical reaction with virtually any other substance, feed and draw juices from any other human emotion or activity. ... Only in such a liberated and detached version may eroticism sail freely under the banner of pleasure-seeking, undaunted and undiverted from its pursuits by any other [sphere]. It is free now to establish and negotiate its own rules as it goes. (Bauman 1998: 21, 26)

## Social Causes

There are social reasons for this radical change in sex. They are the same processes that we have pointed to throughout this book, processes that gradually are transforming modern into postmodern society:

✓ *Urbanization and mobility.* As small towns and villages continue to give way to large urban, suburban, and exurban sprawls, anonymity increases. There is less surveillance of individual lives and thus more opportunity for sexual "deviance" or, in more positive terms, sexual exploration. As impersonal legal regulation replaces "small-town morality," regulation of extramarital sex breaks down, and "no-fault" divorce becomes possible. As individuals more frequently travel away from home for business and leisure, the link between sex and marriage becomes strained and nonprocreative sex becomes more widely available (Hearn and Parkin 1987: 80).

✓ *Postindustrial economy.* The movement from production to consumption correlates with this shift in public legitimacy from exclusively procreative to more broadly nonprocreative sex. As the physical burdens of work decrease, the body becomes less a natural given and more a focus of the social, often sexual public imagination. As leisure, service, and entertainment become major new industries, sexual excitement, expressed in myriad realms from media to clothing, becomes a major economic focus.

✓ *Extended socialization.* Postmodern societies require ever longer periods of secondary socialization. One result is the emergence of a growing amount of time between sexual puberty and the assumption of clearly defined adult roles. This new period of being an "adult single" provides an opportunity for sexual experimentation without the responsibilities of making a living, raising children, or maintaining marital fidelity. Lifelong marriage to the same person has long since ceased being regarded as an inevitable, natural, or even particularly desirable human phenomenon. "The development of the singles culture in the '60s was still seen as a temporary stage before marriage," says Stephanie Coontz, author of *The Way We Never Were.* "Now, marriage seems to be a temporary interruption of the singles culture" (Coontz 1992). Since there are so many more people today who have never married or are divorced than in the '60s, kids have fewer visible role models for committed, long-standing intimate relationships. It's no wonder that, for today's adolescents, uncommitted sex seems to be no big deal. "Kids today live in an environment where sex is an everyday thing between two people," explains one 16-year-old boy. "They just think it is something to pass the time, or to have fun with, so let's do it" (quoted in Hersch 1993: 25).

✓ *Feminism.* Because the public-private split depended so heavily on patriarchal controls and female self-inhibition, the empowerment of women has been critical in changing these modern sexual practices. In short, women's demand for sexual equality with men has permeated the public sphere.

✓ *Globalization and multiculturalism.* As Western colonial power and racist prejudices have begun to fade, it has become much less feasible to maintain the simplistic split between "normal" and "abnormal" sexual practices by projecting repressed sexual desires onto an excluded and dominated third party. As diverse images of sexuality circulate rapidly around the globe, the superiority of modern Western sexual practices is challenged. And as multiculturalism confronts centuries of racial and ethnic domination inside of Western societies, stereotypes that project "abnormal" sexual practices onto excluded groups and separate them from "normal" people become less persuasive.

✓ *Expressive individualism.* Postmodern social organization has the effect of highlighting creativity over regulation, of legitimating the expression of emotions over self-control and inhibition. During the modern period, the counterculture of eroticism had linked nonroutine sex to the idea of expressing the "true" self against "false" social regulation. But with postmodernity, what the philosopher Charles Taylor (1992) calls the "cult of authenticity" is given much freer reign. The result is that erotic sexuality has become central to public life. Forms of sexuality once stigmatized as promiscuous and perverse are now legitimated.

## Sex Tourism

An increasingly significant form of economic activity in the postmodern world is **sex tourism**—a form of leisure travel for the purpose of engaging in sexual activity. As shown in Figure 6.4, this category encompasses a range of sexual encounters, from couples on holiday to the hiring of prostitutes.

Sex tourism combines many of the legacies of modernity, especially those from the Anglo-Saxon world. To begin with, the very idea of "going away on holiday" was an invention of the industrial capitalism of the nineteenth century, when regulated work schedules were introduced and time off from

**Sex tourism** Leisure travel for the purpose of sexual activity, ranging from couples on holiday to the hiring of prostitutes. Sex tourism remains a gendered and racialized activity and can contribute to sex trafficking exploitation.

work became commodified. Although a variety of leisure-time pursuits were developed and marketed for both men and women during that era, tourism in general was significantly more oriented toward men. According to Victorian notions of masculinity, it was acceptable and even desirable for men to venture abroad to "see the world" while women were expected to tend to the home. It was also during the nineteenth century that colonialism was in full force and Western Europeans were encountering new cultures. As we have seen in this chapter, Europeans often interpreted these societies according to their own cultural standards of what constituted normal and abnormal sexual behavior. The sexualization of nonwhite races in-

**FIGURE 6.4 Varieties of Sex Tourism Encounters**

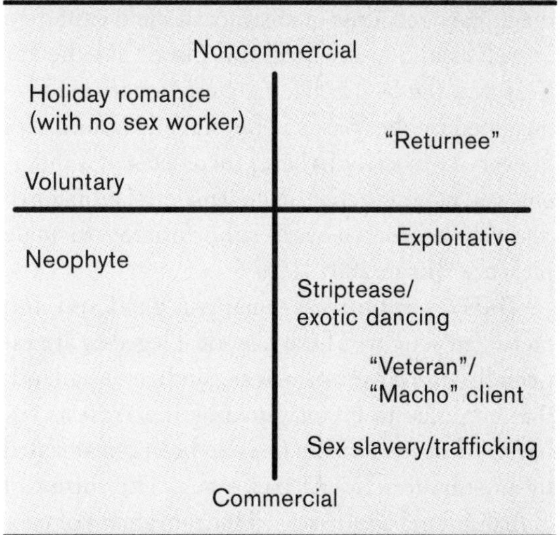

*Source:* Ryan (2001: 62).

Amsterdam is known worldwide for its legal prostitution; shown here is the red light district with a prostitute in the window in the background. (iStockphoto)

**TABLE 6.2  Sex Trafficking: Regional Distribution of Forced Labor**

| Region | Number of People in Forced Labor |
| --- | --- |
| Asia and Pacific | 9,490,000 |
| Latin America and Caribbean | 1,320,000 |
| Sub-Saharan Africa | 660,000 |
| Industrialized countries | 360,000 |
| Middle East and North Africa | 260,000 |
| Transition countries | 210,000 |
| World | 12,300,000 |

*Source:* ILO (2005).

volved not only the projecting of fears but also the fantasizing about all that was forbidden both culturally and sexually in their own society. Through the literary accounts of missionaries and explorers as well as in popular literature, places like the Far East and the South Pacific were "exoticized"—imagined by the West as "beyond the boundaries of everyday society [where] there existed a different way of conducting male-female relationships; one where women were subordinated to male pleasure" (Ryan 2001: 12).

Today, sex tourism remains a gendered and racialized activity. These historical legacies are especially significant in places, such as Thailand, that continue to be imagined by the West as sex havens. But sex tourism has also been transformed by postmodern social processes. The forces of globalization have increased the movement of people across borders, whether for "business, war, or pleasure" (Wonders & Michalowski 2001: 548).

At the same time, the postindustrial global economy has contributed to greater disparities between developed and developing countries. In other words, more people from wealthy countries are going abroad looking for adventure and self-discovery, while more people from developing countries are crossing borders in order to escape war, genocide, or desperate poverty. Together, these forces have expanded the number of sex workers and those interested in engaging their services. As Table 6.2 and Figures 6.5 and 6.6 make clear, sex tourism is both a major industry and a social problem for developing economies.

Contemporary society needs neither mass industrial labor nor mass (conscript) armies. The era when factories and troupes were the decisive order-sustaining institutions is (at least in our part of the world) over. ... The great majority of people—men as well as women—are today integrated through seduction rather than policing, advertising rather than indoctrinating, need-creation rather than normative regulation. Most of us are socially and culturally trained and shaped as sensation-seekers and gatherers, rather than producers and soldiers. Constant openness to new sensations and greed for ever new experience, always stronger and deeper than before, is a condi-

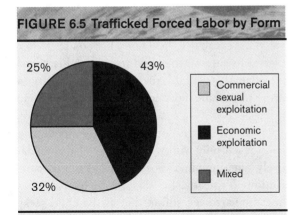

**FIGURE 6.5 Trafficked Forced Labor by Form**

- 43% Commercial sexual exploitation
- 32%
- 25%
- Commercial sexual exploitation
- Economic exploitation
- Mixed

*Source:* ILO (2005).

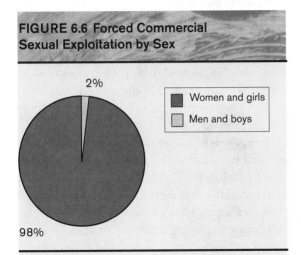

**FIGURE 6.6 Forced Commercial Sexual Exploitation by Sex**

- 98% Women and girls
- 2% Men and boys

*Source:* ILO (2005).

tion sine qua non of being amenable to seduction. It is not "health," with its connotation of a steady state, of an immobile target on which all properly trained bodies converge—but "fitness," implying being always on the move or ready to move, the capacity for imbibing and digesting ever greater volumes of stimuli, flexibility and resistance to all closure, that grasps the quality expected from the experience-collector, the quality she or he must indeed possess to seek and absorb sensations. And if the mark of "disease" was incapacity for factory or army life, the mark of "unfitness" is the lack of elan vital, ennui, acedia, inability to feel strongly, lack of energy, stamina, interest in what the colourful life has to offer, desire and desire to desire. ... Eroticism cut free from its reproductive and amorous constraints fits the bill very well; it is as if it were made to measure for the multiple, flexible, evanescent identities of postmodern men and women. (Bauman 1998: 23, 27)

## HISTORICAL DEVELOPMENTS

The social forces pushing beyond the modern construction of sexuality are brought into play by individuals and groups. Social actors have free will. They are agents, subjects not objects. Postmodern social forces create a new "external environment" for social actions: They offer different resources, different opportunities, different rewards, different sanctions. Yet postmodern social forces also change the "internal environment" of individuals and groups. By changing socialization and culture, postmodernism has created new personalities and needs. In short, over the course of time, new sexual selves have emerged.

### Freudianism

The first significant challenge to naturalistic thinking about sexuality actually left the medical framework of normal/abnormal in place. Sigmund Freud (1930: 74) defined the **libido** as an individual's inborn sexual desire and energy, and he made it central to his psychoanalytic theory of personality. Through working with psychiatric patients, Freud developed the notion of a sexual trajectory. At birth, he said, the personality of the infant con-

**Libido**  As defined by Freud, an individual's inborn sexual desire and energy.

sists almost entirely of the **id** (the "it" in German), which he described as a bundle of unfocused, "polymorphous and perverse" libido. The drive to release this energy propelled psychic development. Freud strongly criticized Victorian society for making people feel ashamed about their desire for sexual pleasure. At the same time, he deeply believed that civilization depended on sublimating the sex drive. With sublimation, sexual energy would be transformed into such "aim-inhibited" activities as Platonic friendships, artistic endeavors, and economic enterprise.

According to Freud, primitive libido could be released in three ways. The healthy forms of release were direct sexual pleasure and sublimation. Direct sexual release was unproblematic, though the form it assumed was shaped by an often rocky socializing process. Sublimation was much more important in the long run, but it depended on even more complex social and cultural arrangements. If these two outlets were blocked, sexual energy would take a pathological turn, finding a distorted, self-destructive release via neurosis. Moving beyond primitive sexuality had to be learned, and the learning depended on appropriate parenting and socialization.

People are not, for Freud, "inherently" heterosexual or even genitally oriented. Rather, the body contains *three* equally powerful erogenous zones: the mouth, the anus, and the genitals. The infant first concentrates on oral needs. The erotic pleasures of sucking coincide both with the need for simple nourishment, provided by the mother's breast, and with social support for intense mother-child bonds. Psychological development beyond the "fused" emotional needs that are generated by orality depends on a similar combination of physi-

cal, psychic, and social factors. Parents decide that it is time for the child to stop nursing and to develop the capacity to feed himself. Soon after, they place pressure on the child to control his bowel movements, to inhibit the pleasures of anality in order to gain the independence that toilet training brings.

At the end of this long process, the developing child is left only with what Freud called the relatively "aim-inhibited" possibilities of genital satisfaction. Typically, he said, these possibilities become narrowed still further as the child seeks adult substitutes for the much-loved parent of the opposite sex. When this happens, genital sexuality becomes expressed in a heterosexual way.

As the nature and outlets of sexual satisfaction are narrowed and channeled, the **ego** (the "I" in German) and the **superego** (the "overself" in German) develop alongside the id. The repressive and controlling superego and the rational and independent ego together make sublimation not only possible but desirable.

Freud's psychoanalytic approach profoundly affected twentieth-century thinking about sexuality. On the one hand, its insistence on sublimation reinforced the diminution and control of sexual "instinct" upon which modernity was based. By vigorously employing a medical vocabulary, moreover, this new psychoanalytic psychology seemed to give scientific legitimacy to the Victorian notion that deviations from genital heterosexuality were symptoms of disease, perversions for which medical figures had to develop a cure.

In other respects, however, psychoanalytic theory sharply challenged the Victorian age. Freud showed that sexuality was not an automatic, natural thing. To the contrary, he demonstrated that society, in the form of parenting, played a critical role in shaping and organizing sex. In so problematizing sexuality, psychoanalysis broke with essentialism. Anatomy is important, but it enters consciousness and informs behavior, Freud believed, only as a result of the symbolic meanings attached to it by the unconscious mind. Adult sexual iden-

**Id, ego,** and **superego** Again, as defined by Freud, three parts of the human psyche. The id is the unfocused energy that drives the libido; it is inborn and initially unchecked. The ego and the superego develop alongside the id, controlling and repressing its urges and desires.

tity, far from being a given, is thus explained as a product of internal conflict—a process that begins with a bisexual nature whose sexual object is not predetermined.

Psychoanalysis thus challenged sexual modernity not only as a scientific theory but also as a cultural and social movement. The resulting controversy undermined the insistence that sexuality must be confined to the privacy of married life. Freud himself insisted on the healthy importance of public sex discussion. From the 1920s on, "Freudianisms" entered powerfully into artistic and intellectual discourses, into journalism, and, eventually, into the common sense of everyday life.

## The Kinsey Report

At the beginning of the second half of the twentieth century, just as American society was entering a period of rapid, postwar social change, the appearance of the "Kinsey Report" in 1948 (see also Kinsey et al. 1953) intensified the public nature of sexuality. In this respect, the report's effect complemented that of Freud. In another respect, however, Kinsey's findings actually undermined the modernist sex regime, for they called directly into question the normal/abnormal split.

Trained as a natural scientist of animal behavior, Alfred Kinsey conducted thousands of interviews with randomly selected Americans. He reported the results in a detached, objective, and assertively nonmoralistic way. Kinsey found that the sexual practices labeled "abnormal," "immoral," or "perverse" were so widely practiced among Americans that they would have to be considered normal in the statistical sense. He found that American women were highly interested in sex, and often wanted more frequent sex than their husbands allowed. He also discovered that masturbation was rampant among adolescents and adult women and men, that oral sex was unexpectedly common, and that more than two-thirds of American men had committed adultery. Most con-

troversially, Kinsey reported that one-third of American men had experienced a homosexual encounter sometime during their lifetime, that 10 percent had been exclusively homosexual for a period in their lives of not less than three years, and that 4 percent considered themselves exclusively homosexual at the time they were interviewed (cited in Michael et al. 1994: 173).

These empirical facts about mid-century sexual practices were shocking revelations, and they created a kind of public sexual frenzy. Kinsey's first book, on male sexuality, was published in 1948, and it sold 200,000 copies in two months. "Hotter than the Kinsey Report" became a popular figure of speech. Kinsey's statistics were worked into comedy routines. Kinsey himself was asked to endorse a range of products from religious works to new brassiere styles. Celebrities lined up at his door.

Kinsey's second volume, on female sexuality, appeared on August 20, 1953—a date that "would be known as K-day, the moment that sex became front-page news in almost every newspaper in the country" (Peterson and Hefner 1999: 222). This time around, the American public was even readier, paying for 200,000 copies in the initial weeks after publication. Brooklyn congressmember Louis Heller demanded that the post office stop shipments of the book. A paperback explaining its findings topped the best seller charts the following year. *Life* magazine wrote that Kinsey's interviews constituted a "mass confession that American women have not been behaving at all in the manner in which their parents, husbands and pastors would like to think, and doubtless a great many people will even be loath to believe that Kinsey got his facts straight" (Peterson and Hefner 1999: 223).

## The Sexual Revolution

In the midst of this normalization and pluralization of sexuality, its new and deepening public status, and the growing understanding of its historically shifting character, Americans began to experience what contemporaries eventually came to describe as the **sexual revolution.** Historians later described the sexual revolution in this way: "An overlapping set of beliefs that detached sexual activity from the instrumental goal of procreation, affirmed heterosexual pleasure as a value in itself, defined sexual satisfaction as a critical component of personal happiness and successful marriage, and weakened the connections between sexual expression and marriage by providing youth with room for some experimentation as preparation for adult status" (D'Emilio and Freedman 1988: 241).

### Hugh Hefner

In December 1953, Hugh Hefner published his first issue of *Playboy* magazine. An influential social critic of the time, Max Lerner, wrote that whereas Kinsey was the researcher of the sexual revolution, Hefner was its pamphleteer: "What Kinsey did was give the American male permission to change his basic way of life, his basic lifestyle. And what Hefner did was show the American male how to do it" (quoted in D'Emilio and Freedman 1988).

*Playboy* featured graphic, glossy photographs of naked women, along with columns and articles preaching sexual libertinism and the pursuit of pleasure without commitment. The magazine was marketed to upwardly mobile male adolescents and young male professionals. It had more than a million subscribers by 1960, mostly single men, and it peaked at 6 million readers in the early 1970s. Portraying marriage as a financial trap for men, and encouraging emotional distance from sexual activity, the magazine also tried to redefine

**Sexual revolution** The process and time period in which sexuality was pluralized. The sexual revolution separated sexual activity from the purpose of procreation, placed new value on heterosexual pleasure, and gave youth the space for sexual experimentation.

Gloria Steinem, shown here in 1960, became instantly famous when she wrote a feminist exposé of her work as a Playboy bunny in Hugh Hefner's Playboy Club. (Bettmann/Corbis)

women's sexuality as compatible with men's, suggesting that the "girl next door" had sexual interests that went beyond "love and marriage."

### Helen Gurley Brown

In the early 1960s, this public equation of sexuality with eroticism did, in fact, broaden to include the "sexually liberated" woman. In 1962, Helen Gurley Brown burst on the public scene with her best seller *Sex and the Single Girl*. Brown described marriage as "insurance for the worst years of your life," advising that "during the best years, you don't need a husband" (quoted in D'Emilio and Freedman 1988: 303). Having separated female sexual desire from the morality of marriage, Brown advised women to use sex as the "powerful weapon" it really was. She championed the "live by your wits" type of woman, suggesting that sex before marriage was fine even for "nice, single girls" and that adultery was not immoral. "Use them in a perfectly nice way just as they use you," she advised her readers, adding that "one married man is dangerous," but "a potpourri can be fun." Brown declared that "it's a question of taking married men, but not taking them seriously." The point, she said, was to give equal access to **free-floating eroticism**: "An affair between a single woman and her lover can be unadulterated, cliffhanging sex" (quoted in D'Emilio and Freedman 1988: 304). When, two years later, Brown assumed editorial control of the American women's magazine *Cosmopolitan*, she had a vastly expanded audience for her postmodern views.

### The Cosmo Girl

In July 1965, Helen Gurley Brown became the editor of *Cosmopolitan*. A noticeable shift occurred in its themes. More emphasis was placed on intimate lifestyle issues—in particular, sex and romance. Images of sexuality appeared that valued it as a site of pleasure and self-expression, even apart from a committed relationship:

> In a provocative piece, Edna O'Brien offered "a defense of the brief encounter." She describes this as "one of my most shattering pleasures." The brief encounter is not meant, she says, to be a substitute for a love affair or marriage. Instead, it should be an occasional adventure valued for its erotic exuberance that women should not pass up. In the brief encounter, the individual "lives for the moment" and "has a beautiful sense of celebration. Her openness is touching, her appetite unconcealed." [Another writer] Alma Birk debunks the myth that women only enjoy sex as an expression of intimacy or love. "The modern argument goes: a woman cannot enjoy a sexual relationship unless it is also deeply emotional. ... Needless to say, more men than women utter these propositions." This notion, she argues, disempowers women; it stigmatizes women who find

pleasure in sex apart from love. (Seidman 1991: 145–146)

## The Singles Culture

Hefner and Brown became cultural entrepreneurs and ideologues of the sexual revolution. Through their writings and publications, they promoted a new sexual ethic to increasingly unmarried generations of young Americans. This audience created the **singles culture**, whose members sought partners in sex rather than marriage. The postindustrial economy gave men and women more disposable income and leisure time than ever before. Creative economic entrepreneurs helped think of ways for them to spend it. They opened singles bars, started dating services, and reframed a series of products—from the miniskirt and stereos to cigarettes, soft drinks, and cars—by connecting them to the titillating eroticism of unmarried sex. They also published guidebooks for those who were not yet sexually initiated. Constructing sex as a series of technological gestures whose aim was to stimulate and receive erotic pleasure, these sex manuals became much-talked-about best sellers. Alex Comfort, the editor of *The Joy of Sex* (1972), described his goal as teaching Americans "to use sex as play." And in *Everything You Always Wanted to Know About Sex but Were*

**Free-floating eroticism** Sexuality that is no longer hard-wired, rigid, and morally stigmatized as a result of having become less regulated, minimized, and moralized in the late twentieth century, when the erotic sphere moved into the center stage of public life.

**Singles culture** An aspect of the sexual revolution whereby single people sought partners in sex rather than marriage—specifically, at a time when publications such as *Playboy* and *Cosmopolitan* promoted a new sexual ethic and the postindustrial economy provided men and women with more free time.

*Afraid to Ask* (1969), Dr. David Reuben described the rationale for "funsex" as "the sheer physical and emotional exhilaration of feeling all the good feelings that come from a complete sexual experience," the goal of which is "to obtain the maximum of pleasure from sexual activity without doing damage to anyone" (quoted in Seidman 1991: 127).

## The Pill

During the late 1960s, the sexual revolution was helped along by new social movements and by technological developments alike. The youth "counterculture" responded to such postmodern developments as postindustrialism and extended socialization, its roots having been formed in the cauldron of rock-and-roll music and antiwar criticism. (See the related discussion in Chapter 5, on socialization and the life cycle.) These alienated young people rejected what they regarded as their parents' culture of sexual denial and sublimation. Through their music, their experimentation with drugs, their dressing styles, and their most intimate practices, the members of the counterculture devoted themselves to an erotically centered way of life: "A movement to uncouple eros from love might not have developed had there not existed a culture that increasingly celebrated self-expression as a valued path to self-fulfillment. With a rising generation already focused on personal and expressive concerns and embroiled in a generational conflict, there materialized a social stratum motivated to spearhead a movement to unbound eros from love" (Seidman 1991: 126). This radical eroticism quickly bubbled up to the adult mainstream. Sexual retreats providing privacy for sexual experimentation, such as Sandstone in the Santa Monica mountains, sprouted up like spring clover in the late 1960s and early 1970s. Novelists such as Gay Talese (*Thy Neighbor's Wife,* 1980), John Updike (*Couples,* 1968), and Erica Jong (*Fear of Fly-*

*ing,* 1973) memorialized swinging adults breaking apart the modernist sexual package.

The cultural and social possibilities for separating sex from the responsibilities of marriage and parenting were undergirded by a revolution in reproductive technology (see Table 6.3). The invention and inexpensive distribution of the birth control pill allowed women to block the fertilization of their eggs. For the first time, women could exercise independent control over whether they became pregnant as the result of sex. (For further discussion of this subject, see Chapter 7, on marriage and the family.)

> Due to the "pill" and an increase in mutually expected self-restraint (mutual consent) in interactions, the dangers and fears connected with sex diminished to such a degree that there was an acceleration in the emancipation of sexual emotions and impulses. Women's sexual desires were taken more seriously: men became more strongly directed at clitoral stimulation and their aversion to oral sex diminished considerably—from more than 50 percent reported in the early 1970s to about 20 percent 10 years later. This means that increasing numbers of men learned to enjoy the woman's enjoyment and that many women opened up to sexual fantasies and titillations. The dominant image of single females ... changed accordingly from "failed-as-a-woman" and "sexually deficient" into the opposite: sexy and independent. In a relatively short period of time, the relatively autonomous strength of carnal desire became acknowledged and respected. (Wouters 1998: 190–191)

It was this kind of liberation from historical sexual and moral constraints that Erica Jong expressed in her description of the "zipless fuck," the central sexual scene in her best-selling novel *Fear of Flying* (1973). Despite Jong's admission that she herself had "never had one," the zipless fuck immediately entered the American popular

**TABLE 6.3 Trends in Contraceptive Use**

| Current Contraceptive Status and Method | 1982 | 1995 | 2002 |
|---|---|---|---|
| Female sterilization | 12.9 | 17.8 | 16.7 |
| Pill | 15.6 | 17.3 | 18.9 |
| Condom | 6.7 | 13.1 | 11.1 |
| Other methods | 20.5 | 16.0 | 15.2 |
| Nonusers | 44.3 | 35.8 | 38.1 |

| Year of First Sexual Intercourse | Used Any Method | Pill | Condom |
|---|---|---|---|
| Before 1980 | 43.0 | 12.5 | 21.7 |
| 1980–1989 | 61.3 | 19.9 | 38.1 |
| 1990–1994 | 70.3 | 16.3 | 57.9 |
| 1995–1998 | 72.8 | 18.8 | 61.1 |
| 1999–2002 | 78.8 | 21.1 | 67.3 |

*Source:* Adapted from Mosher et al. (2004).

ties. By concentrating and segregating homosexuals, it allowed individuals to feel less isolated and provided a separate and relatively protected space for their sexual activity. By the eve of the 1960s sexual revolution, homosexuality had become a new form of identity and a source of solidarity:

Under the impact of a socially influential medical-scientific discourse, "the homosexual" stepped forward as a unique human figure imagined to possess his/her own distinctive psychic and social nature. ... Documents indicate the existence of nascent homosexual networks as early as the 1880s; the heightened self-consciousness implied in the homosexual label greatly facilitated the formation of homosexual lifestyles and subcultures. By the 1940s and 1950s, homosexuality was a basis of individual identity and group life that was widely acknowledged in American culture. (Seidman 1991: 123)

What changed with postmodernity was that this underground identity emerged from the shadows into full and sometimes shocking public view. Reframed as simply another form of nonprocreative, consensual sexuality, it became much less subject to stigma and sanction. During the 1960s and 1970s, homosexuals became symbolically reconfigured as "gays" and "lesbians." The free-floating eroticism of gay men fit well with the expressive individualism of the sexual revolution, and the female-oriented sexuality of lesbians followed naturally from one strand of radical feminism. In the wake of the civil rights and antiwar movements, homosexuals formed a mass-based political movement of their own. They demanded legal recognition for their now very public departures from heterosexuality. In the 1980s, the HIV/AIDS epidemic threatened to reverse this postmodernizing process, causing homosexuality to be stigmatized as the source of a new, rapidly

lexicon as a revolutionary feminine ideal: "The incident has all the swift compression of a dream and is seemingly free of all remorse and guilt; because there is no talk of her late husband or of his fiancée; because there is no rationalizing; because there is no talk at all. The zipless fuck is absolutely pure. It is free of ulterior motives. There is no power game. ... No one is trying to prove anything or get anything out of anyone. The zipless fuck is the purest thing there is" (Jong 1973: 14).

## Homosexuality

Just as modern asceticism had the unintended effect of creating a powerful oppositional eroticism, so its emphatic and exclusive legitimation of heterosexuality had the effect of creating "the homosexual." Despite historical restrictions, the actual practice of male and female homosexuality remained constant during the modern period. In fact, modern repression created *new* opportuni-

The "sexual revolution," when the pill became available in the 1960s and abortion was legalized in the 1970s, changed life for American women. (Bettmann/Corbis)

spreading, and dreaded disease. In the long run, however, the reaction to the epidemic actually contributed to less reactive, more public, and more responsive approaches to both hetero- and homosexuality. To prevent HIV infection, public health officials campaigned for "safe sex" practices. Sex education classes became required for elementary school children across the nation. Condoms were widely advertised and often publicly distributed. As the HIV virus spread into the heterosexual community as well, safe practices, not sexual choice, became the concern of the day.

## THE WOMEN'S MOVEMENT

As the transition from Helen Gurley Brown to Erica Jong suggests, the revolution in women's roles was intrinsic to the sexual revolution. The transfor-mation of women's position in modern society had begun already in the nineteenth century (again, see Chapter 7) when female activists drew attention to such "women's issues" as male drunkenness and female prostitution and, soon after, when suffragettes initiated a mass movement demanding the women's vote. By 1920, women had received the right to vote, and changes in sex roles had already proceeded to the point where 400,000 women were members of the professional labor force, albeit mostly employed in gender-typed occupations such as teaching. By 1930, fully half of America's professional workforce were women. Between 1900 and 1940, the percentage of married white women employed outside the home had increased 300 percent, from 4 percent in 1900 to 12 percent forty years later (Seidman 1991: 68).

As a result of these political, cultural, and economic developments, the carefully wrought boundary line that had excluded sexuality from public life began to show signs of disintegration. With the two sexes coming into public contact so much more frequently, the social circulation of eros became greatly intensified.

Sociologists have found the proximity of male and female co-workers within organizations to be a strong determinant of sexual relationships (Hearn and Parkin 1987). It is much more difficult to maintain sexual taboos in the context of continuous face-to-face relations. As women entered the economy, workplaces became permeated by implicitly sexual behavior, such as "gazing" (eyeing from a distance), suggestive dressing and personal gestures, sexual jokes, and secret personal communications. Even today, workplaces remain "the prime area for making social/sexual contacts, especially for a newcomer to a city" (Miles 1985: 112), and "the most common place for affairs to start is at work" (Laming 1985). During the years of the sexual revolution, as female work participation more than doubled, one sociologist observed that "the amount of sexual energy circulating in any office is awe-inspiring, and given the slightest sanction and opportunity it bursts out" (Korda 1972: 108).

If the growing economic independence of women made it harder to maintain patriarchal control, the enlargement and empowering of the female libido during the sexual revolution made it that much more difficult. The second wave of American feminism emerged in the late 1960s. In these early years, feminist consciousness was often demonstrated via public dramas that intertwined women's demands for political power with their attacks on sexual control. At the 1968 Miss America pageant, the women's liberation movement protested by dumping symbols of what they called "female enslavement"—bras, girdles, high heels, false eyelashes, hair curlers—into a giant "freedom trashcan" (D'Emilio and Freedman 1988: 302).

The relationship between the transformation of women's roles and postmodern sexuality was by no means linear and straightforward. By the early 1970s, advocates of an influential version of radi-

cal feminism began to complain that the ethic of **sexual liberation** might simply be perpetuating female subordination in a new form. True female liberation, these critics argued, would entail more, not less, control by women over their bodies, and sex would be limited to ethically controlled, loving relationships. The mainstream public voice of this new kind of radical feminism, *Ms.* magazine, which first appeared in 1972, prominently displayed these concerns. In its first issue, for example, a feminist criticized the new postrevolutionary sex rules because they "created unpredictable bonds," adding, "I didn't realize that intimacy, physical intimacy … created [such] highly unprogressive … bursts of possessiveness and jealousy." The next year, another *Ms.* magazine contributor condemned *The Joy of Sex* as a "very male-oriented marriage manual," and still another writer reacted to female-authored sex manuals with this declaration: "I hear echoes of the sexual revolution battle cry all over again: let's free women sexually so that they'll be more available for fucking" (in Seidman 1991: 145).

In several respects, the sexual revolution ended towards the end of the 1970s, as the voices raised against sexual violence became louder and louder. At that time … in addition to sexual assault and rape, sex with children—incest in particular—and pornography also came to be included in the category of sexual violence. In the early 1980s, sexual harassment was added. As the women's movement turned against sexual violence, attention shifted

**Sexual liberation** The separation of sex from procreation. The pluralizing and normalizing of sexual activity—and especially the increased sexual freedom of women—have been described as sexual liberation. But to some observers, particularly feminists, sexual liberation was viewed as sexual oppression on the grounds that it contributed to higher rates of sexual violence and did little to reduce or challenge patriarchy and status inequality.

from differences between generations [in regard to sexual emancipation] to differences between the sexes. Opposition to the sexual practices and morality of older generations diminished, while opposition to those of the dominant [male] sex gained momentum. ... In the women's movement, heterosexuality was sometimes branded as "having sex with your oppressor." (Wouters 1998: 192–193)

By the late 1980s, this strand of stridently anti-erotic feminism had begun to fade, though the problems to which it referred very much remained. Insofar as men continue to occupy more powerful and prestigious social positions, the detached, free-floating character of postmodern sexual life will continue to be riskier for women than for men. Meanwhile, with the decline in radical feminist opposition to eroticism, its equation of male domination with heterosexuality has laid the basis for the growth of lesbian social movements.

## CONCLUSION

According to the most recent systematic sociological survey on the subject of sex (Laumann et al. 1994), most Americans no longer believe that only married people should have sex. Their practices match their words, for most also report that they have not been sexually monogamous over their lifetimes. A sizable minority rejects almost any restriction on nonmarried heterosexual sex, except for the partner's consent (see Table 6.4).

Nothing could more emphatically illustrate how sex has changed than a story recently published under the headline "Study Finds That Women Pressure Many Fraternity Pledges into Sex":

Among students pledging Greek groups, men are almost as likely to be victims of women's sexual coercion as women are to have unwanted sex with men, according to a study by the University of

**SURVEY QUESTION:** There's been a lot of discussion about the way morals and attitudes about sex are changing in this country. If a man and woman have sex relations before marriage, do you think it is always wrong, almost always wrong, wrong only sometimes, or not wrong at all?

Washington's Addictive Behaviors Research Center. In a survey of 165 men and 131 women at the Seattle institution—all of them new members of fraternities or sororities—34 men and 36 women said they had experienced unwanted sexual contact. An additional 17 men and 7 women said they had instigated such sexual contact. The research [was] published in the current issue of *Sex Roles*, a quarterly journal. ... "Our culture in general has a hard time believing that young men can have sex they don't want," says Mary E. Larimer, principal investigator on the study, an assistant professor of psychology at Washington. "We simply fail to ask the question of whether men can be recipients of sexual coercion." Most of the male victims reported giving in to sexual arousal or verbal pressure by women. The women were more likely to have been subjected to physical force or plied with alcohol or drugs. ("Study Finds" 1999: A51)

Once fundamentally restricted, sexuality in postmodern society has become infused with eroticism. And sex itself, no longer emphatically gendered, is now regulated less by power than by a kind of "communicative ethic" (Seidman in Smelser and Alexander 1999: 168–189). This new ethic is exemplified by the "sexual consent" workshops that Antioch College required of every entering student:

They had heard about Antioch's sexual offense policy. ... Were the 13 pages of legalistic "do's and "don'ts" as preposterous as [some] reports, the new students wondered, or were they as liberating as their hall advisers promised? ...

At the lectern was Karen Hall ... facing her first audience, an auditorium full of suspicious

**TABLE 6.4  American Attitudes Toward Premarital Sex**

| | Sex before Marriage | | | |
|---|---|---|---|---|
| | Always Wrong | Almost Always Wrong | Sometimes Wrong | Not Wrong at All |
| 1974 | 33.0% | 12.7% | 23.6% | 30.7% |
| 1994 | 26.0% | 10.1% | 20.4% | 43.5% |
| 2004 | 27.0% | 8.9% | 17.8% | 46.3% |

*Source:* Davis, Smith, and Marsden (2005).

single," or having a sexually transmitted disease presented a defining aspect of personhood that society had to recognize. But today that is precisely what is being demanded. As Weeks (1998: 36–37) points out, "It is commonplace for many previously marginalized people—those belonging to sexual minorities—to define themselves both in terms of personal and collective identities by their sexual attributes, and to claim recognition, rights, and respect as a consequence."

People do not go around saying "I want to be a sexual citizen." It is not an identity which people aspire to, nor is it an explicit project which people usually group around. Nevertheless … the idea of sexual or intimate citizenship is a sensitizing concept which alerts us to new concerns, hitherto marginalized in public discourse: with the body, its possibilities, needs and pleasures; with new sexualized identities; and with the forces that inhibit their free, consensual development in a democratic polity committed to full and equal citizenship. … It has a positive content, in the articulation of new claims to rights and "sexual justice." But it also offers a sharp critique of traditional discourses on citizenship, and on the occlusions and hesitations of contemporary debates. (Weeks 1998: 37–38)

boys. Ms. Hall told them that the Antioch policy required "willing and verbal consent" for each individual sexual act. She told them that "asking do you want to have sex is not enough" because sex means something different to different people. … "Each step of the way, you have to ask," said Ms. Hall. … If you want to take her blouse off, you have to ask. If you want to touch her breast, you have to ask. If you want to move your hand down to her genitals, you have to ask. If you want to put your finger inside her, you have to ask."

"Whaaat!" the boys cried, in a bleat of fear and anger.

"Really?" the girls inquired, in a rising inflection of embarrassment and relief. …

The code, revised several times amid much overheated rhetoric and some abridgment of civil rights, is largely the product of discussion among students and requires young people to talk about sex, even as they do it. (Gross 1993: 1)

Once regarded as a natural, unalterable fact, sexuality has been "sociologized." It has become part of the more inclusive, more democratic culture of postmodern times. In contemporary societies, people are demanding what Jeffrey Weeks calls **sexual citizenship.** Thirty years ago, nobody would have suggested that "being queer," "being

**Sexual citizenship** A term, coined by Jeffrey Weeks, referring to the efforts of previously marginalized sexual minorities who wish to define themselves by their sexual identities and thereby claim social status and recognition. Sexual citizenship grants the individual a number of rights, including but not limited to the right to contraceptive technologies, the freedom of sexual choice, and spousal, parental, and grandparental rights regardless of orientation.

As a result of the movement toward sexual citizenship, the phrase "regardless of sexual orientation" has been added to the demand that people be respected "regardless of race, religion, or gender," and agencies have become more open and truthful about sexually transmitted diseases. Sexual citizenship means the right to be protected from such diseases if at all possible, regardless of one's wealth. It means the right for every person to have access to old and new reproduction technologies, from condoms to birth control pills to Viagra. It means freedom of sexual choice, but also freedom from sexual violence and coercion. It means having the same right to be parents as heterosexuals have, and having the same right to be grandparents as do heterosexual parents:

> Across the country ... open homosexuals cut an unprecedented profile in politics, on television and movies, and in the mundane vicissitudes of even small-town America ... More couples are having or adopting children, and so engaging in the civic life of schools, day-care centers and sports leagues. Employers are increasingly extending health benefits to same-sex partners. For gay teens, whose experience has often been one of dark isolation, about 700 high schools now have gay-straight alliances. (Leland et al. 2000: 46)

As gay parents and their children are becoming more visible in the grocery store, at the P.T.A. and on television shows ... some gays and lesbians say they are starting to feel a new element in the family weather: The Nudge. Parents who once resigned themselves, however painfully, to what they assumed would be a life without grandchildren are now starting to do something about it. ... "My mother keeps telling me, 'come on, where's the grandchild?'" said Cyndi Harrison, a nurse practitioner who lives with her [female] partner in Los Angeles. Ms. Harrison, who is undergoing artificial insemination, ... added[,] "Even my stepmother says, 'You guys would make such good parents, you have good careers. What's taking you [so long]? It would make your father so happy." (Leland 2000: F1)

Sexual citizenship means, finally, the equal right to be viewed as attractive and cool: "Gay content and gay characters—increasingly common accessories on shows aimed at trendy young adults—serve as a sort of coolness shorthand, bestowing hipness on their shows and audience, serving as a conduit to cred for the majority group, just as racial minorities have in the past. From Norman Mailer's White Negro [in the 1950s] we've gone to the Gay Hetero" (Poniewozik 1999: 117).

The emergence of postmodern forms of sexuality hasn't swept aside everything in its path. Some of the attitudes, organizations, and legal sanctions that constructed modern sexuality not only remain but have fought against the new ways. The result is a tensely divided society, with sexual backlash confronting sexual revolution. In 1994, a firestorm of conservative public opinion forced Democratic president Bill Clinton to fire his longtime political associate Joycelyn Elders, the Surgeon General of the United States, because she made public remarks about the legitimacy of masturbation. Surveys of gay college students conducted in the late 1980s showed that about a fifth had been threatened with violence and more than half verbally harassed (Brooke 1998: A19). Despite the growing legalization of gay parenting, more than half of America's states have adopted laws prohibiting gay marriages. And in Wyoming specifically, voters have defeated a law outlawing discrimination against homosexuals on three separate occasions. As we saw at the beginning of this chapter, the tragic case of Matthew Shepard demonstrates that it is still very dangerous in some parts of even a postmodern society to be openly gay.

As summarized in Table 6.5, a total of 1,792 incidents of anti–lesbian, gay, bisexual, and transsexual (LGBT) violence were reported to the National Coalition of Anti-Violence Programs (NCAVP) in

2006. The total number of victims was 2,131. Both of these figures represent a 4 percent increase from the previous year. Sadly, the actual frequency of violent incidents is likely much higher. Statistics on hate crimes (criminal acts motivated by prejudice) are inaccurate because of underreporting. Victims hesitate to report offenses to the police or community service agencies (such as the Anti-Violence Project) because they fear further retaliation from offenders, abuse from the police, or being "outed" to friends and co-workers. As also indicated in Table 6.5, 10 percent of victims are heterosexual. The NCAVP has suggested two explanations for this surprisingly high proportion: (1) A large number of transgendered people identify their orientation as heterosexual, and (2) many heterosexuals become victims of anti-LGBT violence because they are perceived to be LGBT (Patton 2005).

But the problems generated by postmodern sexuality are not limited to the backlash against it. They are also related to the ambiguity of free-floating sexuality itself. The very fact that contemporary sexuality is regulated by a communicative ethic means that there are no clear standards regarding the "how," "with whom," or "when" of sex. As Zygmunt Bauman (1998: 31) puts it, "the specter of sex" now haunts "every offer of friendship and every manifestation of a deeper-than-average interest in another person … [whether it be a] casual remark on the beauty or charm of a workmate … [or even] an offer of a cup of coffee." When sex becomes free-floating, it can emerge at any time in "company offices and college seminar rooms" and be read into "every smile, gaze, [and] form of address" (Bauman 1998: 31).

Sexuality has become separated not only from the restrictive bindings of religion and gender domination but also from morality and love. And, indeed, the liberation of sexuality has made it more difficult to maintain the kinds of long-term, committed relationships that foster the morality of love. As one sociologist has observed: "In these years, increasing numbers of women and men will

**TABLE 6.5  Hate Crimes Reported to the NCAVP**

| Crime or Offense | Number of Incidents[a] in 2006 |
|---|---|
| Murder | 11 |
| Sexual Assault/Rape | 63 |
| Vandalism | 115 |
| Discrimination | 409 |
| Assault/Attempted Assault | 551 |
| Intimidation | 737 |
| Verbal Harassment | 842 |
| **Total Number of Incidents** | **2,728** |

| Sexual Orientation of Victim | % |
|---|---|
| Lesbian or Gay | 78 |
| Heterosexual | 10 |
| Organization[b] | 2 |
| Bisexual | 5 |
| Self-Identified[c] | 3 |
| Questioning/Unsure | 2 |

*Notes:*

[a]A single incident can include multiple offenses.

[b]The category "organizations" refers to LGBT community organizations and advocacy groups that are also targets of violence.

[c]"Self-identified" is an open category on the NCAVP incident report form that allows victims to describe their own sexual orientation if they do not feel that the available five categories (gay, lesbian, bisexual, heterosexual, questioning/unsure) adequately describe them.

*Source:* Patton (2007).

have experienced with greater intensity that the relationship between carnal desires and the longing for enduring intimacy is an uneasy one, and that the continuation and maintenance of a (love) relationship has on the whole become more demanding" (Wouters 1998: 192).

Another sociologist has linked this splitting of sex and love to the contemporary preoccupation with the "love affair." She writes that "the 'affair' is related to the transformations undergone by sexuality after the Second World War," suggesting that "in its intrinsic transience and affirmation of pleasure, novelty and excitement, the affair may be dubbed a postmodern experience" (Illouz 1998: 176). An embodiment of free-floating sexuality, affairs provide "experiences of pure sensation, desire, [and] pleasures," yet such experiences are often viewed by lovers as "nonmediated by reason." The very intensity of affairs, moreover, makes them highly discontinuous, thereby fragmenting "the experience of love into separate emotional units." This conclusion may be overly pessimistic but it points, nonetheless, to the ambiguities that continue to beset sexuality, even in a postmodern society: "The contemporary romantic self is marked by its persistent, Sisyphus-style attempt to conjure up the local and fleeting intensity of the love affair within long-term global narratives of love (such as marriage), to reconcile an overarching narrative of enduring love with the fragmentary intensity of affairs" (Illouz 1998: 178).

Sexuality remains a social rather than an individual story, even when it has been freed.

# EXERCISES

## Exercise 1

In this chapter, we have seen how an advance in reproductive technology—the pill—gave women control over when or whether they became pregnant and contributed to the "sexual revolution" of the 1960s. Although new contraceptive technologies have since been introduced, the pill remains the most common method used by women today (again, see Table 6.3). But what would happen if a pill for men were introduced? Would you expect it to become a popular method of birth control for heterosexual couples, equaling or surpassing the current rate at which the female pill is used? Why or why not? Do you think feminists would view the male pill as an advance for women or as a step backward?

## Exercise 2

Recall a few classic or current movies in the popular culture genre of the "teen movie" (e.g., *Sixteen Candles*, *American Pie*). Do you think these movies represent or promote a free-floating sexuality liberated from the restrictions of modernity? Or do some modernist assumptions still lurk in the background of such films? As you ponder your answers, consider some of the issues we have covered in this chapter: naturalism, attitudes toward nonprocreative sex, the portrayal of homosexuals, gender.

## Exercise 3

An important concept introduced in this chapter is that of sexual citizenship. What claims to sexual citizenship have you seen on campus? In what ways have sexual minorities at your university organized to claim the right for recognition? What strategies are they implementing to achieve equal rights? Have any of these initiatives provoked controversy or met with resistance?

# STUDY QUESTIONS

1. Describe the difference between naturalist and constructivist approaches to sexuality. What is the role of society in each approach?

2. Which of these two approaches—naturalism or constructivism—has been characterized as essentialist? What is essentialism, and on what grounds has it been criticized?

3. Briefly describe the ancient Greek concept of "self-cultivation." In what ways did this ideal of ethical conduct apply to sexual relations? How does it help explain the status of male homosexual relationships in ancient Greek society?

4. According to Max Weber, how did the Protestant Reformation make modernity possible? How did Puritanism transform both the private bedrooms and the public sphere of early-modern Europe?

5. What is the erotic sphere? How was it created, how are nonprocreative sexual practices viewed from within it, and how does it create a tension within modernity?

6. Describe the emerging postmodern understanding of sexuality. What does it have in common with the modern understanding of sexuality, and how is it different? What are the social causes contributing to the rise of postmodern sex?

7. How did Freud's psychoanalytic theory and Kinsey's research on sexual behavior help unravel modernist understandings about sexuality?

8. What is sexual citizenship? What rights accompany the claim to sexual citizenship?

## FURTHER READING

Bem, Sandra Lipstiz. 1995. "Dismantling Gender Polarization and Compulsory Heterosexuality: Should We Turn the Volume Down or Up?" *Journal of Sex Research* 32, no. 4: 329–334.

Chauncey, George. 1995. *Gay New York: Gender, Urban Culture, and the Making of the Gay Male World, 1890–1940.* New York: Basic Books.

Fausto-Sterling, Anne. 2000. *Sexing the Body: Gender Politics and the Construction of Sexuality.* New York: Basic Books.

Foucault, Michel. 1978–1986. *The History of Sexuality*, 3 vols. New York: Pantheon.

Heasley, Robert, and Betsy Crane, eds. 2002. *Sexual Lives: A Reader on the Theories and Realities of Human Sexualities.* McGraw-Hill Humanities/Social Sciences/Languages.

Seidman, Steven. 2002. *Beyond the Closet: The Transformation of Gay and Lesbian Life.* New York: Routledge.

Wonders, Nancy A., and Raymond Michalowski. 2001. "Bodies, Borders, and Sex Tourism in a Globalized World: A Tale of Two Cities—Amsterdam and Havana." *Social Problems* 48, no. 4: 545–571.

# chapter 7

# Marriage and the Family

In May 1992, the vice president of the United States, Dan Quayle, gave a speech to the Commonwealth Club of California (Rosenthal 1992). It became a widely reported media event and, later, a minor scandal.

The second most powerful public official in the nation did not address any pressing economic, political, or international issues on this occasion. Nor did he lay out any new policy proposals of the Republican administration. Instead, he launched an attack on Murphy Brown, the famous lead in an Emmy-winning situation comedy bearing her name.

Murphy Brown was played by former model Candice Bergen. In real life, she was married at the time to avant-garde French film director Louis Malle, with whom she had one daughter. In her television life as Murphy Brown, Bergen was still beautiful but now single and without children. An ambitious and successful television news reporter, Murphy had only one weakness: a fondness for pontification.

In the show's most notorious subplot, Murphy had become pregnant by a man she never intended to marry, and decided to continue the pregnancy and raise the child herself. These developments brought high ratings, and Murphy-the-single-mother's frustrations and satisfactions became a mainstay in the still-popular program's final years.

Yet the same fictional events produced outrage among many other Americans, perhaps even among some otherwise loyal viewers. Vice President Quayle gave voice to this conservative anger when he attacked Murphy Brown for not getting married to her fictional baby's father:

It doesn't help matters when prime-time TV has Murphy Brown—a character who supposedly epitomizes today's intelligent, highly paid, professional woman—mocking the importance of fathers, by bearing a child alone, and calling it just another "lifestyle choice." ... Ultimately, marriage is a moral issue that requires cultural consensus

and the use of social sanctions. Bearing babies irresponsibly is, simply, wrong. Failing to support children one has fathered is wrong. We must be unequivocal about this. (Quoted in Rosenthal 1992)

Quayle accused Murphy of being not only foolish but morally irresponsible for choosing to raise her child without a father, assailing the "dangerous" decision as setting a course that could only hinder the future development of the child, whether girl or boy.

This conflict between a fictional character in a television sitcom and the vice president of the United States spoke volumes about the tense standoff over "family values" developing throughout the industrialized and now postmodernizing

When Murphy Brown, a popular television character, chose to bear a child out of wedlock, many conservative Americans felt it offended their "family values." (Bureau L.A. Collection/Corbis)

world. Media representatives pounced on this high-powered public attack on a television character, characterizing it as not just unjustified but unfair interference in the freedom of artistic expression. A segment of the American public agreed, finding it mindlessly reactionary, or just plain mindless. But for many other Americans, Mr. Quayle's attack on Murphy Brown made him a hero.

Responding to the "family values" attack, Murphy Brown in her television show, and Candice Bergen in her real life, campaigned against the Bush-Quayle Republican ticket in the 1992 presidential election. The Republicans lost, and the "baby-boomer" generation came to power for the first time. The baby-boomer-in-chief was President Bill Clinton, married to an ambitious career woman, father of one. He would later prove to be famously susceptible to the kinds of temptations that have made marital and family stability so fragile in this postmodern world.

## AN INDIVIDUAL OR A SOCIAL STORY?

This tale of politics and entertainment surely can be seen as the product of two unique individuals, each dealing forcefully with specific situations. Both the character Murphy Brown and the actress Candice Bergen were headstrong and independent women. They had successful careers and were admired by the men whose institutions they helped sustain. Murphy's decision not to get married seemed consistent with her character. As the situation comedy made abundantly clear, there had never been a man who could "tame" this larger-than-life, beautiful, and brilliant career woman. And as implied by the feminist values that informed the show, there was no man who deserved to become her husband. Murphy's decision to carry her baby through pregnancy and raise the child on her own, moreover, seemed not only in

character but appropriate to her time of life. Her biological clock was ticking; there might not be much time left. The decision was also financially viable. Murphy was wealthy and could hire all the extra help she would need.

If Murphy turned out to be right in her decision as a sitcom figure—she, her baby, and the show's ratings flourished—such an outcome might be taken simply as testimony to the brilliance of the show's writers and producers. If Candice Bergen were right in her real-life decision to attack the vice president, it might be taken as a demonstration of her individual political smarts.

The vice president's orientation to this fictional situation can be seen as following in just as likely a manner from his individual character. Dan Quayle had been raised and had prospered in a Midwestern "heartland" family. He was happily married to a woman who had given up her legal career to raise the couple's three children and to help her husband in his career. Just as Murphy Brown generalized from her own personal decisions, Mr. Quayle presented his own life story as an appropriate model for other Americans. He and his fellow Republicans wore their "family values" on their political sleeves: Doing so helped them rally the party faithful, and conservative independents as well, to their political side. Turning Murphy's "wildness" and "indiscretion" into a political issue seemed to be in Quayle's political self-interest. If he ended up having been wrong in this judgment, it would have been possible to see this mistake simply as the result of political misjudgment.

But this immortal all-American encounter surely transcended the individual characters involved in it, both real and fictitious. For their personal decisions took place against the background of fundamental, unexpected, and, for many Americans, deeply unnerving changes in the nature of marriage and family. It was only in the context of such drastic institutional and cultural change that their decisions as individuals made sense. There was, in other words, not only an individual but a sociological side to the fight between Vice President Quayle and Murphy Brown.

One way of getting some perspective on these changes is to look back at the America of the 1950s—specifically, at an equally popular situation comedy called *The Ozzie and Harriet Show*. It was a story about the life and times of a perky and cheerful all-American family. The happily married parents consisted of Ozzie, a hardworking and earnest father with a dry sense of humor, and Harriet, a dedicated and modest but resourceful stay-at-home mom. They had two gregarious sons, David and Ricky, who got into a lot of trouble but, by the end of each episode, showed themselves to be grateful, obedient, and, for the most part, high

The stereotypical American white, middle-class nuclear family was portrayed on many television shows in the 1960s, such as *The Ozzie and Harriet Show*. (AP Photo/ A & E)

achieving. What a contrast this faithful representation of the ideals of American marriage and family in the 1950s presented to the shrunken but quite possibly equally representative snapshot of 1990s marriage and family life portrayed by *Murphy Brown!*

## MARRIAGE AND FAMILY: THE SOCIAL FORCES OF CHANGE

There are many statistics pointing to the social forces that changed the "Ozzie and Harriet family" into "Murphy Brown." They suggest that, no matter what his individual motives or abilities, Dan Quayle probably was bound to fail in his campaign against the fictional heroine. For although the vice president tried to define Murphy Brown as singular and deviant, in reality she was anything but.

Today, more children in the United Sates live with single mothers than in families with a breadwinner father and a homemaker mom (Stacey 1996: 45). From 1940 to 1990, in fact, the proportion of single-income families in the United States declined from nearly 70 percent to about 20 percent. Another figure that would have astonished Ozzie and Harriet and their millions of loyal 1950s viewers is that, at the end of the twentieth century, one-third of all children in America are born to unwed mothers, as often by choice as by necessity.

Single motherhood is not just a luxury pursuit for such bored celebrities as Madonna and Rosie. It has become a widespread phenomenon among twenty- and thirty-something women impatient with the dwindling marriage market.

The National Center for Health reported this week that births to unwed mothers are at an all-time high. The mothers of almost a third of the 3.94 million babies born in 1998 were single women. Many weren't the prototypical unwed teenage moms—teens' birth rates were down—but women in their 20s and 30s. Donna E. Shalala, secretary of the federal Health and Human Services Department, calls this trend toward single motherhood "troubling." … Not long ago, Madonna occupied the fringes of social trends. Now she seems almost normal. (Holmes 2000)

## Was the Ozzie and Harriet Family "Natural"?

In the 1950s, and for at least a century before, the "all-American family" of Ozzie and Harriet fame was considered *natural*—both quintessentially modern and traditional at the same time. As an immensely popular 1950s song put it, "Love and marriage, love and marriage, go together like a horse and carriage. … You can't have one without the other!" It was natural for people who loved each other to get married, just as it was unnatural for loving people to have sexual relations outside of marriage. It was natural for a man and a woman—but unnatural, abnormal, and unstable for two people of the same sex—to be bound permanently to each other through sexual love. Heterosexual married lovers would naturally have children. They would naturally stay married, and their families would naturally consist only of their children and themselves.

Recent social changes have cast doubt on just how "natural" these modern models of marriage and family were. In 1970, there were just over 500,000 unmarried heterosexual couples living together in the United States, a figure already higher as a result of the cultural revolution of the '60s. By 1980, that figure had tripled, and by 1990 it had doubled again. In 2000, the U.S. Census Bureau (2001) recorded 3.8 million "unmarried partner" households, more than six times the figure of just two decades before. During the same period, the number of single-parent families headed by women more than tripled (3 million in 1970 increased to 10 million in 2000). The number of same-sex persons living together also soared.

Not only "marriage" but also what was considered a family had dramatically changed. In 1960, 75 percent of all households consisted of married couples, and more than half of these included children (Ahlburg and De Vita 1992). By 2000, only 53 percent of households consisted of married couples, only a quarter of which included children. Today, the proportion of unmarried-partner households with children under 18 is about the same as that of married-couple households (41 percent of cohabiting couples compared to 46 percent of married couples). The number of persons living alone or with unrelated other persons has sharply risen in turn. By a ratio of three to one, people surveyed in a 1990 *Newsweek* magazine poll defined the family as "a group of people who love and care for each other" rather than, as in earlier times, "a group of people related by blood, marriage, or adoption" (Stacey 1996: 9). (Figure 7.1 summarizes the changes that households, by type, underwent between 1970 and 2000.)

## After Naturalism: Postmodern Constructions

In the last three decades, as modern society has fitfully become postmodern, the patina of "naturalness" that characterized postwar marriage and family patterns has gradually been scraped away. It is now clear that such patterns were historically specific arrangements rather than "modern" ones in the sense of being rational, universal, positive, and adaptive in a for-all-time way. The departure from these modern forms of marriage and family has involved extraordinary transformations, a process that we are right in the middle of now. This process has responded to political, economic, and cultural shifts, but, above all, it involves changes in the **micro-institutions** that structure socialization and affectual life. These are institutions that relate to our sense of personal security and shape the kinds of satisfaction we experience in our personal

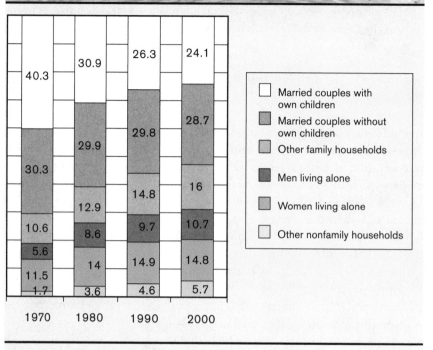

FIGURE 7.1 Households by Type: Selected Years, 1970–2000 (percent distribution)

Source: Fields and Casper (2001).

**Micro-institutions** Institutions that structure socialization and the affectual life. These institutions, such as the family, tend to be personal and private; they relate to our sense of personal security and shape the satisfaction we find in our personal interactions.

interactions. It is hardly surprising that deep and unexpected changes in such structures have caused immense confusion and anxiety.

Our goal here is to sort out this confusion. The chaos of transition should not obscure the fact that new structures are continually being created. There is not only decline and loss but also progress and construction. What is happening to all the other institutions in our postmodern age is happening also to marriage and family. What were once thought to be their "naturally given" identities have been stripped away, and their cultural and constructed quality has become evident. This revelatory process has created enormous problems and pain, as we struggle to sort out situations we never before imagined. But it has also allowed an extraordinary opening up of these central social

institutions to broad cultural reconsideration and to radical social change. Men and women, parents and children, grandparents and aunts and uncles, government agencies and new kinds of professional caretakers—all are party to the fundamentally different postmodern patterns of marriage and family that are struggling to emerge.

## Modern Sociology: Naturalizing Marriage and Family

In the 1950s and 1960s, and indeed for many decades before, modern sociology reflected the same naturalistic approach to marriage and the family as Ozzie and Harriet did. One textbook defined marriage, for example, as "(a) socially legitimate sexual union, begun with (b) a public announcement, undertaken with (c) some idea of permanence, and assumed with a more or less explicit (d) marriage contract, which spells out reciprocal obligations between spouses and between spouses and their future children" (Stephens 1963: 7). Definitions of the family reflected a similar sense that its contemporary form was the most effective possible adaptation to the conditions of modern life. According to one classic definition, "the family is a social group characterized by common residence, economic cooperation, and reproduction," and it further stipulated that the family "includes adults of both sexes at least two of whom maintain a socially approved sexual relationship, and one or more children, own or adopted, of the sexually cohabiting pair" (Murdock 1949: 1). In the **functionalism** approach developed by Talcott Parsons during the 1950s, the **gendered division of labor** that underlay the family was explicitly defined as the most highly evolved adaptation to the demands of modern life. The division between the father working at economic tasks outside the home and the mother dedicating herself to domestic and socializing roles within it was taken to represent the same division of labor and role specialization that allowed for efficiency in industrial production. It was also analogized to the separation of instrumental and expressive roles that characterize high-functioning small groups (Parsons and Bales 1955).

Today, these modernist understandings appear incredibly old-fashioned. Indeed, it seems that virtually every feature of marriage and the family taken to be natural and universal in the 1950s and 1960s has been called into question. Do sexual relations necessarily involve love? Does love necessarily lead to marriage? Does a loving couple need to be married to live together in a committed relationship? Is a couple itself needed to form a family? Is heterosexuality the only basis for marriage and parenting? Is biological relatedness the only basis for family ties? Do instrumental and expres-

**Functionalism** An analytical perspective that views society as a system composed of various interdependent parts, such as actors, institutions, and the state. These parts have particular functions to serve within society and are assumed to work together with a tendency toward stability. For example, a functionalist might describe the gendered division of labor as a required role specialization whereby men work outside the home, thus supporting the economy, and women remain at home, bearing responsibility for the socialization of children.

**Gendered division of labor** The differing ways that work and responsibility are divided up in the family between husband and wife. For a long time, husbands worked outside of the home whereas wives dedicated themselves to domestic tasks at home. With our movement toward an increasingly postmodern experience, however, the gendered division of labor has changed as well.

**Rates** The number of times a particular phenomenon takes place in a specific period of time. For example, the divorce rate might be measured as the number of divorces that take place in one year.

sive roles need to be gendered and divided between inside and outside?

## MARRIAGE AND THE TRANSITION FROM MODERN TO POSTMODERN SOCIETY

The **rates** at which people actually get married vary widely. In the United States, they reached their highest point right after World War II and hit their lowest point in 1958, in response to an economic recession and the relatively small number of young adults reaching marriageable age. Rates remained low in the 1960s and rose quickly in the 1970s and 1980s, as baby boomers—persons born in the years after World War II—entered their prime marrying years. In the 1990s, the rate declined slightly once again—this time owing to the smaller size of the marriageable cohort (see Figures 7.2 and 7.3).

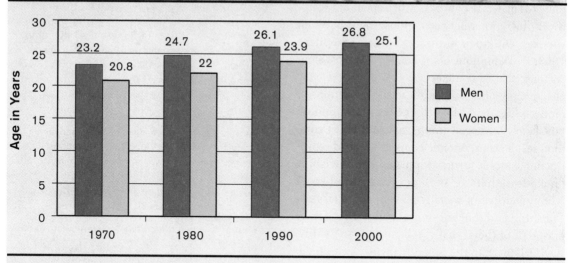

**FIGURE 7.2** Median Age at First Marriage of the Population 15 Years and Over by Sex: Selected Years, 1970 to 2000

*Source:* Fields and Casper (2001).

## Putting Off Marriage

What matters to us, in our concern with the changing nature of marriage, is not the frequency of marriage but its permanence and longevity. In a postmodern society, as we saw in Chapter 5, the life cycle loses its rigid, lockstep sequence. And, indeed, an important aspect of the more flexible and open-ended sequencing of the life cycle has been the increasing delays in the age at which young people decide to start a marriage. Today, the median age of marriage in the United States is at an all-time high. In 1980, the median age for first marriage was 22.0 years for women and 24.7 years for men; by 2000, those figures had shifted upward to 25.1 and 26.8, respectively. This was true despite the fact that the marriage rate in the United States remained at a higher level than that in any other industrialized country (Hutter 1991: 7). In earlier generations, people got married and started their own families between the ages of 18 and 24. According to the 2000 census, however, 56 percent

of men and 43 percent of women in that age group were still at home living with one or both of their parents. It was the next age group, 25- to 34-year-olds, for whom married life became the typical living arrangement, with 50 percent of men and 57 percent of women falling into that category (U.S. Census Bureau 2001). (Figures 7.4 and 7.5 summarize the marital-status shifts that occurred during the period 1970–2000.)

## The Marriage Crunch for Older Women

This unprecedented postponement of marriage—what sociologists call the "aging of marriage"—might seem relatively unimportant, but, in fact, it has been both the cause and the consequence of a series of other fundamental social changes. One outcome it has led to is the **marriage squeeze** for women (also referred to as the *marriage crunch* or *marriage gap*). In 1960, 75 percent of women from 20 to 24 were married. But in 1990, two-

**FIGURE 7.3 Median Age at First Marriage, United States, 1890–2004**

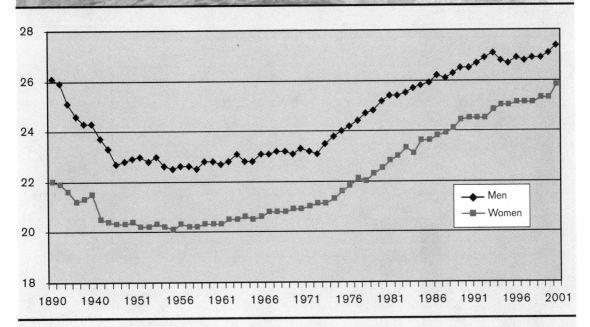

*Source:* U.S. Census Bureau (2005).

thirds of women in this age group had never been married—a figure that, by 2000, had risen to 72.8 percent. Two factors contributing to the "squeeze" have been the persisting cultural belief that women should not marry younger men and the tendency among men to marry women a few years younger than themselves. Logically, then, the older the woman, the fewer potential marriage partners she has compared to a man of the same age. So, for example, in 1990, for every 100 single women from 40 to 45 there were only 83 "available" men (U.S. Census Bureau 1991).

Looking at such figures, you might assume that the declining number of married older women, if not the declining number of married women with children, is simply the unintended (and presumably unwanted) result of demographics. In other words, given the gender cultural bias we noted above, the decision to marry later in life might simply be seen as a response to changes in supply and demand: Because there are more "older" single women and fewer eligible men, the marriage prospects of women have been undermined. There is some truth to this proposition. But you would be mistaken if you believed this is all that's involved.

## Women Making Choices

If you thought about *delayed marriage* only as an unintended consequence of demographics, you

**Marriage squeeze** The restricted supply of available partners that results when a woman chooses to delay marriage. Because cultural norms suggest that women should not marry younger men, and men have a tendency to marry women several years younger than them, women who choose to marry later may be caught in a "squeeze."

**FIGURE 7.4 Marital Status of the Male Population 15 Years and Over, Selected Years, 1970–2000**

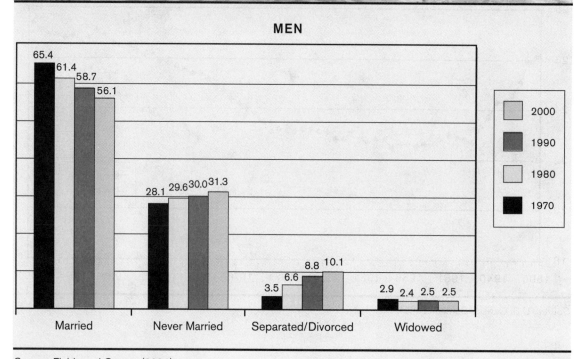

*Source:* Fields and Casper (2001).

would end up missing one of the most essential and importantly new aspects of postmodern life. It is certainly the case that some women want to marry but are inhibited by the restricted supply of available partners, but many others are delaying marriage until college or even graduate school is finished and their career is in place. There are also many women who choose a career instead of marriage. And there are many couples who set up households without marrying, an arrangement that is far more structured than a casual relationship but far less institutionalized than a marriage.

In short, the postponing of marriage can be seen as a response to the extraordinarily different role that women play in postmodern as compared to modern societies. We will explore this extremely significant change below, when we examine the transformation of family life. It is primarily because of this new female role that the aging of marriage is accompanied by the increasing frequency with which couples, married or not, decide to remain childless. According to a 1990 Roper survey, an "overwhelming majority" of Americans stated that children were not a necessary element in the making of a good marriage. This trend is another example of how postmodernity has provided women with a wider range of choices: Now they can opt for new marriage patterns rather than having old rules forced upon them.

## Postmodern Divorce

Another cause, as well as effect, of changing marriage patterns that reflects choice rather than necessity is the increasing frequency of divorce

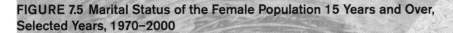

FIGURE 7.5 Marital Status of the Female Population 15 Years and Over, Selected Years, 1970–2000

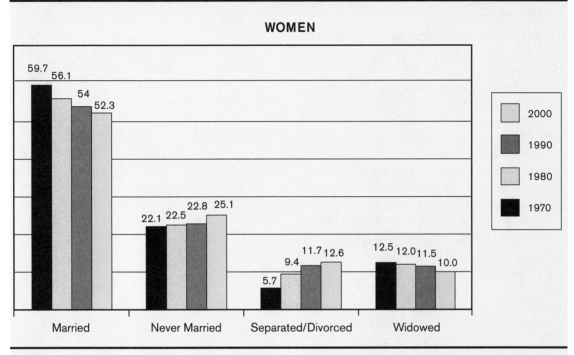

WOMEN

Married  Never Married  Separated/Divorced  Widowed

*Source:* Fields and Casper (2001).

(Jacobson and Jacobson 1959). During the Civil War (1860–1864), only 1.2 married Americans in 1,000 became divorced. By the turn of the century, that figure had more than tripled to 4.2. Twenty-five years later it was 7.6 per 1,000, a rate that remained stable throughout the Great Depression and World War II. After the war, long-delayed decisions about absent partners sent the rate soaring to 13.7, but it declined to 9.4 during the 1950s. The rate began to climb dramatically over the next decade, more than doubling to 22.8 divorces per 1,000 marriages in 1979.

By the late 1980s, the divorce rate had dropped to just under 21 percent, but many more people in long-term relationships were choosing not to marry than ever before. In 1970, couples in their 20s accounted for 42.9 percent of the divorce rate, a share that fell to 30.7 percent in 1990. If break-ups of long-term nonmarried relationships were included in divorce statistics, the current rate would undoubtedly far surpass the peak divorce rate of 1979. As it is, there are about 1.1 million divorces among the approximately 55 million married people each year. (See box titled "False Starts.")

Of course, the divorces granted in any single year involve couples who have been married at various times in the past. By calculating the percentage of all marriages that eventually end in divorce, we arrive at the so-called annual ratio of marriages to divorces. This is a striking figure. In 1960, there were 258 divorces granted per 1,000 recorded marriages, or about 1 in 4. By 1994, the ratio had almost doubled, to 504 in 1,000, or about 1 in 2. The widely circulated assertion that "half of all marriages end in divorce" is true, and

## media moments

### False Starts: The "Starter Marriage" Trend

Divorce has long been common within the first five years of marriage, but today marriages are ending progressively earlier. And the new young [divorcées and] divorcés are a bit different from their predecessors; rather than becoming single moms and alimony dads, we're divorcing before having children. Because while we still marry relatively young, we increasingly delay childbirth. The average age of first-time mothers has been steadily rising since 1972, and more couples are delaying children for three, four, five years into their marriages. First marriages aren't exactly new, but starter marriages are more prevalent.

Pop culture is packed with new starter marriage icons. Drew Barrymore, Uma Thurman, and Angelina Jolie all jumped in and out of marriage and are already onto their seconds. Courtney Thorne-Smith, former *Ally McBeal* star, divorced her husband after seven short months of marriage—while still posing on the cover of *InStyle Weddings* magazine. Milla Jovovich was married for two months, alongside such temporarily committed people as Jennifer Lopez and Neve Campbell. Even Hollywood's reigning bride, Julia Roberts, had a starter marriage. Starter marriages have practically become trendy. *Self* magazine described the phenomenon with the snappy headline "Just Married, Just Split Up." And in September 2000 *Entertainment Weekly* included "divorcing in your 20s" on its list of "in" things to do. In 2000 more than four million twenty- to thirty-four-year-olds checked the "divorced" box. *Jane* magazine heralded the trend in April 2001 with the headline, "Young, Hot, and Divorced."

But starter marriages are not to be glamorized or trivialized. To those who've had one, the very term "starter marriage" can sound dismissive and, frankly, demeaning. Some people still use the expressions "training marriage," "practice marriage," or "icebreaker marriage"; others prefer the generic umbrella "first marriage." ... Whatever they're called, these are marriages—in every sense except "till death do us part." A starter marriage isn't a whim or a fantasy or a misbegotten affair—it's a real marriage between a man and a woman, bound together by love, personal belief, state law, and, often, religious oath. A starter marriage doesn't feel like one when you're engaged or when you're inside it. It is charged with all the hope, expectations, and dreams that inspire almost all marriages. All [participants in] starter marriages truly believe they are getting married forever.

*Source:* Paul (2002: 29–30).

the couples in question part during various times of the life cycle. More than one-third of husbands and more than one-quarter of wives divorce in their 40s or older.

The figures are higher in the United States, but the intensification of the divorce rate has occurred in most industrial countries (see Table 7.1). Between 1890 and 1974, divorces per 1,000 marriages increased from 24.3 to 117.0 in France, from 17.6 to 186.0 in Germany, and from 12.9 to 380.0 in Sweden. At the same time, it's important to note that most divorced people eventually remarry. In 1990, nearly half of all marriages in the United States were remarriages for one or both partners.

# TABLE 7.1 Divorce Rates in Selected Countries

| | Number of Divorces per 100 Marriages | | | | | | | | | Mean Marriage Duration at Divorce[a] | |
|---|---|---|---|---|---|---|---|---|---|---|---|
| | 1970 | 1975 | 1980 | 1985 | 1990 | 1995 | 1998 | 1999 | 2000 | 1995 | 1999 |
| Australia | 11.0 | 57.5 | 36.4 | 34.3 | 35.3 | 43.4 | 48.1 | 46.5 | 46.0 | 7.6 | 7.8 |
| Austria | 19.6 | 23.1 | 28.7 | 34.5 | 36.0 | 42.4 | 45.7 | 46.9 | 49.8 | 10.9 | 10.1 |
| Belgium | 8.7 | 15.3 | 21.8 | 32.0 | 31.5 | 68.1 | 59.7 | 59.8 | 59.8 | 14.0 | 11.2 |
| Canada | 15.8 | 25.6 | 32.5 | 33.7 | 41.8 | 48.4 | 45.1 | .. | .. | 13.2 | 13.7 |
| Czech Republic | 23.7 | 26.9 | 34.7 | 37.8 | 35.2 | 56.7 | 58.1 | 44.2 | 53.7 | .. | .. |
| Denmark | 26.2 | 41.7 | 51.4 | 49.1 | 43.6 | 37.4 | 37.8 | 38.1 | 37.5 | 11.9 | 9.8 |
| Finland | 14.8 | 29.7 | 32.2 | 35.2 | 52.6 | 59.1 | 57.6 | 57.8 | 53.2 | 13.1 | 11.7 |
| France | 9.9 | 14.4 | 24.3 | 39.9 | 36.9 | 46.8 | 42.9 | 40.9 | .. | 13.2 | 11.6 |
| Germany | 18.1 | 28.1 | 28.4 | 36.1 | 30.0 | 39.4 | 46.1 | 44.3 | .. | 12.0 | 5.2 |
| Greece | 5.2 | 4.9 | 10.7 | 11.9 | 10.2 | 17.2 | 14.1 | 15.7 | 15.4 | 11.7 | .. |
| Hungary | 23.6 | 25.1 | 34.6 | 40.0 | 37.5 | 46.5 | 57.4 | 56.3 | 49.9 | .. | .. |
| Iceland | 15.5 | 23.5 | 33.8 | 42.1 | 41.5 | 38.1 | 31.7 | 30.3 | 30.7 | 14.7 | 11.9 |
| Ireland | .. | .. | .. | .. | .. | .. | .. | .. | .. | .. | .. |
| Italy | .. | 2.8 | 3.7 | 5.2 | 8.7 | 9.3 | 12.1 | 12.5 | .. | 17.9 | 13.7 |
| Japan | 9.3 | 12.7 | 18.3 | 22.6 | 21.8 | 25.1 | 31.0 | 32.9 | 33.1 | 10.0 | 10.3 |
| Korea | 3.9 | 5.7 | 5.9 | 10.3 | 11.4 | 17.1 | 31.1 | 32.5 | 35.9 | .. | .. |
| Luxembourg | 10.1 | 9.4 | 27.1 | 33.9 | 32.9 | 35.1 | 49.9 | 49.9 | 48.0 | 12.9 | 11.5 |
| Mexico | 8.7 | .. | 4.4 | .. | 7.2 | .. | .. | 6.6 | 7.4 | .. | .. |
| Netherlands | 8.3 | 20.1 | 28.5 | 41.1 | 29.7 | 41.9 | 37.3 | 37.5 | 39.3 | 12.1 | 11.7 |
| New Zealand | 12.0 | 17.5 | 27.3 | 36.3 | 37.6 | 44.8 | 48.9 | 50.0 | 47.1 | 12.4 | 12.2 |
| Norway | 11.7 | 21.5 | 29.8 | 40.6 | 46.4 | 47.8 | 40.0 | 38.7 | 39.7 | 13.4 | 10.5 |
| Poland | 12.3 | 12.5 | 13.0 | 18.4 | 16.6 | 18.4 | 21.6 | 19.2 | 20.3 | .. | .. |
| Portugal | 0.6 | 1.5 | 8.1 | 13.1 | 12.9 | 18.7 | 22.9 | 26.0 | 30.0 | 14.5 | 9.9 |
| Slovak Republic | 9.5 | 14.0 | 16.8 | 20.0 | 21.9 | 32.7 | 33.9 | 35.4 | 35.8 | .. | .. |
| Spain | .. | .. | .. | 9.2 | 10.5 | 16.5 | .. | .. | .. | .. | .. |
| Sweden | 29.9 | 57.6 | 52.9 | 51.6 | 47.8 | 67.0 | 65.7 | 58.9 | 53.9 | 12.3 | 10.2 |
| Switzerland | 13.7 | 25.3 | 30.5 | 29.4 | 28.3 | 38.5 | 46.2 | 51.2 | 26.4 | 12.7 | 12.2 |
| Turkey | .. | .. | 4.3 | 5.1 | 5.6 | 6.2 | 6.6 | 6.6 | .. | 9.4 | 9.3 |
| United Kingdom | 13.4 | 30.0 | 38.2 | 44.6 | 44.1 | 52.8 | 52.5 | 52.7 | .. | 11.2 | 7.8 |
| United States | 32.8 | 48.1 | 49.7 | 49.3 | 48.4 | 50.0 | 50.6 | .. | .. | 7.2 | .. |
| **OECD average** | **14.7** | **23.5** | **28.1** | **32.8** | **32.5** | **40.2** | **41.9** | | | **12.3** | **10.6** |
| **EU average** | **13.7** | **21.4** | **27.4** | **32.9** | **32.1** | **41.2** | **41.4** | | | **12.9** | **10.4** |

.. Data not available.

*Notes:* Australia: 1972, 1977, 1982, and 1987 data. France, Korea, Mexico, Spain, and Turkey: 1997 data. Italy: 1971 data. Mexico and United States: 1996 data; (*a*) Median duration between marriage and final separation for Australia. Data for 1998 in France, Italy, and United Kingdom. Data for 1990 in the United States.

*Sources:* All countries except for following: EUROSTAT, Demographic data, NewCronos database 2002; Australia: Australian Bureau of Statistics, Social trends, catalogue n°4102, 2001; Canada: Statistics Canada; Japan: Ministry of Health and Welfare, Vital statistics, 2000; Korea: Annual report on vital statistics, National Statistical Office, Republic of Korea, 2001; Mexico: INEGI, Dirección General de Estadística, Dirección de Estadísticas Demográficas y Sociales, 2001; New Zealand: Statistics New Zealand, Demographic Trends 2001; Turkey: State Institute of Statistics, Prime Ministry, Turkish Republic; United States: U.S. Census Bureau, Statistical Abstract of the United States, Vital Statistics, 2001.

*Source:* OECD (2002).

## Postmodern Alternatives to Marriage

As we have seen, marriages are being postponed. Fewer persons are getting married. Fewer marriages involve reproduction. And more marriages eventually end in divorce. With such changes, the possibility of maintaining a "naturalistic" approach to the institution of marriage disappears. The statistics make it clear that there are many different ways to couple, to love, to maintain sexual relations, to make long- and short-term commitments of an emotional kind.

With sexual love now separated from marriage, and procreation separated from coupling, there has been increasing support for the legitimation of nonheterosexual relationships. For example, the state of Hawaii allows what are called "same-sex unions" to be legalized short of marriage. And in March 2000, the Vermont House of Representatives approved the most sweeping set of rights for same-sex couples in the continental United States. The legislation, later approved by the state senate and signed by Vermont's governor, allowed gay and lesbian couples to enter legal unions that gave them virtually all the economic and social benefits of marriage. This trend is hardly confined to the United States. In 1989, Denmark became the first nation in the world to recognize same-sex partnerships, and nowadays almost all Scandinavian

Gay and lesbian couples are fighting for the civil right of legal marriage; many consider the alternative of civil unions "second-class citizenship." (David Schneer and Gregg Drinkwater)

**Contracts** Binding relationships, often regulated or enforced by law, that specify and negotiate particular behaviors. Marriage is a type of contract. For many, it is a contract between a man and a woman that is legally binding and lifelong. In today's postmodern society, some have suggested that the marriage contract ought to be revised. Rather than requiring a lifelong, all-purpose, legally binding relationship between a man and a woman, they argue, it should be extended to include various types of relationships.

countries do so, along with Holland, Switzerland, and Belgium. Such unions are also recognized in certain localities within Germany, Italy, and Spain.

The legal recognition of same-sex unions has not been without its opponents. On February 24, 2004, President George W. Bush declared his support for an amendment to the American Constitution that would ban gay marriage. In a five-minute announcement from the Roosevelt Room of the White House, Bush echoed the sentiment guiding Dan Quayle's speech twelve years earlier, declaring that "the union of a man and a woman [is] 'the most fundamental institution of civilization' and that it cannot be separated from its 'cultural, religious and natural roots' without weakening society." Preserving marriage had become a matter of national importance because "activist judges" had made aggressive efforts to redefine it. Bush said that "America is a free society, which limits the role of government in the lives of our citizens," but that "this commitment of freedom … does not require the redefinition of one of our most basic social institutions" (Bumiller 2004: A1). Despite conservatives' efforts to portray the amendment as "crucial to preventing societal decline," it was soundly defeated in the Senate (Hulse 2004: A1). However, the issue of gay marriage is far from resolved and will likely continue being debated in the American public sphere.

The decomposition of the elements of the modernist marriage package, and its statistically demonstrable shorter and shorter life, have led some to argue not only for allowing homosexual partnerships but for altering the format of heterosexual vows as well. For example, it has been suggested that the very idea of a lifelong, all-purpose, legally binding relationship should be discarded and replaced by a series of specific, time-limited contracts. One contract, for example, could be made between two persons who wish to share the lifelong responsibility of raising shared children. This kind of contract would emphasize friendship, mutual respect, and financial partnership but does not necessarily involve romantic love, sexual relations, or fidelity. Other kinds of contracts might be developed for romantically involved couples who do not wish to raise children. Young couples could enter into very short-term contracts that would create obligations but allow thorough reconsideration after six months or one or two years. And older couples might choose to enter into legally binding relations for five or ten years and, at some point, even sign old-fashioned lifelong marriage agreements. Even these non-child-bearing-couple contracts could differ in their stipulations regarding sexual fidelity and financial cooperation.

Such a plethora of different kinds of marriage contracts would substitute purposively adapted cultural constructions for the unthinking obligations generated by naturalist institutions. At first glance, of course, the whole idea might seem rather far-fetched to you. But if that's the case, it will probably surprise you to learn that one of the most advanced and sophisticated countries in the world has already initiated exactly this kind of postmodern marital change (see box titled "French Couples Take Plunge That Falls Short of Marriage").

## THE MODERN FAMILY

As the French example suggests, the **transformation of marriage** is not something peculiar to the United States and its cultural politics. Indeed, the **denaturalization** of marriage is an ongoing process in many contemporary societies. It is not a product of short-term history, the 1960s, a moral decline, or this or that political regime; it is rather a gradual, often tentative and halting, but apparently unstoppable social process. This evolution has deeply affected what were once considered the

**Transformation of marriage**  A term that refers to postmodern efforts to denaturalize marriage and redefine the nature of the marriage contract. The movement in favor of gay marriage in the United States is perhaps the clearest example of this transformation.

**Denaturalization**  The process by which something assumed to be normal, universal, and accepted is challenged or modified and thus no longer seems obvious or natural. For example, marriage has long been defined as a relationship between a man and a woman recognized by law (and often religion); however, the contemporary debates surrounding gay marriage have challenged and denaturalized this definition.

## French Couples Take Plunge That Falls Short of Marriage

Montpellier, France—Aline Fesquet, a 27-year-old school teacher, and Frank Embert, a 29-year-old doctoral student, have been together for eight years, but say they do not feel ready yet for marriage. Both are children of divorce and they think marriage is a burdensome institution, weighed down by religious connotations [and] likely to end badly and at enormous expense.

But when France last year created a new form of legal partnership, originally intended for gay couples, it seemed just right to them.

On a recent day, dressed casually in slacks and baggy sweaters, they waited for their turn to enter into a civil solidarity pact, or *Pacte civil de solidarité*, known here as a "PACS."

The event took only a few minutes. A court clerk, Hélène Belin, flipped through their file, noting that neither was married, a parent or already "PACS-ed" with anyone else. Then, she put a stamp on their contract and closed the folder. "That's it?" said Ms. Fesquet. It was.

Creating the PACS—which gives couples some of the benefits and responsibilities of marriage, but not all—was no easy feat. No law has been so debated in Parliament since France remade its Constitution in 1958. Begun as an effort to legalize gay unions, it set off furious protests and demonstrations before finally passing in November 1999 as an alliance open to couples of any kind.

But in the four months since the law went into effect it has proved wildly popular. Experts [had] predicted that perhaps 10,000 couples would be interested in such unions in the first year. But already the numbers are higher than that, and show no sign of slowing down. ... Some advocates have estimated that about 40 percent are heterosexual couples ... [who] tend to see the union more as a trial run for a marriage. ... "For us, it is a step forward in our relationship," said Ms. Fesquet, "but without the family and all that baggage. And it is better because everything is spelled out at the beginning so we would never need lawyers, we wouldn't have to go in front of a judge. Maybe we will marry later. But this is just a way of acknowledging a further step in our relationship without going that far."

Under the law, when a couple is joined in such a union both parties are responsible for financially supporting each other. Any purchases and debts are theirs jointly, unless otherwise specified. In three years they can file a joint income tax form and get the same tax break as married couples. They are usually eligible immediately for the other person's work benefits.

But a PACS is much easier to dissolve than a marriage and does not require a lawyer to do so. ... The PACS also does not speak of fidelity or children or inheritance. ...

On a recent day in Montpellier, where the number of PACS has been high, Ms. Belin performed the ceremony for five couples, all of whom were heterosexual. Four of the couples were young people under the age of 30, almost all highly critical of marriage and its pitfalls. They hoped without exception that the PACS might be the answer to acknowledge a loving relationship, without making the same mistakes their parents made. ...

The French law met fierce opposition from conservatives and the Catholic Church, but surveys showed that nearly half the French people supported PACS for homosexuals and even more wanted it for heterosexual relationships. Supporters of the law argued that it would not undermine marriage in a country where two million heterosexual couples already live outside marriage and 40 percent of the children are born to unwed parents.

*Source:* Daley (2000: 1A).

equally and obviously related "natural structures" of family life.

## Nuclear Versus Extended Families

Socialization in the modern societies of the late eighteenth and nineteenth centuries, and for most of the twentieth century, was organized around the **nuclear family,** a form of family organization in which the most compelling, long-term, and intimate relationships consisted of a husband, a wife, and the children who were their offspring. During the heyday of modernist sociology, various attempts were made to argue for the universality of the nuclear family (Zeldich 1955), or at least for its necessity in all posttraditional societies (Goode 1963). Anthropologists, by contrast, were more sensitive to the fact that, before industrialization at least, extended rather than nuclear family arrangements had generally been the rule. **Extended families** combine several generations and a variety of different kinds of kinship relations.

### Consanguineal Families

When these relations include such indirect relatives as grandparents, uncles, aunts, nieces, nephews, and in-laws, they are referred to as **consanguineal families; conjugal nuclear families,** by contrast, emphasize the marital bond. In consanguineal arrangements, as compared with conjugal nuclear families, the nuclear relationships created by the marital bond and its immediate offspring have less autonomy. Moreover, in preindustrial societies, as compared with modern societies, the conjugal unit was less isolated from the larger family kinship network. One consequence of this arrangement is that people entered marriages not by choice, based on romantic love, but through arrangements established by negotiations between various kinship networks. From a modern perspective, and even more so from a postmodern

one, most people would find such restrictions on their personal freedom intolerable. Yet consanguineal systems have the great advantage of providing considerable stability.

### Family Units Versus Family Systems

In traditional societies, the stability that consanguinity provides comes at the cost of individual freedom; but because it restores a kind of balance to the instability of conjugal relations, it raises certain tantalizing possibilities for those concerned about the instabilities that marriage and family are undergoing today. Is it feasible to combine some aspects of consanguineal families with the protean and expressive individualism we have come to expect in postmodern life?

As we ponder this question, it is helpful to recall a distinction made by the most insightful modern sociologist of the family, William J. Goode (1963, 1976, 1993). Goode introduced a distinction be-

---

**Nuclear family** A form of family organization typically consisting of a husband, wife, and the children who are their offspring. Traditionalists would argue that this is the most natural form of family organization and should remain universal.

**Extended family** A form of family organization that combines several generations and a variety of different kinship relations, as when grandparents, aunts, or uncles live together with a traditional nuclear family.

**Consanguineal family** A form of family organization that includes the conjugal nuclear family as well as a larger kinship network of grandparents, uncles, aunts, nephews, nieces, and cousins. Consanguineal families are more common in traditional societies than in modern and postmodern ones, and they tend to be more stable, remaining intact even after a disruption such as divorce, death, or financial difficulty occurs.

**Conjugal nuclear family** A form of family organization that emphasizes the marital bond and the nuclear family. Conjugal nuclear families are less stable than consanguineal families owing to their lack of a close kinship network, but they tend to have more autonomy and independence.

A consanguineal family includes many relatives, as this large family demonstrates. (iStockphoto)

tween **family unit** and **family system.** He did so to highlight the differences between traditional and modern families. In doing so, however, he also implicitly pointed to a way of thinking about combining features of consanguinity with the conjugal emphasis produced by modern individualism.

In looking at more traditional societies, Goode observed that high divorce rates did not necessar-

**Family unit** A term introduced by William Goode that refers to the modern understanding of the family as a self-sustaining group.

**Family system** A term introduced by William Goode that refers to the traditional understanding of the family as an interdependent group of individuals who work together as a microsocial system.

**Patriarchal** An adjective referring to the organization of the family around father-rule and, more broadly, to the organization of a society or social system around the idea of male dominance, superiority, and power.

ily indicate the same kind of family breakdown as that produced by divorce in modern societies. Strictly speaking, divorce involves the disappearance of a unit within the broader family system, not the decline of family as such. From this perspective, Goode suggested that rising divorce rates may represent a "sifting device," whereby the society in question makes greater use of an already established social procedure to deal with, or "tame," disruptions in other parts of the social system.

In the contemporary case, these "disruptions" are created by what we later refer to as the denaturalization of gender, reproduction, and parenting, all of which are related to the transition from modern to postmodern society. But traditional societies also underwent sharp episodes of unexpected change, which in turn produced increased, if temporary, rates of divorce. In such situations, the split between family unit and family system that characterized consanguineal kinship cushioned the effects. Divorce worked successfully as a sifting device, and the stability in marriage and family patterns could once again be achieved.

In traditional Japan, the **patriarchal,** male-dominated family system organized arranged marriages whereby the new bride came to live with her husband's family. If the bride didn't satisfy the husband's family—for example, if she showed too little respect or didn't bear any male children—a divorce could easily be arranged. Despite the humiliation and dislocation experienced by the conjugal couple, particularly the in-marrying woman, such divorces did not place great strain on the extended kinship network that formed the family system.

Later, when Japan began industrializing in the late nineteenth century, more impersonal and mobile social relationships developed, and mutually satisfactory marriages became much more difficult to arrange. Yet patriarchal controls and the consanguineal system remained in place. The result was a sharp increase in the divorce rate, though not in the instability of the family and socialization systems. Eventually, stability in marriage arrangements was reestablished, and the Japanese divorce rate declined during the early 1900s. It began to rise again only after postwar Japanese modernization made it impossible to continue the consanguineal system of extended families and arranged marriages.

In *consanguineal families*, the kinship-based system of primary socialization is not dependent on the continuing health of the conjugal unit formed by the marriage bond. Death, financial disruption, or a spouse's decision to leave the marital relationship may result in the dissolution of the conjugal family. In *consanguineal systems*, however, this dissolution can be handled within the wider kinship frame, and primary socialization can easily be maintained.

### Conjugal Families

Despite the obvious advantages of this cushioning between family unit and family system, we can see why such consanguineal arrangements were fated to give way in the course of modernization. A situation in which extended kinship communities exerted more influence over parents and children's lives than did the individuals themselves also had its advantages. But this influence could be maintained without difficulty only in small-scale, preindustrial societies, where immobility was the rule, childhood virtually nonexistent, and socialization sharply limited in its complexity and length.

With the increasing demands for individuality that characterized modernity, the willingness to sustain extended families declined. Privacy became much more important in order to ensure the wide freedom of intimate actions. As a result, conjugal arrangements became much more the rule. Marital bonds became more important relative to other kinds of adult kinship ties. Marriages were much less frequently arranged and ordered by communities, and became increasingly responsive to freedom of choice as expressed in feelings based on romantic love. The residences of married cou-

A conjugal family consists of two parents and children. (iStockphoto)

ples became separated, often by wide distances, from those of other kin. Family decisions generally, and socialization more particularly, became centered on the conjugal family rather than on the extended family and community.

## Creating the Modern Nuclear Family

The results of this historic transformation in family structure were mixed. On the one hand, individuals became much more autonomous, for the conjugal family relieved them of automatic, unbreakable obligations to other members of the kinship unit. On the other hand, the price for this freedom was increasing fragility in the intimate sphere, in the emotional lives of parents and children, and in the socialization that transpired between them. Cut off from the broader kinship unit, the nuclear family became more transitory, more

The modern homemaker was supposed to have an overweaning interest in things such as Tupperware parties. (AP Photo/Tupperware)

susceptible to disruption due to the departure of a parent through illness, death, or divorce. It is not surprising that in such an isolated and vulnerable family unit the risk of divorce would increase, and that the consequences of such changing marriage and separation patterns would be felt in a particularly perilous way. Nor is it surprising that institutions of secondary socialization beyond the family—schools, for example—began to be formalized during the historical period in which the conjugal family initially held sway.

The conjugal family was formed during the industrial revolution. For the first time, work and socialization became sharply separated spheres. In traditional agricultural societies, economic production had taken place within the confines of the home, thus providing an incentive for extending the home well beyond the nuclear unit. The family became multigenerational and included a wide swath of cousins and in-laws; as a consequence, home and family life became multigenerational as well. It also extended geographically and in terms of kinship. The geographically spread clans that resulted were the pillars of the larger community.

With industrialization, economic production began to take place in specialized institutions whose market-related, instrumental relationships were fundamentally incompatible with family ties.

Family relations became separated from work and community, even as they became more emotionally intense. The new concentration on the conjugal nucleus increased the intimacy of family relationships, encouraging individuation and more emotional self-expression. For the first time, men and women married more for love than for purely practical reasons, and they made their own decisions, refusing obedience to the traditional hierarchies of parents and other kin.

### Gender Inequality in the Modern Family

This arrangement increased individuality and the length and complexity of socialization, but it also restricted autonomy. Specifically, by increasing the distance between male and female role behavior, it intensified the sense, and possibly the actual rigidity, of gender difference. While in the early factories, women and children worked long hours, the restrictive protective legislation of modern societies quickly separated these "vulnerable" groups entirely from economic life. In the home-centered agricultural production of more traditional societies, women had been able, despite their child-rearing and domestic duties, to play important economic roles. After the early years of industrialization, women were relegated to the home, which had changed from a production unit to a place for homemaking. Left by themselves with their children, women took on the vital task of primary socialization. Yet, although they specialized in the emotional and expressive skills these tasks required, and even as they were lauded for performing them, women were criticized for not possessing the qualities required for active participation in public life. Men began to define their homebound, emotional, and expressive partners, who were completely dependent upon them economically, as inferior in other ways as well. And women themselves often adopted deferential and self-abnegating forms of behavior. As they became radically subordinated to their husbands, wife beatings increased, as did male drunkenness.

### Strains on the Modern Nuclear Family

From this historical perspective, it becomes clear that such marriage and family structures were not the highly evolved, highly adaptive institutions of modernist sociological folklore but, rather, institutions that created and bore serious strain. Love was now emphasized, and romantic sexuality was encouraged, but they were tied to child-rearing and to permanent and unbreakable connections—through marriage—that would inevitably attenuate them. Autonomy was gained, yet men continued to dominate women and gender became even more sharply differentiated. The modernist package became naturalized, and divorce, except in the most unusual circumstances, was out of the question.

Many modern analysts of this conjugal and nuclear family structure were, at the same time, apologists who denied its frequently dire and demeaning results. The separated and emotion-laden modern family, to which the exhausted workingman returned each evening, was nostalgically described by one contemporary historian as a "haven in a heartless world" (Lasch 1977). Evolutionary theorists described the development of this modern family as the very embodiment of progress. It had arrived at the ideal state of monogamy through earlier, primitive stages of promiscuity, group marriage, and polygamy. Rather than being subordinated to community and kinship, it had become proudly independent. The *ideal modern form of the family* contained two adults who had been married before having children and who performed all parental and marital tasks by themselves. Adults and children belonged to only one nuclear family with boundaries that were geographically, legally, and biologically explicit and distinct.

### Feminist Criticism

Criticism of this modern familial progress crystallized even as it triumphed in its Ozzie and Harriet form. Tranquilizers were developed in the 1950s in response to a need that family physicians viewed as explicitly female. In the year after they were introduced in 1955, the amount of tranquilizers consumed soared from almost zero to 1.15 million pounds. Commentators also noticed a sharp increase in women's drinking and smoking during this decade (Coontz 1992). In 1963, Betty Friedan published *The Feminine Mystique,* the pathbreaking trigger of modern **feminism** in which Friedan documented what she called the "problem that has no name." What she meant by this was the emotional frustration of middle-class women, and she attributed it to their subjugation to men and their isolation from the public sphere.

Friedan became the founding intellectual of the feminist revival, which became a vast social movement in the late 1960s. During those years, young college-age women began to broaden the lessons about equality that were being broadcast by the civil rights movement, and to apply the consciousness-raising techniques and protest tactics they had picked up from their participation in it.

Thus began a cultural shift in women's expectations for themselves that was without historical precedent. Among its repercussions were the changes in marriage and family we have discussed here. Most men responded to feminism with only partial and grudging acceptance, though eventually male roles also began to change in fundamental ways. When these shifting gender relations combined with the other broad shifts we are documenting in this book, modern marriage and family institutions entered the period of crisis and change that we are living through today.

**Feminism** A set of ideologies that emerged from the women's movement with the aim of promoting women's equality and ending sexist practices; and, more broadly, a framework used to observe and interpret how gender and gender inequality are employed and enforced in society.

## THE POSTMODERN FAMILY: EMERGING POSSIBILITIES

In recent decades, intellectuals and sociologists are not the only ones who have changed their views about the natural status of modern marriage and families. Members of the general public, too, have found out through their own experiences—often the hard way—that these structures are neither wonderfully adaptive nor fixed and unchangeable. As postmodern society has developed, people have become all too aware that love, sex, and kinship relations are *culturally constructed* rather than natural, and many have tried to push them to change, or have been pushed to change them.

Today, we are experiencing vast, rapid, and often disconcerting shifts in marriage and family structures. These changes are destroying older patterns and the security they generated, but they are also creating new forms of interpersonal relations, including two-parent working families and stepfamilies, multigenerational families and adoptive families, unmarried families, childless families, same-sex-parent families, and surrogate-mother families. These new forms, though often laden with difficulty, have been created because they can, and sometimes do, provide emotional security and socialization in ways that are compatible with postmodern life.

In the box titled "A Postmodern Family Form," we see a clear example of the denaturalization of family forms. In the following sections, three related processes are discussed: the degendering of social life, the denaturalization of reproduction, and the denaturalization of parenting. These processes have destroyed what were once taken to be the natural, biologically given forms of marriage and family. They have also stimulated efforts to create new and better forms of cultural control and more satisfactory and responsive institutions of intimate life.

We have seen that feminism developed one of the most cogent criticisms of modern marriage and

# A Postmodern Family Form: "Living Apart Together"

Susan and Simon are a couple, and have been so for more than 10 years. The difference between Susan and Simon and many other couples is that they do not share their everyday lives together. They have both been married before and have children from these previous relationships. Susan lives with her children in a neighboring town and meets Simon every weekend and during holidays. Simon lives alone in the same town as his children, who live with their mother. Simon wants to be close to his children so that he can meet them as often as possible. By living in this current arrangement, Simon can have both a couple relationship with Susan and a parenting relationship with his children. Susan also likes the current situation because she does not have to choose between a partner and her children or make her children move away from their friends in order for her to keep her relationship with Simon.

Susan and Simon are living in a living apart together or LAT relationship—a historically new family form. LAT relationships are a result of changes in our living arrangements. These changes have occurred, little by little, during the past 30 years as a result of changing norms. Previously, it was expected that one would be married in order to live together. Only in marriage was a couple considered to be a "real" couple. Now, however, one can choose to live with one's partner without being married—what we call cohabitation (Trost 1979; Heimdal and Houseknecht 2003; Kamp Dush et al. 2003). ...

The question ... is whether two people may be considered to be a couple *without* having a common home. In recent times the answer has become "yes" and a new family form has appeared. To be a couple is no longer dependent upon sharing a common household. It is no longer important for one to be married or to be living in the same household—one can still be a couple, and it is that to which the new term, LAT relationship, refers.

The term "LAT" was first used in the Netherlands, where a Dutch journalist, Michel Berkiel, wrote an article in the *Haagse Post,* in 1978, about a phenomenon he had observed, and in which he lived himself with the person he loved. ... In France, a different term has been used in a study by Caradec (1996) who uses *cohabitation intermittente* and *cohabitation alternée.* ... In Germany, Schneider (1996) refers to "partners with different households" or *Partnerschaften mit getrennten Haushalten* in German. ... The study is rather special as it contains a majority of "young adults who are in education, mainly studying, or who are in their early period of gainful employment" (Schneider 1996: 96; my translation). In this study more than 10,000 people, aged 18–61, were interviewed in 1994. He found that 9 percent of the respondents were living in LAT relationships. In the USA, the discussion about LAT relationships is just beginning.

*Source:* Levin (2004: 223–228).

family forms, in which patriarchy played such a significant role. The elimination or at least diminution of patriarchy has been fundamentally involved in every one of these denaturalizing processes. But it has not been the only force involved. Feminism's effects have been interwoven with the broad, multidimensional texture of postmodern change.

## The Degendering of Social Life

With the rise of modern feminism, women have made persistent demands for economic equality and full participation in the public sphere. They have also struggled to gain access to the forms of expressive individualism—sexuality, romance, artistic creativity, and emotional self-fashioning—that emerged in modernity and that have been vastly expanded in the years since.

One effect of this powerful social and cultural movement has been an extraordinary increase in *women's workforce participation*. Women have insisted, moreover, on continuing this newfound economic participation during marriage. In 1940, only 14 percent of wives were in the workplace. In 1980, slightly more than 50 percent were employed. Today, 80 percent of married women under 35 years of age hold jobs.

In addition, increasing numbers of women have insisted on maintaining their capacity for economic independence after having children, opting to work even during their early child-bearing years. In 1950, only 12 percent of women with children under 6 years of age worked outside the home. In 1991, when more than two-thirds of women were part of the labor force, 58 percent of women with children under 6 were employed. Of these, two-thirds were employed full-time (Ahlburg and De Vita 1992). Additional economic indicators are summarized in Tables 7.2 and 7.3, which provide comparisons of selected countries.

Although women make up nearly half of the workforce in the new millennium, they still do a disproportionate share of the domestic labor such as child care, prompting some to refer to it as the "second shift." (Getty Images)

This degendering of social life has undermined one of the primary supports for the patriarchal structure of the modern nuclear family. It has meant that women no longer need to be married in order to stay alive: "Many more wives can now imagine surviving economically on their own, and so have much less incentive to stay in lousy marriages. Since women are more likely than men to initiate divorce, and have been so for much of this century, any change in their status that makes it easier for them to walk out the door will inevitably jack up the divorce rate" (Talbot 1997: 30).

Owing to this new economic independence from men, and the rapidly rising expectations that women have for their lives more generally, life in the modern patriarchal family has become less satisfying to both women and men. Many men postpone marriage because they see that women's domestic roles have changed in a manner that gives them less incentive to get married. They no longer gain the benefits of a "homemaker" that earlier, modern marriage provided, nor are they eager to assume the new and more demanding domestic responsibilities of postfeminist married and family life (Hunt and Hunt 1982). For their part, women are less interested in assuming roles in marriages or child-rearing that would inhibit their growing sense of entitlement to self-expression and independence: "Under postmodern family conditions throughout the postindustrial world, women enjoy greater access to education and employment, and a greater need for both, than ever before. As women become less dependent upon male earnings, they are freer to leave or avoid abusive or hostile relationships" (Stacey 1996: 50).

In the context of these newly constructed circumstances, the data that we reported earlier regarding the increasing tendency toward postponement of marriage and child-rearing make perfect sense. So does women's increasing tendency to choose to have children on their own, outside of marriage and often outside of any long-standing love relationship. The number of single-parent families headed by women tripled in the United States between 1970 and 2000, and almost one-third of today's children are born to unmarried women. Another result of this increasing freedom over marriage and child-rearing is the growing distinction regarding family versus career lifestyles: "The movement of women into careers and of men into family involvement will break down the inte-

gration of these spheres and promote the evolution of more distinct lifestyles organized around either careers or families" (Hunt and Hunt 1982: 508).

Family-oriented couples are curbing their career aspirations, choosing not to compete with couples who give priority to their respective careers. In turn, those in career-oriented couples are beginning to have more in common with one another, even across gender lines, than with those in family-oriented couples. This self-segmentation is allowing the work world to become increasingly gender-neutral.

## The Denaturalization of Reproduction

The sweeping shifts in family structure stimulated by the denaturalization of gender have been intensified by complementary changes in reproduction. For one thing, women now exert far more control over sexual life, simply because they are more in control of their lives. What once was an area in which women were more or less subjugated to men has become an arena much more subject to negotiation.

But however significant this change, it is only the tip of the iceberg. Its effects have been multiplied many times by radical shifts in **reproductive technology** that have allowed sex to be separated entirely from child-bearing.

Contraception was widely available in modern society, but it was only in the 1960s that the birth control pill enabled women to completely prevent the possibility of their own pregnancies. This new

**Reproductive technology** Technological developments, ranging from contraception to artificial insemination, that have allowed sex to be entirely separated from child-bearing.

**TABLE 7.2 Percentage of Mothers Who Work Part-Time: A Comparison of Selected Countries, 2001**

| | Mothers with at Least One Child Under 6 | Mothers with at Least One Older Child | All Women | All Mothers |
|---|---|---|---|---|
| Australia | 66.7 | 55.2 | 41.6 | 18.3 |
| Austria | 50.4 | 34.0 | 24.8 | 6.7 |
| Belgium | 45.0 | 36.2 | 33.4 | 9.0 |
| Czech Republic | 12.0 | 8.7 | 5.4 | |
| Denmark | 5.1 | 8.3 | 20.8 | 59.6 |
| France | 36.7 | 28.9 | 23.8 | 42.1 |
| Germany | 57.1 | 39.8 | 33.9 | 18.8 |
| Greece | 8.0 | 6.8 | 8.5 | 71.2 |
| Hungary | 9.1 | 4.7 | 4.0 | 45.4 |
| Italy | 25.0 | 17.1 | 23.7 | 28.2 |
| Luxembourg | 35.0 | 26.1 | 29.9 | 7.0 |
| Netherlands | 89.4 | 66.7 | 58.1 | 38.0 |
| Portugal | 11.0 | 20.4 | 14.3 | 37.1 |
| Slovak Republic | 4.1 | 4.8 | 2.8 | 18.1 |
| Spain | 19.4 | 17.8 | 16.6 | 4.7 |
| United Kingdom | 66.4 | 41.0 | 40.8 | 5.2 |
| United States | .. | .. | 18.2 | 30.4 |
| **OECD 16** | **33.8** | **26.0** | **23.9** | **27.3** |

Source: OECD (2002).

technological control complemented the feminist desire to participate more fully in expressive individualism. Consensual, unforced, and unpaid sexuality became more independent from the kinds of deep emotions associated with long-term commitments. It also became more separated from marriage, whose identification with long-term love commitments had legitimated modern sexual relations. The new technological control over pregnancy undermined the monopoly of marriage over sexuality in yet another sense as well: by eliminating one of the major risk factors of extramarital affairs.

In this way, sexuality and reproduction entirely lost their seemingly natural connection with marriage. This separation obviously had significant repercussions for family life, for it allowed families to be separated from reproduction, too. But the denaturalizing implications of the new reproductive technology have gone further than allowing the new institution of childless families. Birth control represents a "negative" reproductive control in the sense that it allows women to prevent pregnancy. New techniques of fertilization that make it possible for sperm and eggs to be combined outside the womb of the "natural" mother offer a more radical possibility—that of controlling reproduction in a "positive" rather than just a negative way. The reproductive dimension of family life can now be achieved via reproduction that takes place outside of it. Indeed, parents can have children independently of their own sexual lives.

We are only just beginning to see the implications of this denaturalization of reproduction. One of these, which we pursue in Chapter 6, on sexuality, is that heterosexuality is no longer necessary for the old-fashioned "parents and children" family to be obtained. Another is that such naturalizing pressures as a woman's "biological clock" may eventually become relatively unimportant. One consequence of the latter would be a further opening up of the sequencing of the life cycle.

The denaturalization of reproduction means that child-rearing can take place at any time in adult life. This implication undermines the idea that families can exist only with children, even while it increases the possibility that every family can have them. The centrality of child-rearing to family life is reduced still further by the lengthening of the life span. Persons do indeed live longer today, decades beyond as well as before the child-raising time. Scientific advances in gynecology have made childbirth itself a much less traumatic experience, but birthrates have declined throughout postmodern societies, averaging well less than the "maintenance rate" of two children per couple.

## The Denaturalization of Parenting

In our discussion of socialization, we noted that the role of the family has become increasingly diminished—specifically, as the significance of primary socialization has given way to such institutions of secondary socialization as schools, peer groups, and mass media. The kinds of denaturalizing processes we are documenting in this chapter point to deep changes in primary socialization itself.

In modern societies, primary socialization was considered women's work and was linked to the biologically determined—"natural"—structures of reproduction. Today, the denaturalization of gender has meant that fathers are assuming increasing responsibility for primary socialization. While women continue to do a disproportionate amount of household work—despite their increased participation in the workplace—husbands' participation in child care is much greater than ever before, averaging 40 percent of the total parenting time of both partners (Goldscheider and Waite 1991). (See box titled "For Many Blue-Collar Fathers, Child Care Is Shift Work, Too.")

But parenting has become denatured and postmodernized in other, perhaps even more far-reaching ways as well. For one thing, as the divorce

rate has skyrocketed, single parents have drawn upon, and helped to create, new resources for socialization that go well beyond the possibilities of biological parenting. Single mothers have formed friendship networks in which the duties, pleasures, and travails of parenting duties are shared. Companies have developed child-care programs to allow single parents to bring preschool children to work. Governments have created programs that provide daycare for children that begins shortly after they are born. New helping professions have emerged in which young men and women are trained to work in these new institutions.

**TABLE 7.3 Employment Rates of Mothers Who Work: A Comparison of Selected Countries, 2001**

| | Mothers with at Least One Child Under 6 | Mothers with at Least One Older Child | Women |
|---|---|---|---|
| Australia | 45.0 | | 61.6 |
| Austria | 66.0 | 45.5 | 59.8 |
| Belgium | 66.2 | 39.8 | 50.7 |
| Czech Republic | 32.5 | 51.7 | 57.0 |
| Denmark | 74.3 | 79.1 | 71.6 |
| France | 58.6 | 45.3 | 55.2 |
| Germany | 52.8 | 45.6 | 71.4 |
| Greece | 46.6 | 30.1 | 41.2 |
| Hungary | 32.9 | 43.7 | 49.8 |
| Italy | 46.9 | 28.4 | 41.1 |
| Luxembourg | 56.8 | 41.4 | 50.8 |
| Netherlands | 66.4 | 49.6 | 65.3 |
| Portugal | 69.8 | 51.2 | 61.1 |
| Slovak Republic | 40.9 | 47.3 | 51.8 |
| Spain | 43.3 | 28.2 | 43.8 |
| United Kingdom | 55.5 | 51.2 | 64.7 |
| United States | 61.2 | 75.4 | 67.1 |
| **OECD 17** | **53.9** | **47.1** | **56.7** |

Source: OECD (2002).

**data**

## For Many Blue-Collar Fathers, Child Care Is Shift Work, Too

Christopher Heib rises before dawn to get to his day job as a power line worker for the Los Angeles Department of Water and Power. But just as important to him is his second shift—taking care of his sons Rudy, 6, and Thomas, a newborn.

Like many other men his age, Mr. Heib, 33, of Long Beach, California, regrets having spent so little time with his father growing up. But unlike fathers who hold professional or managerial jobs that occupy 50 or more hours a week, Mr. Heib's job allows him the flexibility to be the father he wishes he'd had.

"I like coming home to take care of the kids," said Mr. Heib, who takes over at 4:30 when his wife, Sandra, 31, leaves for her job as a 911 dispatcher for the Los Angeles Police Department. Her shift runs from 6 P.M. to 2:30 A.M. "I feel I can talk to my son. He's closer to me than I was to my parents. I can come home every single night and be with him."

The number of children being cared for by their fathers is "the best-kept secret in American child care," said James Levine, [co]author of *Working Fathers* (Addison-Wesley 1997) and director of the Fatherhood Project at the Families and Work Institute in New York.

Moreover, it is not upper-middle-class professionals or corporate managers who are leading the trend toward more-involved fatherhood; it is lower-paid, blue-collar men. "Most people think of the stereotype of Mr. Mom, the guy who quits his job and stays home," said Mr. Levine, "when in fact most guys who are primary care givers are in families with two working parents on split shifts."

Fathers in municipal and service jobs—firefighters, police officers and maintenance workers, for example—are twice as likely as those in professional, managerial or technical jobs to care for their children while their wives are working, according to Census Bureau data.

In 1993, among all married fathers of children younger than age 5, some 1.6 million—about 25 percent—cared for their children while the mothers worked. In service occupations, the numbers were far higher: 42 percent of fathers cared for preschoolers, the Census Bureau found, versus 20 percent of fathers with professional or managerial jobs. ...

Even working men who are not the primary providers of care for their children were spending significantly more time with their children than they did 20 years ago. The National Study of the Changing Work Force, a survey of more than 3,500 working men and women in 1997, found that fathers spent an average of 2.3 hours each workday with their children, a half-hour more than the average reported by a Department of Labor survey in 1977. ...

Not all the forces driving the "daddy shift" are economic. Some two-income families do not believe in outside child care, and some men simply see their work at home as part of being a father.

"The expectation of young first-time marrying couples now is that fathers and mothers will co-parent," said Kyle Pruett, a professor of psychiatry at Yale University's Child Study Center who has studied the stay-at-home father's role in child development. "That was not the assumption their mothers and fathers made."

*Source:* Lawlor (1998: 11).

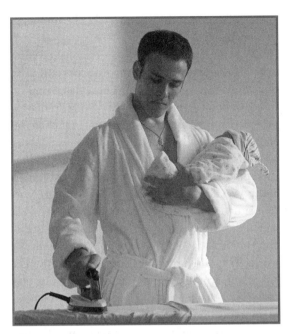

As women have entered the workforce in greater numbers, men have taken on more nontraditional roles at home, such as this father taking care of his baby and ironing. (iStockphoto)

Yet it is important to remember that, despite the large and growing percentage of single parents, the remarriage rate remains high. Remarriage is taking the denaturalizing process still further, for more and more children are being raised by non–biologically related adults. As early as 1990 the U.S. Census had counted 2.3 million "blended" families. Stepparents are now helping to raise their partner's children, while their own biological offspring are being parented by other stepparents in their ex-partner's home. And in response to the growing vulnerability of the conjugal unit, grandparents maintain increasingly strong relationships with their grandchildren. In many cases, these relationships continue even after the grandchildren have separated from their own biological parents. Grandparents are thus constructing new kinds of postnuclear family relations with former sons- and daughters-in-law (Cherlin 1981).

## THE CONSERVATIVE BACKLASH

The changes we have tried to sort out in this chapter are not only confusing but fiercely contested in political and moral terms. They have led, in fact, to one of the defining public debates of our era—witness our opening story of Vice President Quayle's attack on the television character Murphy Brown.

One way to describe this debate is to say that everybody agrees the family unit of modern times is undergoing fundamental and stressful change, but there is widespread disagreement about whether these new strains mean that marriage and the family are being destroyed or being reconstructed. As one commentator put it, "The recent collapse, or near collapse, of the traditional family in the United States and other Western societies is well documented, though whether that change is decline or merely transformation to a viable postmodern family system is much debated" (Glenn 1998: 1755–1756).

This great debate has been carried out in movies, in television dramas and situation comedies, in popular songs, in political campaigns, in policymaking forums—and, indeed, in the private dramas of our everyday lives. A phalanx of "traditionalist" critics has bemoaned the **loss of family values.** They engage in hand-wringing, apocalyptic discussions about the "breakdown of the family," usually placing blame on what they see as a pathological growth of selfish individualism. Robert Bellah (1985) decries the weakness of collective attachments, whether to families, communi-

**Loss of family values** The supposed postmodern phenomenon whereby the family is breaking down and its significance is declining. The loss of family values is a critique of postmodernity often lodged by traditionalists in response to various postmodern trends, including the transformation of marriage and changes in the gendered division of labor.

ties, or nations, and sees individualism as having run amok. Richard Gill (1997) laments "the decline of the family," observes that the "processes of progress" have undermined the "promises of progress," and attacks what he sees as the "parental neglect of child-raising responsibilities" at the heart of contemporary problems. David Popenoe (1988) attributes the "decline of marriage and fatherhood" to "the cultural shift toward self-fulfillment" that he defines as a "serious threat" not only to the family but "to the social order, and even—ironically—to the goal of self-fulfillment itself." And Harriet Whitehead (1997: 195) criticizes "the divorce culture" that "undermines the foundation of our public commitment to children." She attributes it to the rise of an "extreme individualism" that encourages people to seek personal happiness without incurring obligations to others. As a solution, she recommends that Americans recapture "a sense of the purposes of marriage that extend beyond the self" and create a new culture in which the "wholeness of self is found in service and commitment to others."

It seems to us, as the authors of this book, that the proper response to such critical claims is not to deny that an expansion of expressive individualism has occurred (it has) but, rather, to insist that this individualism has led to the creation of new forms of community. Nor would it make any sense to deny that a breakdown of traditional arrangements has taken place. Indeed, in many instances it has involved wrenching instability and pain. Yet this process has not been entirely disintegrative: On the contrary, it has been accompanied by reconstruction and new progressive institutional forms.

To say that the current flux and strain of marriage and family are the products of a new egoism or selfishness is to tell an individual story. But the position we have taken in this chapter is that the story is a sociological one. Individuals do make choices to end marriages, to bring children into the world without husbands, and to enter the workforce full-time while balancing domestic re-

sponsibilities. But they don't make these choices in a sociological vacuum.

Every decision to destroy an established form or to create something new involves loss and pain, not simply pleasure and gain. These new forms do not develop in some magical way. They do not appear as pristine "functional adjustments" to an unstable system. They are the result of wrenching adjustments to struggle and loss, of trials and errors, of conflicts and struggles over the resources and power to initiate change. To look at the current situation without engaging in hand-wringing and, ultimately, a merely reactive "discourse of discontent" is not to suggest that all is right with the world. What doing so does suggest is that there is no getting around the contested, ambivalent, and undecided character of our contemporary cultures of coupling and family. As Judith Stacey asserts, postmodern family arrangements "are diverse, fluid, and unresolved." They "admix unlikely elements in an improvisational pastiche of old and new," such that the postmodern family "incorporates experimental and nostalgic dimensions as it lurches forward and backward in an uncertain future" (Stacey 1996: 7–8).

## CONCLUSION

The sociological story we have told in this chapter looks not to the failure of individuals but to a vast transformation in the form of society. In the transition to postmodern society, the Ozzie and Harriet marriage and family have become less the norm than the exception to the rule. Fewer Americans live within families than at any other time in this century. Only one-quarter of American households consist of couples with children, down from just under one-half in the past. And only slightly over half of America's 100 million households consist of married couples, down from close to three-quarters a generation ago. Of American homes with children, almost one-quarter are headed by single mothers, and only about one-third of Americans over 25 years of age have children living with them. Nearly 30 percent of children live with only one parent.

Perhaps even more significant than the fact that there are more families without children than ever before is the fact that families with children are no longer the isolated conjugal units of earlier modern times. Intimate life in traditional societies was stabilized by overarching consanguineal structures that took most decisions out of the nuclear family's hands. In modern societies, the conjugal bond of married parents and their biological offspring assumed center stage, and the authority and support of the wider family system virtually disappeared.

What we see in the transition to postmodernity is that these two earlier family forms are beginning to merge. The many *new conjugal forms* of marriage and parenting represent radical changes in the family *unit*. The *new linkages* between these conjugal forms, on the one hand, and stepparents, grandparents, surrogate parents, friends, daycare centers, government programs, and the new child-care professionals, on the other, represent the re-creation of the family *system*. The latter elements come together in an intricate network to provide support and regulation of the new conjugal forms. This network modulates the wide and sometimes wild swings of love and coupling that characterize the postmodern age by providing sustaining relationships for both members of the conjugal pair—relationships that predate their relationship and will postdate it if and when it falls apart. The nodes of this new network provide emotional connections, beyond the immediate parents, for the children that the couplings may produce. And the network itself provides a stabilizing safety net that supplements socialization for the dual-career family, a factor that becomes particularly important when divorce breaks the conjugal unit apart.

What we have described here might be thought of as a new kind of consanguineal family system. This new consanguinity does not pretend to es-

Changes in the family system, including increased divorce, more never-married mothers, and blended families have led to new child-care arrangements. (iStockphoto)

tablish the authority wielded by the earlier, traditional form of extended family. Far from being arranged without reference to individual desires, contemporary marital and coupling relations reflect an intensification of expressive individualism. Yet, even as the instability of modern conjugality has increased, stabilizing mechanisms have emerged in the conjugal unit's wider environment. In short, a new family system has developed as a bottom-up network of relationships that provides some of the benefits of consanguinity in a postmodern form.

This is a sociological way of looking at the millions of individual decisions that are changing the face of marriage and the family today.

# EXERCISES

## Exercise 1

Are you married, or do you plan to marry? Do you have children or plan to have any? How does your situation compare with the marriage and family lifestyle patterns of your parents' and grandparents' generation? How does it compare with the marriage and family lifestyles of your friends?

## Exercise 2

In this chapter, we have seen that coupling and family relations can take many forms in postmodern society other than the nuclear family, from cohabiting partners to stepfamilies to same-sex unions. What about your family? Are any of your relatives (siblings, uncles, aunts, cousins) members of a "postmodern family form"? How typical, in your experience, is the nuclear conjugal family?

## Exercise 3

We have also seen in this chapter how representations of the family in popular culture can become the center of controversy and public debate. Recalling what you learned about television in Chapter 4, on media and communication, think about the portrayal of the nuclear conjugal family on television since the 1950s. Is it still assumed to be the "natural" family form? How unusual are characters like Murphy Brown? Is there a significant difference between "Ozzy and Harriet" and "The Osbournes"?

## STUDY QUESTIONS

1. What does it mean to have a "naturalistic" approach toward marriage and the family? What are the limitations of this view?

2. How did modern sociology define marriage and the family? Why were they viewed as highly evolved adaptations to the demands of modern life?

3. What four trends in marriage statistics in the last three decades have posed a major challenge to the naturalistic view of marriage?

4. What is the difference between the consanguineal family and the conjugal nuclear family? What terms did William J. Goode introduce to make a similar distinction?

5. What is the advantage of the consanguineal family?

6. How did modernization, in terms of both its values and the transformation of economic production, contribute to the decline of the consanguineal family?

7. In what ways did industrialization transform gender relations and the economic role of women?

8. What is meant by the "degendering" of social life? What other related processes are transforming and denaturalizing the family in postmodern society? What are some of the effects or results of these processes?

## FURTHER READING

Baker, Maureen. 2001. *Families, Labour and Love*. Crows Nest, New South Wales: Allen and Unwin.

Beck-Gernsheim, Elisabeth. Trans. Patrick Camiller. 2002. *Reinventing the Family: In Search of New Lifestyles*. Malden, MA: Polity Press.

Coontz, Stephanie, with Maya Parson and Gabrielle Raley, eds. 1999. *American Families: A Multicultural Reader*. New York/London: Routledge.

Hays, Sharon. 1996. *The Cultural Contradictions of Motherhood*. New Haven: Yale University Press.

Hochschild, Arlie. 1989. *The Second Shift: Working Parents and the Revolution at Home*. New York: Viking.

Manning, Wendy D., and Pamela J. Smock. 2004. "Living Together Unmarried in the United States: Demographic Perspectives and Implications for Family Policy." *Law and Policy* 26, no. 1: 87–117.

Shelley, Budgeon, and Sasha Roseneil, eds. 2004. Special Issue: "Beyond the Conventional Family." *Current Sociology* 52, no. 2.

Stacey, Judith. 1990. *Brave New Families: Stories of Domestic Upheaval in Late Twentieth Century America*. New York: Basic Books.

# PART FOUR

# Inequalities and Identities

# chapter 8

# Inequality

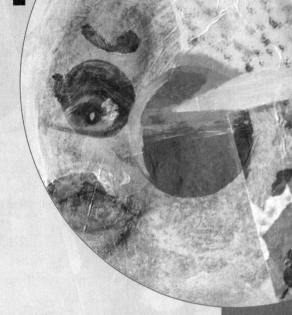

theory

## Why Only Some Make It

There are a few people who make it. They're the ones that's blessed or that has intelligence. The rest of us just have to make do. (Edna from North Carolina, quoted in Luttrell 1997: 28)

In high school I had signed up for commercial, but I got sent to kitchen practice.

*What was kitchen practice?*
Being a waitress, cook chef. That was the worst course in school. There was really the low life in that course.

*How did people get placed into kitchen practice?*
I think they just went down and said, well this is a poor one and she's not going to do good; she probably doesn't have the mentality. Look at the income, look where she lives, she's not going to amount to anything so stick her in there. Once you get into ninth grade you ran into a lot of problems. It didn't matter how smart you were anymore, they didn't take that into consideration. It was where you lived and how much money you had backing you. There were academic courses where I went to high school, you know English and history and all. Only some of us were put into academic—I wasn't one of them.

*Even though you were this really good student in Junior High? (She had made the honor roll every semester.)*
That's right. You know at the time I just didn't think anything of it. I accepted it. Then afterwards I thought about it, why did that happen? I could have been put into academic. If only I had pushed harder. I remember that I had wanted to become something professional, like a lawyer maybe. I did. I wanted to be somebody when I was younger. (Peggy from Philadelphia, quoted in Luttrell 1997: 46–47)

## AN INDIVIDUAL OR A SOCIAL STORY?

The Nike advertisement calling upon Americans to "just do it" illustrates the American belief that individuals can achieve anything they want to, if they have intelligence and motivation. Even those who have not achieved the "American dream"—such as Edna, a black woman in North Carolina, and Peggy, a white woman from a poor section of Philadelphia, both of whom were featured, among others, in a study by Wendy Luttrell (1997)—sometimes tell their life stories in ways that suggest they must have lacked the right kind of intelligence or had not tried hard enough (see box titled "Why Only Some Make It"). If they look beyond themselves, it is often to praise or blame other individuals—teachers or mothers—who had helped or blocked them. And even when they look beyond the people in their lives to the system in which they operate, they believe that a certain kind of intelligence and motivation is what divides people and sustains social inequality: "The important point is that the system is not working. People's mobility is very limited. People need education in order to get out of the ruts. The system keeps people in their place, in their class. You need intelligence to get out of your place" (Cheryl, a Philadelphia woman, quoted in Luttrell 1997: 28).

This phenomenon has been described as the **American individualistic success model**—a cultural model that combines individualism with optimism and a belief in self-discipline and hard work (the "work ethic"). All Western societies share elements of this model, but Americans are more inclined than others to explain success or failure in individualistic terms. For example, when asked the question "Why are there people in this country who live in need?" more Americans chose "personal laziness" (39 percent) over "societal injustice" (33 percent) as an answer. In France the figures were 15 percent and 42 percent, respectively (World Values Study Group 1994).

Does it matter what people believe about inequality? Americans' celebration of freedom, individualism, and the quest to "become somebody" may seem a worthy cause, but not when it leads to indifference toward inequalities among groups and the differences in power that perpetuate those inequalities. Knowledge and beliefs—the ingredients of culture—play a vital part in shaping and reproducing the patterns of inequality and power. Twentieth-century sociology developed useful methods for mapping the structures of inequality, and the "cultural turn" is now furthering our understanding of the part played by knowledge and beliefs.

In the first part of this chapter we examine some of the main concepts and theories concerning social inequality that are common to sociology as a whole, irrespective of different national traditions. Next, we describe some of the main findings about patterns of inequality in America and in other parts of the globe. Finally, we look at developments in the cultural approach to inequality and at forecasts about what kinds of inequality will develop in the future. For example, we consider the question of whether old social divisions based on position and occupation in the system of economic production (class) are becoming less important than cultural differences based on consumption (lifestyle), gender, or ethnicity. An even more radical suggestion is that we are now entering a postmodern era in which there are no fixed social positions and identities—"all that is solid melts into air."

## SOCIAL STRATIFICATION

The focus on individual responsibility for inequality can be seen as a reflection of American culture, but it is also an example of nonsociological thinking more generally. As individuals, we are all unique. And, of course, each of us is different from others in various ways. At the same time, we are all alike in certain respects. At the most fundamental level, we are all human. Below that level of shared likeness, however, we begin to encounter a rich variety of differences—some based on physical attributes, such as skin color, body type, and male or female sex organs, and others based on social and cultural characteristics, ranging from wealth and occupation to lifestyle and consumer tastes. The sociologist becomes interested when these various differences appear in patterned combinations that persist and get reproduced from one generation to the next and, ultimately, have significant social effects.

Social differences become **social stratification** when people can be ranked hierarchically along some dimension of inequality, such as wealth, income, prestige, power, gender, sex, religion, or eth-

**American individualistic success model** The cultural model shared by many Americans whereby success and failure are believed to be the result of individual qualities and efforts, and inequalities are assumed to be based on merit and personal shortcomings.

**Social stratification** The hierarchical ranking of people on the basis of social difference—specifically, with regard to their access to desirable resources, their life chances, and their social influence. Various theories of social stratification have proposed different understandings of how these strata are defined and arranged. Marx, for example, maintained that class was the basis of stratification in modern capitalist society. Weber, on the other hand, distinguished among three different types of strata—class, status, and power. Other theories of stratification might consider gender or race to be the basis of stratification.

nicity. People at each of the levels constituting the stratification hierarchy tend to have **life chances** in common; in other words, they have similar chances of sharing in material or cultural goods. Members of the same social stratum may have similar lifestyles, such as going to the opera or taking vacations overseas. They may even have a sense of shared identity with "people like us." On the other hand, the chances of getting a higher education and of living into old age are examples of life chances that are unequally distributed in society.

An important factor in maintaining hierarchies and inequalities is power—the capacity to get things done even against the wishes of others. The possession of power depends on the unequal distribution of resources such as wealth, prestige, strength, and force. Sometimes power is given institutional recognition and becomes "authority," which denotes a formal position or official status, as in the case of organizational officeholders—chief executive officer, governor, police chief, and so on. At other times, power becomes much broader than a particular organization and is accumulated in a social stratum, such as an elite. When power gains acceptance in the eyes of those subject to it, we may say that it has secured "legitimacy." The question of how this legitimacy is achieved is a subject addressed by the sociology of culture (Chapter 3) and by the cultural approach to politics (Chapter 17).

It is important to recognize that an objective **social structure** of inequality may exist independently of people's conscious awareness of it. To an extent, structure and consciousness have to be kept analytically separate. However, consciousness—what people think—is a significant factor in the creation and maintenance of social stratification, even though the latter may involve mere acceptance of the routine necessities of everyday life rather than an active endorsement of the social order. Alternatively, acceptance of the unequal social order may be due to a lack of knowledge of any possible alternative, and acceptance of the way things are ordered, whether positive or passive and fatalistic, may be the result of the persuasive influence of an ideology—a set of assumptions and beliefs justifying the existing social order. This ideology does not have to be set out in formal documents as a set of doctrines; indeed, it can be implicitly conveyed through popular culture, as in the individualist sentiments of a popular song such as Frank Sinatra's "I Did It My Way" or in the "rags-to-riches" theme of many TV game shows and soap operas.

## Dimensions of Stratification

One way of thinking of social stratification is to see it in terms of how individuals fit into set positions or locations in a pre-given structure of hierarchies. The hierarchies may take various forms, with different degrees of opportunity for movement up or down the hierarchy.

The most rigid form of stratification is that of **caste,** and, historically, India has provided the best illustration of how caste should be understood (Milner 1994). Indian society still has traces of the caste system, according to which one's lifestyle and possible occupation are set from birth on the basis of the family's societal status. The caste system was supported by Hindu scripture, which identified a hierarchy of castes separated by rules of ritual pu-

**Life chances**  The opportunities for sharing in material or cultural goods during one's lifetime. Life chances are affected not only by personal merit and accomplishment but also by race, gender, and socioeconomic status.

**Social structure**  The enduring, orderly, and patterned relationships among elements of society that shape and, at times, regulate social behavior. Social structure influences not only our actions and behavior but also our possibilities for action and behavior. The enduring theoretical debate, of course, is that between social structure and human agency.

Social inequality can become social stratification when it is maintained by a powerful elite, such as whites in the American South during racial segregation. (Bettmann/Corbis)

rity. Each caste was ritually purer than the one below it, and members of one caste could not marry someone from a lower caste. At the bottom of the hierarchy were the "untouchables"—so called because they were excluded from rituals that conferred religious purity. They were denied the right to enter Hindu temples or to draw water from the same wells as members of higher castes, who feared they would suffer ritual pollution if they came into contact with an untouchable. The Enlightenment values that inspired India's anticolonial struggle against Britain informed the new nation's decision to officially abolish caste—indeed, the Indian Constitution officially abolished "untouchability"—

and an untouchable was elected president in 1997. As noted earlier, the caste system still exercises an influence on Indian social stratification; however, that influence is diminishing in the face of India's rapid economic expansion in recent years, accompanied by increasing levels of higher education and

**Caste** The most rigid form of stratification. In a caste system, individuals are born into their social position and have few, if any, opportunities for upward or downward mobility. Traditional Indian society, in which the Hindu religion was dominant, is often cited as an example of a caste system.

social mobility—not least in the regions where the expanding computer industry is located.

An interesting feature of the caste system is that it represents a hierarchy of social statuses based on **prestige**—in this case, religious prestige. Members of the higher castes do not necessarily have greater economic standing or power than those below them, although it is often the case that they do. It was perhaps because Max Weber had so thoroughly studied India that, upon turning his attention to modern societies, he emphasized the need to distinguish among three hierarchies or dimensions of stratification: class, status, and political power. These categories were often related, but sometimes they were clearly separate. For example, a minister of religion might have high status based on prestige, but low income from his or her class position and little political power.

## Class, Race, and Gender

The three hierarchies of stratification that have drawn the most attention and controversy are class, race, and gender. (1) The class structure is composed of positions in the system of economic production. (2) In the racial structure, people are distinguished according to their skin color. Race is distinct from ethnicity, which refers to a shared cultural identity, often involving shared language, religion, and other cultural factors that lead people to believe they have a common origin, as in the case of immigrant groups such as Italian-Americans and Polish-Americans. Race and ethnicity may overlap, and various ethnicities exist within racial categories. For example, both Italian-Americans and Polish-Americans would be classified within the category of the white race. Some ethnic groups have been found to be more difficult to categorize, such as Hispanics in the United States, who may choose to classify themselves as "white." The increasing numbers of Asian ethnic groups present a similar problem. Apart from skin color, which itself is variable (no group is really "white" or "black"), it is difficult to find a physical factor that would differentiate so-called races. (3) Finally, a gender structure exists to the extent that people are distinguished according to whether they have a set of characteristics that lead them to be classified as either male or female and are expected to behave in ways deemed appropriate to their gender.

A key question is whether class is the fundamental source of modern stratification (see Table 8.1). In the nineteenth century, when the modern industrial system was being established, large numbers of former rural agricultural workers moved to the growing cities to become factory workers. Their living and working conditions were often harsh and they were subjected to tough work disciplines, with wage stoppages as punishment for lateness or slowness. Women and children worked in conditions that would now be unacceptable in Western societies, although they are still widespread in some developing countries. Violent conflict often erupted between owner-managers (capitalists) and their workers—one group attempting to increase production and reduce costs, the other group trying to resist **exploitation.** It was in these circumstances that Karl Marx developed an analysis of modern society that viewed social classes and the conflicts between them as the most important determinants of stratification (Marx and Engels 1848/1964).

Much of the discussion of social class in twentieth-century sociology could be described as a de-

**Prestige**  The esteem, honor, or deference assigned to one's social position.

**Exploitation**  The manipulation of one person or group by another for the latter's own benefit and profit. Marx argued that exploitation is inherent to modern capitalism. The wages of workers, he said, are always lower than the value of their contribution to the finished product, thereby benefiting the capitalist at the expense of the workers.

bate with the ghost of Marx. This is especially true of the Weberian approach, which has been so formative for analyzing stratification in modern sociology (Parkin 1979; Weber 1968). The debate hinges on whether Marx was right to single out class divisions, based on relations in the production system, as the most fundamental source of stratification in modern society. Weber and his successors have argued that other sources of stratification, such as prestige (status) and political power (party), can be equally important. In recent years some commentators have argued that class is declining in importance compared with gender, race, and consumer lifestyles; others disagree (Grusky 1998; Lamont 2000).

Those who follow Marx's approach to class insist that the central feature of the capitalist economic system is the exploitation of workers by capitalists. By *exploitation* Marx meant a situation in which wages were consistently lower than the value that workers contributed to the finished product, and the capitalist pocketed part of the workers' "share" (the surplus value) as profit. Consequently, there was always some conflict between the capitalist class (the bourgeoisie) and the working class (the proletariat). Exploitation, according to Marx, had existed in various forms in all types of economic systems (modes of production)—including ancient slavery (in the relations between slaves and their owners) and feudalism (in the relations between landowners and serfs). Although there were more than two classes in capitalist society, including intermediate classes such as the petit-bourgeois class composed of the self-employed and others who mainly exploited their own or their family's labor, the main division was between the exploiting class of capitalists and the exploited class of workers. (Some contemporary sociologists have also attempted to distinguish subclasses according to such criteria as how much autonomy and power workers have in their employment situation [e.g., Wright 1985].)

For Weber, too, property ownership and lack of property were basic categories of all class situations (Weber 1948: 182). However, he also maintained that class situation could vary within those broad groupings, depending on what the individuals in question had to offer in the market (e.g., skills, labor, and property). In practice, this approach has been used to develop a list of classes that, in turn, consist of lists of occupations at similar income levels. This multiple-classes categorization is useful to policymakers who need to know how various income groups are faring and whether opportunities for **social mobility** exist. The amount of social mobility may be affected by state policies aimed at increasing opportunities for individuals—for example, by providing more educational facilities. It is also affected by the ability of occupational groups to practice *closure*, which involves closing off access to new entrants by raising barriers, as when higher educational qualifications are demanded (Parkin 1979). Randall Collins (1979) refers to this practice as "credentialism." (For more information about education and social mobility, see Chapter 13, on education.) Alternatively, a group may seek to usurp the position of a more highly ranked occupation and secure recognition within it, as in the case of nurses in the medical profession.

The result of these different starting points is that sociologists who follow Marx's lead are concerned with revealing how the changing capitalist economic system is affecting class relations and whether his prediction of increasing polarization of the two main classes—capitalists and proletarians—

**Social mobility** The ability of individuals or groups to change their social position or status, either for better or for worse, within a social hierarchy. Societal myths such as the "American dream" imply that society is open and meritocratic, and that social mobility for the better is simply the result of hard work; however, long-standing inequalities suggest that this is not the case.

## TABLE 8.1  Social Inequality in the United States

### Wealth and Poverty

| | |
|---|---|
| U.S. median household income [1] | $40,816 |
| Average household net worth of the top 1% of wage earners | $10,204,000 |
| Average net worth of the bottom 40% of wage earners [2] | $1,900 |
| Definition of middle-class in terms of income [3] | $32,653 to $48,979 |
| Percentage of U.S. children who live in poverty [4] | 20% |
| Percentage of U.S. adults who live in poverty [5] | 12% |
| Percentage of single mothers who live in poverty [6] | 37.4% |
| Rank of the United States among the seventeen leading industrial nations with the largest percentage of their populations in poverty [7] | 1 |
| Portion of U.S. stock owned by the wealthiest 10% of Americans [8] | 9/10 |
| Median hourly wage of a former welfare recipient [9] | $6.61 |
| Percentage of former welfare recipients who have no access to a car [10] | 90% |
| Bill Gates's hourly wage [11] | $650,000 |

### Attitudes About Wealth and Poverty

| | |
|---|---|
| Percentage of those earning $15,000 a year who call themselves middle-class | 36% |
| Percentage of those with incomes between $35,000 and $49,999 who call themselves middle-class | 49% |
| Percentage of those with incomes above $75,000 who call themselves middle-class [12] | 71% |
| Percentage of 5,000 American adults polled who cited "lack of effort" as a reason people are poor | 43% |
| Percentage who cited "strong effort" as a reason some people are rich [13] | 53% |

### Effects of Class, Race, and Gender on Income

| | |
|---|---|
| Median net worth of a white American | $81,700 |
| Median net worth of an African-American [14] | $10,000 |
| Number of white people living in poverty | 21,922,000 |
| Number of black people living in poverty [15] | 8,360,000 |
| Percentage of men earning poverty-level hourly wage | 19.5% |
| Percentage of women earning poverty-level hourly wage [16] | 31.1% |
| *Males* | |
| White-collar | 47% (of workforce), avg hourly wage = $22.20 |
| Service | 10.4%, avg hourly wage = $10.92 |
| Blue-collar | 40.1%, avg hourly wage = $13.71 |
| *Females* | |
| White-collar | 73.4%, avg hourly wage = $14.90 |
| Service | 15.2%, avg hourly wage = $8.17 |
| Blue-collar [17] | 9.6%, avg hourly wage = $9.94 |
| *Median income by type of household* | |
| Family households (all) | $49,940 |
| Married couple families | $56,827 |
| Female householder, no husband present | $26,164 |
| Male householder, no wife present [18] | $41,838 |

*(continues)*

## Education

In October 1996, 48.6% of 16- to 24-year-old high school completers in lower-income families were enrolled in college, compared with 62.7% from middle-income families and 78% from higher-income families.[19]

| | |
|---|---|
| Mean verbal SAT score for children in households with income below $10,000 | 427 |
| Mean verbal SAT score for children in households with income above $100,000 | 559 |
| Mean math SAT score for children in households with income below $10,000 | 446 |
| Mean math SAT score for children in households with income above $100,000[20] | 572 |
| Median household income for those with less than a ninth grade education | $17,261 |
| Median household income for those with a ninth to twelfth grade education (no diploma) | $21,737 |
| Median household income for high school graduates | $35,744 |
| Median household income for college graduates, B.A. | $64,406 |
| Median household income for college graduates, M.A. | $74,476 |
| Median household income for professional degree holders[21] | $100,000 |

## Housing

| | |
|---|---|
| Number of American households that spend more than 50% of income on housing[22] | 14 million |
| Number of families or primary individuals who live in mobile homes or trailers[23] | 6.8 million |
| Percentage change in the number of rural Americans living in mobile homes between 1980 and 1990[24] | + 52 |
| Number of U.S. households earning less than $10,000/year | 7.6 million |
| Number of affordable housing units available[25] | 4.4 million |
| Number of gated communities in America[26] | approx 20,000 (housing approximately 8.4 million people) |
| Number of gated communities in 1950[27] | 2,500 |

Interesting fact: In 1995, homeowners earning more than $100,000 a year received a total of $28.9 billion in federal income tax deductions on mortgage interest payments. The entire 1996 budget of the U.S. Department of Housing and Urban Development was only $19 billion.[28]

Sources:

[1] U.S. Census Bureau, 1999.

[2] Edward N. Wolff, "Recent Trends in Wealth Ownership, 1983–1998," April 2000.

[3] Economy.com, "The Dismal Scientist," 1999.

[4] U.S. Census Bureau, 2000.

[5] U.S. Census Bureau, 2000.

[6] U.S. Census Bureau, 1999.

[7] UN Human Development Report 1998.

[8] Economic Policy Institute, Washington, D.C., 1999.

[9] Urban Institute, 2000.

[10] Surface Transportation Policy Project, 2001

[11] Bill Gates's net worth page, average since 1986.

[12] National Center for Opinion Research, 2000.

[13] Gallup Poll Social Audit, 1998.

[14] Edward N. Wolff, "Recent Trends in Wealth Ownership, 1983–1998," April 2000.

[15] U.S. Census Bureau, 1999.

[16] Economic Policy Institute, 2000.

[17] "The State of Working America 2000–2001," Economic Policy Institute; statistics are for 2000.

[18] U.S. Census Bureau, 1999.

[19] U.S. Department of Commerce, Bureau of the Census, Current Population Survey.

[20] SAT Program information, 1998.

[21] U.S. Census Bureau, 1999.

[22] Habitat for Humanity, 1999.

[23] U.S. Census Bureau, American Housing Survey, 1999.

[24] Housing Assistance Council, Washington, D.C.

[25] Low Income Housing Information Service, 1995.

[26] Fortress America: Gated Communities in America, Edward J. Blakely and Mary Gail Snyder, Brookings Institution Press, 1997.

[27] Fortress America, 1997.

[28] "The New Politics of Housing," Peter Dreier, Journal of the American Planning Association 63, no 1 (winter 1997).

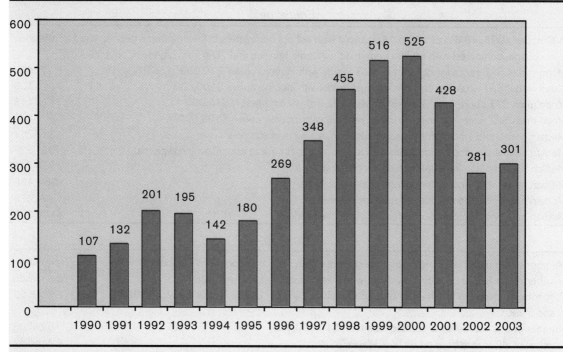

**FIGURE 8.1  Average Executive to Average Production Worker Pay Ratio, 1990–2003**

*Note:* Total executive compensation: Includes salary, bonus, restricted stock, payouts on other long-term incentives, and the value of options exercised (*Business Week* annual compensation survey, 1991–2005). Average worker pay: Bureau of Labor Statistics, Employment, Hours, and Earnings from the Current Employment Statistics Survey, Table B-2.

*Source:* Anderson, et al. (2005).

is occurring. Three developments that might bring this about are (1) an increasing concentration of wealth in the hands of the rich and in large corporations (see Figure 8.1); (2) the de-skilling of labor as a result of new technology in which the skills are built into the machinery (Braverman 1974); and (3) a weakening of labor's position through changes in the market, such as increased employment of nonunionized workers or foreign labor. It can safely be stated that (1) and (3) have been occurring in U.S. society in the last ten years or so, whereas with regard to (2) the evidence is more mixed, varying among occupations and sectors of the economy. (For further discussion of these topics, see Chapter 12, on work and the economy.)

The twelfth annual CEO compensation survey by the Institute for Policy Studies and United for a Fair Economy yielded these findings:

✓ In 2004, the average total compensation for CEOs of the 367 leading U.S. corporations was $11.8 million, up 45 percent from $8.1 million in 2003 and $2.0 million in 1990 (Anderson et al. 2005: 2).

✓ If the minimum wage had risen as fast as CEO pay since 1990, the lowest-paid workers in our country would be earning $23.03 an hour today, not $5.15 an hour (Anderson et al. 2005: 2).

✓ Since 1990, the cumulative pay of the ten highest-paid CEOs in each year together has totaled more than $11.7 billion (Anderson et al. 2005: 3).

✓ Of the 150 possible slots for the highest-paid executives over the same period, not a single one was filled by a woman, and only one non-white male appeared on the list: Charles Wang, founder and former CEO of Computer Associates (Anderson et al. 2005: 3).

Based on their analysis of CEO compensation-package information, Sarah Anderson and her colleagues (2005) concluded that the current ratio of CEO compensation to worker pay is 301:1.

In contrast to sociologists influenced by the Marxian approach to class, those in the tradition of Weber are concerned with mapping the changing market positions (e.g., level of qualifications and skills) of different groups of occupations that constitute classes and investigating how these changes affect "life chances," such as educational attainment, health, and income. Professionals and managers tend to have higher qualifications and can command higher incomes than workers in blue-collar occupations. Similarly, skilled workers are more marketable and earn higher incomes than workers in unskilled occupations. Given the importance of the possession of qualifications and skills (credentials), a key topic is that of educational opportunities. Are educational opportunities increasing for the lower classes, and is there more social mobility as a result? "Weberian" questions like these, concerning social mobility, have occupied American sociologists to a greater degree than "Marxian" questions.

## SOCIAL MOBILITY

Most Americans accept a certain amount of inequality as functional for society. Inequalities are thought to supply motivation to work hard and get ahead—high earnings should go to those with skills and talent, low earnings to those who have less to offer. This is consistent with the structural-functional view of social stratification, whereby various occupational roles are rewarded according to their perceived worth in line with society's values (Parsons 1949). The structural-functional view is sometimes referred to as the Davis-Moore Thesis, because it was first presented by Kingsley Davis and Wilbert Moore (1945). Critics, such as Melvin Tumin (1953), have asked how such estimates of worth could be related to social values. For example, are society's values upheld if a basketball player is paid more than the president of the United States? Or is there a gap between the economic market mechanism and other sets of values?

Criticisms of inequalities occur when it is thought that people are being denied opportunities for social mobility, because of either discrimination against certain groups (e.g., race or sex discrimination) or lack of facilities (e.g., inadequate schools and scarcity of good teachers). Policymakers have been sensitive to this issue of equality of opportunities for social mobility, so a great deal of effort has gone into developing measures of social mobility, especially in relation to education.

The first major study in America was carried out in 1967 by Peter Blau and Otis Dudley Duncan in association with the U.S. Bureau of Census (Blau and Duncan 1967). Using a sample of more than 20,000 men between the ages of 20 and 64, the authors compared respondents' occupations with those of their fathers. Initially, they drew up a list of occupational categories, which they ranked in a hierarchy of prestige, using as the mean indicator of prestige the level of income in each occupation. What they found were a high level of upward mobility from blue-collar to white-collar occupations and a low level of downward mobility. The high level of upward mobility was seen as a consequence of the massive growth in the number of white-collar and service jobs. Most of the mobility was short-range, between manual and white-collar jobs, and there was only a small amount of long-range upward mobility from the bottom of the occupational hierarchy to the top—from "log cabin to riches." The most important factor correlating with upward mobility was education—both the father's level of education and that of the son. Another finding was that African-Americans were disadvantaged in terms of securing upward mobility, with respect to both educational opportunities and competition for jobs with similarly qualified white Americans.

Blau and Duncan's findings regarding social mobility in the 1960s have been found to hold true in subsequent periods, with little change. Moreover, comparative studies of social mobility in other Western societies show rates of social mobility that are broadly similar to those in the United States (e.g., Erikson and Goldthorpe 1994).

In the past, findings about social mobility between classes tended to be based on changes in men's occupations over their lifetime or compared with their father's occupation. Women's social mobility was often ignored on the grounds that many women were not in paid employment or because married women were assumed to share the class position of their husbands. However, now that many more women are in the workforce, it is important to investigate patterns of inequality and opportunity as they relate to women. (For further discussion of these trends, see Chapter 7, on marriage and the family, and Chapter 9, on gender.) One of the main avenues of upward mobility is education. The more education people receive, the bigger their paychecks are likely to be (U.S. Census Bureau 2002). However, at each level of education, women earn less than men do and the inequality shows little variation (U.S. Census Bureau 2002). Among professional-degree holders, for example, women earned on average half the salary of men in 1993, although the gap appears to be narrowing a little (U.S. Census Bureau 1993, 2002). Moreover, some degree fields are dominated by men (e.g., engineering) and others by women (e.g., nursing). The earnings of people with bachelor degrees in engineering were at the top of the earnings league, while those with the equivalent degree in education were next to the bottom. So, although educational opportunities

Some of the highest-paid professions, such as civil engineering, are still primarily filled by men in the new millennium. (iStockphoto)

Female-dominated professions such as teaching and nursing historically have been lower paid than those dominated by men. (iStockphoto)

have increased for women, their incomes still lag behind those of men with comparable levels of education.

Race and ethnic background also affect one's chances of getting a good education and experiencing upward social mobility. Poor, black, and Hispanic students are more likely than white, middle-class children to be physically punished, suspended, expelled, or forced to repeat a grade (Eitzen and Baca-Zinn 1991). Even the standardized intelligence tests used to measure supposedly innate intelligence have been found to be culturebound, tapping into an individual's familiarity—or unfamiliarity—with a range of white, middle-class experiences (Curran and Renzetti 1996). The schools and educational facilities available to racial and ethnic minorities in poor school districts tend to receive much lower funding than those in predominantly white, middle-class districts with higher property values. Consequently, black Americans do less well in terms of securing upward social mobility through education than whites and certain other ethnic groups, such as Asians. (For more discussion of this topic, see Chapter 13, on education.)

## The Class Gap

Arguably, the really major inequalities of opportunity are not in the middle of the social stratification hierarchy but at the top and the bottom. It is certainly more difficult to gain entry to the top positions and to escape from the bottom than to move up or down a few positions in the middle. Accordingly, many sociologists have felt it necessary to focus on what distinguishes those at the top from those at the bottom. As we will see, it is not class position alone that accounts for this distinction but also the factors that Weber referred to as power and status. Ownership of property is always an important source of power, but it is not the only source. It has been argued that, on the one hand,

there is an **elite** whose power grows out of corporate hierarchies—chief executives of corporations, top government officials, senior politicians, military leaders—and that these constitute a power elite and, on the other hand, that at the bottom of the stratification system are groups below the working class whose constituents have the status of welfare recipients—the so-called **underclass.**

## The Elite

The idea that society is divided between a small and organized power elite and an unorganized and powerless mass was offered as a response to the rise of fascist and communist dictatorships in Europe during the first half of the twentieth century. The fascist regimes of Germany and Italy in the 1930s and 1940s, and the communist states of the Soviet Union in the 1920s and then of China and Soviet-dominated Eastern Europe after 1945, subjected property and markets to the control of the political power elite.

The elite-mass model of stratification was also used by some sociologists to describe the post–World War II American power structure. According to Columbia University sociologist C. Wright Mills (1956), the fusion of executive-governmental, corporate, and military power during the Cold War gave rise to a power elite that reached the top of the corporate hierarchies of the state-military-industrial complex—and, from there, ruled Amer-

**Elite**  A social group that occupies a position of prestige and power in society and is dominant as a result.

**Underclass**  A segment of society that, unlike other classes that are defined by property ownership or occupation, is composed of people who are underemployed or unemployed and may be dependent upon welfare benefits from the state. It is because of their dependency that members of the underclass are often negatively stigmatized.

ica. Although Mills accepted Marx's ideas about the power of property and the importance of class relations, he was also influenced by Weber's insistence that organizational-political power could, to some extent, operate independently of class.

Has the existence of such a power elite been verified? In fact, during the Cold War period, which lasted from the end of World War II in 1946 until the fall of the East European communist regimes in 1989, there was plenty of evidence of close decisionmaking ties between corporate elites in the state-military-industrial complex. This is probably not surprising in view of the perceived threat posed by the nuclear arms race and the need for secrecy in matters of strategic importance. Since the end of the Soviet regime and its military power, the issue of the military's role in the American power structure has become less prominent. Concerns about a power elite have become more focused on the question of whether the super-rich and those in charge of large corporations have too much influence, especially over major institutions (including universities), politicians, and the mass media (Domhoff 1998). It is easy to find examples to support this view. The most obvious ones are multimillionaires, such as H. Ross Perot and Steve Forbes, who used their vast wealth to fund their presidential campaigns (in 1992 and 1996, respectively). Wealthy donors to political campaigns have also gained privileged access to the White House and to high-level members of Congress (Van Natta and Fritsch 1997). However, we can also cite examples of divisions within the ranks of the rich, suggesting that there may not be a single power elite. For example, even the great wealth and influence of Bill Gates of Microsoft were not enough to spare him the federal court proceedings that led to a judgment requiring the partial breakup of his company. Nor did the corporate riches of Enron and its close connections to local and national political power prevent its corrupt executives from being prosecuted and spending a good part of their adult lives in jail.

The claim that the power elite manipulates the masses through the mass media has also been disputed. Although those who control large media corporations exercise great influence, their power is often limited by the competition and diversity that exist in the media themselves. There is strong evidence, moreover, that the professional ethics of news journalists provide a powerful counterweight against the temptation for newspaper owners to manipulate their stories. And, finally, there is reason to believe that the consumers of the mass media are not passive receivers of the media's messages but, rather, play an active role in selecting and interpreting them. (For further discussion of the media's role and of related issues such as audience reception, see Chapter 4, on media and communication.) In sum, the problems with the power elite thesis are (1) that it overemphasizes the consolidation of stratification to the neglect of its multidimensionality and fragmentation, and (2) that it moves directly from this distorted characterization of inequality to make claims about political governance. We explore the first of these problems in the present chapter. And we discuss the second one in Chapter 17, on politics, publics, and the state.

## The Underclass

A key development in twentieth-century industrial societies was the expansion of state activity, including the growth of the welfare state. As a response to political pressure from organized labor and other groups, the state began to provide a "safety net" of welfare benefits to the unemployed, who suffered disproportionately from illness, homelessness, and old age. Eventually, such benefits were directed not only to the unemployed but also to the underemployed (in part-time or irregular employment), the physically and mentally disabled, many female heads of households, and all elderly people. Once people become part of this underclass, they tend to remain in it, as do their families. This is especially true in cases where membership intersects with age, female gender, race, or ethnicity.

Strictly speaking, the underclass is not a class, because it is defined neither by property or non-property ownership (Marx) nor by occupation (Weber). Rather, it is defined by status: the status of being a citizen dependent on welfare benefits. Because of the prestige attached to wealth and consumption in society, those who have little to spend except for welfare "handouts" are negatively stigmatized. This, in turn, may combine with the stigma attached to their race, gender, or family circumstances (e.g., single mothers), causing them to experience further discrimination and exclusion. Indeed, they can become stuck in a "culture of poverty," which makes it hard for them to break out (Lewis 1961). Educational opportunities are less available to them than to those in families that are not dependent on welfare. And the situation is made even worse when an area, such as the inner city, is deserted by members of the community who have managed to prosper and move out. The effects of this isolation of the inner-city black underclass from the more affluent parts of the black community is the focus of William Julius Wilson in his book *The Truly Disadvantaged: The Inner City, the Underclass, and Public Policy* (1987), which we discuss further in Chapter 10, on race and ethnicity. The removal of the more successful members of a community from an area also removes their spending power, leadership abilities, and the chance for them to be seen as role models.

The concept of the underclass is controversial because it can be used as a blanket label covering people with a variety of circumstances and needs (e.g., single parents, low-paid part-time workers, the elderly, the physically or mentally sick, the unemployed). It also has the potential to stereotype people, implying that their poverty is their own fault rather than possibly the result of absent economic and educational opportunities.

The populations most vulnerable to poverty are single mothers and their children, like this mother who receives welfare to support her five children. (David Butow/Corbis)

## BELIEFS AND ATTITUDES

Sociologists who have conducted surveys of beliefs about inequality in America have found that there is a "dominant ideology" involving three key beliefs: first, that opportunity for economic advancement is widespread in America today; second, that individuals are personally responsible for their circumstances; and third, that the overall system of inequality is therefore equitable and fair (Bullock 1999; Cozzarelli, Wilkinson, and Tagler 2001; Kluegel and Smith 1986: 23).

This dominant ideology is said to dispose people to a conservative evaluation of welfare policies, inasmuch as these policies are deemed unnecessary on the grounds that the stratification system presents ample opportunities to better oneself through individual effort. However, social liberalism has increased somewhat in response to social and political struggles and events of the past forty years, such as the civil rights movement and the women's movement. Social liberalism entails an attitude of acceptance of social and political equality with groups such as blacks and women, although without necessarily calling into question the fundamental bases of economic inequality. As a result, beliefs and attitudes regarding some aspects of poverty, race relations, and women's role in society have become markedly more liberal. The growth of social liberalism has not been uniform, however; some groups—such as the "baby-boom" generation—are more liberal than others. In addition, there are regional differences with regard to social liberalism and conservatism, as indicated by the use of terms such as *red states* and *blue states* to distinguish among the prevailing attitudes and values of voters in the 2004 presidential election.

People in different social positions in the hierarchy of inequality react differently to the social inequalities affecting them; hence the mix of beliefs about inequality is likely to vary from group to group (Bullock 1999). In other words, although certain key beliefs are widespread, the overall set of ideas or beliefs is not internally consistent and may include contradictory elements. A person's set of beliefs serves more than one function. For example, some beliefs are based on individual experience or the accepted wisdom of the group, whereas others may act as defense mechanisms to bolster the individual's or group's interests. A belief in one thing (say, that the poor are generally the helpless victims of unfortunate circumstances) may coexist with a contradictory or inconsistent belief (that the poor could lift themselves from poverty if they tried hard enough). Facing up to such inconsistencies of this sort and attempting to resolve them may be too psychologically costly for the individual, whereas just living with the potential contradictions carries few if any costs in everyday life. It is perfectly possible to live with such inconsistencies because the different beliefs come to mind only in response to cues that trigger them. For example, thoughts about the "helpless poor" might be triggered by television images of racial minorities facing job discrimination, just as images of welfare recipients driving Cadillacs may bring to mind the belief that poor people are undeserving.

Americans of all classes and ethnic groups generally accept the ideology of individualism and the American dream, both of which advance the belief that hard work, perseverance, individual achievement, and upward mobility are inherently linked (Hochschild 1995). When the members of a group succeed, the ideology behind the American dream attributes their upward mobility to individual effort, hard work, and grit. However, when people feel that a certain group has violated the traditional American value of individualism, prejudice against this group is a likely result. For example, the persistence of anti-black prejudice among whites has been found to be based in part on whites' perception that blacks violate the principle of individualism in cases where they are believed to have received preferential treatment in the form of government set-asides or affirmative action (Kinder and Sears 1981; Lamont 2000; Lipset and Schneider 1978). But the question of who is deserving and who should legitimately receive preferential treatment varies enormously with respect to the various groups. Most white Americans do not object to preferential treatment for veterans or those who have disabilities, but they firmly draw the line when it comes to blacks. And whereas whites in mainstream middle-class America feel that blacks violate the tenets of individualism, in black, urban America it is not African-Americans but rather foreign-born individuals who may receive the blame. Indeed, resentment is often directed against foreign-born store owners, such as Koreans and Asian Indians, who set up shop in black communities. The (mistaken) belief is that they must be receiving preferential treatment from the government or from U.S. banks, and this violates the belief in the link between American individualism and upward mobility (Lee 1999).

To summarize: The interpretation and application of the ideology behind individualism, meritocracy, and the question of who is "deserving" vary according to the circumstances—they are context- and group-specific (Skrentny 1996).

## INEQUALITY:
## PAST, PRESENT, AND FUTURE

The various models of social stratification discussed here have been developed over a period of more than 150 years, and societies have changed considerably during that time. Attempts have been made to adapt these models to take account of economic and social changes. However, their greater usefulness is in drawing attention to inequalities that offend people's values and enabling policymakers to pinpoint some of the main causes of inequality. The model of class conflict derived from Marx's ideas in the nineteenth century highlighted a recurring source of social division—the conflict between the desire of capitalists to cut labor costs and workers' interest in increasing their wages. Originally developed to explain the bitter class divisions between bosses and workers in the harsh conditions of the nineteenth-century industrial revolution, this class model did not envisage the extensive growth of the welfare state or give much attention to nonclass divisions such as those based on gender or race and ethnicity. Thus it had to be adapted in an effort to take account of some of these new developments and changed circumstances.

Weber's model of stratification points to various sources of social division and inequality, including status/prestige and political power. It also yields a multiclass approach based on positions in the economic market; specifically, it classifies groups in terms of the type of resource they possess (e.g., land, capital, skills, and labor) and ranks them according to their market value. The model draws attention to the ways in which a group may try to achieve "closure" against new entrants who might dilute the group's position—as when a profession raises the level of credentials required of those wishing to enter. A combination of Marx's and Weber's ideas still provides much of the framework used by sociologists to explain structures of inequality. But in addition to elaborating and refining this framework, sociologists are ask-

ing whether new ideas are needed to explain social and cultural differences and inequalities in the twenty-first century. Some of the old class divisions and inequalities remain, but we cannot ignore the structural and cultural changes that are taking place on a global scale and having an effect on inequalities.

## Structures of Inequality

The facts about the structures of inequality in America up to the end of the twentieth century have been well documented (see Figures 8.2 and

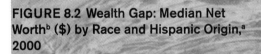

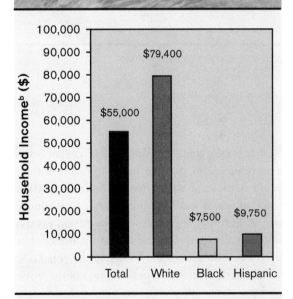

**FIGURE 8.2 Wealth Gap: Median Net Worth[b] ($) by Race and Hispanic Origin,[a] 2000**

[a]Excludes residents of group quarters

[b]Quintile upper limits for 2000: lowest quintile $1,304; second quintile $2,426; third quintile $3,813; fourth quintile $5,988. Quintile upper limits for 1998: lowest quintile $1,194; second quintile $2,006; third quintile $3,463; fourth quintile $5,417.

*Source:* Orzechowski and Sepielli (2003).

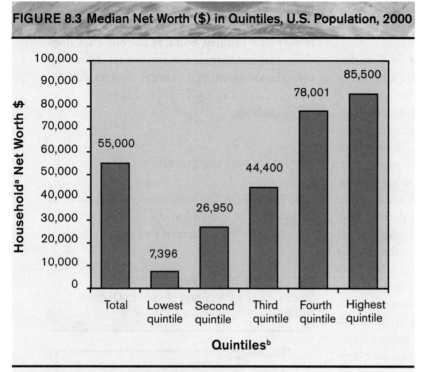

FIGURE 8.3 Median Net Worth ($) in Quintiles, U.S. Population, 2000

ᵃPeople of Hispanic origin may be of any race.

ᵇExcludes residents of group quarters.

*Source:* Orzechowski and Sepielli (2003).

8.3). It is clear that, even during the long period of economic boom that led up to the new millennium, significant social inequalities still existed, some of which were widening rather than diminishing. Indeed, the gap between the class at the top of the wealth hierarchy and that at the bottom has been expanding since the 1980s. In the year 2000 the share of U.S. wealth in the hands of the top 5 percent—more specifically, the top 1 percent—had reached levels not seen since before the stock market collapse of 1929, and company chief executives were receiving 475 times as much in annual remuneration as the average blue-collar worker— an all-time record disparity (Phillips 2000). Since 1969, the share of household income controlled by the bottom 20 percent decreased from 4.1 per-

cent to 3.6 percent in 1997, while the share controlled by the highest 20 percent increased from 43 percent to 49.4 percent. Even more notably, the share of income controlled by the top 5 percent of households increased from 16.6 percent to 21.7 percent (U.S. Census Bureau 1999). Insofar as the average family's income went up in the 1990s, the increase was largely due to the fact that people—specifically women—were working longer hours (Uchitelle 1997). Even the decreases in profits and share prices in 2002–2003 failed to reduce the pay gap between America's chief executives and its average workers. In March 2003, *USA Today* reported that the chief executives of the top 100 U.S. companies were earning an average of $1,017 an hour, compared with $16.23 for the average worker (reprinted in Teather 2003). The average compensation package for these executives was $33.4 million, but nearly one-third banked more than $50 million in salaries, bonuses, and shares. Moreover, their salaries and bonuses rose 15 percent higher in 2002, whereas workers received pay raises of only 3.2 percent.

Although most ethnic groups gained ground during the economic boom of the 1990s, research revealed that in one ethnic group, Latinos, the net worth of a median household actually fell by 24 percent during the period 1995–1998 (Walsh 2000a). This finding was particularly ominous in light of the fact that Latinos were the fastest-growing ethnic group, making up 11.5 percent of the population at the time of the report. Two explanations were offered: an accelerating influx of poor immigrants and a population ill-equipped to meet the challenges of economic restructuring. In the past, immigrant families in an area such as California could get jobs in the aerospace or clothing industries, but many of these jobs had moved off-shore or disappeared and the state's new jobs were in the information industries.

The structuring of inequality is complicated. To fully understand it, we must trace the differential impact of social and economic changes on various sections of the population—regional, occupational, ethnic, male or female, young or old. It is only by making such distinctions that we can account for the apparent contradiction whereby, during a period of prolonged economic boom such as that at the end of the twentieth century, some sections of the population were worse off and inequalities increased. This is not a new phenomenon. More than seventy-five years ago, during another economic boom, husband-and-wife sociology team Robert and Helen Lynd picked Muncie, Indiana, as the quintessential American town for their study of economic growth's impact on middle America. The Lynds produced an exhaustive account, under the title *Middletown* (1929), of how the Roaring Twenties had enriched some and left others poor. At the beginning of the twenty-first century, it was a *Los Angeles Times* journalist, Mary Williams Walsh, whose follow-up story reported that the same thing seemed to be happening again. Eighty years before, the Lynds had found that the arrival of large-scale manufacturing promoted inequality by bringing poor, nonunionized workers to town. Later the workers became unionized and were able to negotiate rates of pay that lifted them out of poverty. When market competition increased in the 1970s and 1980s, manufacturers sought to reduce labor costs by substituting machinery for workers, where possible, or by transferring the work to countries where labor costs were lower, such as Mexico. Muncie mirrored this national trend. Services overtook factories as the chief source of employment in

**TABLE 8.2 Share of Global Income Going to Richest 20% and Poorest 20% of World Population**

| Year | Share of Richest 20% | Share of Poorest 20% | Ratio of Richest to Poorest |
|------|----------------------|----------------------|-----------------------------|
| 1960 | 70.2% | 2.3% | 30 to 1 |
| 1970 | 73.9% | 2.3% | 32 to 1 |
| 1980 | 76.3% | 1.7% | 45 to 1 |
| 1989 | 82.7% | 1.4% | 59 to 1 |

*Source:* United Nations (1992).

the late 1980s, and since the 1998 departure to Mexico of a big automotive gearshift plant, the town's two biggest employers have been the local hospital and the university. These pay good rates to highly qualified workers, but less-educated people receive much lower rates or find it difficult to secure full-time employment.

To a greater degree than ever before, the structuring of inequalities has become globalized (see Table 8.2). There have always been international movements of workers and capital; even in Muncie many of the first factory workers were from immigrant families, fleeing poverty in Europe. But now, owing to developments in communications and transport and the growth of multinational enterprises, globalization pressures have increased. The UN *Human Development Report* (UN Development Program 1999) showed that the income gap between the richest fifth of the world's people and the poorest fifth, measured on the basis of average national income per head, increased from 30:1 in 1960 to 74:1 in 1997. In the same year, the fifth of the world's peoples living in the highest-income countries had 86 percent of the world gross domestic product (GDP), 82 percent of the world export markets, 68 percent of foreign direct investments, and 74 percent of world telephone lines; the bottom fifth, in the poorest countries, had about 1 percent in each sector. Obviously, the wider the gap between poor and rich countries, the more pressure there is for people to migrate or to be prepared to work for lower wages in order to attract jobs or to keep the one they have.

According to a 1997 report by the World Bank, industrial development (particularly in China, Indonesia, South Korea, and Singapore) is the reason that poverty in East Asian nations has declined by more than half over the past two decades. However, 21 percent of these populations remained in poverty in 1995, with evidence of widening gaps between the rich and the poor. And that was the good news. In 1999, according to the Economic Policy Institute, the richest 10 percent of the world population's income was roughly 117 times higher than the poorest 10 percent, up from 79 times higher in 1980. Take China out of the equation and the 1999 ratio becomes 154:1. In 2004, according to the Worldwatch Institute (2004), "the 12 percent of the world's population that lives in North America and Western Europe accounts for 60 percent of private consumption spending, while the one-third living in South Asia and sub-Saharan Africa accounts for only 3.2 percent." And Anna Tibaijuka, executive director of UN-Habitat, warned in 2004, before the release of her *The State of the World's Cities*, that "extremism is likely to flourish in the world's rapidly spreading slums if governments do not tackle the poverty that fuels it." In 2030, an estimated 5 billion people will be urban dwellers, 2 billion of whom will live in slums.

But globalization is not simply a matter of economic structures. The people affected by these structural developments also embody their culture and carry it with them. Culture, too, is on the move.

## Culture and Inequality

When the Lynds began their *Middletown* research in the 1920s they described a town split into two distinct classes, with the well-heeled managerial class on the north side and the factory hands in a south-side slum called "Shed Town." At the beginning of the twenty-first century, a reporter found that a class division still existed there, but the ways in which it was symbolized and perceived were different: "Today, no one would dream of uttering 'Shed Town' in polite conversation, but the north-south class boundary remains intact" (Walsh 2000b). Muncie's entire shopping district had fled the south side and consumers now shopped in the new shopping malls on the north side, even if the wealth gap meant that they lived in segregated areas. This scenario illustrates an important cultural development. America has been described as a **consumer society,** where people think of themselves more as consumers than as producers. Billions of dollars are invested in shopping malls and mass advertising, which address us as individual consumers, not as members of separate occupations or social classes. We are said to think of ourselves primarily as part of one big middle class—**middle America.** Advertisers portray their products as part of a middle-class lifestyle. Not surprisingly, most Americans, when asked to think about social class and to describe their own class, identify themselves as part of the middle class or upper-middle class.

For example, in 1999, a Gallup survey posed this question: "If you were asked to use one of these words to describe your social class, which would you say you belonged in?"

| Results | Percent |
| --- | --- |
| Working | 36 percent |
| Lower | 2 percent |
| Lower-middle | 5 percent |
| Middle | 38 percent |
| Upper-middle | 15 percent |
| Upper | 2 percent |
| No answer | 1 percent |

When asked about the circumstances that may be keeping them from having a more satisfying life, very few (6 percent) mentioned factors affecting them as a member of a group, such as class or race. Only a few more (10 percent) chose this option: "The circumstances in the United States that now restrict the chances of people who are in my station." The most common factors mentioned were individual factors, such as lack of training and education (47 percent), not getting the right breaks in life (23 percent), lack of ability (18 percent), and lack of any clear and positive aim in life (13 percent) (Gallup 1999).

When marketing companies strategize about how best to target potential consumers, they seem to employ a Weberian rather than Marxian approach, coming up with niche-like status groups whose behaviors vary according to consumption patterns and cultural tastes. Table 8.3 shows an example from the United Kingdom of how the population might be classified along social class dimensions other than pure income. Table 8.4, based on U.S. demographics generated by a company called Claritas, shows a different way of categorizing a population, using sixty-six distinct lifestyle types—among which five were randomly selected for appearance in the table.

Of the various cultural forces in society, the mass media are arguably the most influential in terms of molding public consciousness. It has been estimated that Americans spend, on average, twenty-eight hours per week watching television. They spend a substantial number of additional hours reading periodicals, listening to the radio, and going to the movies. Both the broadcast and print media address their audiences as individuals, but also as members of a like-minded audience. The flip side of creating a sense of "we" or "us" is establishing a perception of the "other." The other is made up of "deviants," the problem groups in society, which may comprise the immoral, the underclass, the poor, or any other category of people who are not part of the mainstream.

The media tend to distinguish the majority "middle-class" from the blue-collar segment, which is declining in size. The hardships of blue-collar workers are often portrayed as inevitable (due to "progress"), as a result of bad luck (chance circumstances in a particular industry), or as a product of the workers' own doing ("they priced themselves out of a job"). In view of this media presentation it is not surprising that few people see themselves as part of the working class. Yet if manual, supervised, unskilled, and semiskilled workers were included in this classification, more than 50 percent of the adult working population would be categorized as working-class (Mantsios 1995; Navarro 1992). As it is, the working class has been relegated to the ranks of the "other" along with poor people and minorities, a "social problem" marginal to the mainstream of society. The mainstream is depicted as a kind of universal middle class, in which the same concerns are shared by all of us—concerns about safeguarding our wealth, health, and security. The media give us the impression that we are victimized by the poor ("who drive up welfare costs and taxes"), by minorities ("who commit crimes against us"), and by workers ("who are greedy and drive companies out and prices up") (Mantsios 1995: 414–415). By contrast, the broadcast and print media love to celebrate the doings of the rich and successful ("who help keep the American dream alive"). Indeed, the misdeeds of the rich and powerful are chalked up as the excesses of individuals rather than portrayed as products of the system.

The "other"—in the form of the working class, minority groups, and the poor—is rendered invisible not only by the mass media (except as social problems) but also by the segregation of communities along income or ethnic lines. The number of gated communities in America has increased con-

**Consumer society** A society whose inhabitants think of themselves more as consumers than as producers. America is often described as a consumer society.

**Middle America** The "one big middle class" that many Americans identify themselves as part of.

## TABLE 8.3  A Classification of Residential Neighborhoods, United Kingdom, 2005

| Category | Group | Type |
|---|---|---|
| **Wealthy Achievers** | Wealthy Executives | 1. Affluent mature professionals, large houses<br>2. Affluent working families with mortgages<br>3. Villages with wealthy commuters<br>4. Well-off managers, larger houses |
| | Affluent Greys | 5. Older affluent professionals<br>6. Farming communities<br>7. Old people, detached houses<br>8. Mature couples, smaller detached houses |
| | Flourishing Families | 9. Larger families, prosperous suburbs<br>10. Well-off working families with mortgages<br>11. Well-off managers, detached houses<br>12. Large families and houses in rural areas |
| **Urban Prosperity** | Prosperous Professionals | 13. Well-off professionals, larger houses, converted flats<br>14. Older professionals in detached houses or apartments |
| | Educated Urbanites | 15. Affluent urban professionals, flats<br>16. Prosperous young professionals, flats<br>17. Young educated workers, flats<br>18. Multiethnic young, converted flats<br>19. Suburban privately renting professionals |
| | Aspiring Singles | 20. Student flats and cosmopolitan sharers<br>21. Singles and sharers, multiethnic areas<br>22. Low-income singles, small rented flats<br>23. Student terraces |
| **Comfortably Off** | Starting Out | 24. Young couples, flats and terraces<br>25. White-collar singles/sharers, terraces |
| | Secure Families | 26. Younger white-collar couples with mortgages<br>27. Middle-income, home-owning areas<br>28. Working families with mortgages<br>29. Mature families in suburban semis<br>30. Established home-owning workers<br>31. Home-owning Asian family areas |
| | Settled Suburbia | 32. Retired home owners<br>33. Middle-income, older couples<br>34. Lower-income people, semis |
| | Prudent Pensioners | 35. Elderly singles, purpose-built flats<br>36. Older people, flats |
| **Moderate Means** | Asian Communities | 37. Crowded Asian terraces<br>38. Low-income Asian families |
| | Postindustrial Families | 39. Skilled older family terraces<br>40. Young family workers |
| | Blue-Collar Roots | 41. Skilled workers, semis and terraces<br>42. Home-owning, terraces<br>43. Older rented terraces |

| Category | Group | Type |
|---|---|---|
| **Hard-Pressed** | Struggling Families | 44. Low-income larger families, semis |
| | | 45. Older people, low-income, small semis |
| | | 46. Low-income, routine jobs, unemployment |
| | | 47. Low-rise terraced estates of poorly off workers |
| | | 48. Low-income, high unemployment, single parents |
| | | 49. Large families, many children, poorly educated |
| | Burdened Singles | 50. Council flats, single elderly people |
| | | 51. Council terraces, unemployment, many singles |
| | | 52. Council flats, single parents, unemployment |
| | High-Rise Hardship | 53. Old people in high-rise flats |
| | | 54. Singles and single parents, high-rise estates |
| | Inner-City Adversity | 55. Multiethnic, purpose-built estates |
| | | 56. Multiethnic, crowded flats |

*Note:* A Classification of Residential Neighborhoods (ACORN) categorizes all 1.9 million U.K. postal codes, which have been described using more than 125 demographic statistics within England, Scotland, Wales, and Northern Ireland, along with 287 lifestyle variables.

*Source:* ACORN map from CACI Ltd. http://www.caci.co.uk/acorn/acornmap.asp (accessed April 15, 2006).

siderably in recent years (Blakely and Snyder 1995; Kennedy 1995; Reich 1991). Many such communities, which are located mainly in middle-class and upper-class white areas, employ private security guards to keep out "unwelcome" visitors. And many residents, though they spend considerable money improving their own facilities within the gated community, they complain about their obligation as citizens to pay taxes that help those outside.

At the same time, there is a general tendency in the United States toward increased **privatization,** whereby people think of themselves as individual consumers. Or, if they think in terms of collective identity, they identify with particular consumer lifestyles. Even ethnicity, sexuality, and gender are defined as matters of cultural style by the mass media. For example, black rap is both the lifestyle fashion of a particular ethnic group and a commercialized commodity that has spread to other groups. And in the context of sexuality and gender, entertainers such as Michael Jackson have blurred the clear distinctions that once existed and encourage us to buy into more ambiguous forms.

Marx believed that the structures of economic production and class relations form the basis of society and determine the form taken by culture. Class differences would eventually widen, he said, and so would the cultural differences between them, leading to a greater sense of class consciousness. But in fact, the evolution of capitalism has resulted in an apparent fragmentation into

**Privatization** The process by which people make the transition from identifying as part of a class or occupational group to thinking of themselves as individuals—specifically, as individual consumers.

## TABLE 8.4  PRIZM Lifestyle Types, United States

### 2005 Statistics

| Type | Description | Households | Median Household Income |
|---|---|---|---|
| 09 Big Fish, Small Pond | Older, upper-class, college-educated professionals, the members of Big Fish, Small Pond are often among the leading citizens of their small-town communities. These upscale, empty-nesting couples enjoy the trappings of success, belonging to country clubs, maintaining large investment portfolios, and spending freely on computer technology. | 2,451,435 (2.21%) | $78,915 |
| 24 Up-and-Comers | Up-and-Comers is a stopover for young, midscale singles before they marry, have families, and establish more deskbound lifestyles. Found in second-tier cities, these mobile twentysomethings include a disproportionate number of recent college graduates who are into athletic activities, the latest technology, and nightlife entertainment. | 1,357,887 (1.22%) | $47,961 |
| 35 Boomtown Singles | Affordable housing, abundant entry-level jobs, and a thriving singles scene—all have given rise to the Boomtown Singles segment in fast-growing satellite cities. Young, single, and working-class, these residents pursue active lifestyles amid sprawling apartment complexes, bars, convenience stores, and laundromats. | 1,347,018 (1.21%) | $38,239 |
| 41 Sunset City Blues | Scattered throughout the older neighborhoods of small cities, Sunset City Blues is a segment of lower-middle-class singles and couples who have retired or are getting close to it. These empty-nesters tend to own their homes but have modest educations and incomes. They maintain a low-key lifestyle filled with newspapers and television by day and family-style restaurants by night. | 1,892,142 (1.7%) | $37,088 |
| 47 City Startups | In City Startups, young, multiethnic singles have settled in neighborhoods filled with cheap apartments and a commercial base of cafes, bars, laundromats, and clubs that cater to twenty-somethings. One of the youngest segments in America—with ten times as many college students as the national average—these neighborhoods feature low incomes and high concentrations of Hispanics and African-Americans. | 1,605,824 (1.45%) | $22,891 |

*Source:* MyBestSegments.com. PRIZM NE, a segmentation system from Claritas, Inc., available at http://www.claritas.com/ MyBestSegments/Default.jsp?ID=30&SubID=&pageName=Segment%2BLook-up (accessed April 15, 2006).

## Demographic Traits

| Lifestyle Traits | Ethnic Diversity | Family Types | Age Ranges | Employment | Education | Income |
|---|---|---|---|---|---|---|
| 1. Go cross-country skiing<br>2. Own a vacation/wknd home<br>3. Read *Southern Living*<br>4. Listen to classical radio<br>5. Drive a Cadillac de Ville | Mostly White | Couples | 45+ | College Grad+ | Professional | Upscale |
| 1. Use Internet for job search<br>2. Shop at Ann Taylor<br>3. Read *Shape*<br>4. Watch MTV<br>5. Drive a Mitsubishi Eclipse | White, Asian | Mix | <35 | High School or College | Professional, White-Collar | Midscale |
| 1. Buy alternative music<br>2. Play soccer<br>3. Read *Muscle & Fitness*<br>4. Watch MTV<br>5. Drive a Daewoo | White American Indian | Singles | <35 | HIgh School or College | White-Collar, Service | Lower Middle |
| 1. Collect coins<br>2. Eat at Olive Garden<br>3. Read mature-market magazines<br>4. Watch *People's Court*<br>5. Drive a Buick Century | White | Singles or Couples | 65+ | High School | Blue-Collar, White-Collar, Service | Lower Middle |
| 1. Go to nightclubs<br>2. Order pizza from Papa John's<br>3. Read *Rolling Stone*<br>4. Watch *Mad TV*<br>5. Drive a Kia Spectra | High Asian, Black, American Indian | Singles | <35 | High School or College | White-Collar, Service | Poor |

Gated communities, mostly in wealthy white neighborhoods, have introduced another form of social segregation. (Dan Lamont/ Corbis)

multiple income, occupational, and consumer groupings, along with a proliferation of groupings distinguished by other cultural differences such as ethnicity, sexuality, and gender—although the latter are becoming increasingly fluid and negotiable.

## CONCLUSION

In the context of the North Carolina and Philadelphia women whose stories we referred to at the beginning of this chapter, it is now clear that the cultural construction of class and other stratification identities is a fluid and negotiated process. It matters a great deal which labels we attach to other people and to ourselves. For example, it is significant that in Wendy Luttrell's study, the women from North Carolina referred to themselves and their families as "black" whereas the Philadelphia women never once referred to themselves as "white." Moreover, the North Carolina women described their families as "poor" and as having "country ways" whereas most of the Philadelphia women described their family backgrounds in terms of religion (Catholic), ethnicity (Irish or Polish), and class (such as "working-class," "blue-collar," or "union"), yet some simply referred to themselves as being "working" or "neighborhood" women (Luttrell 1997: 127). The author concluded that, in the process of identifying themselves as the subjects of their stories, the two groups of women were drawing on different stocks of relevant knowledge. It was knowledge based on personal experience. If, say, a sociologist told *her* story, she would likely tell it differently and attach different labels. None of these stories necessarily involves false consciousness in the Marxian sense. Rather, people's subjective sense of their identity is an ongoing construction that they undertake in relation to other people and the given circumstances.

It is still the case that the poor die young and suffer more illnesses than those who are relatively rich. And structural inequalities will undoubtedly remain in the future; they may even continue to widen, especially on a global scale between rich and poor countries. However, as a result of globalization, mass communication of cultural products, and the increasing variety of consumer lifestyles, older class divisions are likely to decline as the basis of shared culture and group solidarity. Consumer lifestyles have not yet displaced occupation as a source of identity, but they have become disconnected from it. It is only in rather isolated enclaves of "company towns," mining settlements, and rural communities that class subcultures continue to exist. Indeed, when people today are asked about their main sources of identity, class tends to rank behind occupation, family role, national citizenship, gender, ethnicity, age, region of residence, and even the local sports team (Emmison and Western 1990).

The sociology of inequality underwent three phases, which we summarize as follows:

✓ The earliest phase was marked by a focus on the emerging divisions of industrial capitalism based on ownership (the capitalist class) and nonownership (the working class) of the means of production, identified as the dominant form of stratification. Marx's "dominant ideology" thesis emphasized that the control of the ideational world is essential to the exercise of domination. His concept of "false consciousness" pointed to the connection between material position and worldview and to the legitimization and universalization of specific worldviews.

✓ In the twentieth century, American textbooks dealing with the topic of social stratification focused almost exclusively on the structural factors that determine the position of individuals in systems of inequality as well as on the extent of social mobility and the obstacles to it. As we have seen, sociologists of this period typically offered a discussion of the types of stratification systems, the structure of modern stratification, the degree of inequality in the distribution of a given asset (e.g., income), the criteria used to define social classes, and the determination of social mobility. In addition to mapping changes in the relative standing of classes and subclasses (e.g., on the basis of income) and the rates of mobility between classes, they included groupings created by the actions of the state and organizations (e.g., power elites, managers, bureaucrats, welfare recipients, and the underclass). In some respects, these lines of inquiry took their direction from Weber's writings on stratification in *Economy and Society* (1968). Twentieth-century sociologists also focused on status groups, on the role that common lifestyles and worldviews played in closure and monopolization of resources, and on the cultural bases of stratification (i.e., how cultural characteristics are mobilized as bases of exclusion). Weber's discussion of the formative impact of ideas on economic developments in *The Protestant Ethic and the Spirit of Capitalism* (1904) provided inspiration for those who wished to stress the relative autonomy of culture.

✓ Another shift in thinking occurred during the transition between the twentieth and twenty-first centuries, when sociologists began concentrating on the formation of groupings based on lifestyle and value commitments. This category includes consumer lifestyle groupings, ethnic cultural groups, and groups committed to certain cultural values propagated by social movements, such as gays and lesbians or feminists. Correspondingly, the earlier focus on economic classes, and on the operations of the ruling class or power elite, seems to have declined. The recent "cultural turn" in sociology has brought about an outpouring of research in four areas: self and identity, cultural practices, representations of groups, and the impact of the mass media. These topics are addressed in numerous ethnographies and interview-based studies of the subculture of various classes, genders, and ethnic and racial groups; in studies of the interface between subcultures and institutions; in studies of how cultural signaling and the drawing of boundaries contribute to the reproduction of inequality; and in studies of how the media contribute to the construction of reality.

The issue of how inequality is subjectively perceived and judged is obviously important. Tied in with Americans' strong belief in the equal moral worth of all people is the belief that their country is a land of equality of opportunity and fairness. In the post–World War II period, a few sociologists provided scathing critiques of American "boosterism," or what C. Wright Mills called the "American Celebration." Many others, however, were only too ready to share in the optimism propagated by figures like Arthur Burns, the director of the National Bureau of Economic Research (later chair of the Federal Reserve Board), who concluded in 1951 that the U.S. economy had achieved "one of the great social revolutions of history"—a revolution in which economic growth had produced a more equitable income distribution (Burns 1951). Many people continue to believe that inequalities are healthy, manifesting rewards for intelligence, hard work, and creativity. But many others are concerned about inequality's human cost, questioning whether inequities need to be as great as they are to induce economic growth.

As in earlier periods, inequality continues to occupy a central place in sociological investigation, just as it continues to matter greatly to those who experience its consequences. What may have changed is the variety of ways in which inequalities are perceived and responded to by different social strata or categories of people. In order to study those changes, sociologists of postmodernity are paying increasing attention to media representations of such differences, as well as engaging in detailed studies of groups' attitudes and lifestyles.

# EXERCISES

## Exercise 1

What social class do you come from? Think about the characteristics of your own family background—your parents' education, occupation, income, lifestyle—and consider which of these is most important in determining your family's social class. Have your parents been socially mobile, in the sense of having risen or descended in the social scale compared with their parents' class location?

## Exercise 2

Draw up a list of occupations and rank them in a scale of prestige—first, according to your own judgment, and then, based on how you think society in general ranks them. Would the ranks change very much if they were based solely on income, or on power and influence?

## Exercise 3

Make a list of the main lifestyle groupings in your hometown, taking into account factors such as cultural activities and consumer choices. How separate and distinctive are such groupings from each other in terms of social relations? For instance, do the people in one grouping socialize with those in another during their leisure time? Also think about some of your favorite TV programs and films: What social strata do the main characters come from, and how do they relate to characters from other strata?

## Exercise 4

Ask a few relatives and friends what they consider to be the main reasons for the inequality in American society. Do they believe there is too much inequality, too little, or the right amount? Do their responses vary according to their own attributes, such as age, experience of unemployment, and income level?

# STUDY QUESTIONS

1. What is the *American individualistic success model*, and how does it color Americans' perception of inequality?

2. How do Karl Marx's theories of social stratification differ from those of Max Weber?

3. Is class still the fundamental source of stratification, as suggested by Marx? What other dimensions of stratification have attracted the attention of sociologists in recent years?

4. Do Americans tend to believe that more social mobility exists than is actually the case, and has there been much change in rates of social mobility in recent decades?

5. What impact has the "cultural turn" had on the ways in which social stratification is perceived?

6. What is globalization? Are global inequalities increasing or decreasing?

## FURTHER READING

Dines, G., and J. M. Humez. 1995. *Gender, Race and Class in Media*. Thousand Oaks, CA: Sage.

Grusky, David, ed. 1994. *Social Stratification: Race, Class, and Gender in Sociological Perspective*. Boulder, CO: Westview Press.

Hochschild, Jennifer. 1995. *Facing Up to the American Dream*. Princeton, NJ: Princeton University Press.

McMichael, Philip. 2000. *Development and Social Change: A Global Perspective*. Thousand Oaks, CA: Pine Forge Press.

# chapter 9

# Gender

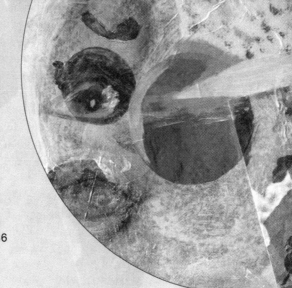

Helen Mather did not suspect she was any different from other women her age. But two factors worried her. At 19, she'd never had a period. And penetrative sex had always been impossible.

Mather went for tests at the Elizabeth Garrett Anderson Hospital for Women. Here it was discovered that she did not have a vagina or uterus, fallopian tubes or ovaries. She was told she had a rare genetic condition called androgen insensitivity syndrome (AIS). She would have been born a boy, but an insensitivity to androgens, or male hormones, caused the fetus to develop along female lines. Tests showed that she was biologically male and had XY chromosomes, but in every outward way she appeared female.

"It would be grotesque to suggest I'm anything other than female," says Mather, now 46. "I wouldn't know how to be a man" (D'Silva 1996).

## AN INDIVIDUAL OR A SOCIAL STORY?

Helen's is an exceptional case but it raises some interesting issues that are more widely relevant. Her dilemma about her sex seems to contradict one of our basic assumptions about identity—that we are either male or female. It is the most taken-for-granted belief that we have about ourselves. But might there be grounds for questioning that certainty? Like many other aspects of identity, ideas about male and female, masculine and feminine, are becoming less clear and certain in the twenty-first century. It seems as if more questions are raised as we acquire more knowledge. But there can be no turning back; we have to learn to live with uncertainties and go on examining the questions that arise in the light of new knowledge as it becomes available.

What makes men and women different? Is it something that is biologically determined, or is it the result of social and cultural processes? One way social scientists went about answering that

question in the twentieth century was to make a distinction between sex and gender. The term *sex* was taken to refer to the biological characteristics associated with maleness and femaleness, whereas *gender* was used to refer to the social and cultural characteristics of masculinity and femininity. For twenty-first-century sociology, however, the distinction between sex and gender appears likely to become less clear because, as we will see, the cultural processes of gendering have been found to have a multitude of effects on biology. As philosophers have begun to conclude, body and mind cannot be separated. Most people still believe that biological differences are what determine social and cultural characteristics, though they may also be aware that the latter vary among different societies. But there is growing acceptance of the idea that, apart from the chromosome difference (a male embryo develops when an X and a Y chromosome are paired whereas a female embryo results when two X chromosomes are paired), even biological differences between males and females are not always distinct or universal. The development of male genitalia depends on the body's production of testosterone—and if this does not occur, for any reason, then female genitalia develop. In some cases, a hormone imbalance before birth produces a body with a combination of both male and female genitalia (a hermaphrodite), which some societies, such as the Navajo of North America, have regarded with positive feelings of awe. Yet in mainstream American society, it is reason to perform "corrective" surgery.

Helen Mather's case was, as noted, a rare one: She had the XY chromosomes of a male but failed to fully develop the genitalia of either sex. Because she had *learned* to be a female, and others had interacted with her as a female, she could not imagine herself as a male. This tells us something about the importance of cultural factors and socialization in the formation of gender identities. It is not just the possession of certain biological characteristics that is significant but also how they are regarded—

## When Gender Isn't a Given

At the moment after labor when a mother hears whether her new child is a boy or a girl, Lisa Greene was told she had a son. She named her baby Ryan and went home. Ms. Greene learned five days after the birth that her baby was really a girl.

Doctors who ran tests diagnosed congenital adrenal hyperplasia, a condition that, put simply, can make baby girls' genitals look male. As the young mother struggled to get over her shock, to give explanations to relatives and put away the blue baby clothes, she also had to make a decision: whether to subject her daughter to surgery to reduce the enlarged clitoris that made her look like a boy, or leave it alone.

Thus Ms. Greene, a 26-year-old cashier in East Providence, R.I., was thrown into a raging debate over a rare but increasingly controversial type of cosmetic surgery.

For decades, parents and pediatricians have sought to offer children whose anatomy does not conform to strictly male or female standards a surgical fix. But the private quest for "normal" is now being challenged in a very public way by some adults who underwent genital surgery and speak of a physical and emotional toll.

Some of them gave tearful testimony at a hearing last May before the San Francisco Human Rights Commission, which has taken up the surgeries as a human rights issue and is expected to announce recommendations before the end of the year. They spoke of lives burdened by secrecy, shame and medical complications: some said the surgeries robbed them of sexual sensation and likened the procedures to mutilation; others said they were made to feel like freaks when nothing was really wrong with them.

*Source:* Navarro (2004: 1).

and this latter consideration varies within and among societies.

Comparisons of different societies show wide variations in the ways in which masculinity and femininity are represented and perceived. Historical studies indicate that some North American native peoples, including the Cheyenne, Ojibwa, Navajo, and Iroquois, allowed the practice of *berdache* among individuals who were biologically male but preferred doing women's work and dressing as women; they were even permitted to take husbands. Although they had male genitals, they ceased to be males in other respects (Whitehead 1981). In contrast, although Western societies today tend to tolerate transvestites (men who like to dress as women, or women as men), in

the case of transsexuals, who believe their anatomy is out of synch with their gender identity, there is often pressure to undertake psychiatric or surgical treatment to bring them into line with their anatomy (see box titled "When Gender Isn't a Given").

In a study comparing three societies in New Guinea, anthropologist Margaret Mead (1936)

**Transvestites** Men who prefer to dress as women or women who prefer to dress as men. Compared with transsexuals, transvestites are more commonly tolerated in modern Western society. Both transvestites and transsexuals challenge the notion that gender and sex are natural and identical.

found very different gender patterns. Among the Arapesh both sexes appeared to be sensitive and cooperative, exhibiting traits that we might consider typically "feminine." The Mundugumor were much fiercer, and both sexes seemed selfish and aggressive—patterns of behavior regarded as "masculine" in our society. And among the Tchambuli (or Chambri), male and female behaviors were clearly distinguished, but the women were rational and dominant whereas the men were submissive, emotional, and nurturing. Mead's accounts of these three societies have been criticized on the grounds that the contrasts were too neat. For example, one author countered that the Tchambuli men were not normally as submissive as Mead claimed, suggesting that she had observed them at a time when they were reconstructing their homes after losing property in tribal wars (Gewertz 1981). Nevertheless, the main point of this anthropological evidence remains valid: Gender behavior patterns sometimes vary across societies.

On the other hand, one of the most extensive surveys of anthropological evidence from different societies seemed to stress uniformities in gender behavior. In a survey of 224 societies around the world, anthropologist George Murdock (1937) claimed to have found evidence that biological differences between men and women led to a similar division of tasks in all societies. His argument was that as men tend to be stronger and women bear children, it is natural that societies should divide tasks in a way that takes these biological differences into account; and in his view there was evidence showing that women were responsible for

**Transsexuals** Individuals who believe their anatomy is out of synch with their gender identity. For example, an individual might have male sex organs but identify as a woman. Often, transsexuals are pressured to undertake psychiatric or surgical treatment to bring their gender identity into line with their anatomy.

gathering vegetables, cooking, and caring for children, and men for hunting, mining, and warfare. However, feminist sociologist Anne Oakley (1974) argued that Murdock's account was flawed. She found 38 societies in his sample where cooking was shared equally between the sexes, and she pointed to a number of societies, not in his sample, where women's roles didn't fit the pattern Murdock had proposed. As an example of the latter she discussed the Mbuti Pygmies of the Congo rainforests, where men and women hunted together and shared child care. Additional examples include societies where women have worked as miners (e.g., Latin America) and undertaken combat roles in the armed forces (e.g., Cuba, China, and Israel in recent times).

Historical studies also reveal wide variations in gender patterns. Even in the relatively short period of the last fifty years, it is possible to find striking changes in movie portrayals of male and female characters. For example, in the 1950s, actors such as James Stewart and John Wayne were admired for their masculine qualities. Stewart represented the sober-suited, breadwinning family man, and John Wayne was the tough guy looked up to for being strong and protective. In the 1960s, however, these stereotypes came under critical attack and new versions of masculinity began to appear, epitomized by the agonized and sensitive characters played by actors such as James Dean and Montgomery Clift.

The rise of the women's movement, and of social movements promoting the rights of ethnic minorities and gays and lesbians, also raised questions about gender stereotypes, leading to an increased consciousness of diversity in gender patterns and behavior. Indeed, historians have shown that even as far back as the nineteenth century, gender models varied among different sections of the population. In America, for instance, the dominant model of femininity emphasized delicacy and women's need for male protection. But this model was much less applicable to working-class and black women. At a women's rights convention in Ohio in 1852, a group of men jeered at the participants and insisted that women needed protection, not the vote. A former slave, Sojourner Truth, mounted the platform and declared:

> That man over there says women need to be helped into carriages, and lifted over ditches, and to have the best place everywhere. Nobody ever helps me into carriages, or over mud-puddles, or gives me the best place! And ain't I a woman? Look at me! Look at my arm! I have ploughed, and planted and gathered into barns, and no man could head me! And ain't I a woman? I could work as much and eat as much as a man—when I could get it—and bear the lash as well! And ain't I a woman? I have borne thirteen children, and seen most of them sold off to slavery, and when I cried out with my mother's grief, none but Jesus heard me! And ain't I a woman? (Quoted in hooks 1981: 160)

Auguste Comte (1798–1857), the sociologist who gave sociology its name and laid many of its foundations, believed that the division of tasks between males and females was based on biological differences, especially those of a "mental" nature. He maintained that women were naturally more emotional and caring, whereas men were more rational. Although Comte was criticized for this **biological determinism** by a former admirer—the champion of women's rights John Stuart Mill (see Thompson 1976)—the idea that there is a special affinity between women and expressive emotional behavior prevailed in a more sociological form for a long time. In the 1950s the foremost American sociologist of the time, Talcott Parsons, spoke of the "expressive female" and argued that modern society functioned more effectively with a clear sexual division of labor: women giving emotional support and socialization to children in the private sphere of the family and men undertaking the more "instrumental" task of breadwinner in the

**Biological determinism** The idea that certain characteristics are inherently distinct as a result of biological factors. For example, early sociologist Auguste Comte believed that the division of labor between males and females was biologically determined. He maintained that women were naturally more emotional and caring and thus more suited to manage a household, and that men were naturally more rational and thus better suited to work outside the home.

public sphere of the economy. (For more discussion of family and gender roles, see Chapter 7, on marriage and the family.) Feminist sociologists in the 1970s took issue with both biological and sociological determinism of gender when they challenged the idea that a gendered division of labor was necessary. They pointed out that child-care arrangements had varied in different societies, as had the work tasks undertaken by women (Oakley 1974). Feminist sociologists also charged that male social scientists had simply reinforced traditional ideas about relationships between men and women, while not admitting that the social role ascribed to women—that of wife and mother—served the interests of men and maintained their power.

Sociologists today regard gender not as an inevitable outcome of biology but as a *process* and *product* of social construction. From the moment of birth, gendering takes place through interaction with parents and other family members, teachers, and peers (*significant others*). Through socialization and gendered personality development, the child is encouraged to develop a gendered identity that, in most cases, reproduces the values, attitudes, and behavior that the child's social environment deems appropriate for a girl or a boy. (Chapter 5, on socialization and the life cycle, considers this topic in greater detail.)

Even as babies, boys and girls are handled and responded to differently by parents and other caregivers. Infant boys are likely to be handled more robustly and infant girls more gently (Mc-Donald and Parke 1986), possibly accounting for the faster early development of physical confidence and motor skills in boys. Studies of communication between infants and caregivers show that when little boys demanded attention by behaving aggressively (e.g., by screaming or crying loudly) they tended to get it, whereas little girls elicited responses from adults when they attempted to use language or made gentle gestures. By the age of 2, girls become more talkative and boys more assertive in their communication styles (Fagot et al. 1985). Subsequently, little boys accept the gender ideal of exercising strength or skills. In contrast, girls learn to value "appearance" and to manage themselves as "ornamental objects" (West and Zimmerman 1987).

Another subtle aspect of the process of gendering personalities through socialization concerns the emotional bonding between parents and children. Borrowing from the psychoanalytic theory of Sigmund Freud, Nancy Chodorow (1978) argues that because mothers usually provide most early child care, infants bond more closely with them. The formation of the self entails separating from the mother, with whom the infant is psychologically merged. Girls can separate gradually and maintain a continuous relationship with the mother, whose gender is the same. But for boys the separation entails repressing feminine characteristics and rejecting the emotional tenderness of the early relationship. The sense of maleness is achieved at some emotional cost. The result is that boys develop a more autonomous sense of self and exhibit greater competitiveness and instrumentality, but have difficulty expressing their emotions and accepting intimacy. Girls develop qualities that are associated with being feminine, such as having greater empathy and being able to sustain relationships. In adult relationships, men may regard women as a threat to their independence and masculine sexuality because they remind them of their dependence on their mothers. At the same time, however, men may feel that they need women for the emotional support and intimacy that they rarely get from other men. Their mixed feelings toward women may take the form of the love-hate relationships often depicted in the media; extreme versions of such relationships may involve pornography, domestic violence, and sexual abuse of women. Peer-group relations are also important for the construction of gender characteristics and identities. On the playground, girls and boys tend to divide up into separate groups. Within the group, girls appear more cooperative and play people-based games. Boys, by contrast, tend to play competitive, rule-based games.

## HARDLY FAIR PLAY: GENDER AND SPORTS

The sports realm presents another opportunity in which to observe the reproduction of gender differences. Traditionally, school sports and professional sports have given greater prestige to manly prowess, such as strength. (See Tables 9.1 and 9.2 for related information regarding sports news coverage.) Where women did gain recognition it was often because they combined skill with feminine attractiveness. For example, *Sports Illustrated* has rarely featured women on its front cover apart from the (highly lucrative) annual swimsuit issue. But it made an exception for the then fifteenth-ranked tennis player Anna Kournikova in its June 5, 2000, issue, running a cover story that unabashedly celebrated her sexual attractiveness more than her athletic abilities. In the two years leading up to this story, the magazine had featured only five female athletes on its cover—which amounts to 4 percent of 123 issues. The relative absence of women athletes from the pages of *Sports Illustrated* during this time is explained in part by the introduction of *Sports Illustrated for Women* in 1997. While a magazine devoted to the accomplishments of female athletes is in many re-

**TABLE 9.1  Minutes and Proportion of Sports News, by Gender, on ESPN *Sports Center***

|  | Number of Stories | Total Minutes | Percentage |
|---|---|---|---|
| Men's sports | 551 | 991.8 | 96.7 |
| Women's sports | 24 | 22.1 | 2.2 |
| Neutral or both men and women | 10 | 11.9 | 1.1 |

*Note:* These statistics are based on analysis of three weeks of one-hour 11 p.m. ESPN *Sports Center* broadcasts. Three two-week periods were selected in order to include a range of different sports: March 15–28, July 12–25, November 8–21. *N* = 251 news broadcasts, fifteen hours of airtime; *N* = 21 *Sports Center* broadcasts, approximately seventeen hours of airtime.

*Source:* Adapted from Duncan and Messner (2006).

**TABLE 9.2  Percentage Distribution of Sports News, by Gender**

|  | 1989 | 1993 | 1999 | 2004 |
|---|---|---|---|---|
| Men | 92.0 | 93.8 | 88.2 | 94.3 |
| Women | 5.0 | 5.1 | 8.7 | 4.7 |
| Neutral or both men and women | 3.0 | 1.1 | 3.1 | 1.0 |

*Note:* These statistics are based on analysis of six weeks of TV sports news (6 p.m. and 11 p.m.) on three local network affiliates in Los Angeles. Three two-week periods were selected in order to include a range of different sports: March 15–28, July 12–25, and November 8–21. *N* = 251 news broadcasts, approximately fifteen hours of airtime.

*Source:* Adapted from Duncan and Messner (2006).

spects a positive development for women's sports, its existence has excused the parent magazine from printing more responsible coverage of women's sports. With women safely confined to a "media ghetto" on the margins, *Sports Illustrated* can remain the "cultural center" of print media with an authoritative voice that ostensibly transcends gender. After all, *Sports Illustrated* was never renamed "Sports Illustrated for Men" (Messner 2002).

Recently, increased opportunities for women in sports have led to changes in images of femininity. One overlooked fact is that, although men have greater short-term strength, women can outperform men in some tests of long-term endurance. As their opportunities to compete at the top level in athletics have increased, women have been closing the performance gap in marathon races. In 1925 the record for men was under two hours and thirty minutes, whereas for women it was over three hours and forty minutes; by 1998 fewer than fifteen minutes separated the world marathon records for women and men. In soccer, the success

of the United States' team in the 1999 Women's World Cup made media stars of the players to a degree never attained by the national men's team. At the same time, the team members took the opportunity to present a new image of the attractive female athlete—one that featured muscles (see box titled "Strong Signals"). Perhaps this reflects wider changes whereby women are asserting their independence and strength. Yet the media treatment of these women soccer players was still cast in terms of their attractiveness, even if that image now included muscles.

The downside of this concern with developing the body and its appearance is that it can lead to eating disorders and other worrying conditions. Such circumstances are not confined to athletes: "Research studies consistently reveal that between four and nine percent of female college students meet the criteria for clinical eating disorders of anorexia nervosa and bulimia. ... Between 60 and 80 percent of college women have been found to engage in regular binge eating and other abnormal

**Body image**   A person's perception of his or her own appearance. Body image is not a neutral perception but, rather, is heavily influenced by cultural and social norms and values regarding what is beautiful, masculine, feminine, strong, and so on. For example, in contemporary society there is a high emphasis placed on being physically fit, thin, and strong.

**Body image disorder**   A condition characterized by excessive emphasis on the development and appearance of one's body. Individuals with body image disorders have inaccurate perceptions of their appearance and act in accordance with these distorted perceptions. For example, people who suffer from anorexia nervosa perceive themselves as fat, even when underweight, and starve themselves to lose weight.

The winning U.S. Women's World Cup soccer team marked a turning point in sports: The generation of girls who benefited from Title IX came into its own. Here Brandy Chastain celebrated the team's win over China in 1999. (AP Photo/San Francisco Examiner/Lacy Atkins)

eating behavior that falls short of the clinical criteria. Many college women who are at normal weights continue to express a strong desire to be thinner and hold beliefs about food and body image that are similar to those of problem eaters" (Hesse-Biber, Marino, and Watts-Roy 1999: 385). The idealized **body image** that women students feel pressured to live up to is not associated exclusively with high school or college. Indeed, it is implanted at a much earlier stage as part of the socialization process; recall our earlier discussion of the effects of gendered socialization on preschool girls, such as learning to value "appearance." Studies of college women with **body image disorders** reveal the importance of the messages that young girls receive from their parents and siblings. A number of women who have suffered from eating disorders relate the fact that, as they were growing up, their families exhibited an overemphasis on physical appearance, especially the importance of being thin. Examples of the tension sparked by this emphasis on physical appearance include the following:

JOAN: My brothers and sisters would go around and make pig noises. ... My dad would say, "You need to lose weight." And I'd try and I'd be successful.

BECKY: My brothers would mention to my mother and she would say, "Tommy thinks you are getting fat" and then she'd say, "Maybe you should stop eating so much." He (father) commented a lot. Never bad. Always good. He'd say, "You look good, you lost weight." He was always commenting on pretty young girls. So I knew it was important to him that I look good too. I wanted him to see that I could be as pretty as all the girls he was commenting on. I wanted him to be proud of me for that, and I knew he was.

FLORENCE: I was sitting at the table and he (father) would just turn to one of the girls ... and he would say, "You're getting a little fat belly."

## media moments

### Strong Signals

Skinny is out, muscles are in. Today's female athletes are helping shape the way we feel about our bodies—for the better.

If there's a poster girl for positive body image, it's Brandi Chastain, who achieved instant celebrity last summer when she made the winning penalty kick in the Women's World Cup, then whipped off her jersey and celebrated with abs bared and biceps cocked.

Adding to the media frenzy was the fact that Chastain had just posed in *Gear* magazine, proudly baring her buffness in, well, the buff. Women aren't supposed to have muscles, are they? If they do, they aren't supposed to show them off, right?

Wrong. Today's female athletes are challenging society's perceptions of femininity and the ideal female body type. "Anybody in their right mind would rather be Mia Hamm than Barbie," says Emily Hancock, Ed.D., author of *The Girl Within* (Ballantine). "Girls these days realize that muscles are something to admire." …

Sadly, many female athletes, especially teens, struggle with negative body image. Says Diane G. Sanford, Ph.D., president of the Women's Healthcare Partnership in St. Louis, "There's more pressure for them to focus on their appearance, in terms of how muscular they are and how much they weigh."

It's a paradox fraught with danger: Athletes must be in tune with their bodies, yet obsessing about appearance can lead to problems ranging from eating disorders to steroid abuse. A 1994 Norwegian study found that 29%–35% of female athletes in esthetic sports (such as gymnastics, figure skating and diving) have eating disorders. At the opposite end of the spectrum, use of steroids has doubled among teenage girls since 1991, reports the National Institute on Drug Abuse. …

As for Chastain, 31, she admits she has come a long way from her junior prom, when she wouldn't dance because the sleeves of her dress kept falling down and exposing her big shoulders. "I'm much more comfortable because society has finally accepted the notion that women can be athletic and feminine," she says.

That positive feeling contributes to success on the field. "People should find confidence in their uniqueness," Chastain says. "My uniqueness just happens to be in my athleticism. I feel good when I go onto the field. I stand taller, I push myself more—and I don't get knocked around."

*Source:* Rasmusson (2000).

MARY: My dad used to call me fat. I wouldn't have noticed on my own. … I was three years old when my dad was calling me fat." (Hesse-Biber, Marino, and Watts-Roy 1999: 399)

The socialization process plays a large part in reproducing gender differences, including how we shape and view our bodies. The male or female body is not something that is just "given," with gender a gloss that is added. On the contrary, the body is molded and shaped by culture. However, as we have noted, the picture varies among societies and within societies. We should also be on guard against accepting too deterministic a view of this process and underestimating the capacity of men and women to vary or change their behavior.

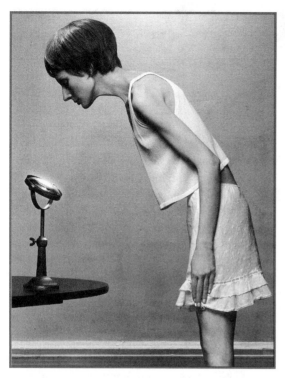

An overemphasis on slenderness as the ideal body size has led to an epidemic of eating disorders among young American women. (Dennis Galante/Corbis)

**Gendering** The process by which individuals take on gender identities, behaviors, and actions. There is no such thing as a single, fixed gender identity, such as "man" or "woman." Rather, gendering is a fluid process that intersects with other identities or aspects of identity, including class, status, ethnicity, and sexuality.

**Stereotype** An oversimplified (and often exaggerated) belief that is applied to an entire social category and/or the individuals within it. For example, a gender stereotype might characterize all women as overemotional and thus unfit for physically demanding, rigorous jobs.

**Horizontal segregation** Gender segregation across occupations. For example, nursing and school teaching are jobs typically held by women, whereas construction work and engineering are jobs typically held by men.

There is no such thing as a single, fixed gender identity, such as that of "woman" or of "man." Rather, **gendering** is a fluid process—one that is always intermingling with other identities or aspects of identity, including class, status, ethnicity, sexuality (gay, lesbian, heterosexual), and so on. Furthermore, although studies of gender acquisition may tell us about how gender differences are formed, they do not always reveal the inequalities and power relations between males and females—especially that of male dominance (*patriarchy*). For such analyses we need to look at some of the main social institutions, such as the economy, the family, and the mass media.

## GENDER AT WORK

Whether or not they have fully internalized the social construction of gender differences or tried to rebel against gender **stereotypes,** adults encounter a gendered work world (see Tables 9.3, 9.4, 9.5, and 9.6). In industrialized and postmodern societies, many of the workplaces that adults enter are either predominantly or completely single-gender. This situation is referred to as **horizontal segregation.** During the 1970s and 1980s, as part of the shift in Western economies from manufacturing to services, there was a massive influx of women into the labor force, rising from 39 percent of American women working in 1965 to 60 percent in 1998. At the same time, women were staying longer in paid work and taking shorter career breaks when their children were young. (See Chapter 7, on marriage and the family, for more on this subject.) These were decades in which women were thought to have made inroads into many occupations previously dominated by men in the United States. Yet, only about 6 percent of occupations saw an increase of women workers that was significantly more than the general increase of women in the paid labor force during that period. Rather than bringing about desegre-

**TABLE 9.3  Selected Occupational Groups by Gender, United States, 2000**

|  | Total (%) | Men (%) | Women (%) |
|---|---|---|---|
| Management, professional, and related occupations | 33.6 | 31.4 | 36.2 |
| Service occupations | 14.9 | 12.1 | 18.0 |
| Sales and office occupations | 26.7 | 17.9 | 36.7 |
| Farming, fishing, and forestry occupations | 0.7 | 1.1 | 0.3 |
| Construction, extraction, and maintenance occupations | 9.4 | 17.1 | 0.7 |
| Production, transportation, and material moving occupations | 14.6 | 20.5 | 8.0 |

*Note:* These data are based on a sample. For information on confidentiality protection, sampling error, nonsampling error, and definitions, see www.census.gov/prod/cen2000/doc/sf3.pdf.

*Source:* Adapted from Fronczek and Johnson (2003).

**TABLE 9.4  The Ten Occupations Employing the Most Women, United States, 2000**

| Occupations | Number | Percentages |
|---|---|---|
| Employed civilian females 16 years and over | 60,630,069 | 100.0 |
| Secretaries and administrative assistants | 3,597,535 | 5.9 |
| Elementary and middle school teachers | 2,442,104 | 4.0 |
| Registered nurses | 2,065,238 | 3.4 |
| Cashiers | 2,030,805 | 3.3 |
| Retail salespersons | 1,775,889 | 2.9 |
| Bookkeeping, accounting, and auditing clerks | 1,526,803 | 2.5 |
| Nursing, psychiatric, and home health aides | 1,469,736 | 2.4 |
| Customer service representatives | 1,396,105 | 2.3 |
| Child-care workers | 1,253,306 | 2.1 |
| Waiters and waitresses | 1,228,977 | 2.0 |

*Note:* These data are based on a sample, and the occupations are based on the most detailed level of occupations available in Census 2000 (509 occupations). Confidence intervals are not displayed because they round the percentages shown in the table.

*Source:* Adapted from U.S. Census Bureau (2000).

gation of occupations, most of the new women workers went into occupations where most of the employees were women. Those who chose occupations whose employees were predominantly men often found that men then left those occupations. Among the U.S. occupations that went from mostly male to mostly female were personnel, training, and labor relations specialists; computer operators; and insurance adjusters, examiners, and investigators. In effect, these occupations had resegregated. When women join men in previously all-male occupations, gender stereotypes are symbolically maintained, as when policewomen view their work as social work or male nurses empha-

**TABLE 9.5 The Ten Occupations Employing the Most Men, United States, 2000**

| Occupations | Number | Percentages |
|---|---|---|
| Employed civilian males 16 years and over | 69,091,443 | 100.0 |
| Driver/sales workers and truck drivers | 2,925,936 | 4.2 |
| First-line supervisors/managers of retail sales workers | 1,606,310 | 2.3 |
| Retail salespersons | 1,605,860 | 2.3 |
| Laborers and freight, stock, and material movers | 1,448,035 | 2.1 |
| Carpenters | 1,317,690 | 1.9 |
| Janitors and building cleaners | 1,308,889 | 1.9 |
| Managers | 1,253,965 | 1.8 |
| Construction laborers | 1,066,404 | 1.5 |
| Sales representatives, wholesale and manufacturing | 1,026,745 | 1.5 |
| First-line supervisors/managers of production and operating workers | 1,008,876 | 1.5 |

*Note*: These data are based on a sample, and occupations are based on the most detailed level of occupations available in Census 2000 (509 occupations). Confidence intervals are not displayed because they round the percentages shown in the table.

*Source:* Adapted from U.S. Census Bureau (2000).

size the technical and physical strength aspects of the job.

Gender is not the sole source of discrimination in job allocation. Race and ethnicity are also involved. The concept of "queues" has been used to analyze this process. In *Job Queues, Gender Queues,* Barbara Reskin and Patricia Roos (1990) argue that the processes that sort women and men of various racial or ethnic groups into different types of work involve a matching of ranked workers and jobs, or queues of workers and jobs. Workers are ranked by employers from their first picks to their last. Jobs are similarly ranked by workers. Lower-ranked workers get the chance to move into better jobs than they previously held when these jobs are abandoned by favored workers, or when there are too few of these workers to go around, as in wartime. The process works the other way, too: When there are too few of the best jobs for preferred workers, as in a recession, only the best qualified or experienced will be hired; conversely, those with fewer credentials and less seniority move down the queue, bumping out lesser-ranked workers. When workers are moving up, workers who occupy the most preferred race, ethnicity, and gender categories usually get the better jobs. In some cases, the job may be so rigidly stereotyped as "women's work" that men will not apply or be hired; thus, certain jobs in service, sales, and clerical work continue to remain female, even when men are available owing to the decline in manufacturing jobs.

The main factor that redistributes workers of different genders and races is changes in the structure of the work process and in the quality of particular jobs within occupations. This is a factor that can be manipulated by employers. That is, jobs can be automated and de-skilled or made part-time or home-based to bring about a reduction in labor costs, with a few better-paid workers (often white men) retained in supervisory positions. Shifts in labor queues up and down the job

**TABLE 9.6  Annual Median Earnings of Americans by Gender, 1955–2001**

| Year | Men | Women | % of Men's Earnings |
|------|-----|-------|---------------------|
| 1955 | 4,241 | 2,735 | 64 |
| 1960 | 5,434 | 3,296 | 61 |
| 1965 | 6,598 | 3,816 | 58 |
| 1970 | 9,184 | 5,440 | 59 |
| 1975 | 12,934 | 7,719 | 60 |
| 1980 | 19,173 | 11,591 | 60 |
| 1985 | 24,999 | 16,252 | 65 |
| 1990 | 28,979 | 20,591 | 71 |
| 1995 | 32,199 | 23,777 | 74 |
| 2001 | 40,136 | 30,420 | 76 |

*Note:* Sample consists of people 15 years old and over as of March 1980, and people 14 years old and over as of March 1981. Income is represented in current and 2001 CPI-U-RS adjusted dollars.

*Source:* U.S. Census Bureau (2004).

ladder may be accompanied by conflict between women and men or among ethnic groups. Dominant men generally want to maintain the work conditions that justify their high pay. And employers who want to reduce labor costs may degrade the working conditions so they can hire cheaper labor, at which point these new workers are often accused of depressing the job's qualifications and skills. Reserving some of the better jobs for men is one of the ways employers keep their male workers satisfied, while expanding the number of cheaper workers.

In situations characterized by **vertical segregation,** women are concentrated at lower levels of the occupations hierarchy in terms of rewards and status. On the whole, women's work tends to entail lower levels of pay, prestige, and fringe benefits, such as health insurance. Researchers have estimated that if wages were used to compensate for unattractive nonmonetary characteristics, women's jobs would have to pay four times as much as men's jobs (Jencks, Perman, and Rainwater 1988). Indeed, even the lower pay that women receive for full-time work is not compensated for by allowing them better opportunities to undertake child care. Control over the timing of tasks and the flexibility of scheduling is more likely to be the prerogative of male managers than of their female secretaries.

The best-paid jobs are still modeled on the ideal image of the traditional male career—long-term, continuous work in the same occupation, with steady pay raises and a pension at retirement. Men are expected to earn more when they marry and have children, so employers tend to view them as better workers than women; by contrast, women are often thought of as earning only supplementary income, whether they are married or single, inasmuch as they are viewed primarily as daughters, wives, or mothers. Yet research has shown that, in actuality, married women with children work harder and are more productive than married men with children (Bielby and Bielby 1988).

What is regarded as "women's work" or "men's work" has a sense of normality and naturalness, sometimes accompanied by a moral justification. Men are expected to fill jobs that seem designed to enable them to exercise their skills or use their strength, while women's jobs may appear to allow them to express a "natural" capacity, such as caring for others. The justification for such cultural typifications is usually an after-the-fact rationalization. The assumption is that the skills, compe-

**Vertical segregation**  Gender segregation within an occupation. In situations characterized by vertical segregation, one gender is concentrated at lower levels of the occupations hierarchy in terms of status and pay—a pattern that results in part from differential and unequal opportunities in hiring, training, and promotion. For example, unlike their male counterparts, women in the corporate world frequently encounter barriers to promotion, particularly to the level of CEO.

tence, strength, and other qualities needed to do a job are tied up with masculinity and femininity, but in fact the gendering of job identities is socially constructed, imparted during primary socialization and reinforced by secondary socialization (again, see Chapter 5), training, and organizational sociability, such as women making the coffee and men playing in company golf games and sports teams. Within gender-typed occupations there may be specific specialties that are gender-typed in the opposite direction. For example, the majority of physicians are men in the United States and women in Russia, but in both societies the same specialties are gender-typed—pediatrics for women and neurosurgery for men. These culturally informed hierarchies are reinforced by economic structures. It is no coincidence that in both societies neurosurgery pays better and has more prestige than pediatrics. And opportunities for promotion within occupations tend to be greater for men than for women, with women bumping up against a "glass ceiling"—a lid on their progress up the ladder beyond a certain point. Even in professions where women are in the majority, such as elementary school teaching, men are more likely to rise to positions such as superintendent—a phenomenon dubbed the "glass escalator."

Exceptions to this gender-based hierarchy in the sphere of work and the economy are given widespread publicity, as in cases where a woman is the chief executive of a major corporation. But these are still exceptions to the general rule whereby males occupy the best jobs and positions of authority. At the bottom of it all is a cultural reason for which so few women are in top positions: What we think of as an "authoritative" character is often conflated with "masculinity" (Kanter 1977). True gender equality would mean that women have access to the same professional and occupational training, and are distributed in the same proportions within occupations and hierarchical positions. Instead, women in most industrialized countries are overrepresented in clerical and service jobs, low-prestige professional and technical work, and sales; in developing countries, and in areas of industrialized societies with large numbers of poor people and recent immigrants, women tend to be concentrated in labor-intensive factory work, agriculture, and the informal (off-the-books) economy. In short, despite the emergence of feminism and the disappearance of "objective" or natural reasons for economic gender hierarchies, significant cultural stereotyping remains.

## Women in the Global Economy: Is Any Job Better Than No Job?

Street vendors, roadside barbers, domestic workers, garment makers, food processors, cigarette rollers, assemblers of electronic parts: These are examples of jobs in the informal economy. But whether they involve self-employment in small, home-based enterprises or wage-paid day labor or piecework, all such jobs are without secure contracts, benefits, or social protection.

As Table 9.7 demonstrates, the informal sector is a major part of the economy in developing countries, accounting for one-half to three-quarters of employment outside of agriculture. This table further shows that women are disproportionately involved in the informal sector. This is partly due to structural inequality. Disadvantaged in terms of ed-

**Gender ideologies** Sets of cultural beliefs, values, and attitudes about the genders that contribute to the rationalization of inequalities in society. For example, gender ideologies about women's roles and the lower value of their work help to perpetuate the lower wages they receive relative to men.

**Reserve army of labor** A pool of workers who are available for full-time work in times of scarce labor and can easily be fired or put on part-time schedules when there is less work. Typically, the reserve army of labor is composed of women and minorities.

ucation, training, wages, and occupational segregation, women continue to be a source of cheap labor. But culture also plays a role. **Gender ideologies** about women's roles and the lower value of women's work contribute to the rationalization of low wages and insecurity. Since women are not expected to be the major breadwinners in families, there is no social pressure on employers to pay them a living wage. Some women, furthermore, prefer to think of their work as a hobby to avoid contradicting traditional gender roles. For others, working part-time or in the home is an attractive option because it allows them to make money without disrupting their domestic responsibilities (see Table 9.8).

To understand why this pattern of gender inequality is reproduced we must examine not only fundamental cultural patterns (see Chapter 3, on cultural structures) but also the functioning of institutions that sustain inequality in public life, complementing the gendered patterns of domestic labor (see Chapter 7, on marriage and the family, and Chapter 13, on education). Low pay, uninteresting jobs, and the glass ceiling encourage single women to marry and married women to devote energy and attention to child-rearing and domestic work. And, in turn, the way the economy works encourages the development of a **reserve army of labor**—a pool of workers who are available for full-time work in times of scarce labor and can easily be fired or put on part-time schedules when there is less work. Women and immigrants make up the majority of the reserve army of labor. More stable jobs are offered to men of the dominant racial and ethnic groups to encourage them to give their all to the job. Employers, most of whom are men them-

**TABLE 9.7** Informal Employment in Nonagricultural Employment, by Gender, 1994–2000

| Region/ Country | Informal Employment as % of Nonagricultural Employment | Women's Informal Employment as % of Women's Nonagricultural Employment | Men's Informal Employment as % of Men's Nonagricultural Employment |
|---|---|---|---|
| North Africa | 48 | 43 | 49 |
| Algeria | 43 | 41 | 43 |
| Morocco | 45 | 47 | 44 |
| Tunisia | 50 | 39 | 53 |
| Egypt | 55 | 46 | 57 |
| Sub-Saharan Africa | 72 | 84 | 63 |
| Benin | 93 | 97 | 87 |
| Chad | 74 | 95 | 60 |
| Guinea | 72 | 87 | 66 |
| Kenya | 72 | 83 | 59 |
| South Africa | 51 | 58 | 44 |
| Latin America | 51 | 58 | 48 |
| Bolivia | 63 | 74 | 55 |
| Brazil | 60 | 67 | 55 |
| Chile | 36 | 44 | 31 |
| Colombia | 38 | 44 | 34 |
| Costa Rica | 44 | 48 | 42 |
| El Salvador | 57 | 69 | 46 |
| Guatemala | 56 | 69 | 47 |
| Honduras | 58 | 65 | 74 |
| Mexico | 55 | 55 | 54 |
| Dominican Republic | 50 | 47 | 48 |
| Venezuela | 47 | 47 | 47 |
| Asia | 65 | 65 | 65 |
| India | 83 | 86 | 83 |
| Indonesia | 78 | 77 | 78 |
| Philippines | 72 | 73 | 71 |
| Thailand | 51 | 54 | 49 |
| Syria | 42 | 35 | 43 |

*Source:* ILO (2002).

**TABLE 9.8 Wage and Self-Employment in Nonagricultural Informal Employment, by Gender, 1994–2000**

| Region/ Country | Self-Employment as % of Nonagricultural Informal Employment | | | Wage Employment as % of Nonagricultural Informal Employment | | |
|---|---|---|---|---|---|---|
| | Total | Women | Men | Total | Women | Men |
| North Africa | 62 | 72 | 60 | 38 | 28 | 40 |
| Algeria | 67 | 81 | 64 | 33 | 19 | 36 |
| Morocco | 81 | 89 | 78 | 19 | 11 | 22 |
| Tunisia | 52 | 51 | 52 | 48 | 49 | 48 |
| Egypt | 50 | 67 | 47 | 50 | 33 | 53 |
| Sub-Saharan Africa | 70 | 71 | 70 | 30 | 29 | 30 |
| Benin | 95 | 98 | 91 | 5 | 2 | 9 |
| Chad | 93 | 99 | 86 | 7 | 1 | 14 |
| Guinea | 95 | 98 | 95 | 5 | 2 | 6 |
| Kenya | 42 | 33 | 56 | 58 | 67 | 44 |
| South Africa | 25 | 27 | 23 | 75 | 73 | 77 |
| Latin America | 60 | 58 | 61 | 40 | 42 | 39 |
| Bolivia | 81 | 91 | 71 | 19 | 9 | 29 |
| Brazil | 41 | 32 | 50 | 59 | 68 | 50 |
| Chile | 52 | 39 | 64 | 48 | 61 | 36 |
| Colombia | 38 | 36 | 40 | 62 | 64 | 60 |
| Costa Rica | 55 | 49 | 59 | 45 | 51 | 41 |
| El Salvador | 65 | 71 | 57 | 35 | 29 | 43 |
| Guatemala | 60 | 65 | 55 | 40 | 35 | 45 |
| Honduras | 72 | 77 | 65 | 28 | 23 | 35 |
| Mexico | 54 | 53 | 54 | 46 | 47 | 46 |
| Dominican Republic | 74 | 63 | 80 | 26 | 37 | 20 |
| Venezuela | 69 | 66 | 70 | 31 | 34 | 30 |
| Asia | 59 | 63 | 55 | 41 | 37 | 45 |
| India | 52 | 57 | 51 | 48 | 43 | 49 |
| Indonesia | 63 | 70 | 59 | 37 | 30 | 41 |
| Philippines | 48 | 63 | 36 | 52 | 37 | 64 |
| Thailand | 66 | 68 | 64 | 34 | 32 | 36 |
| Syria | 65 | 57 | 67 | 35 | 43 | 33 |

*Source:* ILO (2002).

selves, benefit from women's cheap labor and from the fact that the private needs of male workers are met in the home by the unpaid domestic labor of women. Female employees still perform the majority of household tasks, returning home from a day's work to put in a "second shift" (Hochschild 1989) of cleaning, shopping, and cooking that, on average, amounts to 19.5 hours a week for married women in the United States. Housework within the "private sphere" of the family is not considered "real work" in our market-based economy, because it does not have a market price in the form of wages (Walby 1990). Better-paid and professional women workers may find that, in order to compete with male colleagues, they have to hire "wives"—other women to do their domestic work. This pool of paid domestic labor—usually made up of poorer women and recent immigrants—is increasingly in demand in many areas.

## The Division of Domestic Labor: The Ambiguous Result of the "Chore Wars"

It could have something to do with the success of second-wave feminists, or perhaps because standards in the struggle to balance work and family have been relaxed—but either way, women are spending less time doing housework than they did in the 1960s. As shown in Tables 9.9 and 9.10, women in 1995 spent 17.5 hours a week doing housework, down from 30 hours a week in 1965. Men have started pulling more of their own weight, but women still do two-thirds of most kinds of housework. The disparity is most apparent when it comes to cleaning, the

**TABLE 9.9  Trends in Average Weekly Housework, United States, by Gender, for Individuals Aged 25–64**

|  | All Women | | | | All Men | | | | Ratio of Women's Time to Men's Time | | | |
|---|---|---|---|---|---|---|---|---|---|---|---|---|
|  | 1965 | 1975 | 1985 | 1995 | 1965 | 1975 | 1985 | 1995 | 1965 | 1975 | 1985 | 1995 |
| Total housework | 30.0 | 23.7 | 19.7 | 17.5 | 4.9 | 7.2 | 9.8 | 10.0 | 6.1 | 3.3 | 2.0 | 1.8 |
| Core housework | 26.9 | 21.0 | 16.3 | 13.9 | 2.3 | 2.5 | 4.0 | 3.8 | 11.9 | 8.3 | 4.0 | 3.7 |
| Cooking meals | 4.5 | 2.4 | 1.9 | 0.7 | 0.5 | 0.3 | 0.4 | 0.1 | 9.9 | 9.4 | 4.9 | 5.4 |
| Meal cleanup | 7.2 | 7.3 | 5.0 | 6.7 | 0.5 | 0.5 | 1.3 | 1.7 | 15.5 | 14.0 | 3.9 | 3.8 |
| Housecleaning | 7.2 | 7.3 | 5.0 | 6.7 | 0.5 | 0.5 | 1.3 | 1.7 | 15.5 | 14.0 | 3.9 | 3.8 |
| Laundry and ironing | 5.8 | 3.2 | 2.4 | 1.9 | 0.3 | 0.2 | 0.3 | 0.3 | 22.1 | 13.5 | 7.5 | 6.9 |
| Other housework | 3.1 | 2.7 | 3.4 | 3.6 | 2.6 | 4.7 | 5.7 | 6.2 | 1.2 | 0.6 | 0.6 | 0.6 |
| Outdoor chores | 0.3 | 0.7 | 0.5 | 0.8 | 0.4 | 1.0 | 1.3 | 1.9 | 0.7 | 0.7 | 0.4 | 0.4 |
| Repairs | 0.4 | 0.6 | 0.5 | 0.7 | 1.0 | 2.0 | 1.8 | 1.9 | 0.4 | 0.3 | 0.3 | 0.4 |
| Garden and animal care | 0.6 | 0.8 | 0.8 | 0.8 | 0.2 | 0.7 | 0.9 | 1.0 | 2.4 | 1.1 | 0.9 | 0.8 |
| Bills, other financial | 1.8 | 0.7 | 1.6 | 1.3 | 0.9 | 1.0 | 1.6 | 1.5 | 2.0 | 0.7 | 1.0 | 0.9 |
| *N* | 579 | 927 | 1,725 | 493 | 469 | 783 | 1,405 | 359 | | | | |

*Note:* Authors' calculations, time diary sample (1965–1995).

*Source:* Bianchi et al. (2000).

**TABLE 9.10  Trends in Average Weekly Housework, United States, by Gender, for Married Couples Aged 25–64**

|  | Married Women | | | | Married Men | | | | Ratio of Women's Time to Men's Time | | | |
|---|---|---|---|---|---|---|---|---|---|---|---|---|
|  | 1965 | 1975 | 1985 | 1995 | 1965 | 1975 | 1985 | 1995 | 1965 | 1975 | 1985 | 1995 |
| Total housework | 33.9 | 26.1 | 21.9 | 19.4 | 4.7 | 6.7 | 10.4 | 10.4 | 7.2 | 3.9 | 2.1 | 1.9 |
| Core housework | 30.4 | 22.9 | 18.4 | 15.8 | 1.8 | 1.9 | 4.0 | 3.7 | 16.6 | 12.3 | 4.6 | 4.3 |
| Cooking meals | 10.7 | 9.0 | 7.9 | 5.3 | 0.9 | 1.0 | 1.9 | 1.4 | 11.5 | 8.8 | 4.1 | 3.8 |
| Meal cleanup | 5.0 | 2.8 | 2.2 | 0.9 | 0.4 | 0.3 | 0.4 | 0.2 | 12.2 | 10.0 | 5.4 | 5.2 |
| Housecleaning | 8.1 | 7.3 | 5.6 | 7.1 | 0.4 | 0.4 | 1.4 | 1.9 | 21.7 | 16.2 | 4.1 | 3.8 |
| Laundry and ironing | 6.6 | 3.8 | 2.7 | 2.4 | 0.1 | 0.1 | 0.3 | 0.3 | 55.3 | 32.4 | 9.4 | 9.5 |
| Other housework | 3.6 | 3.1 | 3.5 | 3.7 | 2.9 | 4.9 | 6.4 | 6.7 | 1.2 | 0.6 | 0.6 | 0.5 |
| Outdoor chores | 0.4 | 0.7 | 0.5 | 0.8 | 0.5 | 1.0 | 1.5 | 2.1 | 0.7 | 0.7 | 0.3 | 0.4 |
| Repairs | 0.5 | 0.9 | 0.6 | 0.8 | 1.3 | 2.2 | 2.1 | 2.2 | 0.4 | 0.4 | 0.3 | 0.3 |
| Garden and animal care | 0.6 | 0.8 | 0.8 | 1.0 | 0.3 | 0.6 | 1.1 | 0.8 | 2.2 | 1.3 | 0.8 | 1.3 |
| Bills, other financial | 2.0 | 0.8 | 1.6 | 1.1 | 0.8 | 1.0 | 1.8 | 1.6 | 2.5 | 0.7 | 0.9 | 0.7 |
| *N* | 452 | 722 | 1,175 | 416 | 678 | 1,041 | 211 | | | | | |

*Note:* Authors' calculations, time diary sample (1965–1995).

*Source:* Bianchi et al. (2000).

**TABLE 9.11  Division of Domestic Labor Index by Employment Status of Partners, United Kingdom**

| | Proportion of Domestic Work Time Contributed by Women in Couples | | | | | |
|---|---|---|---|---|---|---|
| | 1975 | 1987 | 1997 | 1975 | 1987 | 1997 |
| All | 0.77 | 0.67 | 0.63 | 680 | 388 | 175 |
| Both full-time | 0.68 | 0.62 | 0.6 | 158 | 104 | 57 |
| Husband full-time, wife part-time | 0.8 | 0.7 | 0.69 | 199 | 120 | 34 |
| Husband full-time, wife not employed | 0.82 | 0.73 | 0.73 | 294 | 118 | 23 |
| Other | 0.61 | 0.55 | 0.59 | 29 | 46 | 61 |

*Source:* Sullivan (2000).

**TABLE 9.12  Division of Domestic Labor Index by Employment Status of Partners and Socioeconomic Class, United Kingdom**

| | Proportion of Domestic Work Time Contributed by Women in Couples | | | |
|---|---|---|---|---|
| | Manual/Clerical | | Professional/Technical | |
| | 1975 | 1997 | 1975 | 1997 |
| All | 0.78 | 0.63 | 0.74 | 0.66 |
| Both full-time | 0.69 | 0.6 | 0.62 | 0.62 |
| Husband full-time, wife part-time | 0.8 | 0.68 | 0.74 | 0.71 |
| Husband full-time, wife not employed | 0.82 | 0.73 | 0.8 | 0.73 |
| Other | 0.58 | 0.53 | 0.72 | 0.65 |

*Source:* Sullivan (2000).

most despised task. Things are not much better in the United Kingdom, according to Oriel Sullivan (2000; see Tables 9.11 and 9.12). Even in households where both the man and the woman work full-time, the women still do more housework.

A United Nations report in 1980 estimated that women do two-thirds of the world's work, receive 10 percent of the world's income, and own 1 percent of the world's property. This imbalance in the relations of men and women has been described as the "patriarchal dividend"—the benefit that men gain from women's unpaid work maintaining homes and bringing up children, and from women's low-paid work in servicing hospitals, schools, and many other workplaces.

## A UNIVERSAL PROBLEM: EXPLOITATION AND VIOLENCE

Women's subordination at work is manifested not just in the abstract structure of the economy but also in interaction. During the 1990s, the issue of sexual harassment became so prominent that the rules of the workplace were literally rewritten for private corporations, government agencies, and educational institutions alike. Although women are not the only victims of harassment, they are the most common ones. As many as 50 percent of women at work are estimated to have been subjected to unwelcome sexual attention (Loy and Stewart 1984). Sociologist Carol Brooks Gardner (1994) has described this abuse as contributing to the situational disadvantage of women. The public sphere, she notes, is a territory where men hold and display certain rights, but women are more likely to experience a variety of unfavorable

## FIGURE 9.1 Percentage of Adult Women Reporting Physical Assault by a Male Partner

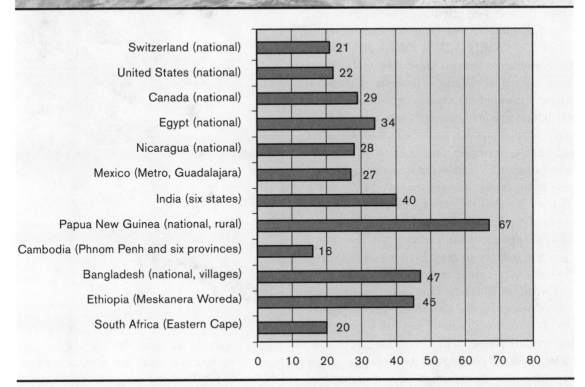

*Note:* The reference to "partner" includes any form of intimate relationship.

*Source:* Heise, Ellsberg, and Gottemoeller (1999).

circumstances, handicappings, drawbacks, and abuses. Having been made to feel unwelcome, women are faced with a choice: Either they retreat back to the private sphere or they develop strategies that reduce their appearance in public and ensure their safe passage through this hostile terrain (Gardner 1994).

Gender inequality is not confined to the sphere of paid work. Women experience domination and exploitation in other areas of life as well. Some are subjected to abuse, ranging from sexual harassment in the form of comments, gestures, or touching to rape and physical disfigurement, often at the hands of male relatives or friends (see Figure 9.1). Others are forced to bear children or are sterilized against

their will. It is girls who are most often abandoned in countries with overpopulation. And it is the bodies of girls that are most frequently used in sex work through prostitution and pornography.

It is difficult to arrive at accurate figures for the extent of **gender abuse** and exploitation throughout the world—in part because many victims are

**Gender abuse** Exploitation and violation of people (more often women than men) on the basis of their gender. Gender abuse includes but is not limited to sexual harassment, sexual assault, rape, and genital mutilation.

ashamed or afraid to report abuse, and in part because gender abuse is not universally considered a crime. Estimates suggest that, in the years since the Fourth United Nations Women's Conference in 1995 gave priority to these human rights violations, as many as one-quarter of the world's women have suffered some form of domestic violence—a frequent cause of suicide among women. At least 60 million girls are "missing" from the world's female populations due to sex-selective abortions, infanticide, or neglect, and as many as 2 million girls from 5 to 15 years of age are introduced every year to the commercial sex trade (UNFPA 2000). Women are also targets of extreme violence in times of conflict. Systematic rape, for the purpose of humiliating and demoralizing the enemy, is a common military strategy. Between 250,000 and 500,000 women were raped during the genocide in Rwanda in 1994, and rape figured prominently in Serbia's genocidal wars in the 1990s. Women are also vulnerable to abduction and forced sexual slavery during times of war. Trafficking rings benefit from reduced policing and the desperate poverty resulting from displacement. The International Migration Organization estimates that 2 million women are trafficked across borders every year (Rehn and Sirleaf 2002).

Estimates of gender abuse are further clouded by the fact that many violent acts are culturally defined. For instance, Western societies consider the practice of female genital surgeries to be morally abhorrent. Feminist advocacy groups have been outraged by this practice, condemning it as an act of brutality in which young girls are coerced, their sexual satisfaction denied, and their bodies maimed by their own families. Accordingly, they have sought the eradication of what they call "female genital mutilation." For many of the women who have actually undergone such surgery, however, the practice is not understood in terms of human rights or the denial of sexual pleasure. Rather, "female circumcision" is frequently defended as an important part of their cultural heritage, and the

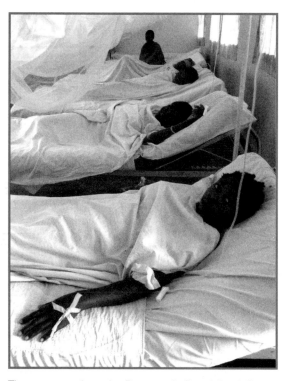

These women from the Democratic Republic of Congo have received surgery to repair their genitals from the brutal rapes they endured during the ongoing insurgency there. (Wolfgang Langenstrassen/dpa/Corbis)

practice itself is described in terms of cleanliness, beauty, and adulthood (Shweder 2000). The Muslim practices involving headscarf wearing and the veiling of women in public have similarly provoked ire from Western society and have been the focus of major controversies in Europe and the Middle East since the 1980s.

Pornography, which has spread beyond magazines and films to colonize large parts of the Internet with soft-porn websites, has been described by some feminists as central to the way in which men subordinate women (MacKinnon 1987), turning women into objects to be used and exploited by men. Pornography is said to incite violence toward women: "Pornography is the theory, and rape the practice" (Morgan 1980: 139). In 1983, Andrea Dworkin and Catharine MacKinnon proposed a draft ordinance to the Minneapolis city council to make the production or dissemination of pornography a civil offense on the grounds that it constituted a violation of women's civil rights. Whereas some feminists have accepted support from political conservatives in measures to censor material that they considered pornographic, other feminists have opposed such censorship, arguing that pornography is not central in maintaining women's subordination and that feminists should not be involved in campaigning for legal reform that restricts freedom of speech (Kelly 1988).

The debate about pornography raises questions about the ways in which women and men are represented by the mass media and in everyday cultural practices, ranging from advertisements to dating behavior and makeup (see also Chapter 4, on media and communication, and Chapter 5, on socialization and the life cycle). Such forms of communication are central to the focus of the "cultural turn" in the social sciences and humanities. But this emphasis on the media of communication and cultural practices in no way diminishes sociologists' certainty that women (especially ethnic minority women) face "real" structural inequalities, such as inferior pay and working conditions. As we have seen, such inequalities do exist, and they are substantial. The significance of the cultural construction and maintenance of gender differences is that contemporary societies proclaim values of equality and yet sanction images and practices that help to reproduce inequality. How does this happen?

## EVERYDAY CULTURE AND MASS MEDIA

All of us are skilled at seeing things, and ourselves, through the eyes of others. We have a stock of practical knowledge that enables us to know what behaviors are expected of us—what will receive a positive response or elicit a negative one. Of course, we make choices before acting, but these choices are not usually random. On the contrary, they tend to follow a pattern—and for each of us it is our particular version of a socially and culturally derived pattern. The main sources of our knowledge of such a pattern are our everyday life experiences at home, work, and leisure. We must always remember that our experiences are precoded by cultural structures as well as reinforced by our exposure to media of communication, which use visual symbols and verbal or written languages to make seemingly practical points. Gender differences are expressed through all of these communication media—which most definitely include the commercial structures of advertising.

An obvious example is that languages such as English and Spanish have gendered nouns (e.g., *chairman*) and pronouns (e.g., *he*). Over the last thirty years, feminists not only have worked to reveal the masculine dominance and gender discrimination that are subtly built into everyday speech but, indeed, have campaigned for the substitution of **gender-neutral language.** As a result, *humankind* has gradually replaced *mankind, police officer* has been substituted for *policeman, flight attendant* has replaced *stewardess,* and *head of department* or *chair* is now more commonly used than *chairman* or the more awkward *chairperson.*

Everyday life practices, such as etiquette on dates, also tend to be consistently patterned along gender lines. Research into young singles' dating practices has found that male and female partners consistently follow a **cultural script** that governs

**Gender-neutral language** Language that avoids gendered nouns and pronouns such as *mankind* and *he*. Many feminists have argued that gender inequalities and discrimination are promulgated by terminology that subtly implies masculine dominance and, accordingly, have campaigned in favor of everyday speech that employs gender-neutral language such as *humankind* and *they*.

their behavior. For example, one study of young heterosexual adults' expectations of behavior on their first date revealed a high level of agreement, even though the scripts for women and men differed considerably: The scripts for women emphasized the private sphere (concern about appearance, conversation, and controlling sexuality), whereas those for men focused on control of the public domain (planning, paying for, and orchestrating the date). This particular study also examined eight guides to adolescent dating behaviors representing the period from 1957 to 1988, finding little change in such behaviors throughout those years (Rose and Frieze 1989). However, other research has shown that, during the 1980s, the double standard of behavior implicit in traditional courting patterns was starting to disappear among college students. Evidence suggested that male and female dating partners were exhibiting equal power when signaling sexual interest during the flirtation phase of relationships and that women were freer to have premarital sex than in the past (McCormick and Jesser 1983). In addition, many young women were beginning to share date expenses (Korman and Leslie 1982), and a majority of young men reported having been asked for a date by a woman. The trend in this area of gender relations seems to be toward a lessening of male dominance and female submission.

**Cultural scripts** Patterned norms, values, and behaviors that serve as guidelines for social interaction. Cultural scripts are different for different "characters" such as men and women. For example, because cultural scripts for men differ from those for women, there are different expectations for single males and females on a first date.

**Cultural dopes** Unthinking followers of fashions and trends. Feminist theorists, in particular, caution against labeling women who adopt beauty regimes as cultural dopes who unconsciously subscribe to a trend that keeps them subordinate to men.

In the box titled "Dating Controversies of the Past: Going Dutch," masculinity and femininity are definitely the relevant issue. *Co-ediquitte*, a 1936 etiquette book for college students, warned: "Dutch treats have not worked. Too much independence on a girl's part subtracts from a man's feeling of importance if he takes her out and can do nothing for her. … The man unconsciously resents her masculine assumption of initiative." A 1948 advice book aimed at the "young man about town" said flatly that any man who allows a girl to pay for her own entertainment "deserves to lose her respect," and the 1954 classic, *How to Be a Woman,* advised, "It's custom for him to pay the way, and it helps him feel masculine to do so." The most horrifying vision was summoned by a Philip Morris ad in the *Massachusetts Collegian* in 1955. The ad's hero was seeking a girl who could "appreciate the equity of Dutch treat"—and he found her. "Today," the ad copy read, "Finster goes everywhere and shares expenses fifty-fifty with Mary Alice Hematoma, a lovely three-legged girl with sideburns. Three 'legs'?" (Bailey 1988: 109–111).

Other everyday cultural practices, too, have been considered to indicate male dominance and female submission. For example, French sociologist Michel Foucault maintained that the body is a central location for the expression and reproduction of power relationships. Through self-surveillance and everyday disciplinary practices, he argued, individuals internalize and reproduce hierarchies of social status and power, transforming their bodies into "carriers" or representatives of relations of domination and subordination (Foucault 1979). Some feminists have used this insight to emphasize women's resistance to oppressive beauty regimes, such as dieting and wearing makeup (Bartky 1990; Bordo 1993). Other feminists have warned against regarding women who adopt these beauty regimes as **cultural dopes**—unthinking followers of fashions that keep them subordinate to men (Davis 1995). Although it is important to acknowledge inequalities of power,

## Dating Controversies of the Past: Going Dutch

When a culture insisted, as this one [in mid-twentieth-century America] did, that insofar as a man was feminine or a woman masculine, to that extent he or she was "repulsive" to the opposite sex, and when it also defined adherence to etiquette as an important way to demonstrate masculinity or femininity, it added great weight to an otherwise arcane field. Rules clothed in the language of gender seemed not merely records of convention, but matters of great significance. In this world, etiquette was more concerned with roles than with politeness, and, as young people learned from many sources, these prescribed roles could be transgressed only at great risk to one's masculinity or femininity. …

When this "preemption" [the preemption of the properly masculine] took place in a sphere more directly related to women's changing roles, it seemed even more threatening. Dutch dating was probably the most condemned such breach of etiquette. Because, by convention, men paid for dates (and dates in general had to be paid for), the centrality of men's money in dating conferred power—and control of the date—upon men. When women paid their own ways on dates, men lost that extra power. They were no longer the

provider, no longer in control. Beyond that, women's handling of money forcibly reminded men of women's entrance into the economy, encroaching upon a man's world and even attempting to compete with him, to challenge his control. Dutch dating, both symbolically and literally, threatened to undermine the whole system of courtship that had grown up in modern America.

The advice and etiquette books almost universally condemned the practice, and graphically depicted the dangers of going Dutch:

[Dutch dating] sounds wonderful, but almost always it flops. Boys usually like the system at first, but after a few dates in which they play second fiddle, they begin to feel like sissified heels and their eyes begin to wander to the glamour girls (not gold diggers) who make them toe the mark.

In the beginning the girl feels important and useful but about the third date she begins to feel she is not out with a masterful, masculine boy, but a real Caspar Milktoast. Can she idolize this sort of boy? No! Emphatically no! Soon she's looking down her nose at him and admiring the fellow who will date her half as much but will take the lead in everything.

*Source:* 1954 teen advice book.

women have to be treated as "active and knowledgeable agents" in the construction of social life.

Just as countless articles in women's magazines have insisted that wearing makeup enhances a woman's career, some researchers have found that conventionally "attractive people are perceived as having greater occupational potential than are less attractive people" (e.g., Jackson 1992: 97). Other

studies, however, have argued that organizations' tendency to define women in terms of their sexuality often has a negative impact on their careers (Gutek 1985; Kanter 1977). Overall, it seems that women have to negotiate a difficult line between presenting a good appearance and avoiding being defined primarily in sexual terms. In a study seeking to understand women's use of makeup in the workplace, Kirsten Dellinger and Christine Williams (1997) found that appropriate makeup use was strongly associated with assumptions and norms about health, heterosexuality, and being perceived as a competent worker. According to the authors, the responses of women workers illustrated the degree to which appearance standards are internalized and self-imposed, in order to avoid negative judgments from other people. Yet it's not solely because of the pressures imposed by institutionalized norms concerning appearance that women wear makeup to work. Indeed, some women point to the pleasure they receive by talking about makeup with other women and getting compliments on their appearance. Others claim that they actively bend the rules by wearing the minimum and refusing to monitor their cosmetics throughout the day.

Studies of women's magazines, including their advertisements, provide insights into the ways in which a gendered subjectivity is formed through mass-media texts. In this context, subjectivity refers to "the conscious and unconscious thoughts and emotions of the individual, her sense of herself and her ways of understanding her relation to the world" (Weedon 1987: 32). The notion that women's magazines exert an influence on women's social subjectivity is consistent with the observation of French feminist author Simone de Beauvoir that "one is not born, but rather becomes, a woman" (de Beauvoir 1953: 9). Indeed, owing to their ability to shape consensual images and definitions of femininity, women's magazines have been said to exert "cultural leadership" in struggles surrounding what it means "to be a woman" (McCracken 1993). A study of magazines for teenage girls found that the type of discourse used in such magazines revolved around topics such as "romance," "jealousy," and "problems" (McRobbie 1978), and that it is through these topics that the readers derive meanings for their experiences as "girls." Subsequent research on teen magazines characterized them as promoting the socialization of girls into traditional womanhood through messages that emphasize physical beautification and heterosexual romance (Evans et al. 1991; Peirce 1990). Content analysis demonstrated that the messages in both women's and teenagers' magazines have not kept pace with social changes accompanying "women's liberation."

Although many girls and women read such magazines, it does not follow that they automatically accept everything they read or see themselves in those terms. It would be elitist for any of us to think that we alone read such texts in a knowledgeable way, while other readers are just "cultural dopes" who are fooled into uncritically accepting everything the texts represent. According to a study of women who read romance novels, for example, many such readers are not only selective in what they read but also conscious of taking emotional pleasure from the fantasies (Radway 1984). Similarly, a study of adolescent girls' reactions to advertisements in teen magazines found that, instead of passively accepting the images presented, the girls actively selected the ads they enjoyed, while criticizing and rejecting others. And instead of viewing the magazines as vehicles of fantasy and pleasure, as many middle-aged critics do, the teenaged girls experienced them as an everyday reading practice. Moreover, the girls favored texts that addressed their concerns and interests as teenagers in a "realistic" manner but, at the same time, seemed to accept as natural a self-image based on white, middle-class femininity (Currie 1997). And although they often criticized the magazines' use of beautiful models with "perfect" bodies, they seldom challenged the cultural mandate for women to look good. Indeed, many of the girls used the magazines to get ideas about how they could improve their appearance—a clear indication of how deeply everyday culture is structured around dominant images and values about gender that are accepted as natural and realistic.

In the field of television, too, gender images have been slow to change. A survey of American prime-time television from 1967 to 1998 showed that women continued to be the "second sex" (Signorielli and Bacue 1999). There was little change in the proportion of male-to-female characters: three to two. And female characters were much more restricted than male characters in terms of appearance and age, in that the majority of them were young, thin, and attractive (Silverstein et al. 1986). However, the growing prominence of female television celebrities such as Oprah Winfrey and the ironical treatment of male-female relations in series like *Friends* suggest that television has responded to cultural shifts in the broader society. These changes involve a greater awareness of the culturally constructed character of what were once thought to be natural and normal gender characteristics. The implication is that the mass media can both reflect and help to push forward the increasing variability of cultural identities.

## CONCLUSION

Questions concerning gender at the beginning of the twentieth century were mainly about civil rights for women—and, indeed, the first wave of feminists fought for the vote (achieved in the United States in 1920). The second wave of feminists, in the second half of the century, were concerned with women's struggle to overthrow society's view of their primary role as that of housewife and mother. They fought for access to formerly all-male occupations and for equal pay. Substantial gains were achieved, but the struggle continues as women still tend to work in less prestigious jobs and receive less pay than men. However, feminists have also been addressing broader cultural issues about gender identities—what have been referred to collectively as **identity politics**. Among these are issues such as mass-media images of women, attitudes toward sexuality (both heterosexuality and lesbianism), and appearance (including body shape). It is becoming clear that

there's not just one gender difference—between men and women—but multiple differences. For example, black feminists have criticized white, middle-class feminists for glossing over the differences between them (Tang Nain 1991; see also Patricia Hill Collins [1990] and bell hooks [1984] on black feminist thought), and lesbian feminists have criticized much of the feminist movement for accepting heterosexuality as "normal," maintaining that heterosexuality is just one more institution bent on ensuring male domination (Rich 1994).

Insisting on equality with men remains a central tenet for all feminists. But some assert that it is possible for women to be equal with men without becoming like them. For example, Carol Gilligan (1982) argues that women and men have different moral viewpoints: Women tend to deploy an interpersonal "ethic of care," while men tend to conceive of morality in impersonal terms of "fairness" and "justice" as part of a system of rights for individuals. Other feminists have criticized this notion of an "essential" difference between men and women, claiming that socialization accounts for whatever variance exists. If men were socialized to care for others in ways similar to those influencing women's behavior—such that looking after children was seen as gender-neutral parenting—then the gap between moral viewpoints would narrow. On the other hand, there are mothers who insist that their experience of "mothering" could not be experienced by a man (Manne 2005). In their view, the issues of equality and difference should be separated, men's and women's tasks and identities should be equally valued, and women need to be free to make life choices for themselves (Pateman 1992).

**Identity politics** A category of cultural issues being addressed by feminists that concerns gender identities and includes such topics as mass-media images of women, attitudes toward sexuality, and physical appearance.

Progress is being made in reducing the inequalities between men and women. Ever since they secured the vote, women have been expanding their political clout; however, they are still poorly represented at the highest political levels. In the United States there are few female senators or state governors, and there has yet to be a woman president; and elsewhere in the world, women hold far fewer parliamentary seats than men (see Table 9.13). Economically speaking, women have benefited from the shift away from occupations where men have predominated (e.g., mining and manufacturing) and from the growth of occupations in the service sector; however, as we have seen, they have yet to break through the glass ceiling in large numbers, and their pay lags behind that of men. Public opinion polls show a considerable decline in the number of people who believe it is better if the man is the main achiever outside the home and the woman takes care of the home and family; how-

ever, the majority of household chores are still performed by working women who have to work a second shift in the home. The "New Man," who "cares and shares" to the same degree that women do and is not afraid to express his emotions, is not yet typical (Connell 1995). The dominant image of masculinity is still tied to dominant forms of heterosexuality as part of a competitive struggle connected to individual achievement and power (Seidler 1989). There has even been a male backlash against changes in ideas of masculinity (Bly 1991; Doyle 1989) and against feminism (Faludi 1992), although the extent of the backlash is probably much smaller than would appear from the amount of publicity it has received.

Strategies for bringing about further change vary, depending on the perspective adopted. For liberal feminists, who emphasize the classical liberal philosophy of individual rights, the main task is to increase women's freedom of choice and provide more opportunities to exercise their talents. Socialist feminists advocate more fundamental changes, especially in the economic system, where the exploitation of women's labor, whether through low-paid employment or unpaid housework, is seen as just one aspect of the drive to make profits by keeping down labor costs. Radical feminists want fundamental changes as well, but they believe that male dominance (patriarchy) will be abolished only when our cultural ideas and practices based on gender are eliminated altogether. Their goal is a "gender-free" society. The main resistance to these strategies comes from those who like things the way they are (or see the alternatives as worse) or who are convinced there is evidence that men and women are basically so different that we should let evolution (or God's will) take its course. The so-called culture wars of recent years (again, see Chapter 3) have frequently been about "family values" and

**TABLE 9.13 Women in National Parliaments: Regional Averages, 2005**

| Region[1] | Single House or Lower House | Upper House or Senate | Both Houses Combined |
|---|---|---|---|
| Nordic countries | 39.9% | – | 39.9% |
| Europe–OSCE member countries, including Nordic countries[2] | 19.0% | 16.8% | 18.5% |
| Americas | 18.7% | 18.5% | 18.6% |
| Europe–OSCE member countries, excluding Nordic countries | 16.9% | 16.8% | 16.9% |
| Asia | 15.0% | 13.5% | 14.9% |
| Sub-Saharan Africa | 14.9% | 14.0% | 14.8% |
| Pacific | 11.2% | 26.5% | 13.2% |
| Arab states | 6.7% | 5.6% | 6.5% |

Notes:
[1] Regions are classified by descending order of the percentage of women in the lower or single house.
[2] OSCE stands for Organization for Security and Cooperation in Europe.
Source: Inter-Parliamentary Union (2005).

opposition to changes that some see as threatening the traditional family and women's roles as wife and mother.

Finally, there are those who, while supporting efforts to change women's position in society, insist that the focus on gender is mistaken. Postmodern feminist Judith Butler (1990) argues that in seeking to be equal with men, women would need to construct themselves in men's image, having taken as their norm of equality the character and position of men. What she advocates, instead, is avoiding the dichotomy of the categories *male* and *female*. Feminists such as Butler, Donna Haraway (1989, 1991), Jane Flax (1990), and Marjorie Garber (1992) challenge the concept of gender categories that are based on this opposition between just two identities, insisting that sexuality and gender should be seen as much more fluid and shifting categories. An inclusive, monolithic concept of *woman,* they argue, denies the multiplicity and complexity of genders. Indeed, for such feminists the task of the sociology of gender is to take apart ("deconstruct") the different aspects of gendering and show how each of them operates—through symbols, everyday routines and practices, socialization and education, sexual relations, work allocation and rewards, mass media and popular culture. By exposing how gendering occurs, sociology can raise people's consciousness about ways of thinking and acting that are not inevitable and unchangeable.

It is tempting to see the future of gender optimistically, with continuing progress toward greater equality, building on the undoubted achievements made by feminists and reformers in the twentieth century. However, it is far from inevitable that gender categories will gradually blur under the weight of evidence about the similarities of women and men, or that gender will stop being a major determinant of how work and rewards are allocated, and of how tasks are divided in the home. Pendulum swings are common, and it is all too easy for events to occur that seem to justify turning the

clock back to a more traditional pattern of gendering. This happened to American women after World War II, when those who had been filling men's jobs in the defense industries were fired and daycare centers were abandoned (Milkman 1987). As Judith Lorber (1994: 9) points out, "The 1950s were conservative, family-oriented and gender-segregated." And in Islamic countries that have become more fundamentalist, women have had to abandon Western clothing and go back to wearing the veil, often losing their civil rights at the same time (Kandiyoti 1991). In the long run, changes are unlikely to be deep-rooted unless the sociological imagination becomes deeply ingrained and people become conscious of how genders are constructed and determined to remove the inequalities that are reproduced.

Looking back at Helen Mather's story at the beginning of this chapter, we might now conclude that what appeared to be an extreme case involving one individual's choice of identity was in fact a symptom of a wider problem raised by gender divisions. The problem is that gender involves social status, power, and inequality. And although today's culture offers more varied images of sexuality and gender than ever before, resistance to change continues. As Lorber puts it: "When we no longer ask 'boy or girl?' in order to start gendering an infant, when the information about genitalia is as irrelevant as the color of the child's eyes (but not the color of skin), then and only then will women and men be socially interchangeable and really equal. And when that happens, there will no longer be any need for gender at all" (1994: 302).

## EXERCISES

### Exercise 1

We have seen in this chapter that gender is not a simple biological category but a fluid social identity. Through the process of socialization and the daily navigation of social life, we gain a practical knowledge of what is expected and appropriate for men and women in our society. In other words, gendered behavior is guided by norms. Our actions, intentional and otherwise, will always be performed and interpreted within this framework of gender norms. What are some examples of gender-norm violations today? What are the consequences of violating gender norms? Are female athletes violating gender norms or changing them? Are they creating a realm in which women can be valued for something other than their attractiveness or just setting a higher standard for female beauty?

## Exercise 2

We have also seen that the definition of masculinity is historically variable, and that gender identity is shaped in relation to other social categories, such as race and class. How has masculinity been represented in hip-hop and rap music? How does this compare with the construction of masculinity in country music? How has the image of masculinity changed throughout the history of these genres?

## Exercise 3

Think of the television programs you've watched in the last week. Are women still the "second sex" in prime time? Are female characters still restricted in terms of age and appearance? How are women portrayed? Are the jobs held by female characters horizontally and vertically segregated? Do the plot-lines involving female characters differ significantly from those involving men? Would radical feminists approve or disapprove of any shows in particular? (For example, what would they think of *Buffy the Vampire Slayer* or *Sex in the City*?) Do women fare any better in reality television when they are supposedly playing "themselves"?

# STUDY QUESTIONS

1. What is the difference between "sex" and "gender"? Why was this distinction introduced? How has it become problematic?

2. What was the major finding from George Murdock's survey? In what way does his work resonate with classical sociology's understanding of the social division of labor?

3. How has biological determinism been challenged? What kind of evidence contradicts its claims? What accusations have been made about its proponents?

4. How is gender understood in current sociology?

5. What is the difference between horizontal and vertical gender segregation in the workplace?

6. What is the reserve army of labor? Why do women and immigrants make up the overwhelming majority of this reserve army?

7. Discuss feminists' use of Foucault's theories to condemn diet and beauty regimes as symbolic of female submission. Why have other feminists been reluctant to do so?

8. How do liberal, socialist, and radical feminists differ in terms of their strategies for achieving gender equality?

# FURTHER READING

Allen, Beverly. 1996. *Rape Warfare: The Hidden Genocide in Bosnia-Herzegovina and Croatia.* Minneapolis: University of Minnesota Press.

de Beauvoir, Simone. 1953. *The Second Sex.* New York: Vintage. (Reprinted in 1989.)

Dworkin, Shari. 2001. "Holding Back: Negotiating a Glass Ceiling on Women's Muscular Strength." *Sociological Perspectives* 44: 333–350.

Ehrenreich, Barbara, and Arlie Hochschild, eds. 2004. *Global Woman: Nannies, Maids, and Sex Workers in the New Economy.* New York: Metropolitan.

Enloe, Cynthia. 2001. *Bananas, Beaches, Bases.* Berkeley: University of California Press.

Fausto-Sterling, Anne. 1985. *Myths of Gender: Biological Theories about Women and Men.* New York: Basic.

Feree, Myra Marx, Judith Lorber, and Beth Hess, eds. 2000. *Revisioning Gender.* New York: AltaMira.

Friedan, Betty. 1963. *The Feminine Mystique.* New York: Laurel.

Ghorayshi, Parvin, and Claire Belanger, eds. 1996. *Women, Work, and Gender Relations in Developing Countries: A Global Perspective.* Westport, CT: Greenwood.

Messner, Michael. 2002. *Taking the Field: Women, Men, and Sports.* Minneapolis: University of Minnesota Press.

Rosen, Ruth. 2000. *The Whole World Split Open: How the Modern Women's Movement Changed America.* New York: Penguin.

# chapter 10

# Race and Ethnicity

The story of race and ethnicity, as told by sociology, has as its theme the social and cultural construction of racial and ethnic differences.

Scarcely more than two decades ago, in 1982, a 48-year-old woman named Susie Phipps stood up in a New Orleans courtroom and declared that she had the right to be white. Five years before, when Mrs. Phipps applied for a birth certificate, she had learned that Louisiana's Bureau of Vital Statistics identified her as "colored." Mrs. Phipps told the court that she was "flabbergasted" and "sickened" upon hearing this news. Pointing to her face, she said, "I'm not light, I'm white!" Mrs. Phipps told the court that she had "married white twice," and she produced a family photographic album, going back through three generations of blue eyes (*New York Times*, September 19 and 20, 1982).

Why was Mrs. Phipps in court? She was asserting not just her race but also the right to define it—herself. Her husband, a white man, agreed with her view, and so did her family and friends.

## AN INDIVIDUAL OR A SOCIAL STORY?

Is race a matter of personal identity? Is it something that each individual can decide?

Apparently, Louisiana did not think so. Since 1970, state law had held that, if a person had just 1/32 of "Negro blood," he or she was legally black. Before that, "a trace" of Negro ancestry had made a person black in the eyes of the state. But in the late 1960s, when the South squared off against the national demand for black civil rights, this ambiguous restriction was judged unacceptable by white society.

To defend itself against Mrs. Phipps's suit, Louisiana spent $5,000 to hire a genealogical researcher to analyze her racial ancestry. He traced it back 222 years to a black slave named Margarita, who was Mrs. Phipps's great-great-great-grand-

mother. Her great-great-great-grandfather was a white planter named John Gregoire Guillory. This made Mrs. Phipps 3/32 black.

During Mrs. Phipps's trial, an anthropology professor at Tulane University, Dr. Munro Edmonson, testified on her behalf. He stated that, based on such purely genealogical calculations, white Americans themselves would have to be classified as black. On the average, long-settled American whites have 5 percent traceable black genes.

The Louisiana court ruled against Mrs. Phipps. She did not have the right to decide her race. To many, this view would seem to reflect a fact of life. After all, they might argue, biology and genes determine the color of one's skin. Sociologists take a different view, though we are just as skeptical about individual volition. For us, race is a social fact. It is determined not by biological forces but by social ones more powerful than any individual will. Biologically, race is an arbitrary classification, but it is the "logical" outcome of social life—of interracial history and group contact. Determined by history, race is patterned by deep and arbitrary cultural prejudices, and, if necessary, it is enforced by the state.

## THE SOCIAL CONSTRUCTION OF "RACE" AND "ETHNICITY"

### Race: Biology or Society?

Race would be difficult to get a fix on if it were defined in purely biological terms. If it were, there would be thousands of "races." Owing to migrations, conquests, and intermarriages, continuous intermingling has occurred throughout human history. In fact, however, such genetic intermixing affects only the most superficial of physical traits. As recent genetic research has demonstrated, the human genome stopped evolving several hundred thousands of years ago and is virtually identical across all regional, national, and cultural outcroppings of the *Homo sapiens* (human) race. In any meaningful sense, then, the purely biological categorization of different physical races is impossible.

Sociology challenges the notion that biological or genetic differences "naturally" relegate people to a distinctive race. As Pierre Van den Berghe put it, race happens when a "human group … *defines itself* and/or *is defined by* other groups as different from other groups by virtue of innate and immutable physical characteristics" (quoted in Feagin 1978: 7, italics added). If race is a matter of definition, it is a social rather than biological categorization. It is culture that leads the members of a society to perceive differences in race and to believe that these differences matter. And it is social structure that causes these cultural evaluations to appear to be true. Members of stigmatized racial groups usually end up on the lower rungs of the social and economic ladder. If they sometimes act differently from members of dominant groups, it is because they are compelled to lead different, and much less privileged, lives.

### Race and Modernity

Today, many liberal and progressive people think of racially based classification as a kind of irrational throwback to primitive thought. Certainly, as we have just seen, from a truly scientific perspective, it is. Yet the idea of a racial biology arose only with modern society. Before the nineteenth century, the concept of *race* was used to refer to descendants of common ancestors. Its meaning, in other words, was similar to that ascribed to the concept of **ethnicity** today. People spoke of the Christian race, the European race, the Italian or American or French race. Skin color was not an issue. Casual encounters between Mediterranean whites and black Africans in the premodern period were generally cordial, resulting in friendships and intermarriages.

Racial stereotypes about skin color came later, as a response to European expansion, which began in the 1400s. When white Europeans plundered the "new world" of the Americas—both the North and the South—for its gold and silver, and gradually colonized it, they justified their domination in terms of the superiority of their race. When white Europeans, and later white American settlers, sailed to Africa and enslaved millions of healthy young men and women to work in their fields back home, racial coloration became an even more important cultural justification.

It was in the sixteenth century that François Bernier first began to theorize about the need to sort the world's people according to physical traits—primarily facial characteristics and skin color. A widely accepted hierarchy of "racial types" emerged soon after that, with European and American settler whites sitting comfortably on top. Africans were ranked at the bottom, condemned not only for their skin color and facial structure but also for what was supposed to be the inevitably associated inferiority of their native culture.

This new kind of cultural classification did not emerge all at once. As Winthrop Jordan points out in *White over Black* (1968), which traces the emergence of racial thinking in American society, the colonists were initially identified in religious terms. National and political demarcations followed. In response to the rapidly growing slave trade, however, skin color soon became a domi-

> **Race** Biologically speaking, an arbitrary classification assigned on the basis of genetic characteristics (notably, skin color). From a sociological perspective, however, race is socially constructed. Its meaning in society is a cultural process. If members of stigmatized racial groups behave differently from those in the majority or occupy lower social positions, it is not their innate worth that is implicated but, rather, social structures and culture.
>
> **Ethnicity** Group distinctiveness based on a common territory, history, and tradition.

When European explorers arrived in North America in the fifteenth century, they viewed the indigenous peoples, such as this Apache girl celebrating a centuries-old rite of passage into womanhood, as inferior "races" and thus justified conquering them. (Anders Ryman/Corbis)

## Racial Classification and the Origins of Modern Philosophy

Even the rational and democratic Enlightenment, the great movement of ideas in the latter part of the eighteenth century that inspired the American and French revolutions, was scarred by this new kind of primitive thought. Immanuel Kant was the major thinker associated with this movement. More than any other philosopher, he insisted on rationality and the independence of the intellectual from dogmatic belief. Yet Kant's ideas were embedded in racial classification. This demonstrates the tragic and primitive misperceptions about difference that permeated modern life.

In one essay, ironically titled *Observations on the Feeling of the Beautiful and Sublime*, Kant insisted that "the Negroes of Africa have by nature no feeling that arises above the trifling." He claimed that David Hume, another Enlightenment philosopher, had shown irrefutably that "among the hundreds of thousands of blacks who are transported elsewhere from their countries, although many have been set free, still not one was ever found who presented anything great in art or science or other praiseworthy quality" (Kant 1764a: 110–111).

From this Kant concluded that the "difference between these two races of man" is so "fundamental" as "to be as great in regard to mental capacities as in color." In his *Anthropology from a Pragmatic Point of View*, Kant claimed to have learned from other scientific observations that "blacks are ... so talkative that they must be driven apart from each other with thrashings." No wonder he believed that "the intermixture of races (caused by large-scale conquests), which gradually extinguishes their characteristics, does not seem beneficial to the human race" (Kant 1764b).

In response to the Enlightenment there developed Romanticism, a movement of art and ideas that formed the other foundation of modern philosophical thinking. The great philosopher of Romanticism was Friedrich Hegel. Though he had

nant reference: "From the initially common term *Christian*, at mid-century there was a marked shift toward the terms of *English* and *free*. After about 1680, taking the colonies as a whole, a new term of self-identification appeared—*white*" (Jordan, quoted in Omi and Winant 1994: 64). By the eighteenth century, *race* had come to refer to distinct categories of people with physical characteristics transmitted by descent. In the early nineteenth century, biologists and physical anthropologists picked up the idea of physically different races, employing it to differentiate among plants and animal groups.

probably never met a black person in his life, Hegel claimed that the "want of self-control distinguishes the character of the Negroes." Because of this character flaw, he claimed, black people were "capable of no development or culture." He concluded that "the only essential connection between the Negroes and the Europeans is slavery" (Gilroy 1993: 41).

### The Racial Fallacy

Writings from as far back as the beginning of modern society provide us with vivid examples of **racism.** Racism exists when a physical difference between human groups, believed to be hereditary, is connected with differences in social and cultural behavior. When behavioral difference is attributed to such physical qualities, groups are held to be different in some inherent, irreversible way. This leads to the belief in the inevitable inferiority of one and the inherent superiority of another. When inequality is attributed not to social causes but to innate incapacities in intelligence and character, the element of human responsibility is eliminated and moral judgment becomes difficult. When inequality is understood in a sociological rather than a racial manner, things look completely different.

In a fascinating series of studies on how the race of an applicant affects employment opportunities, researchers have shown that race continues to be a significant factor.

For example, a study by Devah Pager (2003) focused on the impact of incarceration on employment opportunities, but the results also demonstrate that the race of job applicants, despite their criminal record, affects the chances of being hired. Using a novel methodological approach called an "experimental audit," Pager arranged for matched pairs of equally qualified candidates to apply for entry-level jobs. Four "testers" at a time—two black males and two white males—went, in person, to a job site to fill out applications and seek interviews for jobs advertised in the local newspaper. Selected on the basis of similar physical ap-

pearance, presentation of self, and other background characteristics such as education and prior work experience, each set of testers was partnered together by race and randomly assigned in terms of who had a criminal record and who did not—a factor that changed from week to week during the job-application process. The two white testers applied for 150 jobs over the course of the study (in other words, they completed 150 audits), and the two black testers completed 200. The outcome measured was how many callbacks each applicant received.

Pager found that both race and criminal record have an interaction effect on employment opportunities. She also found that a criminal record affects blacks and whites differently. Among the white participants, 34 percent without criminal records received callbacks, compared to only 17 percent of those with criminal records. Therefore, a criminal record reduced the likelihood that a white applicant would receive a callback by 50 percent. Among the black participants, 14 percent without criminal records received callbacks, compared to only 5 percent of those with criminal records. Comparing the callback rate for blacks *without* criminal records (14 percent) with those whites *with* criminal records (17 percent) clearly shows an effect of race (see Figure 10.1).

Pager, along with Bruce Western, repeated this study on a larger scale in New York in 2005 and found similar results: Once again, black applicants with no criminal record were no more likely to receive a callback for a job than a white applicant with a criminal record, and white applicants were twice as likely to receive a callback as an equally qualified black applicant.

**Racism** Behavior based on the belief that a group is inferior because of inherited physical differences that are inherently connected with behavioral differences.

## FIGURE 10.1 Discrimination in Hiring Practices by Race and Criminal Record

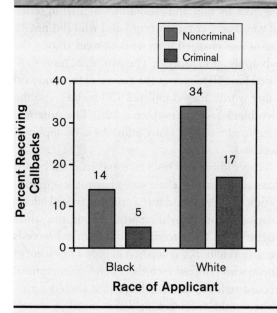

Source: Pager (2003: 958, Fig. 6).

## TABLE 10.1 Average Callback Rates by Racialized First Name

| White Female Name | Average Callback | Black Female Name | Average Callback |
|---|---|---|---|
| Emily | 8.3% | Aisha | 2.2% |
| Anne | 9.0% | Keisha | 3.8% |
| Jill | 9.3% | Tamika | 5.4% |
| Allison | 9.4% | Lakisha | 5.5% |
| Sarah | 9.8% | Tanisha | 6.3% |
| Meredith | 10.6% | Latoya | 8.8% |
| Laurie | 10.8% | Kenya | 9.1% |
| Carrie | 13.1% | Latonya | 9.1% |
| Kristen | 13.6% | Ebony | 10.5% |

| White Male Name | Average Callback | Black Male Name | Average Callback |
|---|---|---|---|
| Neil | 6.6% | Rasheed | 3.0% |
| Geoffrey | 6.8% | Tremayne | 4.3% |
| Brett | 6.8% | Kareem | 4.7% |
| Brendan | 7.7% | Darnell | 4.8% |
| Greg | 7.8% | Tyrone | 5.3% |
| Todd | 8.7% | Jamal | 6.6% |
| Matthew | 9.0% | Hakim | 7.3% |
| Jay | 13.2% | Leroy | 9.4% |
| Brad | 15.9% | Jermaine | 11.3% |

Source: Bertrand and Mullainathan (2004).

Economists Marianne Bertrand and Sendhil Mullainathan (2004) conducted a similar though narrower study by responding to help-wanted ads with the same résumé whose only difference was a randomly assigned name at the top: either one common among blacks or one common among whites. According to the study, which was titled "Are Emily and Greg More Employable Than Lakisha and Jamal? A Field Experiment on Labor Market Discrimination," 10.1 percent of the applicants who had been assigned a "white-sounding" name were called back for job interviews, compared to only 6.7 percent of those with a "black-sounding" name. In short, white applicants were 50 percent more likely to be called back for job interviews than were black applicants (see Table 10.1). This finding is all the more ironic in light of the data in Tables 10.2 and 10.3, which we summarize in the list below:

✓ Black men with a master's degree make 81 percent as much as their white counterparts.
✓ Black women with a master's degree make 93 percent as much as their white counterparts.
✓ Black women with a bachelor's degree make 68 percent as much as white men with a bachelor's degree.

Empirical research has demonstrated that the very idea of what makes up a race differs greatly from one society to another. The physical characteristics that receive heightened attention in one

## TABLE 10.2  Annual Median Earnings of African-Americans by Gender, 1955–2001

| Year | Men | Women | % of Men's Earnings |
|------|-----|-------|---------------------|
| 1955 | 1,865 | 653 | 35 |
| 1960 | 2,260 | 837 | 37 |
| 1965 | 2,847 | 1,174 | 41 |
| 1970 | 4,157 | 2,063 | 50 |
| 1975 | 5,560 | 3,107 | 56 |
| 1980 | 8,009 | 4,580 | 57 |
| 1985 | 10,768 | 6,277 | 58 |
| 1990 | 12,868 | 8,328 | 65 |
| 1995 | 16,006 | 10,961 | 68 |
| 2001 | 21,466 | 16,282 | 76 |

*Note:* Sample consists of people 15 years old and over as of March 1980, and people 14 years old and over as of March 1981. Income is represented in current and 2001 CPI-U-RS adjusted dollars.

*Source:* U.S. Census Bureau (2005).

## TABLE 10.3  Wage Gap by Education and Race, 2004

| | High School Diploma | Bachelor's Degree | Master's Degree |
|------|------|------|------|
| White Men | 36,224 | 57,842 | 70,657 |
| White Women | 26,560 | 41,403 | 50,160 |
| Gap | 73% | 72% | 71% |
| | | | |
| Black Men | 30,409 | 46,024 | 57,006 |
| Black Women | 23,956 | 39,394 | 46,931 |
| Gap | 79% | 86% | 82% |
| | | | |
| Hispanic Men | 28,530 | 45,088 | 61,320 |
| Hispanic Women | 22,596 | 37,387 | 50,331 |
| Gap | 79% | 83% | 82% |

*Note:* Figures represent median earnings of workers over age 25, full-time, year-round. Race categories used are white and black alone or in combination.

*Source:* U.S. Census Bureau (2004).

culture or nation may well go completely unnoticed in another:

✓ In South Africa, during the apartheid regime that ended in 1994, there were actually four legally defined racial categories: white, black, colored, and Indian. In many Latin American countries today, "racial" boundaries are drawn in relation to hair texture, eye color, and social status rather than skin color and nose or lip shape.

✓ In Brazil, mixed-race people, who would be seen as black in the United States, are commonly perceived as white (Winant 1994). For Brazilians, such rigidly defined racial boundaries simply do not exist.

✓ In France, people of African origin are significantly less racially stigmatized than Arab Muslims from North African countries. The latter are much more likely to form an economic underclass, and they occupy the decaying outskirts of French cities. These Arab Muslim outsiders are frequently referred to as *les noirs*, the blacks, though physiologically their skin color is lighter than that of French African immigrants.

✓ In Great Britain, impoverished Arab Muslim and Asian youth are often classified as black. And the latter, including many resentful young Pakistanis, often classify *themselves* as black.

### Racism and Genocide

The focus on racial coloration may have originated in modern European society, but the belief in genetic superiority reflected in physical appearance is nearly universal. In Burundi, a country in Central Africa, racial classification centers on physical stature rather than skin color. The Tutsis are tall and slender, averaging six feet in height. A warrior people, they invaded and conquered the Hutus between 400 and 600 years ago, and forced them into agricultural labor and serfdom. To justify their domination, they gloated over the supposedly natural inferiority of the Hutus, who looked

In South Africa, dark-skinned people—legally divided into three races: black, colored, and Indians—could not vote until 1994, when the apartheid regime ended; this elderly man proudly voted for the first time. (Peter Turnley/Corbis)

different from them and typically were not more than four feet tall.

When the Belgian government took over the colonial reins in 1916, it supported this supposedly racially based subjugation, forcing each group to carry identity cards and the Hutus to obey a nearly godlike Tutsi king. Liberated from Belgium in 1962, the area became divided into Rwanda, where Hutus were the majority, and Burundi, where the Tutsis remained in control. After decades of racially charged conflict, during a few short weeks in 1994, Hutu militants in Rwanda murdered at least a half-million Tutsis—the most gruesome **genocide** since the Nazis' mass murder of Jews during World War II.

There can be no doubt that racial thinking played a major role in instigating this genocide. Testimony during a subsequent Rwandan war crimes tribunal made this graphically clear, as documented in an article titled "'Hate Radio' Urged Hutus to Break 'Small Noses,' Expert Witness Testifies":

Journalists at the Radio Libre Des Mille Collines (RTLM) broadcast messages describing the physical features of the ethnic Tutsi and calling for their extermination, an expert witness today testified before judges at the International Criminal Tribunal for Rwanda (ICTR). Language expert Matthias Ruzindana, the 43rd witness, [quoted the following excerpt], which he claims called for the extermination of Tutsi: "The Inyenzi [cockroach] have always been Tutsi. We will exterminate them. One can identify them because they are of one race. You can identify them by their height and their small nose. When you see that small nose, break it." … [T]he prosecution alleges [that this message] was used to incite genocide in Rwanda. (Kimani 2002)

## Ethnicity: From Biology to Origins

Racial classification focuses exclusively on visible physical qualities. Ethnicity is subtly different. While the latter often points to physical qualities, it emphasizes common territory and origins, and is based on the notion that these supposedly "unmeltable" social factors define an unwavering solidarity that makes an ordinary group into a "people." In short, ethnicity suggests a sense of belonging, the distinctiveness of a group's culture, and the overriding importance of shared tradition.

While it is impossible, from a democratic perspective, to say anything positive about racism, this is not the case with ethnicity. Certainly there is something positive and sympathetic about a collective identity that is constructed in this way. Indeed, in their best-selling work on the disappearance of community feelings and obligations in America, Robert Bellah and his colleagues look regretfully at the passing of strong ethnic communities. They describe ethnicity as a pattern of commitment that defines the loyalties and obligations that keep a community alive:

We can speak of a real community as a "community of memory," one that does not forget its past. In order not to forget that past, a community is involved in retelling its story, its constitutive narrative, and in so doing, it offers examples of the men and women who have embodied and exemplified the meaning of the community. [While] there are

[such] ethnic … communities, each with its own story and its own heroes and heroines, [it] has been hard to sustain in our restless and mobile society. (Bellah et al. 1985: 153–143)

This sympathetic view, however, is one-sided. It is important to remember that every in-group is defined in relation to an out-group. "There can be no ethnicity," Van den Berghe (1978: xvii) once remarked, "without some conception and consciousness of a distinction between 'them' and 'us.'" It is not just love of those who are of a similar origin, but also hatred, or at least dislike, of those who are not that allows people to feel part of the same ethnic group.

### Ethnocentrism
This exclusionary element turns ethnicity into **ethnocentrism:** the tendency to interpret, critique, and evaluate other groups according to the standards and values of one's own. To the degree that a group of people are ethnocentric, they believe that their own particular way of life is "natural," and that any really worthy person probably would eat, drink, dress, or speak in the same way. As Edna Bonacich and John Modell define the former term, "Ethnicity is a communalistic form of social affiliation, depending, first, upon an assumption of a special bond among people of like

**Genocide** The systematic mass murder of a group of people. Perhaps the most famous example is the Nazis' mass murder of Jews during World War II; however, race and ethnicity have also been the basis of genocide, as was the case in Rwanda in the 1990s.

**Ethnocentrism** An attitude based on a belief in the cultural superiority of one's own ethnic group above all others. People are ethnocentric if they tend to naturalize their own cultural practices while looking down on the cultural practices of others.

origins, and, second, upon the obverse, a disdain for people of dissimilar origins" (1980: 1).

Ethnic difference is real, in the sense that it refers to cultural practices that form around symbolic objects such as food, dress, language, family patterns, recreation, and sexual activities. It influences who one's friends are, whom one marries, even where one might work. But there is a great deal that is imagined, too. Those inside of the ethnic group place a romantic spin on their own particular cultural practices. But this belief in their cultural superiority is arbitrary. Ethnocentric people believe that their cultural practices are better—simply because they are their own!

This superiority complex is revealed in the very origins of the word *ethnos*. It is derived from the Greek word for *people*, and its earliest known English usage has been traced to the year 1470, to the beginnings of European expansion. Europeans used it to refer to the inhabitants of "heathen" nations—most likely Africans and Muslims who were neither Christian nor Jewish. However, it was only in the latter part of the nineteenth century that the term *ethnic* came into common usage in the United States. At that time, new and heavy waves of immigration from Eastern and Southern Europe seemed to threaten the identity of the Anglo-Saxon groups who had formed America's founding core.

The racial and ethnic composition of the United States is changing (see Table 10.4). Assuming current trends, the U.S. Census Bureau projects that, by 2050, minorities and Hispanic-origin groups will comprise almost half of the American population. Immigration, changing definitions of racial and ethnic identifications, and intergroup marriage are factors that contribute to this shift.

### Nativism in America

Despite the United States' democratic political structure and distinctly modern identity, its culture and institutions have been distorted by racism and ethnocentrism since the nation's beginnings. Indeed, throughout the first part of its history the United States actively encouraged racial domination. Because we still live in the aftermath of the civil rights movement, most Americans are well aware of this racist past. But many of us do not realize that ethnocentrism, too, has deeply marked the history of American life.

We like to think of the United States as the land of opportunity, as a nation built on voluntary immigration. However, many **immigrants** to this country have not been welcomed with open arms. And in many cases those who did become settled have resisted the next wave of newcomers in turn. The basis for this resistance is ethnocentrism—an antagonism that has focused on the various parts of Europe from which immigrants came, and on the religious and lifestyle qualities associated with each place.

Most seventeenth- and eighteenth-century American settlers came from Calvinist areas of Great Britain and Holland. They believed strongly that their culture was superior, and that other peoples and religions were distinctly less suited to America's democratic life. In the nineteenth century, as American territory pushed westward and the U.S. economy expanded and industrialized, massive waves of immigrants were drawn to Amer-

**Immigrants** Individuals who have relocated from their native country to another country. Many immigrants leave their homes in the hopes of finding a new or better lifestyle with increased opportunities. Immigration is a complicated social issue. On the one hand, diversity is an eagerly expected characteristic of postmodern life. On the other hand, several countries have strict policies that restrict immigration, often on the ethnocentric basis of protecting the national culture as well as opportunities for native-born citizens.

**Nativism** The ethnocentric attitude of a native-born population toward immigrants. In the United States, this attitude was particularly prevalent during the 1850s—a time when American nativists believed that the beliefs and customs of certain European groups would undermine the culture upon which the United States was founded.

TABLE 10.4  Percentage Distribution of the Population by Race and Hispanic Origin, 1990 to 2050

| Year | Total | Race | | | | | Not of Hispanic Origin | | | |
| | | White | Black | American Indian[1] | Asian[2] | Hispanic Origin[3] | White | Black | American Indian[1] | Asian[2] |
|------|-------|-------|-------|----------|-------|----------|-------|-------|----------|-------|
| **ESTIMATE** | | | | | | | | | | |
| 1990 | 100.0 | 83.9 | 12.3 | 0.8 | 3.0 | 9.0 | 75.6 | 11.8 | 0.7 | 2.8 |
| **PROJECTIONS** | | | | | | | | | | |
| **Middle Series** | | | | | | | | | | |
| 1995 | 100.0 | 83.0 | 12.6 | 0.9 | 3.6 | 10.2 | 73.6 | 12.0 | 0.7 | 3.3 |
| 2000 | 100.0 | 82.1 | 12.9 | 0.9 | 4.1 | 11.4 | 71.8 | 12.2 | 0.7 | 3.9 |
| 2005 | 100.0 | 81.3 | 13.2 | 0.9 | 4.6 | 12.6 | 69.9 | 12.4 | 0.8 | 4.4 |
| 2010 | 100.0 | 80.5 | 13.5 | 0.9 | 5.1 | 13.8 | 68.0 | 12.6 | 0.8 | 4.8 |
| 2020 | 100.0 | 79.0 | 14.0 | 1.0 | 6.1 | 16.3 | 64.3 | 12.9 | 0.8 | 5.7 |
| 2030 | 100.0 | 77.6 | 14.4 | 1.0 | 7.0 | 18.9 | 60.5 | 13.1 | 0.8 | 6.6 |
| 2040 | 100.0 | 76.1 | 14.9 | 1.1 | 7.9 | 21.7 | 56.7 | 13.3 | 0.9 | 7.5 |
| 2050 | 100.0 | 74.8 | 15.4 | 1.1 | 8.7 | 24.5 | 52.8 | 13.6 | 0.9 | 8.2 |
| **Lowest Series** | | | | | | | | | | |
| 2050 | 100.0 | 75.7 | 15.7 | 1.2 | 7.4 | 22.0 | 55.8 | 14.2 | 1.0 | 7.0 |
| **Highest Series** | | | | | | | | | | |
| 2050 | 100.0 | 73.5 | 15.8 | 1.0 | 9.7 | 25.7 | 50.5 | 13.8 | 0.8 | 9.2 |

*Notes:*

[1] American Indian represents American Indian, Eskimo, and Aleut.

[2] Asian represents Asian and Pacific Islander.

[3] Persons of Hispanic origin may be of any race. The information on the total Hispanic population shown in this report was collected in the 50 states and the District of Columbia and, therefore, does not include residents of Puerto Rico.

*Source:* U.S. Census Bureau (1996).

ica from other areas outside Northwestern Europe and from religions other than Calvinist Protestantism.

Nativism is the descriptive term applied to the ethnocentric reactions against this new immigration. Its intellectual leaders and agitators defended what they believed to be America's "native" or founding culture. They insisted that immigrants who came to America from other regions would undermine American life. For example, nativists were virulently anti-Catholic, whether the new Catholic immigrants were from Ireland, Poland, or Italy. In the 1850s, the nativist movement created the "American Party," which their opponents quickly labeled the "Know-Nothing" party. Its aim was to prevent Catholics—who at that time were predominantly Irish—from immigrating to the United States. For a while, this ethnocentric party made extraordinary inroads into the American political structure. Eight "Know-Nothing" governors were elected, along with more than 100 congressmen and 3 mayors (those of Philadelphia, Chicago, and Boston). As a consequence of the ethnocentric rage that swept through America, Catholic citizens were burned and priests were tarred and feathered. Only the beginning of the Civil War, in 1860, brought an end to these dangerously antidemocratic activities of the American Party.

Nativism relegated many European Catholic immigrants to harsh industrial labor, such as 10-year-old Secondino Libro, a factory worker in Lawrence, Massachusetts, in 1911. (Library of Congress)

But immigrants did not have to be Catholic to be victims of American nativism. In 1886, in Haymarket Square in Chicago, a bomb exploded during a radical political demonstration. Five German immigrants were immediately arrested. Without evidence, in a climate of almost hysterical suspicion, they were convicted by a jury and hanged. Throughout the trial, American newspapers were filled with descriptions of relentless attacks on the "foreign element" that was supposedly undermining good old-fashioned American life: "These people are not Americans, but the very scum of and offal of Europe ... an invasion of venomous reptiles ... long-haired, wild-eyed, bad-smelling, atheistic, reckless foreign wretches, who never did an honest hour's work in their lives. ... Crush such snakes ... before they have time to bite. ... Europe's human and inhuman rubbish" (quoted in Higham 1963: 55).

Large segments of the new Russian and Polish immigrants were Jewish, providing American nativism with another shameful theme: anti-Semi-

tism. Just before World War I, in Atlanta, Georgia, a female factory worker was found murdered. The rumor spread that she had also been sexually molested, and popular suspicion focused on the factory manager, Leo Frank, who happened to be the son of a wealthy Jewish businessman from New York. Without any real evidence, Frank was convicted by a local jury and sentenced to death. Responding to public indignation outside the South, and to the shoddy nature of the legal case, Georgia's governor commuted Frank's sentence to life in prison. Enraged by the governor's decision, a mob of working-class Georgians snatched Frank from prison, carried him 175 miles across the state, and slaughtered him in their own backyard. To explain these actions, one working-class leader, Tom Watson, offered the following classic example of ethnocentric, nativist thinking: "From all over the world, the Children of Israel are flocking to this country, and plans are on foot to move them from Europe en masse ... to empty upon our shores the very scum and dregs of the Parasite Race" (quoted in Higham 1963: 186).

In 1917, when the United States joined Britain and France in their war against Germany, nativism reached its apogee. Theodore Roosevelt and Woodrow Wilson, two of the most distinguished and respected Americans of that time, railed against what they called "hyphenated Americans." Roosevelt agitated in support of the war effort by campaigning for what he called the "simple and loyal motto"—"America for Americans." The former president claimed that he was not fighting against "Americans of German origins" but, rather, against "German-Americans who *call* themselves such." In other words, Roosevelt was attacking immigrants who were continuing to express pride in their non-American national origins. He viewed this pride as proof that they would "spiritually remain foreigners in whole or in part."

Woodrow Wilson, who was president at the time, at first resisted such ethnocentric hysteria. But when he needed to rally support for defense appropriations to support the war, he too began calling attention to "alien sympathies." He cruelly attacked immigrants "who have poured the poison of disloyalty into the very arteries of our national life" and called for severely repressive measures against them: "Such creatures of passion, disloyalty, and anarchy must be crushed out" (quoted in Higham 1963: 199–200).

The war ended in 1918, but the nativist uproar continued. Powerful and intimidating, it forced the American government to close the spigot on immigration—for the first time in history. In 1924, the government placed tight controls upon immigration, virtually ending the influx for the next forty years. It was not until the 1960s that the idea of the United States as a "white Christian nation" became confined to the ravings of a few extremist groups. Indeed, the arrival of some 20 million immigrants over the past several decades has revived the collective representation of America as a "nation of nations." This "new immigration" is far more diverse than earlier waves, thanks to the 1965 Hart-Celler Act, which abolished the national origins system favoring groups from Northern and Western Europe. Now all nations, regardless of region or size, are placed on an equal footing, with the result that two-thirds of all post-1965 immigrants have come from Asia and Latin America. Large waves have also flowed in from Africa, the Middle East, and the Caribbean. As suggested earlier, demographers have noted that if present trends continue, whites will constitute only 52 percent of the national population in the year 2050 (Martin and Midgley 1994: 9). America is becoming more diverse than ever before, a truly inclusive nationality encompassing the spectrum of the world's population. This is not to say, of course, that tensions among recent and earlier immigrants have disappeared. In fact, America is presently undergoing a new polarization around Hispanic immigration, as we will see below.

Figure 10.2 shows how the composition of America's immigrant population has changed over

One of the worst examples of nativism in U.S. history was the U.S. Supreme Court–ordered internment of Japanese-Americans in concentration camps during World War II. (iStockphoto)

the last three decades. In the 1970s, for example, the majority of immigrants came from Asia. In the 1990s, that trend began to shift, with most immigrants coming from areas such as Africa, Oceania, Bermuda, and Canada.

## MINORITY GROUP THEORY

In the early part of the twentieth century, in response to the difficult period of ethnocentric abuse, American sociologists developed a more

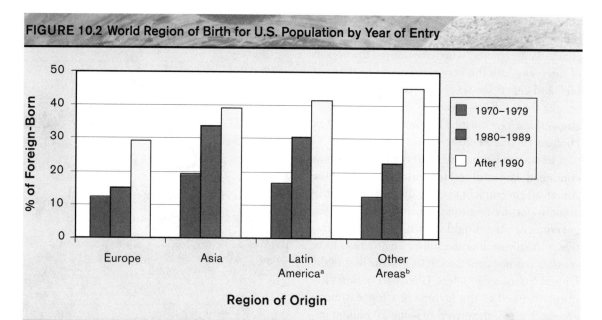

FIGURE 10.2 World Region of Birth for U.S. Population by Year of Entry

Notes:

[a]The majority of those born in "Latin America" are from Mexico.

[b]bThose born in "Other Areas" are from Africa, Oceania, Bermuda, and Canada.

Source: U.S. Census Bureau (2001).

general theory that would rise above the particularities of the American situation. In contrast to theories that emphasize class, this approach—known as *minority group theory*—highlights status inequality, especially the noneconomic and non-political dimensions of race and ethnicity. (Recall the distinction between class and status stratification discussed in Chapter 8, on inequality.) This theory is still considered one of the singular contributions of American sociology.

**Minority group** As defined by Louis Wirth, a group of people within society who are subordinated on the basis of their physical or cultural characteristics. The status of *minority* refers not to numbers but to power differentials between racial and ethnic groups.

According to Louis Wirth, one of the most influential of these early American sociologists, every society contains both minority and majority groups. The status of *minority* refers not to actual numbers but, rather, to power differentials between ethnic and/or racially defined groups. As Wirth put it, a **minority group** is "[a] group of people who, because of their physical or cultural characteristics, are singled out from others in the society in which they live for differential and unequal treatment and who therefore regard themselves as objects of collective discrimination" (quoted in Feagin 1978: 11). The very concept of minority group implies, of course, that there is a majority group in turn. This is the group that has more power, more resources, and more rights and that feels justified in this dominant position by virtue of its culture or physical appearance.

Prejudice flows from the tension between minority and majority groups. Defined as a negative attitude toward members of a racial or ethnic group, prejudice reflects a hasty and biased judgment, and can be seen as a premature or faulty generalization from a small number of observations.

Of course, nobody goes around making judgments solely on the basis of proven observations! We are all cultural creatures, embedded in traditions. What distinguishes prejudice from other cultural attitudes is the fact that it not only stigmatizes but also is tenaciously held "no matter what." As Gordon W. Allport once asserted, "prejudgments become prejudices only if they are not reversible when exposed to new knowledge" (Allport 1954: 18).

Another way to put this is to say that prejudice rests upon stereotypes. Originally referring to a method of duplicate printing, the term stereotype was introduced into social thought by Walter Lippmann in *Public Opinion* (1922). Lippmann himself employed a neutral understanding of the word. He suggested that stereotypes are fixed, cognitive preconceptions that are essential for managing reality in modern societies. In this sense, without stereotypes we would find it impossible to deal with the complexity of everyday life, inasmuch as all our judgments and perceptions presuppose cultural frames.

American social scientists, however, soon applied the term *stereotype* to the perceptions that relate minority and majority groups. For example, in an article titled "Racial Prejudice and Racial Stereotypes" (1935), Daniel Katz and Kenneth Braly discussed their finding that American college students tended to evoke stigmatizing clichés whenever they were asked about minority ethnic groups. The stereotype of blacks included such traits as "superstitious" and "lazy"; that of Jews, "mercenary" and "grasping"; that of Turks, "cruel" and "treacherous."

Psychological explanations for stereotyping abound, no doubt because in everyday life we are inclined to look at prejudiced behavior in individualistic ways. Psychologists have said, for example, that stereotyping represents "externalization," a defense mechanism that allows an individual to get rid of emotional anxiety by scapegoating somebody else. And Theodor Adorno and his colleagues (1950) related prejudice to what they called the "authoritarian personality." Prejudiced people, they found, tended to be emotionally insecure, submissive to authority, and conformist in their opinions.

The more sociological approach to stereotypes regards them as cultural structures that simultaneously facilitate and rationalize a majority's domination over minority groups. Stereotypes are effective because they supply the supposedly "factual" basis for racism and ethnocentrism.

Prejudices are stigmatizing attitudes that rely on stereotypes, which, as noted, are cultural beliefs. Taken together, they define the subjective elements that inform minority-majority relations. Discrimination, by contrast, refers to actual behavior, regardless of the motivation. It is objective, not subjective. Joe Feagin (1978: 14) defines discrimination as "actions or practices carried out by members of dominant groups, or their representa-

---

**Prejudice** A negative attitude toward members of an ethnic or racial minority group. Prejudices are often based on the premature or faulty generalization of a small number of observations.

**Stereotypes** A neutral term, introduced by Walter Lippmann, referring to fixed, cognitive preconceptions that are necessary for understanding modern society. Eventually, stereotypes came to carry a negative connotation. Based on stigmatized beliefs, they facilitate and maintain a majority's domination of the minority.

**Discrimination** Behaviors based on cultural beliefs that stigmatize members of a minority group, harmfully impact them, and reinforce their lower status in relation to the majority group. Discrimination can be individual or institutional, conscious or unintended.

tives, which have a differential and harmful impact on members of subordinate groups."

Discrimination varies along two axes: scope and intentionality. *Scope* refers to whether discrimination is individual or institutional in origin; *intentionality* refers to whether it is conscious or unintended. In cases of individual discrimination, a member of a minority group is stigmatized by somebody acting in isolation. Such stigmatizing encounters can occur even when the majority culture is free of prejudice and stereotypes. At the opposite end of the spectrum is institutional discrimination. Historically, highly unequal group relations have undermined the life chances of minority groups as a result of both individual and institutional discrimination. Think of what it means to be born into one of the impoverished ghettoes in America's inner cities. In such isolated urban areas, African-American children are exposed to decaying neighborhoods, failing and ineffective schools, and socialization processes often undermined by broken families and criminal peer behavior. These circumstances represent institutional discrimination at its worst—discrimination that exists regardless of the prejudice or intention of any white individual or group. We speak at length about the sources of this structural situation in the next section.

**Racial underclass** Collectively, the large number of African-Americans who are impoverished and much more likely than mainstream groups to be out of work, to be sick, to have dropped out of high school, to live in single-parent households, and to have been incarcerated. William Julius Wilson argues that the racial underclass has come about as the result of a combination of external (exogenous) and internal (endogenous) factors. An exogenous factor might be a political process such as affirmative action that increases the physical and social separation from the poor, between black working and middle classes, whereas an endogenous factor might be a demographic variable such as urban migration, limited access to societal institutions, or lack of neighborhood resources.

Another form of discrimination exists as well. Neither individual nor institutional, but still systematic and conscious in scope, it occurs when members of one racial or ethnic group—usually but not always from the majority—act in concert against members of another, without the support of the surrounding community. An example is the rash of African-American church burnings that occurred during the 1990s in the American South, despite a significant decline in stereotyping and prejudice in that region in the decades after the civil rights movement of the 1950s and 1960s. Indeed, a vast decrease in actual discrimination had also occurred. This explains why the church burnings, though clearly a product of group action, did not set off a wider backlash against black progress among Southern whites.

## THE GREAT DEBATE: ORIGINS OF THE RACIAL UNDERCLASS IN AMERICA

These different theoretical possibilities play out in sociological research on the origins of America's **racial underclass**. There is wide agreement among liberals and conservatives, whites and blacks, and sociologists of every theoretical stripe that the centers of America's large cities continue to be home to a significant percentage of impoverished African-Americans (see also Chapter 8, on inequality, and Chapter 16, on urbanism and population). These citizens are much more likely than their white counterparts to be out of work, to be sick, to be high school dropouts, to be in single-parent-headed households, and to have been in and out of jail. The question is why.

The scramble for an answer has set off *the* great debate in American sociology. At the center of this debate is the work of America's best-known black sociologist, William Julius Wilson. He has published two of the most cited and debated publications in American academia in the past thirty years: *The Declining Significance of Race: Blacks and Changing American Institutions* (1979) and *The Truly Disadvantaged: The Inner City, the Underclass, and Public Policy* (1987), following these up with the synthetic work *When Work Disappears* (1996). The first of these books caused great controversy because some critics mistakenly interpreted it as arguing that racial discrimination (and hence race itself) was of declining importance when compared with class factors in explaining the situation of blacks. But, in fact, what Wilson was arguing was that both racial discrimination and class position affect life chances and that it is the changing character of their interaction that is important for understanding the present situation. Among the key changes he noted were the growing differences within the black population itself, especially between the now substantial black working and middle classes, on the one side, and the large black underclass, on the other. Wilson still insists that the long history of institutionalized racism helped to shape these differences and that large average interracial differences continue to exist. What has changed in more recent times, however, is the fact that economic class has become more important than race in determining *job placement* and *mobility between occupations*.

In the early twentieth century, the expansion of the economy facilitated the movement of black families from the rural areas of the South to the industrial centers, where greater job opportunities led to greater occupational differences within the black community. In particular, an increasing percentage of blacks moved into white-collar positions and semiskilled and skilled blue-collar positions. The civil rights movement and black political mobilization lowered racial barriers to employment even further. Together, these economic and political changes created a pattern of black occupational upgrading that resulted, for example, in a substantial drop in the percentage of blacks in low-paying service, unskilled-labor, and farm jobs. Specifically, the proportion of black

Black single mothers are represented disproportionately on the welfare rolls for complex reasons, including the legacy of poverty inherited from slavery and historically institutionalized racial discrimination. (Shepard Sherbell/Corbis Saba)

men in such jobs declined dramatically from close to 80 percent in 1940 to only 36 percent in 1970 (Wilson 2003: 1098).

As Wilson argued in *The Declining Significance of Race* (1979), these changes also resulted in a closer, more "sociologically normal" association between black occupational mobility and class affiliation. Black access to good-paying jobs is now increasingly based on the educational achievement required for participating in postmodern as compared to industrial economies. Ironically, however, this more recent association among class position, education, and economic mobility—in itself a welcome and healthy development—threatens to stymie attempts by poorly educated, low-income blacks to improve their economic position.

These changes inside the African-American occupational structure have coincided with a drastic decline in manufacturing jobs nationally, which means that less-educated job applicants have much less access to high-wage but low-skilled jobs. The result is a *segmented* labor market, with very different mobility opportunities for different segments of the black population. On the one hand, poorly trained and educationally limited blacks from the inner city, including growing numbers of black teenagers and young adults, see their job prospects increasingly restricted to the low-wage sector, their unemployment rates soaring to record levels, their movement out of poverty slowing, and their presence on the welfare rolls increasing. On the other hand, better-educated and -trained blacks are experiencing increased job opportunities in the corporate and government sectors owing to the expansion of salaried white-collar positions and the pressures of widespread and continuing affirmative action programs in both the public and private spheres.

In *The Truly Disadvantaged* (1987), Wilson continued his analysis of historical trends that have subjected poor blacks to circumstances in which they found it difficult to better themselves. In particular, he explored the social transformation of the inner city—the ghetto. Historical discrimination combined with migrations from the rural South to large metropolises kept the urban black population relatively young and created a problem of weak labor-force attachment that made them particularly vulnerable to the industrial and geographic changes in the economy since the early 1970s. Innovations in technology, the shift from goods-producing to service-producing industries, the relocation of manufacturing industries out of central cities, the increasing polarization of the labor market into low-wage and high-wage sectors, and periodic recessions have elevated the rate of black joblessness—despite the passage of legislation against discrimination and the creation of affirmative action programs. This higher rate of joblessness, in turn, has led not only to a higher concentration of poor blacks, leaving greater numbers of single-parent families dependent on welfare, but also to a significant outmigration of working- and middle-class families from inner-city ghetto neighborhoods. The groups who have remained in the ghetto are largely the poor, who—given the diminishing presence of middle-class

and working-class families—now also lack an important social buffer that served to deflect the full impact of the prolonged high levels of neighborhood joblessness stemming from uneven economic growth and periodic recessions.

To provide some much-needed historical perspective on the current situation, Wilson (2003) has pointed out that, in earlier decades, most of the adults in ghetto neighborhoods were employed. These black working and middle classes provided greater stability in the ghetto. They invested their economic, their social, and, perhaps most important, their cultural resources inside the black community itself, by patronizing neighborhood stores, banks, and churches; by participating in community organizations; by sending their children to the local public schools; and, in general, by providing role models for less privileged members of their stigmatized community. In the process they reinforced societal values and norms, and made it meaningful for the disadvantaged in these segregated enclaves to envision the possibility of upward mobility.

Today, by contrast, the inner-city ghetto is made up of groups of poor residents whose major predicament, as we noted above, is rising joblessness—a trend that is strengthened by growing social isolation. The contact between groups of different class and racial backgrounds has decreased because of the outmigration of higher-income families, further exacerbating the adverse effects of living in impoverished neighborhoods. These effects were created, in the first place, by inadequate access to jobs, lack of informal job networks and quality schools, decreasing availability of suitable marriage partners, lack of exposure to conventional role models, and limited contact with "mainstream" social institutions.

In arguing about the recent increases in social dislocations in the inner-city ghetto, Wilson has aimed at reaching a balance between structural and cultural factors and at showing how these factors interact. He maintains that this discussion cannot be reduced "to the easy explanations of racism advanced by those on the left" (2003: 1101) or to the "culture of poverty" argument posited by those on the right. (The latter attributes black impoverishment to cultural defects, such as an alleged lack of moral values that emphasize the virtues of married life, education, hard work, and enterprise.) Rather, Wilson's goal is to combine the above-noted structural and cultural factors with economic factors: "Although historic racism created the ghetto and although contemporary discrimination has undoubtedly aggravated the economic and social woes of its residents, an adequate understanding of the sharp increase in these problems requires the specification of a complex web of additional factors, including the impact of shifts in the modern American economy" (2003: 1101). A formal model of Wilson's theoretical framework subdivides this web of factors into those that are external to the ghetto (exogenous factors) and those that are internal (endogenous factors), as follows:

✓ Exogenous factors represent the sources of the concentration of black ghetto poverty and include racial discrimination, changes in the economy that have restructured occupations and relocated industries, and political processes (affirmative action programs and antibias legislation) that have contributed to the increased physical and social separation of the black working and middle classes from the black poor.

✓ Endogenous factors are created by the exogenous factors and include demographic variables such as urban migration, changes in the age structures, the pool of marriageable men, and economic factors such as employment and income distribution. They also include social isolation, which [not only] deprives ghetto residents … of access to institutions in the broader society and to economic and social resources, including conventional role models to buffer

the impact of joblessness, but also limits access to mainstream social networks that facilitate economic and social mobility. The limited access to societal institutions, lack of neighborhood and social resources, declining presence of conventional role models, and circumscribed cultural learning produce outcomes that restrict social advancement. Some of these outcomes are structural (weak attachment to the labor force and lack of access to informal job networks) and some are cultural and behavioral (limited aspirations and negative social dispositions). (Wilson 2003: 1102)

The importance of Wilson's interest in culture, and not just in structural factors, is well illustrated by a *New York Times* op-ed article written in 2004 by his Harvard colleague Henry Louis Gates under the title "Breaking the Silence." The silence he referred to was the alleged failure of many black scholars and politicians to speak publicly about the culturally motivated behaviors that contribute to black poverty. As Gates explained: "Scholars, such as my Harvard colleague William Julius Wilson, say that the causes of black poverty are both structural and behavioral. Think of structural causes as 'The devil made me do it,' and behavioral causes as 'The devil is in me.' Structural causes are faceless systemic forces, like the disappearance of jobs. Behavioral causes are self-destructive life choices and personal habits. To break the conspiracy of silence, we have to address both of these factors" (Gates 2004: 11).

Gates drew on his own experience, as well as on statistics, to illustrate his argument that black values and behavioral choices are as important as structural factors in explaining black poverty. He quoted his father, aged 91, saying to him, as they drove past a packed inner-city basketball court at midnight, "If our people studied calculus like we studied basketball, we'd be running M.I.T." Gates added, "When my brother and I were growing up in the '50s, our parents convinced us that the

Although many black children aspire to follow role models like Kobe Bryant into professional sports or entertainment, very few opportunities in those fields are available. (Paul Buck/epa/Corbis)

'blackest' thing that we could be was a doctor or lawyer. We admired Hank Aaron and Willie Mays, but our real heroes were people like Thurgood Marshall, Dr. Benjamin Mays, and Mary McLeod Bethune." Yet, in many black neighborhoods today, he claimed, "academic achievement has come to be stigmatized." Too many black children, he argued, now believe that it is easier to become a black professional athlete than a doctor or lawyer. "Reality check: according to the 2000 census, there were more than 31,000 black physicians and surgeons, 33,000 black lawyers and 5,000 black dentists. Guess how many black athletes are playing professional basketball, football and baseball combined. About 1,400. In fact, there are more board-certified black cardiologists than there are black professional basketball players."

In conclusion, Gates suggested that many African-Americans hesitate to discuss this issue in public because they think that doing so lets the larger society off the hook:

> We're stuck in an either/or mentality—that the problem is either societal or it's cultural. It's important to talk about life chances—about the constricted set of opportunities that poverty brings. But to treat black people as if they're helpless rag dolls—swept up and buffeted by vast social trends—is a supreme act of condescension. Only 50 per cent of all black children graduate from high school; an estimated 64 per cent of black teenage girls will become pregnant. (Black children raised by female "householders" are five times as likely to live in poverty as those raised by married couples.) Are white racists forcing black teenagers to drop out of school or to have babies? (2004: 11)

Structural factors are important, and opportunities need to be created for inner-city blacks to get out of poverty. "But values matter too. We can't talk about the choices people have without talking about the choices people make" (Gates 2004: 11).

If, as Wilson argues, securely employed working-class families and middle-class professional and business people are no longer visible in the inner city, then where are young black male ghetto-dwellers to get their role models? The answer would appear to be the media, which mainly feature successful blacks in sports or entertainment rather than in the traditional professions. And where in the ghetto are young black women going to find role models? Glamorous media images are likely to draw their attention, too. Consider the case of the young black woman (a single mother) who won the TV competition *American Idol* in 2004. It was a great personal achievement for her and was held up as an example for others to follow, but it may not have provided a realistic model for other young black women to follow.

Some of the self-destructive cultural tendencies in black ghetto life may exacerbate the hardships of underclass social structure—but does this justify the old game of "blaming the victim"? Many Americans would answer in the affirmative. They believe that if ghetto residents would only try harder in marriage, work, and family, and learn to "just say no" to antisocial and illegal temptations, their lives would be happier. But, in fact, bad behavior locks people into the bottom rungs of society only when they are faced with the structural barriers of an underclass. When working- and middle-class Americans (white or minority) make mistakes, they are usually given second and even third chances, and they can fall back on community institutions. But there are no second chances, no institutional safety nets, in the black underclass. Given the current conservative political climate in the United States, it is morally tempting for the relatively well-off majority of Americans to put the blame on the "character failings" of black individuals—certainly this is politically and economically easier than trying to remedy the structural factors that formed the underclass in the first place (Steinberg 1995). But eliminating welfare payments will not bring jobs back into the ghetto, provide good education to young black people, or fix the tears in the fabric of their primary and secondary socialization.

As bad as it is, the situation has grown worse as a result of the further exodus of college-educated blacks from the North and West to the South. A study by the Brookings Institution, released in 2004, found that black Americans were moving back to the Southern states in increasing numbers, causing a "full-scale reversal" of the great migration that occurred when they fled segregation. Southern cities such as Atlanta, Dallas, Houston, and Charlotte showed the greatest increases in black migrants during the 1990s, whereas New York, Chicago, Los Angeles, and San Francisco showed the steepest declines. Georgia, Texas, and Maryland attracted the most college-educated

Latino/as have surpassed African-Americans as the largest minority group; many immigrants from Mexico, Central America, and South America work in agriculture. (Bob Sacha/Corbis)

graduates from 1995 to 2000, whereas New York suffered the largest net loss during that period.

To some extent these migrants are following job opportunities. However, such **reverse migration** may also reflect the desire of African-Americans for voluntary segregation—a wish to be the dominant "racial minority" rather than one more "ethnic minority" alongside Hispanics and Asians in an increasingly diverse West and North. In fact, the census of 2003 revealed that Hispanics had overtaken African-Americans as the United States' largest minority. As a result of higher birthrates and immigration, the Latino population stood at 37 million; the figure for black Americans in that year was 36.2 million. Even Los Angeles County

**Reverse migration** A recent trend whereby black Americans are moving back to the South in high numbers (having originally fled the South after the Civil War). Some sociologists argue that reverse migration is a result of the availability of job opportunities in the South. Others argue that it is evidence of voluntary segregation—the desire to be the dominant racial minority in a region rather than one of many ethnic minorities.

Racial intermarriage, which was once called miscegenation and was illegal in the United States, is on the increase today. (iStockphoto)

saw a fall in its black population—for the first time in its history.

Most fundamentally, these potentially seismic shifts in minority demographics are the product of two factors. The first is the impressive long-term progress toward black incorporation, despite the glaring and troubling exception of the underclass. The second is the massive immigration of Hispanic people from Mexico and Central America to the United States, which has occurred over roughly the same period.

At the same time, the politics of race and ethnicity may also be changing, from a focus on discrimination and inequality to a concern over

**Multiculturalism** A value based on the principle that many cultures can, and should, coexist in a particular region. Quite often, multiculturalism is in conflict with the push for assimilation of many cultures into one dominant culture. This conflict is illustrated by the tension between the concepts of *melting pot* and *mosaic*. The former term suggests the combination of many cultures into one; the latter, a cluster of many cultures.

assimilation and fragmentation. Consider, for example, the argument of outspoken conservative political scientist Samuel P. Huntington regarding what he calls "The Hispanic Challenge." Huntington denies that discrimination and institutional blockages are problems facing new immigrants. Instead, he claims, Hispanic immigrants resist assimilation and want to remain outside core American culture and institutional life: "The persistence of Mexican immigration into the United States reduces the incentives for cultural assimilation. Mexican Americans no longer think of themselves as members of a small minority who must accommodate the dominant group and adopt its culture. As their numbers increase, they become more committed to their own ethnic identity and culture" (Huntington 2004a: 44).

This attitude toward Hispanics is reminiscent of the nativism of the nineteenth and early twentieth centuries, which we discussed earlier in the chapter. By the mid-twentieth century, however, American citizens and sociologists alike had become more concerned with issues of inequality and discrimination than with "essentialist" arguments about the supposedly inherent divergence between out-group culture and American traditions. The new immigration from south of the American border has weakened this commitment, but so, indirectly, has the powerful postmodern movement toward diversity and multicultural rights. Even as the civil rights movement of the 1960s was succeeding in making integration a partial reality, there arose the Black Power movement, which focused not on incorporation but on preserving the integrity and independence of African-American culture. Thus began the broader interest in diversity and identity politics—in **multiculturalism**—that, as we have seen, sits at the center of postmodern life.

It was in the context of this post–civil rights movement toward multiculturalism that sociologists began to criticize the idea that ethnic groups could or should be assimilated into the tradition-

**data**

## Racial Intermarriage in the United States

✓ Racial intermarriage has increased from less than 1 percent of all married couples in 1970 to more than 5 percent of couples in 2000.

✓ The typical interracial couple is a white person with a nonwhite spouse. Intermarriage between two people from minority racial groups is relatively infrequent.

✓ Whites and blacks have the lowest intermarriage rates, while American Indians, Hawaiians, and multiple-race people have the highest. Asians and people reporting some other race have intermediate intermarriage rates.

✓ Black men are more likely to intermarry than black women, while Asian women are more likely to intermarry than Asian men. Men and women from other racial groups are equally likely to intermarry.

✓ About one-fourth of Hispanic couples are inter-Hispanic, a rate that has been fairly stable since 1980.

✓ Younger and better-educated Americans are more likely to intermarry than older and less-educated Americans.

✓ U.S.-born Asians and Hispanics and foreign-born whites and blacks are more likely to intermarry than foreign-born Asians and Hispanics and U.S.-born whites and blacks.

✓ More children are growing up in either interracial or inter-Hispanic families. Between 1970 and 2000, the number of children living in interracial families increased nearly fourfold—from 900,000 to more than 3 million—while the number in inter-Hispanic families increased nearly threefold—from 800,000 to 2 million.

*Source:* Lee and Edmonston (2005: 7).

ally dominant white Anglo-Saxon Protestant (WASP) culture. What should change, they suggested, was the dominant culture itself. A prominent contemporary sociologist, Douglas Massey (2004: 408), has recounted how, when he first came into sociology in the late 1970s, the very idea of assimilation was suspect and under relentless attack. Books such as Nathan Glazer and Daniel P. Moynihan's *Beyond the Melting Pot* (1963), Michael Novak's *The Rise of the Unmeltable Ethnics* (1972), and Andrew Greeley's *Ethnicity in the United States: A Preliminary Reconnaissance* (1974) stressed the resilience of immigrant cultures and pointed to the remarkable persistence of ethnicity as evidence that refuted assimilation the-

ory and its supposed prediction of Anglo conformity and cultural absorption.

In a series of papers published during the 1980s and 1990s, however, sociologists such as Richard Alba and Victor Nee (2003) kept finding results that confirmed "America's dirty little secret" of assimilation (as they called it), not only for immigrants but for excluded racial groups as well. By the end of the twentieth century it seemed that descendants of earlier European immigrants had indeed assimilated across a variety of social, economic, and cultural dimensions. Moreover, there was some evidence that the children and grandchildren of the new immigrants from Asia, Latin America, and the Caribbean were largely following suit. Sociologists have also noted, however, that groups from different national origins differ with respect to patterns and rates of assimilation, depending on such factors as their level of skills and the extent to which they were geographically dispersed. Groups with a large proportion of members with low levels of skill and who are concentrated within a geographical area—such as Mexican immigrants in the Southwest region of America—tend not to assimilate quickly (Perlmann and Waldinger 2000).

In a 2005 study conducted for the Population Reference Bureau, Sharon Lee and Barry Edmonston analyzed the Public Use Microdata Sample files from the 1970, 1980, 1990, and 2000 censuses to produce a statistical summary of trends over the last three decades in the rate of intermarriage among the U.S. population. Their results are summarized in the box titled "Racial Intermarriage in the United States" as well as in Table 10.5.

Social assimilation is now recognized to be highly contingent and segmented; that is, it depends on the varying incidence of a combination of factors such as skills and geography. Cultural assimilation, too, is dependent on a variety of factors—especially the strength of ethnic cultural institutions, such as radio stations and television channels broadcasting to that community, and the presence of ethnic associations that keep community links alive. So, while sociologists do insist that assimilation is proceeding, their understanding of it has changed. They no longer assume it to be a one-way process in which immigrants move toward Anglo-American values and behaviors but, rather, describe it as a two-way process in which ethnic groups often maintain significant elements from their home culture—in part because mainstream U.S. culture has become less homogeneous and prejudiced (see box titled "Ethnicity Redefined"). Witness the widespread interest in Asian and Hispanic food and entertainment, from sushi and tacos to the martial arts. This two-way process inspired Alba and Nee to title their study "*Remaking* the American Mainstream." (For a broad overview of this new sociological approach, see Kivisto 2005.)

This is not to say that the new pathways into American society are smooth and well paved! Changing the American mainstream is never conflict-free. Members of America's old core groups, and their political representatives and ideological spokespersons, often resent what they regard as threats to their cultural styles and values. This resentment can be bitter, and it can lead to reactive social movements. Huntington and other conservative intellectuals believe that an actual culture war is under way in the United States, between those who believe the country should become multicultural and those who believe new arrivals should identify with what Huntington calls "Anglo-Protestant culture." Anti-immigrant move-

### TABLE 10.5 U.S. Interracial Marriage Rates[1] by Race, 1970 to 2000

| Race | 1970 | 1980 | 1990 | 2000 |
|---|---|---|---|---|
| White | 0.4 | 1.0 | 1.5 | 2.7 |
| Black | 1.1 | 2.4 | 4.1 | 7.0 |
| American Indian | 37.6 | 53.1 | 59.7 | 56.7 |
| Asian | 19.9 | 21.1 | 17.7 | 16.0 |
| Hawaiian | 50.1 | 58.0 | 50.7 | 45.6 |
| Some Other Race (SOR)[2] | N/A[3] | 15.8 | 15.7 | 17.7 |
| Multiple Race | N/R[4] | N/R | N/R | 56.0 |

Notes:

[1] The interracial marriage rate is the percentage of married people within each group with a spouse of another race. Multiple Race was reported only in the 2000 Census.

[2] Nearly all SORs also identified as Hispanic, but not all Hispanics identified as SOR.

[3] Not applicable. The 1970 composition of the SOR race category was not comparable with later years.

[4] Not reported. The Multiple Race category was reported only in the 2000 Census.

Source: Adapted from Lee and Edmonston (2005).

## theory

### Ethnicity Redefined

The American ethnic mosaic is being fundamentally altered; ethnicity itself is being redefined, its new images reified in the popular media and reflected in myriad and often surprising ways. Immigrants from a score of nationalities are told that they are all "Hispanics," while far more diverse groups—from India and Laos, China and the Philippines—are lumped together as "Asians." There are foreign-born mayors of large American cities, first-generation millionaires who speak broken English, a proliferation of sweatshops exploiting immigrant labor in an expanding informal economy, and new myths that purport to "explain" the success or failure of different ethnic groups. Along "Callo Ocho" in Miami's Little Havana, shops post signs to reassure potential customers that they'll find "English spoken here," while Korean retailers in Los Angeles display "Se habla español" signs next to their own Hangul script, a businesslike acknowledgement that the largest Mexican and Salvadoran communities in the world outside Mexico and El Salvador are located there. In Brooklyn, along Brighton Beach Avenue ("Little Odessa"), signs written in Cyrillic letters by new Soviet immigrants have replaced old English and Yiddish signs. In Houston, the auxiliary bishop is a Cuban-born Jesuit who speaks fluent Vietnamese—an overflow of 6,000 faithful attended his recent ordination and he addressed them in three languages—and the best Cuban café is run by Koreans.

*Source:* Rúmbaut (1991: 209).

ments have formed in recent years, and the U.S. Congress is sharply divided over immigration reform. Should the continuing flow of new immigrants be supported if regulated with enlarged quotas, citizenship opportunities for illegal workers, and beefed-up border controls? Or should immigration be brought to a halt, followed by the deportation or imprisonment of those whose entry into the country was illegal?

It is the moral and intellectual responsibility of sociology to respond to this clarion call for culture war. Is there, in fact, any agreement about what constitutes the American cultural identity into which all immigrants and their descendants in different ethnic groups should assimilate? Is there, as Huntington and his concerned conservative colleagues suggest, an unchanging and essential American cultural core?

In attempting to answer such questions, sociologists have begun to use terms like *hybridity* and *diaspora*. In the current globalizing and increasingly pluralistic postmodern society, the idea of a single homogeneous identity into which all ethnic groups can be integrated is passé. The core American values that do remain are not ethnic, sexual, religious, or racial but political and civil. They are values that relate to democracy, to a belief in independence, mutual concern, and the capacity for human beings to be tolerant and sympathetic in their feelings toward others. Such "universalistic" values transcend the emotions that separate groups and provide the basis for a broad solidarity that manifests itself in public civility and private tolerance and is furthered through participation in schools, voting, and consumption of shared media.

Women who wear the veil, whether from Africa, the Indian diaspora, or the Middle East, have experienced discrimination and racial profiling in the United States, especially after 9/11. (iStockphoto)

Another critical factor of postmodern life is the fact that globalization makes it much easier for immigrant groups to maintain their betwixt and between "diasporic" status. A disapora is an ethnic or religious group that, while residing outside the homeland for short or long periods of time, continues to nurture strong feelings for, and beliefs in, the possibility for return. And today, because international travel is easy and relatively cheap, simultaneous communication around the world has been made possible by the Internet, and songs, movies, and products from hundreds of different cultures and nations circulate rapidly around the globe, cultural identity may be best thought of as a hybrid—as a mixture or combination of equally cherished cultural components, drawn from and looking toward diverse sources and places. The

point here isn't that new immigrants and their children may not regard themselves as "American" but, rather, that their perception of what it is to be American may differ from others' (Portes and Rúmbaut 1996; Portes and Zhou 1993).

The diaspora of peoples whose origins are in the Indian subcontinent (South Asia) and who are now living in Western countries—especially in English-speaking United States, Canada, and Britain—exemplify this new situation. These immigrants constitute one of the fastest-growing minority groups in the United States, but they are also among the best educated and most professionally qualified. As far back as the time of the 1990 census, the median family income of Indians in the United States, at $49,309, was well above that of non-Hispanic whites, at $37,630 (Waters and Eschbach 1999: 315); 43.6 percent were employed either as professionals, mostly doctors and engineers, or as managers; and 58.4 percent held at least a bachelor's degree (Shinagawa 1996: 113, 119). This latter characteristic also holds for young female members of Indian ethnic groups (Muslim, Christian, and Hindu).

These South Asian populations bring with them cultures that are highly developed and historically durable; in other words, they are not easily swamped or eroded by contact with Western cultures. But it is their use of postindustrial technology that is most striking in the new process of hybrid assimilation. Kenneth Thompson's (2002) research on the media use and leisure practices of Asian-originating mothers and daughters in Britain and North America found that many of the daughters (in particular, those between the late teens and 30 years of age) used the Internet as a vehicle for creating and maintaining a "virtual community" of members of their ethnic peer group.

Another researcher, Ananda Mitra (1997), analyzed postings to the soc.culture.indian Usenet group and identified three categories of messages. The most common were general postings, primarily informational in character. Typically, users were looking for someone and, through the network, reestablished contact; relationships severed by the geographical move from India were reconnected on the Internet. Most users were in the United States, with a few in Europe and even fewer in India. Mitra identified a national critical discourse—postings that addressed religion and issues about contemporary Indian identity. Postings of this kind were often contested, and some of the discussions that ensued were antagonistic. Finally, Mitra identified a group of postings concerning the Indians' negotiation of roles in the United States—in short, discussions of immigrant identity. Overall, the study found that, to a greater degree than the press and broadcasting, the Usenet allowed the expression of a diversity of voices, producing a picture of both division and cohesion. At the same time as such internal ethnic fragmentation occurred, the mutual support manifested in the first set of postings brought its participants together—permitting a sense of community rooted in the original homeland to be transferred to the West, where belonging is more problematic and where the space to develop community is virtual space. As in other such cases, a more unified ethnic identity emerged only when the group felt attacked or underappreciated by other groups. The unifying pressure arose when the Internet discussions began to center on the precarious nature of the participants' immigrant identity against what they perceived as "the Other"—either majority white America or other immigrant groups who seemed more favored. Postings that had a unifying effect included those with such themes as the proposition in California to deny public services to illegal immigrants, the portrayal of an Indian rapist on *NYPD Blue*, and a discussion of Christian TV channels' references to Hindu religion as "pagan" (Mitra 1997: 67).

The new media, such as the Internet, videos, and cable television, like the new possibilities for international travel, enable diasporic ethnic cultures to flourish within a postmodern multicultural society. Even older sources of ethnic culture,

Indian-American women are one of the most educated and economically well-off minorities in North America, often not conforming to traditional roles and dress codes. (iStockphoto)

such as religion, may thrive. Indeed, religion is generally found to play a central role in constructing ethnicity among immigrants because it serves as a vehicle for the transmission of culture and also provides the institutional framework for community formation. According to sociologist of religion Stephen Warner (1993), this is particularly the case in the United States, inasmuch as Americans view religion as the most acceptable and nonthreatening basis for community formation and expression. But there is a two-way flow of influence between the immigrant religion and the host culture, within which the diasporic ethnic religion may be transformed. Whereas in India "children breathe in the values of Hindu life" (Fenton 1988: 127) and of "Indianness," in the immigrant situation the meaning and content of religion and culture have to be explicitly articulated and explained. Much of this task is found to be performed by women (Rayaprol 1997). The idealized family based on traditional gender images from Hindu religion is a central icon in the construction of American Hinduism. However, this idealized image contains a strong patriarchal bias, with the woman seen as a virtuous and self-sacrificing homemaker, enabling the professional success of her husband and the academic achievement of her children through her unselfish actions on their behalf. This image is difficult to reconcile with the reality that Indian-American women are among the most highly educated and professionally active groups in the population—a disparity that leads to tensions and even to gender abuse (DasGupta and DasGupta 1996). However, there is evidence that, because women are the primary transmitters of religious and cultural traditions within households and local ethnic associations, at these levels they are able to reinterpret patriarchal images in their favor as well as construct a model of gender that is egalitarian and emphasizes the importance of male responsibilities (Kurien 1999: 650). This reinterpretation reveals how hybridity not only sustains difference but also allows cultural integration into the kinds of egalitarian values that form the nonethnic core of democratic societies.

The Great Seal of the United States carries the motto *E pluribus unum*, "From many, one," which seems to suggest that "manyness" must be left behind for the sake of oneness. But the Great Seal presents another image as well: the "American" eagle holding a sheaf of arrows. Here there is no merger or fusion but only a fastening, a putting together: many in one (Waltzer 1990). Rather than resembling Israel Zangwell's classic image of a "melting pot," America seems to have become more like this sheaf of arrows—or, as Thompson (1994) has put it, a "salad bowl"—in which various ethnic cultures can coexist without being merged into a single "American" ethnicity. For example, some Asian Indians living in the United States may feel that they have more than one identity, or that their identity is made up of elements drawn from Indian as well as WASP culture, embracing at the same time "American" democracy as a culture that encourages such pluralism and mixing. This notion of hybrid culture and democratic

American identity is similar to the old idea of hyphenated Americanism—Italian-Americans, Irish-Americans, Greek-Americans. But there's a difference, too: Contemporary multiculturalism does not restrict ethnicity (the left side of the hyphen) to the private sphere, in contrast to a presumed common identity of political citizenship and economic status (the right side of the hyphen) in the public sphere. Ethnic groups carry their demands for recognition and respect into the public sphere. And, indeed, the aforementioned "culture war" often involves efforts by politicians to mobilize such support from ethnic groups. For example, appeals to "family values" and "pro-life values" may have enabled President Bush to secure more votes from Catholic Hispanics in the 2004 presidential election than would normally be expected for a Republican candidate.

## CONCLUSION

Oscar Handlin's famous portrait of America as an immigrant society, *The Uprooted,* opens with these lines: "Once I thought to write a history of the immigrants in America. Then I discovered that the immigrants were American history" (Handlin 1951: 3). Two decades later, in a postscript to the second edition, he wrote that immigration was already "a dimly remote memory, generations away, which had influenced the past but appeared unlikely to count for much in the present or future," and that ethnicity now seemed "a fading phenomenon, a quaint part of the national heritage, but one likely to diminish steadily in practical importance" (Handlin 1951: 274–275).

Even as Handlin was writing these words, however, the complacency about American national identity was changing. Civil rights protests had already brought the problems of stigmatized racial groups into the center of American consciousness, the black underclass had become an extraordinary focus of national concern, and, antidiscrimination laws, powerful affirmative action programs, and long-term economic transformations were working together to transform the status of the African-American working, middle, and professional and business classes. At about the same time, legal barriers to immigration were being lifted, with the result that tens of millions of new immigrants (legal and illegal) were arriving in the United States not from Europe but from Asia and Latin America. These changes posed strong challenges to America's traditional racial and ethnic identities.

Some have predicted that, if postmodern social forms continue to develop, strong cultural identities will disappear—an outcome that would involve a fragmentation of cultural codes, a multiplicity of styles, and a new emphasis on the ephemeral and impermanent. Culturally pluralist societies would emphasize difference rather than solidarity and integration—resulting in a postmodern cultural mosaic rather than a strong community. The main sources of identity would be not the strong nation-state cultures characteristic of modernity but, rather, fleeting and multiple consumer and mass-media styles, with ethnicity reduced to matters of fashion and taste.

As things stand now, however, such a radical shift seems unlikely, or at least very far away. Even in postmodern societies, cultural identities involve more general and less ephemeral attachments than those associated with consumer and mass-media styles. Regional, national, and even what might be called "civilizational" styles remain strong. Postmodernity and deepening democracy do not wash away particular attachments, whether religious, gender-based, political, or ethnic. They simply make it likely that people will seek to hold multiple and varying attachments at the same time. The nation-state has not withered away, and racist and nativist reactionary movements have not disappeared. The conflicts that marked the tragedies of modern society have been transformed, but they continue to divide and animate the postmodern societies we are living in today.

# EXERCISES

## Exercise 1

As Table 10.4 shows, the Hispanic population is becoming an increasingly large presence in American society. To what extent do you think Hispanics have achieved cultural and structural assimilation, and to what extent has their acculturation influenced American society? Have you noticed any influence in popular culture, tastes, and fashions? In the economy? In public policy? In your opinion, which of these three sets of factors is the most meaningful indicator of Hispanics' incorporation into mainstream society?

## Exercise 2

Take a closer look at Table 10.5, which provides statistics concerning interracial marriage rates in the United States between 1970 and 2000. Why do you think some groups (i.e., American Indians and Hawaiians) are more likely to intermarry than other groups (i.e., blacks and whites)? Why do you think black men and Asian women are more likely to intermarry than Asian men and black women? Have you noticed similar patterns in interracial dating on your campus? List some of the stereotypes involved in interracial dating. Do you think multicultural societies are more or less tolerant of interracial dating and marriage?

# STUDY QUESTIONS

1. Why is race a social rather than a biological categorization?

2. Define *racism*. What is the difference between a racial and a sociological explanation of inequality?

3. Is racial classification universally based on skin color?

4. Explain the difference between *race* and *ethnicity*. What is *ethnocentrism*?

5. What is *nativism*? Describe the role that nativism played in American history. What did American nativists perceive as a threat? To what extent did nativism influence American politics?

6. What effect did the Hart-Celler Act have on American immigration patterns?

7. Describe Louis Wirth's concept of the minority group. What is *prejudice*, and how is it different from other cultural attitudes?

8. What is the original meaning of the word *stereotype*? How was this concept first used in social theory? How has it been used to explain race and ethnic relations?

9. What is *discrimination*, and how does it differ from *prejudice*? Describe the two axes of discrimination.

10. Describe the exogenous and endogenous factors in William Julius Wilson's theoretical framework on the origins of the racial underclass in the United States. What is the relationship between these factors, and what outcomes do they produce?

# FURTHER READING

Alba, R. D. 1990. *Ethnic Identity: The Transformation of White America*. New Haven, CT: Yale University Press.

Bertrand, Marianne, and Sendhil Mullainathan. 2004. "Are Emily and Greg More Employable Than Lakisha and Jamal? A Field Experiment on Labor Market Discrimination." *American Economic Review* 94, no. 4: 991–1013.

Bobo, L. 1997. "The Color Line, the Dilemma, and the Dream: Race Relations in America at the Close of the Twentieth Century." In *Civil Rights and Social Wrongs*, edited by J. Higham. University Park: Pennsylvania State University Press.

Bonilla, Frank, Edwin Meléndez, Rebecca Morales, and Maria de los Angeles Torres, eds. 1998. *Borderless Borders: U.S. Latinos, Latin Americans, and the Paradox of Interdependence*. Philadelphia: Temple University Press.

Collins, Patricia Hill. 1990. *Black Feminist Thought: Knowledge, Consciousness, and the Politics of Empowerment*. Boston: Unwin Hyman.

Du Bois, W.E.B. 1903. *The Souls of Black Folk*. Boston: Bedford Books. Reprinted in 1997.

Fredrickson, G. M. 1988. *The Arrogance of Race: Historical Perspectives on Slavery, Racism, and Social Inequality*. Middletown, CT: Wesleyan University Press.

Gans, H. J. 1979. "Symbolic Ethnicity: The Future of Ethnic Groups and Cultures in America." *Ethnic and Racial Studies* 2: 1–20.

Lee, Jennifer, and Frank Bean. 2004. "America's Changing Color Lines: Immigration, Race/Ethnicity, and Multiracial Identification." *Annual Review of Sociology* 30: 221–242.

Lieberson, Stanley, and Mary C. Waters. 1988. *From Many Strands: Ethnic and Racial Groups in Contemporary America*. New York: Russell Sage Foundation.

Pager, Devah, and Bruce Western. 2005. "Discrimination in Low Trust Labor Markets." Paper presented at the American Sociological Association Annual Meeting, Philadelphia.

Portes, A., and R. G. Rúmbaut. 2001. *Legacies: The Story of the Immigrant Second Generation*. Berkeley: University of California Press.

Waters, Mary. 1990. *Ethnic Options: Choosing Identities in America*. Berkeley: University of California Press.

# chapter 11

# Crime and Deviance

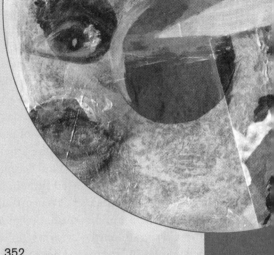

What leads someone to be labeled a deviant or a criminal? Take the case of John Walker Lindh, a once apparently "normal" Californian young man who suddenly became branded as a deviant and even a criminal because of his association with the Moslem Taliban regime in Afghanistan, which supported the Al-Qaeda terrorist destruction of the World Trade Center in New York on September 11, 2001. At what point did John Walker's harmless eccentricity become deviance and then criminality? And what was the cause?

According to the newspaper article reprinted in the box titled "John Walker's Restless Quest Is Strange Odyssey," Walker seemed a fairly normal American teenager "who had a basketball hoop in his driveway" and a "collection of more than 200 hip-hop and rap CDs." But the article also notes that there was already a hint of eccentricity or deviance, in that he "showed little interest in predictable teenage pastimes." When Walker began to take an interest in the Muslim religion, got rid of his CDs, and started wearing an ankle-length white robe, he was indeed deviating from his peer group of white, middle-class teenagers in Mill Valley, California. He did, however, find acceptance and respect in the Islamic Center of Mill Valley, even though a fellow member admitted that "[n]o one like him had ever come here before." When his devotion to his religion led him to fight for a foreign army that supported terrorists against his own country, it was left to the U.S. courts to judge whether the "deviant" had become a "criminal." Walker was eventually found guilty and sentenced to twenty years' imprisonment.

## AN INDIVIDUAL OR A SOCIAL STORY?

Whatever else you may think of John Walker's story, it certainly raises many questions about the life journey or "odyssey" in the course of which we develop or are given an identity that may be labeled normal, deviant, or criminal. And it seems that this journey to identity is becoming increasingly influenced by the impressions we gain from the mass media in postmodern culture. A common feature of the stories and explanations we hear in this culture is that they tend to be posed in individualized terms, such as those of individual psychology—Walker was "brainwashed," or a "rebel."

In the postmodern era, newspapers, bookstores, television channels, and cinemas are full of "Gothic horror" stories of violent assault and shocking murders. Fiction and fact vie with each other in representations of dangers that lurk around every corner, whether in the form of the serial murderer in the movie *The Silence of the Lambs,* the killers in the Columbine school massacre, or the destroyers of the World Trade Center. What is striking about many of these stories is that violence and murder are portrayed as occurring in ordinary and "respectable" settings, suggesting that they represent the risks and dangers of everyday life in postmodern society—ranging from the office (the World Trade Center) to the school, park, or home. Such stories have at least one thing in common: They usually present some type of individualistic account—that is, of the *individual criminal.* One version is that of an individual acting under the influence of evil—the evil "Other," an agent of drives or forces outside society as we know it. President Bush repeatedly branded the people responsible for the destruction of the World Trade Center in New York, especially their alleged leader, Osama Bin Laden, as extraordinarily "evil" individuals. (Most Americans agreed with that moral judgment, although they were still left wondering "Why do they hate us and act in this way?") Another version is that of the criminal personality or criminal mind, whereby an individual's biological or psychological abnormalities are said to predispose him or her to commit violent acts.

Postmodern culture (see Chapter 3) presents a confusing mixture of cultural discourses about crime, including religion, science, and various mass media genres. The practices of labeling individuals

# John Walker's Restless Quest Is Strange Odyssey

Before he became known on battlefields in Afghanistan as the holy warrior Abdul Hamid, or had shocked his doting parents by adopting the Muslim name Suleyman, John Walker Lindh [hereafter "Walker"] walked into a mosque in this foggy hillside town near the Golden Gate Bridge five years ago eager to learn a religion that would soon dominate his life.

He was shy and studious, a lanky 16-year-old who had a basketball hoop in his driveway but showed little interest in predictable teenage pastimes. And his strange odyssey was about to begin.

"He was a good person, a quiet person," said Abdullah Nana, 23, who often prayed with Walker on the red carpet of the Islamic Center of Mill Valley and gave him rides home because he did not have a driver's license. "He was accepted and respected for his dedication. No one like him had ever come here before."

As his devotion grew, Walker would get rid of his coarse collection of more than 200 hip-hop and rap CDs and begin wearing an ankle-length white robe.

He would forsake an easy path to college to travel alone to remote villages in Yemen and Pakistan. He would try to memorize the Koran.

And he would scorn the peace-and-love precepts of his parents to take up arms with the harshly conservative Taliban.

"When he left, he just said that he wanted to learn Arabic and follow Islam full time," Nana said. "We thought it would be beneficial for our community, because no one else here had gone to study overseas the way he wanted to. We thought he would be a pioneer."

Instead, Walker had become a puzzling prisoner of war, the lone American caught with en-

John Walker Lindh (aka Abdul Hamid), an American convert to the Taliban, became infamous for that association after the terrorist attacks of September 11, 2001. (AP Photo)

emy forces in the aftermath of the Sept. 11 terrorist attacks, dragged filthy and wounded from a medieval fort with other defiant al Qaeda fighters last month. U.S. military officials have Walker in custody, and President Bush is preparing to decide his fate. He could be prosecuted for treason or aiding terrorists, charges that could bring the death penalty or many years in jail.

But much of Walker's journey is still a mystery. Was he just an innocent abroad, an impressionable young scholar swept up in a movement he did not fully understand—"brainwashed," as his mother, Marilyn Walker, has suggested?

Or was he a teenage rebel with a cause, renouncing the have-it-all, progressive suburban culture from which he came and duping his parents into believing they were supporting, and financing, a purely spiritual quest?

*Source:* Sanchez (2002: A01).

as "evil" and "born to be bad" have long histories. The former idea dates back to traditional societies, where religious language was dominant. The latter idea—that some people are born to be criminals—came to prominence in the sociobiological evolutionary theories of the nineteenth century, when scientists believed they could find physical differences between criminals and the general population, such as skull shape, showing that criminals were a throwback to a more "primitive" stage in human evolution. More recently, some scientists have sought to link criminal behavior to genetic inheritance or some other biological cause (Samenow and Yochelson 1976; Wilson and Herrnstein 1985). An example of defense lawyers' use of this kind of explanation can be seen in the case of California murder defendant Carl Stayner:

> Carl Stayner is California's most notorious murder defendant, accused of last year's Yosemite slaying. He confessed to slitting the throat of one victim, burning the bodies of two others and beheading a fourth. But was Stayner destined from birth to commit those gruesome crimes? Was he predisposed—by biology or perhaps some childhood injury—to murder? Stayner's defense team hopes to find answers to such provocative questions with a radioactive brain scan performed at U.C. Irvine that can detect if the motel handyman suffers some sort of cerebral abnormality. (Bailey 2000: A3)

As noted, the common thread among these widely publicized horror stories is that they all focus on the individual and reflect a return to theories about the abnormal, criminal mind, whether possessed by evil or by biological abnormalities. It follows that the most popular solutions are incarceration, medical treatment, and execution, and that the favored prevention policies include not only deterrence through tough sentencing but also increased surveillance measures, medical treatment of potential offenders, and insurance against personal risk. Indeed, such individualistic and "commonsensical" discourses about crime are enjoying renewed prominence in contemporary society. In some respects they represent a reaction against the sociological accounts of crime and deviance in modern society that began to gain currency in the middle of the twentieth century.

Although sociologists have differed in their theories about crime and deviance (see our discussion on theories later in this chapter), they tend to unite in focusing on social and cultural factors rather than on individual factors. In the middle of the twentieth century the focus was on factors such as class inequalities in wealth, housing, education, and family circumstances as well as on the consequent failure to socialize everyone into following the same norms of behavior as those associated with mainstream (white, middle-class) cultural values. Later, in the 1960s, sociological studies of crime and deviance began to focus not so much on crime and its causes as on the processes of social interaction that lead to the constructing or labeling of certain behaviors as crimes, and on the social reactions that such behaviors and crimes provoke (Becker 1963; Lemert 1967). In the twenty-first century, sociologists are still interested in those social factors, but they are also turning their attention to such issues as postindustrialism, consumer society, multiculturalism, and the media-saturated postmodern culture. Not all of these developments are new—many started in the earlier phases of modernity—but, as we will see, they are becoming increasingly significant.

In this chapter we examine five issues:

1. *The nature of deviance and crime.* What forms of behavior constitute deviance and crime, and how have these terms been defined? Are such definitions universal, or do they vary according to time and place?
2. *The extent of crime.* What are the statistics on crime and punishment? Is crime increasing or decreasing?

3. *Responses to crime.* What are the different views about the best ways to deal with crime and criminals?
4. *Explanations of crime.* How do different theories explain crime? How are these explanations related to public opinion and "commonsense" notions about crime in different periods?
5. *Representations of crime.* How do the mass media represent crime? What do people involved with crime have to say about it?

## DEFINING AND DESCRIBING DEVIANCE AND CRIME

The terms **deviance** and **crime** seem fairly straightforward at first glance. Deviance refers to behavior that clearly departs from what the majority of a community or society considers to be "normal"—that is, in line with norms. *Norms* are prescribed forms of behavior. *Values* are the more general cultural goals toward which norms are directed (again, see Chapter 3). Whereas a norm prescribes actual behavior, a value justifies that behavior and provides the reason for which some actions garner more approval than others. Crime is any behavior that the law forbids. But what is deviant is not quite so straightforward to determine. It all depends on who is doing the defining in any particular case. For example, what a rich, upper-middle-class white man regards as deviant behavior might not be regarded as such by a poor, lower-class black youth. Even what gets categorized as a criminal act can vary depending on the circumstances. For example, physician-induced suicide and hate crime are two categories of crime about which judgments vary in different jurisdictions.

In the mid-twentieth century, in the midst of the more homogeneous integration that characterized modern society, it seemed reasonable to concentrate on instances of "deviance" from widely observed social norms—such as the ethnic gangs whose conflict is featured in the movie musical

**Deviance** Any behavior that departs from what the majority of a community or the whole society considers to be "normal." Not all deviance is forbidden by law, nor is all of it criminal. Deviance can be as minor as not addressing an authority figure by his or her proper title or as significant as killing another human being. Moreover, deviance is not a permanent category but, rather, changes over time and between groups with regard to what is considered "normal."

**Crime** Any act forbidden by law. As with deviance, the definition of crime shifts across time and with respect to different groups.

from that time, *West Side Story*. But postmodern society is increasingly characterized by cultural diversity and disagreement about what is normal. Alongside values that continue to be shared are the much more loosely integrated networks of subcultures and lifestyles. The latter are particularly evident in the case of youth subcultures, which often vary even within a school or college.

Take the example of Columbine High School. The boys who slew their fellow students were allegedly members of a subcultural group, the Trench-Coat Mafia, who apparently saw themselves as radically different from the more mainstream or "normal" culture of the school, especially that associated with the school's athletes. But some commentators have questioned whether there really was such a clear separation. After all, some of the stylistic elements to which the Trench-Coat Mafia subculture adhered had a wider following within contemporary youth culture. As an expert commentator in *Time* magazine put it:

The "normal" culture of adolescence today contains elements that are so nasty that it becomes hard for parents (and professionals) to distinguish between what in a teenager's talk, dress and taste in music, films and video games indicates psychological trouble and what is simply a sign of the times. Most kids who subscribe to the trench-coated Gothic lifestyle, or have multiple body piercings, or listen to Marilyn Manson, or play the video game Doom are normal kids caught in a toxic culture. (Garbarino 1999: 51)

As noted earlier, *crime* refers to any act explicitly forbidden by legislation (specifically, as interpreted by the courts). This definition seems fairly unproblematic. In practice, however, it is not always so clear-cut. There are variations over time, and even within the criminal justice system, as to what acts are judged to be illegal and worthy of prosecution. For example, the treatment of witches has undergone changes throughout American history. In seventeenth-century Salem, Massachusetts, young girls allegedly indulging in witchcraft were condemned to death (Erikson 1966). But today, witches can practice their rites with impunity, and this postmodern form of *Pagan* or *Wicca* spirituality has close links with New Age religion and some feminist groups (Lewis 1996). Or take the example of racial hate crimes. Until the twentieth century, whites in the South who lynched blacks often suffered no consequences. But in postmodern society, ethnic and cultural differences are more likely to be accorded tolerance and respect—in part, because the criminal justice system now gives more attention to crimes involving discrimination or hate. Since 1990, when President George H.W. Bush signed into law the federal Hate Crime Statistics Act (HCSA), there has been

Marilyn Manson, who takes his stage name from screen idol Marilyn Monroe and murderer Charles Manson, has been blamed for inciting violence in his fans. (AP Photo/Franco Greco)

an apparently clear definition of **hate crime:** "crimes that manifest evidence of prejudice based on race, religion, sexual orientation or ethnicity" (quoted in Perry 2001: 7). Implicit in the use of this term is the assumption that there is agreement about what would constitute the commission of a recognized criminal offense and the existence of the motivation of prejudice. But not all states recognize the same categories of prejudice in their hate crime legislation: Some, for instance, exclude the category of sexual orientation, whereas others include that of "whistle blowers" (Perry 2001: 12). Inconsistencies of this sort have implications for the reliability of statistics about hate crimes. Not only do law enforcement agencies vary in their recording of such crimes, but the victims of such crimes may be reluctant to report them. Gay vic-

**Hate crime** A particular type of crime involving discrimination against or hateful acts toward particular groups in society (e.g., African-Americans and homosexuals). Hate crimes are difficult to define owing to lack of agreement regarding the designation of prejudice as a motivation. In addition, some states do not recognize certain categories of prejudice, such as sexual orientation. This discrepancy can have a serious impact on hate crime statistics, inasmuch as some individuals are afraid to go to the police or may be discredited by the police when reporting these crimes.

tims as well as sexually abused women, children, and ethnic minorities may fear the consequences of going to the police.

Given the questionable reliability of hate crime statistics, it may be wise to look carefully at the media's claims about trends in crime. As we have seen, some crimes may be underreported by victims or unrecorded by the police. The prosecution of crimes may vary as well. Émile Durkheim's famous work *Suicide* (1897) made generalizations about variations in social solidarity between societies and groups on the basis of official statistics about their suicide rates—for example, there were higher rates of suicide for Protestants than for Catholics. But critics have pointed out that this disparity may reflect the fact that Catholics view suicide more severely than Protestants and are thus more inclined to record death at a person's own hand as "accidental" or due to a "disturbed state of mind" than as a "deliberate" suicidal act. Clearly, statistics for the crime of suicide need to be interpreted with this difference in reporting practices kept in mind.

Although it is important to read crime statistics with some caution, there is no avoiding the conclusion that Americans have the dubious distinction of living in the world's most violent industrial nation (see Table 11.1). Violent crime skyrocketed in the United States starting in the late 1960s, a trend that continued into the early 1990s. In view of this, it is no wonder that crime has consistently been one of the public's major concerns over the past three decades. But since the mid-1990s, most parts of the country have witnessed a sharp drop in violent crime (see Figure 11.1). The FBI's 2000 survey of crimes (see *Public Agenda* 2005), which is reported to the police, showed the overall murder rate at its lowest level since 1967. (Even so, the United States still had higher rates of murder than any other industrial society.) Similarly, the National Crime Victimization Survey, designed to measure both reported and unreported crime, found the lowest overall **crime rate** since the sur-

vey began in 1973. The crime rate fell for the ninth straight year in 2000, declining 3.3 percent from 1999, 18.9 percent from 1996, and 30.1 percent from 1991 (Rennison 2001). Criminal justice experts attribute this trend to three possible causes: the decline in cocaine use; the fact that more criminals are in prison, and are serving longer sentences; and the temporary drop in the number of young males, the group most prone to violent crime. (For additional data on the declining crime rate, see Figures 11.2 and 11.3.)

Despite the falling crime rate, public opinion surveys show that most Americans do not feel much safer (see Tables 11.2 and 11.3). In a 2000 survey, fewer than half of Americans said they felt safe at school or walking in their neighborhood after dark. Their concern may be justified in view of the fact that a majority of Americans, sooner or later, will be victims. Taking into account both violent crime and property crime, the FBI reports that 83 percent of Americans can expect to be a victim of crime at least once in their lifetimes (*Public Agenda* 2000).

There is no doubt that Americans are preoccupied with crime. Crime is prominent as a subject in television series, news programs, and newspaper reports. It's also listed near the top of citizens' concerns in opinion surveys. Some experts argue that the level of fear of crime in America is a reasonable response to the extraordinary volume of crime in the United States. For example, American homicide rates are consistently many times those of comparable industrial nations (Currie 1985). One researcher has suggested that the fear may be due in part to the changing nature of violence in

**Crime rate**  The number of incidents of crime (typically violent crime) within a particular area across a given time period (usually one year). As with any statistic, crime rates have to be carefully interpreted. For example, even when a crime rate is declining, people may not feel safer in their neighborhoods.

## TABLE 11.1 International Comparison of Selected Crime Statistics, 2000[1]

| Country | Crimes Recorded by Police[2] | Violent Crimes Recorded by Police[3] | Homicide Rate per 100,000 Population[4] | Imprisonment Rate per 100,000 Population[5] |
|---|---|---|---|---|
| England & Wales | 5,170,843 | 733,374 | 1.50 | 124 |
| Northern Ireland | 119,912 | 24,323 | 3.10 | 60 |
| Scotland | 423,172 | 27,047 | 2.19 | 115 |
| Austria | 560,306 | .. | 0.90 | 84 |
| Belgium | 848,648 | 59,791 | 1.79 | 83 |
| Bulgaria | 127,659 | .. | | .. |
| Cyprus | 4,358 | 113 | 0.6 | 43 |
| Czech Republic | 391,469 | 21,996 | 2.78 | 208 |
| Denmark | 504,231 | 15,748 | 1.00 | 61 |
| Estonia | 57,799 | 1,158 | 11.43 | 325 |
| Finland | 385,797 | 34,291 | 2.60 | 56 |
| France | 3,771,849 | 243,166 | 1.68 | 80 |
| Germany | 6,264,723 | 187,103 | 1.19 | 97 |
| Greece | 369,137 | 9,105 | 1.55 | 76 |
| Hungary | 450,673 | 29,144 | 2.47 | 157 |
| Ireland (Eire) | 73,276 | 3,312 | 1.37 | 76 |
| Italy | 2,205,782 | 74,136 | 1.50 | 94 |
| Latvia | 50,199 | .. | 6.51 | .. |
| Lithuania | 82,370 | 6,176 | 8.91 | 257 |
| Luxembourg | 22,816 | 4,280 | 0.87 | 92 |
| Malta | 17,016 | .. | 1.68 | 68 |
| Netherlands | 1,173,688 | 90,944 | 1.40 | 87 |
| Norway | 330,071 | 20,582 | 0.93 | 56 |
| Poland | 1,266,910 | 90,062 | 2.04 | 170 |
| Portugal | 363,294 | 19,780 | 1.35 | 124 |
| Romania | 353,745 | 20,818 | 2.36 | 222 |
| Russia | 3,001,748 | 97,153 | 20.52 | 729 |
| Slovakia | 88,817 | 13,549 | 2.54 | 132 |
| Slovenia | 67,617 | 1,414 | 1.14 | 57 |
| Spain | 923,269 | 119,923 | 2.77 | 114 |
| Sweden | 1,214,968 | 74,646 | 2.06 | 64 |
| Switzerland | 270,733 | 8,152 | 1.09 | 79 |
| Turkey | .. | .. | 2.54 | 74 |
| Australia | 1,431,929 | 181,999 | 1.87 | 113 |
| Canada | 2,353,926 | 301,875 | 1.79 | 123 |
| Japan | 2,443,470 | 64,418 | 1.06 | 47 |
| New Zealand | 427,230 | 44,887 | 2.28 | 149 |
| South Africa | .. | .. | 54.25 | 385 |
| United States | 11,605,751 | 1,424,289 | 5.87 | 685 |

*Source:* Adapted from Barclay and Tavares (2003).

*Notes:*

[1] Definitions of offenses, legal systems, and statistical recording procedures vary between countries and comparisons should be interpreted with caution.

[2] More serious offenses. Excludes misdemeanors.

[3] Includes violence against the person, robbery, and sexual assault.

[4] Intentional killing of a person (murder, manslaughter), excluding attempted murder and death by dangerous driving.

[5] Based on estimates of the national population.

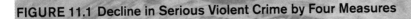

## FIGURE 11.1 Decline in Serious Violent Crime by Four Measures

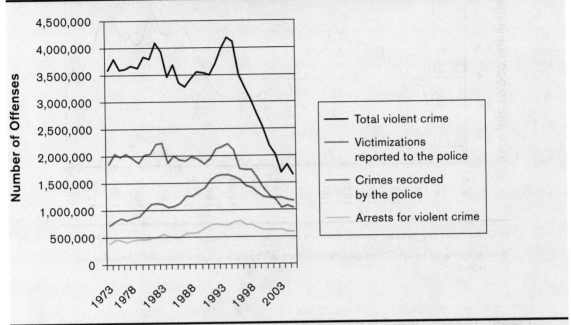

*Note:* The category of serious violent crimes referred to in the figure title includes rape, robbery, aggravated assault, and homicide. Two sources of data were used to create the measures. The first source is the National Crime Victimization Survey (NCVS), a household survey started in 1972 that interviews approximately 75,000 people age 12 and above in 42,000 households twice a year about their victimizations from crime. This method tends to report higher rates of crimes because it includes incidents never reported to the police. The second source is the Uniform Crime Reports (UCR), which collect information about crimes and arrests reported to the Federal Bureau of Investigation by law enforcement.

*Total violent crime* consists of the estimated number of homicides of persons age 12 and older reported to the police plus the number of rapes, robberies, and aggravated assaults from the NCVS, whether or not they were reported to the police.

*Victimizations reported to the police* consists of the estimated number of homicides of persons age 12 and older recorded by police plus the number of rapes, robberies, and aggravated assaults from the NCVS that victims said were reported to the police.

*Crimes recorded by the police* consists of the total number of homicides, forcible rapes, robberies, and aggravated assaults recorded in the Uniform Crime Reports, excluding commercial robberies and crimes involving victims under age 12.

*Arrests for violent crime* consists of the number of persons arrested for homicide, forcible rape, robbery, or aggravated assault as reported by law enforcement agencies to the FBI.

*Source:* Bureau of Justice Statistics, available online at http://www.ojp.usdoj.gov/bjs/glance/cv2.htm (accessed January 26, 2006).

the United States—specifically, to concerns that it is becoming more "random" and that many offenders are younger than they used to be (Young 1994). Other analysts argue, however, that the high levels of fear and concern besetting Ameri-

cans are largely caused by media imagery and the rhetoric of enterprising politicians who have an interest in exploiting fears about crime. Indeed, the amount of time devoted to television viewing correlates strongly with fear of crime (Gerbner and

340

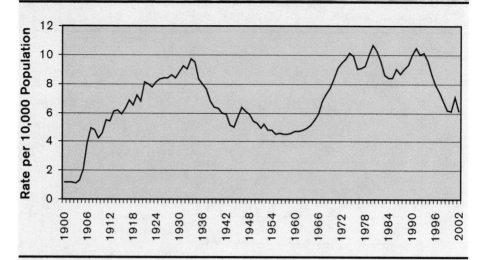

FIGURE 11.2 Recent Decline in Homicide Rate, 1900–2002

*Note:* The 2001 rate includes deaths attributed to the terrorism attacks of September 11, 2001.

*Source:* Bureau of Justice Statistics, available online at http://www.ojp.usdoj.gov/bjs/glance/tables/hmrttab.htm.

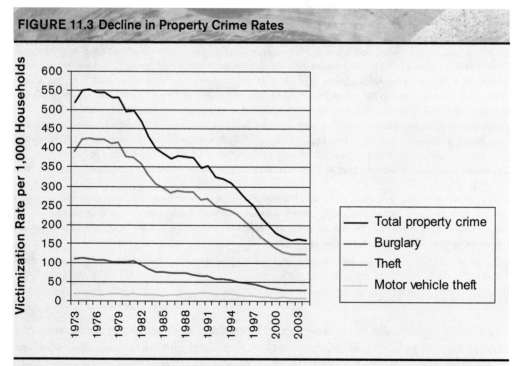

FIGURE 11.3 Decline in Property Crime Rates

*Note:* The National Crime Victimization Survey (NCVS) on which this chart is based was redesigned in 1993. The data before 1993 have been adjusted to make them comparable to the data collected since the redesign.

*Source:* Bureau of Justice Statistics, available online at http://www.ojp.usdoj.gov/bjs/glance/house2.htm (accessed February 2, 2006).

**TABLE 11.2 Percentage of Respondents Reporting Concern about Crime Victimization, by Sex and Race, United States, 2003**

| SURVEY QUESTION: How often do you, yourself, worry about the following things—frequently, occasionally, rarely or never? | Total | Male | Female | White | Nonwhite | Black |
|---|---|---|---|---|---|---|
| Your home being burglarized when you are not there | 48 | 42 | 52 | 47 | 47 | 54 |
| Having your car stolen or broken into | 45 | 43 | 47 | 44 | 49 | 49 |
| Being a victim of terrorism | 38 | 31 | 44 | 36 | 42 | 41 |
| Having a school-aged child of yours physically harmed while attending school | 35 | 31 | 38 | 32 | 46 | 51 |
| Your home being burglarized when you are there | 30 | 23 | 35 | 28 | 34 | 40 |
| Getting mugged | 28 | 21 | 34 | 27 | 32 | 46 |
| Being attacked while driving your car | 26 | 22 | 30 | 26 | 28 | 30 |
| Being sexually assaulted | 23 | 5 | 39 | 21 | 26 | 35 |
| Getting murdered | 18 | 15 | 21 | 17 | 24 | 35 |
| Being the victim of a hate crime | 17 | 14 | 18 | 13 | 30 | 35 |
| Being assaulted or killed by a coworker or other employee where you work | 9 | 9 | 9 | 7 | 14 | 21 |

*Note:* "Nonwhite" includes black respondents.

*Source:* Pastore and Maguire (2003).

**TABLE 11.3 Percentage of Respondents Reporting Whether They Engage in Selected Behaviors Because of Concern over Crime, by Sex and Race, United States, 2003**

| SURVEY QUESTION: Next, I'm going to read some things people do because of their concern over crime. Please tell me which, if any, you, yourself, do or have done. | Total | Male | Female | White | Nonwhite | Black |
|---|---|---|---|---|---|---|
| Avoid going to certain places or neighborhoods you might otherwise want to go to | 49 | 43 | 55 | 47 | 57 | 62 |
| Keep a dog for protection | 31 | 28 | 34 | 32 | 27 | 25 |
| Bought a gun for protection of yourself or your home | 27 | 32 | 22 | 26 | 32 | 36 |
| Had a burglar alarm installed in your home | 25 | 25 | 25 | 22 | 37 | 44 |
| Carry mace or pepper spray | 19 | 8 | 29 | 17 | 28 | 31 |
| Carry a gun for defense | 12 | 17 | 9 | 11 | 16 | 23 |

*Note:* "Nonwhite" includes black respondents.

*Source:* Pastore and Maguire (2003).

Gross 1976; Gerbner et al. 1980). And there is evidence that trends in popular concern about drugs match trends in the amount of prominence given to this issue by politicians (Beckett 1994).

Media portrayals make it difficult to separate the "reality" of crime and the criminal justice system from the ways in which they are perceived. However, we can get a sense of how far the two sorts of information match up by looking more closely at both the relevant statistics and the media portrayals themselves.

## Crime and Punishment Statistics

Although the incidence of some types of crime has declined in recent years, the U.S. criminal justice system has been growing rapidly for several decades. Its expansion from the 1970s onward has been dramatic. Between 1972 and 1988, nationwide spending on criminal justice reportedly grew by 150 percent, and between 1969 and 1989, per capita state expenditures on police and correction increased tenfold (Chambliss 1994). This spending financed a doubling in the size of the nation's police force between 1980 and 1990 as well as a massive expansion of the state and federal prison systems. On December 31, 2000, as the United States was entering the twenty-first century, the number of people in prison had reached 1,381,892. Between 1990 and 1999, the average annual growth of crime was 6 percent (Beck and Harrison 2001). And by year's end in 2003, the prison population had increased to 1,470,045, having grown at an annual rate of 3.4 percent (Harrison and Beck 2004). Ethnic and gender differences remain significant. In 2000 there were an estimated 478 prison inmates per 100,000 U.S. residents—up from 292 in 1990. In the same year, the number of women prisoners reached 91,612, compared to 1,290,280 men. And at the end of that year, there were 3,457 sentenced black male inmates per 100,000 black males in the United States, compared to 1,220 sentenced Hispanic male inmates per 100,000 Hispanics and 449 white male inmates per 100,000 white males. Here are some additional statistics to consider:

✓ If **imprisonment rates** remain the same, one of every fifteen persons in the United States (6.6 percent) will serve time in prison during their lifetime.

✓ Lifetime chances of going to prison are higher for men (11.3 percent) than for women (1.8 percent) and higher for blacks (18.6 percent) and Hispanics (10 percent) than for whites (3.4 percent).

✓ Based on current rates of first incarceration, an estimated 32 percent of black males will enter prison during their lifetime, compared to 17 percent of Hispanic males and 5.9 percent of white males. (Adapted from U.S. Department of Justice, Bureau of Justice Statistics 2001)

Surveys show that many Americans want tougher policing and sentencing (see Figures 11.4–11.6). However, statistics reveal that some sections of the population suffer both more crime and more imprisonment than others. Poor blacks and Hispanics are the ones most at risk. It is also the case that they live in inner-city areas, where there is more social breakdown than elsewhere, as indicated by higher male unemployment, more single-parent families, and a higher frequency of failing schools. (For further information on this topic, see Chapter 8, on inequality; Chapter 10, on

**Imprisonment rate** The number of individuals imprisoned in a particular year. The U.S. imprisonment rate has steadily increased since the 1990s—a trend that has serious implications when we consider the racial breakdown of the individuals incarcerated: Men are more likely than women, and racial minorities are more likely than whites, to be incarcerated. When considering structural causes for social inequalities, we find that these statistics may be seen as indicators of the varying life chances of categories of individuals.

**SURVEY QUESTION:** Do you favor or oppose the death penalty for persons convicted of murder?

### FIGURE 11.4 Attitudes Toward the Death Penalty

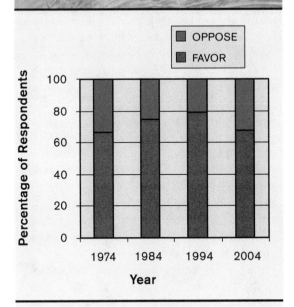

*Source:* Computer-assisted Survey Methods Program (2006).

**SURVEY QUESTION:** In general, do you think the courts in this area deal too harshly or not harshly enough with criminals?

### FIGURE 11.5 Attitudes Toward Court Sentencing of Criminals

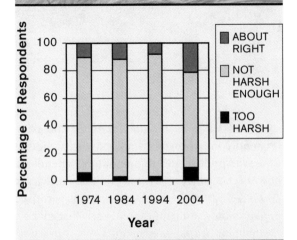

*Source:* Computer-assisted Survey Methods Program (2006).

**SURVEY QUESTION:** We are faced with many problems in this country, none of which can be solved easily or inexpensively. I'm going to name some of these problems, and for each one I'd like you to tell me whether you think we're spending too much money on it, too little money, or about the right amount. Halting the rising crime rate: are we spending too much, too little, or about the right amount on halting the rising crime rate?

### FIGURE 11.6 Attitudes Toward Spending on the National Crime Problem

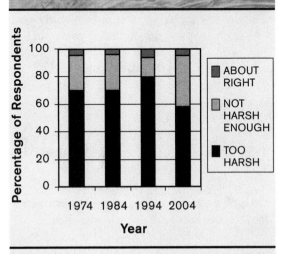

*Source:* Computer-assisted Survey Methods Program (2006).

race and ethnicity; and Chapter 16, on urbanism and population.) Sentencing policy has hit offenders from these communities hardest—particularly since the introduction of the "three strikes and you're out" policy.

### Representations of Crime

The "cultural turn" in sociology has been important for the study of crime and deviance since the 1970s. It played a key part in the development of a "constructionist paradigm" for social problems research. The theoretical perspective known as the social construction of reality or social constructionism is particularly helpful in understanding the impact of the pervasive mass media in defining and

## media moments

### Three Strikes and You're Out: Human Rights, U.S. Style

The scene is a battered old green and white bungalow in the heart of South Central, Los Angeles, which serves as the local Quakers' meeting house. There are around 20 people here, heads bowed and holding hands as one of their number, Carmen Ewell, asks the Lord for his help in the mighty task facing them.

That task involves changing one of the most controversial statutes in the U.S., the three strikes law, so that people now serving prison sentences of 25 years to life for offences including stealing four cookies and possession of $10 worth of drugs will be able to return to their lives. ...

The law was introduced after the horrific murder of a 12-year-old girl named Polly Klaas in 1993. Her abductor and murderer, Richard Allen Davis, was a three-time offender who was on parole. In the wake of the outrage over the crime, Californians voted for an initiative, which called for three-time felons to be jailed for a minimum of 25 years. The initiative became law, and now more than 30 states in the U.S. have adopted their own versions of it.

Under three strikes, violent criminals like Davis have been locked up for life. But it has also been used to sweep thousands of homeless people, drug addicts and petty offenders off the streets and into jail with sentences that bear little relationship to the crime. Critics of the law claim it has created a Siberia of forgotten prisoners, mainly black and Latino, who are the victims of cruel and unusual punishment. ...

"The United States is a very unforgiving country at the moment," says Gail Blackwell, who works at the FACTS office in South Central. Her friend, Joey Buckhalter, was jailed for 75 years to life for stealing a wallet with $24 in it. "People are more interested in punishment and revenge than in rehabilitation. People don't even care about the 2 million people in jail in their country in terrible conditions." ...

The Los Angeles district attorney, Steve Cooley, agrees that the law has been wrongly applied in the past, but says there is little chance of retrospective action to free those jailed for minor nonviolent offences because few politicians want to be accused of being soft on crime.

There is also a powerful prison-industrial complex, which has a very clear financial incentive in maintaining the three strikes law. California spends $5.7 billion a year on its prisons and there would be fierce lobbying against any reduction in the budget.

*Source:* Campbell (2002: 3).

interpreting social problems in postmodern society. Constructionist researchers focus on how problems come to be constructed or "framed" in particular ways. For example, Joseph Gusfield (1981) examined the cultural factors that contribute to the framing of "drinking and driving" as a problem stemming from morally defective individuals rather than from public transportation policy or the design of automobiles. In the context of fear and concern over crime, the issue's significance for politics and public policy depends on how it is socially constructed and framed (Sasson 1995: 3–4). In other words, the way it is perceived depends on the mental framework that gives it meaning for people—a framework that is based on people's own experiences but also is influenced by the pronouncements of opinion leaders such as politicians and the media. On this score the conventional wisdom is that Americans, in the mass media but also in everyday conversation, construct crime as a threat "from below" (Reiman 1990). The offender is often imagined as black and, even more often, as poor and male. Many people reject the notion that crime is caused by poverty or racial discrimination, instead blaming either individual moral failure or a poorly functioning criminal justice system. They believe that the problem would be solved if the police cracked down on offenders and the courts "got tough." This perspective is referred to as **volitional criminology** (Scheingold 1991), and its advocates are described as having a "law and order" orientation (Dahrendorf 1985; Gordon 1990). It reflects a widespread tendency in America to believe that crimes are the result of individuals' moral failings and their decisions to act illegally—a tendency evidenced by the observation that many Americans attribute responsibility for a whole range of behaviors to individuals rather than to societal forces (Gans 1988). Although American values tend to stress individual choice and responsibility, there are variations in the ways in which these values are framed, leading to differing interpretations of social problems such as crime. (See box titled "Three Strikes and You're Out.")

A survey by Theodore Sasson (1995) on the kinds of discourses about crime used by opinion leaders in the media, such as politicians and journalists, found that such discourses could be reduced to five basic "frames": *Faulty System, Blocked Opportunities, Social Breakdown, Media Violence,* and *Racist System.* Sasson describes each of these as follows:

1. The *Faulty System* frame is typified by what is referred to as the "law and order" perspective, which maintains that people commit crimes because they know they can get away with it. Advocates of this perspective claim that there are insufficient resources for law enforcement and prisons, that judges are too liberal, and that too many technicalities and loopholes make it possible for criminals to escape justice. It is a view held by many conservative politicians and commentators, as well as by many criminal justice professionals. By failing to take sufficient action, in the ringing words of conservative political scientist James Q. Wilson, "[w]e thereby trifle with the wicked, make sport of the innocent, and encourage the calculating" (Public Agenda Foundation 1993: 15).

2. The *Blocked Opportunities* frame depicts crime as a consequence of inequality and discrimination, especially in the forms of unemployment, poverty, and inadequate educational opportunities. People commit crimes when they discover that legitimate means of attaining goals are blocked. Certain sections of the population have always suffered from these disadvantages, particularly black Americans. The problems of blocked opportunities worsened with deindustrialization from the 1970s onward, as good-paying blue-collar jobs disappeared and were replaced by lower-paid and insecure service jobs. Increasing desperation and frustration promote property crime and violence; "[i]f you're going to create a sink-or-swim society," says criminologist David Bruck, "you have to expect people to thrash before they go down" (quoted in Public Agenda Foundation 1993: 22). This view is put forward by many liberal and Left policy analysts and some liberal Democrat politicians. It is symbolized by references to the only kind of jobs available to inner-city youth—dead-end jobs such as "flipping burgers at McDonald's."

**Volitional criminology** A particular way of framing crime as a social problem. From this perspective, the public understands crimes to be the result of individuals' moral failings and their decisions to act illegally, rather than the effect of social forces such as poverty or racial discrimination.

3. The *Social Breakdown* frame depicts crime as a consequence of family and community disintegration. As evidence, supporters of this view cite high rates of divorce and out-of-wedlock births, loss of a sense of community responsibility in the cities, and a general breakdown in the moral and social bonds that previously discouraged crime. This frame is expressed in calls for a return to "family values" and by references to cases such as that of Kitty Genovese, the New York woman who in 1964 was stabbed to death while dozens of her neighbors watched passively from their windows. There are conservative and liberal versions of this frame. Conservative advocates attribute social breakdown to declining "family values," permissiveness and lack of discipline, the protest movements of the 1960s and 1970s (e.g., civil rights, feminism), and government-sponsored welfare programs, whereas liberal advocates point to unemployment and low wages, deindustrialization, and diminished access to blue-collar careers.

4. The *Media Violence* frame focuses on violent crime and sees it as a consequence of violence on television, in the movies, and in popular music. (For a detailed discussion of this issue, see Chapter 4, on media and communication.) Its supporters argue that, to reduce violent crime, it is necessary to reduce the extent of its portrayal and glamorization by the media. This frame is favored by the antigun lobby and groups concerned with the welfare of children as well as by some members of Congress and officials in the Department of Justice.

5. The *Racist System* frame is a minority view. Focusing on the criminal justice system rather than on the issue of who or what is responsible for crime, it holds that the courts and police are racially biased against nonwhite citizens and, in effect, operate a dual system of justice. Advocates point to the fact that, compared to whites, blacks experience higher rates of arrest and conviction and are more likely to receive the death penalty. This frame is used by many civil rights and civil liberties activists as well as by some Left intellectuals. An incident that gave it credibility was the beating of black motorist Rodney King by white Los Angeles police in 1991, which, caught on video and shown on national television, led to a controversial court case that divided blacks and whites, followed by riots when a mainly white jury found the police not guilty.

For instance, it is possible to think of arguments against each of the "frames." *Faulty System* fails to take account of the fact that imprisonment itself "hardens" offenders and frequently leads to reoffending; it also fails to address the causes of crime. The *Blocked Opportunities* view overlooks the fact that most poor people do not engage in crime. *Social Breakdown* is countered by the criticism that it is triggered by nostalgia for an earlier, idealized community that never existed or, at least, was not very widespread, while references to "family values" may disguise a thinly veiled hostility to feminism. *Media Violence* disregards the hypothesis that aggressive behavior is correlated with—rather than necessarily caused by—media violence. And the *Racist System* frame is limited in its usefulness because it directs attention to only one problematic aspect of the criminal justice system (although an important one).

## White-Collar and Corporate Crime

One reason for which crime and prison statistics show a disproportionate number of poor and black people as offenders may be that the crimes they commit—street crimes—are those that are most energetically policed and punished. Americans take for granted that street crime is the worst social problem and that **white-collar crime** is not as dangerous or as costly. Although antitrust violations, false advertising, price fixing, unfair labor practices, embezzlement, and fraud cost society more money and pose greater dangers to public safety than ordinary street crime, the people who commit white-collar crime seldom receive heavy punishment (Reiman 1998). Indeed, white-color offenses tend not to be regarded as "real" crimes; perhaps it is because of their "impersonal" nature that people do not fear them as a threat to themselves. Yet such crimes can have severe effects on individuals, as in the case of the thousands of employees and pensioners who lost their savings as a result of being misled into investing in the energy corporation Enron, which went bankrupt in 2002 after engaging in financial malpractices (see also Chapter 17, on politics, publics, and the state). Although in certain respects Enron was a special case (the seventh-largest corporation in the United States, with ties to politicians in both parties stretching up to Congress and the White House), it was not an isolated one. A considerable number of additional examples of corporate illegal practices could be listed. Below are a just a few from the 1990s that illustrate the scale of the problem and the leniency with which the corporate offenders were treated:

Enron attorneys testify in a hearing to the U.S. House Energy and Commerce Committee Oversight and Investigations Subcommittee about the company's financial fraud. (AP Photo/Dennis Cook)

- ✓ In 1992, the U.S. Justice Department accused Teledyne, Inc., of systematically falsifying tests on an electrical component used in the construction of sophisticated weapons and spacecraft. The company also sold the government a $6 part for $20 and, over a period of one year, defrauded the U.S. taxpayers of about $250 million (Stevenson 1992, cited in Newman 2000: 207). Although the company was caught committing the same kind of fraud on other occasions, the government has continued to do business with it.
- ✓ In 1994, six airlines (American, Delta, Northwest, TWA, Alaska, and Continental) were found to have collaborated illegally to raise airline ticket fares over a four-year period, costing consumers an estimated $4 billion in excess fares. No criminal charges ensued, and the airlines received no formal punishment. They simply agreed not to negotiate ticket-price changes in the future—a settlement that the government was happy to accept.
- ✓ In 1997, Florida justice officials discovered that America's largest insurance company, Prudential, had been engaged in a deliberate scheme to cheat its customers for more than a decade. Rather than being subject to criminal prosecution, the company was allowed to settle with a payment of $15 million—a mere fraction of the $2 billion it had gained by defrauding customers (Treaster and Peterson 1997, cited in Newman 2000: 177)

**White-collar crimes** Crimes that take place within the business and corporate sector, such as false advertising, unfair labor practices, and embezzlement. Although street crime is often assumed to be a more serious social problem, white-collar crimes actually cost society more and affect a wider public.

The perpetrators of these white-collar crimes, even repeat offenders, are seldom subject to the massive law-enforcement efforts directed at street crimes such as those committed by prostitutes, beggars, drug dealers, and thieves. Consider, as just one example, the long jail sentences given to low-income individuals who, having already been labeled as criminals, are convicted for stealing small amounts of money. Inequality and harshness also characterize punishment of more violent crimes and the application of the death sentence. In this post-Enron era, efforts have been made by the U.S. Justice Department to combat this patently unjust situation, at least in terms of its most conspicuous representations. We have been treated to scene after scene of the super-rich and powerful being hauled into squad cars with their heads pushed down and their hands handcuffed behind their backs, and judges and juries have sentenced some of these white-collar criminals to heavy jail time. But whether this handful of cases presages a new relationship between the criminal justice system and white-color crime remains to be seen. It will take a lot more than post-Enron attention to balance the scales of justice fairly.

## Matters of Life and Death

The ultimate get-tough punishment is the death penalty, which was briefly struck down by the U.S. Supreme Court in the 1970s but has gradually been reinstated by many states and the federal government. At the end of 2003 more than 3,300 people were on death row in the United States, and in the last twenty-five years more than 700 prisoners have been executed. Until the end of the 1990s the numbers being executed rose steeply. After 1999, however, a small reduction occurred, accompanied by numerous reports of mistakes whereby condemned or executed prisoners were found to have been innocent. An overview of crime issues published by *Public Agenda* (2005) cited Columbia University research that found two out of three cap-

ital convictions were overturned on appeal, often owing to incompetent defense lawyers or because overzealous prosecutors had withheld evidence. The likelihood of being executed also varies among states; Texas leads the field, accounting for 24 of the total of 65 persons (all men) executed in the United States in 2003. Only eleven states carried out executions that year. Of the persons executed in 2003, 20 were black and 41 white; under sentence of death were 1,418 black persons and 1,878 white prisoners (Bonczar and Snell 2004).

Although there is no evidence that capital punishment deters would-be murderers, the majority of Americans continue to support the death penalty (see Tables 11.4–11.6). At times, public opinion in other Western societies has also shown majority support for capital punishment, but many governments in these societies, such as those of Western Europe, have resisted reintroducing it. The fact that European societies have lower rates of murder could be taken as evidence that capital punishment does not act as a deterrent, but it may simply reflect the different cultural attitude toward the ownership and use of firearms. European societies are not necessarily more law-abiding. For example, a comparison carried out for the U.S. Department of Justice showed that in 1996, Britain had higher rates of assault, burglary, and motor vehicle theft than the United States. However, murder rates in the United States were 5.7 times higher. A significant difference was that guns were involved in crime far more often in the United States than in Britain, where there is stricter gun control (Langan and Farrington 1998). The individual's right to bear arms is something that many Americans believe to be a constitutional right and a part of their culture.

## THEORIES OF CRIME AND DEVIANCE

Sociologists have long sought to dissociate themselves from what they regard as the errors of individualistic approaches to crime and deviance,

**TABLE 11.4 American Attitudes Toward the Death Penalty, 2004**

| | SURVEY QUESTION: Generally speaking, do you believe the death penalty is applied fairly or unfairly in this country today? | | | SURVEY QUESTION: Do you feel that the death penalty acts as a deterrent to the commitment of murder, that it lowers the murder rate, or not? | | |
|---|---|---|---|---|---|---|
| | *Applied fairly* | *Applied unfairly* | *Don't know/refused* | *Yes, does* | *No, does not* | *Don't know/refused* |
| **National** | 55% | 39% | 6% | 35% | 62% | 3% |
| **Sex** | | | | | | |
| Male | 59 | 35 | 6 | 41 | 57 | 2 |
| Female | 51 | 42 | 7 | 31 | 65 | 4 |
| **Race** | | | | | | |
| White | 59 | 35 | 6 | 37 | 61 | 2 |
| Nonwhite | 41 | 51 | 8 | 31 | 64 | 5 |
| Black | 32 | 58 | 10 | 15 | 80 | 5 |
| **Education** | | | | | | |
| College postgraduate | 43 | 50 | 7 | 31 | 65 | 4 |
| College graduate | 56 | 41 | 3 | 33 | 67 | 0 |
| Some college | 59 | 34 | 7 | 28 | 69 | 3 |
| High school graduate or less | 57 | 36 | 7 | 44 | 53 | 3 |
| **Community** | | | | | | |
| Urban area | 42 | 50 | 8 | 32 | 65 | 3 |
| Suburban area | 58 | 36 | 6 | 35 | 62 | 3 |
| Rural area | 64 | 31 | 5 | 40 | 58 | 2 |
| **Region** | | | | | | |
| East | 53 | 40 | 7 | 39 | 58 | 3 |
| Midwest | 52 | 41 | 7 | 36 | 60 | 4 |
| South | 64 | 30 | 6 | 35 | 62 | 3 |
| West | 48 | 46 | 6 | 31 | 67 | 2 |
| **Politics** | | | | | | |
| Republican | 75 | 20 | 5 | 49 | 49 | 2 |
| Democrat | 42 | 51 | 7 | 25 | 71 | 4 |
| Independent | 50 | 44 | 6 | 34 | 64 | 2 |

*Note:* Based on telephone interviews with a randomly selected national sample of 1,000 adults (over the age of 18).

*Source:* Pastore and Maguire (2003).

whereby the causes of crime are located in the individual's nature—as implied by phrases such as *evil nature* and *born criminal* (those who are born with characteristics that predispose them toward criminal behavior). In this respect, sociological theories differ from theological, psychological, and biological theories:

✓ Sociological theories characterize deviance and crime as a response to the society in which they occur.

✓ Psychological theories locate deviance and crime within the psyche or mind of the individual, as the product of inborn "abnormality" or of "faulty cognition processes."

**TABLE 11.5  Reported Reasons for Opposing the Death Penalty for Persons Convicted of Murder, United States, 1991 and 2003**

| | SURVEY QUESTION: Why do you oppose the death penalty for persons convicted of murder? | |
|---|---|---|
| *Reason for Opposing* | *1991* | *2003* |
| Wrong to take a life | 41% | 46% |
| Punishment should be left to God/religious belief | 17 | 13 |
| Person may be wrongly convicted | 11 | 25 |
| Does not deter people from committing murder | 7 | 4 |
| Possibility of rehabilitation | 6 | 5 |
| Unfair application of death penalty | 6 | 4 |
| Need to pay/suffer longer/think about their crime | n/a | 5 |
| Depends on the circumstances | n/a | 4 |
| Other | 16 | 3 |
| No opinion | 6 | 4 |

*Note:* Question asked only to those respondents who answer "no, not in favor" to the question "Are you in favor of the death penalty for persons convicted of murder?" Up to two responses were recorded from each respondent.

*Source:* Pastore and Maguire (2003).

**Strain** A condition experienced when the members of a society lack a sufficient amount of legitimate means to achieve socially approved goals, prompting some individuals to pursue their aims through alternative means, such as deviant or criminal action. For example, people who are impoverished and need to feed their families experience strain. While their goal is socially acceptable, they are unable to meet it through legitimate resources (i.e., personal income or welfare benefits). They might find an alternative means to achieve the goal, such as going to a soup kitchen or soliciting donations on the street. Alternatively, they might turn to criminal activity to earn the income needed to provide for their families.

✓ Biological theories locate deviance and crime within the biological makeup of the individual.

✓ Theological theories locate deviance and crime within the spiritual or moral makeup of the individual.

The sociological theories we discuss in this chapter are functionalist theory, especially that of Emile Durkheim; labeling theory and the symbolic interactionist perspective; conflict theory, particularly that influenced by Karl Marx; and cultural approaches to crime and deviance, including theories relevant to postmodern society in particular.

## Functionalist Theory

Functionalist theory developed in the period from the end of the nineteenth century until the middle of the twentieth. It was based on an analogy between society and the body, with organs or parts that contribute to the smooth functioning of the whole. If any part malfunctioned or became dysfunctional, perhaps as a result of external causes, then the body would react in order to preserve itself—the reaction would be manifested in pathological symptoms, such as sickness and fatigue. According to Durkheim (1893), modern society in his own time was experiencing just such symptoms as a result of the loss of traditional community and the pressures of economic and social change. Whereas traditional society had been bound together by shared group values and norms, people in modern society were becoming less attached to norms (a condition he called "anomie") and thought they could simply pursue their own individual interests. Durkheim recognized that a certain amount of deviation from norms is normal and healthy for any society. It allows for innovation and adaptation to change. Even deviance and crime, in small amounts, could have a reinforcing function in bonding the elements of society together against a common enemy. But too much crime and deviance becomes a problem. He believed this to be the case with excessive individualism in modern society: Too many people thought they could behave as they wanted, ignoring the group and its rules.

The functionalist-based idea of anomie was taken up by Robert Merton (1957), whose interest was in the structural causes of nonconformist (deviant) behavior. He explained crime and deviance as the result of **strain** caused by lack of sufficient legitimate means to achieve socially approved goals. Such goals are symbolized by the American dream, which holds that—provided one works hard—success in the form of a good job, money, a nice house, and an affluent lifestyle can be yours. Americans internalize these values or cultural goals as part of their socialization, but there is a dysfunction or strain resulting from the unequal distribution of the means to achieve such goals. Merton went on to specify five main responses to such strain:

1. *Conformity:* In this scenario, the norms of correct behavior are followed even though the means to achieve them are not available. Conformity is not a deviant response.
2. *Innovation:* Here, the goals are accepted but, because of inadequate means to achieve them, other means are used that have not previously been approved. So-called creative bookkeeping, as practiced by the accountants of large corporations that are not achieving their profit goals, is one kind of innovation that treads a fine line between legality and illegality. (In the Enron crash of 2002, the line was crossed.)

**TABLE 11.6  Reported Reasons for Favoring the Death Penalty for Persons Convicted of Murder, United States, 1991 and 2003**

| Reasons for Favoring | SURVEY QUESTION: Why do you favor the death penalty for persons convicted of murder? | |
| --- | --- | --- |
| | 1991 | 2003 |
| An eye for an eye/they took a life/fits the crime | 40% | 37% |
| Save taxpayers money/cost associated with prison | 12 | 11 |
| Deterrent for potential crimes/set an example | 8 | 11 |
| Depends on the type of crime they commit | 6 | 4 |
| Fair punishment | 6 | 3 |
| They deserve it | 5 | 13 |
| They will repeat their crime/keep them from repeating it | 4 | 7 |
| Biblical reasons | 3 | 5 |
| Serve justice | 2 | 4 |
| Don't believe they can be rehabilitated | 1 | 2 |
| If there's no doubt the person committed the crime | n/a | 3 |
| Would help/benefit families of victims | n/a | 2 |
| Support/believe in death penalty | n/a | 2 |
| Life sentences don't always mean life in prison | n/a | 1 |
| Relieves prison overcrowding | n/a | 1 |
| Other | 10 | 4 |
| No opinion | 3 | 2 |

*Note:* Question asked only to those respondents who answer "yes, in favor" to the question "Are you in favor of the death penalty for persons convicted of murder?" Up to two responses were recorded from each respondent.

*Source:* Pastore and Maguire (2003).

3. *Ritualism:* When people give up hope of achieving goals, even in cases where the means of attaining them are available, they may continue to work within the system but are really only "going through the motions." Ritualism of this sort is common in large bureaucracies,

where workers may observe the rules but lose sight of the goals.

4. *Retreatism:* Those who lack the means and have not accepted the goals may drop out or retreat from society—in some instances, by becoming recluses or turning to alcohol or drugs.

5. *Rebellion:* Some people reject the dominant goals and the means to achieve them, but then replace them with their own set of values. This rebellion response could account for acts of politically motivated terrorism or "freedom fighting."

Some critics have maintained that Merton saw deviance too much in terms of individuals and ignored the communal aspects of some forms of deviance. For example, Albert Cohen (1955) and Richard Cloward and Lloyd Ohlin (1960) insisted that deviance, especially youth delinquency, is the result of excluding groups from opportunities to achieve the goals of society based on their position in the social structure. This, the authors noted, is particularly the case for working-class youths. Cohen said that such youths experience "status frustration," because they increasingly became aware that they are denied the means to achieve their goals. Their reaction is to substitute new and deviant goals, which creates a delinquent subculture. Cloward and Ohlin pointed out that some young people lack even the opportunity of joining a gang or making a career of crime. These individuals are "double failures," and many of them retreat into a life of drug abuse and violence.

## Labeling Theory and the Symbolic Interactionist Perspective

Labeling theory gradually took over from functionalist approaches to crime and deviance in the 1960s and 1970s. It arose out of the symbolic interactionist perspective that developed out of the work of W. I. Thomas, G. H. Mead, and others at the University of Chicago before World War II. Thomas's "theory of the situation" (the so-called **Thomas Theorem**) states: "If men define those situations as real, they are real in their consequences" (1931 [1966]: 301). Mead's contribution was to show how meanings and identities are constructed through social interaction and to explain that we regulate our behavior by taking account of the way we think others will respond. It was these ideas that labeling theory later applied to deviance and crime to demonstrate the ways in which deviant labels are created, imposed, and resisted through interaction (Mead 1934). Three decades later, Howard Becker made the point that no actions are by nature criminal or deviant, nor are people naturally criminal or deviant. Rather, deviance depends on the norms of the society, and on the reactions of members of society in different situations. In his book, *Outsiders: Studies in the Sociology of Deviance*, Becker stated that groups create deviance by making the rules and then applying those rules to particular people and labeling them as outsiders: "The deviant is one to whom that label has successfully been applied" (Becker 1963: 9).

The effect of this perspective on the sociology of crime and deviance was to shift the focus from why people are criminal or deviant onto the question of why and how people come to be *labeled* as criminal or deviant. Becker also described the **deviant career** in terms of the stages that people undergo in internalizing the label that has been applied to them. This idea is useful for elucidating how young people gradually accept the labels such as "oddball" or "delinquent" that have been applied to them, and even see their identities in those terms. It also helps explain what happens to young prisoners whose criminal identities and criminal careers become hardened as a result of their social interactions in jail.

The two main criticisms of labeling theory are that it can appear to doubt the reality and serious consequences of deviant or criminal acts and that it has nothing to say about the structural causes of crime, such as social conditions of poverty and blocked opportunities.

## Conflict Theory

Conflict theory, especially the version influenced by Marx's ideas of class conflict and exploitation (Chambliss 1975; Quinney 1977), points out that inequalities of wealth and power are what lead some people to be branded as deviant or criminal. It is the rich and powerful who make the laws and rules to serve their interests—and anyone offending against these has to be punished and controlled. The state and its agencies—the courts and the police—are simply tools of the ruling class. So it is the system, specifically the capitalist system, that creates criminals. It does this in various ways. First, it punishes any infractions or threats to the functioning of the capitalist economic system itself. Under capitalism the most important value is the right to exploit private property to the fullest so as to make a profit. Crimes against property are severely punished. Second, capitalism is alleged to generate greed and selfishness because it has to create new and bigger markets for its commodities, which entails spending vast sums on advertising and marketing. Third, it stimulates competition for scarce resources, which means that the rich and powerful get and use more than their fair share, to the disadvantage of others. Richard Quinney (1970, 1974), for example, argues that laws in capitalist societies are not about fairness but about forging a tool to control the working class.

The main criticisms of Marxist conflict theory are that it levels blame exclusively against the conflict between the interests of the two classes of capitalists and workers, even though there are laws that protect both capitalists *and* workers. It also ignores other sources of conflict that are not class based.

Not all conflict theorists follow Marx in emphasizing class conflict in discussions of crime and de-

**Thomas Theorem** A theorem stating that if people define a situation as real, it is real in its consequences. The Thomas Theorem parallels the symbolic interactionist perspective, which emphasizes how social actions are the result of shared definitions of a situation.

**Deviant career** The process of internalizing and accepting the label of "deviant." According to labeling theory, no person is a deviant by nature; rather, deviance is a label that is either accepted or resisted.

viance. Indeed, some focus on racial conflict and oppression. They point to the massively disproportionate number of blacks who are stopped by the police and brought to court, and to the more severe sentences they receive compared to whites, including the death penalty. Not just the police and judiciary act on racial stereotypes and prejudices, they argue; even some criminological ideas, such as biological theories, legitimize racism. This was one of the criticisms against Wilson and Herrnstein's best-selling *Crime and Human Nature* (1985), which, along with similar books, was said to have fueled public debates about the supposed links between race and crime (Garland 2001: 136).

## Cultural Approaches to Crime and Deviance

In recent years, sociologists have increasingly turned their attention to cultural factors to explain crime and punishment. This endeavor can take several forms, such as undertaking ethnographic research into deviant subcultures and seeking to understand the meanings that criminals attach to their actions, or examining the portrayal of crime in the media. Neither ethnographic studies nor studies of media portrayals of crime are completely new developments in the sociology of crime and deviance. However, both are likely to become more important in the future because of their relevance to the sociological analysis of trends in crime and deviance in postmodern society.

## Ethnographic Research

Earlier we looked at some of the "facts" about crime and punishment, as represented by statistics. However, it is important to remember that facts do not speak for themselves—they have to be constructed by those who report and collect the information, as well as by those who interpret it. As we have seen, there are sometimes disagreements over statistics and what they mean. Another way of gaining an understanding about deviance and crime is to undertake firsthand observation of those involved and their cultures. Early examples of this kind of ethnographic field research (*ethno* means "people," *graphic* means "description," and *in the field* refers to "the situation") can be found in the studies performed by University of Chicago sociologists—the Chicago School—such as Frederic Thrasher's *The Gang* (1927), Clifford Shaw's *The Jack Roller* (1930), Nels Anderson's *The Hobo* (1923), and John Landesco's *Organized Crime in Chicago* (1929). These first urban ethnographers were essentially following the advice of the chair of the Chicago sociology department, Robert Park, who instructed students to "go get the seat of your pants dirty in real research" (quoted in McKinney 1966: 71).

This type of research went into partial hibernation during the ascendancy of functionalist sociology around the time of World War II and the period immediately following. A number of professional researchers regarded ethnographic research on deviant groups as "unscientific" and too subjective, believing quantitative (statistical) research to be more objective. (For a more detailed discussion of sociological methods overall, consult Chapter 2.) Some sociologists continued in the Chicago School tradition during the postwar era, especially those pursuing the study of juvenile

delinquency. Others focused on individuals who sought to maintain social control by rousing public opinion on moral issues, termed "moral entrepreneurs" (Becker 1963). An example of such a moral crusade—or "moral enterprise" (Becker 1963)—is the Temperance movement against alcohol, described in Joseph Gusfield's *Symbolic Crusade* (1963).

In the 1960s, the main center of ethnographic research moved to California, where the study of deviant, alternative, countercultural, and illegal groups flourished. Researchers studied these groups at close proximity in order to find out what constituted their realities. Readers were treated to in-depth accounts of the underworld of horse racing (Scott 1968), religious cults (Lofland 1966), skid row (Wiseman 1970), and nude beaches (Douglas and Rasmussen 1977).

One work in the Chicago tradition, though carried out largely in New York (with some historical research in England), was Ned Polsky's *Hustlers, Beats, and Others* (1967)—an ethnographic study of poolroom hustlers that demonstrates the advantages of this kind of research in understanding the motivation of those who pursue a risky career (involving deception and illegal gambling) within a deviant subculture. Polsky explains that "hustlers are social deviants, in the sense that they gamble for a living and, in the process, violate societal norms of 'respectable' work and of fair dealing." Yet within their working-class subculture, they are not regarded as particularly deviant and so are not stigmatized as "poolroom bums" by their own subculture's norms. Furthermore, "once embarked in the hustling life, hustlers prefer to stay in it: it's exciting, it has a tradition and ideology that can make them feel heroic, it's fun (the game is enjoyable as such), it's not routine, and so on" (Polsky 1967: 85–86, 90).

During the 1960s it could be said, the hustling career shared deeply, often passionately, in every one of the orientations that sociologists have described as "focal concerns" of American lower-class subcultures—"trouble (with the law), smartness (in the sense of being able to con and of being no one's dupe), excitement, fate, toughness ('heart'), and autonomy" (Miller 1958, quoted in Polsky 1967: 90). But it's important to realize that this was a time when a large, inner-city, blue-collar working class was employed in manufacturing and laboring jobs, and that such jobs were mainly masculine in ethos. This working-class subculture has declined with the rise of the postindustrial economy. There is now a proliferation of consumer lifestyles rather than class-based subcultures, although inner-city ethnic groups may still be said to have distinctive subcultures (containing some of the "focal concerns" earlier attributed to the working class) and to be more tolerant of behavior that the larger society labels as deviant or criminal.

Ethnographic studies of deviant and criminal groups were discouraged by many universities in the 1980s and 1990s on the grounds that they could be judged unethical, especially if they involved a covert role for the observer, lacked parental consent (in cases where deviant youth were being studied), or did not have signed consent forms from those being observed. Government agencies and other organizations have also been unsympathetic to such research, especially when researchers have tried to protect the privacy and confidentiality of their sources. One graduate student researcher, Rik Scarce, at Washington State University, was jailed for six months for contempt of court because he would not divulge information about the members of the radical environmental movement he was studying. Scarce's later request to conduct field research with inmates was denied by his university (Ferrell and Hamm 1998: xv).

Despite the difficulties encountered in doing ethnographic field research on deviants and criminals, there has been a resurgence of such studies in recent years. In *Ethnography at the Edge: Crime, Deviance, and Field Research* (1998), sociologists Jeff Ferrell and Mark Hamm describe the horrors,

perils, and joys of their deep involvement with such diverse groups as skinheads, phone-sex workers, drug dealers, graffiti artists, and homeless people. They recount how doing this kind of research involved such episodes as illegal drug use, drunk driving, weapons violations, assault at gunpoint, obstruction of justice, and arrest. Clearly, ethnographic field research is not for the fainthearted. But it does add a valuable source of data that are not available from more "orthodox" or quantitative research. Indeed, it not only provides an understanding of the meanings and emotions of those under scrutiny in a particular situation—the moments of pleasure and pain, the emergent logic and excitement—but also allows researchers, through attentiveness and participation, to appreciate the specific roles and experiences of criminals, crime victims, crime control agents, and others caught up in the day-to-day reality of crime and deviance.

Among the important results of this kind of research are findings that concern the emotions and the situated logics (what "makes sense" in particular situations) of those involved in specific criminal or deviant cultures. Such an understanding cannot be attained from "outside," solely on the basis of statistical data. In addition, whereas the adrenaline-rush experiences often studied by ethnographic researchers, such as joyriding, drug taking, shoplifting, and gangbanging, might appear to be isolated, individual, or impulsive experiences, ethnographic study shows that they reflect a shared vocabulary of motive—a repertoire of meanings common to those involved in them (Mills 1940). In short, the emotions and the meanings of deviants and criminals are constructed collectively out of the common experiences of subcultural participants and the shared cultural codes of their groups. They cannot be understood solely on the basis of individual psychology or statistics, even though these are the types of explanation favored by media reports and many criminal justice professionals.

Ethnographic studies show that strong emotions, such as the thrill of danger, pleasure, excitement, anger, and frustration—as experienced in instances of shoplifting (Katz 1988), graffiti writing, neo-Nazi skinheads "going berserk" (Hamm 1993), or Latino gang members "going crazy" against rival gangs (Vigil 1988)—are important elements in some deviant and criminal subcultures. As reported by Kenneth Tunnell (1992), even adult property criminals, though operating on the basis of rational calculation about how much they could make, report that stealing gave them a feeling of exhilaration. Another study reveals that many adult burglars are "committed to a lifestyle characterized by the quest for excitement and an openness to 'illicit action'" and that some go so far as to burglarize occupied homes in order to make "the offence more exciting" (Wright and Decker 1994: 117).

As we will see in the next section, the same two themes—pleasure and risk—are prominent in mass-media portrayals of crime and deviance in postmodern society.

### Media Portrayals of Crime and Deviance

Early sociologists viewed modern society in terms of theories of the progressive development of a rational society based on scientific principles, while still allowing for occasional setbacks and persisting pockets of irrational thought and antisocial behavior. Functionalist sociologists conceded, with Durkheim, that a limited amount of crime and deviance could be healthy for society, but they expected that better organization and scientific endeavor could limit the pathological effects. For example, it was thought that better socialization of youth through education would minimize juvenile delinquency or rebellion. Conflict theorists looked to reform or revolution of the social system to cure structural problems of which crime and deviance were symptoms. Labeling theorists' ideas were taken on board by teachers and other professionals, who got the message that sticking a label on someone—for example, "the troublemaker"—

could have the result of causing that person to live up (or down) to that label. Hence, careful calculation of the effects of labeling was needed.

As we have discussed throughout *A Contemporary Introduction to Sociology*, by the second half of the twentieth century the idea of linear social progress had begun to look less convincing, not just in light of horrific events such as the Holocaust and the development of atomic weapons but also because some of the means to progress, including science and the mass media, seemed to be among the causes rather than the cures of these events.

Great faith was placed in the potential of modern communications media to promote social progress. The earliest forms of mass media, such as newspapers, had something of the character of informational and educational channels, with dense columns of sober print communicating information to the literate public. (Note, however, that the first American papers were extremely partisan and short-lived.) Subsequently, with the rise of the popular "penny" press catering to a mass readership (see Chapter 4, on media and communication), the content became more sensational and entertaining, with crime stories predominating. The advent of television carried this development much further. It has been estimated that, from the 1960s to the 1990s, crime and justice programming amounted to one-fourth of all prime-time shows, making it the largest single subject matter on television (Surette 1998: 35–36). In addition to the many fictional crime series now available on TV, crime news has become the mainstay of hybrid news-entertainment (infotainment) shows. One paradoxical result of this extensive crime coverage is that the media are simultaneously perceived as both a major cause of crime and violence and an untapped but powerful potential solution to crime. On the one hand, the media are accused of spreading glamorous images of crime, which can lead to copycat behavior; but on the other hand, the media are expected to aid in reducing crime, assisting in manhunts, and bolstering the criminal justice system. Another paradoxical effect is that the criminal justice system is often not shown positively, yet the solution rate on television exceeds 90 percent (Surette 1998: 21). This results in an unrealistic picture of crime and justice that can only lead to dissatisfaction when real-life crimes are not cleared up or reduced in number.

There are many indications that crime rates have dropped over the past decade, but this fact has hardly caused a decline in crime reporting. If you watch the local news tonight, chances are you will see at least one crime story. Figures 11.7 and 11.8 show some of the findings from an extensive survey of local television news stations across the United States. Crime is by far the most common topic of news stories, by a margin of 2:1 over any other category. Correspondingly, over a quarter of the people you will see on the news are people involved in crime, such as victims, criminals, law enforcement officials, and judges.

A consequence of the all-pervasive nature of mass media in postmodern society is that a large amount of attention is being focused on a few criminal events, producing a kind of spiral effect. The public is led to believe that a certain kind of deviant behavior is spreading rapidly and is a symptom of an underlying moral decline in society, or among certain groups (such as youth). Sociologists have referred to this sequence as **moral panic** (Cohen 1972; Thompson 1998). The term was first used by sociologist Stanley Cohen to characterize the outraged reactions of the media, the public, and agents of social control to the youth disturbances—fights on the beach between "Mods" and "Rockers"—that were occurring during holiday weekends in 1960s Britain:

Societies appear to be subject, every now and then, to periods of moral panic. A condition, episode, person or group of persons emerges to become defined as a threat to societal values and interests; its nature is presented in a stylized and stereotypical fashion by the mass media; the

moral barricades are manned by editors, bishops, politicians and other right-thinking people; socially accredited experts pronounce their diagnoses and solutions; ways of coping are evolved or (more often) resorted to; the condition then disappears, submerges or deteriorates and becomes more visible. (Cohen 1972: 9)

Employment of the phrase *moral panic* to describe such events has been criticized on the grounds that *panic* implies an irrational reaction. However, the usefulness of the concept depends not on the meaning of *panic* but, rather, on the fact that the concept draws attention to the processes by which the media can set in motion a spiral effect that amplifies a threat and plays on people's fears and their sense of being at risk (even if, statistically, they are not). A similar phenomenon is invoked in Philip Jenkins's (1994) description of the social construction of serial murder in the 1980s, in which a few cases were made to appear as an exploding, pervasive social problem.

Indeed, as the mass media have become more pervasive and intrusive in postmodern society, their role in the construction of crime and deviance has become increasingly significant. As noted above, the result is an increased sense of being at risk, even if the objective possibility of risk has not actually increased. Sociologist Ulrich Beck (1992) writes about the new "Risk Society" as if increased danger were literally a fact (see also Adam, Beck, and van Loon 1992). Such a noncultural understanding can hardly do justice to the

**Moral panic** A period or episode of heightened anxiety about what are seen as symptoms of moral decline in society. Moral panics typically include a campaign aimed at mobilizing agents of social control against particular groups that are alleged to be responsible for the moral decline. The pervasive presence of the media in postmodern society can be tremendously influential in terms of amplifying and sustaining these moral panics.

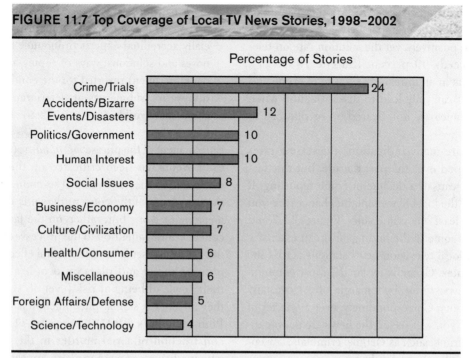

FIGURE 11.7 Top Coverage of Local TV News Stories, 1998–2002

Percentage of Stories

Crime/Trials — 24
Accidents/Bizarre Events/Disasters — 12
Politics/Government — 10
Human Interest — 10
Social Issues — 8
Business/Economy — 7
Culture/Civilization — 7
Health/Consumer — 6
Miscellaneous — 6
Foreign Affairs/Defense — 5
Science/Technology — 4

*Note:* These data are based on content analysis of local news from 154 stations from 15 to 20 markets that were randomly selected with controls for station size and geographic diversity. Weather and sports coverage were not included. Totals may not equal 100 due to rounding.

*Source:* PEJ (2004).

mass media's role in constructing such dangers as crime. It is the media's construction or representation of crime that produces the kind of gothic fascination and emotional involvement that characterize the postmodern imagination and give rise to unrealistic demands for the elimination of crime and other risks.

## THE FUTURE OF CRIME AND DEVIANCE IN POSTMODERN SOCIETY

The emphasis, in recent ethnographic and media studies, on the importance of emotions such as the excitement associated with acts of crime echoes the ideas of one of the leading postmodern thinkers, Michel Foucault. His writings about pleasure (1985), the body (1978), and the changing regimes of discipline and control in different historical periods (1977) led him to pronounce that "power is in our bodies, not in our heads" (quoted in Fraser 1994: 11). By that, Foucault meant that social regulation of people's bodies, including their emotions, is of paramount concern. Each major historical epoch, he argued, is distinguished by a predominant form of regulation or control. In traditional feudal society, physical punishments, including the most ferocious forms of torture and execution, were common. This phase was succeeded in the early-modern, industrializing societies of the late eighteenth and early nineteenth centuries by incarceration of offenders

## FIGURE 11.8 Main Subjects of Local TV News Stories (percentage of stories)

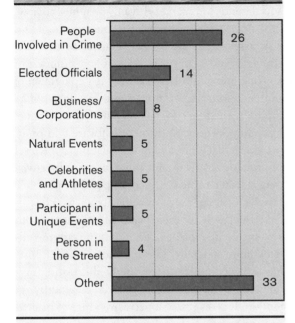

| Subject | Percentage |
|---|---|
| People Involved in Crime | 26 |
| Elected Officials | 14 |
| Business/Corporations | 8 |
| Natural Events | 5 |
| Celebrities and Athletes | 5 |
| Participant in Unique Events | 5 |
| Person in the Street | 4 |
| Other | 33 |

*Note:* These data are based on content analysis of local news from 154 stations from 15 to 20 markets that were randomly selected with controls for station size and geographic diversity. Weather and sports coverage were not included. Totals may not equal 100 due to rounding.

*Source:* PEJ (2004).

in what Erving Goffman, in *Asylums* (1961), called "total institutions," characterized by "barrier(s) to social intercourse with the outside and to departure that is often built right into the physical plant, such as locked doors, high walls, barbed wire, cliffs, water, forest or moors" (Goffman 1961: 4). These institutions used surveillance, discipline, and rituals to strip occupants of their deviant personality features and then to remake them in a common mold.

Foucault described the modern correctional regime as one based on techniques and "scientific" discourses, aimed at disciplining the mind-body of the prisoner. The story that Foucault presented in *Discipline and Punish* (1977) is a history not just of the modern prison but also of the emergence of a more generalized regime of discipline and control in modern society, involving other disciplinary occupations (e.g., doctors, psychologists, and teachers). Foucault's focus was on the emergence of what he termed *power-knowledge*—the complex range of practices and schemes of professional knowledge and everyday "common sense" increasingly put to use in the control of unruly, difficult, or simply disturbingly different (deviant) populations. For Foucault, and those influenced by him, modern society is to be understood through "discourse analysis"—focusing on the specific sets of practices and ideas that provide meaning in specific spheres of social life. Specifically, Foucault's idea was that, instead of permitting the state increasingly centralized control in modern society, social regulation would be decentralized and exercised through institutions such as medicine and education. And not only deviants and criminals would be corrected and reformed through these various disciplines. Rather, in Foucault's account, the whole of modern society would become a disciplinary or "carceral" society. Ironically, Foucault's proposals led many liberals to become extremely critical of community-based policies aimed at reforming and reintegrating offenders, rule breakers, and deviants. When this criticism from the left side of the political spectrum combined with criticisms from the

**Social regulation** The ways in which society regulates our actions and behaviors. Michel Foucault, one of the leading postmodern thinkers, argued that whereas social regulation in traditional society was based on physical punishment, such as torture and execution, the modern correctional regime was dependent upon disciplining the mind and body of the offender. Here, social regulation was located not just in correctional facilities but throughout all social institutions, including medicine and education.

Surveillance cameras are becoming ubiquitous in postmodern society. (iStockphoto)

right, it became easier for politicians, from the 1970s onward, to bow to pressure to concentrate on punishment rather than reform of offenders.

Postmodern society is characterized by diversity and contradiction. If Foucault had been right, imprisonment would have given way to the more subtle techniques of disciplinary control. What we find instead, however, is a parallel growth of the prison population and the reintroduction of capital punishment, alongside other disciplinary techniques such as psychiatry, drug treatments, electronic tagging, private security measures (including armed guards in some schools), and gated communities. Powerful platforms for these new techniques have been provided in the new patterns of consumerism. Today's malls are privatized versions of the old public spaces of inner-city shopping streets and squares, but with their own security forces and electronic surveillance measures. Many residential communities, too, are not only gated and walled off from the surrounding

public spaces but equipped with surveillance systems that identify deviant-looking intruders. The result is one of the fastest-growing dimensions of social control in market-driven, consumer society: "the management of risk." Risk management and risk assessment are indeed central to the new strategies and tactics of policing. Large numbers of key operational decisions about the deployment of police resources are now made by local police forces by reference to data on patterns of criminal offending, produced through software computer programs that deliver such information to the level of individual streets. But this kind of "objective" data doesn't necessarily correspond to people's own "subjective" sense of being at risk, which is affected not only by their personal experiences but also by media representations and the cultural climate more generally. The cultural climate of postmodern society is increasingly fluid and fragmented, a kaleidoscope that is constantly in motion. It gives rise to a pervasive sense of insecurity and risk that no amount of policing can allay.

## CONCLUSION

The case of John Walker Lindh and the publicity given to it, as described at the beginning of this chapter, illustrate some of the main points that have been made about sociological explanations of crime and deviance. Sociology is interested in social trends, and in discovering general social and cultural factors that can be used to explain them. It asks questions such as "Is this case a typical example of a social and cultural trend?" and "What are the social and cultural factors that might account for its occurrence and the ways in which it is perceived?" Indeed, individual cases, such as that of John Walker Lindh, can be examined in this light. If we considered just the bare facts of this case, there would appear to be little to justify the public fascination with it, nor would it seem sufficiently socially typical to be of interest to sociologists. After all, Walker was simply a single young American abroad, who was found fighting on the wrong side in a distant war in Afghanistan. In normal times, people might have accepted the psychological explanation that he was just a mixed-up individual. What made his capture a sensational event, however, was the cultural context that gave it meaning. This context was the heightened sense of insecurity and risk that resulted from searing images of the destruction of the World Trade Center, followed by a campaign on behalf of patriotism and national solidarity. The image of this highly deviant-looking American Muslim fighter, with his filthy robes and straggling beard, symbolized the threats to national security and solidarity.

The John Walker Lindh case and, indeed, September 11 itself were exceptional events; but it was the cultural construction of them, via the media, that tapped into the underlying feelings of horror and fascination that pervade postmodern society. In this respect such events parallel other examples of the social construction of deviance and crime. For instance, Joel Best (1991) describes the media's role in constructing the new "crime problem" of highway violence, news coverage of which is dominated by an emphasis on the random, senseless quality of such incidents, employing terms like *Mad Max*, *Road Warrior*, and *Freeway Rambo*. And in Philip Jenkins's (1994) account of the social construction of serial murders, the author observed that the media immediately linked these shocking homicides to other publicly hyped phenomena—missing children, pedophilia, sexism, racism, and homosexuality—so as to raise the sense of threat. These symbolic linkages fanned public anxieties about the structural stresses and strains in a changing society, such as pressures on the family unit, the changing roles of women, high unemployment in some minority groups, and the greater freedom granted to homosexuals.

Although the media may provide sensationalized accounts of individual criminal acts and help

Different cultures do not regard crime and deviance in the same way; for example, sex work is legal in the Netherlands, whereas prostitution is a crime throughout the United States. (Wolfgang Kaehler/Corbis)

to create "moral panics" about the threats facing society, there are real causes of anxiety that they plug into. People are concerned about the stresses and strains to which the social fabric is being subjected as a result of global and local social changes. And politicians and judges are responding to those perceived anxieties when they introduce or impose the penal sanctions that account for why America has the largest prison population in the developed world. However, although rapid social changes create real strains in the social structures of postmodern societies, comparisons of America with similar developed societies suggest that we have to look to cultural factors in order to explain its higher rates of imprisonment and more severe sentencing policies. Not only is America unique in maintaining capital punishment, it is the only developed country with a large and growing number of prisoners serving life sentences without parole. A survey by the *New York Times* (Liptak 2005a: A1) found that the number of lifers almost doubled between 1995 and 2005 and that the number of prisoners serving life sentences without the possibility of parole had risen and amounted to 28 percent of all lifers in 2005. In 2005 alone, about 9,700 were serving life sentences for crimes committed before they were 18, and more than a fifth had no chance of parole (Liptak 2005b: A1). The cultural reasons underlying America's distinctiveness in this dubious regard are hard to pinpoint, but they merit thinking about. In the *New York Times* article noted earlier, two experts are quoted as attributing it to America's Calvinist religious tradition. Said one commentator: "It's the same reason we're not a socialist welfare state. ... You deserve what you get, both good and bad" (Liptak 2005a: A1).

This argument is probably too simplistic, if only because there are other developed societies with a Calvinist religious tradition that have different attitudes toward crime and its punishment. Furthermore, Calvinist Protestantism is not the only brand of religion that is prominent in America—the Catholic population, for example, is long established and has increased dramatically with Latino immigration. Granted, America is unusually religious for an economically developed society, but a valid explanation will have to account for the full range of other factors that are distinctive to America, such as its particular racial history and its political system and culture. In the final analysis, it is the complex interplay of all these social and cultural factors that will be found to explain the trends in American crime and deviance and society's perception of them.

# EXERCISES

## Exercise 1

Take a close look at Table 11.2. It shows the results of a survey that asked people about their fear of becoming the victim of particular crimes. Do any of these numbers stand out to you? For example, do women fear certain crimes more than men? Do blacks fear certain crimes more than whites? What crimes are feared most overall? How would you explain these findings? How would a conflict theorist interpret the patterns they reflect?

## Exercise 2

A major theme in this chapter has been the portrayal of crime in the media, including such examples as the absurdly high crime-solution rate in fictional dramas, the use of crime details to provide the bulk of material for "infotainment" shows, and the prevalence of crime reporting on local television news (see Figure 11.8). But what about 24-hour news networks, such as CNN? Is their coverage of crime different from that of more traditional formats? And what about "reality television" series about crime, such as *COPS?* What are the dominant discourses on these shows? Discuss how both genres of television programming would be understood through each of Theodore Sasson's "frames."

# STUDY QUESTIONS

1. Briefly define *crime* and *deviance*. Explain why neither of these terms is as straightforward at it seems, especially in postmodern society.

2. What trend in the rate of violent crime has been dominant in the United States over the last ten years? Has the American public's fear of crime mirrored this trend?

3. What trend in the imprisonment rate has been dominant in the United States since 1990? Which demographic groups have the highest chance of going to prison?

4. What is volitional criminology? In what ways does this orientation reflect American values?

5. Which is more costly to society: street crime or white-collar crime? Why does the public perceive street crime as the more serious social problem?

6. What is the difference between sociological and individualist approaches to crime and deviance? Describe where each of the individualist approaches locates the causes of crime and deviance.

7. According to Émile Durkheim, how could deviance have a positive function in society? When did it become a problem? What did he mean by the term *anomie*, and what was the cause of this condition?

8. According to labeling theory, how is deviance created? What is meant by the term *deviant career*?

9. According to conflict theory, how does capitalism create criminals?

10. What is ethnographic field research? What are the risks and limitations of this methodology in researching crime? What are the benefits?

11. What is a moral panic? What role do the media play in it?

12. Describe the forms of social regulation that were dominant in traditional, early-modern, and modern epochs. According to Foucault, what important development in discipline and control emerged during the modern era? In this new regime, which institutions exercised social regulation, and over whom?

# FURTHER READING

Anderson, Elijah. 1978. *A Place on the Corner*, 2nd ed. Chicago: University of Chicago Press. Reprinted in 2001.

Chancer, Lynn S. 2005. *High-Profile Crimes: When Legal Cases Become Social Causes*. Chicago: University of Chicago Press.

Dotter, Daniel L. 2005. *Creating Deviance: An Interactionist Approach*. Walnut Creek, CA: AltaMira Press.

Garland, David. 2001. *The Culture of Control*. Chicago: University of Chicago Press.

Heimer, Karen, and Candace Kruttschnitt, eds. 2005. *Gender and Crime: Patterns of Victimization and Offending*. New York: New York University Press.

Moore, Mark H., Carol V. Petrie, Anthony A. Braga, and Brenda L. McLaughlin. 2003. *Deadly Lessons: Understanding Lethal School Violence*. Washington, DC: National Academies Press.

Pattillo, Mary, David Weiman, and Bruce Westera, eds. 2004. *Imprisoning America: The Social Effects of Mass Incarceration*. New York: Russell Sage Foundation.

# PART FIVE

# Institutions

# chapter 12

# Work and
# the Economy

There are few things more important to us than how we make our living. What are our prospects for finding a good job that pays well and satisfies our ambitions? And does our destiny lie solely in our own hands, or are there social factors that may affect our chances? Sociology is not alone in addressing such questions. Journalists and other media commentators are constantly presenting stories that claim to "tell it like it is." How are we to make sense of these accounts? In answering this question, let us consider the box titled "The Artist in the Gray Flannel Pajamas."

## AN INDIVIDUAL OR A SOCIAL STORY?

In this box is a *New York Times* story that paints a picture of individuals who have become more free and independent in their working lives. The fact that the author, Michael Lewis, begins this article about work in America by comparing 1950s images of work with those in 2000 tells us something about the power of images in postmodern society. As we have seen in other chapters, sociologists simply cannot ignore the power of media images— "the cultural construction of reality"—when discussing any aspect of society. The dominant image in the 1950s was that of the Organization Man, the Man in the Gray Flannel Suit. But much has changed in the last five decades; note, for example, that the image of "the worker" now includes women as well as men. By 2000, the image of a worker willing to subordinate "his" identity to a giant corporation had become so completely unfashionable that it was useless "for cultural purposes." In other words, the media were not interested in that image. What they were interested in, as Lewis's story demonstrates, was the image of workers throwing off their corporate chains and becoming free individual agents at the dawn of a new economy. A century and a half earlier, at the beginning of the modern industrial economy, Karl

Marx asserted that the only way workers would become free was by uniting as a class to overthrow the class of employers: "The workers have nothing to lose but their chains," he wrote (Marx and Engels 1848). So what has happened?

Quite a lot, but probably not entirely along the lines that Lewis believes. The story he tells is one of massive cultural change, involving a "drift away from old-fashioned corporate order and a tendency toward individualism in work life" (Lewis 2000: 45). This "drift" is said to be especially true of those who are image-conscious and in businesses concerned with inventing new lifestyles for others (e.g., the culture industry, such as Hollywood; software consultants in Silicon Valley). Lewis describes such people as "free agents," as "artists" prone to "piercing some highly unlikely body part," "cultivating an air of total independence," and maintaining an "ironic" attitude toward corporations. (Note that irony is one of the attitudes characteristic of postmodern culture.) He also claims that cultural values about work in America have changed significantly since the 1950s and that workers themselves are in the vanguard of that culture change.

The values and attitudes that seem to be coming into prominence are largely associated with individualism and freedom, according to Lewis. This is how he chronicles the shifts that have occurred:

1. The moral authority of corporate executives was undermined in the eyes of their subordinates when top executives in the 1980s began opting for shares rather than salaries and then selling out for a profit. Workers wondered: "Why should I devote my career to a company that my boss treats like a private lotto?"
2. In the boom years, many other workers, too, began to receive remuneration in shares—an increase from 200,000 workers with equity in their companies in 1974 to 10 million in 1999. This might have been expected to increase em-

## theory

## The Artist in the Gray Flannel Pajamas

If you pick up one of the many books written about American business in the 1950s, you will find a typical corporate employee who is unrecognizable today. The Organization Man, the Man in the Gray Flannel Suit—whatever you call him, he seems as freakish today as a bearded lady or a six-toed foot. The worker who is willing to subordinate his identity to some giant corporation is so deeply unfashionable that, for cultural purposes, he might as well not exist. Where did he go? One answer is that he was set free.

A few years ago I began to notice that people I was introduced to were suddenly describing their work, not saying who they did it for. The senior vice president of the Chase Manhattan Bank had somehow vanished. In his place had arisen a number of people with baffling new job descriptions: migrant Web master, kernel hacker, creative director. For about six months it seemed as if half the people I met called themselves software consultants. What the hell was that? As best as I could tell it meant piercing some highly unlikely body part and cultivating an air of total independence.

Actually, what these people all were, or appeared to be, were artists. They kept artists' hours. They wore artists' clothes. They had preserved the sort of odd habits that membership in any group—other than the group "artists"—tends to drum out of people. Maybe the most interesting thing about them was their lack of obvious corporate attachments. Corporations usually paid for their existence, but otherwise seemed to have no effect on their lives. If forced to discuss the companies that paid the bills, these people tended to be dismissive or, at the very least, ironic.

Here were the prosperous children of the great American economic boom, an amorphous, un-pin-downable labor force. They were not full-time employees of big companies, just temps. But there was now sufficient glory in being a temp—rather than a full-time employee with hours and a boss—that a temp was no longer a temp. He was, in new-economy parlance, a free agent.

*Source:* Lewis (2005).

ployee loyalty, but Lewis maintains that it had the opposite effect. Workers who had been paid in stock options could not afford to be loyal: They looked for signs that their stock might sink and then prepared to jump ship.
3. What followed was a new skepticism toward the company's argument that it serves some purpose higher than itself. Lewis claims that economic booms, such as the one that lasted through the 1990s, create new forces of selfishness.
4. The authority of bosses to impose discipline and order declined during the boom: "The boom has turned employers into buyers in a seller's market, and it is tough to sell discipline and order to a newly empowered population imbued with the free-agent spirit" (Lewis 2000: 45).
5. Next came a collapse of the "guild mentality"—the sense of belonging to a self-governing profession, such as medicine, law, and accountancy. Lewis (2000: 45) maintains that

professionals were increasingly following the "business model" whereby making money became the only source of prestige.

6. A new corporate language was invented "to support people's need to believe that their work is actually an endless quest for originality. 'Outside the box,' for instance. These days you cannot spend two hours inside any big American company without some poor sucker telling you how he believes in 'thinking outside the box'" (Lewis: 2000: 45).

7. Nonconformity seemed to have become almost the norm! "There are now many jobs in which it takes more nerve to wear a blue suit than a nose ring. Working from home in the nude is no longer evidence that you are an interesting person, or even a happy one." In other words, "[t]here are limits to the pleasure of individualism" (Lewis 2000: 45).

Working from home is a sign of the new individualism that accompanies the postmodern economy. (iStockphoto)

This is a long list of alleged cultural changes, encompassing not just the values and attitudes of workers but also the culture within organizations. The story told by Lewis is attractive because it incorporates some of the core values that have long featured in American ideology—individualism, freedom, and progress. But unfortunately, from time to time, even the most persuasive stories can be contradicted by events. Lewis admits that the changes he describes were dependent on a booming economy—and, as we know, the boom came to an end in 2001. Technology stocks collapsed, and many investors and workers suffered a loss of income. The tragic events of September 11, 2001, saw a further change in values and attitudes. Blue-collar workers, such as those involved in firefighting and rescue at the World Trade Center, became heroes and the values of public service came back into fashion. Does this mean that the cultural changes described by Michael Lewis were exaggerated, reflecting just a temporary phenomenon restricted to a few occupations? Not entirely, as we will see. But it is important to develop a more balanced sociological story about what has been happening.

Media stories aim to entertain as well as inform their readers, viewers, and listeners, and they have a tendency to exaggerate trends. The picture of work and the economy presented in many television programs is also significantly distorted. Think about some of the popular television programs of recent years and ask yourself what impression you get about work. Aren't the most frequently featured occupations those of professionals in medicine and law enforcement? Indeed, what viewers find entertaining are the dramatic lives of professionals—doctors and nurses, detectives and lawyers—rather than the routine activities of kitchen workers and janitors, who may also be nonwhite and/or immigrants. At the same time, we see little about the working lives of characters in programs focusing on contemporary young people, such as *Friends* and *Sex in the City*. It is their private lives that are featured, not their public lives as workers. In short, apart from these glamorous depictions, television programs and films give little attention to the everyday working lives of large sections of the population. Media impressions of work in our society, outside of our own experience as workers and customers, thus miss some of the most significant developments. Think again about what you have seen in recent TV programs and films, and ask yourself: Have they informed viewers about basic facts such as the massive increase in the proportion of women workers in the economy in recent years, or the new jobs taken by immigrants? These trends toward "feminization" and diversity in the workforce are not just linked to structural changes; they are also significant with respect to work cultures—how work is perceived and "lived."

In this chapter we examine the structural and cultural dimensions of work and the economy, showing how these have developed during various periods. We conclude by asking whether there are trends that might indicate the future shape of this important area of social life. In comparing the past and the present—then and now—we will see that the ways in which work and the economy are organized have undergone major structural changes. For example, in the **division of labor**—how work is divided up between jobs and people—changes have occurred not only at the microlevel of the factory but also between different groups (male and female workers). The national economy has been divided among different sectors (agriculture, manufacturing, and services). Globalization is increasing. And the workforce and the workplace are becoming more culturally diverse as a result of larger numbers of women workers and immigrant workers.

Over the course of the late nineteenth and early twentieth centuries, the American economy transformed from one that was based largely around agriculture and other primary-sector industries to

**Division of labor** The specialization of tasks required to produce goods. The culmination of the division of labor occurred at the original Ford production plant, where thousands of auto workers performed highly specialized tasks on an assembly line.

an economy based on manufacturing and the production of goods. Then, as the twentieth century wore on, these secondary-sector industries experienced a sharp decline, as a tertiary (or "service") sector came to dominate the U.S. economy. Figure 12.1 illustrates how the distribution of the American labor force into these three sectors changed between 1860 and 2000, and Figures 12.2 and 12.3 show the differences in full-time and part-time employment by gender. As discussed in this chapter, men are more likely than women to occupy full-time jobs, whereas women are more likely than men to occupy part-time jobs. We find a similar pattern with respect to the *hours* of labor. By an almost 2:1 margin, women are more likely to occupy jobs with irregular or shorter hours (i.e., between 19 and 39 hours), whereas men are more likely to work regularly long hours (i.e., 40+ hours per week).

## STRUCTURAL AND CULTURAL DIMENSIONS OF WORK AND THE ECONOMY

You might think that the economy is exclusively the subject matter of the discipline of economics. Why should sociologists study such matters? One reason is that they are interested in all the basic activities that make up social life, particularly the ways in which different activities relate to each other and contribute to the social whole that we refer to as society. Other academic disciplines, such as economics or politics, specialize in just

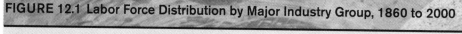

**FIGURE 12.1 Labor Force Distribution by Major Industry Group, 1860 to 2000**

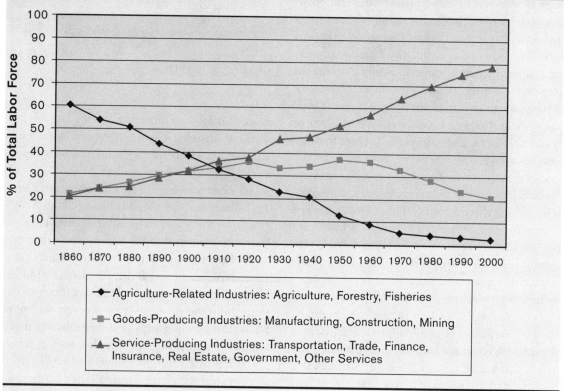

◆ Agriculture-Related Industries: Agriculture, Forestry, Fisheries

■ Goods-Producing Industries: Manufacturing, Construction, Mining

▲ Service-Producing Industries: Transportation, Trade, Finance, Insurance, Real Estate, Government, Other Services

*Sources:* Data for 1860–1940 adapted from U.S. Department of Commerce (1975); data for 1940–2000 adapted from U.S. Department of Labor (2005b).

one sphere of social activity, whereas sociologists take a broader view and do not give priority to any one sphere. Accordingly, the sociological approach to work and the economy proceeds along lines similar to those taken in studying other social institutions. There are two dimensions to the subject of work and the economy in modern society. The first is the structural dimension, which concerns the way work and the economy are organized. The second is the cultural dimension of work and economic organization—a dimension that encompasses values, norms, attitudes, thought, and expression.

The **economy** is the social institution that is primarily concerned with the production, distribution, and consumption of goods and services. Modern economists tend to define *economics* as the study of how people and social groups choose to employ scarce resources to produce various commodities and distribute them for consumption among various persons and groups in society (Samuelson 1947).

**Economy** The social institution primarily concerned with production, distribution, and consumption of goods and services.

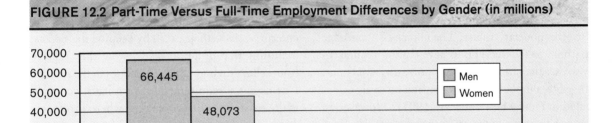

**FIGURE 12.2 Part-Time Versus Full-Time Employment Differences by Gender (in millions)**

*Source:* OECD (2005).

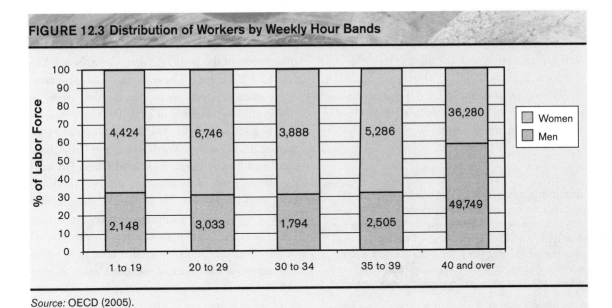

**FIGURE 12.3 Distribution of Workers by Weekly Hour Bands**

*Source:* OECD (2005).

This is a narrower focus than that of sociology, because it gives most of its attention to market processes—the ways in which exchanges of goods and services are organized. In traditional societies, exchange was often carried out through barter—exchange of one good for another, such as a cow for a sheep—whereas in modern market exchanges the primary medium of exchange is money. Hence, economists devote a great deal of their attention to calculating the effects on the price (monetary value) of goods and services due to changes in supply and demand. Sociologists, too, are interested in exchange and have developed their own exchange theories. They have also developed rational-choice theories to understand why people allocate scarce resources to areas not confined to exchanges that involve monetary values. The choice of a marriage partner, or the decision to have children, often involves calculations about opportunity costs and benefits, although the latter may not be easily calculated in money terms (Becker 1997). However, in this chapter we focus on economic institutions—the business sectors of society—and their relations with other institutions and dimensions of social life, such as politics, family and gender, and race and ethnicity. It is this broader, more holistic focus that distinguishes sociology from economics.

## STRUCTURE OF THE ECONOMY: ECONOMIC SYSTEMS

There are two major kinds of modern economic systems: capitalist and socialist. The **capitalist economic system** is one in which people and organizations invest their capital in the production of goods and services so as to make a profit—that is, to accumulate more capital wealth. Unlike the owners or capitalists, the workers receive most of their remuneration in wages. The owners of the enterprise make their profit by keeping their costs, including that of labor, below what they receive from selling their goods and services in the market. One essential requirement of a capitalist economy is the existence of free markets, where producers can compete with each other and freely enter into contracts to buy or sell, with a minimum of restrictive governmental regulation.

The alternative is the **socialist economic system,** in which the capital invested and the gains from production and supply of goods and services are vested in the state. In the twentieth century, from 1917 to 1989, there were socialist economies in Russia, then known as the Union of Soviet Socialist Republics (USSR), and the states it dominated in Eastern Europe (Hungary, Poland, Romania, Bulgaria, and Czechoslovakia) and in other parts of the world (China, Cuba, North Korea, and Vietnam). These state-run economies, sometimes referred to as communist, were, in nearly all cases, moving in a capitalist direction by the beginning of the twenty-first century—although a few, such as North Korea and Cuba, have remained largely communist, and China has kept significant parts of its economy under state direction, with its political life still under the ultimate control of the ruling Communist Party. At various times, such as the period after World War II (1939–1946), capitalist societies have tried to introduce some elements of socialism, such as state ownership of utilities, transport, or basic resources (e.g., electricity, railroads, coal). These **mixed economic systems** were common in Western European countries, such as Britain, France, and Scandinavia. State ownership has declined in favor of privatization since the 1980s, although the state may continue to exercise some regulation of such industries. Regulatory agencies range from ensuring fair competition to acting on behalf of consumers and preventing excessive prices. All of the most advanced economies, including the United

**Capitalist economic system** A type of modern economic system in which people and organizations invest capital in the production of goods and services to make a profit. Workers invest their labor and, in turn, receive wages. Owners, on the other hand, make a profit by keeping their costs low. Capitalism requires a free market in which producers can compete with one another and freely enter into contracts to buy or sell.

**Socialist economic system** A type of modern economic system in which the capital invested and the profits from production and supply of goods and services are vested in the state. The twentieth century witnessed socialist economies in Russia (then the USSR), Eastern Europe, Cuba, and parts of Asia (China, North Korea, and Vietnam). Nearly all of these state-run economies have since been transformed in a capitalist direction; the exceptions are North Korea, China, and Cuba, which have kept significant parts of their economy under the control of the state.

States, can be described as mixed economies if one takes account of the fact that the biggest employer is central and local government.

Capitalism has been the predominant economic system since modern societies emerged from subsistence economies—traditional, agricultural societies in which most items produced were consumed by the producers themselves. These agricultural societies, which existed some 5,000 years ago, were preceded by even simpler hunter-and-gatherer economies. The introduction of the plow, often pulled by horses, began to produce a surplus, which meant that not everyone was needed for food production; some people could now specialize in trades, such as making tools and other articles. At this point, it became possible to build permanent settlements (towns) and conduct trade. The first capitalists were traders and craftsmen, who employed others to work for them for wages. This was the rudimentary form of capitalism that persisted until the Industrial Revolution, which began in the second half of the eighteenth century in Western Europe and North America.

The Industrial Revolution transformed traditional and mainly agricultural economies into the modern form of industrial capitalism, with power-driven machinery in factories engaged in mass production of commodities for sale at a profit. The first factories depended on water power, but the invention of the steam engine by the English engineer James Watt in 1765 increased the power and speed of machines and the rate at which they could produce goods, such as cotton cloth. This kind of factory production led to increased division of labor whereby workers performed very limited and repetitive tasks, in contrast to the broader range of skills of traditional craft workers; factory workers in town were also completely dependent on the employer, having been cut off from other sources of income and food, such as those available in the rural areas. The capitalist owners were at the mercy of the market; any reduction in demand for their goods brought pressure to re-duce prices, which meant cutting costs, especially labor costs. This could be done in several ways: laying off workers, reducing wages, employing cheaper workers (such as women and children), speeding up machinery, and spending less on maintaining tolerable working conditions. Workers attempted to resist these pressures by gathering together in trade unions and threatening to strike. At its peak, trade union membership accounted for almost 25 million non-farmworkers in America. This figure had dropped to 18 million by the late 1990s.

In the first part of the twentieth century, the major change in employment was the decline in the number of workers employed in the primary sector of the economy—agriculture and the extraction of raw materials such as coal, oil, and minerals. The major growth was in the secondary or manufacturing sector, which produced automobiles and household goods. The second half of the twentieth century saw a drop in the number of workers employed in manufacturing and a rise in the number of jobs in the service sector. And the end of the century witnessed the transition from an **industrial economy** based on mass production of manufactured goods to a **service economy** in which the

---

**Mixed economic system** A type of modern economic system in which elements of socialism (e.g., state ownership of utilities) are introduced into an otherwise capitalist society. Britain, France, and Scandinavia are examples of countries with mixed economic systems. Historically, such systems have tended toward capitalism.

**Industrial economy** An economy characterized by the employment of large numbers of workers in the mass production of manufactured goods (e.g., on conveyor-belt-driven assembly lines at factories). The industrial economy reached its peak during the twentieth century.

**Service economy** An economy devoted to supplying services, such as information processing, teaching, nursing, advertising, marketing, or food.

largest part of the economy is devoted to supplying services, such as information processing, teaching, nursing, advertising, marketing, and food. (For further discussion of this topic, see Chapter 18, on social change, collective action, and social movements.) Of course, manufacturing still goes on in what is sometimes referred to as postindustrial America, and the value of its output has increased, but there has been a significant change in employment patterns. At its height, the industrial economy was characterized by the employment of large numbers of workers in the mass production of manufactured goods, working on conveyor-belt-driven assembly lines at factories like the giant Ford motor plant in Detroit. By the end of the twentieth century the U.S. had become a service economy, with 70 percent of the labor force employed in service work. This has been described as the transition from Fordism to post-Fordism.

The history of the modern capitalist economy presents two contrasting pictures: a constant drive to increase organizational efficiency and productivity, on the one hand, and inequalities and conflicts between capitalists and workers, on the other.

## ORGANIZATION OF WORK

How and why work is organized the way it is has been a major issue in capitalist countries such as the United States. Karl Marx emphasized that, despite the conflict it generated, capitalist organization was the most dynamic economic force for bringing about modernization the world had seen. Its ceaseless drive to improve efficiency in order to make profits meant that it was always seeking new technological and organizational solutions. For example, the early textile industry was based on the domestic system, in which most of the production of cotton material was carried out in people's homes on machines provided by the capitalist. Then, some capitalists invested in newly invented,

power-driven machinery that could be most efficiently run continuously in factories. The other great sociological writer on economic life, Max Weber, maintained that the essence of modern capitalism is the rational calculation of monetary profit and loss. This formal rational calculation, he argued, has replaced earlier, less rational motives such as those based on allegiance to traditional values or traditional authority. Weber believed that the coercive organization of economic life typical of slave societies and feudal societies, and even that of early capitalism, was not a viable basis for organizing modern society. The most rational form of organization, in principle if not always in practice, was the modern bureaucracy—*a large hierarchical organization governed by formal rules and having a clear specification of work tasks that are carried out by suitably qualified officials.*

The advantage of bureaucracy, Weber said, is that it's technically more efficient than traditional forms of organization. It also has the advantage of giving workers the sense that power in the organization is based on rational rules and regulations, and that these govern the allocation of duties and rewards. The key characteristics of employees and their work situation in a bureaucracy, according to Weber, are as follows:

- ✓ Employees are personally free, subject to authority only with respect to their impersonal official obligations.
- ✓ They are organized in a clearly defined hierarchy of offices.
- ✓ The office is defined by competence, and candidates are selected for their technical qualifications.
- ✓ The office is filled by a free contractual relationship.
- ✓ Employees are remunerated by fixed salaries in money.
- ✓ The office is treated as the sole, or at least the primary, occupation of the incumbent.
- ✓ This occupation constitutes a career.

In the post–World War II economy, large, hierarchical, bureaucratic offices were thought to be the most efficient form of work organization. (Underwood and Underwood/Corbis)

✓ The official's work is entirely separated from ownership of the means of administration.

✓ Employees are subject to strict and systematic control in the conduct of the office. (Based on Weber 1947: 333–334)

Admittedly, this is not how most people think of bureaucracy today, whatever they may have thought in Weber's time at the beginning of the twentieth century. For example, for much of the post–World War II period, sociological research on this issue was framed by debates about the efficiencies and dysfunctions of bureaucracy. To some people, bureaucracy was dysfunctional because it meant just a lot of red tape that got in the way of real efficiency. As one worker in a bureaucratically organized insurance company put it: "I'm in a framework, a corporate framework, where I have to abide by their rules and regulations for everything, which get to me because of all the bureaucratic junk that I have to go through to complete something. I know there's a faster way to do something, but I have to follow their ways, which is frustrating sometimes" (quoted in Burris 1983: 157).

Organizational sociologists have sought to understand the conditions under which bureaucracy is and isn't an efficient way to organize work (Lawrence and Lorsch 1967; Dimaggio and Powell 1983). Many agree that the formal rules of bureaucracy were originally necessary for avoiding unpredictability and corruption in organizations; but, then, many organizational gurus began to advocate giving workers more independence and

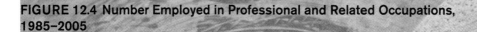

**FIGURE 12.4 Number Employed in Professional and Related Occupations, 1985–2005**

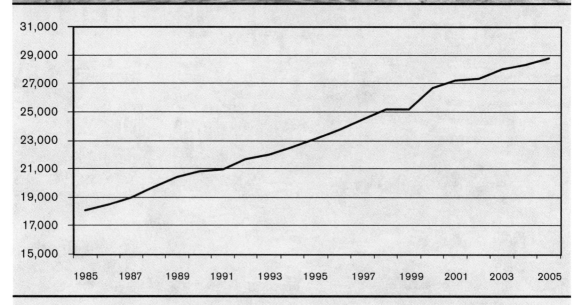

*Source:* Adapted from customized tables, U.S. Department of Labor (2005b).

stripping out hierarchies to make the organization flatter and leaner (Peters and Waterman 1982). The jury is still out on the question of whether the latter is a recipe for greater efficiency, although it is certainly widely believed to be so.

**Professionals** Workers characterized by control of a large body of abstract, formal knowledge; substantial autonomy from supervision; authority over clients as well as subordinate occupational groups; and the claim that they will use their knowledge for the benefit of their clients, putting their clients' interests above their own when necessary.

**Craft workers** Employees who combine an intense pride in their work with a broad knowledge of tools, materials, and processes as well as manual skills acquired by long training and experience.

For a long time, some groups of workers were spared the close supervision and hierarchical management of bureaucracy. This was particularly the case with independent professionals and skilled craft workers. **Professionals** are characterized by (1) control of a large body of abstract, formal knowledge; (2) substantial autonomy from supervision; (3) authority over clients as well as subordinate occupational groups; and (4) the claim that they will use their knowledge for the benefit of their clients, putting their clients' interests above their own when necessary (Hodson and Sullivan 1995). The largest professions, in rank order, are those of teachers, health-related professionals (such as doctors, dentists, and nurses), engineers, writers and entertainers, computer scientists, social workers, and lawyers (Hodson and Sullivan 1995). **Craft workers** constitute about 10 percent of the labor force in advanced economies. They

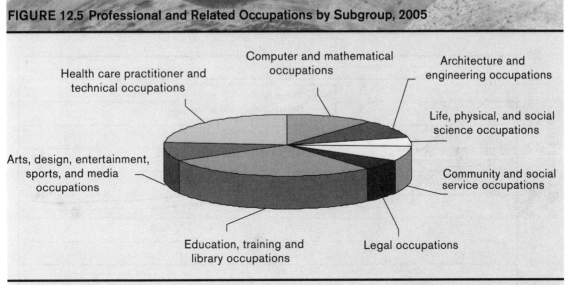

FIGURE 12.5 Professional and Related Occupations by Subgroup, 2005

*Source:* Adapted from U.S. Department of Labor (2005a).

combine intense pride in their work with a broad knowledge of tools, materials, and processes as well as manual skills acquired through long training and experience. Their occupation range includes tool and die makers; power-plant operators; mechanics and repairers; telephone-line installers and repairers; heating, air conditioning, and refrigeration mechanics; heavy-equipment mechanics; and carpenters, electricians, painters, and plumbers. (See Figures 12.4 and 12.5 for additional information concerning professional and related occupations.)

Both professionals and craft workers went through a period in the twentieth century when their independence was gradually reduced as they were absorbed into the bureaucracies and mass-production assembly lines of modern economic organizations. For example, the medical profession was transformed from an organizational structure based on private or group practice to one based on large hospitals (or multiple hospital systems) and health maintenance organizations (Fennell and Alexander 1993). However, it is possible that some

professionals and craft workers may be regaining a certain independence as organizations shed full-time workers and buy the services of self-employed professionals and craft workers as and when needed. These could include some of the computer specialists featured in Michael Lewis's story.

In Figure 12.6, we observe a sharp decline between 1950 and 1980 in the percentage of U.S. workers who were self-employed. By the turn of the century, however, the rate of self-employment seems to have leveled off. Indeed, there is some indication that it may be increasing: From 2002 to 2003, the number of self-employed workers increased for the first time, rising from 7.3 percent to 7.5 percent of the total labor force, and from 6.7 percent to 6.9 percent of the nonagricultural labor force.

## CONFLICT AND CONTROL

In the first half of the twentieth century, social scientists and engineers devoted significant attention

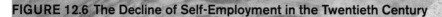

**FIGURE 12.6 The Decline of Self-Employment in the Twentieth Century**

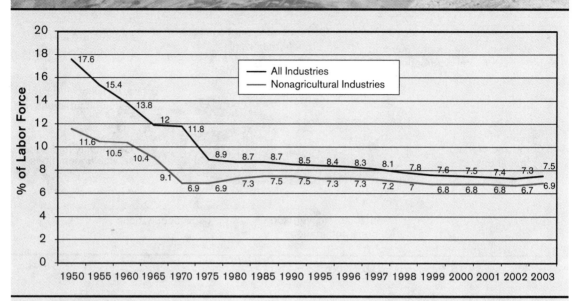

*Source:* U.S. Department of Labor (2003).

to methods of increasing the productivity of manufacturing organizations through the rationalization of work practices. This rationalization process became the focus of American industrial engineer Frederick Taylor (1911), who developed the system of "scientific management" that became known as **Taylorism.** He believed there was "one best way" to do every task. One could discover that way by first carefully observing how the workers do the task and then devising a more efficient way to do it. Taylor was also concerned about

**Taylorism** A system of "scientific management" developed by industrial engineer Frederick Taylor. Taylor believed that there was one best way to perform every task, and that this way could be discovered by observing workers and then developing a more efficient means of accomplishing their work. His ideas were the predecessors to modern quality control as well as the modern industrial ethic behind Fordism.

long-serving workers who resisted working as fast as managers demanded; he recommended firing such workers and training unskilled workers who would accept lower wages. Taylor's ideas were developed into the principles associated with modern quality control and scientific management, which are based on the establishment of uniform practices under close control and scrutiny of management (Scott 1981: 39). Such principles played a role in the design of the automatic assembly line developed by the Ford Motor Company and were copied throughout the world—including communist Russia. This early, modern industrial system—of standardized procedures, assembly-line production, and tight managerial control—is the quintessence of Fordism.

The principles of scientific management took little account of the "human side of enterprise"—the needs, desires, and attitudes of human beings. In *The Functions of the Executive* (1950), Chester Barnard, an American writer on management, ar-

The principle of scientific management used at automobile factories like this one was copied throughout the world in the belief that it would increase economic productivity. (Bettmann/Corbis)

gued that organizations are essentially cooperative systems that serve to integrate the contributions of their individual participants. He defined a formal organization as "that kind of cooperation among men that is conscious, deliberate, purposeful" (Barnard 1968: 4). In order for participants to willingly cooperate and give their fullest efforts they must be induced to do so, not only through material rewards but also through symbolic and emotional inducements such as prestige, personal satisfaction, opportunities for development, and, above all, a sense of common purpose. Indeed, according to Barnard (1968: 87), "the inculcation of belief in the real existence of a common purpose" is the principal duty of every executive.

While Barnard's understanding of the nonmaterial dimensions of organization anticipated the "cultural turn" in postmodern organizational studies, for a long time most sociologists of work and organizations remained focused on the material and vertical structures in the work process. They interpreted even the introduction of computing as reinforcing this emphasis. The publication of Henry Braverman's *Labor and Monopoly Capital* (1974) influenced some sociologists by refocusing the debate on the issue emphasized by Marx: conflict over control in organizations. Braverman argued that owners and managers organize and control work—the labor process—in whatever way will get the most productivity out of workers for the least cost. For example, they will introduce new machinery and organize labor to work with it only if they can be sure that it will increase profits. Braverman maintained that capitalists sought to de-skill workers by building their skills into the machines, with the aim of reducing workers' power.

The debate about whether workers' skills have been upgraded or downgraded as a result of changes in technology and organization is by no means resolved. Perhaps it depends on whether you look at the entire economy, which yields some evidence of upgrading, or at specific occupations that provide evidence of downgrading (Form

**Formal organization** A cooperative system that serves to integrate the contributions of individual participants. Formal organizations have an official structure, with formal rules and sanctions governing the operation of the system. They contrast with informal organizations, which refer to the various unofficial practices that develop within the organization, often initiated by employees.

**De-skill** A term referring to the process by which workers' skills are built into machines, thus removing the necessity and value of the workers themselves. This process originated with the emergence of capitalism and factory labor, and it continues today as a function of the increasing abilities of computers and technologies.

1987; Spenner 1983). Upgrading occurs in occupations when workers develop new skills in order to make use of computerized machines. By contrast, older skilled crafts, such as printing, have suffered a net loss in the breadth of the skills precisely because of computerized processes. Automation and scientific management have de-skilled many production workers, but skilled workers have become even more indispensable in advanced production systems; indeed, skilled craft workers are essential for the operation and maintenance of sophisticated robotics devices and automated production equipment. Moreover, there has also been a continued growth of professional occupations to more than 20 percent of the labor force in the advanced economies of the world. If the growing occupational groups classified as semi-professionals and technicians (such as dental hygienists and laboratory assistants) are taken into account, the share of the workforce rises to 25 percent (Hodson 2001: 31).

Rather than rushing to make wide generalizations about de-skilling and other changes in work and organization, some researchers have preferred to analyze specific factors in terms of how they vary in different occupations and organizations. Toward this end they have carried out ethnographic case studies in particular work locations. One influential sociologist, Michael Burawoy (1979), combined Marxist ideas about the exploitation of workers with ethnographic case studies of the culture of particular workplaces. Rather than appealing to statistical evidence for making generalizations about the effects of economic changes on workers, Burawoy made a case study of how individual workers came to terms with the de-

Playing around on the job is one form of resistance to the demands employers place on workers, which sometimes ignore their human needs. (iStockphoto)

mands that bosses made on them in their particular work situation. Workers consented to labor conditions, Burawoy found, because they were drawn into a game of **making out,** in which they personally felt they had freedom to resist management pressure and to come out ahead.

Subsequent ethnographic studies have tried to determine where it is possible to make generalizations and where not. For instance, sociologist Randy Hodson (2001) made a comparison of studies of ways in which workers are able to put up resistance to management pressures. He categorized the workers' resistance strategies as either passive or active. Playing dumb, withholding enthusiasm, and avoiding work are examples of passive strategies of resistance. Active strategies include various forms of machine sabotage and social sabotage (such as chronically criticizing supervisors in their absence). Other forms of resistance strategy are strikes, absenteeism, making up games, inventing unofficial status hierarchies as al-

**Making out**  Introduced by Michael Burowoy, a term referring to workers' willingness to consent to labor conditions inasmuch as they have the freedom to resist management pressures and still come out ahead.

ternatives to those imposed by management, being a *smooth operator*, and the extreme strategy of theft of company property. The kind of resistance that tends to be put up varies according to occupation and type of organization. Workers with few skills and little job interest often have to resort to trivial forms of resistance in order to transform their regimented work life into something more personal and satisfying. Playing around on the job is one such strategy. An ethnographer noted the aggressive play typical of concrete workers:

> At one sewer plant project, one favorite pastime was ripping the clothes of one of the concrete finishers. Pete's clothing inevitably had some tear or hole. The men always teased him about his tattered work clothing. A number of times, one of the foremen and Pete would engage in a clothes-tearing fight. Each man would try to get his finger into a hole in the other man's shirt or pants and then pull. Away would come a shirt or pants leg, revealing bare limbs that would set off peals of laughter from the other men. (Applebaum 1981: 33)

Another strategy is that of creating an alternative status hierarchy, such as by undermining the authority of superiors through humor or insults. Workers may also engage in a variety of strategies to make their work less burdensome. The expression *making out*, noted above, is often used to describe ways of organizing one's job to get the work done without being exhausted at the end of the day. The strategy of the *smooth operator* is different; it describes workers who manage to get extra rewards through carefully calculated actions. An ethnography of Pullman porters describes one porter as carefully calibrating his answer to a passenger's question, thus increasing his chance of getting a good tip:

> I had Mrs. Will Rogers, practically on her deathbed. I had to lift her from one bed to another, accompanied by a nurse in the room, and I had to pick her up out of this bed and put her over on this bed, and vice versa, as long as we could keep her comfortable. So on one occasion, while I was doing that thing, she asked me, "Porter, how much do you think I weigh?" She didn't weigh but a feather. I said, "You weigh 135 pounds." So she said, "Thank you!" And when she got off, I got 135 skins! Beautiful! (Quoted in Santino 1989: 72)

Of course, some workers, rather than resisting management, engage in cooperative behaviors whereby they give extra effort so as to maintain efficiency. In his review of ethnographic studies, Hodson (2001) was able to distinguish among and measure a number of these recurring forms of cooperative, or citizenship, behavior. These citizenship measures included commitment to organizational goals, pride in work, extra effort, extra time, peer training, insider knowledge, good soldiering, and loyalty to a particular manager. Peer training entailed volunteering to help train co-workers. The *good soldier*, for instance, was a worker who gave full effort in spite of obstacles. And *insider knowledge*, as a form of cooperation, is particularly evident among professional and craft workers, who can draw on sophisticated skills and work practices including significant autonomy from managerial oversight to solve problems. Interestingly, occupations with large numbers of female workers or racial minority workers tended to have less autonomy and creativity (Hodson 2001: 166; see also England 1992).

## THE CULTURAL DIMENSION: VALUES AND ATTITUDES AT WORK

In terms of organizational structure, professional and craft workers enjoy many advantages over other workers in their capacity to resist managerial pressures. They tend to have much greater autonomy and freedom from close supervision. And perhaps more significantly, with respect to the cultural dimension, they have more organization-independent sources to draw on in giving meaning to their work. These sources are based on professional craft ideals of creativity, skill, service, and standards as well as on professional or craft associations that help to maintain such ideals and resist pressures to sacrifice them. However, every type of occupation and organization involves certain forms of "meaning construction." Some physically demanding blue-collar occupations, such as that of construction workers, are given meaning and a sense of identity through the value placed on the following physical characteristics:

> Physical strength and stamina … play a large part in determining construction workers' self respect. … Much construction work involves hard physical labor under trying conditions. Construction men must develop the stamina to persevere through very adverse conditions—extreme cold; arm-weary shoveling; leg-weary sloshing through mud; the chilling effect of high winds; the back-straining pushing and lifting of heavy weights. Men who do this work are proud of their physical capabilities. (Applebaum 1981: 32–33)

Meaning at work can also be attained through the construction of individual and social identities that impart a sense of pride and self-respect, even though these feelings are not directly related to production. For example, both Hodson's (2001) ethnographic study of construction workers and his study of women workers on an assembly line found that work-related identities can take on gender-related aspects. The construction workers' sense of *masculinity* was strengthened by their physical prowess and toughness at work. And the female assembly workers confirmed the importance of their *feminine*, family-based roles through their focus at work on celebrating birthdays, weddings, showers, and other personal events. As noted elsewhere in this book, masculine and feminine identities are cultural constructions that have effects on many social institutions—economic ones included.

National work cultures also vary. In the 1970s, American managers went through a period of wondering whether Japanese work cultures, with their stress on team building and collective responsibility, had something to teach American companies. Some of those ideas and attitudes have been adopted, although they've had to be translated into forms compatible with American values. Americans have always viewed work as central to their lives and as a key source of individual identity. Some historical sociologists have traced this tendency back to its roots in the "Protestant ethic" (Weber 1904), whereby work is deemed an individual's vocation as given by God and one that the individual must pursue in a self-disciplined way. A study by Nancy Morse and Robert Weiss in 1955 showed that work was indeed a central life interest for the vast majority of Americans: Eighty percent of men said that they would continue to work even if they did not have to do so for economic reasons. Since the 1970s as well, the annual General Social Survey (GSS) have consistently shown that about 70 percent of Americans say they would continue to work. Statistics on hours worked confirm these results using behavioral data. Americans work more hours than people in any other country except, significantly, Japan (Schor 1991). Despite this similarity, however, Japanese workers identify with the collectivity of the company and are concerned about how they are regarded by it, whereas American workers appear to be motivated by more individualistic considerations.

An indicator of the meaning of work is what people feel is important in their jobs. Since 1973, responses to the GSS reveal that Americans have consistently rated "intrinsic" aspects of work—having a job that gives them a feeling of accomplishment—as the job characteristic they prefer above all, even more than "extrinsic" rewards such as promotions and income. This finding has been confirmed by other surveys as well (National Academy Press 1999). Clearly, then, in the United States, with its great emphasis on individual autonomy, obtaining intrinsic rewards is important not only for job satisfaction but also in the context of securing a commitment to the organization (Lincoln and Kalleberg 1990).

## THE FUTURE OF WORK, ORGANIZATION, AND THE ECONOMY

As we have seen, ethnographic studies of actual workplaces and of various occupations reveal many factors determining the extent to which workers can take action to maintain their freedom and a degree of autonomy from control. However, the largest scope for such individual freedom is enjoyed by skilled workers and professionals in certain sectors of the economy, such as computer software. One of the generalizations made by Michael Lewis was that growing numbers of such workers were increasing their individual freedom and mobility—either as a result of benefiting from employee stock ownership plans, cashing in, and moving on or because their skills were so much in demand that they could move easily from company to company. In addition, these workers were linked into loose informal networks with friends and colleagues in other firms, allowing them to exchange information and support—another factor making it easy for them to change jobs.

At the beginning of the new millennium, Silicon Valley seemed to represent this "new world" of work, in which the importance of information-age technology in wealth creation surpassed that of the mass-production assembly line—the very embodiment of the transition from Fordism to post-Fordism that we mentioned above. By 1996, Silicon Valley's new economy employed 1.13 million people—a figure approximating that of car manufacturing and exceeding that of many other old-economy industries. Silicon Valley, according

to one observer, exemplified "what people think about when they consider the future of work," describing it as "a useful laboratory because its economy is driven by the new business of the information-age technology" (Osterman 1999: 13). Founded by "people who rejected old bureaucratic or manufacturing organizational models," this economy was essentially "a community of enterprises that sometimes compete and sometimes cooperate" (Osterman 1999: 13). Boundaries between firms were very porous, with people moving easily between companies; and boundaries were blurred between social life and work, firms and local institutions, and managers and workers (Saxenian 1994: 56). The bureaucratic organization, as defined by Weber (1947)—that is, with fixed boundaries and hierarchy as well as predictable career paths through which employees ascended the ladder—was much less prevalent. Indeed, the image of the future economy evoked by Silicon Valley appealed to the ideologies of both Right and Left, presenting a picture of individualism *and* cooperation.

Does this remain an accurate picture today? In important respects it does. But the bursting of the high-tech bubble in 2001 allowed us to see that the rosy image of the new economy was misleading in certain other respects. In fact, the computer industry was only one part of the complex economy of Silicon Valley. Its highly skilled and well-paid computer workers were supported by large numbers of low-paid service workers, and racial economic inequality was significant. A study of the janitorial services industry in the Valley found a substantial shift toward outsourcing, largely to firms heavily staffed by legal and illegal Mexican and Central

**Outsourcing** The process by which corporations and businesses send work to off-site contractors (often outside the country) in order to avoid paying high wages or providing expensive benefits.

Not all workers have access to flexible postmodern work options; many immigrants to the United States are relegated to nineteenth-century-like labor conditions. (Bo Zaunders/Corbis)

con Valley as a model of the whole economy, inasmuch as it tends to attract an above-average number of college-educated workers, even among its ethnic minorities. This is not representative of the American labor market, where roughly three-quarters of employees lack a four-year college degree.

Just how real is the "new economy," then? Have the traditional labors of goods and service production really been replaced by a knowledge industry? For a significant number of native-born American workers, the answer to these questions is certainly yes. As Figure 12.7 shows, members of this group are far more likely to end up in office jobs (14.8 percent) or management positions (11.0 percent) than on an assembly line; indeed, the production occupations that were once synonymous with middle-class America are now no more popular than "education, training, and library" jobs (6.1 percent).

However, when we shift our focus from the top occupations of native-born workers to those of recent American immigrants—particularly Latino immigrants—the twenty-first-century economy suddenly seems a lot less "new." From this perspective, as illustrated in Figure 12.8, the contem-

American immigrants (Zlolniski 1994). Even among the most highly skilled workers, ethnic networks continued to play a big role in linking people to jobs, as evidenced by network names such as the Indian Professionals Association, the Korean American Society of Entrepreneurs, and the Monte Jade Science and Technology Association (Takahashi 1998). Also misleading is the notion of Sili-

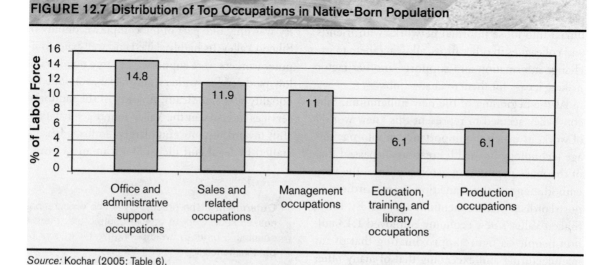

**FIGURE 12.7 Distribution of Top Occupations in Native-Born Population**

*Source:* Kochar (2005: Table 6).

**FIGURE 12.8 Distribution of Top Five Occupations of Foreign-Born Latino Workers**

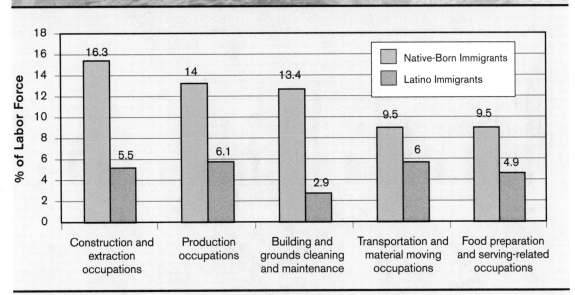

Source: Kochar (2005: Table 6).

porary U.S. economy more closely resembles the nineteenth century. Almost one-third of all foreign-born Latino laborers are employed in construction/extraction and production occupations (30.3 percent), as compared to just 11.6 percent of native-born workers. This asymmetry is even more pronounced with respect to building, grounds cleaning, and maintenance occupations, which employ the third-highest percentage of Latino immigrants (13.4 percent), but only a fraction of non-immigrants (2.9 percent). As Figure 12.9 makes clear, the same patterns can be observed at the industry level as well.

If Silicon Valley was never representative of the American work economy as a whole, we have to ask why its image, as presented in media stories such as that of Michael Lewis, seemed so agreeable. One reason is that it appealed to important elements in American values and ideology, such as individual freedom and enterprise. (See also our discussion of American culture in Chapter 3.) But

did its positive image also stem from presenting the most optimistic version of a more complicated picture? A special issue of the *New York Times Magazine* (March 5, 2000) captured only a few of the contradictory elements through its title "The Liberated, Exploited, Pampered, Frazzled, Uneasy New American Worker." The work situations and attitudes it described were those of what it called the **free agent,** an individual who does not seek jobs but, rather, is on the lookout for projects, new knowledge and information, and connectedness

**Free agent** An individual who does not seek jobs but, rather, is on the lookout for projects, new knowledge and information, and connectedness through the World Wide Web. Free agents do not require a physical location to work; what they do need is a powerful computer, programming languages, and access to the Internet. They have project contracts, not jobs, and run their own business operations.

**FIGURE 12.9 Distribution of Native- and Foreign-Born Populations Across Major Industries**

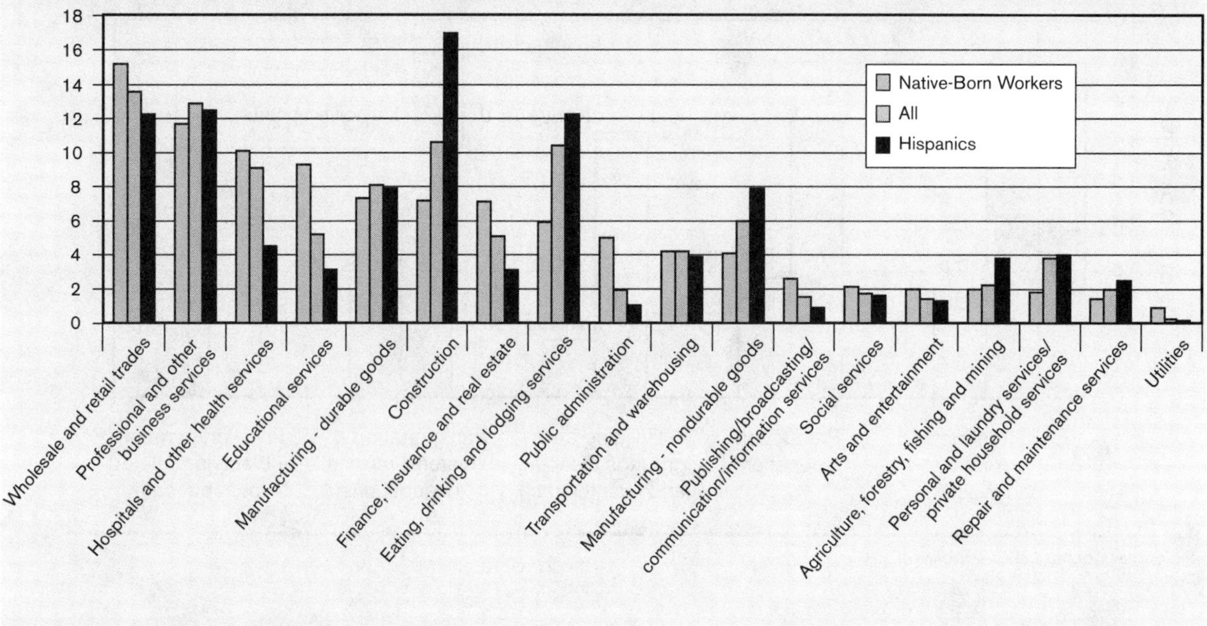

*Source:* Kochar (2005: Table 6).

through the World Wide Web. Such free agents do not require a single physical location in which to work. They simply need a powerful computer, state-of-the-art programming languages and database-management programs, and a password to access the Internet. They have project contracts, not jobs, and they run their own business operations. They are happy to see their start-up companies swallowed up by bigger firms, because they can then regroup and recombine their resources to find the next profitable gap in the market. In short, they are masters of their occupational fates rather than "microserfs" (Smith 2001: 157–158).

This description has at least some validity. But as Vicki Smith explains, it would be an exaggeration to extend it to the overall economy:

[D]espite the encroaching hegemony of this caricature, most American workers are eons away

from the abstract, cutting-edge world of dot.com innovators and agents. The majority of workers, like the photocopiers, the timber workers, and the assemblers, create the infrastructure that makes it possible for free agents to prosper. They continue to serve people in a multiplicity of service jobs; to construct roads, homes, office buildings and factories; to assemble the computers, modems, scanners, fax machines, and servers in those factories; to input and process data in those offices; to care for ill and vulnerable people; and to supervise and manage these legions of employees. They typically carry out these tasks in the employ of an owner or owners and in physical work settings—large and small companies, offices, factories, and other work sites that require bodily presence.

Unlike the mythical free agent, most workers lack the skills, and hence the bargaining power, to make the economy their oyster, to manipulate jobs and labor markets to their advantage. Most workers continue to be located in subordinate positions in hierarchies based on unequal power and to have their activities, efforts, and outcomes measured, evaluated, and disciplined. They are struggling to reach a part of the postindustrial terrain that is far from the territory of the mythical free agent. (2001: 158)

Some of the contradictions in this new work economy were the result of the emergence of postindustrialism—or what some prefer to call **deindustrialization.** Deindustrialization refers to the systematic disinvestment in a nation's manufacturing infrastructure (Bluestone and Harrison 1982). The crisis in profitability among manufacturing firms in the late 1970s and early 1980s, especially those in competition with more productive Japanese and other Far East plants, led to widespread plant closings and relocations. In the process, thousands of manufacturing jobs were eliminated and thousands more were moved to parts of the United States not previously identified with manufacturing (the Southeast and West) or to locations in other countries with lower labor costs, more favorable tax treatment, and lax environmental regulations. Some researchers have shown that communities are rarely able to attain the same income levels once manufacturing jobs are lost (Perrucci et al. 1993). Other researchers have studied the rise of the service sector; their work reveals some of the insecurities and pressures that accompany the growth of temporary work and unstable work careers (Biggart 1988; Hochschild 1983). For example, in *The Managed Heart: Commercialization of Human Feeling* (1983), Arlie Hochschild exposes the strains imposed on service workers such as airline cabin attendants, who must constantly control and manage their emotions in required ways when dealing with customers. And Nicole Biggart's *Charismatic Capitalism: Direct-Selling Organizations in America* (1988) chronicles the efforts of direct-selling agents, such as "Avon Ladies" and Tupperware agents, who were required to sell to their friends and acquaintances, often in their own homes.

It is no accident that some of the best case studies of work in the new economy, such as those by Hochschild and Biggart, are of women workers in service jobs. The most dramatic and far-reaching change in the increasingly diverse American labor force during the twentieth century was the expansion of women's labor-force participation from about 1 in 5 to about 3 in 5 between 1890 and the mid-1990s (National Academy of Sciences 1999). Meanwhile, the overall labor force grew from about 30 million people in 1900 (about 40 percent of the American population) to 145–150 million by the year 2000 (approximately half of the American population). Women's greater representation in the workforce has made some issues more pressing than they were when the labor force was predominantly male and the typical family consisted of a male breadwinner and a wife who stayed at home with the children. For example, issues of how to combine work life and family life occupy an increasingly prominent place on the agenda of managers as well as sociologists of work, who are concerned with how families cope with the stress of dual careers. (See also Chapter 7, on marriage and the family.)

Figure 12.10 shows the long rise in women's labor-force participation over the course of the twentieth century. In 1920, just a little more than 20 percent of women aged 25–44 participated in the labor market; today, that number has more than tripled, to 76.9 percent. Nevertheless, a significant **gender gap** remains with respect to labor-force participation, as evidenced by the 95 percent participation rate of men in that age group.

**Deindustrialization** Systematic disinvestment in a nation's manufacturing infrastructure.

**Gender gap** Broadly speaking, the difference between men's and women's labor-force participation.

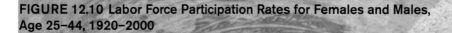

FIGURE 12.10 Labor Force Participation Rates for Females and Males, Age 25–44, 1920–2000

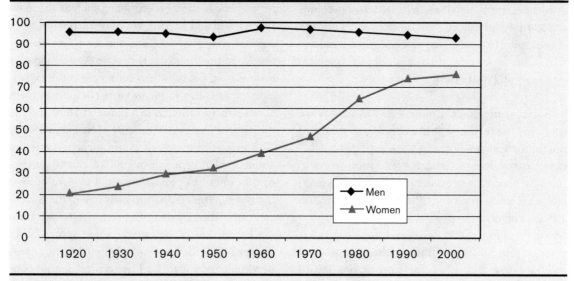

*Source:* Data for 1920–1990 from Goldin (1994); data for 2000 from U.S. Department of Labor (2003).

The growing proportion of nonwhites in the labor force, due to increased employment of women as well as large-scale immigration, has raised questions of how to manage diversity and to accommodate different cultures within the same workplace. It also highlights the disparity between whites and nonwhites in terms of working conditions and incomes. At the opposite end of the scale from the (mainly white) free agents featured in Michael Lewis's story titled "Heartache on Aisle 3: Sweatshop for Janitors" are many nonwhite workers laboring in very different conditions:

Faced with huge debts after a wave of consolidation, large supermarket chains are outsourcing to a shadowy system of subcontractors who recruit recent immigrants.

His name is Guadalupe Flores, and he works the midnight shift seven nights a week, stripping, waxing and buffing the floors of an upscale Fullerton supermarket.

He says he earns far less than the minimum wage, and just laughs when asked about overtime pay for his 56-hour weeks. Strong chemicals make his nose bleed, burn his fingers and eat the soles of his cheap sneakers. He operates powerful, potentially dangerous machines but isn't protected by workers' compensation insurance.

Flores sleeps on the floor of a tiny unfurnished one-bedroom house, where seven other supermarket janitors—all from remote ranching towns in central Mexico—stretch out on the dirty carpet. Most are young and new to California; some are still paying off the $1,500 smuggling fees that got them across the border.

Frightened, desperate and isolated, they and thousands of other vulnerable immigrants constitute a new class of sweatshop labor. Late at night, as unionized stockers tear through cartons of merchandise and a few bleary-eyed shoppers fill their carts, they are the anonymous figures at the end of the aisle, polishing the linoleum. (Cleland 2000: 1)

Outsourcing work to contractors has become a common feature of the new work economy, encompassing both the "knowledge industry" of Silicon Valley and the menial work of cleaning supermarkets. Many jobs that once were filled by a firm's own staff have been contracted out. In the case of janitors' jobs, an official of the Service Employees International Union reported that it now represents only about 20 percent of the supermarket janitors in Southern California, whereas at one time most supermarket janitors were in-house employees earning union wages (Cleland 2000).

These developments suggest that the "ideal type" of modern work organization, as represented by the modern bureaucracy and the Fordist system of production, is no longer dominant in the postmodern economy. Indeed, this new economy is much more varied than its predecessor and even seems to be developing in contradictory directions. Whereas modernization involved increasing separation of the work situation from personal and family life (in contrast to traditional society), the use of computers and other electronic devices (scanners, fax machines, cell phones) has made possible an increase in work outside the bureaucratic office or factory. The home office is where many self-employed workers carry on their business, reflecting an erosion of the boundary between workplace and home. This outcome, which can be described as a postmodern incorporation of premodern conditions, is being matched by an erosion of the boundaries between work life and personal life. This, too, may entail a reinvention of older forms of organization. Nicole Biggart likened the direct-selling organizations featured in her study, such as Tupperware Home Parties, Shaklee Corporation, Amway, and Mary Kay Cosmetics, to "colonial peddlers"—salesmen who sold tools, tea, and liniment from door to door in colonial America. The late-twentieth-century resurgence of peddling, in the loosely organized form of "home office" operations of direct-selling organizations, has gone against the modern trend of bureaucratic

organization. The bureaucratic Organization Man, who was the subject of sociologist William H. Whyte's best-selling critique in 1956, and the Man in the Gray Flannel Suit, based on Sloan Wilson's novel, which became an award-winning movie that same year, were expected to exhibit "masculine" interactional skills as they made their way up the hierarchy. As Biggart notes, "Social action among bureaucratic officials is characterized by aggressive individualism and instrumentalism; the structure of the firm rewards independence and competition" (1988: 88–89). By contrast, interactions in direct-selling organizations incorporate "feminine" or "family" characteristics, stressing mutual caring and support, with networks of cooperation rather than hierarchical control. Such networks, in which family and friends may be recruited by salespeople as co-distributors of goods, break down the boundaries between the firm and its customers as well as between work relations and personal relations.

This tendency is not limited to direct-selling organizations: A similar blurring of boundaries has occurred in other organizations. Professionals and highly skilled craft workers have never taken easily to the rigid controls and hierarchies of bureaucracy. Firms are increasingly seeking to recreate and enhance, within the organization, the "human bonds" and personalistic relations that exist outside work. For example, one General Motors division, reminiscent of direct-selling organizations, held weeklong "family awareness workshops" so that workers and supervisors could practice making decisions together (Schlesinger 1987). Of course, service work cannot be subject to the same kind of direct supervision as manual labor. Some services depend on the creation of a social relationship between a worker and a customer, and this cannot be produced at the turn of a switch. (For example, an airline cabin attendant must create a believable performance of friendliness toward passengers.) The more employees can be persuaded to genuinely embrace the appropriate emotional posture, the better the performance, and the more business interests are served.

> The emotional orientation of much service work, the dedication to standards required of professionals, and the commitment to a fellow employee's success or safety cannot be managed effectively from without. Only the wholehearted complicity of the person of the worker produces quality work. Physical labor can be extracted through supervision, but intellectual, emotional, and morally committed labor is more elusive. It requires commitment to ideals as well as routines and to people as well as positions. (Biggart 1988: 170)

## FROM MODERNITY TO POSTMODERNITY

Modernity was characterized by the differentiation of activities into specialized institutions, such as the separation of the family institution and the economic institution. Each had its particular form of interaction and organization. The modern economy was characterized by relatively impersonal and instrumental interactions, and the typical form of organization was the bureaucracy. The family institution was characterized by broad personal interactions and emotional bonds. However, in postmodernity we are witnessing *dedifferentiation*, whereby these modern separations and boundaries are breaking down. Of course, sociological studies of modern bureaucracies in the mid-twentieth century showed that the separation of formal work relations from informal human relations was never complete (Gouldner 1954). What is different about postmodernity is not just the rising percentage of service work; indeed, it has also witnessed the proliferation of corporate "makeovers" that aim to submit older organizations to cultural changes that blur the boundaries between work and the rest of life. Some efforts at cultural

change in organizations have drawn on New Age spirituality, with its emphasis on self-actualization, and on humanistic therapies to unlock the self's potential. Key figures in this regard include Abraham Maslow, who claimed that "work can be psychotherapeutic or psychogogic (making people grow towards self-actualization" (1965: 1); Douglas McGregor, whose "theory Y" offered management ways "to realize the potential represented by its human resources" (1960: 48); and Frederick Herzberg, who emphasized the "need as a human to grow psychologically" (1966: 71). More recently, sociologist Steven Tipton has commented that "the meaning of mundane work has been redeemed by coupling it with a sacred career," by treating it as a means to the sacred end of "expanding your aliveness" (Tipton 1982: 216). In using the word *career* Tipton is referring not to the modern-era notion of a lifetime career spent in one occupation and probably in one firm but, rather, to the career of developing the self, which is seen as divine or sacred.

Postmodernity is characterized by a confusing and yet symptomatic mixture of old and new forms of work organization. Modern bureaucracies still exist, but they incorporate or coexist with other forms of organization; some of these seem similar to premodern forms (e.g., spiritual motivations), whereas others constitute new developments (e.g., the electronic "virtual" network of coworkers linked only by Internet communication).

This cultural change in the economy is partly a legacy of the counterculture of the 1960s, which, in turn, can be described as a reaction against the regulations and impersonal rationality of modern bureaucratic organization and the alienating conditions of factory work. Although the counterculture appeared to be a revolt against modern capitalism, it also assisted the transition from Fordism to post-Fordism—that is, from industrial to postindustrial society. In *The Coming of Post-Industrial Society* (1974), Daniel Bell links the economic changes that occurred in the late twenti-

The cultural turn in the workplace puts more of a premium on worker interaction and more humanistic employment practices, including concern for equal rights for women and people of color. (iStockphoto)

eth century to cultural changes, especially the development of a more highly educated workforce capable of thinking and acting independently. Indeed, workers are now more flexible and self-regulating; they have their own sources of motivation and are not solely dependent on the organization to motivate and control them. Moreover, the post-Fordist economy, unlike its predecessor, is not dominated by industrial factories engaged in the mass production of standardized goods. Consequently, it has less need of close supervision of workers, who under Fordism had been confined to narrow, repetitive tasks. Under post-Fordism, workers have broader and more flexible skills and are allowed more autonomy and responsibility. The post-Fordist manufacturing process is based on "flexible specialization" (Piore and Sabel 1984), whereby products are varied, by means of flexible computer systems, to suit the demands of different market segments rather than being locked

into the mass production of a few standard models (e.g., the black Model T Ford of the 1930s). Today, the customer expects and is given more choice.

The availability of technology that makes it possible to produce a wide variety of consumer goods and to produce goods more quickly and cheaply has led some commentators to describe postmodern society as *consumer society*. The implication of this term is that affluent Western societies are increasingly being organized around consumption. Yet, while consumerism certainly has spread throughout every social class in advanced capitalist societies, many Americans report that work remains central to their identity. The culture of work has changed, but for most people, whether lower-paid janitors or highly remunerated professionals and executives, work still takes up a large chunk of their time—larger than that devoted to leisure and shopping.

## CONCLUSION

Michael Lewis's *New York Times* story of work in the new economy presented an attractive picture of trends in work patterns that may well become the norm in the future. However, there are many reasons to be cautious about these predictions, as we have seen. The story Lewis told may be accurate for some sections of the population, but it does not cover many others, whose constituents remain the majority. Indeed, for some workers, work is clearly as hard, low-paid, and insecure as ever. This particularly applies to many female and ethnic-minority workers.

There are many terms associated with the new economy, including *post-Fordism, postindustrial society, flexible specialization,* and *consumer society.* All of these terms describe the work changes that characterize the emerging postmodern society, each highlighting a different aspect of the ongoing changes in advanced capitalist economies. They are also linked to wider processes, such as *globalization,* which describes the transformation of capitalism into an integrated global economy, the worldwide spread of common cultural products, and flows of information and people. The most advanced forms of globalization can be seen in the organization of multinational corporations and in the increasingly fast electronic transfers of financial capital around the world. However, globalization also entails an international division of labor, whereby certain economic processes previously carried on within a single economy are now divided up and transferred to other parts of the world, depending on where costs are lowest. Some parts of the global economy are more advanced than others and possess more of the characteristics associated with the various *post-* conditions.

This is not to say that any society, even the highly developed United States, is completely of the *post-* type. Yet, while most *post-* changes are partial and incomplete, it is possible, as we have seen in this chapter, to observe and even measure economic developments along these lines. We must remember, nonetheless, that there is nothing inevitable about the shape of the future, including that of work and the economy.

# EXERCISES

## Exercise 1

Take another look at Figure 12.1, which shows the changes that occurred in the percentages of U.S. workers employed in agriculture, manufacturing, and the service sector during the period 1860–2000. How would you explain the dramatic increase in manufacturing jobs between 1860 and 1920 and the decline of manufacturing and the rise of the service sector in the late twentieth century? In answering this question, try to utilize several of the theoretical concepts and distinctions discussed in this chapter (e.g., division of labor, industrialization, post-Fordism).

## Exercise 2

Figure 12.6 illustrates how the number of self-employed workers in the United States has changed over the past fifty years. Based on our discussions in this chapter, how would you explain the recent rise of self-employment? What might be some of the social and cultural forces driving this change? Given the flexibility involved in self-employment, do you think self-employed workers are predominantly women or men? Why?

# STUDY QUESTIONS

1. What are the main differences between capitalist and socialist economic systems? What are the features of "mixed" economic systems?

2. To what does the term *division of labor* refer? How did the Industrial Revolution transform the division of labor in society?

3. Define Max Weber's concept of *bureaucracy*. What aspects of the modern bureaucracy make it an efficient way to organize work? What aspects make it inefficient?

4. What are the four defining characteristics of "professionals"? List some examples of professional occupations.

5. Henry Braverman argued that capitalists organize the work process in whatever way will minimize labor costs, and thus maximize productivity. Is this a "structural" explanation of the labor process? Or is it a "cultural" explanation? Discuss the implications of both.

6. Why are the concepts of *meaning* and *identity* important for understanding work? What role does gender play in the construction of workers' identities?

7. Have technological changes led to a downgrading or an upgrading of worker skills? Explain why.

8. Describe how outsourcing has changed the way work is organized for supermarket janitors in Southern California. In what way does outsourcing represent the transition from Fordist to post-Fordist production?

9. This transition to post-Fordist production has been described as one of dedifferentiation, which involves the erosion of institutional boundaries. Give three examples of boundaries that have been blurred or undermined under the post-Fordist system.

10. Ethnographic studies of workplace behavior distinguish between strategies of "resistance" and "cooperation." Give three examples of workers' resistance strategies as well as three examples of cooperation.

## FURTHER READING

Bell, Daniel. 1973. *The Coming of Post-Industrial Society: A Venture in Social Forecasting.* New York: Basic Books.

Braverman, Henry. 1974. *Labor and Monopoly Capital: The Degradation of Work in the Twentieth Century.* New York: Monthly Review Press.

Burawoy, Michael. 1979. *Manufacturing Consent: Changes in the Labor Process under Monopoly Capitalism.* Chicago: University of Chicago Press.

Durkheim, Émile. 1893. *The Division of Labor in Society.* New York: Free Press. Reprinted in 1964.

Ehrenreich, Barbara. 2001. *Nickel and Dimed: On (Not) Getting By in America.* New York: Henry Holt.

Hochschild, Arlie Russell. 1997. *The Time Bind: When Work Becomes Home and Home Becomes Work.* New York: Henry Holt.

Lamont, Michèle. 2000. *The Dignity of Working Men: Morality and the Boundaries of Race, Class, and Immigration.* Cambridge, MA: Harvard University Press.

Marx, Karl, and Friedrich Engels. 1848. *The Communist Manifesto.* New York: Monthly Review Press. Reprinted in 1964.

# chapter 13

# Education

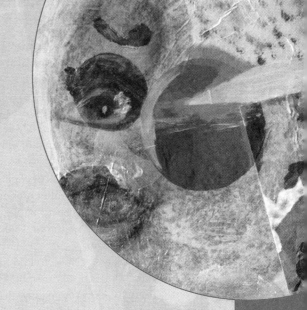

## media moments

### BASD Superintendent Links Academic, Societal Decline

**Thomas Doluisio Tells Rotary That American Youth Can't Compete Globally Without Higher Standards**

A lot has changed since Bethlehem Area School District Superintendent Thomas Doluisio was a student, and he doesn't like much of what he's seen.

Lack of parent involvement, declining academic achievement, disrespectful students, an eroding work ethic and declining social morals have made being an educator more difficult than ever before, Doluisio said.

"I think as a society, we need to look at some of these signals," Doluisio told members of the Bethlehem Rotary Club Wednesday afternoon during their weekly luncheon at the Bethlehem Club on New Street. "They're not good."

Today's educational environment is a sharp contrast to the standards expected when Doluisio graduated from high school in the 1950s.

Back then, he said, the presence of Bethlehem Steel meant few worries about finding a job or pursuing higher education.

"There was always a job available," Doluisio said. "Even high school dropouts were able to fulfill that middle class lifestyle with a home and a car, because the steel company was always there to take care of us."

Doluisio said the decline of Bethlehem Steel in many ways has resulted in a wake-up call for the region's public schools, where academic programs had become stagnant after years of complacency, leaving students ill-prepared for today's high-tech world.

"It's much more competitive out there, and you can't make the income you did at the steel company with very few skills," said Doluisio, who added that today's high school dropouts are more likely to earn $7 an hour at McDonald's than [to find] a middle class job.

"American kids are not competitive internationally anymore. American kids do not work hard enough. Work ethic is in decline, and I think that's a call to arms for public school districts across the nation."

*Source:* Berg (2000: B3).

The livin' promises to be anything but easy this summertime for Lindsay Rosenthal, 17. With senior year and college application season looming, the aspiring doctor from Burlingame, California, plans to shadow two Bay Area rheumatologists on their rounds. She will volunteer to buy groceries for AIDS patients, spend hours being tutored for SATs and, if there's any time left over, look for a paying gig. After a frenzied junior year filled with Advanced Placement courses, standardized exams and varsity tennis matches, what's wrong with whiling away the summer at the beach with a good novel? It just wouldn't wow admissions directors. "I really want to go to a school on the East Coast, and they're really competitive," Lindsay said. Getting into Ivy League and other elite schools has long been tough, but the bar keeps rising as competition intensifies. For stressed-out teenagers in the final throes of high school, that means more testing, more AP classes, more community service—in short, more resume-building. (Groves 2000: 1)

## media moments

### Dispositions Toward (Collective) Struggle and Educational Resilience in the Inner City

Benita (African American, low academic achiever, 16 years of age):

> My friends on the street. ... They say, "What can an education get you? You can sell drugs and get the same amount of money in a couple of days that you can make in a couple of years when you going to school and all that." ... At times I agree with them when I'm thinking of making money. 'Cause it be true. ... They say, "It's ... the White man taking over." They always saying the White man taking over. You can have fifty hundred years of high school and college, and the White man can come up in there with the same thing you got; they going to pick the White man over the Black man. ... We got a White president, a White everything—don't know—everybody they just so down, and they ain't got no self-esteem—they feel like they don't want to go for the president position—go for nothing. Won't hurt to try? Mmmhh! Don't nobody don't even want to go for it. 'Cause like, how they did Jesse Jackson—shouldn't he a been in the place for vice president or something like that? 'Cause ain't he have more votes or something? But you see what happened. Why should we try?

Sharon (African American, high academic achiever, 16 years of age):

> Some Black people still think the White people still got a hold on us. We still got to be less than the White people. Only thing we could do is be their secretaries, take care of their house, and things like that. They don't think like they could—like the White person could one day be their secretary. The White person could be their housekeeper and clean up their house. They don't think like that. The White people do have a hold on us, but the hold ain't full. You know, they own most everything, control most everything, and they got more money. But we can break that hold—we can fight it. If we don't at least try to break that hold, we never going to get nowhere.

*Source:* O'Connor (1997: 594).

What are the goals of education, and how are they achieved? For some students, like Lindsay Rosenthal and other "stressed-out teenagers," education is about working hard to achieve the goal of reaching a good social position in an increasingly competitive race. School District Superintendent Thomas Doluisio has another take on the subject. From his perspective, as summarized in the box titled "BASD Superintendent Links Academic, Societal Decline," the main goal of education should be to train workers so that America can compete successfully in world markets. And for the two African-American students whose stories are told in the box titled "Dispositions Toward (Collective) Struggle and Educational Resilience in the Inner City," the goal of education should be to promote democratic equality, although they differ about whether that goal is attainable.

These three views correspond to three different goals that American education has been expected to serve over the years: democratic equality (schools should focus on preparing citizens), social efficiency (schools should focus on training workers), and social mobility (schools should enable individuals to compete for social positions) (Labaree 1997). These goals represent the issue of education from the perspective of three different social roles, respectively: the citizen, the consumer, and the taxpayer. Sometimes these competing visions and goals come into conflict.

One trend marking the gradual transition from a modern society to a postmodern, consumer society is the growing domination of the social mobility goal, which has reshaped education into a commodity for the purpose of gaining social status. This outcome has strengthened the popular belief that education is a matter of individual choice, and that success is determined solely by talent and motivation. It is widely believed that if individuals are motivated to work hard, provided that they have sufficient intelligence, they will acquire the qualifications that will bring them the rewards they deserve.

## AN INDIVIDUAL OR A SOCIAL STORY?

In the twentieth century, sociologists focused on the goal of democratic equality and investigated whether it was true that educational success is just a matter of individual talent and motivation or more a result of social position. They found evidence that certain aspects of social structure have

an effect on the distribution of educational opportunities and achievement. For example, children from the poorer social classes with fewer material resources at home, such as a good diet and space to study, are likely to be educationally disadvantaged. Schools in poorer districts often have fewer facilities and fewer qualified teachers than those in more affluent areas, and the amount of public money invested per student is up to four times higher in affluent suburban areas than in poorer areas (Ballantine 1997; Carroll 1990). The conclusion might seem obvious: that differences in educational achievement are due to differences in resources.

However, the sociological story does not end here, with a social structural explanation of educational patterns replacing the individualist story. Even when economic and educational resources are improved or more evenly distributed, students vary in their educational achievements. Sociologists have examined factors such as family and group cultures that might account for this variance. For example, James Coleman, the author of *Equality of Educational Opportunity* (Coleman et al. 1966), found inequalities in schools' resources but concluded that the home environment affected students' achievement more significantly than the schools themselves. The family's educational and social background was most important, followed by the backgrounds of other children in the school. It was on the basis of this finding that Coleman recommended the integration of schools so that lower-class students, who were disproportionately black, could share an education with middle-class students and thus be in a value climate more conducive to learning. In a later study, Coleman compared private (mainly Catholic) and public schools and concluded that the value climate in private schools was more favorable to achievement. However, other studies have shown that value climate is also influenced by principal leadership, staff cooperation, student behavior, teacher control over school and classroom policy, and

**Democratic equality** A goal of education that refers to the function of education to prepare good citizens.

**Value climate** The atmosphere in a school. Value climate is influenced not only by the individuals in the student body but also by factors such as principal leadership, student behavior, and teacher morale. The assumption is that if these factors are positively balanced, the value climate will improve, and the school will provide a better learning environment and be more favorable to achievement.

teacher morale (NCHS 1987: 74; Smith et al. 1995: 47, 57).

How we frame the story of what is happening to education in contemporary society depends on the focus we adopt. Early sociologists, such as Émile Durkheim, saw education as a morally unifying force that could counteract the negative effects of social divisions in modern society. But the question now is whether postmodern society is becoming so fragmented into different cultural groupings that the goal of a common education as a source of unity is increasingly difficult to attain. Addressing this issue involves looking at the ways in which postmodernity seems to offer the possibility of greater variety and choice in education, but at the risk of transforming it into just another form of consumption. Indeed, educational institutions are losing some of their old authority, such that they have to sell themselves in the market and be sensitive to consumer demands. Likewise, students and their parents must act like critical consumers. Even knowledge itself is being transformed. You may have seen advertisements that promise to turn the consumption of information into a pleasurable, entertaining pastime. Could it be that all the hard work and discipline associated with learning will become more like playing computer games? And that the organization of education will be radically changed? Already there are signs that information technology, such as online courses, is making it possible for education to break out of the constraints set by conventional educational organizations and to create "virtual" schools and colleges for lifelong learning.

It is certainly the case that the former goals of the education system—to prepare citizens, train future workers, and enable individuals to compete for positions—are being reassessed and redefined in postmodern society. Before trying to answer these questions about what is happening to education in postmodern society, we need to review how education developed as a central feature of modern society.

## EDUCATION AND MODERNITY

We tend to use the terms **education** and **schooling** interchangeably, often forgetting that much education has always taken place outside the walls of schools and colleges (and not just in the form of homework!). Informal processes at home and between friends are a major source of information and training in life skills, ranging from how to behave toward others to how to work appliances. In more traditional societies, the greater part of education took place through such processes, in the absence of a specialized institution devoted to schooling. The various forms of school that we are familiar with came into being at different times and for a number of reasons. In Western societies, primary schools were invented from the early eighteenth century onward by modernizing kings and emperors who wanted to teach basic literacy to their subjects, while at the same time building an identification of young people in distant realms with the language and national heroes associated with the political center. The predecessors of our modern secondary schools can be found in the ancient Greek academies, where the teaching of philosophy and rhetoric was rooted in the life and ideals of the aristocracy, who wished to prepare their sons for public life. And modern universities can find their predecessors in the colleges of the Middle Ages, which prepared young men for the "learned occupations," most of which had some

**Education** A term that refers broadly to the processes by which individuals develop their capacities by acquiring knowledge and receiving training in life skills, varying from how to behave toward others to how to use particular technologies. Education is both an informal and a formal process; it can occur at home and between friends as well as in schools.

**Schooling** A term that refers to the time spent in formal educational institutions, such as elementary and high schools, as well as in colleges and universities.

connection to the church: the clergy, medicine, law, and teaching itself (Brint 1998: 18–19).

A key factor in the development of a separate and specialized institution devoted to education was the rise of the nation-state in the Middle Ages, whose rulers frequently sought to assert their power independent from that of the church. The interests of the state included instilling, through education, a sense of shared identity and loyalty, as well as equipping sufficient numbers of people to carry out such tasks as administration and legal adjudication. Similar social goals—"reasons of state"—influenced the development of modern American schools.

## Democratic Equality and Citizenship

When, in 1779, Thomas Jefferson first devised a system for free education based on intellectual merit, it was conceived less as a means for facilitating social mobility than as a vehicle for ensuring democratic representation (Jefferson 1950).

Aside from facilitating citizenship in a general sense, education affects voting behavior. Education has been shown to be positively and directly related to voter participation in the United States. The more education people have, the more likely they are to register to vote and to cast their vote in a presidential or congressional election.

In the 2000 presidential election, 70 percent of the voting-age citizen population (18 and older) was registered to vote, and 60 percent voted. However, from the perspective of levels of education, we find that only 52 percent of those with less than a high school education were registered to vote compared to 83 percent of those with a bachelor's degree or higher. Moreover, of those who did not complete high school, 38 percent reported voting in 2000 compared to 78 percent of those with a bachelor's degree or higher. Table 13.1 shows similar effects for elections in 1994, 1996, 1998, and 2000.

The goal of training children and young people for citizenship grew out of the process of nation-building—a fact that offers one of the best explanations for the founding and spread of common schools in mid-nineteenth-century America. The new American republic was thought to be at risk from the spirit of individualistic economic striving and cultural fragmentation due to large-scale immigration, unless future citizens could be educated into a common sense of citizenship and devotion to the public good. We can still see the results of this concern in the curriculum of American schools—specifically, in courses such as social studies, civics, government, and American history. The concern for preserving the republic also lay behind the pursuit of equal treatment in the school system, irrespective of religion, race, and ethnic background (although some states would have preferred to keep schools racially segregated, and there was some argument about gender—whether girls and boys should receive different but equal treatment). However, from an early stage, the ideal of providing a common experience for all school students was compromised by tendencies toward stratification on the basis of age, academic achievement, divisions between academic and vocational curriculum tracks, institutional prestige, and social class. These stratifying tendencies were often a response to pressures to promote the goals of social efficiency and social mobility.

## Social Efficiency

It was in the context of social efficiency that the modern economy was believed to require sufficient numbers of suitably qualified workers, leading to the expansion of educational provision to the level of "mass education." In the late nineteenth and early twentieth centuries, there developed a movement called vocationalism, formed by an alliance of leaders from business, labor, and education devoted to moving the curriculum away from academic learning and toward training in skills necessary for carrying out job roles. This shift was noted by the school board president of Muncie, Indiana, who, in the 1920s, told sociological researchers Robert and Helen Lynd: "For a long time all boys were trained to be President. ... Now we are training them to get jobs" (Lynd and Lynd 1929: 194). To some extent vocationalism was manifested in vocational courses at the secondary school level and, later, at the community college level; it was also stratified along gender lines, with boys taking courses relevant to jobs such as lathe operator and mechanic whereas girls were encouraged to develop secretarial skills. However, such specialized courses were never more than a minority part of the curriculum, inasmuch as the main thrust of the social efficiency argument was that future workers should have acquired basic intellectual skills as a result of disciplined effort.

The social efficiency goal came into prominence again as a result of increasing economic competition in the 1980s. An influential National Commission on Excellence in Education report, *A Nation at Risk* (1983), found that only one-fifth of 17-year-olds could write an adequate essay and only one-third could solve mathematical problems requiring several steps. The level of **functional illiteracy** (reading and writing skills inadequate for everyday living) was higher in America than in most comparable countries. The report stated: "Our nation is at risk. Our once unchallenged preeminence in commerce, industry, science, and technological innovation is being overtaken by competitors throughout the world. ... We report to the American people that ... the educational foundations of our society are presently being eroded by a rising tide of mediocrity that threatens our very future as a nation and a

**TABLE 13.1  Percentage of U.S. Citizens Ages 18 and Older Who Reported Being Registered to Vote and Voting, by Educational Attainment, Type of Election, and Year, 1994–2000**

| Education | Presidential Election | | Congressional Election | |
|---|---|---|---|---|
| | 1996 | 2000 | 1994 | 1998 |
| *Reported being registered to vote* | | | | |
| **Total** | **70.9** | **69.5** | **67.1** | **67.1** |
| Less than high school | 54.2 | 52.2 | 51.5 | 51.2 |
| High school diploma or equivalent | 65.5 | 63.9 | 62.4 | 61.9 |
| Some college | 76.1 | 73.3 | 71.7 | 71.4 |
| Bachelor's degree or higher | 85.3 | 83.2 | 81.5 | 80.3 |
| *Reported voting* | | | | |
| **Total** | **58.4** | **59.5** | **48.3** | **45.3** |
| Less than high school | 38.8 | 38.4 | 30.7 | 29.6 |
| High school diploma or equivalent | 51.7 | 52.5 | 42.9 | 39.2 |
| Some college | 63.1 | 63.1 | 51.5 | 48.3 |
| Bachelor's degree or higher | 77.0 | 77.5 | 67.4 | 61.1 |

*Note:* The survey sample includes the civilian, noninstitutionalized population. A presidential election includes those years in which a president is elected as well as congressional, state, and local officials. A congressional election is one that takes place in years when a president is not elected but when congressional, state, and local officials are elected. In this study, information was collected from respondents two weeks after each election. These estimates may differ from administrative data or data from exit polls.

*Source:* U.S. Department of Education (2003).

**Social efficiency** A goal of education suggesting that the purpose of education is to train workers.

**Vocationalism** The shift in educational curriculum away from academic learning toward providing training for skills necessary to carry out job roles.

**Functional illiteracy** The inability to read or write at a level sufficient for everyday living.

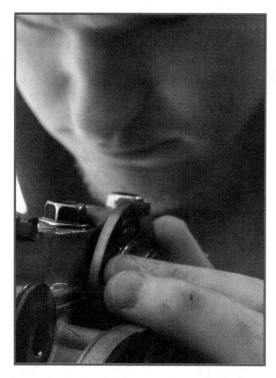

In vocational education, boys are often trained to have mechanical skills, like this auto mechanic. (iStockphoto)

Young women in vocational schools often learn secretarial skills. (iStockphoto)

people" (National Commission on Excellence in Education 1983: 5).

This anxiety gave rise to a concern with raising educational standards by specifying testable competencies and skills that should be attained by students at different levels—an approach that has been very appealing to politicians, public officials, and taxpayers, who like to be able to see value for the money expended on education (often amounting to one-third of all state and local revenues). But the results have not always been encouraging. Scores on the Scholastic Aptitude Test (SAT) declined between 1967 and 1998, from a median score of 516 down to 505 in mathematics and from 543 down to 512 in verbal ability. Compared with their counterparts in other countries, U.S. eighth graders ranked only seventeenth in the world in science and twenty-eighth in mathematics in 1996 (Bennett 1997).

Another aspect of standardized testing is that it facilitates comparisons of the achievements of individuals and schools, thereby intensifying the sense of competition. It also leads to further stratification. Indeed, the educational system has become a kind of obstacle race in which some students fall behind or drop out at each level. Dropout rates are highest in large, urban school systems and for schools with large numbers of African-Americans or Hispanics. This results in a pyramid-shaped educational achievement structure, with percentages decreasing on the way to the top at the higher degree levels (see Figure 13.1). Since this structure reflects the verticality of the job market and its rewards, it seems perfectly logical from the viewpoint of those advocating the social efficiency goal. In principle, the best-qualified candidates should get the best jobs, but in practice it seems to be more a question of where you come from.

## FIGURE 13.1 Highest Level of Educational Attainment of U.S. Population, 2004

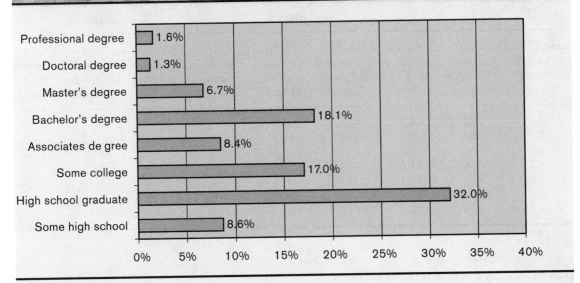

Professional degree — 1.6%
Doctoral degree — 1.3%
Master's degree — 6.7%
Bachelor's degree — 18.1%
Associates de gree — 8.4%
Some college — 17.0%
High school graduate — 32.0%
Some high school — 8.6%

*Note:* Data pertain to persons 25 years and older, with N = 187 million.

*Source:* U.S. Census Bureau (2005).

## Social Mobility

Whereas the social efficiency goal pertains to the collective needs of modern society for trained workers, the **social mobility** goal concerns the needs of individual educational consumers to improve or maintain their social status. The former can be thought of as a top-down view, the latter as a bottom-up one. Both exert pressure toward stratification of education. In the case of the social mobility goal, the individual seeks to gain competitive advantage over others by scoring higher grades and gaining higher qualifications from more prestigious institutions. In fact, there is evidence that much of the upward expansion of education in the United States over the last 150 years has resulted more from consumer demand for this kind of educational distinction than from pressure to meet the needs of society (Brown 1995; Labaree 1988). As

the enrollment of students becomes almost universal at one level—grammar school, then high school, and, recently, even college—the demand for educational distinction shifts to the next level.

The downside of the influence of the social mobility goal is that it can have negative effects in terms of the other two goals of education: democratic equality and social efficiency. Democratic equality is made more difficult by the increasing

**Social mobility** A goal of education pertaining to the ability of individuals or groups to change their social position or status within a social hierarchy. While societal myths such as the "American Dream" imply that society is open and meritocratic and that social mobility for the better is simply the result of hard work, long-standing inequalities suggest that this is not the case.

## TABLE 13.2  Educational Attainment by Race and Hispanic Origin, 1940–2000[1]

| Year | White[2] Less Than 5 Years of Elementary School | High School Completion or Higher[3] | 4 or More Years of College[4] | Black[2] Less Than 5 Years of Elementary School | High School Completion or Higher[3] | 4 or More Years of College[4] | Hispanic Less Than 5 Years of Elementary School | High School Completion or Higher[3] | 4 or More Years of College[4] |
|------|------|------|------|------|------|------|------|------|------|
| 1940 | 10.9 | 26.1 | 4.9 | 41.8 | 7.7 | 1.3 | – | – | – |
| 1950 | 8.9 | 36.4 | 6.6 | 32.6 | 13.7 | 2.2 | – | – | – |
| 1960 | 6.7 | 43.2 | 8.1 | 23.5 | 21.7 | 3.5 | – | – | – |
| 1970 | 4.2 | 57.4 | 11.6 | 14.7 | 36.1 | 6.1 | – | – | – |
| 1980 | 1.9 | 71.9 | 18.4 | 9.1 | 51.4 | 7.9 | 15.8 | 44.5 | 7.6 |
| 1990 | 1.1 | 81.4 | 23.1 | 5.1 | 66.2 | 11.3 | 12.3 | 50.8 | 9.2 |
| 2000 | 0.5 | 88.4 | 28.1 | 1.6 | 78.9 | 16.6 | 8.7 | 57.0 | 10.6 |

Notes: (–) = data not available.

[1] Data pertain to percentage of population 25 years and older, by years of school completed.

[2] Includes persons of Hispanic origin for years prior to 1980.

[3] Data for years prior to 1993 include all persons with at least four years of high school.

[4] Data for 1993 and later years are for persons with a bachelor's or higher degree.

Source: Adapted from U.S. Department of Commerce (2005).

demand for distinctions and hierarchy, and social efficiency is compromised when the scarcity of a particular qualification is what determines how much it is valued, rather than how much usable knowledge it represents. According to some critics, the social mobility goal ultimately results in **overcredentialing** (the overproduction of academic qualifications relative to the occupational need for advanced skills) and **credential inflation** (the rising level of educational attainment required for jobs whose skill requirements remain largely unchanged) (Labaree 1988: 55; Shelley 1992).

Since educational credentials play a role in social stratification and social mobility, we need to look closer at who achieves what. Indeed, as Table 13.2 and Figure 13.2 demonstrate, differences among people based on race and ethnicity are significant and need to be taken into consideration. Consider, for example, the racial and ethnic backgrounds of students who have completed four or more years of college. In 2000, this educational level was attained by 28.1 percent of whites but only 16.6 percent of blacks and 10.6 percent of Hispanics.

As illustrated in Figures 13.3–13.7, educational attainment also varies on the basis of income. In particular, these figures show how earnings in the United States increase with education: Workers with at least a bachelor's degree earn more than those who have had less education. Note, however,

**Overcredentialing** The overproduction of academic qualifications relative to the occupational need for advanced skills.

**Credential inflation** The rising level of educational attainment required for jobs whose skill requirements remain largely unchanged.

## FIGURE 13.2 Four or More Years of College Completed by Race and Hispanic Origin, 1940–2000

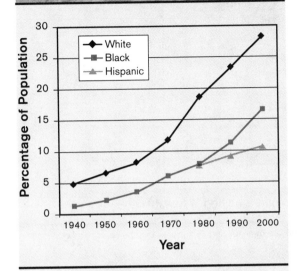

*Note:* No separate data exist for Hispanics prior to 1980.

*Source:* U.S. Department of Education (2004).

that within the various categories of earned-education credentials, there are significant differences by gender. In 2002, for example, males with a bachelor's degree or higher earned $48,955 on average, compared to their female counterparts, who earned only $40,021. This gender gap holds across all categories of education. (For further discussion of gender differences, see Chapter 9, on gender, and Chapter 12, on work and the economy.) How have these trends shifted over time?

## Historical Summary

As detailed above, we can think of American education's development from modernity toward postmodernity in terms of the changing balance among the three major goals of democratic equality, social efficiency, and social mobility (Labaree 1997):

## FIGURE 13.3 Education and Income by Gender, 2002

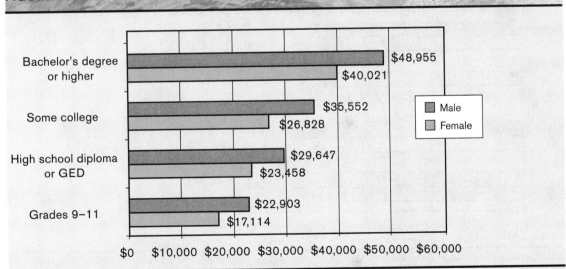

*Note:* Data pertain to median annual earnings in constant 2002 dollars of all full-time, full-year wage and salary workers ages 25–34.

*Source:* Adapted from U.S. Department of Education (2004).

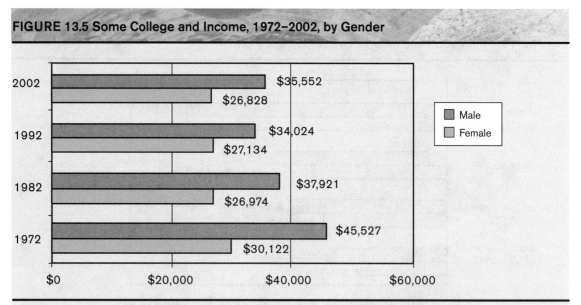

**FIGURE 13.4 Bachelors Degree or Higher and Income, 1972–2002, by Gender**

Male | Female

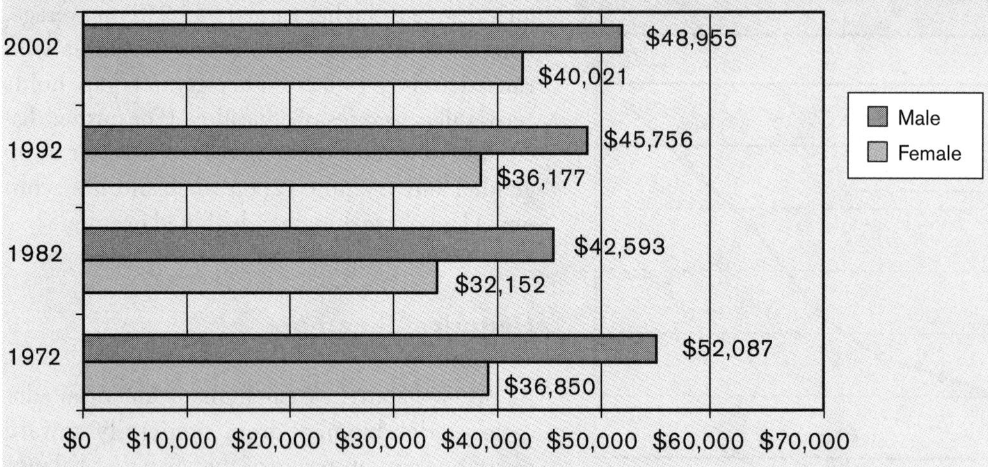

2002: $48,955 / $40,021
1992: $45,756 / $36,177
1982: $42,593 / $32,152
1972: $52,087 / $36,850

$0  $10,000  $20,000  $30,000  $40,000  $50,000  $60,000  $70,000

*Note:* Data pertain to median annual earnings in constant 2002 dollars of all full-time, full-year wage and salary workers ages 25–34.

*Source:* Adapted from U.S. Department of Education (2004).

**FIGURE 13.5 Some College and Income, 1972–2002, by Gender**

Male | Female

2002: $35,552 / $26,828
1992: $34,024 / $27,134
1982: $37,921 / $26,974
1972: $45,527 / $30,122

$0  $20,000  $40,000  $60,000

*Note:* Data pertain to median annual earnings in constant 2002 dollars of all full-time, full-year wage and salary workers ages 25–34.

*Source:* Adapted from U.S. Department of Education (2004).

**FIGURE 13.6 High School Diploma and Income, 1972–2002, by Gender**

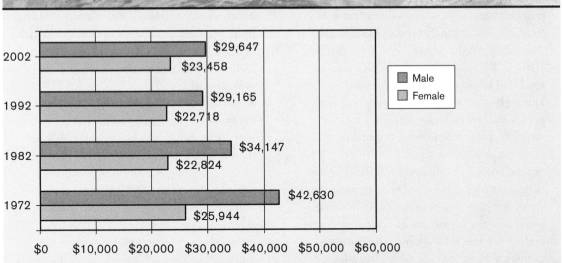

*Note:* Data pertain to median annual earnings in constant 2002 dollars of all full-time, full-year wage and salary workers ages 25–34.

*Source:* Adapted from U.S. Department of Education (2004).

**FIGURE 13.7 Grades 9–11 and Income, 1972–2002, by Gender**

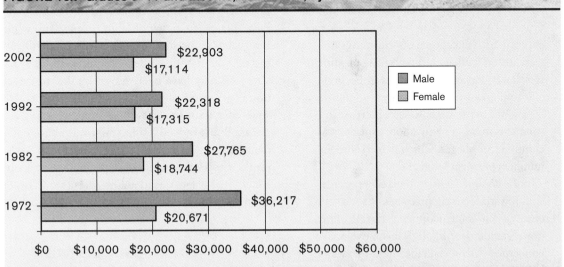

*Note:* Data pertain to median annual earnings in constant 2002 dollars of all full-time, full-year wage and salary workers ages 25–34.

*Source:* Adapted from U.S. Department of Education (2004).

1. In the *mid-nineteenth century*—the era of the common school—democratic equality was the dominant goal. The main outcome expected from education was that it should maintain social stability in the face of social and economic changes. By 1850 half of the U.S. population aged 5 to 19 were enrolled in schools.

2. During the *late nineteenth century and early twentieth century,* social efficiency and social mobility goals became more prominent. Growing numbers in upper elementary grades created consumer demand for distinctive credentials in high school and college, and educational and business leaders were concerned about how to prepare students for an increasingly differentiated workforce. By the mid-1960s a majority of U.S. adults had a high school diploma.

3. In the *1960s and 1970s,* the tide began to turn toward democratic equality (although it was still linked to social mobility). This trend was tied into the more general movements for racial and gender equality—the civil rights movement and the feminist movement. Sociologists focused on questions of social inequality and educational opportunity in relation to class, race, and gender. Educational opportunities policies were introduced, including busing of students to schools outside their own neighborhood and setting quotas for minority students in colleges. And there was a massive increase in enrollments in higher education, especially in community colleges, which tripled student numbers between 1966 and 1976.

4. The *1980s and 1990s* witnessed a political shift toward focusing on issues of social efficiency, such as maintaining or raising educational standards. Although this move was concerned with social efficiency, it was also linked to social mobility, as there were fears that qualifications were being devalued as a result of their greater availability—an outcome seen as a threat to the social hierarchy based on

merit. There were calls to tighten up educational standards, along with a reaction against affirmative action and quota policies that aimed to increase representation of ethnic minorities in higher education. The result was that, in California and some other states, such policies were abolished.

5. From the *end of the twentieth century and into the twenty-first century,* education has increasingly been emphasized as a consumer good. The language of the market is more and more common among educators, students are being addressed as consumers or clients, and schools and colleges are promoting themselves through advertising and public events. This trend has raised people's expectations, as consumers, and they are now demanding that schools satisfy many and various functions.

The problem for postmodern society in trying to satisfy all these demands and goals is that they often come into conflict. The goal of producing citizens with a common educational experience is not helped by an emphasis on achieving a social position by acquiring an education that is somehow "better" than that of other people. And while the goal of increasing social efficiency and educating people only to the level required to fill available jobs may have been served by the introduction of a vocational track, individuals may feel that such education prevents them from achieving social mobility. Indeed, ethnic minorities have complained about being steered into vocational tracks on the basis of racial stereotypes about their unsuitability for more academic studies (see Chapter 8, on inequality).

## DIFFERENT PERSPECTIVES ON EDUCATION

In the twentieth century, sociologists were divided regarding the best perspective to adopt in analyzing the educational system and its goals in modern society. The two main competing approaches were **functionalism** (sometimes referred to as *structural-functionalism*) and the **conflict perspective.** Functionalism concentrated on the functions that education performed in maintaining social integration by passing on shared values and norms and preparing members to take up roles in society, whereas the conflict perspective assumed the existence of a tension in society created by the competing interests of individuals and groups.

## Functionalism and Social Integration

Not just one of the founders of sociology, Émile Durkheim laid the basis for the sociological study of education—clearly believing that education was central to the development and maintenance of modern society. Three of his major works were about education: *Moral Education* (1925), *The Evolution of Educational Thought* (1938), and *Education and Sociology* (1956). In the last of these he gave a definition of education and described its functions: "Education is the influence exercised by adult generations on those that are not yet ready for social life. Its object is to arouse and to develop in the child a certain number of physical, intellectual and moral states that are demanded of him [*sic*] by both the political society as a whole and the special milieux for which he [*sic*] is specifically destined" (Durkheim 1956: 28).

In short, Durkheim saw education mainly in terms of preparing children and young people to take up their positions as citizens and workers. Primarily concerned with the role of schools in transmitting values that would preserve stability in society, he did not consider possible conflicts between the need for stability and the values and skills necessary for living in changing, emerging industrial societies. Later functionalists, such as Talcott Parsons (1959), continued this approach. The functionalist approach was criticized for dis-

regarding conflicts over values and interests, such as those between rival educational goals and different classes.

## Conflicts and Interests

Like the functionalist approach, the conflict perspective attempted to explain how education contributes to the maintenance of the status quo in modern society. However, the latter did so from a critical standpoint, seeking to reveal how education functioned to mold individuals to fit the needs of an unequal society and a capitalist economic system. Its basic premise was that there are conflicting group interests and goals in society.

Max Weber's studies of power in society and the ways in which groups seek to maintain their status inspired one version of the conflict approach to education (Collins 1971). Weber also used cross-cultural examples to shed light on the role of education in different types of society (Weber 1958a). During the preindustrial era, education served the primary purpose of training people to fit into a particular status ("station") in society, whereas in the modern industrial era, pressures were put on education from upwardly mobile members of society competing for higher positions in the economic system.

**Functionalism** The functionalist, or structural-functionalist, perspective focuses on the contribution of the parts of a structure to the maintenance of the whole. It rests on the assumption that there is no fundamental conflict between the demands of the parts.

**Conflict perspective** The view that education contributes to maintaining the status quo by revealing how education molds individuals to fill the needs of an unequal society. The conflict perspective rests on the assumption that there are conflicting groups and interests in society, and that education reflects these conflicts.

Another version of the conflict perspective derived from Marxism. Advocates of this perspective view mass education as a tool of the capitalist class for producing the disciplined workers needed by the economy and for making them think that the system is fair. Specifically, they see the culture and knowledge passed on in education as ideologically biased in favor of maintaining the status quo and preventing workers from developing a class consciousness that would cause them to take collective action to change it (Bowles and Gintis 1976).

American education, in particular, has been portrayed as promoting an ideology that emphasizes individualism and competition, obscuring the fact that only a limited number of individuals can better themselves in the competition, while the majority lose out. According to Samuel Bowles and Herbert Gintis (1976), schools prepare children for the unequal stratification system in society in a way that corresponds to their family background. In other words, schools predominantly attended by blacks and working-class children emphasize behavioral control and rule following, in contrast to schools in the well-to-do suburbs, which employ relatively open systems that favor greater student participation, less direct supervision, and more student choice.

**Macrosocial**  A term describing an approach that looks at the "big picture"—that is, at social structures and their role in the maintenance of a whole social system.

**Microsocial**  A term describing an approach that focuses on individuals, such as students and teachers in the classroom. Microsocial perspectives tend to be interactionist, as they address social relationships and everyday interactions.

**Labeling theory**  A microsocial attempt to explain differences in educational attainment. Labeling theory maintains that students who are given the impression that they are dumb and not expected to succeed may incorporate this label as part of their identity and behave accordingly.

## Interaction

The functionalist perspective and the conflict approach have tended to focus on the "big picture" or **macrosocial** level, viewing education in terms of its contribution to maintaining the social system. A completely different approach that became popular in the second half of the twentieth century focused on individuals in interaction at the **microsocial** level, such as students and teachers in the classroom. The most influential version of this interactionist perspective is **labeling theory** (Becker 1963), which maintains that students who are given the impression that they are dumb and not expected to succeed academically may incorporate this label as part of their self-concept and behave as the label suggests. Studies have found plenty of evidence that this was a common occurrence in schools (e.g., Rosenthal and Jacobson 1968)—particularly in cases involving a division between vocational and academic tracks, leading students to see themselves as either less or more intelligent, depending on which track they were put in.

The interactionist perspective inspired a great deal of research into small-scale interactions in educational settings, providing valuable insights into how students and teachers took their cues from others in developing their self-concepts and ideas about how they should behave. The main criticism of this perspective was that it often failed to show how such interactions linked into the larger structures of the social system.

## Other Perspectives

Beginning in the 1970s, attempts were made to create new syntheses of the macrosocial and microsocial approaches. One effort at synthesis focused on the difference between the speech of working-class students and that of middle-class students (Bernstein 1971). Students from working-class families were found to employ a "restricted speech code," whereas middle-class students exhibited an "elaborated speech code" in addition to a restricted code (as did their middle-class teachers). The restricted code is a kind of shorthand speech whose meanings are limited to a particular social group; they are bound to a specific social context and are not readily available to outsiders. In contrast, the elaborated code explicitly verbalizes many of the meanings that are taken for granted in a restricted code. Its meanings tend to be "universalistic," in that they are not tied to a particular context. It follows that, because schools are concerned with the transmission of universalistic types of meanings, working-class students are at a disadvantage in the educational system.

There is also a relationship between occupations and speech codes. Routine occupations provide little variety, offer few opportunities to participate in decisionmaking, and do not require elaborate verbal skills. By comparison, professional occupations involve more discussion and negotiation in reaching decisions and therefore require elaborate speech patterns.

Speech codes are part of culture, and it is by turning to cultural factors that sociologists of education have attempted to link the microsocial and macrosocial levels. In some cases, however, these cultural factors seem little more than a kind of "message system" through which the macrostructure determines what happens at the microlevel of families, schools, and individuals. This is the criticism leveled at the writings on education by French sociologist Pierre Bourdieu, especially his concept of **cultural capital** (Bourdieu 1977; Bourdieu and Passeron 1977). Bourdieu correctly notes that children of middle-class families arrive at school already possessing many of the cultural qualities that are prized in the educational system, including the "right" language (linguistic capital) with which to unlock the categories used in formal education. Underlying this language are rules that function something like a grammar; they constitute what Bourdieu calls "habitus," the rules of the

> **Cultural capital** A concept introduced by Pierre Bourdieu referring to cultural qualities that are prized in the educational system as well as by society overall. These qualities include the "right" language, access to books, and exposure to cultural forms such as art, music, and theater.

game necessary for success. But, although Bourdieu accepts that schools have a certain amount of autonomy relative to the economy, he seems to suggest that little choice is available—that the education system mainly functions to reproduce the established social order and to make it appear legitimate. And yet he himself is a teacher and presumably thinks he and other teachers like him could make a difference.

The attempts to link the microsocial and macrosocial levels in the sociology of education were based on the assumption that the most important structural feature of modern society was the division between social classes. And social class position was determined by a person's occupation in the system of economic production. In postmodern society, however, other factors have become equally important, if not more so; these are cultural in nature, and they include gender, ethnicity, sexuality, and the consumer lifestyle. Studies of education have begun to focus on these other cultural factors. (Some of these studies are cited in Chapter 6, on sexuality; Chapter 8, on inequality; Chapter 9, on gender; and Chapter 10, on race and ethnicity.)

## EDUCATION IN A MULTICULTURAL, POSTMODERN SOCIETY

### Cultural Deprivation

The focus on class divisions and the cultures associated with them remained a feature of much of the sociology of education until late in the twentieth century. Theories of cultural deprivation were first developed in connection with social class. The argument was that working-class students were being held back by aspects of their culture that were not conducive to academic success. For example, as we discussed earlier, one sociological study found that many working-class families use a restricted code of speech (Bernstein 1971), reliance on which makes it difficult for their children to undertake abstract analytical work. Other studies targeted additional cultural factors, such as lack of self-discipline, lack of parental interest, and a lack of ambition. And when attention was broadened to encompass not just class but also ethnic minorities and educational achievement, similar arguments were made about cultural deprivation or deficiencies in the culture of their families.

Among the studies attempting to evaluate the opportunities and performance of minority students compared with white students, the best known was the Coleman Report (Coleman et al. 1966). It attributed the lower educational achievement of minority students (with the exception of Asian-Americans) to their family background and suggested that one way to improve the academic achievement of poor and minority children would be to integrate the schools, putting minority children in the same classes as white children to produce a climate of achievement and to provide educational role models. This report provided a major impetus for increased efforts to integrate schools in the 1960s and later, especially through the use of busing. In a later study, however, James Coleman and his colleagues (1975) concluded that school desegregation contributed to "white flight" from big cities and was fostering resegregation of

Desegregation of schools in the 1970s by busing plans is thought to have caused the phenomenon of "white flight" out of inner cities into the suburbs. (Owen Franklin/Corbis)

urban districts. In fact, the policy of busing and its effects on educational achievement have remained controversial and unresolved. Programs of compensatory education, dating from the Elementary and Secondary Education Act of 1965, have also been subjected to criticism; some detractors alleged that they showed small results for the billions of dollars spent on them, while others thought they institutionalized a "deficit" view of minority cultures. (On the other hand, some compensatory programs—such as Head Start, aimed at helping disadvantaged children achieve "readiness" for first grade—have been shown to be beneficial.)

The problem with the cultural deprivation or "deficit" view is that it explains the failure of certain groups as the result of their failure to conform to a single model of the good, "educable" student—usually white and middle-class. But it could also be argued that the fault lies in the educational system, which is not sufficiently responsive to different cultures. Accordingly, we need to consider differences

between cultures and how they might be reflected in the curriculum and the processes of schooling.

Originally, standardized tests like the SAT were adopted as a means of sorting students and helping college admissions officers select the best candidates. Questions have been raised, however, about what exactly these tests measure: Is it aptitude and potential, or merely knowledge of the mainstream culture? If the latter, such tests are clearly weighted against students who come from disadvantaged backgrounds.

Consider, for example, the test scores on the SAT I for the class of 1999. As shown in Figures 13.8 and 13.9, there is a consistent difference between male and female test takers, with males scoring higher across all racial/ethnic categories, except for African-Americans in the verbal section. (At the college level, however, females excel at skills requiring verbal aptitude.) The differences across race/ethnicity are also quite stark, with white students scoring significantly higher (verbal:

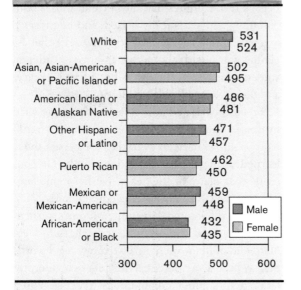

**FIGURE 13.8 Class of 1999, SAT I Scores by Race and Gender: Verbal Scores**

Source: Adapted from Hoff (1999), citing College Board data.

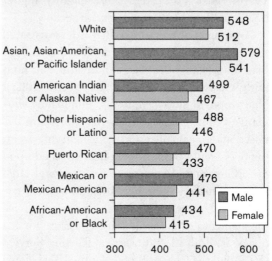

**FIGURE 13.9 Class of 1999, SAT I Scores by Race and Gender: Math Scores**

Source: Adapted from Hoff (1999), citing College Board data.

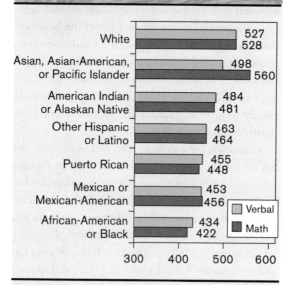

**FIGURE 13.10 Class of 1999, SAT I Total Verbal and Math Scores by Race/Ethnicity**

White — 527 / 528

Asian, Asian-American, or Pacific Islander — 498 / 560

American Indian or Alaskan Native — 484 / 481

Other Hispanic or Latino — 463 / 464

Puerto Rican — 455 / 448

Mexican or Mexican-American — 453 / 456

African-American or Black — 434 / 422

Verbal / Math

*Source:* Adapted from Hoff (1999), citing College Board data.

527, math: 528) than black students (verbal: 434, math: 432). Note as well that, as shown in Figure 13.10, Asian test takers score slightly higher (math: 560) than whites in the math section.

A number of researchers have demonstrated that certain questions on tests such as the SAT are biased against students from nonwhite and non-middle-class backgrounds (e.g., Freedle 2003). The proposed movement toward eliminating affirmative action policies for higher education has raised additional concerns because, in this event, the SAT would be even more heavily relied upon for admissions. At the same time, several large state institutions of higher education—most notably, the University of California system—have threatened to drop the SAT as a measure for admissions. Both the Educational Testing Service (ETS) and the College Board National Task Force on Minority High Achievement maintain that the gap in student performance is based not so much

on the structure of the test as on the gap in student family incomes and resources, on cultural differences, on racial and ethnic prejudice, and on variations in educational policies at the K–12 level (College Board n.d.). Nonetheless, the College Board and the Educational Testing Service have been attempting to revise the SAT to eliminate racial, ethnic, gender, and class bias. The ETS, in particular, announced in 2002 that it would "revamp" the SAT to make it more relevant, in part by replacing the "culture-bound" analogies section with a "writing" section.

However, some critics still believe that a cultural bias will reemerge, inasmuch as "[test] graders no doubt will emphasize stylistically and grammatically Standard English, marking students down whose writing style employs idioms, phrases, or merely word patterns more common to communities of color" (Wise 2002: 7). For such critics, the ETS test designers are "merely gatekeepers for the status quo" (Wise 2002: 9). In a striking study published in 2003, Roy O. Freedle, a research psychologist who had worked at ETS for over thirty years, proposes further corrections to what he calls the SAT's "ethnic and social class bias." Freedle argues that the current SAT is both culturally and statistically biased, and he presents a revised scoring method (the R-SAT) that he claims will positively impact minority students, students for whom English is not a first language, and disadvantaged white students.

Freedle's critique addresses the language used in the SAT, especially the "easy" versus "hard" words—those used in everyday life versus those learned through school-based curricula. He contends that many of the "easy" verbal items "tap into a more culturally specific content and ... are perceived differently, depending on one's particular cultural and socioeconomic background. ... Hard verbal items often involve rarely used words that ... have fewer potential differences in interpretation across ethnic communities" (Freedle 2003: 5). As a result of their different perceptions and life experiences, "whites tend to score better on easy items and African Americans on hard items" (Freedle 2003: 3). Freedle's revised test, the R-SAT, would give thousands of students an additional 100–200 points, which could mean the difference between getting into a selective college or not, or being qualified for a range of scholarships.

## Multiculturalism

It is easy to imagine that, as the American population becomes more heterogeneous as a result of immigration, education will automatically change to reflect that structural fact and become multicultural. However, in doing so we would underestimate the struggles and controversies involved. The civil rights movement of the 1960s had to fight hard to gain acceptance of its demands for desegregation of the nation's schools and for changes in the curriculum to recognize and value the contributions of African-Americans. In the decades that followed, other minority groups have been able to build on that hard-won success and to press their claims for cultural recognition in education under the banner of multiculturalism.

The United States has always been a nation of immigrants, but their numbers and origins have varied over time (see also Chapter 10, on race and ethnicity, and Chapter 16, on urbanism and population). In the last half-century the demographic composition has changed dramatically, with the proportion of whites dropping from 90 percent in 1950 to 75 percent in 1990. Today, most immigrants come not from Europe but from Asia and Latin America. By the late 1980s, many U.S. states (beginning with California in 1987) had added principles in their curriculum guidelines requiring "multicultural and gender-fair" perspectives (Rosenfelt 1994). The transformation was most noticeable in primary schools, where the customs of different lands are studied and walls and hallways are decorated with pictures illustrating the diverse cultures. High schools have added minority writers to the English syllabus, and in some history courses the contributions of minorities are featured. And in higher education, more than half of colleges and universities surveyed have reported efforts to introduce multicultural themes into departmental offerings, although these are largely add-ons to existing curricula rather than replacements for traditional courses (Levine and Cureton 1992: 29). Such moves toward multiculturalism in education have met with resistance, giving rise to ideological controversy that some refer to as the *culture wars*. There has even been a backlash against multiculturalism, with conservatives accusing liberals of introducing a policy of "political correctness"; this, they allege, entails requiring college faculty to follow a political agenda rather than using their own academic judgment in deciding what to teach. An example of a critical account of the introduction of a multicultural policy into a university is Dinesh D'Souza's description of events at Stanford University, California, in 1997–1998 (see the box titled "Multiculturalism at Stanford").

Why has multiculturalism been so controversial? Although the dominant ideology in the United States is market-oriented individualism, it has not been a very unifying ideology in this nation of immigrants. Not surprisingly, there has always been a subtheme of cultural pluralism in the American creed (de Crevecoeur 1783). Multiculturalism could be regarded as simply extending this cultural value to include those who have previously been neglected or excluded. However, some critics take it to be attempting more than that. They accuse its supporters of wanting to jettison the cultural heritage of Western civilization. In defending the core books and authors (the canon) of the traditional curriculum, they quote figures such as the great African-American novelist Ralph Ellison, who wrote that he found mental "freedom" by reading such books as a boy in Macon County, Alabama.

## media moments

### Multiculturalism at Stanford

"Hey, hey, ho, ho, Western culture's got to go," the students chanted on the lawn at Stanford University. They wore blue jeans, Los Angeles Lakers T-shirts, Reeboks, Oxford button downs, Vuarnet sunglasses, baseball caps, Timex and Rolex watches. No tribal garb, Middle Eastern veils, or Japanese samurai swords were in sight. Observers could not recall a sari, kimono, or sarapa. None of the women had their feet bound or bandaged. Clearly the rejection of the ways of the West was a partial one. Nevertheless, it was expressed with great passion and vehemence, and commanded respect for its very intensity.

What were these eager and intelligent students protesting about in early 1988? The weather was beautiful in California, the campus pristine, many of the students hailed from middle-class and privileged families. Yet precisely this comfortable environment seemed to contribute to a vague sense of disquiet. The stu-dents appeared to share a powerful conviction that Western culture is implacably hostile to the claims of blacks, other minorities, women, and homosexuals. When they thought about the West, what entered the protesters' minds were slavery, colonialism, the domestication of women, and the persecution of "deviant lifestyles."

The Stanford administration was faced with a bewildering dispute over the content of the un-dergraduate curriculum being conducted in a manner scarcely different from a political march or a workers' strike. The real targets of the protest—Aristotle, Aquinas, Locke, and other "white males"—had all been dead for hundreds of years. The students resented the fact that the ideas of these men still dominated Stanford's "core curriculum." They shouted slogans and carried placards demanding that the Stanford faculty and administration make major changes in the course offerings.

*Source:* D'Souza (1991: 59–60).

---

The advocates of multiculturalism in the curriculum respond with two arguments. The first is that we are now living in an age when culture changes so rapidly that the idea of a canon—a set of required great books—is outmoded. Clayborne Carson, professor of history and Afro-American studies at Stanford, has been widely quoted as saying: "What's one generation's standard canonical text is the next generation's pulp" (quoted in D'Souza 1991: 62, reprinted in Thompson 1997: 196).

The other argument is that the existing canon is unrepresentative of the various groups who make up the population. This was the view of members of the campus Rainbow Coalition at Stanford, which included black, Hispanic, Asian, and Native American groups:

"Western culture does not try to understand the diversity of experiences of different people," charged Alejandro Sweet-Cordero, a member of the Movimiento Estudiantil Chicano de Aztlan, the Hispanic group on campus. "If you think American culture is centered on the Constitution and the Founding Fathers, then you're going to exclude a major part of what this country is," re-marked Stanford student activist William King, calling for non-Western alternatives to provide students with "a different picture." King added, "It was painful to come to Stanford and find that no member of your race was in the required curriculum." Stacey Leyton, a student member of Students United for Democracy in Education … remarked, "It's a strong statement you're making when the only required readings are by whites and males. You're saying that what's been written by women and people of color isn't worthy of consideration." Freshman Joseph Green wrote in the *Stanford Daily,* "I get tired of reading the thoughts of white men who would probably spit on me if they were alive to face me today. … Stanford is sending many students into the world with no knowledge of the challenges facing people of color." And Black Student Union activist Amanda Kemp protested that the implicit message of Western culture is "Nigger go home." (Quoted in D'Souza 1991: 63, reprinted in Thompson 1997: 197)

Since Stanford took the lead in the late 1980s, many colleges have attempted to make their core curriculum more representative of the cultures of their students. Those critics who claim that multiculturalism goes beyond simply expanding cultural pluralism to include minorities accuse it of adding a dimension of **cultural relativism** and a new ethnocentrism. Cultural relativism sees all cultures as equally valuable and rejects any ranking of cultures and their products in terms of quality. And ethnocentrism occurs when a group wishes to make its own culture the central focus of study. Clearly, the occurrence of such tendencies is an ever-present danger, but they are not inevitable aspects of multiculturalism.

As a nation of immigrants, modern America could establish and maintain its unity only if the various cultural groups merged in the "melting pot," and one of the main goals of education was to promote that process. But postmodern society is more like a "salad bowl" in which different cultures coexist. Multiculturalism is a recognition of that fact. Of course, the nation-state is still important, and it still requires education to serve social

functions such as preparing young people to become responsible citizens and to take up work roles. But other institutions now contribute to those processes: The mass media, political parties, and organized social movements are engaged in informing people about their rights and duties as citizens, and training for work roles is available through a variety of sources, including self-instruction media packages and resources on the Internet. In short, schooling in postmodern society has become less distinct, in time and space, from education in general. If this trend continues, postmodernity will come to resemble premodernity more than it resembles modernity.

## Consumers and Choice

We have suggested that education in postmodern society might be breaking out of the constraints set by formal schooling. The possibilities opened up by online courses, virtual schools and colleges, and the development of lifelong learning could make conventional schooling, as we have known it, less crucial in determining individuals' opportunities to experience social mobility. At present, however, there is often still a lack of options and choices for students and their parents, particularly for poorer or more disadvantaged groups.

Several schemes have aimed at increasing choice. For example, some districts have set up **magnet schools.** This policy is intended to dis-

**Cultural relativism**  In contrast to ethnocentrism, a perspective whose advocates see all cultures as equally valuable and reject any ranking of cultures and their products in terms of quality.

**Magnet schools**  Schools whose aim is to distribute students and desegregate schools on the basis of special interests or talents, such as science, mathematics, art and music, and vocational education.

Charter schools focus on a particular theme or skill, like the KIPP music school in the Bronx, New York. (Neville Elder/Corbis)

tribute students and desegregate schools on the basis of special interests or talents, such as science, mathematics, art and music, and vocational education. Research shows that they achieve a certain amount of success, provided they are well resourced and are not simply the same old schools with a new name (Blank and Archibald 1992). Another scheme involves **charter schools**, which are similar to magnet schools except that they focus on a particular method, theme, or curriculum; they are publicly funded but give parents and students a degree of autonomy in school government (Ballantine 1997: 356, Bennett de Marrais and LeCompte 1995: 298).

An even more market-oriented move toward developing consumer choice has been the intro-

duction of the **voucher system**. Families with school-aged children are given money vouchers that are valid for a year of education at the school of their choice. Toward this end, the school district is required to establish a variety of schools with different educational programs and, at times, different philosophical and discipline approaches. Parents, in turn, are encouraged to become involved in the selection and operation of the schools. In some cases, corporations have sponsored "model" schools, providing money for programs, equipment, and teacher training (Rist 1990; Weisman 1990). A more radical departure from the public school system is schooling for profit. Some school districts have issued contracts to private, profit-making companies to run their schools. The results have been mixed, with some large school boards expressing disillusionment over what has been achieved by the companies to which they gave contracts. Taken together, these various initiatives of the "school choice" movement constitute a departure from the "common school" as well as from the shared-experience goal of education in the earlier stage of modernity. Indeed, there has been a shift toward diversity and cultural fragmentation in the postmodern age.

This increasing diversity in education may be advantageous for the other two goals of education—namely, social efficiency and social mobility. It contributes to social efficiency by providing a wide range of differently equipped newcomers in the employment market, thus fitting the needs of the flexible, postindustrial economy. And for individuals looking for opportunities to improve their social mobility prospects, the increase in educational choices is something to be welcomed. It looks like a "win-win" development.

However, there are problems with the consumer approach to education. First, it often ignores the fact that consumers have varying resources, even if it tries to compensate for these inequalities through schemes such as giving poorer students state-funded vouchers or scholar-

**Charter schools** Schools that focus on a particular method, theme, or curriculum. Charter schools are publicly funded but give parents and students a degree of autonomy in school government.

**Voucher system** A market-oriented approach to education in which families with school-aged children are given money vouchers that are valid for a year of education at the school of their choice.

ships. In practice, such subsidies are seldom sufficient to produce equality. Second, it assumes that people make their choices on the basis of full and equal knowledge about the possible rewards and costs involved. In fact, poorer people are usually less well informed and thus have fewer educational choices. The educational system has been likened to a shopping mall in which consumer information is vital to making the right choices. Students with parents who have insider access to the needed information have an important advantage over those who do not.

The social inequalities reproduced by the educational system in modern society seem likely to persist (and perhaps even to widen) in the postmodern age. As research has shown, the various schemes to increase school choice only perpetuate the gap between wealthy and poor youth (Manski 1992: 1).

## Postmodern Education: A Virtual Revolution

Signs that we may be entering a postmodern educational era are not difficult to find. Every day seems to bring announcements of new online courses and virtual colleges. Some of these involve consortia of prestigious universities and libraries on a global scale, indicating the extent to which information technology is bringing about a globalization of cultural products. A typical example was the October 2000 announcement of the creation of a virtual college by an alliance of Oxford University with Princeton, Yale, and Stanford. Named *The University Alliance for Lifelong Learning*, it aims to provide online courses in the arts and sciences in a distance learning venture for the institutions' 500,000 alumni and, eventually, to make the courses available to the general public.

Despite the potential benefits of globalization, of the revolutions in information and communications technology, and of increased access to educa-

tion, some people are still being left behind, especially women and students in less developed countries. (In this connection, see also Chapter 8, on inequality; Chapter 9, on gender; and Chapter 18, on social change, collective action, and social movements.) Literacy, on a global scale, is a key measure of a society's progress and promise. As a United Nations Educational, Cultural, and Scientific Organization (UNESCO) official has noted, "a lack of literacy skills limits the potential for societies to deal with issues such as discrimination, poor health, social exclusion and powerlessness. Literacy is at the heart of the social, political, cultural, economic and political well-being of individuals, communities, societies and nations, indeed of the world" (UNESCO 2004: 8).

Statistics for literacy on a worldwide basis differ: *The World Factbook* (Central Intelligence Agency 2005) claims that 82 percent of the world's population is literate (87 percent of males and 77 percent of females), whereas UNESCO (2005a: 2) cites data showing 67 percent literate and 33 percent illiterate. (The term *literacy* is loosely defined as referring to those members of the population over the age of 15 who can read and write.) Both organizations nonetheless agree that two-thirds of the world's illiterate population (771 million adults) are women and that the highest rates of illiteracy are concentrated in three regions: South and West Asia, sub-Saharan Africa, and the Arab states. In these regions, only 60 percent of adults are estimated to be literate, of whom two-thirds are men and only half are women (UNESCO 2005b) (see Figure 13.11).

If you are spending long hours in the classroom in order to get an education, you may be skeptical about this book's claims that the world is entering a postmodern age. To you it may seem that nothing much has changed in the system of education that was established to satisfy the needs of modern society for responsible citizens and educated workers. But you would be wrong to underestimate the enormous changes that are taking place.

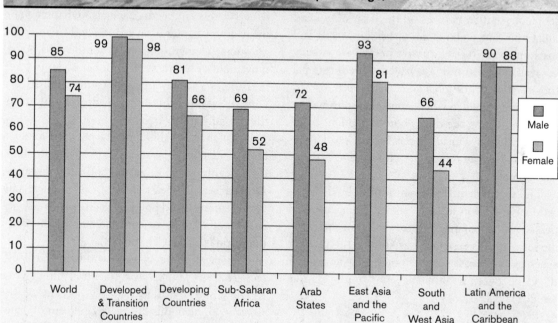

FIGURE 13.11 Adult Literacy Rates by Gender, 2000 (percentage)

*Source:* Adapted from UNESCO (2004).

What was once regarded as a futuristic dream—the classroom without walls—is now becoming widely established. As detailed in the box titled "A Virtual Revolution in Teaching," computers are making it possible for students to receive schooling without entering a building or meeting their teachers face-to-face. But does this mean the end of the distinction between schooling and education?

Clearly, much is changing, yet there are limits to what can be discarded. It is likely that postmodern education will be less spatially confined within the walls of the classroom and that teacher-student communications will be mediated by new technologies. But some functions of schooling can be satisfied only through extensive face-to-face contact between teacher and student. This is particularly the case with socializing young people for their future roles, which will require that they are able to work with others within an organization.

So it is at the higher education level, rather than in the earlier grades, that we are likely to see more emphasis on "distance education," especially as the previously limited period of formal schooling gives way to "lifelong learning." The postmodern economy will necessitate that workers are able to retrain to adjust to rapid changes in the job market and to use advancing information technologies. Within the home and at leisure, technological developments will also require that people have the capacity to learn to operate new systems.

As with the "school choice" movement, the development of "distance education" holds out the promise of widening opportunities for individuals to achieve social mobility and could also have favorable implications for the goal of increasing social efficiency. Less clear, however, is whether these developments will serve the educational goal of promoting democratic equality and citizenship.

## media moments

### A Virtual Revolution in Teaching

With colleges running out of classrooms and companies trying to keep down training costs, online education is a concept whose time may have come. But quality control is high on a list of concerns.

A virtual college campus lives inside the computers of University Access, where thousands of students electronically gather for class inside the stacks of PCs.

Machines abound in the company's ritzy Hollywood offices, where the only physical ties to scholastic tradition are felt pennants from USC and Indiana University that decorate employee cubicles. Clean-cut and perky, the young staffers talk about "digital" this and "futuristic" that with the fervency of Silicon Valley prospectors convinced they've hit upon the next big idea.

Maybe so.

"The way people want to learn is changing," said Tom O'Malia, director of the entrepreneur program at USC's Marshall School of Business.

Hoping to attract everyone from middle managers in Shanghai to teenagers in Sioux Falls, S.D., corporations and colleges have invested at least $300 million in the last few years on the Internet college gamble. One in three U.S. colleges now offers some sort of accredited degree online, more than twice as many as last year.

Demand for online executive training alone—a small piece of the electronic learning pie—will burgeon by 2002 into a $7.1 billion market, according to research analysts at International Data Corp.

"There's so much money to be made doing this," said Jaime McKenzie, editor of the *Educational Technology Journal* in Bellingham, Wash. "Everyone's racing to grab students and their checkbooks."

But although the promise is huge, so are the possible pitfalls.

If schools start mass-marketing their courses online, will they keep their elite reputations? Will students get as good an education as those who physically sit in the lecture hall? What happens as corporations move into the college market and use people with no classroom experience to teach? What's to keep a top professor from freelancing course work to a competing organization? And how much cachet will a "dot-com" degree have in the real world?

No one has answers, but online education just keeps coming.

*Source:* Huffstutter and Fields (2000: 1).

It is a question about which cultural values are most influential in shaping education. Are they values mainly concerned with individual self-interest or with social responsibility? Bear in mind that education was developed in the public sphere and not left to the private sphere in modern society because of the belief that the values of individual self-interest and profit needed to be balanced by the value of social responsibility.

An example of concerns over these trends can be seen in the debate about the controversial book *Creating Entrepreneurial Universities* (1998), written by the distinguished American sociologist of education Burton Clark. One speaker at a recent Organization for Economic Co-operation and Development (OECD) conference in Paris described this work as "higher education's equivalent of Harry Potter" (quoted in Pratt 2000: 9). In his book, Clark invokes an alarming scenario of "institutional insufficiency" in which the demands made of universities—for growth, access, efficiency, and the explosion of knowledge—exceed their capacity to respond. The only solution, he says, is for universities to transform themselves and become more entrepreneurial. At the OECD conference referred to earlier, some senior managers from universities in various countries supported Clark's view, stressing the need for university autonomy, the virtues of strong central management, and the benefits of using information technology to reach new consumers in the global market. However, critics at the conference spoke of the "seamy side" of entrepreneurialism, the dangers it posed to quality, and the need for ethical considerations and consumer protection. A warning also came from Brown University's Frank Newman, who reported research "showing that there are key aspects of higher education that profit-making organizations will not undertake, notably socializing students for their responsibilities in society, contributing to social mobility and maintaining disinterested scholarship and unfettered debate" (quoted in Pratt 2000: 9).

## CONCLUSION

In this chapter we have framed the story of what is happening to education in contemporary society by focusing on three of the competing goals of American education: democratic equality, social efficiency, and social mobility. As we have seen, the balance between these goals and the means for achieving them has varied over time. It has been suggested that the balance is shifting in favor of the goal of social mobility in the emerging postmodern era. However, this goal, like the other two, is being reassessed and reshaped. It is particularly affected by the development of the ideology of individualism in the direction of seeing ourselves, and

our identities, as consumers in a market. Education itself is also increasingly being viewed as a market in which we should be able to exercise individual choice—choosing how we are educated and for what purposes.

A central feature of modern society in the nineteenth and twentieth centuries was the involvement of government (at the federal, state, and local levels) in the institutionalization of education. Schooling was thought to be too important to be left to voluntary bodies or the market; it had to be located in approved forms of organization and subjected to governmental regulation. (Even the several thousand church schools and nonreligious preparatory schools in this country, which together educated fewer than 15 percent of American children during this time period, were subjected to external rules and standards.) It is precisely this capacity of government to occupy the central position in education and to regulate it that may be weakened by postmodern developments.

Changes in education necessitate corresponding changes in the perspectives that sociology has brought to bear on it. Twentieth-century sociologists of education, in considering the macrosocial level, tended to adopt either a functionalist or a conflict perspective. The first approach was concerned with how efficiently education was serving its social functions, such as socializing youth to take up adult roles as parents, citizens, and workers, and attempting to secure social integration by molding a diverse population into a unified society sharing the same norms and values. The second approach, the conflict perspective, focused on revealing how schooling perpetuated inequalities by giving the children of better-off families the best education and assigning students from working-class and minority families to schools and tracks that fitted them for only the most routinized jobs. In addition to these inequalities in education, advocates of the conflict perspective criticized the ideology of individualism and competition, which left students believing that the system was fair and not socially or culturally discriminatory. Other approaches focused either on social interaction at the microsocial level, such as that between teachers and students, or on cultural factors, particularly language.

What these various perspectives had in common was a concern with the social functioning of schooling in modern society and with ways in which government could act to improve it. They addressed such questions as can schools be made more socially efficient through better organization and regulation? and is it possible to achieve greater fairness and equality of opportunities in schooling?

Although the various themes that characterize postmodern sociology have a different focus, concerns about social efficiency and equality remain important. Among these themes are three significant trends in education that have attracted the interest of sociologists and might be said to mark the passage from modernity to postmodernity. The first is the increasing sense of our being "productive" consumers—that is, being able to pick and choose what we want from education. The second is the gradual acceptance of multiculturalism within society, which involves a decline in the dominance of a particular ethnic culture (e.g., WASPs) and the construction of new cultural identities. And the third is the revolution in communications and information technology that is breaking down the walls of the classroom and making lifelong learning possible. Taken together, these trends could bring about a significant "deinstitutionalization" of education—freeing it from some of the narrow constraints of organized schooling and making it more a part of everyday life.

However, there is another way of interpreting these trends. They can be seen as raising more problems. For example, talking about students as customers in a market is viewed by some as a threat to certain educational values and to the goal of preparing students to be responsible and equal citizens. Others argue that multiculturalism is a threat to the educational goal of promoting national efficiency, on the grounds that it reduces the amount of time available in the curriculum for academically challenging subjects. And online education has been accused of undermining the hierarchy of prestige according to which colleges and their qualifications are ranked, making it difficult for "virtual" students to achieve the goal of upward social mobility.

These are just a few of the concerns that we need to consider in assessing what is happening to education in postmodern society.

# EXERCISES

## Exercise 1

On a personal level, you might find it useful to compare your own education with that of your parents and then try to imagine what current trends might mean for education during the rest of your lifetime. Can you imagine what "lifelong learning" might entail—bearing in mind that the proportion of American adults taking courses is growing rapidly and that new online courses are increasingly available? Will this mean that in postmodern society everybody will be consuming education as just another aspect of everyday life?

## Exercise 2

What recent developments in your own college or university seem to be aimed at making it more entrepreneurial? In what ways have such developments affected the balance among the three educational goals discussed in this chapter?

# STUDY QUESTIONS

1. Which of the three examples related in the first paragraph of this chapter is most consistent with the concerns of the functionalist perspective?

2. Which of these examples corresponds most closely to the Weberian conflict perspective?

3. Which example offers evidence supporting the Marxist conflict perspective?

# FURTHER READING

Anderson-Levitt, Kathryn, ed. 2003. *Local Meanings, Global Schooling: Anthropology and World Culture Theory*. New York: Palgrave Macmillan.

Brantlinger, Ellen. 2003. *Dividing Classes: How the Middle Class Negotiates and Rationalizes School Advantage*. New York: Routledge Falmer.

Brint, Steven. 2006. *Schools and Societies*, 2nd ed. Stanford, CA: Stanford University Press.

Central Intelligence Agency. 2005. *The World Factbook*. Entry for category "World," subcategory "Literacy." Last updated March 29, 2006. Available online at http://www.cia.gov/cia/publications/factbook/geos/xx.html (accessed April 15, 2006).

College Board.com. 2005. "National Task Force on Minority High Achievement Report." College Board Office of Academic Initiatives. Available online at http://www.collegeboard.com/about/association/academic/taskforce/taskforce.html (accessed December 28, 2005).

Freedle, Roy O. 2003. "Correcting the SAT's Ethnic and Social-Class Bias: A Method for Reestimating SAT Scores." *Harvard Educational Review* 73: 1–43. Available online at http://gseweb.harvard.edu/hepg/freedle.html (accessed April 15, 2006).

Hodges, Larry V., and Barbara Schneider, eds. 2005. *The Social Organization of Schooling*. New York: Russell Sage.

Hoff, David J. 1999. "ETS Creating Demographic Index for SAT." *Education Week* 19, no. 1: 1–2. Available online at http://search.epnet.com/login.aspx?direct=true&db=aph&an=2280301 (accessed April 15, 2006).

MacLeod, J. 1995. *Ain't No Makin' It: Leveled Aspirations in a Low-Income Neighbourhood*. Boulder, CO: Westview Press.

Patchen, Martin. 2004. *Making Our Schools More Effective: What Matters and What Works*. Springfield, IL: C. C. Thomas Publishers.

Thernstrom, Abigail, and Stephan Thernstrom. 2003. *No Excuses: Closing the Racial Gap in Learning*. New York: Simon and Schuster.

UNESCO (United Nations Educational, Cultural and Scientific Organization). 2004. "The Literacy Decade: Getting Started 2003–2004." Part of the *United Nations Literacy Decade (2003–2012) Report*. Paris: UNESCO. Available online at http://unesdoc.unesco.org/images/0013/001354/135400e.pdf (accessed April 15, 2006).

UNESCO Institute for Statistics (UIS). 2005a. "Literacy Assessment and Monitoring Programme (LAMP)." Pamphlet. Montreal: VIS. Available online at http://www.uis.unesco.org/TEMPLATE/pdf/LAMP/LAMP_EN_2005.pdf (accessed April 14, 2006).

UNESCO Institute for Statistics (UIS). 2005b.

"Women Still Left Behind in Efforts to Achieve Global Literacy." Fact Sheet 6, September. Available online at http://www.uis.unesco.org/template/pdf/literacy/UIS_factsheet_06_EN.pdf (accessed April 15, 2006).

Wise, Tim. 2002. "Failing the Test of Fairness: Institutional Racism and the SAT." *Z Magazine Commentary,* August 12. Available online at http://www.zmag.org/sustainers/content/2002-08/12wise.cfm (accessed April 15, 2006).

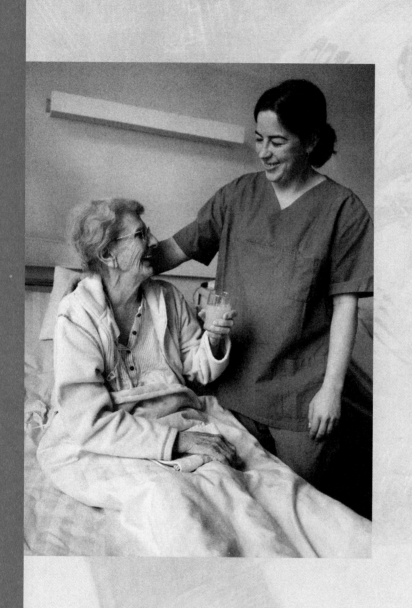

# chapter 14

# Health and Medicine

We tend to think of ourselves as unique individuals, each with a mind and a body that we can call our own. And when something goes wrong with that mind or body, we tend to seek specialist medical help to put it right. A similar approach is taken when something goes wrong with our car: We take it to a mechanic to get it fixed. But are we wise to think in this way about our minds and bodies? Do ideas about health and medicine vary across societies and groups?

Medical journalist Lynn Payer provides some amusing as well as thought-provoking descriptions of the differences in health philosophies, medical diagnoses, and treatments in four Western industrialized countries (see box titled "Medicine and Culture"). A few of these descriptions may too readily call to mind national stereotypes, such as the belief that the French value thinking, eating, and long vacations as sources of good health or that the medical aggressiveness of Americans reflects their long-ago conquest of the vast frontier: "Disease also could be conquered, but only by aggressively ferreting it out diagnostically and just as aggressively treating it, preferably by taking something out rather than adding something to increase the resistance. Disease might even be prevented by cleansing the environment of hostile elements" (Payer 1988: 127).

## AN INDIVIDUAL OR A SOCIAL STORY?

There is probably some truth in these comments, but they are very big generalizations and the idea that individuals act in conformity with a uniform national character in a complex modern society is not easily sustained. Indeed, we may wish to consider a more modest hypothesis: that throughout the history of a national society certain structural and cultural factors are likely to have had an effect on an institution such as health and medicine. It is these structural and cultural factors that sociologists seek to identify and evaluate. For example,

the differences between the French and U.S. health systems may have less to do with "national character" than with differences in political values and the forms of organization to which these gave rise. The political values of the United States emphasize individual responsibility and free enterprise, whereas those of France stress the role of the state in preventing disease and securing near-universal health care. And as shown in *The World Health Organization Report 2000: Health Systems—Improving Performance* (WHO 2000a), although America spent more on health than France in 2000 (14 percent versus 9 percent of GNP), care in America is very unequally spread, with 44 million residents lacking health insurance and high-tech medicine and expensive drugs grabbing a large share of health spending.

The United States spends more than any other country on health care—yet its health system ranks only 37th in the world, according to a report on the quality of health systems released today by the World Health Organization.

The French health system ranks No. 1 worldwide in the study. Italy, Spain, Oman, Austria and Japan are also in the top 10, as well as the smaller nations of San Marino, Andorra, Malta and Singapore.

Most of the lowest-ranking countries are in impoverished sub-Saharan Africa, where diseases such as AIDS contribute to very low life expectancies. Sierra Leone scored worst among the organization's 191 member nations.

The United States, sandwiched between Costa Rica and Slovenia, got top score on the amount it spends on care and also on a multifaceted measure known as "responsiveness," which tries to tally how well people are treated by their health systems.

But it slips elsewhere. It scores poorly (ranked at position 54/55, tied with the nation of Fiji) on whether payment for health care is fair and equitable, based on people's ability to

## theory

### Medicine and Culture

✓ An American opera singer in Vienna consulted an Austrian doctor, who prescribed suppositories for her headache. Not used to receiving headache medication in this form, she ate one.

✓ A British general practitioner took his wife to a North Carolina clinic where he was temporarily working to show her the position American women customarily assume for a pelvic examination. Her judgment: "Why, that's barbaric!" Her husband performed the examination with women lying on their sides and, while he was ridiculed by the other North Carolina doctors, he soon found he had a queue of women outside his office who had heard he examined "the English way."

✓ A French professor on sabbatical in California suffered an attack of angina pectoris, for which his doctors recommended immediate coronary bypass surgery. The professor consented, not realizing that at the time American rates of frequency for coronary bypass were twenty-eight times that of some European countries and that later studies were to show that bypasses rarely have to be done immediately, if at all.

✓ A young American working in Germany was told by her German gynecologist to take mud baths rather than antibiotics to treat her vaginal infection. "I don't want to sit in mud," wailed the woman later to a colleague. "All I want is a couple of pills!"

World travelers who had to see a doctor in a foreign country have usually discovered that medicine is not quite the international science that the medical profession would like us to believe. Not only do ways of delivering medical care differ from country to country; so does the medicine that is delivered. The differences are so great that one country's treatment of choice may be considered malpractice across the border. ...

How can medicine, which is commonly supposed to be a science, particularly in the United States, be so different in four countries [the United States, France, Britain, and Germany] whose people are so similar genetically? The answer is that while medicine benefits from a certain amount of scientific input, culture intervenes at every step of the way.

*Source:* Payer (1988: 23–24, 26).

---

pay. General health of the U.S. population, and the extent to which all citizens share that level of health, also lag[s] behind scores of comparable industrialized countries. (Mestel 2000: A20)

More recent data from the National Center for Health Statistics (2004) show a similar trend: In 2001, America's national health expenditure as a proportion of GDP was the highest in the world at 14.1 percent, followed by Switzerland (11.1 percent), Germany (10.7 percent), Canada (9.7 percent), and France (9.5 percent). Data for additional countries can be found in Figure 14.1.

In 2002, America's spending totaled $1.6 trillion, a 9.3 percent increase from 2001 (National Center for Health Statistics 2004: 4). As noted above, however, Americans' access to health care is highly dependent on their health insurance coverage. In 2002, for example, only 70 percent of the population under age 65 had private health insur-

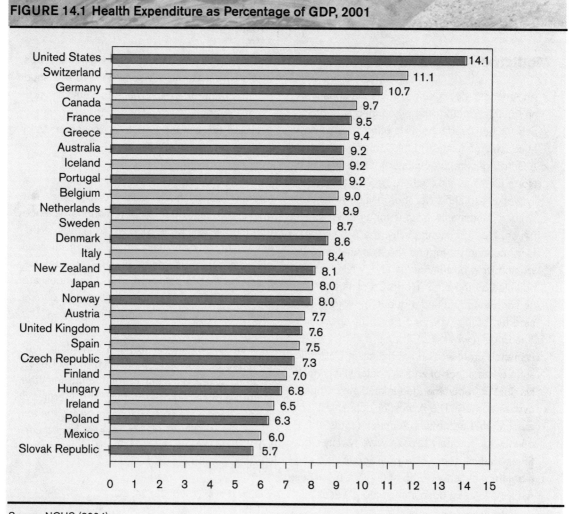

FIGURE 14.1 Health Expenditure as Percentage of GDP, 2001

*Source:* NCHS (2004).

ance—a decline from 72 percent in 2001 and from a high of 77 percent in 1984 (National Center for Health Statistics 2004: 16). As shown in Figure 14.2, access to private health insurance also varies according to an individual's race and ethnicity—a pattern of inequality that has remained similar over the years. In 2006, the proportion of Americans with no health insurance (either private or public) was approximately 15 percent or 43.6 million (National Center for Health Statistics 2007).

## MEDICINE, STRUCTURE, AND ORGANIZATION

The sociological perspective on health and illness—what we refer to as the *sociology of medicine*—takes as a central proposition something that scientific medicine has often ignored—namely, that social inequalities are important in explaining health and illness in modern societies. Indeed, improvements in the living conditions of

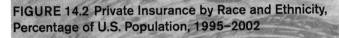

FIGURE 14.2 Private Insurance by Race and Ethnicity, Percentage of U.S. Population, 1995–2002

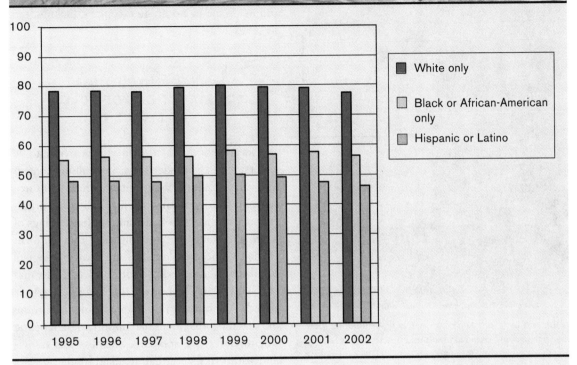

*Source:* Adapted from NCHS (2004).

people, including access to basic health care, may have a more significant impact on illness and death rates than improvements in the treatment of individual patients through developments in drugs or medical technology.

The sociology of medicine is also important for understanding why issues concerning the human body are becoming increasingly prominent in the twenty-first century. Some of the most controversial ethical issues facing society involve medical judgments, such as cloning, abortion, and the use of human embryos. Medical judgments regulate such everyday matters as the competence to work, criminal responsibility, renewal of driving licenses, access to drugs, adoption, reproduction, and the criteria for retirement and access to welfare bene-

fits. In addition, people are feeling increasing pressures to exercise self-regulation over their bodies—pressures not only to avoid risks from overeating, smoking, and drinking but also to keep fit and "look good." The insight that **medicine** is a system of social regulation can be traced back to one of the founders of the sociology of medicine, Talcott Parsons (1951b), who defined *health* as the ability to

**Medicine** A field of science devoted to diagnosing and treating various bodily ailments as well as a social institution that provides opportunities for studying the ways in which cultural processes act as a form of social regulation or control over the body.

In the late twentieth and early twenty-first centuries, people increasingly came under pressure to regulate their health to avoid societal costs, as this 1970s antismoking campaign demonstrates. (Hulton-Deutsch/Corbis)

perform expected roles effectively and viewed the sick person and the doctor as engaged in role performance. More recently, this insight has become prominent in postmodernist sociology through the work of Michel Foucault (1973), who emphasized that medical discourses—language and practices— have the power to regulate the body and its behavior. Indeed, it is precisely because medicine is so tied to issues involving moral regulation and power that it has become an area of conflict and struggle.

In the pages that follow, we consider the ways in which health and medicine are socially constructed and discuss how medicine provides society with a system of control and regulation. This entails, first, examining how the body, its health, and its treatment have been shaped by prevailing ideals about what is normal and desirable; second,

evaluating how social structural (especially economic) inequalities affect health and medicine; and, third, exploring the changing place of health and medicine in twenty-first-century, postmodern societies.

## SOCIAL AND CULTURAL CONSTRUCTIONS OF HEALTH AND MEDICINE

The awareness that **health** and **disease** have to be understood in a broader social and cultural context is not new. Early in the twentieth century, anthropologists were reporting that many so-called primitive societies had categories and understandings of health and illness that were different from our own. Ethnographic field reports by anthropologists Bronislaw Malinowski (1948) and E. E. Evans-Pritchard (1937) showed that such categories played an important role in explaining misfortune and that religious rituals had important therapeutic functions in tribal societies. Sickness was associated with evil forces that attacked human beings through, for instance, the agency of witchcraft and demonic possession. Because illness functioned within such a cosmology of good and evil forces, it served as an important explanatory device, describing or justifying evil and misery. When people fell ill, they had an idea that it was due to some physical cause, but they also may have asked "Why me?" In many societies, notions of health and disease addressed both of these issues.

By contrast, Western medicine has historically tended to concentrate on diagnosing and treating the specific physical causes of illness, paying less attention to social and cultural factors. Partly as a result of social science research findings, however, there is a growing awareness of the social and cultural dimensions of health and illness.

Indeed, it is important that health and illness be seen as social constructions. Although the concepts of *disease* and *sickness* have a technical mean-

**FIGURE 14.3 Percentage of Uninsured by Race and Hispanic Origin, Three-Year Average, 2002–2004**

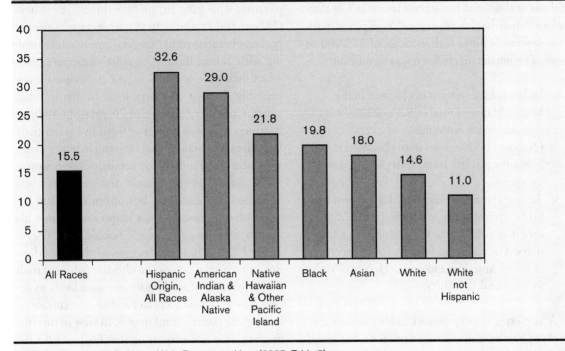

*Source:* Adapted from DeNavas-Walt, Proctor, and Lee (2005: Table 8).

ing in Western medical science, they are also related to more general ideas about health and illness that are at the core of our society's values. Having gone through a period in the twentieth century when medicine became highly specialized, scientific, and professionalized, we now recognize that health issues cannot be viewed in such splendid isolation.

Using Current Population Survey data for the period 2003–2005, researchers at the U.S. Census Bureau derived a number of statistics indicating the significant effect that social structures have on individuals' access to health care (DeNavas-Walt, Proctor, and Lee 2005). For example, in 2004, the number of uninsured people in the United States was 45.8 million—an increase from 45.0 million in 2003. Uninsured people are those who have no private health insurance; no government health insurance such as Medicare, Medicaid, or military health care; no State Children's Health Insurance Program (SCHIP) insurance; and no individual state health plan (DeNavas-Walt, Proctor, and Lee 2005: 16). As illustrated in Figure 14.3, the percentages of uninsured vary according to race and ethnicity.

**Health** The normal functioning of an organism. Examples of health depend on a given society's definition of which functions are "normal," reflecting the society's concept of the good life.

**Disease** A general lack of comfort. Examples of disease depend on a given society's definition of what is "comfortable," reflecting the society's concept of the good life.

They also vary by income level. Specifically, people with more money are likelier to have health insurance. In 2004, for example, only 75.7 percent of those with annual household incomes less than $25,000 had health insurance, compared with 91.6 percent of those with incomes of $75,000 or more. The impact on children was significant:

- ✓ In 2004, 11.2 percent of children in the United States—a total of 8.3 million—were without health insurance.
- ✓ Of those children who were classified at or below the poverty level, 18.9 percent were uninsured.
- ✓ Among Hispanic children, 21.1 percent had no health insurance, compared with 7.6 percent of non-Hispanic white children, 13.0 percent of black children, and 9.4 percent of Asian-American children. (DeNavas-Walt, Proctor, and Lee 2005)

A society's conception of health necessarily tends to involve a moral description of "the good life." Whereas social science attempts to avoid confusing the concepts of *norm* as a prescriptive standard and *normal* as a description of an average state of affairs, in everyday practice these tend to merge, with the description of an average providing a convenient peg upon which to hang measures of morality. The concept of *normal*, then, often acts as a lay benchmark for things that are both healthy and moral (King 1982: 119). For example, *The International Dictionary of Medicine and Biology* defines *health* as "a state of well-being of an organism or part of one, characterized by normal function and unattended by disease" (Becker et al. 1986: 1276). But what counts as normal depends on a particular society's standards. Moreover, the fact that *disease* is derived from the Old French word *aise*, meaning "comfort," suggests that an illness represents discomfort or lack of ease relative to normal standards of what is tolerable or desirable. The moral evaluation of

what is tolerable varies across societies. For example, a study of lower-class women in Scotland found considerable negative moral evaluation of persons who give in, or "lie down," to illness (Blaxter and Peterson 1982), whereas in America, perhaps because of its "can-do" approach to dealing with illness, those who refuse treatment, even when their case is hopeless, are considered unacceptably deviant and may even be hauled into court. Consider the case of 70-year-old William Bartling, who was suffering from five potentially fatal diseases, including an inoperable lung cancer: When he asked to have his ventilator taken away, a judge said his prognosis for recovery was "guarded and cautious, but optimistic," and ordered that he remain on a respirator against his wishes and that his hands remain tied (Payer 1988: 133). It has been suggested that American doctors regard death as the ultimate failure of their skill whereas British doctors are more likely to accept it as a physiological fact and to concentrate on making the patient comfortable. In view of this distinction, it is not surprising that hospices for the dying grew up first in Britain rather than in America (Payer 1988: 121).

The view of health and illness as culturally dependent may have derived from earlier anthropological studies, but it is increasingly the focus of sociologists today. This trend is related in part to the "cultural turn," which has led to a greater interest in the ways that meanings and values are constructed in various social institutions, including medicine. At the same time, globalization of modern forms of knowledge and organization has brought about an awareness of the differences between these modern constructions and traditional forms—differences that can actually be vitally important in understanding and dealing with global threats to health. One such threat is AIDS, which by the year 2000 had killed 19 million people and infected another 34 million. Yet in some of the African nations where it was spreading most quickly, many people refused to believe that an invisible virus could be the cause of such mass death. A report by the United Nations Programme on HIV/AIDS cited a 1999 survey in a hard-hit Kenyan rural community where 72 minors had been orphaned by AIDS. Although they all knew of the disease, none of them believed their parents had died of it; most thought that witchcraft or a curse was to blame (UN Programme on HIV/ AIDS and World Health Organization 2005: 20).

Statistics on the AIDS epidemic are tracked by numerous organizations, most notably the joint United Nations Programme on HIV/AIDS (UNAIDS) and World Health Organization (WHO) (see Table 14.1). In annual updates, data are provided regarding the number of adults and children living with HIV/AIDS, the number of adults and children newly infected, and the number of adult and child deaths attributable to AIDS. As Figures 14.4, 14.5, and 14.6 make clear, these categories vary widely from region to region.

The region hardest hit by the AIDS epidemic is sub-Saharan Africa (see Figure 14.7). Although this area contains only 10 percent of the world's population, it carries the burden of having more than 60 percent of all people living with HIV (UNAIDS 2005b: 1). It is also here that HIV disproportionately affects women: On average, there are 13 women living with HIV for every 10 infected men (UNAIDS/WHO 2004: 24). In 2004, data from South Africa revealed that HIV prevalence among pregnant women had reached its highest levels to date, with 29.5 percent of women attending antenatal clinics testing HIV-positive. Despite these high numbers, as of mid-2005 at least 85 percent of South Africans who needed antiretroviral drugs were not yet receiving them. The same was true of the 90 percent or more of those in need in Ethiopia, Ghana, Lesotho, Mozambique,

Activists with AIDS in Cape Town, South Africa, protested in 2004 against the slow rollout of antiretroviral drugs by their government. (Mike Hutchings/Reuters/Corbis)

**TABLE 14.1  Global Summary of the AIDS Epidemic, as of December 2005**

| Number of People Living with HIV in 2005 | | Range* |
|---|---|---|
| Total | 40.3 million | (36.7–45.3 million) |
| Adults | 38.0 million | (34.5–42.6 million) |
| Women | 17.5 million | (16.2–19.3 million) |
| Children under 15 years | 2.3 million | (2.1–2.8 million) |
| *People Newly Infected with HIV in 2005* | | |
| Total | 4.9 million | (4.3–6.6 million) |
| Adults | 4.2 million | (3.6–5.8 million) |
| Children under 15 years | 700,000 | (630,000–820,000) |
| *AIDS Deaths in 2005* | | |
| Total | 3.1 million | (2.8–3.6 million) |
| Adults | 2.6 million | (2.3–2.9 million) |
| Children under 15 years | 570,000 | (510,000–670,000) |

*Numbers in parentheses indicate ranges around the estimates in this table and define the boundaries within which the actual numbers lie, based on the best available information.

Source: UNAIDS/WHO (2005).

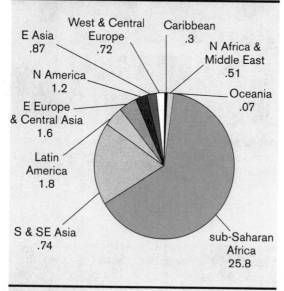

**FIGURE 14.4 Adults and Children Living with HIV/AIDS, 2005 (numbers in millions)**

E Asia .87
West & Central Europe .72
Caribbean .3
N Africa & Middle East .51
N America 1.2
E Europe & Central Asia 1.6
Latin America 1.8
Oceania .07
S & SE Asia .74
sub-Saharan Africa 25.8

*Source:* UNAIDS/WHO(2005).

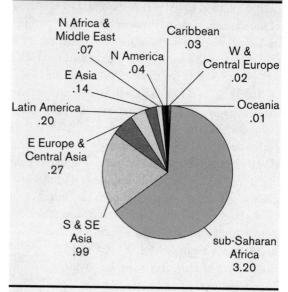

**FIGURE 14.5 Adults and Children Newly Infected with HIV, 2005 (numbers in millions)**

N Africa & Middle East .07
Caribbean .03
N America .04
W & Central Europe .02
E Asia .14
Latin America .20
E Europe & Central Asia .27
Oceania .01
S & SE Asia .99
sub-Saharan Africa 3.20

*Note:* Global total = 4.9 million.
*Source:* UNAIDS/WHO (2005).

Nigeria, the United Republic of Tanzania, and Zimbabwe (UNAIDS 2005b: 2).

The institution of medicine provides an opportunity to study the ways in which cultural processes act as a form of social control or regulation over the body—both the individual body and that of people in particular groups. This observation is all the more relevant now that medicine has taken over some of the functions previously performed by religion and the law in terms of defining what is normal or desirable versus what should count as deviant—a process called the **medicalization of deviance.** The important precedent set by the case of *Durham v. United States* (214 F.2d 863) in 1954, when the court ruled that "an accused is not criminally responsible if his unlawful act was the product of a mental disease or mental defect" (Freund and McGuire 1999: 125), reflected this shift in balance—a shift that corresponded with a period marked by the full professionalization of medicine and increasing esteem for the scientific status and technical achievements of the profession.

This period after World War II was also one in which sociologists began to focus their attention on the professional role of doctors and the social organization of medicine. One of the foremost sociologists contributing to this subject, Talcott Parsons, went on to develop the concept of sickness, and especially the **sick role,** as a form of deviance (Parsons 1951b). He argued that the sick person's incapacity is a form of deviance from social norms and obligations, such as school or work attendance, and that it can be accepted as legitimate only

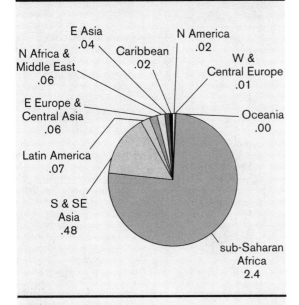

**FIGURE 14.6 Deaths of Adults and Children Due to AIDS, 2005 (numbers in millions)**

E Asia .04
N Africa & Middle East .06
Caribbean .02
N America .02
W & Central Europe .01
E Europe & Central Asia .06
Oceania .00
Latin America .07
S & SE Asia .48
sub-Saharan Africa 2.4

*Note:* Global total = 3.1 million.

*Source:* UNAIDS/WHO (2005).

if the person has an intent to get well and fulfills the obligation of attempting to get well, particularly by seeking help from a professional physician.

This concept has been helpful in terms of illuminating medicine's social control functions and the extent to which definitions of sickness reflect larger cultural values (Parsons 1972: 124). However, Parsons's model of the sick role was itself a reflection of mid-twentieth-century American values, such as individual achievement and responsibility, which emphasized the sick person's intention to get well and his or her responsibility for cooperating with the physician. As such, critics have charged, the model is problematic. Its four main shortcomings have been summarized by Peter Freund and Meredith McGuire (1999) as follows:

1. The sick role is not necessarily temporary. Parsons seemed to have in mind *acute illnesses*, such as influenza and measles, which occur suddenly, peak rapidly, and run their course in a relatively short time. In the case of *chronic illnesses* (e.g., multiple sclerosis, epilepsy, and heart disease), which entail steady deterioration of body functioning, the "intent to get well" is irrelevant. Some chronic illnesses, unlike acute illnesses, may also be considered the fault of the sufferer's own lifestyle, as with lung cancer caused by smoking or cirrhosis of the liver due to drinking. Other conditions that differ from the acute-illness pattern (e.g., physical handicaps, injuries resulting from accidents, mental illness) raise questions as to whether they should be treated as a sickness. Similarly, we must ask whether such normal conditions as pregnancy or menopause should be treated as sickness.

2. The sick role is not always voluntary. Some people cannot afford to be sick. Others resist being labeled as sick because of the stigma attached to the illness, as in the case of epilepsy (Schneider and Conrad 1980). Some are placed in care by others, irrespective of their wishes, as is sometimes the case with children and the dependent aged, or in situations where the court decides an individual needs to be committed for medical treatment. Conversely,

**Medicalization of deviance** The process by which medicine has taken over some of the functions previously attributed to religion and the law in terms of defining what is normal or desirable versus what is deviant.

**Sick role** As defined by sociologist Talcott Parsons, a role governed by social expectations. On the one hand, the sick role is a form of deviance insofar as it enables a person to ignore his or her social obligations and responsibilities; on the other, it is legitimate if the individual expresses a desire to be well again and seeks out appropriate treatment.

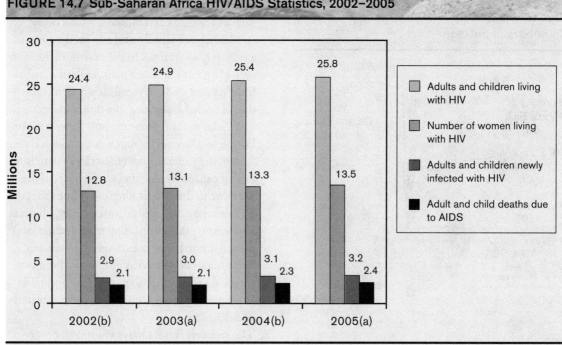

**FIGURE 14.7 Sub-Saharan Africa HIV/AIDS Statistics, 2002–2005**

Legend:
- Adults and children living with HIV
- Number of women living with HIV
- Adults and children newly infected with HIV
- Adult and child deaths due to AIDS

*Sources:* UNAIDS/WHO (2004); UNAIDS/WHO (2005).

some people are denied access to the sick role by a "gatekeeper" such as the school nurse or the company doctor.

3. The selection process by which people are classified as sick varies according to gender, social class, and subcultural expectations. Many unskilled workers, for example, have no paid sick leave, whereas most white-collar workers are given an annual allowance of "sick days." Until recently, sickness was often grounds for dismissal from a job—and for some workers without legal protection, it still is. Historically, the meaning of sickness itself has varied across groups: In the nineteenth century, for instance, upper-class women were expected to be "delicate" and to retire to bed when suffering from "nerves," whereas lower-class women were expected to be more robust in keeping with their "coarser" or less civilized nature (Ehrenreich and English 1978). Cultures also vary in terms of the degree of legitimacy they accord particular illnesses. For example, neurasthenia is more likely to be regarded as a legitimate basis of the sick role among Taiwanese than among Americans (Kleinman 1980).

4. Contrary to Parsons's model, responsibility for sickness is sometimes attributed to sick people themselves. Examples include those suffering from sexually transmitted diseases and from conditions relating to substance abuse. In addition, there are categories of illness that, although not officially considered the fault of the person, are nevertheless stigmatized. **Stigma** is a label that changes the way an individual is viewed (Goffman 1963). Because AIDS has become associated with homosexuals and drug users, it carries a stigma, even though its sufferers include newborn babies.

The fact that the imputation of responsibility and stigma to sick persons is so widespread and variable suggests that Parsons's sick-role model underestimates the moral judgment and social control aspects of medicine (Freund and McGuire 1999: 125).

Another aspect of medicine that attracted sociologists' attention in the mid-twentieth century had to do with the professional role of the doctor and the ways in which medical students were socialized into taking a particular view of patients and their illnesses. Parsons defined the physician's role in relation to the patient as being specifically limited to concern with matters of health and to be carried out in an "impersonal" manner without emotional involvement. In short, the physician's authority rests on his or her scientific training (Merton et al. 1957; Parsons 1951b). This rather bland view of the professionalization of medicine was subsequently criticized by sociologists and historians for ignoring the political, economic, and ideological processes through which the medical profession had established a monopolistic control over the field of health and the treatment of illness (Freidson 1970).

The American Medical Association (AMA) was established in 1847 on the basis of a program designed to create internal professional cohesion and standardization by controlling requirements for medical degrees and by enacting a code of ethics that would exclude "irregular" practitioners such as those using homeopathic treatments or other traditional healing arts—for example, bone-setters, barbers (who performed minor surgery), and folk and religious healers. The physicians who formed the AMA adhered to the medical belief system dubbed *allopathy*, which, at the time, was characterized by "heroic" and invasive treatments such as bloodletting, purging, blistering, vomiting, and medicating with powerful drugs such as opium and poisons such as mercury and arsenic (Freund and McGuire 1999: 207). Although these allopathic physicians called themselves orthodox or "regular" physicians, many of the public were attracted to the less dangerous forms of medicine practiced by competing approaches, such as homeopathy, naturopathy, and hydropathy. It was not until the early decades of the twentieth century that the AMA achieved a dominant position through its strategy of insisting on a scientific approach to medicine and on rigorous standards of education. It invited the Carnegie Foundation to investigate the existing medical colleges in the United States and Canada, and the ensuing Flexner Report in 1910 led to the closing of many medical colleges based on insufficiently high scientific education standards. Unfortunately, this had the effect of limiting access to the profession by women, blacks, working-class people, and others who could not afford the newly required four years of college and four full-time years of medical school (Freund and McGuire 1999: 208–209).

One consequence of the cultural construction of health and illness is that a certain set of beliefs, values, and assumptions—the **biomedical model**—became dominant. This model is widely accepted,

---

**Stigma** A label that changes the way an individual is viewed in society, typically in a negative manner. For example, because AIDS has become associated with homosexuals and drug users, it carries a stigma—despite the fact that its sufferers include newborn babies.

**Biomedical model** The dominant set of beliefs, values, and assumptions in Western medicine. The biomedical model assumes that a separation exists between mind and body, whereby illness is in the body in isolation from the mind. It concentrates primarily on the body and its functions with very little account of social, psychological, or behavioral factors in disease. It asserts that every disease is caused by a single agent that can be treated with the correct remedy. And it likens the human body to a machine whose broken parts are to be repaired or replaced. Individuals seeking to maintain or regain health according to the biomedical model are expected to exercise self-control and regulate themselves, as well as to submit themselves to the authority of medical experts.

but it does not necessarily produce better health care. It has been criticized for deflecting attention from nonmedical measures for promoting health in areas such as nutrition and public health, and for leading to difficulties in doctor-patient communication. The main components of the biomedical model are the dichotomization of mind and body, physical reductionism, the doctrine of specific etiology, the machine metaphor, and an emphasis on bodily regimen and control (Freund and McGuire 1999: 212–214). Let us consider each of these in turn.

1. Physicians who endorse the notion of the *dichotomization of mind and body* tend to presume that physical diseases are located within the body and that the body can be treated in isolation from other aspects of the person, including the mind. The foundations of this presumption probably stem from the shift toward emphasis on clinical observation that took place at the end of the eighteenth century and the development of pathological anatomy that occurred early in the nineteenth century—a shift toward what Foucault referred to as the "clinical gaze" (Foucault 1973). Previously, physicians had viewed the body indirectly through patients' descriptions of their experience of an illness. The new emphasis on physical observation and examination was aided by technological inventions such as the stethoscope, which emerged in 1819. Critics have charged that this medical perspective saw the body as "docile"—as something physicians could observe, manipulate, and change (Armstrong 1983; Foucault 1973).

**Physical reductionism** The process by which the medical model and medical professionals exclude social, psychological, and behavioral dimensions of illness in favor of concentrating solely on the individual's body and bodily functions.

2. *Physical reductionism* in the medical model excludes social, psychological, and behavioral dimensions of illness, such that attention is directed narrowly to the individual's bodily functions.

3. The doctrine of *specific etiology* refers to the belief that each disease is caused by a specific, potentially identifiable agent, such as a virus. This approach leads to searches for a drug or remedy that will be the "magic bullet" to "shoot and kill" the disease.

4. The *machine metaphor* evokes an image of the body as functioning like a machine. Illness is seen as due to the malfunctioning of one or more parts, which then need repair or replacement—a rather instrumental and manipulative view. Other societies have advanced different metaphors, such as the image of a balance of elemental forces (yin and yang) in the Chinese tradition and the image of a river in ancient Egyptian thought (Osherson and Amara Singham 1981). Of course, the prominence of the machine metaphor in Western thought has been based on great technological achievements, including medical triumphs such as transplants, artificial joints, and pacemakers.

5. In turn, the machine metaphor in the Western medical model conceptualizes the body as the proper object of *regimen and control*. Individuals are expected not only to subject themselves to self-control and regulation in order to maintain or restore health but also to submit to the authority of experts and accept their advice, whether it relates to "healthy sex," diet and exercise regimes, or hygiene.

There was nothing inevitable about the way medicine developed. It was the result of a combination of social, economic, and political factors, which in turn have varied across the cultures of the world. Globalization processes, however, have led in some cases to convergences of medical ideas and technologies.

Backed by strong scientific, bureaucratic, and commercial forces, the Western medical model is not easily adapted to local and traditional cultural practices of healing. Yet some Western societies have witnessed a revival of interest in forms of healing other than those offered by scientific medicine. For example, in a nationwide Gallup survey conducted in 1996 for the Harvard Medical School's Mind/Body Institute at Deaconess Hospital, 30 percent of the respondents reported experiencing a "remarkable healing" of a physical or psychological problem. The majority credited either a "higher power," such as God, or the action of prayer, and many said that these perceptions of healing changed their health habits, such as diet, and increased their interest in alternative medicine (Gallup 1997).

A later survey (Barnes et al. 2004) produced by the National Center for Complementary and Alternative Medicine (CAM) as part of the National Institutes of Health revealed that, in 2002, 36 percent of Americans claimed to have used some form of alternative therapy within the prior year. When prayer was included in the question format, as many as 62 percent of Americans acknowledged using alternative therapies.

In the United Kingdom, as the use of CAM became widespread, so did concerns about new forms of regulation to protect the public. Several questions were raised: How could research on CAM be accumulated, and what would constitute a suitable evidentiary base? What agencies could make reliable information about CAM available? Who would train and license practitioners? Would CAM therapies be covered through the publicly funded National Health Service? These concerns prompted an inquiry by the House of Lords in

**TABLE 14.2  Use of Complementary and Alternative Medicine (CAM) in the United Kingdom and United States**

|  | U.K.[a] 1999 (%) | U.S.[b] 1990 (%) | U.S.[b] 1997 (%)[c] |
|---|---|---|---|
| Use of any CAM in past 12 months:[d] | 20 | 34 | 42 |
| Acupuncture/acupressure | 14 | 0 | 1 |
| Aromatherapy | 21 |  |  |
| Chiropractic | 3 | 10 | 11 |
| Herbal medicine | 34 | 3 | 12 |
| Homeopathy | 17 | 1 | 3 |
| Massage | 6 | 7 | 11 |
| Osteopathy | 4 |  |  |
| Reflexology | 6 |  |  |
| Relaxation techniques |  | 13 | 16 |
| Spiritual healing |  | 4 | 7 |

Notes:

[a] Data from nationally representative random telephone survey of 1,204 British adults, commissioned by the BBC (Ernst and White 2000).

[b] Data from two nationally representative random household telephone surveys of 1,539 American adults in 1990 and 2,055 American adults in 1997 (Eisenberg et al. 1998).

[c] Table shows selected figures relating to the top five therapies based on the 1997 survey, plus (for comparison with the UK statistics) figures for homeopathy and acupuncture.

[d] Percentages of those who had used CAM. Some individuals used more than one therapy, so the numbers do not add up to 100.

Source: Adapted from UK House of Parliament (2000).

2000. The results of their survey and comparisons with rates of CAM use in the United States are shown in Table 14.2.

Much of the popularity of **alternative medicine** derives from a revival of interest in Eastern forms of spirituality and traditional healing that

**Alternative medicine**  Forms of treatment that fall outside of conventional scientific medicine, including prayer, homeopathy, and acupuncture.

began in the 1960s counterculture movement—a popularity strengthened by research showing that many visits to doctors' offices concern stress-related problems such as headaches, backaches, depression, fatigue, high blood pressure, insomnia, digestive complaints, and other "mind-body" ailments that often resist standard treatments. Medical researchers have begun to study how people's style of life affects their health; what they have found is that those who lack supportive relationships exhibit a higher incidence of untimely death from all illnesses (Goleman and Gurin 1993).

This social factor may help to explain why simply attending religious services seems to have a healing effect (Marwick 1995). In one federally funded survey, researchers at Duke University's medical school found that among nearly 2,000 older people, some healthy and others infirm, those who visited a church or temple weekly were much less likely to have high blood levels of inter-leukin-6—a biochemical produced by the immune system that is associated with many diseases, including cancer, and even with difficulties in managing routine tasks. The research team suggested that religious participation may have enhanced immune functioning by evoking feelings of belonging and togetherness (Koenig et al. 1997). This hypothesis supports the sociological thesis of Émile Durkheim's classic work *Suicide* (1897) concerning the beneficial effects of social integration.

## SOCIAL STRUCTURE AND HEALTH CARE INEQUALITIES

Durkheim was the only one of the founding fathers of sociology in the late nineteenth century who specifically addressed the relationship between health and society. In this connection, he argued that the way a society reacts to deviance, such as how it punishes criminals or treats the sick, serves to reaffirm and revitalize its core values and maintain solidarity. (For more detailed discussion of this topic, see Chapter 11, on crime and deviance.) According to Durkheim, variations in certain mortality rates, such as suicides, could be regarded as signs of whether a society had a healthy or "pathological" level of social integration. His hypothesis was that both excessive individualism and excessive social integration were pathological. In *Suicide*, he demonstrated that high rates of suicide occurred in societies in which, or during periods when, there was too much or too little integration of the individual into the community. Among the forms of pathological integration in modern societies, the two most common were those in which individuals were left without moral support, giving rise to "egoistic suicide," and those in which individuals were given too little guidance about attainable norms and thus were likely to have unrealistic goals, resulting in "anomic suicide." In both cases there was a lack of "moral community." Contrary to the belief that suicides would rise only in situations of poverty and economic depression, Durkheim was able to show that rates also increased during periods of rapid economic boom, when income inequalities increased and there was a loss of moral community.

This reasoning has also been applied to explain differences in morbidity and mortality rates across regions and societies at various times. One example studied by sociologists was that of the small town of Roseto, in eastern Pennsylvania, which attracted attention for its low death rates—particularly from heart attacks (Bruhn and Wolf 1979). The fact that death rates from heart disease were initially over 40 percent lower in Roseto than in neighboring towns could not be explained by the usual risk factors such as diet, smoking, and exercise (Wolf and Bruhn 1993).

The population of Roseto mainly comprised Italian-Americans descended from immigrants who in the 1880s had come from the southern Italian town of the same name. What appeared to distinguish the Pennsylvanian Roseto from the neighboring towns was its close-knit community and egalitarian ethos. For instance, "[t]he local priest emphasized that when preoccupation with earning money exceeded the unmarked boundary it became the basis for social rejection, irrespective of the standing of the person" (Bruhn and Wolf 1979: 80). It was only when the community ties began to loosen, as inequalities increased and young people moved away, that Roseto lost its health advantage.

Another example of the relationship between social structure and health has been provided by a study of several regions of Italy itself, in which the author, Robert Putnam (1995b), explains local government effectiveness between the regions in terms of whether the **civic community** was strong. Putnam measured civic community on the basis of involvement in local public life (e.g., in voluntary associations), as contrasted with little or no involvement in public affairs unless in pursuit of direct self-interest of oneself or one's family. He uses the concept of *social capital* to describe this scenario: "By 'social capital' I mean features of social life—networks, norms, and trust—that enable participants to act together more effectively to pursue shared objectives" (1995b: 664–665). Although Putnam was interested in neither health nor income distribution, his findings show that civic community is related to both. In particular, there is a significant correlation between civic community and lower infant mortality rates as well as between civic community and narrower income inequalities (Wilkinson 1996: 121).

Similar positive effects on health as a result of strong moral community and low rates of income inequality have been found in Britain during the two world wars (Wilkinson 1996), whereas in the case of America, according to Putnam, participation in voluntary groups and organizations has declined since the 1950s. Americans, he says, are becoming ever more isolated, cynical, and anomic and as a consequence are detached from civic life and deprived of social networks. The title of Putnam's book—*Bowling Alone: The Collapse and Revival of American Community* (2000)—is based on the rueful example that Americans still bowl, but less so in leagues. They were lonely bowlers now, making their strikes without benefit of a hearty clap on the back or a beer bought by the guys. His thesis has been criticized for ignoring new forms of voluntary association, such as youth soccer leagues, environmental organizations, book clubs, prayer fellowships, and support groups, and, from a gender point of view, for underestimating the extent to which women are now working, with less time to devote to developing and maintaining voluntary organizations. Indeed, if there *has* been a decline in social capital and civic community, it may be due to this economic development.

Putnam's concept of *civic community*, like Durkheim's concept of *moral community*, suggests that the degree to which people are socially integrated has an effect on health and illness. However, as Durkheim also demonstrated, too much integration can have pathological effects. If people are too tightly bound into a group and see little prospect of improving their situation, they might become fatalistic and depressed, even to the extent of committing suicide as the only way out. The key sociocultural factors that appear to account for differences in rates of illness and death across groups—that is, differences in **morbidity rates**

**Civic community** A sense of solidarity within a society. Robert Putnam, who coined the term, measured civic community on the basis of individuals' involvement in public life. Like Durkheim's concept of moral community, Putnam's civic community suggests that a relationship exists between social integration and the health and success of an individual.

**Morbidity rates** The amount of illness in a given society during a particular time frame. Morbidity rates are not strictly biological statistics but, rather, are closely related to social inequalities. Individuals who lack access to jobs, proper nutrition, and healthy living and work conditions are more susceptible to illness as well as less likely to have access to health care.

and **mortality rates**—are (1) the amount of stress experienced and (2) the degree of social support available.

Of course, material deprivation also has a significant effect on morbidity and mortality, especially at the extreme poverty level, where the risks from poor housing and inadequate diet increase susceptibility to disease. Children in poor families are three times as likely to die from disease, accidents, or violence during their first year of life than those born into higher-income families. Adults with above-average incomes are twice as likely as low-income people to describe their health as excellent. And rich people live seven years longer, on average, because they eat more nutritious foods, live in safer and less stressful environments, and receive better medical care. In the less developed countries of the world, the effects of poverty on morbidity and mortality are even more evident, with 1 billion people suffering from serious illness due to poverty (WHO 2000a). Clearly, malnutrition and poor sanitation increase susceptibility to disease. And it is often the case that, even where public health measures and health technologies do manage to prevent infectious diseases and reduce infant deaths, population growth outstrips the available resources, leading to more poverty and illness. This vicious circle is broken only when health measures are accompanied by birth con-

Malnutrition is fatal for thousands of people in Africa; this parent and child in south Sudan are threatened by death from starvation. (Liz Gilbert/Corbis Sygma)

**Mortality rates** The number of deaths in a given society in a particular time frame. Mortality rates, like morbidity rates, are closely linked to social factors.

**Life expectancy** A measure that refers to the average number of years individuals are expected to live. Just as social factors influence morbidity and mortality rates, life expectancy varies with respect to racial and gender structures. For example, compared with more affluent people, those beset by poverty are more likely to contract diseases due to poor living conditions and nutrition as well as lack of access to medical treatment.

trol—a solution that requires not just medical advice and low-cost contraceptives but also changes in cultural values and attitudes.

**Life expectancy,** a measure that refers to the average number of years people are expected to live, was traditionally used to gauge the overall quality of life in a given country (Central Intelligence Agency 2005). However, in 2000, the World Health Organization announced a new measure, "healthy life expectancy," which is based on a calculation of disability adjusted life expectancy (DALE)—essentially the number of years of healthy life minus the number of years of ill health. Not surprisingly, this new WHO measure shows that years lost to disability are much higher in poorer countries, largely owing to the diseases and other conditions that affect such populations (e.g., malaria, AIDS, tuberculosis, pneumonia, diarrheal disease, injury, and blindness) coupled with a severe lack of resources (WHO 2000b).

Japan ranks highest among 191 countries, with a healthy life expectancy of 74.5 years. The remainder of the top ten nations are Australia, 73.2 years; France, 73.1 years; Sweden, 73.0 years; Spain, 72.8 years; Italy, 72.7 years; Greece, 72.5 years; Switzerland, 72.5 years; Monaco, 72.4 years; and Andorra, 72.3 years (see Figure 14.8). The United States ranks only 24th, with an average of 70.0 years of healthy life—in part because the members of certain minority groups as well as many residents of inner cities in this country have extremely poor health, comparable to the status of those living in poor countries. In addition, many Americans are suffering from the effects of the HIV epidemic, cancers related to tobacco, coronary heart disease, and high levels of violence (WHO 2000b). All of the bottom ten countries are in sub-Saharan Africa, where the overall life expectancy has dropped significantly over the past decade—primarily as a result of the AIDS epidemic (WHO 2000b). These countries are Sierra Leone, 25.9 years; Niger, 29.1 years; Malawi, 29.4 years; Zambia, 30.3 years; Botswana, 32.3 years; Uganda, 32.7 years; Rwanda, 32.8 years; Zimbabwe, 32.9 years; Mali, 33.1 years; and Ethiopia, 33.5 years (see Figure 14.9). Populations in Africa seem particularly vulnerable: Among those countries with a DALE of less than forty years, 32 out of 33 are in Africa. (The only outlier is Afghanistan, with a DALE of 37.7.)

## RACE, ETHNICITY, AND GENDER

Rates of morbidity and mortality vary across racial and ethnic groups. Some of the variation is due to genetically transmitted illnesses, such as sickle-cell anemia among blacks and Taylor-Sachs syndrome

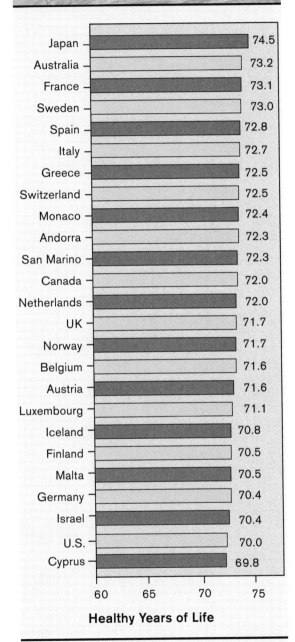

FIGURE 14.8 Healthy Life Expectancy, Highest 25 Countries, 2000

*Source:* WHO (2000a: Table 5).

## FIGURE 14.9 Healthy Life Expectancy, Lowest 25 Countries, 2000

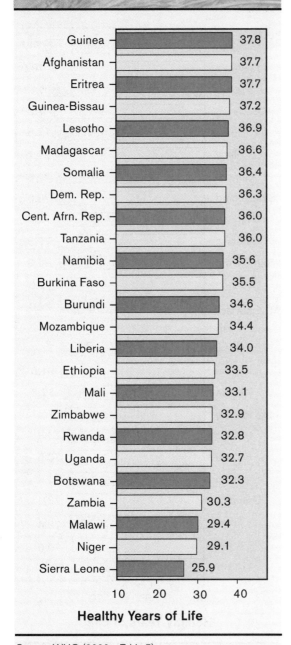

| Country | Healthy Years of Life |
|---|---|
| Guinea | 37.8 |
| Afghanistan | 37.7 |
| Eritrea | 37.7 |
| Guinea-Bissau | 37.2 |
| Lesotho | 36.9 |
| Madagascar | 36.6 |
| Somalia | 36.4 |
| Dem. Rep. | 36.3 |
| Cent. Afrn. Rep. | 36.0 |
| Tanzania | 36.0 |
| Namibia | 35.6 |
| Burkina Faso | 35.5 |
| Burundi | 34.6 |
| Mozambique | 34.4 |
| Liberia | 34.0 |
| Ethiopia | 33.5 |
| Mali | 33.1 |
| Zimbabwe | 32.9 |
| Rwanda | 32.8 |
| Uganda | 32.7 |
| Botswana | 32.3 |
| Zambia | 30.3 |
| Malawi | 29.4 |
| Niger | 29.1 |
| Sierra Leone | 25.9 |

**Healthy Years of Life**

*Source:* WHO (2000a: Table 5).

among persons of Eastern European Jewish origin. Genetic factors may also combine with stressful living and working arrangements to produce disproportionately high rates of diabetes among Mexican-American migrant workers (Angel 1985; Scheder 1988). Often, patterns of variation are linked indirectly to ethnicity through factors such as nutrition, housing, unsanitary living conditions, types of occupation, family situation, and lifestyle. Such factors may account for some of the variation between the members of an ethnic group still in the country of origin and those living in the United States. For example, research indicates that the incidence of coronary heart disease is higher among Chinese-Americans than among Asian Chinese, apparently because of differences in diet and stress levels (Gould-Martin and Ngin 1981).

Black Americans have a significantly lower life expectancy than white Americans, although the gap has been narrowing—down from 45.3 years for blacks and 54.9 years for whites in 1920 to 72.3 years for blacks and 77.7 years for whites in 2002 (Arias 2004). A major reason for the difference is the high rate of infant mortality among blacks. Although overall infant mortality rates in America have been declining, the disparity between blacks and whites has grown: The rate for blacks is now nearly 2.4 times that for whites. Even allowing for greater poverty and other material inequalities, experts are now suggesting that some of the difference may be attributable to the stress of racial discrimination and minority status experienced by black mothers. (See box titled "A Racial Gap in Infant Deaths, and a Search for Reasons.")

Black women are not the only group who suffer higher morbidity rates. It is still the case that women in general experience a higher incidence of illness than men—or at least they consult a doctor more often. The situation is reversed with respect to mortality rates among women and men. Although in the nineteenth century, women died younger than men owing to frequent pregnancies and the risks to health associated with childbirth,

**data**

## A Racial Gap in Infant Deaths, and a Search for Reasons

Ethelyn Bowers had a master's degree, an executive level job and a husband who was a doctor with access to some of the best medical care available. But her accomplishments and connections seemed to make little difference when she endured the premature births and subsequent deaths of three babies, two of whom were in a set of triplets. ...

"At the time of the loss, you really don't dissect out the reasons; all you really think about is the tremendous sorrow," said her husband, Dr. Charles H. Bowers, chief of obstetrics and gynecology at Kings County Hospital Center in Brooklyn. "In retrospect, I think you need to look at psychosocial causes—the euphemism I use for racism. If in fact my counterpart, a white physician making six figures, had a wife the same age and her likelihood of losing their child was less than half of my wife's chances of losing my child, why should that be?"

It is a mystery that consumes not only Dr. Bowers but also a growing field of researchers struggling to explain a persistent racial gap in American infant mortality rates. For years, the number of babies who die before their first birthday has been a source of shame for public health advocates; in international comparisons of infant mortality, the World Health Organization has ranked the United States 25th, below Japan, Israel and Western Europe. But even as infant mortality rates improve—to a record low average of 7.2 deaths per 1,000 live births—the disparity between blacks and whites has grown, from 2 to nearly 2.4 times the number of infant deaths.

Especially troubling is evidence that this is not simply because of poverty. While college-educated black women do better than impoverished ones, they are still twice as likely to bury their babies as their white counterparts. And immigrants have better pregnancy outcomes than assimilated minorities. What happens to their health once they settle here, and why haven't education, better jobs and prenatal care made a bigger difference in closing the infant mortality gap? ...

Because premature deliveries and low birth weights account for two-thirds of infant deaths, much recent research has focused on the causes of early labor. Medical complications from diabetes and high blood pressure, more prevalent illnesses in African-Americans, can be blamed for some of the cases but do not account for the huge disparity. So researchers have begun exploring more subtle factors, like crime, pollution and family support. Another hypothesis is that chronic stress caused by racial discrimination can elevate the hormones that set off premature labor.

*Source:* Berger (2000: 13).

by the 1920s women were living longer than men. In fact, this is now the case in all Western societies, whereas in some less developed countries male life expectancy remains higher—again, due mainly to the risks that women face in pregnancy and childbirth (Doyal 1995; Waldron 1981). The implica-

tion is that the male-female mortality difference, which exists across all societies, is due to physiological rather than to social or cultural factors.

Where social and cultural factors do seem to have significance is in accounting for the greater frequency of medical consultations among women and their use of medically prescribed drugs. A U.S. health survey performed by Lois Verbrugge (1985) found that, among people 17–44 years of age, visits to the doctor and hospital stays are twice as frequent among women as among men. In addition, women's use of medically prescribed drugs is approximately 50 percent higher than men's use of such drugs. It may be that women are more willing than men to express and report their symptoms to others, reflecting their greater acceptance of sickness as a complaint that can be verbalized or their greater adherence to the sick role within a culture that expects women to verbalize their health problems. Or perhaps women are socialized in ways that lead them to be more focused on health matters and therefore more knowledgeable about basic health issues as a consequence of their maternal role. There may also be a difference in the "vocabulary of illness" available to women compared with men. Some sociologists have even suggested that doctors are trained into a medical culture that emphasizes and highlights the health problems of women, thereby constructing women patients.

Indeed, there is evidence suggesting that, in contemporary medicine, women's disorders are conceived to be psychogenic in character, relating to women's supposedly "neurotic" tendencies and the hazardous character of reproduction. The medical responses to and social construction of premenstrual syndrome provide a useful illustration of medical science's categorization of "women's complaints" (Parlee 1994). There may be a vicious cycle connecting the fact that women report their symptoms more frequently than men and the fact that male medical practitioners have been trained to expect women to describe and discuss their symptoms. Paradoxically, concern is now being expressed over the apparent failure of doctors to diagnose men as suffering from clinical depression, whereas they are prepared to diagnose women more readily. (See box titled "Depression Comes out of Hiding.")

The issues concerning gender inequalities and health are complex. One empirical finding, first reported early on in sociology by Durkheim (1897), is that the health of men who are married is better than that of men who are single. In other words, the support provided by marriage and domestic stability is an important factor in men's health. But empirical data also show, by contrast, that women's health tends to be compromised by childbearing and by the burdens of domestic labor. These results are controversial—in part, because men and women are reported to have different types of physical and mental illness. Moreover, whereas women exhibit higher rates of morbidity, they generally enjoy lower mortality rates, surviving beyond men into old age; men, in turn, exhibit higher rates of death from accidents and violence. Some commentators have suggested, however, that with female emancipation and women's increasing tendency to adopt male behavior, such as overconsumption of alcohol and tobacco, their illness profile may come to resemble that of men.

On the one hand, the debate about gender and health has at times led to political polarization between women's and men's lobby groups. The former have argued that women's health has been neglected and that more research is needed regarding the forms of sickness suffered by women, such as breast cancer. The latter have argued that the health of men has been taken for granted, because they visit physicians less, and that more research is needed regarding illnesses such as prostate cancer, one of the principal causes of death among older men. On the other hand, a good deal of social science research in recent years has been devoted to improving the understanding of behavior among gay men with the aim of controlling the spread of HIV through better sex-education programs. This might seem a male concern, but in fact the problem of HIV/AIDS is now a global one that affects men, women, and even young children (again, see Figures 14.4–14.7).

The AIDS scenario is just one more example of the profound inequalities between rich and poor

**theory**

## Depression Comes out of Hiding

For much of his adult life, Beck Weathers, a Dallas pathologist, suffered from crushing depressions. "It makes physical pain look like a cakewalk," he said not long ago. "It dominates every moment of your existence. Not even a minute goes by that you don't have a sense of profound sorrow."

But Dr. Weathers, now 53, didn't discuss his depressions with anyone, not even his wife. "I'm the John Wayne generation," he said. "'It's only a flesh wound'[−]that's how you deal with it. I thought depression was a weakness—there was something disgraceful about it. A real man must just get over it."

Instead, he became a workaholic, growing more and more remote from his wife and children. He plunged passionately into sailing as a hobby. Then he discovered mountaineering.

"It's the ultimate way of doing work," said Dr. Weathers, one of the climbers who almost died in the 1996 storm on Mount Everest chronicled in Jon Krakauer's best-selling book *Into Thin Air*. "All you do is focus all day, because you can't think of much of anything else. It is just a wonderful way to take away thought."

To those who counsel or treat depressed men, Dr. Weathers' story is more than familiar. For years, researchers interested in gender and depression have tended to focus on how the disease affects women, whose rate of depression is twice that of men. Men have been studied mainly to find out what "protects" them from the illness.

But in any given year, according to the National Institute of Mental Health, three million to four million men in the United States suffer from clinical depression, and the rate may be rising slightly. And while definitive statistics are hard to come by, most experts agree that men are less likely than women to seek help.

Yet depression appears to take a greater toll on men. They commit suicide at four times the rate women do [although more women attempt it], and a new study from Ohio University suggests that depression increases men's—but not women's—risk of dying from heart disease.

Some mental health experts have begun to ask if, in their zeal to respond to women, men have been given short shrift.

"In focusing a tremendous amount on the gender gap, we may have lowered our sights for how to better identify the condition in males," said one researcher, who insisted on anonymity for fear of sounding unsympathetic toward women. "I think we ought to pay more attention to depression in men."

Even some of those who defend the traditional emphasis wonder whether depression ought to be approached differently in men and women. Some say the mental health profession may be significantly underestimating the rate of depression in men, or it may be ignoring a new universe of symptoms of the kind Dr. Weathers displayed.

"I'm convinced we're missing a lot of depression in men," said Dr. Jean Endicott, a psychologist at the Columbia University College of Physicians and Surgeons, in New York. "I do think women may have depressive disorders more frequently, but not in a 2-to-1 ratio."

Dr. Endicott believes, for example, that men's significantly higher rates of alcoholism and drug abuse obscure their real rate of depression: "It's often hard to diagnose depression with alcohol or drug abuse confusing the issue," she said.

*continues*

**theory**

## Depression, *continued*

Whether men drink and use drugs because they're depressed or are depressed because of the substance abuse is uncertain. But in either case, the depression itself needs treatment.

Other researchers point out that men who do seek help sometimes do not get it. "Doctors have to see past their own bias," said Dr. Susan Kornstein, a psychiatrist at Virginia Commonwealth University, in Richmond. "They tend to see depression more easily in women because they think more to the emotional side for women, more to the physical side for men. We're socialized to be much more comfortable with women crying and expressing emotional distress, than with men."

Doctors and clinicians may unintentionally rebuff male patients in other ways. Depression is diagnosed through a checklist of symptoms that include fatigue and sleep disorders, as well as feelings of sadness and hopelessness. Many researchers think that fewer men might [fall] through the net if examiners used different language to ask about mood.

"I think there are men who will deny ever having had a period of two weeks or more where they felt sad, blue or down in the dumps," said Dr. Ellen Frank, a University of Pittsburgh psychologist. "I think adding irritability to the criteria can be extremely helpful."

*Source:* Wartik (2000: 1).

---

societies throughout the world. Many AIDS victims in Western societies enjoy relatively good prospects of survival because they can afford the new drugs that have been found to delay the development of the disease; the poverty-stricken victims of AIDS in Africa, Asia, and Russia are not so fortunate. At the same time, globalization, which involves increasing international travel, is contributing to the rapid spread of diseases around the world. This problem pertains not just to AIDS but also to the reappearance in Western societies of diseases that once seemed to have been eliminated, such as tuberculosis. Globalization brings great benefits, but it also increases risks.

### HEALTH AND MEDICINE IN THE TWENTY-FIRST CENTURY

The twentieth century saw great progress in the professional training of medical personnel, scientific knowledge about the causes of diseases, and the development of pharmaceutical and surgical treatments. Sociologists provided valuable research on these processes of modernization, addressing such issues as the nature of scientific medical knowledge, the roles of physician and patient, the professionalization of medical practice, and inequalities (especially class differences) in health care. The ways in which sociologists interpreted these developments varied according to their theoretical perspective: Functionalist sociologists such as Talcott Parsons focused on the roles of physician and patient within the institution of medicine; sociologists engaged in the symbolic interactionist tradition of American sociology provided detailed studies of interactions within health settings such as hospitals (Glaser and Strauss 1965; Glaser and Strauss 1968; Goffman 1961); and sociologists with a conflict perspective emphasized inequalities in health care between classes and the uneven distribution of medical resources (Navarro 1976).

In the postmodern societies of the twenty-first century, we are facing new medical issues in addition to some of the old ones. Interest in alternative, non-Western medical beliefs and practices is undergoing a renewal. The very success of the scientific medical model of disease and the organization of the modern medical institution has entailed the erosion of a more "holistic" view of the sick person. Sociologists are retracing the historical development of Western medicine and asking whether it might be changing direction. And there is a new emphasis on the unity of mind and body, which, in turn, is leading to a greater interest in the question of whether particular states of feeling, such as stress or lack of social solidarity and support, might have physical effects.

As noted earlier, the most severe inequalities in health care are those between poor and rich nations. Globalization may lead to even wider inequalities if the poor nations, especially those in the Southern Hemisphere, continue to be economically exploited by multinational companies seeking profit for their investors in the richer countries of the Northern Hemisphere. There is evidence that many corporations have behaved irresponsibly in matters such as promoting cigarette sales in the developing world and offloading drugs that have been either criticized or banned in the West. Environmental pollution, too, has been inflicted on poorer nations by multinational companies that are more highly regulated in developed countries and so transfer their polluting processes overseas.

Harvard researcher Supinda Bunyavanich and her colleagues (2003) have demonstrated not only how environmental change, climate change, and ecological change are interconnected but also how their related outcomes are affecting child health. They point out, for example, that increased air pollution and UV radiation (environmental changes caused by human activity) can lead to respiratory diseases and melanoma; that climate changes related to environmental changes, such as thermal extremes or weather disasters, can cause heat stroke, drowning, gastrointestinal diseases, or psychological trauma; and that ecological shifts (as a result of climate change), such as alterations in food supply or the emergence of new allergens, can result in higher rates of cancer or birth defects as well as in malnutrition and developmental delays (see Figure 14.10).

Children are a particularly vulnerable subpopulation "because of their developing physiology and anticipated long-term exposure. Internationally, two thirds of all preventable ill health due to the environment occurs in children" (Bunyavanich et al. 2003: 44). Consider, for example, the increased health risks to children posed by environmental changes. Children frequently play outdoors and therefore are exposed to high levels of air pollution and UV radiation. Their respiratory systems are still immature and, when exercising, they breathe rapidly and with open mouths, so the pollutants go straight to their lungs. And their skin is susceptible to sunburn, early episodes of which significantly increase chances of melanoma later in life (Bunyavanich et al. 2003: 45). In light of these concerns, Bunyavanich has called for further research, pediatrician action, and policy changes at both the local and global levels.

As we have also seen, health care remains unequal even in developed societies, with the poor suffering higher morbidity and mortality rates than the more affluent. Differences in working conditions (hazardous occupations and hard physical work) and lifestyles (diet and substance abuse) account for much of this variation in morbidity and mortality. One-third of the U.S. population is not covered by medical insurance. And rich and poor people experience markedly different levels of access to quality medical treatment. Even for-profit health management organizations (HMOs) are implicated in such inequalities. As a result of their spread, chronically ill patients have been denied access to the doctor of their choice in cases where the physician's HMO was not prepared to pay for such expensive patients.

Future debates about health and inequality are likely to raise fundamental questions about citi-

**FIGURE 14.10 Relationship Among Environmental Change, Climate Change, Ecological Change, and Child Health**

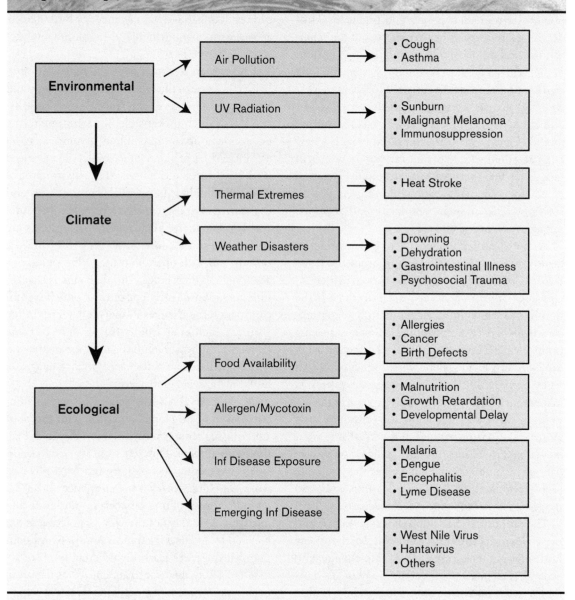

*Source:* Bunyavanich et al. (2003).

zens' rights and how these may conflict with the individual freedoms of consumers and sellers. Globalization, the commercialization of medical care, and the creation of free markets in body parts could have important consequences for the health care system that came to prominence in the twentieth century. Indeed, the model of the professional doctor that Talcott Parsons described, in which the doctor enjoyed autonomy to make medical decisions without commercial considerations or corporate pressure, could become obsolete. That independent doctor may well be transformed into the hired employee of a profit-making commercial enterprise in the form of an HMO or private hospital. Furthermore, the contemporary development of health care in the United States has brought about a new emphasis on specialization, which poses a threat to the professional coherence and solidarity of medicine as a whole.

The Human Genome Project, introduced here in 2001 by Dr. Robert Waterston of the Washington University Genome Sequencing Center, helps find cures for disease by mapping its origins in human genes. (Reuters/Corbis)

## CONCLUSION

Postmodern society is likely to see fundamental changes in the relationships among the self, body, and society. Medical technology and microbiology hold out the promise of freeing us, as individuals, from pain, aging, and death through such developments as the Human Genome Project (which has mapped the DNA structure of the genes in the body), cloning, transplantation, various "wonder drugs," and microsurgery. These medical possibilities have given rise to utopian visions of a world free from disease, in which the human body stands in an entirely new relationship to self and society. Such possibilities have major implications for family life, reproduction, work, and aging. They also raise important issues about the ownership and use of our bodies. Should people be free to sell parts of their bodies for commercial gain? A world market in kidney sales from poor to rich countries already exists. Will there be a need for a system of global governance over all matters affecting disease

and medicine, including threats to health from pollution? Such a system could come into conflict with the values of individual freedom, free enterprise, national sovereignty, and freedom from regulation. Yet it may be the only way of reducing everyone's risks in an increasingly interdependent global society.

# EXERCISES

### Exercise 1

In this chapter, we have discussed how different forms of social inequality affect morbidity rates. Take a closer look at Figures 14.4 through 14.7, which chart the global incidence of HIV/AIDS. What social factors help to explain why the percentage of people living with AIDS is higher in North America and Europe than in sub-Saharan Africa and Southeast Asia? What social factors account for the higher infection rate among women in sub-Saharan Africa? Agencies that gather such statistics warn that the number of deaths from

AIDS reported in developing countries is probably greatly underestimated. What structural and cultural factors might contribute to this underreporting?

### Exercise 2

We have also discussed health and illness as cultural concepts. Is this also true of *disability* and *ability*? How, for instance, is disability understood according to the biomedical model? To what extent does Parsons's model of the sick role apply to the conventional medical treatment of disability, and how has it been resisted? Why are some disabilities more stigmatized than others? To what extent does it matter whether someone is born with a disability as opposed to acquiring it later in life?

# STUDY QUESTIONS

1. What is the difference between the sociological and medical approaches to health and illness? What evidence supports the sociological argument that health is a social construction?

2. Explain why *health* and *disease* are moral as well as medical concepts.

3. Explain Talcott Parsons's perspective on sickness as a form of deviance. Under what circumstances is this deviance legitimate? What have been the main criticisms of Parsons's model of the sick role?

4. How did the American Medical Association help the medical profession establish a monopolistic control over the field of health and the treatment of illness in the United States? What medical belief system did its first members ad-

here to? How did the AMA's rise to dominance create gender, race, and class disparities in the medical profession?

5. Briefly describe the main components of the biomedical model. What criticisms have been directed against it?

6. According to Emile Durkheim, what is the relationship between social integration and mortality rates? What did he consider a "pathological" level of integration, and which two forms of such integration were most common in modern society? How did his study contradict the conventional wisdom about suicide?

7. What social factors contribute to the lower average life expectancy and high infant mortality rate among black Americans?

8. Why are women more likely than men to seek medical consultation and to take medically prescribed drugs? How do doctors contribute to this pattern?

# FURTHER READING

Albrecht, Gary L., Ray Fitzpatrick, and Susan C. Scrimshaw. 2003. *The Handbook of Social Studies in Health and Medicine*. Thousand Oaks, CA: Sage Publications.

Barnes, Patricia M., Eve Powell-Griner, Kim McFann, and Richard L. Nahin. 2004. "Complementary and Alternative Medicine Use among Adults: United States, 2002." *Advance Data Report* 343. Hyattsville, MD: National Center for Health Statistics. Available online at http://nccam.nih.gov/news/report.pdf (accessed April 16, 2006).

Brown, Phil, ed. 2000. *Perspectives in Medical So-*

*ciology*, 3rd ed. Prospect Heights, IL: Waveland Press.

Bunyavanich, Supinda, Christopher P. Landrigan, Anthony J. McMichael, and Paul R. Epstein. 2003. "The Impact of Climate Change on Child Health." *Ambulatory Pediatrics* 3: 44–52. Available online at http://www.med.harvard.edu/chge/buny.pdf (accessed April 16, 2006).

Central Intelligence Agency. 2005. *The World Factbook*. Notes and definitions for "Life Expectancy" entry; last updated March 29, 2006. Available online at http://www.cia.gov/cia/publications/factbook/docs/notesanddefs.html (accessed April 16, 2006).

Cockerham, William G. 2003. *Medical Sociology*. New York: Prentice-Hall.

Conrad, Peter, ed. 2005. *The Sociology of Health and Illness: Critical Perspectives*, 7th ed. New York: Worth Publishers.

Eisenberg, D. M., R. B. Davis, S. L. Ettner, S. Appel, S. Wilkey, M. Van Rompay, and R. C. Kessler. 1998. "Trends in Alternative Medicine Use in the United States, 1990–1997: Results of a Follow-Up National Survey." *Journal of the American Medical Association* 280, no. 18: 1569–1575.

Ernst, E., and A. White. 2000. "The BBC Survey of Complementary Medicine Use in the UK." *Complementary Therapies in Medicine* 8, no. 1: 32–36.

Riska, Elianne. 2005. *Masculinity and Men's Health: Coronary Heart Disease in Medical and Public Discourse*. Lanham, MD: Rowman and Littlefield.

Sen, Gita, Asha George, and Ostlin Piroska, eds. 2003. *Engendering International Health: The Challenge of Equity*. Cambridge, MA: MIT Press.

UNAIDS (United Nations Programme on HIV/AIDS). 2005. "UNAIDS Epidemic Update 2005: Sub-Saharan Africa Fact Sheet." Geneva, Switzerland: UNAIDS. Available online at http://data.unaids.org/Publications/Fact-Sheets04/FS_SubSaharanAfrica_Nov05_en.pdf (accessed April 16, 2006).

UNAIDS/WHO (United Nations Programme on HIV/AIDS and World Health Organization). 2004. "AIDS Epidemic Update: December 2004." Available online at http://www.clintonfoundation.org/pdf/epiupdate04_en.pdf (accessed April 16, 2006).

———. 2005. "AIDS Epidemic Update: December 2005." UNAIDS/05.19E. Available online at http://www.who.int/hiv/epi-update2005_en.pdf (accessed April 16, 2006).

United Kingdom House of Parliament. 2000. Sixth Report: "Complementary and Alternative Medicine." House of Lords, Select Committee appointed to consider Science and Technology, November 21. Available online at http://www.parliament.the-stationery-office.co.uk/pa/ld199900/ldselect/ldsctech/123/12301.htm (accessed April 16, 2006).

Weitz, Rose. 2004. *The Sociology of Health, Illness and Health Care*, 3rd ed. Belmont, CA: Wadsworth.

White, Kevin. 2002. *An Introduction to the Sociology of Health and Illness*. London: Sage.

WHO (World Health Organization). 2000a. *The World Health Organization Report 2000: Health Systems—Improving Performance*. Geneva, Switzerland: World Health Organization, p. 5. Available online at http://www.who.int/whr/2000/en/whr00_en.pdf (accessed April 16, 2006).

———. 2000b. Press Release, June 4. "WHO Issues New Healthy Life Expectancy Rankings." Washington, DC/Geneva, Switzerland: WHO. Available online at http://www.who.int/inf-pr-2000/en/pr2000-life.html (accessed April 16, 2006).

# chapter 15

# Religion

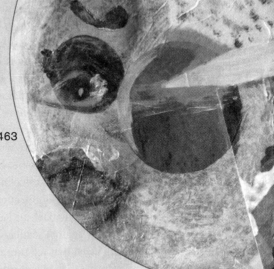

Religion is one of the oldest social institutions. There has never been a society without some beliefs and practices that most people would recognize as in some way religious. However, most of the early sociologists of modernity believed that religion would steadily decline as societies modernized. Science, they predicted, would take over the authority once possessed by religious thought, and other institutions would take over most of its social functions. Religion would be reduced to a private leisure activity and a purely individual matter. The question for sociology at the beginning of the new millennium is whether this prediction of the decline of religion has come true. As we will see, there are several perspectives on this issue. Some commentators agree that religion has declined. Others maintain that some types of religion, such as fundamentalist groups, are fighting back and are engaged in a kind of culture war against secular cultural influences. Still others insist that religion is changing or restructuring in ways that reflect other cultural trends in postmodern society, ranging from the formation of exotic cults to mainstream religion's adaptations to local demands.

A glance at some of the newspaper stories featuring religion in recent years might suggest that it is far from dying out or retreating to the quiet backwaters of private life and leisure. Consider what happened during the Columbine High School massacre, as detailed in the box titled "The Teenage 'Martyr' of Columbine High."

## AN INDIVIDUAL OR A SOCIAL STORY?

This account of an alleged religious martyrdom provides an example of the "social construction of

**Culture wars** Tensions over religious and sacred values that have arisen as a result of efforts to separate church and state. An example is the abortion debate, typically framed with religious values on one side and secular values on the others.

reality" through media stories—in this case, concerning religion. Whether or not this was an accurate account (the later official investigation cast some doubt on it), many people were predisposed to believe it. Even for those who do not share Cassie Burnall's specific religious beliefs, the story appealed to values commonly held by Americans—values relating to heroic individualism and freedom of belief. The question remains, however: Was this simply the story of an exceptional individual, or does it reflect wider social and cultural trends?

In fact, closer examination of Cassie's story does reveal certain more general social and cultural factors. The newspaper account we've just read places it in the context of culture wars—the struggle between Christian believers and "liberal secularism." The view represented here is that America is an arena or battleground in which religion is fighting desperately for survival. An alternative view, however, posits a market situation in which religion is diversifying and thriving, whether in the form of newly developed cults or fundamentalist belief in the literal truth of the Bible.

From this angle, it is not surprising that newspaper articles about the Columbine High School massacre drew attention to conflicting pressures from competing religious groups and subcultures. Evangelicals were opposing not just liberals but also satanic cults and witchcraft. Media stories about the killing of Cassie seemed at one point to be creating a cult around the young "martyr" herself; in the British *Daily Telegraph*, for instance, it was reported that "around 73,000 teenagers flocked to an evangelical rally in Michigan to hear sermons about her death" (*Daily Telegraph*, May 8, 1999). So, we find not only that the actions of individuals at Columbine High School can be set within a wider context of contending social and cultural forces but also that these individual actions had social and cultural effects themselves.

We will return to Cassie's story later in the chapter, but for now we need to ask what is meant

## The Teenage "Martyr" of Columbine High

Cassie Burnall was in the library of Columbine High School when the Trenchcoat Mafiosi, Eric Harris and Dylan Klebold, burst in brandishing guns and bombs.

Like others, Cassie ducked under her desk and prayed. One of the teenage killers pointed a semi-automatic pistol to the side of her head and asked: "Do you believe in God?" Cassie looked back at him and answered, "Yes." He pulled the trigger.

Survivors' accounts vary. One remembers that the gunman said, "There is no God" before he executed Cassie.

As America emerges from the horror and desolation of that day, when 12 pupils and a brave schoolteacher were mindlessly killed, Cassie's story has resonated throughout the Christian community.

However her death may now be embellished—and that process has already started—no one doubts that Cassie died asserting her faith and probably for it. Approaching the 2,000th year of the Christian era, America has found a Christian martyr. The 17-year-old girl from Columbine was typical of her age. She wore scruffy flares and Doc Martens, worried about her looks and wanted to be several pounds lighter. But Cassie is now being compared with Perpetua and Felicity, who were beheaded by the Emperor Septimius Severus in 203 for refusing to deny their Christian faith.

Nearly 1,800 years ago, Perpetua consoled her father in a letter saying: "It shall happen as God shall choose, for assuredly we depend not on our own power but on the power of God."

Just last June, Cassie Burnall wrote to a friend: "Some people become missionaries and things, but what does God have in store for me? ... Isn't it amazing this plan we're part of? I mean, it's a pretty big thing to be part of God's plan."

American Christians, fighting what they see as a "culture war" against liberal secularism, are embracing a girl whose death exemplified for them the fight of good against evil. Even if Cassie's only word to her killer was "yes," one local minister said: "Why did they ask her? Because they knew what she was."

The killers—who dabbled in Satanism and chose Hitler's birthday for their rampage—appear to have been looking for Christians to kill. ...

America's imagination has been captured not simply by the manner of that death, but also by recent revelations from her parents that in early adolescence Cassie herself was angry and dabbling in witchcraft, drugs and alcohol.

The clique she belonged to is said to have been sinister, brooding, suicidal and angry—much like the Trenchcoat Mafia.

Dave McPherson, a local pastor, told the *Weekly Standard* that when he first met Cassie, he feared she was "lost irredeemably to sin," for she "was into black magic, the dark stuff."

But, her parents say, they took her out of school, cut off the phone, and kept her in the house, allowed out only to go to church. Evangelical Christians themselves, they enrolled her in a Christian school and sent her to a Christian summer camp. There, other children gathered round her and prayed over her.

Cassie later recalled: "I don't know what happened, but I was changed. I felt this huge burden lifted off my heart."

After being "born again" two years ago, Cassie, now attending the evangelical West

*continues*

media moments

### The Teenage "Martyr" of Columbine High, *continued*

Bowles Community Church, in Littleton, asked to leave her Christian school so she could go to Columbine and be a "witness" for Christ.

So she returned to "spread the Word" in a secular school, and there died rather than deny

God to killers representing the nihilism she had so recently rejected. "I think young Cassie's life is going to probably have a more phenomenal impact upon young people over the next 10 years than anything I've seen in the past 10 or 15 years," said Josh McDowell, a Texan minister.

*Source: Daily Telegraph* (England), May 8, 1999.

by religion, as this is necessary to our understanding of what is happening to it.

## WHAT IS RELIGION?

There are many ways of defining religion, and it matters which one we choose. First, let us consider the two types of definition: *substantive* and *functional*. A substantive definition restricts the label of religion to a system of beliefs and practices that has a particular kind of content, usually a god or supernatural force. However, whether a particular set of beliefs and practices actually does refer to a supernatural being or force is not always clear. For example, many New Age beliefs and practices are concerned with developing the potential of the self by tapping into various ill-defined cosmic powers. And like traditional religious phenomena, these

**Religion** As substantively defined, a system of beliefs and practices that has a particular kind of content, usually a god or supernatural force; as functionally defined, a system of beliefs and practices that answers otherwise unanswerable questions or binds people together through a shared commitment to something sacred.

cosmic powers elude scientific testing. But many New Age believers see them as natural forces rather than as "supernatural" ones. (For an overview of religious adherence worldwide, see Figures 15.1 and 15.2 as well as Table 15.1.)

As a way of avoiding the problem faced by a substantive definition, which stipulates what religion *is*, others have used a functional definition, defining it in terms of what it *does*. For example, religion may serve the existential function of answering otherwise unanswerable questions ("What is the meaning of life?") or the social function of binding people together through a shared fundamental commitment to something held sacred.

In practice, many sociologists seem to operate with a mixed definition, but with different emphases. French sociologist Émile Durkheim, in his book *The Elementary Forms of the Religious Life* (1915), adopted a mainly functionalist definition but included a substantive element that he called the *sacred* as distinct from the *profane* (see Chapter 3, on cultural structures). The sacred refers to things set apart as exceptional and worthy of awe and reverence, whereas the profane consists of the common things of everyday life, whose value rests in their practical usefulness. Durkheim's definition of religion is especially interesting given the context under discussion: "A religion is a unified sys-

## FIGURE 15.1 Religious Adherence Worldwide

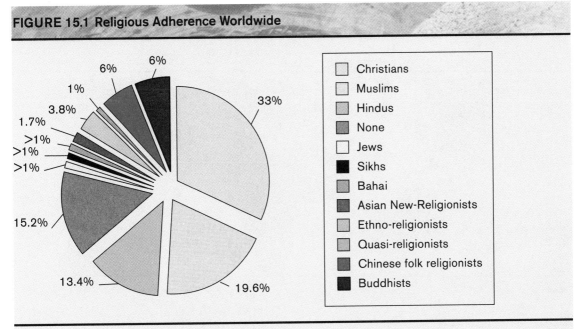

*Note:* "Quasi-religionists" includes secular movements that are partly or virtually religious, as well as religious movements that have negative effects on their members. "Asian New-Religionists" includes sects and offshoots of Hindu or Buddhist religions that combine Christian and Eastern religions.

*Source:* Adapted from Barrett, Kurian, and Johnson (2001: 7).

tem of beliefs and practices ... which unite into one single moral community called a Church, all those who adhere to them" (1915: 62).

The emphasis here is on religion's function of binding those people together who share a commitment to the same sacred symbol, and who are then united in a moral community. It is the bonding on the basis of shared beliefs that is significant, not the particular object of devotion. Anything can become a sacred symbol—ranging from a sacred animal as a totem for a Native American clan to the bread and wine as the Body and Blood of Christ in the Catholic Church. Some sociologists have suggested that even football could be seen as a religion if it functioned to bind together into a community those who regarded it as their ultimate commitment. Probably not many people would give sport or a sports team such a total commitment, al-

though some might! A more likely candidate is nationalism, as many people have shown a willingness to give their lives for their country and an inclination to regard its symbols (such as the flag) as sacred. Even a secular state such as the United States has its sacred rituals and ceremonies, such as swearing allegiance to the flag, inaugurating presidents, and celebrating Memorial Day and Thanksgiving. Such practices have collectively been described as a *civil religion* (Bellah 1970), a topic we discuss more fully later in the chapter.

According to this version of the functionalist perspective, it is society that needs these religious functions to be served. Another, more interpretive or "phenomenological" approach emphasizes the functions that religion serves for the individual rather than for society. It starts with the individual's need to have answers to questions about the

## FIGURE 15.2 World Religions Map

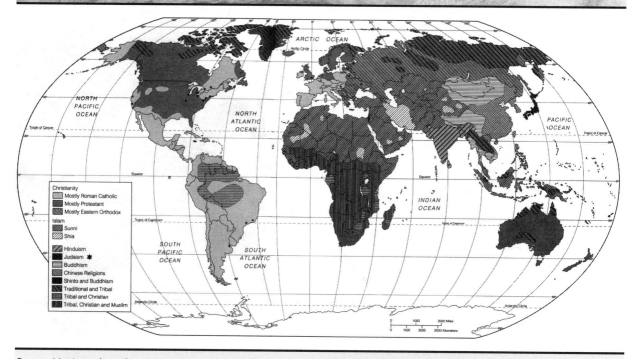

Christianity
Mostly Roman Catholic
Mostly Protestant
Mostly Eastern Orthodox
Islam
Sunni
Shia
Hinduism
Judaism
Buddhism
Chinese Religions
Shinto and Buddhism
Traditional and Tribal
Tribal and Christian
Tribal, Christian and Muslim

*Source:* Matthews (1998).

basic meaning of things—to see the world as a meaningful, ordered, and coherent place—and it proceeds on the assumption that the search for such deep existential meaning can be fruitful only in religious terms. Human existence throws up apparently inexplicable challenges, such as suffering, misery, and "bad luck," and religious beliefs give meaning to these challenges. Such beliefs help us to cope, and may also offer ways of behaving that allow us to represent and express our desire for meaning and order. For example, the tragic death of young Cassie Burnall at Columbine High School was given meaning through the symbols and ceremonies at her memorial service. From an interpretive perspective, religious ritual can be seen as a kind of language, one that allows individuals to express their feelings about the world sym-

bolically—articulating through action the way they would like the world to be.

From the functionalist perspective, which emphasizes collective needs, religion is universal because it performs an essential integrative function for society—binding everyone and everything together. And from the interpretive perspective it is universal because it fulfills the human need to make otherwise senseless things meaningful. Peter Berger, in *The Sacred Canopy* (1967), argued that religion provides a shield or "sacred canopy" against meaninglessness. While acknowledging that there are other meaning systems, including science, he noted that religion is distinguished by the fact that it covers all phenomena (the cosmos) and also tells us how to behave toward them. Its sheltering quality is particularly important in the

## TABLE 15.1  Numbers of Religious Adherents Worldwide

| Religious Denomination | Estimated Number of Adherents |
|---|---|
| Christians | 2,000,000,000 |
| Muslims | 1,188,000,000 |
| Hindus | 811,000,000 |
| None | 918,000,000 |
| Jews | 14,000,000 |
| Sikhs | 23,000,000 |
| Baha'i | 7,000,000 |
| Asian New-Religionists | 102,000,000 |
| Ethno-religionists | 228,000,000 |
| Quasi-religionists | 80,000,000 |
| Chinese folk religionists | 385,000,000 |
| Buddhists | 360,000,000 |

*Source:* Adapted from Barrett, Kurian, and Johnson (2001: 7).

marginal situations in individuals' lives, where taken-for-granted definitions of reality are called into question. Of course, the marginal situation par excellence is death. It is in witnessing the deaths of others (especially significant others), and in anticipating their own deaths, that individuals are often led to question their ordinary ways of thinking.

There are close links between the different definitions of religion and the different sides taken up in the debate as to whether religion is inevitably declining in modern society—the "secularization thesis." Those who define religion in substantive terms—pointing to statistics about declining church attendance or traditional belief, particularly in Europe—are more likely to argue that Western society is becoming increasingly secular. Those who define religion in functional terms tend to be less inclined to accept the secularization thesis. And, indeed, as we have noted in our earlier discussions of culture, many examples of things

held to be sacred can be found even in postmodern society.

## RELIGION, MODERNITY, AND THE SECULARIZATION THESIS

The three thinkers who most profoundly influenced the development of sociology in the nineteenth and early twentieth centuries—Karl Marx, Max Weber, and Émile Durkheim—all had something to say about the issue of the future of religion in modern society.

For Marx, the form of religion and its functioning were determined by the structure of economic relations. Christianity, he argued, is ideally suited to the needs of the capitalist economic system because it is an ideology that disguises the exploitative nature of the relations between capitalists and workers, while at the same time legitimating these inequalities. For the individual, religion provides consolation and comfort—it is "the opium of the masses." And it will inevitably weaken, he said, because it is a "false consciousness"; but its decline will be completed only when the social structure that produced it (capitalism) has disappeared.

Compared to Marx, Weber gave more independence to religious culture in relation to social structures, especially at the point when a new religion first emerges. Weber demonstrated that the subsequent development of a religion is often influenced by the needs of the social group (or "stratum") that becomes its main carrier—small traders and urban artisans, in the case of Christianity. In his most famous work, *The Protestant Ethic and the Spirit of Capitalism* 1904), he traced the process by which one form of Christianity, the Calvinist version of Protestantism, preceded and contributed to the development of capitalism. According to popular belief among Calvinists in the sixteenth and seventeenth centuries, a person's business success resulting from conscientious work and investment of savings could be interpreted as a sign that he or she was predestined to salvation—one of "God's elect." This belief, known as the **Protestant Ethic,** was ideally suited to the development of early capitalism, especially through its emphasis on individual responsibility and striving as well as a compulsion to save and not spend. The only problem for religion was that, once this religious principle had done its work, it became absorbed into the general spirit (or culture) of capitalism. Weber quoted Benjamin Franklin's statement, "Time is money," as an example of an essential element of the spirit of modern capitalism and of the Protestant Ethic itself, although by Franklin's time it had lost its religious basis. Religion was no longer needed by the economy or other social institutions after they developed their own rational systems of thought about the best means to achieve their specific ends.

Weber's key idea about modern society was that it was marked by increasing *rationalization*—by which he meant a process wherein precise calculation of means, ends, and goals would spread into all areas of social life. Rational thinking, he argued, involves the systematic breaking down of an

object for study into smaller parts, which can then be classified and analyzed. But this kind of thinking would bring about a "loss of enchantment," **disenchantment,** with the modern world. Whereas traditional society had been characterized by a belief in magic, myth, and religion, rationality and science would dominate modern society. Disenchantment and rationalization would inevitably result in the decline of religion—that is, **secularization.** The only exceptions to this trend would be occasional breakthroughs in the form of new movements—including religious sects or cults—consisting of followers of a charismatic leader. (For a discussion of charisma, see Chapter 17, on politics, publics, and the state.) Weber followed his colleague, sociologist Ernst Troeltsch, in making this distinction among various forms of religious organization: church, sect, and the mystical cult. The *sect* sets itself apart from the social and religious mainstream and is exclusive in its membership—often stipulating that members must have had a conversion experience. The *church*, in contrast, is a large-scale organization with a broadly inclusive membership; it is also more hierarchical than the sect. An obvious example is the Catholic Church, with its hierarchy of professional officeholders (priests, bishops, archbishops, cardinals, and the Pope). Troeltsch maintained that secularization began when the Catholic Church took on this bureaucratic form of organization (Troeltsch 1931: 94). The *mystical cult* is even more a matter of personal experience; it lacks any permanent form of organization, as in the "Heaven's Gate" cult led by Marshall Herff Applewhite (who called himself "Do"). In 1997 this charismatic leader led thirty-eight followers to commit mass suicide at Rancho Sante Fe, California, in the belief that they would be boarding a spacecraft that would take them to a higher level of existence.

Durkheim was much less inclined than Weber to talk about the prospect of secularization. Although he accepted that science would take over

**Protestant Ethic**  The belief that worldly successes stemming from individual responsibility and a compulsion to save and invest are a sign of God's favor. While this Protestant Ethic to earn God's favor was initially religious in nature, Max Weber argued that it was absorbed into the general spirit of capitalism and thus perpetuated the development of capitalism.

**Disenchantment**  As defined by Max Weber, a process in which previously religious concepts, values, and ideals become detached from their religious roots and secularized. For example, as modernity became increasingly rationalized and capitalism developed, the Protestant Ethic—though initially religious in motivation—became separated from this early religious setting and its enchantment was lost. Weber saw disenchantment as being the accomplice to rationalization and thought that it would inevitably lead to the decline of religion.

**Secularization**  The declining significance of religion in social institutions, culture, and individual experience.

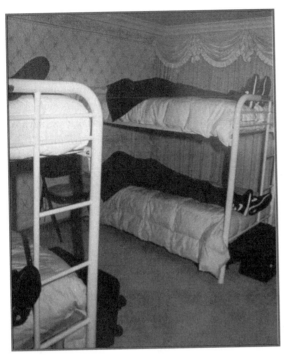

Cult leaders are sometimes charismatic enough to lead their followers into mass suicide, as in this photo of the bodies of some of the members of Heaven's Gate who followed Marshall Applewhite into death. (AP Photo/Nick Ut)

ing an identity that transcended their individual selves. In modern societies, too, there would still be a need for sacred symbols; rituals and ceremonies would be used to stir up a sense of awe and shared identity, even after the old religious symbols had faded away. Oft-cited examples include the symbol of the national flag and ceremonies such as presidential inaugurations.

In modern sociology, it was Talcott Parsons and his functionalist school that elaborated Durkheim's belief in religion's continuing relevance for modernity (Parsons 1967: 1–34, 385–421; see also O'Dea 1966). He did so by suggesting that, while the individual need for religion remained vital, the institutional and cultural reach of religion has greatly diminished. Churches have become denominations, relinquishing their efforts to control political, familial, and economic life. And theology overall has relinquished its interest in cognitive explanations that compete with science, concentrating instead on purely spiritual and moral concerns.

While there was some support for Durkheim's and Parsons's theories, throughout most of sociology's classical and modern history sociologists tended to follow Weber's lead, finding evidence of religion's decline to be integral to the development of modern society. This was particularly the case in Europe, where churchgoing seemed to be rapidly declining. Even in postwar America, sociologists were prepared to interpret higher rates of religious involvement as simply a manifestation of community attachment. For example, Will Herberg, in his book *Protestant, Catholic, Jew* (1955), suggested that church attendance in America was largely a way of identifying with a wider community and of being American, and not necessarily an indication of "religiousness." If people had more worldly motives for attending, such as a desire for respectability, then the churches were arguably becoming secularized from within. The problem with this interpretation, however, is that it is very difficult to investigate motives directly. One kind of

some of religion's intellectual authority, he characterized religion as having an everlasting quality, on the grounds that it serves an essential social function: "Thus there is something eternal in religion which is destined to survive all the particular symbols in which religious thought has successively enveloped itself. There can be no society which does not feel the need of upholding and reaffirming at regular intervals the collective sentiments and the collective ideas which make its unity and its personality" (Durkheim 1915: 474–475).

In simpler forms of society, such as the clans of Native American peoples and Australian aborigines, the unity of the society was reproduced in periodic assemblies where the clan met to perform rituals associated with their particular sacred totem—a bird, for example, or a plant. At these times, the members rekindled their sense of shar-

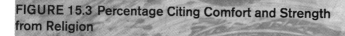

**FIGURE 15.3 Percentage Citing Comfort and Strength from Religion**

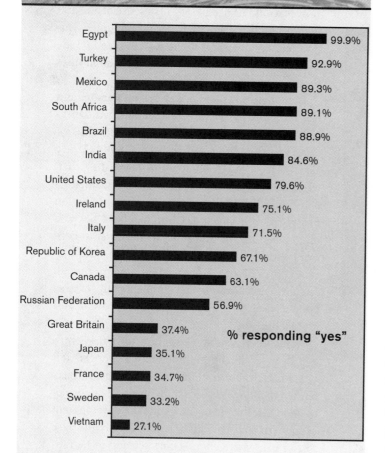

% responding "yes"

| Country | % |
|---|---|
| Egypt | 99.9% |
| Turkey | 92.9% |
| Mexico | 89.3% |
| South Africa | 89.1% |
| Brazil | 88.9% |
| India | 84.6% |
| United States | 79.6% |
| Ireland | 75.1% |
| Italy | 71.5% |
| Republic of Korea | 67.1% |
| Canada | 63.1% |
| Russian Federation | 56.9% |
| Great Britain | 37.4% |
| Japan | 35.1% |
| France | 34.7% |
| Sweden | 33.2% |
| Vietnam | 27.1% |

**Do you find that you get comfort and strength from religion?**

Source: Adapted from European Values Study Group and World Values Survey Association (2005).

within this group can correctly name the first book of the Bible, and even fewer (one in three) can name who preached the Sermon on the Mount (Chaves 2004: 20). Of course, this kind of ignorance is not confined to religion. It is just as evident in responses to questions about politics or geography, a phenomenon frequently exploited by comedians on late-night television.

Sociologists have recently begun to revise their ideas about secularization, as the overall picture is more complicated than was once thought to be the case. Many surveys and reports in the mass media seem to suggest that religion is not in decline in America. And, although there has always been a constitutional ban on government sponsorship of religion in the United States, presidents and other politicians frequently invoke God and take part in public religious events as part of their duties. Indeed, compared with many European societies, America appears to be extremely religious. In a survey conducted in 2003, nearly 80 percent of Americans respond "yes" to the question "Do you gain comfort and strength from religion?" compared with 37 percent in Great Britain and 33 percent in Sweden (World Values Study Group 2003). Moreover, 32.7 percent of Americans say that they attend religious services on a weekly or almost weekly basis (National Opinion Research Center 2004). This figure, too, is much higher than in most European societies. (See Figures 15.3, 15.4, and 15.5 for additional survey results.) So, we must ask: Is America just an exception to a general trend about religion in modern societies, or do we need to rethink the link between modernity and religion?

The advocates of one sociological view maintain that America is just as secular as Europe, but in a

evidence that has been offered takes the form of religious-knowledge surveys, which appear to reveal widespread ignorance about basic factual questions concerning the Bible. For example, a third of Americans believe that the Bible is the actual word of God and is to be taken literally. Yet only half different way. They claim that while Americans may appear to be more religious, their religion is superficial (Wilson 1966: 89). This view is shared by many conservative religious believers, who accuse the mainstream churches of compromising and becoming too liberal; in particular, they point to the churches' alleged failure to stand up for traditional beliefs and values, especially belief in the literal truth of the Bible and obedience of traditional family values. They take some consolation from the fact that some of the more liberal mainstream Protestant churches (e.g., Presbyterian, Methodist, and Protestant Episcopal) seem to be declining in membership whereas conservative churches (e.g., Southern Baptist) have done better (Kelley 1972; Roof and McKinney 1987; Roozen and Hadaway 1993).

According to adherents of another sociological view, what is happening to the mainstream churches is simply part of a wider restructuring of religion. Rather than declining, they argue, such churches are diversifying and decentralizing—that is, catering to numerous subcultures at the local level, and without much regard for central church organization (Warner 1993).

In Europe the decline of religion is often traced back to the intellectual, industrial, and political revolutions of the eighteenth and nineteenth centuries, although some periodic religious revivals occurred during the nineteenth century. In the twentieth century, religious decline in Europe led many sociologists of religion to conclude that the secularization thesis had been confirmed. On July 12, 1999, *Time* magazine's front cover featured the headline "Is God Dead?" followed by the comment "In Western

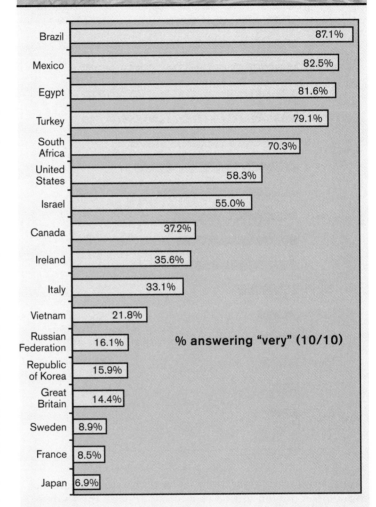

FIGURE 15.4 Percentage Citing Importance of God in Their Lives

% answering "very" (10/10)

| Country | Percentage |
|---|---|
| Brazil | 87.1% |
| Mexico | 82.5% |
| Egypt | 81.6% |
| Turkey | 79.1% |
| South Africa | 70.3% |
| United States | 58.3% |
| Israel | 55.0% |
| Canada | 37.2% |
| Ireland | 35.6% |
| Italy | 33.1% |
| Vietnam | 21.8% |
| Russian Federation | 16.1% |
| Republic of Korea | 15.9% |
| Great Britain | 14.4% |
| Sweden | 8.9% |
| France | 8.5% |
| Japan | 6.9% |

How important is God in your life? Please use this scale to indicate—10 means very important and 1 means not at all important.

Source: Adapted from European Values Study Group and World Values Survey Association (2005).

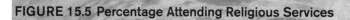

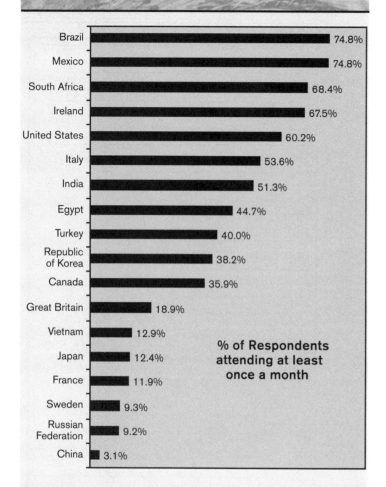

FIGURE 15.5 Percentage Attending Religious Services

| Country | % |
|---|---|
| Brazil | 74.8% |
| Mexico | 74.8% |
| South Africa | 68.4% |
| Ireland | 67.5% |
| United States | 60.2% |
| Italy | 53.6% |
| India | 51.3% |
| Egypt | 44.7% |
| Turkey | 40.0% |
| Republic of Korea | 38.2% |
| Canada | 35.9% |
| Great Britain | 18.9% |
| Vietnam | 12.9% |
| Japan | 12.4% |
| France | 11.9% |
| Sweden | 9.3% |
| Russian Federation | 9.2% |
| China | 3.1% |

% of Respondents attending at least once a month

**Apart from weddings, funerals, and christenings, about how often do you attend religious services these days?**

*Source:* Adapted from European Values Study Group and World Values Survey Association (2005).

Europe it sure can look that way." The article cited statistics for regular church attendance as low as 2 percent in East Germany and 4 percent in Norway, with a middle rate of 11 percent in Britain and a higher rate of 29 percent in Catholic Italy. On the whole, the Catholic countries of Southern Europe (Italy, Spain, and Portugal) were more traditional in the sense of having high rates of church attendance, while the mainly Protestant countries of Northern Europe (such as Norway, Denmark, and Sweden) exhibited low rates. However, the European Values Study (cited in Davie 2000) has found that, even in Northern Europe, belief in traditional religious values remains higher than one would expect based on the low rates of church attendance there, suggesting that many people may still be believing without belonging. This observation has led some sociologists to insist that the secularization thesis should be broken down into separate dimensions so as to highlight whether particular societies are experiencing decline on one dimension (e.g., religious belonging) but not on another (e.g., believing).

What does it take to be a "good Catholic" today? Recent surveys have revealed that American Catholics are neither very strict nor very traditional when it comes to their religion. For example, one survey found that only 26 percent of respondents were certain that the Pope is infallible on matters of faith or morals (GSS 2004). Another survey tried a different approach, listing a number of beliefs and practices and asking which are required for being a "good Catholic." Table 15.2 ranks these items in order of importance. As you can see, creedal doctrines (belief in the resurrection and belief in transubstantiation) are considered very important, whereas obeying church authority on matters like birth control and divorce are not. Of all the items listed, regular church attendance is considered the least important.

The case of America has always been a challenge to the secularization thesis. Over the long term, religion seems to have fared much better in

**TABLE 15.2  Laypersons' Definitions of a Good Catholic, 1999**

| SURVEY QUESTION: *Please tell me if you think a person can be a good Catholic without performing these actions or affirming these beliefs.* | % Who Answered Yes |
|---|---|
| Without believing that Jesus physically rose from the dead | 23 |
| Without believing that in the Mass, the bread and wine actually become the body and blood of Jesus | 38 |
| Without obeying the Church hierarchy's teaching regarding abortion | 53 |
| Without donating time or money to help the poor | 56 |
| Without donating time or money to the parish | 60 |
| Without obeying the Church hierarchy's teaching on divorce and remarriage | 64 |
| Without their marriage being approved by the Catholic Church | 67 |
| Without obeying the Church hierarchy's teaching on birth control | 71 |
| Without going to church every Sunday | 76 |

*Source:* Adapted from D'Atonio, Davidson, Hoge, and Meyer (2001).

America than in other Western societies. In contrast to its apparent long-term decline in Europe, membership in religious organizations in America seems to have started at a low base, increasing from about 17 percent of the population on the eve of the Revolution in 1776 to 37 percent at the start of the Civil War and then to 56 percent in 1926, 59 percent in 1952, and 62 percent in 1980 (Finke and Stark 1992). The proportion has continued to inch upward since then, but bear in mind that comparing numbers of members is problematic, as denominations have different ways of defining and counting "membership." Meanwhile, national surveys have shown that as many as 90 percent of adults are prepared to state that they have a religious preference. A majority of U.S. adults (53 percent) identify with a Protestant denomination, 25 percent say they are Catholic, 2 percent are Jews, and other religious groups—such as Buddhists, Muslims, and Hindus—are growing in size. Only 14 percent of respondents said they had no religious preference (National Opinion Research Center 2004: 124–125).

One explanation for the relative vitality of religion in America is that this country developed a kind of open market for religion, in which there

has been a greater diversity of religions competing with each other. By contrast, many European societies historically had a single church occupying a monopoly position, such as the state-established Church of England, the state-supported Lutheran churches in Scandinavian countries, and the Catholic Church in Spain. This "market" view of the religious situation has been developed by two sociologists into the **Rational Choice Theory (RCT)** of religion, which is similar to an economic theory about consumers making choices among different goods on the basis of calculations about rewards and costs (Stark and Bainbridge 1987). This version of Rational Choice Theory assumes that humans have a constant need for compensa-

**Rational Choice Theory (RCT)** Developed from an economic model, a theory that maintains that human beings are rational, calculating individuals who act so as to maximize their benefits while minimizing their costs. In the context of religious participation, RCT assumes that humans have a need for compensations about the uncertainties of life and death, and that such participation is one way of making up for these uncertainties.

tions for the uncertainties presented by the imponderable issues of life and death. What varies is the supply of such compensations. Other (nonreligious) compensations may be available, but religion offers the most comprehensive array, ranging from fellowship and forgiveness to supernatural sources of meaning and power. RCT asserts that the greater the number of religious sources providing such compensations, the greater will be the vitality of religious activity. However, although many empirical studies have attempted to verify this claim, the findings are mixed (see the summary in Ellway 2006). In addition, RCT has been criticized for neglecting cultural factors that might explain the varied reasons for which some people—and, for that matter, groups and societies—turn to religion while others do not. But the fact remains that RCT has served the useful purpose of stimulating sociologists to look again at the data on religious vitality. If, in the final analysis, these data indicate that religion is not declining but simply changing and offering a greater variety of choices, then we may have to revise the claim of

the earlier sociologists of modernity that society is becoming increasingly secularized—the so-called secularization thesis (Wilson 1966).

## THE AMERICAN CHRISTIAN MOSAIC

The overwhelming majority of Americans identify their religious preference as "Protestant," but this is a large category encompassing many different religious organizations. If we were to consider the membership of each congregation separately, we'd find that the largest church in the United States by far is the Catholic Church, which reported more than 67 million adherents in 2004 (see Table 15.3).

Despite this statistical appearance of high **religiosity,** the personal impression of many older people, looking back to their childhood in the 1950s, is that a significant weakening of religion has occurred since that time. This view seems to be supported by a piece titled "The Brooklyn Sunday School Union Parade," set in 1940s New York:

**TABLE 15.3  The Ten Largest Churches in the United States: Ranking by Membership, 2004**

| Denomination | # of Members | Increase/Decrease from Previous Year (%) |
|---|---|---|
| The Catholic Church | 67,259,768 | 1.28 |
| Southern Baptist Convention | 16,439,603 | 1.18 |
| The United Methodist Church | 8,251,175 | 0.002 |
| The Church of Jesus Christ of Latter-Day Saints | 5,503,192 | 1.71 |
| The Church of God in Christ | 5,499,875 | 0 |
| National Baptist Convention of America, Inc. | 5,000,000 | 0 |
| Evangelical Lutheran Church in America | 4,984,925 | −1.05 |
| National Baptist Convention of America, Inc. | 3,500,000 | 0 |
| Presbyterian Church (U.S.A.) | 3,241,309 | −4.87 |
| Assemblies of God | 2,729,562 | 1.57 |

*Note:* There is some variation in the definition of membership and adherence. If no membership report was submitted, the yearbook uses the number of adherents reported for the previous year.

*Source:* Adapted from Lindner (2005: Table 2).

Marchers filed past the reviewing stand hour after hour. The day was Thursday, June 6, 1946; the place, Prospect Park in Brooklyn, New York. Two years to the day since the Allies landed on the Normandy beaches, the nation now paused to give thanks and reflect on its collective heritage. But the marchers were not soldiers or war heroes. They were children: little girls in starched pinafores, wearing white dress gloves and carrying bouquets of spring flowers; little boys in neatly ironed white shirts with clip-on bow ties and paper hats. Together they marched, accompanied by brass bands and floats, past rows of admiring parents and grandparents. In the reviewing stand Brooklyn's mayor, the governor of New York, and a justice of the U.S. Supreme Court gave their approval. By public declaration all schools were closed for the day. In all, approximately 90,000 youngsters participated. The event was the 117th annual Sunday School Union parade. (Wuthnow 1988: 3)

Today the world of the Brooklyn Sunday School Union Parade seems to belong to a distant age. The idea of a public holiday in which thousands of people turn out for a Sunday school parade now appears strange to most of us. Many social scientists would suggest that this shows the extent to which American society has become secularized. The ever-increasing prominence of science and technology, rising levels of higher education, greater affluence, and more secular system of government that characterize this country give the impression that religion has become a less significant part of American life. The public festivals that attract attention today are national holidays, rock concerts, and sports events; religion does not provide the major public spectacles. In all likelihood, a borough like Brooklyn was able to make religion part of its public life only during a period when its neighborhood and ethnic ties were strong and deeply rooted in tradition. Since that time, Brooklyn has experienced the ravages of

**Religiosity** The amount of "religiousness" in society, usually measured by such variables as attendance of religious services, church membership, individual (financial) contributions to a church or religious institution, and belief in God.

urban decay and urban revival, the population has become more atomized and pluralistic, and many members of the older traditional churches have fled to the suburbs. Then, too, the religion of the suburbs has sometimes been criticized for resembling a private leisure activity.

However, the impression that religion has declined is not supported by other evidence. Earlier we noted the numbers reflecting church membership, which remain high. And there continue to be large gatherings of Christians in the public sphere. For example, on April 29, 1980, more than a quarter-million evangelical Christians packed the Mall in the nation's capital to proclaim "Washington for Jesus," and other such large gatherings have since occurred. Even in Brooklyn, contrary to the image of decaying neighborhoods and closed churches, the number of churches was actually 10 percent

Recent huge rallies on the Washington, D.C., Mall demonstrate that religion is not in decline in the United States. (Eric Freeland/Corbis)

higher in the 1980s than in the 1940s. During the same five decades, moreover, church membership had held steady as a percentage of the borough's population, and membership in theologically conservative churches had risen fivefold (Wuthnow 1988).

But it would be wrong to jump to the opposite conclusion and claim that nothing has changed. For example, whereas a national gathering like the "Washington for Jesus" rally was organized by television preachers who brought in busloads of people from all over the country, the Brooklyn parade was a real neighborhood event, organized as a Protestant show of strength against the local Catholic minority. The Washington rally, by contrast, played down denominational differences and was targeted against secularism and liberalism rather than Catholicism. In short, the Brooklyn parade was evidence of a taken-for-granted alliance between church and state at the local level, while the Washington march seemed more a matter of religion bringing pressure to bear on the government (Wuthnow 1988).

Structural changes in postmodern society have restructured religion and generated new cultural controversies. Population changes in the United States have included a movement from city centers to the suburbs, and from the Northeast to the Southwest. In addition, the country has seen an increase in immigration from South and Central America, as well as from Asia, and a relative decline in West European immigrants. These trends have resulted in the enlargement of certain ethnically based religious groups such as Mexican-American Catholics, Korean Christians, Indian Hindus, and Middle Eastern Muslims.

Probably the most important structural change has been a massive increase in the role of government. As a consequence, many of the controversial issues in which religion has become embroiled now pertain to the problematic boundary between church and state—the sacred and the secular. One

commentator has summarized this state of affairs with a series of questions:

> Does government have the right to keep prayers and other forms of religious activity out of the public schools? What should churches do if they disagree with the Supreme Court's position on the legality of abortion? Is the Internal Revenue Service justified in requiring religious groups to make full disclosure of their financial affairs? Given the enlarged position of government as a provider of social welfare services, how should religious values concerned with justice, equality and peace be articulated to have the greatest effect? (Wuthnow 1988: 7)

These controversial issues have contributed to the conditions that gave rise to the culture wars over conflicting religious and secular values that flared up in the last part of the twentieth century, to the astonishment of those sociologists who had thought religion was in retreat. The controversies range from abortion to "evil" lyrics in rock music. But for an understanding of why the culture wars have become so prominent and bitter, we need to examine what has been happening to culture itself in this period. The box titled "Church Versus State in Europe's Culture Wars" provides a particularly interesting perspective on this issue.

## RELIGION AND CULTURAL CHANGE

As we explained in Chapter 4, the mass media occupy center stage in postmodern societies in ways not true of the earlier modern period. It should come as no surprise, then, that the media have had a significant effect on religion. In the 1960s, for example, they gave publicity to the youth counterculture, a rebellion that brought about shifts in many aspects of culture, including religion. And in the 1980s, televangelists used the media to build

## Church Versus State in Europe's Culture Wars: "L'affaire foulard" in France

A teenage girl wearing a turquoise pantsuit and a flowered head scarf crowded behind class-mates at the entrance to Jacques Brel High School in a Paris suburb Thursday. When she arrived at the door, she showed a monitor a photo identification card and slid the kerchief from her head.

It was a scene played out at many public schools around the country on Thursday, the day 12 million students returned for a new semester. By pulling off her head scarf as she rushed into the building, past a phalanx of reporters, the girl was in compliance with a new law banning Muslim head coverings in public schools. The ban also prohibits all other overtly religious garb, including crucifixes, Jewish skullcaps and Sikh turbans.

The ban triggered massive demonstrations in France and protests in several cities around the world earlier this year. Critics condemned the law as an attack on religious freedom and said it would stigmatize the estimated 5 million Muslims in France. Some Muslim groups pledged further protests, calling the restriction anti-Islamic.

But Thursday, the first day of school with the ban in effect, went quietly. Muslim groups called for compliance with the law, and there were no reports of public demonstrations. The matter had become a life-and-death issue when kidnappers in Iraq threatened to kill two French journalists if France did not rescind the law. ...

"I wear the scarf for my religion, but I will re-move it because it's the law," said Jubaida Mohammed, 17, born in France to Indian immi-grants. She arrived at school wearing a black head scarf but let it drop to her shoulders as she chatted with friends in an outer courtyard.

"I don't think the law is right. I don't think we do any harm," she said. "It seems aimed at Mus-lims and makes us uneasy."

Another young woman who arrived at Jacques Brel wearing a scarf said she was undecided about whether to challenge the ban. The teen-ager, of Tunisian descent, had come to pick up material for a vocational course in accounting she would begin Friday. "I've been wearing it for a month," the girl, who declined to provide her name, said of the scarf. "My father is against it. My mother's on vacation and hasn't seen me. I wear it because I had a mystical feeling. If I wear it to school, I risk losing my education. I'm not against France, just in favor of my religion."

France, with its relatively large Muslim com-munity, has become the epicenter of a pan-Euro-pean struggle to come to terms with growing Islamic immigration and its cultural ramifications. Religious symbolism and teachings have be-come battlegrounds.

France is the only country in Western Europe that has banned head scarves in public schools. The government has a strong tradition of secu-larism and promotes restrictions on religious symbols as a means of promoting integration in a diverse society.

*Source*: Williams (2003: A11).

Because most of the world's major religions consider homosexuality a sin, gays and lesbians have started their own churches, like this Christian church bearing the rainbow flag stating "All are welcome." (iStockphoto)

up large audiences and attracted large funds (in some cases, attracting scandalous publicity as well, for sexual and financial wrongdoing).

Beginning in the mid-1960s, religion has undergone a major shift in emphasis from main-stream Protestant denominations to conservative, evangelical religious bodies. These denominations had experienced an almost artificial prosperity in the 1950s, marked by record growth in numbers and influence. During this period, mainstream Protestantism was criticized for being something of a "culture-religion," captive to middle-class values and so wedded to majority beliefs, values, and behavior as to be virtually indistinguishable from secular culture. When that culture itself came under attack from several fronts, including the youth counterculture of the 1960s, these denominations were unable to hold on to the younger generation or attract new members. It was during the same period that Protestant evangelicalism and fundamentalism became more visible and started to grow. These entities were religiously and culturally identifiable; known for their distinctive beliefs and moral teachings, they offered an experiential faith centered on belief in salvation through personal commitment to Christ. An indication of the change in fortunes occurred in 1967, when the Southern Baptist Convention surpassed the Methodists to become the nation's largest Protestant denomination. Evangelicalism has continued to grow, setting new records of prosperity. In one short period, 1970–1978, the proportion of people who believed that religion was "increasing its influence on American life" tripled, rising from 14 percent to 44 percent (Gallup 1977–1978). A Gallup poll in 1977 revealed that one out of every three persons in the United States claimed to have been "born again," leading George Gallup, Jr., to suggest that the country was in an "early stage of a profound religious revival" (Gallup 1977: 50–55). And in 2006, an estimated 26.3 percent of all white Americans classified themselves as Evangelical Protestants, with black churches (often themselves evangelical) making up another 9.6 percent and Latinos 2.8 percent. Today, white mainstream Protestants amount to only 16.0 percent of the population (Luo 2006: 5).

Much of conservative religion's visibility and success is due to media involvement, including the so-called electronic church and its network of religious programming and television evangelists. One of the great ironies is that televangelists have used the latest marketing techniques and sophisticated electronic technology to attack modernity and secularism, while proclaiming "old-time" religion as the answer to the nation's ills. This form of cultural reinvention, along with nostalgic evocation of the past, is typical of postmodern culture.

Responding to a hunger for certainty and moral absolutism, revivals of "old-time" religion have provoked bitter disputes with more liberal bodies of opinion, both secular and religious, across a wide spectrum of issues ranging from abortion and the Equal Rights Amendment to gay rights and various environmental and consumer concerns. Moral and religious attitudes have crystallized around the two camps—members of the conservative Religious Right and advocates of the liberal free-will, prochoice position (labeled "secular humanism," or simply "liberal," by its opponents).

Rather than insisting on a deep division, Wade Clark Roof and William McKinney (1987) see an enormous increase in cultural pluralism, including religious individualism. They point to the fact that American values, influenced by the Protestant Ethic, have always included an emphasis on individual autonomy. However, since the 1960s another development has occurred—the growth of **expressive individualism**—whereby the pursuit of a free, gratified, and fulfilled self is seen as the key value. Finding oneself has become a central quest, opening up a range of possible identities and bringing to prominence new cultural heroes—spiritual gurus and therapists. According to some critics, the old balance in American religion between community and individualism has been upset, giving way to a less socially restrained and

**Expressive individualism** A term relating to the increased emphasis since the 1960s (in both the secular and the religious context) on the pursuit of a free, gratified, and fulfilled self. Some sociologists have argued that this trend accounts for religion's loss of force as an integrative institution in American society.

more personally expressive mode of religiosity. As a result of this trend, religion has lost its force as an integrative influence in America. In short, it has become more divisive than integrative (Roof and KcKinney 1987).

Such diversity is not without pattern or causes. At the most general level, the market economy in which we live, the individualism that has always characterized American culture, and the prominence of the mass media and the entertainment industry are factors that have encouraged this diversity. The journalistic portrait of American religion shows this diversity, but only in stylized ways. News reports tend to emphasize stereotypes, conflict, and the bizarre or extreme, ranging from mass rallies of Promise Keepers to mass suicides among cult members. At the same time, sociologists have talked about this subject in terms of very broad tendencies and general categories, focusing on testing the secularization thesis through surveys of belief or membership statistics. Only in recent years have sociologists started to pay more attention to understanding people's own stories about their spiritual experiences and how they construct their identities (Wuthnow 1997).

## PERSONAL STORIES AND ETHNOGRAPHIES

Among the most fascinating recent studies of religion are those pertaining to religion's central concern with the construction of identity, which certainly is a distinctive point of focus in postmodern society. As the life cycle has elongated, not just high school students but people of all ages experience difficulty in sorting out who they are and negotiating the various pressures that pull the self in different directions. The quest for identity has been examined by sociologists in terms of people's own stories about their spiritual experiences; it is also the subject of ethnographies of religious groups. Both types of research reveal the restructuring and complexity involved in religious discourses and identities.

An **ethnography** is a study involving in-depth description. One such study tells the story of a weekly Gospel Hour in a gay bar in Atlanta. It demonstrates how the Gospel Hour provides a safe haven for gays with evangelical and other conservative Christian backgrounds. The songs remind them of the comfort they once found in their faith, while drag performances mark the time and space as uniquely gay. The participants use cultural models from both gay and evangelical subcultures to negotiate a new identity as well as new relationships with Christianity, gay culture, and even God (Gray and Thumma 1997). Another ethnography explores how some women manage to negotiate the apparent opposition between their identity as feminists and their identity as members of a conservative evangelical denomination (Stocks

1997). Yet another reveals how a group of Messianic Jews combine elements of Judaism and Christianity, inventing a tradition for themselves by claiming continuity with the first-century Christian Church (Feher 1997).

Although such studies have no direct bearing on the previously discussed topics of secularization and modernization, they enrich our understanding of contemporary religion and spiritual experience. Indeed, by focusing on cultural meanings and questions of identity construction, these sociological examinations of religion reflect not only the "cultural turn" but also the interest in issues that have come to prominence in postmodernity, as distinct from those prominent during the earlier periods of modern society.

## NEW AGE

Another set of beliefs and practices cited as evidence of the emerging postmodern culture is that labeled **New Age** (see Chapter 5, on socialization and the life cycle). This is an umbrella term covering a mix of beliefs, practices, and ways of life, including esoteric and mystical beliefs drawn from Buddhism, Christianity, Hinduism, Islam, and Taoism; pagan teachings of the Native American and European Celtic cultures; and procedures such as Zen meditation, witchcraft, spiritual therapies, encounter groups, and intensive self-development seminars. The element in common to all of these has been described as "self-spirituality." New Agers share the belief that the self itself is sacred. As New Age practitioner and movie star Shirley MacLaine once put it: "If everyone was taught one basic spiritual law, your world would be a happier, healthier place. And that law is this: Everyone is God. Everyone" (quoted in Burrows 1986: 18). Many New Agers also emphasize the spirituality of nature as a whole. But the main emphasis of this orientation is on making contact with the spirituality within us and shifting from a

**Ethnography** A research method that involves immersing oneself in a natural research setting in order to develop an understanding of the people, culture, and society being studied.

**New Age** An umbrella term that covers a mix of beliefs, practices, and ways of life, all of which share the element of "self-spirituality." New Age beliefs and practices, considered by some to be evidence of the emerging postmodern culture, emphasize making contact with the innate spirituality in people and shifting from a contaminated, artificial sense of being (brought about by socialization) to one representing pure and authentic nature.

contaminated and artificial mode of being—caused by socialization—to that which represents our authentic nature (Heelas 1996: 2).

The development of New Age beliefs and practices toward the end of the twentieth century seemed to mark a radical break with modernity, inasmuch as it involved a resurgence of teachings and practices usually associated with the mystics and magicians of premodern societies. Many reasons have been given for this resurgence. Some commentators attribute it to the sense of uncertainty that characterized modern society. The development of modern society involved the overthrow of traditional authorities—a process known as *detraditionalization*—but the new modern authorities were limited to their own areas of technical expertise. This circumstance led to the fragmentation of knowledge as well as the loss of a sense of identity, unity, and purpose for the individual. Many people, especially those who were educated and relatively affluent, were dissatisfied with what they had and who they were, and asked, "Is this all there is?" In seeking to answer that question they drew on whatever cultural resources they could find, whether in the form of ancient practices or way-out, speculative forms of science.

## PUBLIC RELIGION

The secularization thesis maintained that religion would decline in social significance as an inevitable consequence of modernization. Recall that in the sociological accounts of Marx, Weber, Durkheim, and Parsons, the relevance of religion to traditional societies lay in the integration and legitimation functions it served; that is, religion helped hold societies together (integration), notably by conferring authority on their principal institutions (legitimation). However, according to these classic sociological accounts, modern societies do not need religion to perform these functions, which are increasingly being fulfilled in

other ways. Religion may continue to perform a private, psychological function for individuals, but it would cease to have any wider social significance. Secularization, then, was seen as the process by which religious institutions, practices, and beliefs lose their social significance as a result of the differentiation of society into separate spheres, each with its own specialized way of thinking and organizing life: economic, political, legal, and educational. Differentiation is closely related to many of the features associated with modernity, including the expansion of the capitalist system, the emergence of nation-states, the development of bureaucracy, the spread of industrialization, and the breakdown of face-to-face communities (*Gemeinschaft*) by urbanization, leading to a modern form of society (*Gesellschaft*) made up of strangers and characterized by loss of shared norms (*anomie*).

But the secularization thesis was based on European experience, especially in societies where modernization could take place only by violently separating religion from politics and economics. It did not take account of possibilities in other cultural contexts. In America, on the other hand, the formal separation of religion from government was accepted early on, and so there was little animosity toward religion, which has continued to flourish at many levels. Indeed, religious beliefs and cere-

*Gemeinschaft* A term used to describe societies that have a strong feeling of cohesiveness. *Gemeinschaft* is often thought to be characteristic of premodern societies.

*Gesellschaft* A term describing relationships characterized by individualism and impersonal connections between people. *Gesellschaft* arose in opposition to *Gemeinschaft* as a result of urbanization.

*Anomie* A term referring to lack of cohesion and loss of shared norms and values in society. In his work *The Division of Labor in Society*, Émile Durkheim identified *anomie* as one of the potential problems of modern society.

monies still appear in the political sphere here. This close association of religion and politics, especially as manifested in national ceremonies and in beliefs about the special destiny of America, has been described as constituting a **civil religion** (Bellah 1967). A civil religion serves social functions in that it

1. facilitates and sustains widespread acceptance by a people of a sense of their nation's history and destiny;
2. relates their society to a realm of absolute meaning—the sacred;
3. enables them to regard their society and community as special;
4. provides a vision that ties the nation together as an integrated whole; and
5. provides beliefs, values, rites, ceremonies and symbols that give sacred meaning to the life of the community and thus sustain an overarching unity that transcends internal conflicts and differences. (Pierard and Lindar 1988)

American civil religion, in serving its functions of integrating various groups in society and legitimizing the authority of political and other institutions, was probably at its height in the 1950s. By the time Robert Bellah began to write about it in 1967, it was already being called into question.

**Civil religion** Societal practices reflecting a close association of religion and politics whereby the nation becomes a sacred entity, with its own sacred symbols and ceremonies. Robert Bellah described presidential inaugurations and the flag as examples of sacred ceremonies and symbols maintaining American civil religion.

**Deprivatization** The process by which religion has reemerged from the private sphere. Following deprivatization, religious beliefs are no longer purely personal preferences but, rather, become the topic of public argument; in addition, public matters are remoralized.

The youth counterculture of the 1960s and the socially divisive Vietnam War were just two of the developments, highly publicized by global media, that put it under pressure. The effect on civil religion can be illustrated symbolically by the controversy that flared over the Vietnam War memorial. Whereas previous war memorials had been publicly sponsored and uncontroversial, the Vietnam Veterans Memorial erected in Washington, D.C., was the result of a private initiative and attracted great controversy. Even its unconventional design (a plain dark slab) raised objections; subsequently, a more conventional figurative memorial of three soldiers with a flag was added (Katakis 1988; Lopes 1987; Palmer 1987; Powell 1995; Scruggs and Swerdlow 1985).

However, though religion may have lost some of its taken-for-granted character in America since the 1960s, this is not to say that it has been relegated to the private sphere in the way predicted by the secularization thesis. On the contrary: In America, as in many other parts of the world outside Europe, religion has reemerged from the private sphere in a process referred to as **deprivatization** (Cassanova 1996). Deprivatization has been described as "a dual interrelated process of repoliticization of the private religious and moral spheres, and renormativization of the public economic and political spheres" (Cassanova 1996: 359). In other words, religious beliefs have ceased to be a matter of purely personal preference and have again become the subjects of public argument, while concurrently, public matters such as the economy and politics have been remoralized, partly through challenges from religious groups. Typical instances include the role of Catholic bishops in leading the opposition to abortion in the United States and the role of Evangelical Protestant Christians in the mobilization of the Moral Majority to promote "family values." (See Table 15.4 for additional examples.)

The deprivatization of religion refers to its reappearance in the public spheres of economics

## TABLE 15.4  Differences in Political Activities by Religious Tradition

| Activity | Moderate and Liberal Protestants | Conservative and Evangelical Protestants | Black Protestants | Roman Catholics | Jews |
|---|---|---|---|---|---|
| Told people at worship services about opportunities for political activity (within the past 12 months) | 34 | 28 | 47 | 45 | 60 |
| Have ever distributed voter guides | 20 | 32 | 28 | 26 | 25 |
| Of those distributing voter guides, percent distributing Christian Right voter guides | 33 | 70 | 8 | 14 | 17 |
| Have had a group to organize a demonstration or march | 11 | 14 | 15 | 42 | 10 |
| Have had a group to get people registered to vote | 5 | 7 | 35 | 16 | 20 |
| Have had a group to lobby elected officials | 9 | 5 | 10 | 23 | 20 |
| Have had someone running for office as a visiting speaker | 5 | 2 | 27 | 3 | 35 |
| Participated in at least one of these political activities | 57 | 52 | 71 | 68 | 90 |

*Note:* "Black Protestants" include churches whose regular participants are at least 80 percent African-American. The sample of Jewish congregations was small (*N* = 20).

*Source:* Adapted from Chaves (2004: 114–115).

and politics. But this process has also been termed **dedifferentiation,** because it involves a reversal of the trend toward increasing differentiation into specialized institutions that were thought to be aspects of modernization. Now it is becoming clear that there is no single pattern or set of stages of modernization that all societies must go through. If for a long period modernization seemed to necessitate the differentiation of religion from other institutions, in many non-Western "traditional" societies religion continues to play a prominent public role. Modernization of such societies happens much more quickly than it did in the Western world, in large part precisely because it is spreading from there. This continuing role for traditional religion can be found in many Muslim societies today, such as Indonesia, Pakistan, and Kuwait. The same is true of Japan, Korea, and India.

As a result of globalization, we cannot discuss

**Dedifferentiation** Reversal of the trend toward increasing differentiation into specialized religious institutions that were thought to be aspects of modernization.

Religion can serve as a form of resistance against the cultural homogenization brought by globalization; the Hindu Jagannath Temple is an important repository of East Indian culture. (Lindsay Hebbard/Corbis)

what is happening to religion in one society without considering its connections around the world. Yet this phenomenon also seems to leave room for different rates and kinds of change, as well as providing a way of talking about resistance to cosmopolitanism in ways that avoid references to cultures that are "backward" or "behind the times." Religion, often in combination with ethnicity and nationalism, has played a considerable role in articulating resistance to global cosmopolitanism. One recent example is the Serbian Orthodox nationalism in parts of what was once Yugoslavia; another is the Hindu nationalism in India. Islamic fundamentalism, too, has spread rapidly in combination with the assertion of nationalism in many Muslim countries, of which Iran and Iraq are two of the most obvious. In these cases, the relationship between the local and the global takes the form of "resistance identities," whereby people react to global pressures by reemphasizing local or particularistic (religious) bases of identity (Castells 1997; see also Chapter 18, on social change, collective action, and social movements). Contrary to the secularization thesis, this version of globalization theory suggests that, rather than constituting a mere residual resistance to modernization, religious forms of resistance identity are likely to be an ongoing feature of contemporary societies.

## CONCLUSION

Let us now return to the tragic story of Cassie, the alleged teenage martyr. First, what were the main factors mentioned in her story? As an American citizen, Cassie lived in a society where a formal separation exists between church and state, the religious and the secular. She was a student at Columbine, a state high school, where religion was supposed to be a private matter (a clear example of this separation of church and state). We can assume, given that she lived in a relatively affluent middle-class suburb of Denver in the western state of Colorado, that she did not turn to religion as the "opium of the masses," as Marx suggested poor people might do in an attempt to find comfort in their poverty. However, her community was an area with a highly mobile population; many residents had moved there from other areas and had no long-standing community roots. As an adolescent, Cassie experienced problems that made her angry and from which she sought escape in witchcraft, drugs, and alcohol. After she joined a somewhat "deviant" youth subgroup, her parents took her out of Columbine, confined her to the house for a time (allowing her out only to attend church), and then enrolled her in a Christian school and a Christian summer camp. There she was subjected to strong peer pressure, which led to a religious conversion experience. At that point Cassie saw herself as having a mission to return to the state school and spread the religious message. Upon her return there, she became a member of a subgroup very different from the one she had left, although still in the minority and deviant from the norm. The heavily armed young man who shot her was alleged to be a member of the kind of "deviant" subgroup that she had renounced.

A social structural explanation of Cassie's story would draw on some of the factors listed above, emphasizing the tension between public and private spheres—public education and supposedly private religion. Also present were tensions in social relations, with divisions in the form of subgroups, peer-group pressures, strains associated with the adolescent period of the life cycle, and failures in the performance of institutions such as the family, education, and religion. Cassie's missionary activities might be explained as a reaction to changes in the boundary between religion and government, given that government had taken over many of the functions once performed by religion—thus offending religious sentiments.

Alternatively, a cultural explanation might be developed in terms of the culture wars under way at the time, involving conflict between "liberal secularism" and evangelical Christianity as well as wide differences between various youth subcultures in terms of values and lifestyles. Even more important, such an explanation would focus on issues of meaning and identity, on the stories and narratives presented by the media, and on the ways that symbols were used and interpreted. Bearing in mind that the media present stories according to their own journalistic styles and criteria, sociologists taking this cultural perspective would want to carry out in-depth interviews that allowed participants to tell their own stories in their own words.

Cassie's story has significance for the larger story—the "big picture"—of what is happening to religion today and what it might become in the future. Her experience points to two major trends:

1. The reaction to modernization and globalization in the form of *deprivatization* and a return to traditional beliefs and practices, as in the example of fundamentalism.
2. Competition between many brands of religion and spirituality, in a kind of market of faiths, drawing on old and new beliefs and practices, sometimes mixed with nonreligious elements, as in the rich mix of ingredients referred to as *New Age*.

It seems that religion is proving much more adaptable than sociologists of modernity imagined.

# EXERCISES

## Exercise 1

In this chapter we have examined some of the arguments and evidence for and against the secularization thesis, which maintained that religion would inevitably decline in modern society. Does your observation of religion in your own hometown provide evidence in favor of this thesis or against it? What kinds of religion are growing and which are declining? Ask some members of your parents' or grandparents' generation what changes they have seen in their lifetime.

## Exercise 2

Is religion mainly a private matter, or should it play a prominent role in the public sphere? Think of some recent controversies concerning religion in the public sphere, such as the wearing of religious dress or insignia in a public school, or the posting of the Ten Commandments on the wall of a courthouse. Do such controversies suggest that religion is becoming more prominent in the public sphere or that the boundaries between the private and public are changing?

## Exercise 3

Can some of the revivals of religion in the contemporary world be seen as reactions against globalization and aspects of modernity? Consider the implications of the use of the term *fundamentalist* to describe some forms of religion.

# STUDY QUESTIONS

1. What are the two main types of definition?

2. In what respect did Emile Durkheim operate with a mixed definition of religion?

3. What is a *civil religion*?

4. Describe the main ideas contained in Weber's *Protestant Ethic* thesis.

5. Why did Durkheim think that there can be no society that does not have some kind of religion?

6. How did Parsons elaborate Durkheim's belief in religion's continuing relevance for modern society?

7. What might account for the higher levels of religiosity in America compared with many European countries?

8. What do Wade Clark Roof and William McKinney mean when they talk about an increase in "expressive individualism" since the 1960s?

9. Discuss what is meant by the terms *deprivatization* and *dedifferentiation* in the context of describing the changing place of religion in late modern (or postmodern) society.

## FURTHER READING

Berger, Peter L. 1967. *The Sacred Canopy*. New York: Anchor.

Beyer, P. 1994. *Religion and Globalization*. London: Sage.

Cassanova, J. 1994. *Public Religions in the Modern World*. Chicago: University of Chicago Press.

Griffith, M. 1997. *God's Daughters: Evangelical Women and the Power of Submission*. Berkeley: University of California Press.

Warner, R. S., and J. G. Wittner. 1998. *Gatherings in Diaspora: Religious Communities and the New Immigration*. Philadelphia: Temple University Press.

# PART SIX

# Politics, Globalization, and Social Change

# chapter 16

# Urbanism and Population

Today, at the beginning of the twenty-first century, the possibilities and problems posed by cities are among the most important issues facing the planet. For the first time in history, more than 3 billion people—over half of humanity—are living in cities, many in **megacities** (urban agglomerations), each composed of several million inhabitants (Massey, Allen, and Pile 1999: 1). Each year, 20–30 million people throughout the world leave the countryside and move into towns and cities. These population movements are producing a concentration of the world's population never before experienced (see Figures 16.1 and 16.2).

Many of these new urbanites live in megacities (sometimes referred to as *megalopolises*). Among the world's largest cities (see Table 16.1), not a single one is European, and the majority are in less developed countries (LDCs). This noteworthy statistic demonstrates that there is no simple and direct relation between size and power. São Paulo may be bigger than New York, but it is not more powerful; nor is Bombay (now called Mumbai) more powerful than Los Angeles. The British capital, London, which is also one of the top three international financial centers (the others are New York and Tokyo), does not figure in the list, nor does Washington, D.C., the world's most important political city.

Obviously, growth in population size is not the only relevant factor here. Definitions of the term *city* often emphasize size and density of population, but some of the most interesting sociological aspects of cities concern their particular cultures and mentalities. Nevertheless, the problems pre-

**TABLE 16.1 World's Largest Urban Agglomerations, 2005**

| Rank | Agglomeration | Country | Population (thousands) |
|---|---|---|---|
| 1 | Tokyo | Japan | 35,327 |
| 2 | Mexico City | Mexico | 19,013 |
| 3 | New York–Newark | U.S. | 18,498 |
| 4 | Mumbai (Bombay) | India | 18,336 |
| 5 | São Paulo | Brazil | 18,333 |
| 6 | Delhi | India | 15,334 |
| 7 | Calcutta | India | 14,229 |
| 8 | Buenos Aires | Argentina | 13,349 |
| 9 | Jakarta | Indonesia | 13,194 |
| 10 | Shanghai | China | 12,665 |
| 11 | Dhaka | Bangladesh | 12,560 |
| 12 | Los Angeles | U.S. | 12,146 |
| 13 | Karachi | Pakistan | 11,819 |

*Source:* Adapted from UN Department of Economic and Social Affairs/Population Division (2004).

sented by population growth cannot be ignored: Some cities really do seem to have too many people, who are squeezed together into too small a space. The poor long to break out of the inner-city ghettos, where they and their fellow citizens experience many risks and threats to life, property, and peace of mind. On the other hand, the growth of cities has always had its positive side. Even in the ancient world, cities were seen as the apex of civilization and the centers of trade. And in the modern industrializing world, cities provided accommodation for the large numbers of workers needed by factories, along with the shops and other services that sustained them. Today, the emerging postmodern cities are those with postindustrial economies—such as New York, Los Angeles, London, Paris, and Rome—where financial services, mass media and communications, tourism and entertainment, and affluent retailing are more important than manufacturing. The postmodern city presents itself as something to be consumed—a

**Megacities** Large urban areas encompassing a number of formerly separate towns. An example is Los Angeles, which comprises not only Los Angeles proper but also nearby suburbs, such as Long Beach. Megacities (sometimes referred to as *megalopolises*) are a postmodern phenomenon, often characterized by their diverse populations.

## FIGURE 16.1 Total Population by Metropolitan Status: 1910–2000

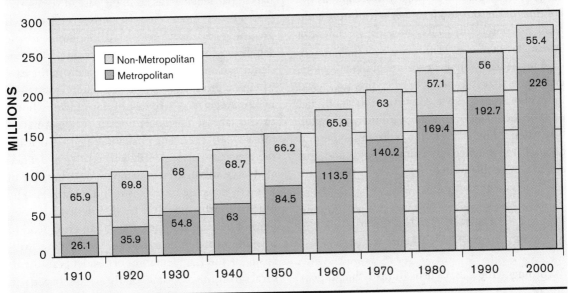

*Source:* U.S. Census Bureau, Population Division, available online at http://www.census.gov/population (accessed June 1, 2006).

## FIGURE 16.2 Percentage of Metropolitan Population Living in Central Cities and Suburbs

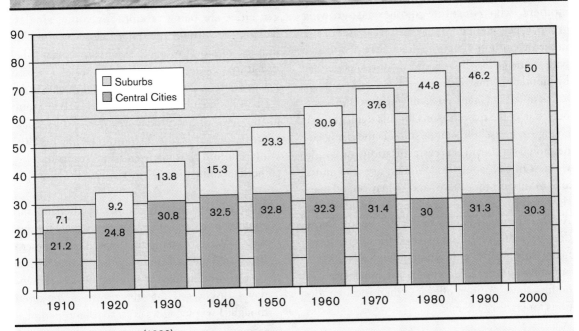

*Source:* Gibson and Lennon (1999).

dazzling and constantly changing display of opportunities for thinking, seeing, and doing new things. Los Angeles is frequently described as the epitome of the postmodern megacity, but it is far from the only global city presenting itself as a "dream factory."

A particularly attractive feature of the postmodern city is that it appears to offer the individual more choices of lifestyle. However, this is not just an individual matter. Indeed, as illustrated in the box titled "The Bridget Jones Economy," such choices are influenced by cultural trends and give rise to new problems in turn.

## AN INDIVIDUAL OR A SOCIAL STORY?

According to the U.S. Census Bureau, the proportion of 20- to 24-year-old American women who are not married doubled from 36 percent to 73 percent over the last three decades, and that of 30- to 34-year-old women more than tripled, from 6 percent to 22 percent (Hobbs and Stoops 2002). Some of these singles, although not all, are single mothers, who constitute another fast-growing group. The same period has also witnessed a rise in the proportion of households where people live with someone to whom they are not related, either by blood or by marriage.

As noted in Chapter 12, on work and the economy, one of the main reasons for this demographic change in household composition is the rising educational levels and career aspirations of young women in rich societies. Women are now more able to support themselves and so may put off marriage and having a baby until later in the life cycle. As life expectancy is now in the 80s, people know they probably could be married for a long time; many thus postpone the commitment. Also, while pursuing a career and living in the inner city can be fun, these options offer less than ideal conditions for starting a family.

A distinctive feature of the postmodern city is the geographical clustering of like-minded individuals in particular areas, as in the case of young singles in the inner city. In earlier cities, such groupings typically consisted of people in the same occupation, class, or ethnic group. This tendency can still be seen today, especially in the case of ethnic groups swollen by new immigrants—as in Los Angeles, where east of downtown is home to the largest Latino *barrio* in Anglo-America (Soja 1989: 242). The postmodern city, especially the megacity or megalopolis (the latter is defined as a large urban area encompassing a number of formerly separate towns), is rich in contrasts. The outer suburbs may still be distinguished along lines of income and race, but urban areas tend to be quite varied. A characteristic of this new "tribalism" is the fragmentation of residents into cultural groupings. Some of these are based on ethnicity and language, especially urban areas that are home to new immigrants—and, obviously, urban underclass ghettos are still defined by race (see Chapter 8, on inequality). Nonetheless, other kinds of cultural networks are increasingly emerging, and it is along these networks that postmodern cities are being rebuilt. For young singles, lacking the support of families close by, the like-minded support groups they join are almost tribal in nature—as depicted in the TV series *Friends*. Ethan Watters, a writer living in San Francisco, described his membership in one such urban group in an article for the Sunday *New York Times* magazine titled "My Tribe." Upon entering his 30s, Watters found that his friendship group had become something more:

> After a few years, that group's membership and routines began to solidify. We met weekly for dinner. ... We traveled together, moved one another's furniture, painted one another's apartments, cheered one another at sporting events. ... One day I discovered that the transition period I thought I was living wasn't a transition period at

## media moments

### The Bridget Jones Economy: How Young Singles Shape City Culture, Lifestyles, and Economies

One of the funniest films of 2001, *Bridget Jones's Diary*, depicts the life of a young woman who fails over and over again to keep the new year's resolutions that open the book on which the film is based. "I will not," Bridget promises herself:

- ✓ Drink more than 14 alcohol units a week
- ✓ Smoke
- ✓ Spend more than earn
- ✓ Fall for any of the following: alcoholics, workaholics, commitment phobics, people with girlfriends or wives, misogynists, megalomaniacs, chauvinists, freeloaders, perverts
- ✓ Sulk about having no boyfriend

Bridget lives alone in London, worries constantly about being 30-something but still single, resents "Smug Marrieds," lives mainly on chocolate, cigarettes and wine, and occasionally tries to dump the resulting cellulite with a trip to the gym. When her affair with her dreadful boss ends in the inevitable disaster, she is propped up by her gang of friends: two single women and a gay man.

Bridget may be a caricature, but only just. Her creator, Helen Fielding, has drawn someone much more human and recognizable than the elegant and wealthy young New York singles in the TV shows "Friends" and "Sex and the City." Yet all three portray the people who now dominate and shape the rich world's city life, not just in New York and London, but increasingly in Tokyo, Stockholm, Paris and Santiago: well-educated, single professionals in their 20s and 30s.

Moralists fret about them; marketing folk court them; urban developers want to lure them. They are the main consumers and producers of the creative economy that revolves around advertising, publishing, entertainment and media. More than any other social group, they have time, money and a passion for spending on whatever is fashionable, frivolous and fun.

Bridget and her friends have begun to show up in the census figures. Spotting them is tricky: many of those who live alone are not Bridgets, and many Bridgets share a pad with someone else. However, the evidence adds up. In America's 2000 Census, one-person households outnumbered for the first time married families with children. Many of these households consist of divorced, widowed or elderly people. But the biggest rise in the 1990s was in the proportion of young people who are living alone.

*Source:* "The Bridget Jones Economy" (2001: 32)

all. Something real and important had grown there. I belonged to an urban tribe. (Watters 2001)

This slightly ironic use of the word *tribe* pertains to a network of individuals who believe they are distinguished by their cultural affinities and lifestyle. A related concept, **neotribalism,** has been

**Neotribalism** As defined by Michel Maffesoli, a characteristic form of postmodern social relations, found particularly in urban settings. Based on the root word *tribe*, neotribalism refers to networks of individuals who share a distinctive lifestyle and cultural affinities.

Gay neighborhoods such as the Castro in San Francisco are examples of neotribalism, where people choose to live in proximity with those like them. (AP Photo/Marcio Jose Sanchez)

defined by sociologist Michel Maffesoli (1996) as a characteristic form of postmodern social relations. Watters noted one example; another can be found in urban concentrations of gays and lesbians. For them, the postmodern city, such as San Francisco, New York, or London, is a place where their cultural identity can be publicly asserted and their chosen lifestyle lived out. However, the coexistence of various cultural groups, whether the difference is ethnic or lifestyle related, is not without tension, even in the postmodern city. To cite just two examples, the AIDS epidemic triggered strong hostility toward gays, and recent terrorist attacks have brought suspicion on Muslims.

Throughout history the city has been the destination of individuals seeking a better life, and it has been the subject of their dreams and nightmares, hopes and fears, utopia and its opposite—dystopia. Ancient cities may have originated as religious centers, where priests and officials controlled the peasants in the surrounding countryside and extracted a surplus from their agricultural production. Having begun as modest shrines, they became elaborated into complexes of monumental architecture: temples, pyramids, palaces, and courts. This sacred origin can still be seen in Jerusalem, which since the time of the ancient world has been a sacred site for Jews, Christians, and Muslims. As Roger Friedland and Richard Hecht demonstrate in their book, *To Rule Jerusalem* (1996), this Israeli city is not just a material place but also a cultural "imaginary." Of course, Jerusalem is conspicuous for its loaded imagery; but in fact every postmodern city rests inside vivid symbolic forms. Even before they are built, urban buildings exist in the minds of architects and investors, and they continue to take on various meanings for the inhabitants and visitors who use or "consume" them. They can also inflame the imagination if they symbolize divisions, inequalities, and threats. In this way the postmodern city, like the megacities of the LDCs, can turn into a nightmare for people. The terrorists who destroyed the twin towers of the World Trade Center chose those targets because of what they believed those buildings symbolized—namely, the wealth and power of America and of Western capitalism. The terrorists themselves were not poor and uneducated. They acted as ideological warriors who knew that by destroying those particular city buildings (and their inhabitants) they could send a powerful message. In short, September 11 represented an attack not just on the American nation, capitalism, or imperialism but also on the diversity, wealth, and innovation of the postmodern city.

## THE GROWTH OF CITIES

The importance of the city for sociology lies in the fact that it provides a kind of laboratory for studying different kinds of social relations and cultures within one location. For instance, research on the growth of cities shows that they depend on favorable material factors. The process of **urbanization** has a very long history and, at each stage, has been closely linked to economic, political, and geographical factors.

The first important factor was increased agricultural production, which freed a potential urban population from remaining on the farm. By 4000 B.C.E. the fertile crescent between the Tigris and Euphrates rivers, in what is now Iraq, was producing enough food to support the first large cities. Similar urban developments took place in fertile areas along the Indus River (areas that now make up Pakistan) and the Nile River in Egypt between 2500 and 1500 B.C.E. and in Central and South America around 1500 B.C.E. In Europe it was the ancient Greeks who began urbanization around 1800 B.C.E.; this period was succeeded in 500 to

**Urbanization** The historical and social process by which cities grew and became the center of social life. The most important condition underlying urbanization has been increased agricultural production. Expansion of the number of people living in cities, not producing their own subsistence, is possible only when agricultural surpluses are available.

400 B.C.E. by the golden age of city-states, such as Athens, which became famous for their philosophy schools and artistic products. As of the first century C.E., it was Rome and its empire that saw the greatest growth of urbanization—an era that lasted for four centuries, until wars led to a defensive shrinking back of its cities. The subsequent Dark Ages persisted for almost 600 years, and it was not until the eleventh century that European cities began to revive and engage in international trade and commerce. There was then a great flowering of trading cities, such as London, Paris, Florence, and Venice. In addition to the merchant class, these cities contained separate sections of workers in specific crafts, such as leather workers, carpenters, goldsmiths, and jewelers, often with their own guild organizations. Other groups—those made up of socially marginalized peoples—were restricted to specified urban areas, as in the case of the Jews, who were pushed into ghettos.

In the second half of the eighteenth century, the first modern industrial cities began to develop—first in Britain and other European countries, and then in America. The British city of Manchester can lay claim to being the first major industrial city, its population having grown from tens of thousands in the early eighteenth century to hundreds of thousands by the 1840s. In 1844, Friedrich Engels, Karl Marx's friend and fellow socialist, wrote a description of the appalling conditions confronting the new urban working class in Manchester:

The couple of hundred houses, which belong to old Manchester, have been long since abandoned

The Roman Forum was part of the urbanization of ancient Rome, when Caesar brought the city to its peak of prosperity and cultural accomplishment. (AP Photo/Andrew Medichini)

by their original inhabitants: the industrial epoch alone has crammed into them the swarms of workers whom they now shelter; the industrial epoch alone has built up every spot between these old houses to win a covering for the masses who it has conjured hither from the agricultural districts and from Ireland; the industrial epoch alone enables the owners of these cattle-sheds to rent them for high prices to human beings, to plunder the poverty of the workers, to undermine the health of thousands, in order that they alone, the owners, may grow rich. (Quoted in Tucker 1978: 584)

In America, there were similar developments in the nineteenth century. The earlier colonial towns—such as Dutch New Amsterdam (later to become New York), founded in 1624, and English Boston, founded in 1630—had been little different from the village-like medieval European towns. It

was during the first half of the nineteenth century that new transportation systems and industrialization led to urban expansion and large cities such as Buffalo, Cleveland, and Detroit. The second half of the nineteenth century saw the growth of the major metropolises. As the massive influx of immigrants swelled their numbers, industrial metropolises such as New York and Chicago had millions of inhabitants by the end of the nineteenth century. Gradually, the more affluent classes moved to the outer zones of the city, so that the zones radiated outward, becoming progressively more affluent toward the perimeter. By the middle of the twentieth century, the movement of **urban decentralization** was fully under way. The middle classes were moving out of the city and into new suburbs. And as the suburbs created their own facilities, ranging from shopping malls to medical centers, suburban residents felt little need to go into the downtown

Urban decentralization led to the proliferation of huge suburbs, such as the Mount Davidson neighborhood near San Francisco. (Morton Beebe/Corbis)

areas. The inner cities became synonymous with social problems: poverty, overcrowding, bad schools, and crime.

By the 1970s, more Americans were living in suburban areas than in the central cities. The flight of the more affluent sections of the population, which in some cases was racially motivated "white flight," left the central cities starved of tax income. Federal government agencies attempted to develop urban renewal policies to stop the urban decay, but the results were very uneven: Subsidizing low-cost housing could not be a solution if job opportunities remained scarce. The old manufacturing cities of the Northeast and Midwest—in the "Snowbelt" region—were losing jobs as their industries declined in the face of economic developments such as competition from newly industrializing countries with lower labor costs. The Snowbelt became known as the Rust Belt. Meanwhile, in the South and West, the new "Sunbelt" cities, which had avoided the problems of aging industrial plants and crumbling public infrastructure, were able to attract new investment and workers. They expanded outward in a vast urban sprawl, as in the cases of Los Angeles and Houston.

The extended economic boom of the 1990s gradually had an effect in terms of slowing down and, in some cases, turning back the decline in the old industrial Snowbelt cities. In 1998, the U.S. Department of Commerce Bureau of the Census published an article with the title "'Rust Belt'

**Urban decentralization** The movement of the middle classes out of inner cities and into the suburbs. Urban decentralization is sometimes referred to as "white flight."

Rebounds." It reported that many Rust Belt cities had followed the trend in shifting from a mostly goods-related economy to a service-based economy and that more flexible, market-oriented companies had generated hundreds of thousands of new jobs. In many Rust Belt metro areas, especially in the Midwest, unemployment, welfare rolls, and crime were down; wages were up; and population figures were either stable or rising as well (U.S. Department of Commerce 1998). This trend seems to have been sustained over the last decade, despite economic downturns; in fact, many of the old Rust Belt cities remain in difficult straits. It's a trend, of course, that is consistent with the shift from an industrial to a postindustrial economy.

## URBAN SOCIOLOGY IN THE TWENTIETH CENTURY

From its beginning, the sociology of the city was very much concerned with the ways in which urban culture produced a modern kind of consciousness that differed from the rural mentality. In the second half of the nineteenth century, and throughout much of the twentieth, as sociology devoted itself to analyzing the emergence of modernity and its problems, both theoretical and empirical research found urbanization to be central. The changes associated with industrialization and urbanization brought many benefits, but they also presented many problems. Writing at the beginning of the twentieth century, Emile Durkheim saw the modern city as a place where social relations were impersonal and involved limited commitments, somewhat like the relations among the specialized organs of the body. These **organic relations** were very different from the much more personal and broadly based commitments of traditional social relations, which, known as **mechanical relations,** proceeded almost automatically and in a mechanical fashion. Durkheim observed that

"in large cities, the individual is a great deal freer of collective bonds" (Durkheim 1893: 297–298). Because individuals were freer they could be more culturally innovative than in the traditional rural village or small town, but they were also less subject to norms of behavior and more likely to suffer from *anomie*. This state of anomie led to pathological conditions, such as higher rates of suicide. A German contemporary, sociologist Ferdinand Tonnies (1887), drew a similar contrast between the relations of "community" (*Gemeinschaft*) in rural villages and small towns and the contractual, "societal" relationships (*Gesellschaft*) that were more common in the cities. (Recall the related discussion of these parenthetical terms in Chapter 15, on religion.) This difference in social relations corresponded to a difference in the cultural characters of those relations: *Gemeinschaft* relations appeared to be "natural" and were based on beliefs and emotions about shared characteristics and bonds, as in the family, whereas *Gesellschaft* relations were based on rational calculation about what was needed to achieve a specific goal, as when making a purchase or doing a job.

Another German sociologist of the time, Georg Simmel, in a classic essay titled "The Metropolis and Mental Life" (1903), also focused attention on the culture of the city. He emphasized what he called the "neurasthenia" characteristic of city existence—the almost neurotic sense of anxiety and stress that pervades the urban way of life. He also talked about the social distance and "indifference" between individuals in the city, where people often encounter one another as relative strangers. Around the turn of the century Simmel published a number of articles in American sociological journals, including the *American Journal of Sociology* (founded at the University of Chicago in 1905). His work was a major influence on the Chicago School, which developed a distinctive body of social research based on analyses of the city of Chicago in the 1920s. A leading member of the sociology department at the University of Chicago,

Robert Park (1864–1944), had briefly been Simmel's student in Germany in the early 1900s, and his writings on the new field of urban sociology owe a great deal to his former teacher. The subject of his doctoral thesis was "the mass and the crowd," a popular theme among sociologists concerned about what they viewed as the impersonality and fragmentary character of social relations in the modern city.

A strong characteristic of Chicago sociology was its tendency to treat the city itself as a kind of social laboratory. Park told his students to look for their research subjects on the street corners, in the dance halls and bars, and in the "hobo" (homeless persons) areas that had become a feature of every large industrial city. Chicago sociologists produced a number of fascinating accounts of everyday life in the city, such as Nels Andersen's famous study *The Hobo* (1923) and Frederic Thrasher's *The Gang* (1927), which examined the ways in which boys' street gangs functioned as a kind of community for their members.

The most influential statement summarizing the findings of the Chicago School studies of the city and setting out a distinctive sociological theory of urbanism was provided by Louis Wirth in his essay "Urbanism as a Way of Life" (1938). Wirth offered a "minimum sociological definition of the city" as "a relatively large, dense and permanent settlement of socially heterogeneous individuals." From these prerequisites he then deduced the major outlines of the urban way of life. As he saw it, such factors as number, density, and heterogeneity created a social structure in which primary-group relationships were inevitably replaced by secondary contacts that were impersonal, segmental, superficial, transitory, and often predatory in nature. As a result, the city dweller became anonymous, isolated, secular, relativistic, rational, and sophisticated. In order to function in the urban society, the city dweller was forced to combine with others to organize corporations, voluntary associations, representative forms of government, and the impersonal mass media of communication. These replaced the primary groups (such as the family or clan) and the integrated way of life found in rural and other preindustrial settlements.

There have been many criticisms of such generalizations about the city's tendency to produce certain cultural or mental characteristics. One of the strongest such criticisms was launched in a famous essay by Herbert Gans titled "Urbanism and Suburbanism as Ways of Life: A Reevaluation of Definitions" (1962). Gans's main objection was that Wirth's emphasis on "ecological" factors in defining the city (large numbers of people, high density, and heterogeneity) made it seem as if all city dwellers ended up sharing the same mentality as a result of these factors. Wirth did not distinguish among various groups in the city but, rather, simply contrasted the city with the preindustrial society. According to Gans, although certain transient groups in the inner city (e.g., recent migrants) may have the characteristics Wirth described as typical of city dwellers (e.g., impersonality and detachment), the factors that led to differences in lifestyle and culture were related more to social class and position in the life cycle. These characteristics might be exhibited by affluent cosmopolitan individuals and young singles who chose to live in the inner city, but other groups had their own subcultures that sheltered

**Organic relations** Social relations that were characteristic of the modern city. As described by Emile Durkheim, individuals in organic relations performed specialized roles, and their interdependence was based on exchange of specialized services. Compared to people in mechanical relations, they were less tightly bound by a shared mentality or collective bonds.

**Mechanical relations** Social relations that were characteristic of traditional, premodern social life. According to Émile Durkheim, mechanical relations were based on the like-mindedness of individuals and involved a low degree of specialization of roles.

them from such tendencies. This was particularly the case with "ethnic villagers," as in the Puerto Rican villages of the Lower East Side of New York in the 1960s.

Gans's main attention was devoted to the suburbs that were spreading rapidly in post–World War II America. His own studies of Italian-American urban villagers and of suburban Levittown led him to conclude that people who had moved out from the inner city did not experience a transformation in their values and ways of life. Although some critics had lampooned the suburbs for their alleged conformity and dullness—"Little boxes, little boxes," as a contemporary song described them—Gans found them to be strong on the kind of neighborly relations that characterized "quasi-primary group" communities (Gans 1962, 1967). Gans was writing during a period when the suburbs were growing at the expense of the inner cities, whereas the earlier sociologists at Chicago and in Europe had been concerned about the movement of rural populations and immigrants into the expanding industrial cities. In each period, sociologists' generalizations about the city and its typical cultures and mentalities were affected by the predominant demographic movement at the time. The early sociologists emphasized the effects of increasing urbanization—namely, detachment and impersonality. And the postwar sociologists were concerned about the effects of movement to the suburbs, such as cultural conformity and the segregation of classes and ethnic groups; but they assumed that "[a]s soon as they can afford to do so, most Americans head for the single-family house and the quasi-primary way of life of the low-density

**Edge cities** Industrial and commercial centers situated just outside the old downtown. Edge cities contrast with suburbs, which are mainly residential developments outside the inner city.

neighborhood, in the outer city or the suburbs" (Gans 1962: 644).

Gans suggested, however, that certain developments could alter this pattern. One such development is industrial decentralization, whereby economic enterprises move out of the city, opening up space for the kind of postmodern urbanism that we considered above. In the new edge cities, for example, industrial and business centers are situated just outside the old downtowns and contain a mixture of offices, factories, shopping malls, and entertainment complexes (Garreau 1991). Distinct from the suburbs, which contain mostly homes, they are part of the urban expansion that results in megacities, stretching for many square miles. Often the edge cities have no clearly marked boundaries. For example, Greater Los Angeles, including Orange County, has been described as consisting of a sprawl of edge cities—or, in Edward Soja's words, as a postmodern exopolis, with "*exo* … referring both to the city growing 'outside' the traditional urban nucleus and to the city 'without,' the city that no longer conveys the traditional qualities of cityness" (1997: 26).

In fact, the megacity of Los Angeles County comprises almost ninety smaller cities, which have been incorporated around the central city of Los Angeles since its founding in 1850. Some of these satellite cities, such as Long Beach (pop. 461,522), are as large as the midsized metropolitan centers of the East Coast. In 2000, Los Angeles County had a population of more than 9.5 million people, only a third of whom were living in the city of Los Angeles proper. Figure 16.3 illustrates the increases that occurred in the number of incorporated cities in Los Angeles County between 1850 and 2000.

Another factor luring people back from the suburbs to the inner city, according to Gans (1962), was that rising numbers of college graduates were swelling the ranks of the "cosmopolites" (professionals and intellectuals) who wanted to be near the cultural facilities located in the center of the city. This has been especially true of cities

**FIGURE 16.3 The Development of Los Angeles County: Increases in the Number of Cities by Year of Incorporation, 1850–2000**

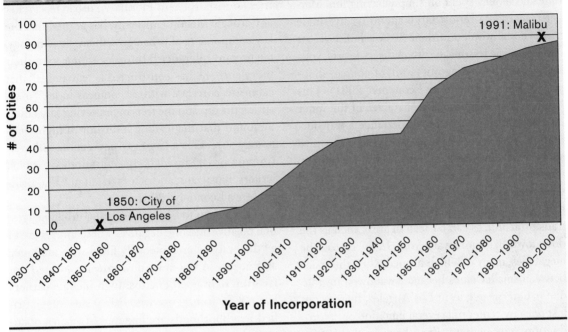

Source: Los Angeles Almanac, available online at http://www.laalmanac.com.

whose central areas have undergone redevelopment to attract not only "cosmopolites" themselves but also the kinds of economic enterprises that employ them and cater to their needs.

## THE CITY OF THE FUTURE: POSTMODERN URBANISM

Today's megacities are notable for the contrasts they contain within their ever-expanding and permeable borders—as will likely continue to be the case in the future. The inner cities contain some of the poorest and most troubled sections of the population, including recent migrants from the countryside and abroad. But the inner city is also home to affluent singles and wealthy "empty nesters" (parents whose children have grown up and left

home). The young singles, especially, have been referred to as "shock troops of creativity and culture" who "drive gentrification" because they are willing to live in the lofts of inner cities and bring with them lots of restaurants and nightlife. They are also held accountable for what has been called "the anesthetization" of the city and the evolution of "the city as spectacle" ("The Bridget Jones Economy" 2001: 34). Not surprisingly, the city is increasingly being constructed as a cultural product to excite the imagination, to be "consumed" and enjoyed. City planners are indeed eager to redevelop the city center as an attractive and exciting landscape, or cityscape, that can compete with other major cities in attracting not just tourists and prosperous young professionals but also private investment in offices, up-market retailers, and entertainment venues.

One thing that distinguishes the affluent young singles who choose to live in the inner city (like the fictional character Bridget Jones) is the amount of time and money spent on simply having fun. Market researchers report large spending by single professional women in their 30s on holidays, art classes, music lessons, health clubs, concerts, yoga classes, movies, eating out—and, of course, shopping ("The Bridget Jones Economy" 2001). This factor has an effect on the character of the inner city, which soon begins to experience a transformation of certain formerly decaying areas into spectacular up-market culture and leisure centers. Out-of-towners and tourists are then drawn in to view the spectacle and to sample what is on display. Town planners are happy to help shape this transformation, as can be seen in areas such as the downtown Baltimore waterfront. In the case of the megacities, many of which formed when the space between smaller cities became swallowed up into one **urban sprawl,** as in Los Angeles, there is not just one city center but several imitation or "reproduction" city centers. Even back in the 1980s, Greater Los Angeles was described as being composed of a sixty-mile circle covering the thinly sprawling "built-up" area of five counties, a population of more than 12 million people, and at least 132 incorporated cities (Soja 1989: 224). Today it is far larger, stretching almost to San Diego in the south.

The relative tolerance of diverse lifestyles in the city is attractive to minorities and to those whose lifestyle deviates from convention. Indeed, it has been argued that the most creative cities in the United States are those with the highest proportion of gay households. One reason is that such households often have the large spending power of two earners without the expense of children. The presence of gays is also compatible with the sort of open, diverse city culture in which creative industries flourish. Richard Florida, an urban researcher at Carnegie Mellon University, has argued that the key components of urban growth are "technology, talent, and tolerance." In order to measure their prevalence, he has constructed a "gay index" that claims to correlate with a "coolness index" measuring the hip and the trendy. Surveying fifty cities, he found that the leading indicator of high-technology success is a large gay population, followed (in rank order) by high concentrations of artists, writers, musicians, and actors (cited in "The Bridget Jones Economy" 2001).

There seem to be two coexisting urban images, one positive and one negative. These images are of a "dual city" simultaneously filled with affluence and misery. A booming downtown is located not far from depressed ghettos; high-income earners live not far from those who barely survive; gentrified neighborhoods are juxtaposed against abandoned, neglected ones (Laska and Spain 1980; Mollenkopf and Castells 1991; Smith and Williams 1986). Recent scholars have described the rising fortunes of outward-looking "tourist cities," while others see insular cities immersed in ethnic conflict (Bollens 1998, 2000; Fainstein, Gordon, and Harloe 1992; Judd and Fainstein 1999).

Even more surprising in its contrasts is the view that links together tourism and terror. In a remarkably timely article, the first draft of which was written before the terrorist attack in New York City on September 11, 2001, H. V. Savitch and Grigoriy Ardashev (2001) analyzed the combination of factors believed to increase the likelihood that such attacks would occur in certain types of cities. As the article went to press after September 11, the authors were able to revise some of its calculations to give greater weight to the symbolic value and global message-sending capacity of successful terrorist attacks on major tourist cities—what Savitch

**Urban sprawl** The process by which smaller cities and the space between them are engulfed into one megacity, where there is not just one city center but several city centers.

and Ardashev called "international message cities" (IMCs). Along with New York in the IMC category were London, Paris, Jerusalem, Tel Aviv, and Athens. Half of the international message cities—specifically New York, London, and Paris—are at the nerve center of the new global economy, where any attack would have ramifications throughout the world because it would upset the flow of international finance, the value of capital equities, and the management of multinational corporations. Two of the other cities in this category—Jerusalem and Athens—are flashpoints of international tension in the sense that they contain sacred religious sites and are known for their unique geopolitical proximity to sources of conflict. The presence of transnational ethnic communities in IMCs—for example, radical Muslims in New York, Irish nationalists in London, and Algerian dissidents in Paris—is an important component for successful attack because terrorists require some base of local support. Also, the contrast between the great wealth in these cities and the poverty of their fellow nationals gives terrorists a rationale for retribution. Finally, international message cities play a prominent role in eroding borders in the world, as they attract populations and finance from abroad in order to compete against rival cities, whether in the context of hosting multinational companies or the Olympic Games. In this respect, IMCs reflect the twin pressures of global economics and global warfare: "While cities are increasingly free-floating and delinked from their national economies, so too has terrorist warfare become 'borderless,' similarly transcending national locations" (Lever 1997, quoted in Savitch and Ardashev 2001: 2529).

Another negative aspect of the postmodern megacity has to do with the tendency of communities that feel at risk, physically or culturally, to separate and protect their territory. The extreme example is that of **gated communities,** whose numbers have increased in the United States, especially in the cities of the Southeast and Southwest.

Gated communities—residential areas with restricted access and privatization of public space—have been described as an expression of a "fortress mentality" (Blackely and Snyder 1997). Within their walls, the influences of the outside world are carefully controlled and "ideal" living spaces are constructed. Gated communities were rare in the earlier modern cities, but their growth has been particularly rapid since the 1980s. Here is yet another paradox presented by postmodern society: Threats of crime, violence, diversity, poverty, and economic uncertainty—combined with shared values of solidarity, identity, and mutual support—increase people's use of physical markers and institutions in order to underline social boundaries. Behind these can be discerned attempts to symbolize superior status through conspicuous (affluent) consumption, leisure style, and the exclusion of others. Based on their research, Edward James Blackely and Mary Gail Snyder (1997) have identified three major types of gated communities: lifestyle, prestige, and security zone. *Lifestyle* communities, as the expression of conspicuous consumption and a new leisure class, are exemplified by retirement communities, golf communities, and new towns. *Prestige* communities, which reflect the desire for status of the well-to-do and upwardly mobile, have the aim of distinguishing themselves from the surrounding areas (especially if these are poorer). And *security zone* communities, which have been described as "enclaves of fear," are socially constructed and symbolized by walls, gates, closed streets, and various security systems as protections against crime and out-

**Gated communities** Residential areas with restricted access and privatization of public space. Gated communities are a paradox of postmodern society; on the one hand they are enclaved to protect their residents from threats of crime and violence, but on the other hand they are "ideal" living spaces with a shared sense of community and identity.

Gated communities demonstrate a "fortress mentality," whereby wealthy communities try to isolate themselves from less affluent groups perceived as more likely to commit crime. (iStockphoto)

siders. The main criticism of gated communities is that, by excluding on the basis of class, race, and cultural differences, even as they contribute to high levels of community feeling inside the gates, they may undermine the ideals of civic community and the interconnectedness of neighborhoods. The box titled "Fortress America" takes this criticism one step further.

Another strikingly paradoxical characteristic of contemporary cities is the variety of ethnic cultures they contain. As noted, early twentieth-cen-

**Assimilation**   The process by which immigrants adopt the values, norms, and behaviors of their new country of residence. Assimilation is another paradox of postmodern life; whereas ethnic plurality is a defining characteristic of the postmodern city, the expectation of a common national culture persists.

tury sociologists viewed ethnic plurality from the modernist perspective of potential assimilation, whereas many sociologists today see the city as a kind of international crossroads—a container for the spread of various ethnic cultures, as exemplified by downtown restaurants specializing in different cuisines. Possibly accompanying this more open and multicultural prospect, however, is a tendency for ethnic groups in the postmodern city to resist not only assimilation but incorporation itself—for example, by maintaining close links with their countries of origin.

This tendency has been plotted as a movement along a continuum stretching from globalization to deglobalization and then to reglobalization. Immigration and the **assimilation** of immigrants into a common, national culture—*American* culture—were once regarded as a one-way process from globalization to deglobalization. The global move-

## media moments

### Fortress America

One of the most familiar sounds in the U.S. these days is the clanging gate. Not the garden gate or the alley gate, but the gate that closes off the street, the block, and increasingly the entire neighborhood. An estimated one-third of all communities in Southern California are now gated. ...

Terrified of crime and worried about property values, Americans are flocking to gated enclaves in what experts call a fundamental reorganization of community life. ...

Walls are only the beginning. Inside may be surveillance cameras, infra-red sensors, motion detectors, and sometimes armed guards. St. Andrews, a gated community in Boca Raton, Florida, spends over $1 million a year on helicopters and canine patrols. Hidden Valley, a private community north of Los Angeles, installed anti-terrorist bollards two years ago to keep non-residents at bay. ... The bollards rise up to impale vehicles that try to defy them. The tally so far: 25 cars and four trucks. ...

Ironically, the rush to gated communities coincides with widely reported decreases in violent crime statistics. ... Developers of gated communities exploit this anxiety by marketing their projects as safer, friendlier, and more economically stable than traditional urban, or even suburban, neighborhoods. Their ads and brochures are sprinkled with words like "village," "community," and "cozy" to suggest a friendliness and manageable scale that [are] supposedly missing outside. ...

Gated communities are part of a broader privatization movement, which in turn is linked to a growing skepticism about government's ability to police streets, stabilize neighborhoods and property values, and generally look after the public realm. ... People are responding by taking matters in their own hands. ... Private security guards now outnumber public police three to one. ...

This desire for control could have dangerous consequences for American cities—and for the world, says urban critic Jane Jacobs. ... "It's a gang way of looking at life, the institutionalization of turf. And if it goes on indefinitely, and gets intensified, it practically means the end of civilization."

*Source:* Dillon (1994: 8–12).

ment of immigrants, from one part of the world to another, is followed by **deglobalization** as those immigrants become assimilated into their new country's culture. And **reglobalization** occurs when an ethnic group relinks itself to its society of origin and begins to reaffirm its original culture. In his study of Asian groups in San Francisco, Michael Laguerre (1999) illustrates this process as it applies to Japanese-Americans. Laguerre maintains that the international needs of the booming Japanese economy after 1968 led some Japanese-

**Deglobalization** The movement away from a society that is pluralistic, diverse, and globalized toward one that shares a common national identity and culture. Deglobalization entails the assimilation of recent immigrant groups.

**Reglobalization** The process by which an ethnic group reconnects itself to its society of origin and begins to reaffirm its original culture and values.

Americans to become more closely relinked with their country of origin. He makes similar claims for the ethnic communities of Chinatown and Manilatown in San Francisco. In short, Laguerre is arguing against the modernist view of the unilinear assimilation of foreign-born communities into American society, and for the postmodernist possibility that the direction of assimilation will actually be changed.

Taken to its extreme, this perspective would suggest that Chinatown belongs to China, of which it is a distant outpost—and, likewise, that Japantown and Manilatown belong to their mother countries. Postmodern sociologists such as Paul Gilroy (1993) have introduced the concept of "diasporic communities" to emphasize just this point. The term **diaspora** first emerged to describe the condition of world Jewry in the 2,000 years since their expulsion by the Romans from their Israeli homeland. In the face of discrimination and exclusion, and sometimes brutal repression, Jewish communities retained their religious and cultural distinctiveness, their methods of communication, and their connection to their ancient homeland. The empirical question confronted by this postmodern theory is whether such diasporic conditions exist in multicultural cities today. For example, are Asian and Hispanic immigrants to the United States partially assimilated Americans, or are they "diasporic" Asians and Hispanics?

Of course, the assimilationist view made more sense in the preglobalization era, when migration still entailed severing many ties with homelands because opportunities for return travel were less available than they are today, and real-time long-distance communication was equally rare. Indeed, the availability of cheaper air travel, along with electronic communications such as the Internet and e-mail, now makes it much easier to maintain and strengthen links with the homeland. Thus the globalization of communications systems does not necessarily erode "local" cultures, such as ethnic cultures; it may even make possible their revival. Some scholars, such as Laguerre, stress the global links that are strengthened and refer to reglobalization. Others emphasize the fact that local cultures, including ethnic cultures, may react to globalization by reemphasizing their distinctiveness—a process sometimes referred to as "glocalization" (e.g., Roudometof 2005). For example, the New York Irish see their St. Patrick's Day parade as an opportunity not just to emphasize their links with Ireland but also to display their distinctive cultural identity. The prominence given to occupations such as police and fire service in the parade marks the fact that these are occupations in which the New York Irish have traditionally been heavily represented (whereas such occupations are not particularly associated with Ireland or Irish identity).

The postmodern city is indeed full of paradoxes. We noted one of these a few lines up—namely, the fact that globalization processes are sometimes accompanied by elements of "glocalization." Ethnic and other minority groups and lifestyles jostle with each other, and some of their cultural characteristics are taken up more widely into the multicultural spectacle that attracts consumers and visitors to the city. At the same time, these groups may reaffirm their difference from others, retreating into their own areas or even into gated communities. The Internet makes it possible for these separate communities to communicate with wider "virtual communities" inside their own diasporic communities. For example, Indian Americans originating from South Asia have their

**Diaspora** A term referring to a people who believe they have common roots but who have been scattered outside their place of origin. In spite of this, they still seek to maintain or create a sense of common identity. Jews were the first group to be described in this way, but the term *diaspora* is now used to refer to other dispersed peoples as well—for example, those who trace their roots to Africa, such as African-Americans, or immigrant groups who seek to link back to their culture of origin.

The St. Patrick's Day parade in New York City emphasizes the distinctiveness of the Irish-American culture; its participants are exhibiting a form of "glocalization." (AP Photo/Mike Albans)

own Internet sites and chatrooms where they can communicate with other Indians about common cultural and social matters. This resource serves to strengthen the links between the homeland and the Indian diaspora. At the same time, however, it can lead to the construction of an idealized diasporic version of Indian culture and identity, emphasizing certain traditional and religious aspects that are contested in India itself. It may also entail emphasizing differences from other cultures and groups, such as secular and materialistic Western culture or, in the case of Hindu Indians, their conflict with Muslims and especially Pakistani Muslims (Kurien 2001; Thompson 2002). In this way, a city such as Los Angeles is rendered borderless, and can be drawn into cultural tensions and social conflicts that emanate from far away.

It is not difficult to see how, under certain very unusual conditions, this broad postmodern tendency toward emphasizing difference and virtual community can facilitate terrorist attacks and stoke fears of reprisal. A good example of diasporic incorporation is the Islamic community of East London. While for the most part multiculturalism and assimilation thrive side by side in this area, there are small pockets of Islamic immigrants who have been responsive to calls for *jihad* against Britain itself. Postmodern cities, with their dualistic identities, can indeed create susceptibility to xenophobic conspiracies and even, on rare occasions, to violent attacks.

Some futuristic commentators have suggested that the new communications technologies will replace the very fabric of face-to-face social, economic, and cultural exchanges that sustain cities and urban life. City residents, they say, might use new technologies to free themselves from their dependence on the city as a place, as everything they require will be "one click away" and accessible via the Internet. Nicholas Negroponte, during the time he was director of the MIT Media Lab, predicted: "Digital living will include less and less dependence upon being in a specific place at a specific time, and the transmission of place itself will start to become possible. If I could really look out the electronic window of my living room in Boston and see the Alps, hear the cowbells, and smell the (digital) manure in summer, in a way I am very much in Switzerland" (Negroponte 1995: 165).

This prospect might be especially appealing to those affluent groups most troubled by the tensions of city life—the same groups who are moving into gated communities in areas such as Southern California and the Southwest. Does this mean that postmodernity will be marked by a backward move to the countryside and out of the city, which was the emblem of modernity—just as an earlier generation, described by Gans and other post–World War II sociologists, moved out of the inner city and into the suburbs? It might be tempting to conclude that global information and communications technologies will result in the displacement of place-based connections by the wider electronic connections and that, as a consequence, the city itself will be "stretched" out of existence. (In fact, Internet shopping has already taken some business away from city shops and malls, at the same time escaping local sales taxes and depriving the city of revenue.)

It is unlikely, however, that delocalization will unfold in this one-sided way. As we have seen in the case of groups like the young singles in San Francisco, New York, and London, some people enjoy combining intense face-to-face interactions with the "stretched-out" interactions made possible by new technologies. Postmodern city dwellers are avid users of electronic communication, yet they remain appreciative of the density and fluidity of urban interactions. For them, space and time are compressed, though certainly not eliminated. Nevertheless, it is clear that postmodern cities are sites that combine diverse relational worlds and that relations mediated by Internet technology (IT) have become subtly combined with the relational worlds within the spaces and places of the city (Amin and Graham 1999: 29).

The term *postmodern* became popular in the 1970s as a description of the architecture featured in the eclectic designs of certain new buildings in cities such as Las Vegas and Los Angeles. As Robert Venturi claimed in his influential manifesto *Learning from Las Vegas* (1977), postmodernist architecture favors the popular and even tacky or "fake" styles symbolized by Las Vegas over modernist "soulless" buildings like the Manhattan skyscrapers or the residential blocks and suburbs of postwar urban planning. Las Vegas is famous (some would say notorious) for its retro buildings, such as imitations of the Grand Canal in Venice and of Paris's Eiffel Tower. And some residential developments in Orange County, Southern California, echo nearby Disneyland in Anaheim. For that matter, Disneyland's Main Street has been described as a crystallization of idealized community more "real" than any actual nineteenth-century small American town. Joel Garreau (1991: 270) calls Irvine "deep kin" to this Disney conception.

Since the 1980s, some of the new residential developments in places like Mission Viejo and Laguna Niguel, in Orange County, Southern California, have adopted retro styles of architecture, such as "California Mission" style or "French Eclectic."

But unlike the fantasy buildings of Las Vegas—or, as discussed earlier, the renovated inner cities inhabited by "cosmopolites"—these residential developments were affected by the same economic logic that led to the mass production of modernist styles in the postwar suburbs. In order to keep costs down, hundreds of houses were built in the same style with mass-produced components. As a result, they have attracted some of the same reputation for conformity and dullness that attached to the modernist, post–World War II suburbs. In order to escape them, young singles (including even the fictional Bridget Jones) and affluent older couples alike have been tempted to move to the renovated inner cities, or to live outside the urban area altogether.

In the chapter on "Southern California" in his book *Edge City: Life in the New Frontier* (1991), Garreau describes one couple, the Maxwells, who decided to leave Laguna Niguel in the Irvine area of Orange County, after having lived and raised their children there for more than twenty years. The Maxwells complained about the lack of neighborly feeling in Laguna Niguel. Their sense of community, it turns out, emerged not from the neighborhood but from a network of family and friends scattered over large distances, with whom they kept in touch by electronic means, mail, and travel. The Maxwells were now buying a truck–mobile home combination, plus a Colorado country house, and will divide their time between the two. "Their personal sense of community," Garreau (1991: 278) explains, "is dependent on microchip connections." When in need of support, they turn to that electronically linked community—"their tribe"—rather than to actual neighbors (1991: 279). Cases like the Maxwells' raise the question as to whether postmodern edge cities, such as those in Irvine, are as successful as modern Levittowns in re-creating a sense of community. Garreau has his doubts. "Homes in Irvine," he says, "are far more repetitive than those in the old Levittowns. The old Levittowns are now

interesting to look at; people have made additions to their houses and planted their grounds with variety and imagination. Unlike these older subdivisions, Irvine has deed restrictions that forbid people from customizing their places with so much as a skylight" (1991: 271).

In fact, when Garreau interviewed John Nielsen, the son of one of the main developers of Irvine's edge cities, the developer confessed that he had spent his own adult life fleeing from those same developments! As Garreau puts it: "Nielsen loves neighborhoods that 'seethe.' He loves places where you can walk to work and if you regularly stop at a little joint on the way to pick up a carton of coffee, soon everybody in the neighborhood knows you. He likes to talk to people in different strata of society. He likes areas that are full of surprises. He thinks the whole point of cities is to bring diverse people together" (1991: 266–267).

## CONCLUSION

While the cultural and symbolic significance of the postmodern city is a central focus in contemporary sociology, the hard realities of **demography** cannot be forgotten. It has been one of the most interesting topics in the sociology of the past and is likely to remain so in the future. From Durkheim to Wirth, classic figures in modern sociology considered the relative density of urban population to be a vital factor in modern cities, and in much else besides. We have learned from the cultural turn that every material factor is mediated by symbolic

**Demography** The study of the growth, size, composition, distribution, and movement of the human population. All of these topics are informed by the "cultural turn" in sociology. For example, a declining birthrate might be explained in terms of a declining adult population, or in terms of changing cultural values in relation to gender and sexuality.

life, and population is no exception. Large numbers of immigrants do not necessarily produce future large populations: The outcome depends on their cultural conceptions of marriage and fertility. This point should be kept in mind as we examine the demographic facts that follow. Some of the key facts are set out in Figure 16.4.

Here is a vital claim regarding the U.S. Census 2000 Report:

> Census 2000 improves our understanding of the ways in which the U.S. population is evolving as we enter the new millennium. It also underscores the commonalities, and a number of important differences, between the United States and other national populations. Recognizing the difference between U.S. population size, growth, and structure and those of other world regions and countries strengthens our understanding of America's place in today's world and the relative opportunities, constraints, and challenges we will face in coming years. (McDevitt and Rowe 2002: 1)

With a total of 298 million people, the United States had a larger population in 2005 than all other countries except China and India. Even so, it comprised less than 5 percent of the world's population of 6 billion. During the 1990s the population of the United States grew by 13 percent—five times the average percentage increase in other more developed countries (MDCs) during the same period. A major reason for this difference is that the United States has had much higher rates of immigration than other MDCs, especially immigration from less developed countries (LDCs) such as those of Latin America and the Caribbean, whose cultures encourage large families and in some cases discourage birth control. On average, women in the United States give birth to more than two children over the course of their reproductive lives, while women in most other MDCs exhibit much lower fertility rates. In fact, during the 1990s the United States added more people to its population than all other MDCs combined. Eleven MDCs in Eastern Europe and the former Soviet Union actually lost population during this decade.

Figure 16.5 compares the population growth and projections of MDCs, LDCs, and least developed countries between 1950 and 2030. Note the difference in trajectory between the United States and all the other MDCs. Unlike the latter, whose

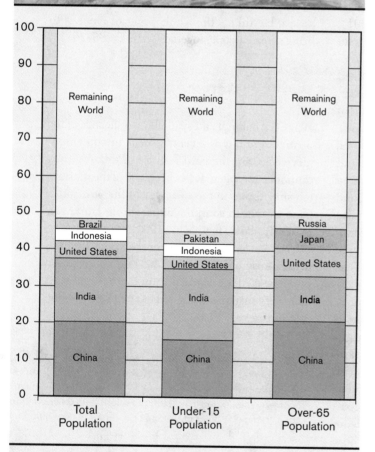

**FIGURE 16.4 Distribution of the World Population, 2005**

Source: McDevitt and Rowe (2002).

# FIGURE 16.5 Projected Population of MDCs, LDCs, and Least Developed Countries, 1950–2030 (in millions)

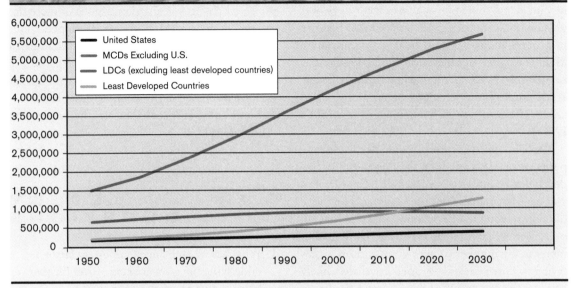

*Source:* Adapted from UN Department of Economic and Social Affairs (2004).

populations have been declining since the 1990s, the United States is projected to grow in size over the next thirty years. As noted earlier, this is largely a consequence of immigration to the United States from less developed countries.

A country's population growth rate and age-sex composition indicate the challenges it faces in providing health care for its children, education for its youth, employment opportunities for its young adults, and medical as well as financial support for its elderly. The problem in the future for most LDCs is that they have increasing numbers of children to support with health and education services and decreasing or static economic opportunities for those of working age. And in the MDCs, the problem is that there will be a smaller proportion of working-age people to support growing numbers of elderly people. The United States, although it has large numbers of older people, is fortunate in that it has a larger proportion of children and young people than most other

MDCs. About 10 million more people entered the United States than left it during the 1990–2000 period, adding to the young adult groups of the population.

Over the course of the next quarter-century, according to the U.S. Census 2000 Report (summarized in McDevitt and Rowe 2002), world population is expected to increase by 29 percent, with nearly all growth occurring in LDCs. The world's population will also have larger numbers of older people—a rising median age and a higher percentage of those aged 80 and above. Excluding the United States, MDCs are likely to see a decrease in population of about 1 percent by 2025, whereas LDCs as a group will grow by 35 percent over the same period. The sex ratio will also change. In 2000 there were about 101 men for every 100 women worldwide. The ratio of men to women was lower in the world's more developed regions (96:100 in the United States and 94:100 in the other MDCs) than in the LDCs (103:100).

There are two major explanations for this outcome. The first is that MDCs have more elderly people and that women tend to outlive men. The second is that some LDC cultures favor boys over girls, not only out of gender bias but also because boys in traditional societies are economically more useful. However, this bias is declining. Predictions suggest that, by 2025, there will be approximately equal numbers of men and women globally and about 101 men per 100 women in the world's LDCs.

Global population pressures are likely to be experienced most strongly in the megacities of less developed countries as well as in MDC megacities that have large immigrant populations. The introduction of commercial farming methods that require less agricultural labor in LDCs will further increase the number of immigrants and refugees trying to enter more developed countries, likely swelling the proportion of ethnic minorities in the inner cities of more developed countries. Thus, although the United States is advantaged in having a relatively balanced population—with a larger proportion of children and young people than other MDCs—it will not be immune to the effects of global population pressures.

# EXERCISES

## Exercise 1

Figures 16.1 and 16.2 show the changes in the distribution of Americans across urban, suburban, and rural spaces during the twentieth century. What trends and patterns do you observe in the data? Do your observations fit with the theories of urbanization and decentralization described in this chapter?

## Exercise 2

Take another look at Figure 16.5, which shows the projected changes in the populations of more developed countries (MDCs), less developed countries (LDCs), and least developed countries between 1950 and 2030. Delineate some of the patterns you observe in these data. Based on what we have discussed in this chapter, describe the social and cultural forces that may be underlying these patterns.

# STUDY QUESTIONS

1. What has been the most important factor underlying the growth of cities over the past seven thousand years? Explain why.

2. One distinguishing feature of the postmodern city is the geographic differentiation of social and cultural groups within the urban center. What distinguishes these clustered groups from the ones in earlier cities? What are some of the social forces behind this phenomenon?

3. Describe the movement of urban decentralization that occurred in the United States in the mid-twentieth century. What were some of the social forces underlying this movement?

4. Emile Durkheim differentiated between communities based on "organic" relations and communities based on "mechanical" relations. Is the modern city characterized by organic or mechanical relations? Are city dwellers more or less likely to suffer from anomie than non–city dwellers?

5. What did urban researcher Richard Florida find to be the leading indicator of high-technology success in major cities? What are the economic and cultural explanations for his findings?

6. Describe the three types of gated communities identified by Edward James Blackely and Mary Gail Snyder. How do the symbols that characterize these communities vary across the three types? What has been the main criticism of gated communities?

7. Explain the movement from globalization to deglobalization, and from deglobalization to reglobalization, that has been attributed to the immigrant populations of cities like Chicago and New York. How does this three-part model differ from earlier unilinear theories of assimilation? What social changes have allowed "reglobalization" to occur?

8. In which major respect do the demographic trends of the United States contrast with those of other more developed countries (MDCs)? What are the reasons for this difference?

## FURTHER READING

Anderson, Elijah. 1976. *A Place on the Corner* (Studies of Urban Society). Chicago: University of Chicago Press.

Gans, Herbert J. 1967. *The Levittowners: Ways of Life and Politics in a New Suburban Community*. New York: Vintage Books.

Hobbs, Frank, and Nicole Stoops. 2002. *Demographic Trends in the 20th Century*. U.S. Census Bureau. Available online at http://www.census.gov/prod/2002pubs/censr-4.pdf.

Kasinitz, Philip, ed. 1995. *Metropolis: Center and Symbol of Our Times*. New York: New York University Press.

Massey, Douglas S., and Nancy A. Denton. 1993. *American Apartheid: Segregation and the Making of the Underclass*. Cambridge, MA: Harvard University Press.

McFalls, Joseph A. 2003. "Population: A Lively Introduction." *Population Bulletin* 58, no. 4. Washington, DC: Population Reference Bureau.

Sennet, Richard. 1971. *The Uses of Disorder: Personal Identity and City Life*. New York: Vintage Books.

Simmel, G. 1903. "The Metropolis and Mental Life." In *Georg Simmel on Individuality and Social Forms*, edited by D. N. Levine. Chicago: University of Chicago Press.

Wilson, William Julius. 1987. *The Truly Disadvantaged: The Inner City, the Underclass, and Public Policy*. Chicago: University of Chicago Press.

# chapter 17
# Politics, Publics, and the State

In mid-January 2002, America's preoccupation with the war against the Taliban in Afghanistan was abruptly pushed off the nation's front page. Fast-breaking economic news was what replaced it. Enron Corporation, the seventh largest company in the United States, was facing imminent bankruptcy, with thousands of its workers not only out of a job but out of their retirement savings. While most of Enron's white-collar employees went from riches to rags, its mink-collared top executives walked off with millions in last-minute bonuses.

The "Enron scandal" soon mushroomed across the nation's newspapers. The juxtaposition of tragic economic deprivation with the sordid display of naked greed was massive and depressing. But this was not enough, in itself, to create a scandal. Politics and the state had to come into the picture and, with them, a growing sense of danger to something called "the public interest."

The "public interest advertisement" tells it all. The ad ran in the *New York Times* opinion section on January 23, 2001. At its center is a sardonic political cartoon depicting Washington's power brokers as if they were "totally wired" into Enron's power lines. There they stand, Democrat and Republican, white and black, male and female—politicians all. They are portrayed as being bound to cover up for Enron and defend its narrow corporate interests. The words below the drawing tell of politicians on the take, who assume a tepid political stance that is too little and too late.

According to this political broadside, greed is afoot at the center of the nation, and corrupt individuals are to blame. When the president's press secretary questioned whether the threatened congressional investigations into the scandal were really necessary, an "incredulous" reporter is said to have asked, "We should just trust you on that?" The advertisement points fingers not only at corporate greed but at the attorney general of the United States and at powerful U.S. senators, along with some 250 other "friends" on Capitol Hill—all

of whom had taken money from Enron. The demand is that these wired individuals "recuse" themselves from any further involvement in the Enron case. Because of their conflict of interest, they must withdraw from playing any further political role. They eventually did so, and over the next five years one after another of Enron's highly placed executives, including the president, CEO, and CFO, were prosecuted, convicted, and jailed.

This editorial ran in the *New York Times* after the Enron scandal broke. (www.TomPaine.commonsense.com)

| TABLE 17.1 Enron Contributions to Federal Candidates and Parties, 1989–2001 | |
| --- | --- |
| Soft Money Contributions | $3,567,260 |
| Contributions from Political Action Committees | $1,146,772 |
| Contributions from Individuals | $1,237,588 |
| Total Contributions | $5,951,570 |

*Source:* Center for Responsive Politics, available at http://www.opensecrets.org/orgs/summary.asp?ID=D000000137&Name=Enron+Corp.

In early 2002, no fewer than ten congressional committees held hearings on the Enron scandal. Of the 248 senators and House members serving on those committees, 212 had received campaign contributions from Enron or Arthur Andersen. Table 17.1 provides an overall breakdown of Enron contributions from 1989 to 2001, and Table 17.2 shows the total amount of money Enron contributed to committee members from 1998 to 2002, along with the total number of hearings held by each committee.

## AN INDIVIDUAL OR A SOCIAL STORY?

Despite the culpability of its leaders and the media focus on big names, the Enron scandal was not simply an individual story. It was not a political crisis created by personal corruption, one that could have been prevented if this or that person had only exhibited more honesty and integrity (though this certainly would have been welcome). Indeed, political life is responsive to collective forces, not just individual ones.

Let's take another look at the political advertisement reproduced in the *New York Times*. Over the despairing headline "TOTALLY WIRED" we find, in an equally large typeface, the name of the organization that paid for the advertisement. It is "TomPaine.common sense," identified as "A Public Interest Journal." The ad concludes with this paragraph, set in bold type: "It doesn't take a cynic to ask if there's enough independence left in Washington to protect the public interest. Wash-

**TABLE 17.2 Enron Campaign Contributions to Members of Congress**

|  | Total Contributions (1998–2002) | Number of Hearings (2002) |
|---|---|---|
| **House:** | | |
| House Energy and Commerce Committee | $133,528 | 7 |
| House Financial Services Committee | $127,431 | 3 |
| House Education and the Workforce Committee | $10,950 | 3 |
| **Senate:** | | |
| Senate Commerce, Science, and Transportation Committee | $115,420 | 7 |
| Senate Energy and Natural Resources Committee | $101,429 | 1 |
| Senate Banking, Housing, and Urban Affairs Committee | $71,279 | 9 |
| Senate Finance Committee | $67,250 | 1 |
| Senate Judiciary Committee | $33,589 | 1 |
| Senate Health, Education, Labor, and Pensions Committee | $23,401 | 1 |
| Senate Government Affairs Committee | $17,000 | 9 |
| **Totals:** | **$701,277** | **42** |

*Note:* Information on the number of Enron hearings in 2002 was taken from the following congressional committee websites: http://energycommerce.house.gov/107/action.htm; http://financialservices.house.gov/hearings.asp?formmode=printed&congress=8; http://www.gpo.gov/congress/house/house06ch107.html; http://commerce.senate.gov/hearings/hearings0202.htm; http://www.senate.gov/~gov_affairs/hearings02.htm; http://help.senate.gov/Hearings/hearings_2002.html; http://banking.senate.gov/hrg02.htm; http://finance.senate.gov/sitepages/february02hearings.htm; http://energy.senate.gov/public/index.cfm; and http://judiciary.senate.gov/hearing.cfm?id=149.

*Source:* Adapted from Kahn (2002).

Many Enron employees lost their livelihoods and all of their savings to the corrupt executives running Enron. (Reuters/Corbis)

ington is wired—the public servants are privately funded by the people they're supposed to oversee. That's the real scandal" (http://www.TomPaine. commonsense 2002).

It wasn't monetary considerations or even financial corruption per se that made Enron front-page news but, rather, the corruption of *politics*. The real issue here was the corruption of the polity, of the institutions of democratic government itself. The financial dishonesty at Enron became a scandal because it was perceived as affecting the public interest. The very ideal of government seemed to have been assaulted—and not just any government, but government of, by, and for the people.

**Public**  A concept that encompasses both civil ideals and institutions. A public is composed of "citizens," who are the critical audience for political events. And politicians are expected to function as the public's "servants." In a political democracy, the public has an honored place.

**Democracy**  Literally, "rule by the people." Unlike monarchy, where political power is vested in a single individual, democracy is a political system in which power is justified and exercised by the people (or the officers they elect).

These considerations point us to an element in the political order that is critical to our discussion in the present chapter. This is the concept of the **public,** which encompasses both civil ideals and institutions. In a political **democracy,** the public has an honored place. It is composed of "citizens," who are conceived as a critical audience for political events. Politicians are supposed to be the public's "servants." And it is the integrity of these servants that is supposed to protect the public from business greed. The public's independence is obviously threatened when its servants—government officials—are on the take. In such circumstances they are doing their jobs not on behalf of the public but at the bidding of some private interest group. When the honesty and responsibility of public officials fail, the public itself becomes threatened. It was just such a threat to the integrity and independence of the public that made Enron a scandal.

In its coverage of the Enron scandal, the *New York Times* ran two news stories that, together, highlight the contrast between the political approaches that were taken toward this unfolding economic tragedy. An individualistic understanding dominates the article reproduced in the box titled "Workers Feel Pain of Layoffs and Added Sting of Betrayal." A more collective, sociological understanding of politics is outlined in an article titled "Web of Safeguards Failed as Enron Fell":

The system of safeguards that was put in place over the years to protect investors and employees from a catastrophic corporate implosion largely failed to detect or address the problems that felled the Enron Corporation. ...

The breakdown in checks and balances encompassed the company's auditors, lawyers and directors ... but it extended to groups monitoring Enron from the outside, like regulators ... [and] the media and Congress, which in the coming week will open a blizzard of hearings into the company's downfall. ...

## media moments

### Workers Feel Pain of Layoffs and Added Sting of Betrayal

This is not just hard times, not just one more company to shut its doors in a sagging economy and leave employees with unpaid mortgages and uncertain retirements. It is not even simple greed, not merely another boss. ...

This, said some of the 4,000 laid-off workers of Enron, was a betrayal by executives who hid the corporation's crumbling finances and fattened their bank accounts while their employees' jobs and retirement funds—built from Enron stock—disappeared.

"What about us?" said Sandra Stone, 51, an executive assistant who lost a $49,000-a-year job and Enron stock rewards that were valued at $150,000 at one point.

As the Corporation floundered, executives told workers it had never been more solid, said Ms. Stone, who said she routinely worked 12-hour days and skipped lunch. ...

"They kept telling us, 'Don't sell, don't sell, it's going to go up.' And they issued more options," Ms. Stone said of the stock. She said that Kenneth L. Lay, Enron's chairman, once told employees, "In a year or two, we'll be laughing at this."

"No," she said, "we won't." ...

Mark Lindquist, a Web designer who lost a $56,000-a-year job and all his benefits, has to figure out how he can pay for therapy for his autistic son. "The upper-level executives got their money," Mr. Lindquist said. "I was let go by voice mail."

*Source:* Bragg (2002).

---

The company's demise seems sure to bring not just legislative changes but sweeping reviews by regulators ... in search of how to [ensure] that investors, employees and other constituencies can have faith in what companies tell them.

In Enron's case, the questions extend to the political influence wielded by the company. But increasingly the focus has turned to the entire framework of legislation, regulation and self-governance in which it operated.

"This was a massive failure in the governance system," said Robert E. Litan, director of economic studies at the Brookings Institution. ... It could be months before criminal, civil, and Congressional investigations unearth all the facts of Enron's collapse. (Stevenson and Gerth 2002)

From the latter point of view, the most dangerous aspect of the Enron scandal was that it represented a massive failure in the "system of governance"—a failure far more frightening than individual fault or even economic breakdown. The system in question was governance—not private interests but the government and the state, not economics but politics and the public interest. This is the issue to which the present chapter is devoted.

## STATES AND IMPERSONAL POWER

### Prepolitical Societies

In the earliest human societies, power did not possess this collective, political dimension. Even in the more complex traditional societies, there was no "state" in the sense in which we conceptualize it today, much less politics and a public sphere.

One way to think about feudal or traditional societies, in fact, is to see them as composed largely of what we might today call private groups—though we must separate the notion of *private* from its modern connections with individualism. Groups in traditional societies could be defined in many different ways: as economic in nature (consisting of lords and peasants), religious (priests and congregants), or military (knights and foot soldiers). But whatever their particular orientation, the members of such groups acted in terms of their own particular, group-specific interests, without any necessary concern for the broader society. Saying that such traditional societies possessed a "government" would not really be accurate. There were no designated institutions responsible for carrying out collective goals, and no civic ideals or binding norms regulating private associations. Indeed, nations as we understand them today had not yet formed; large-scale territorial groupings controlled by a central state simply did not exist.

The ethos of such prepolitical societies was far different from the morality that informs politics, states, and publics today, whether in democratic or in nondemocratic but still modern societies. This difference was captured by Edward Banfield in his classic study, *The Moral Basis of a Backward Society* (1958). Banfield spent a year in Montegrano, a small southern Italian village whose basic social structures had hardly changed for hundreds of years. His initial impressions closely reflect the contrast we are talking about here:

> Americans are used to a buzz of activity having as its purpose, at least in part, the advancement of community welfare. For example, a single issue of the weekly newspaper published in St. George, Utah (population 4,562) reports a variety of public-spirited undertakings. ... [By contrast,] no newspaper is published in Montegrano or in any of the thirteen other towns lying within view on nearby hilltops. Occasional announcements of public interest—"there are fish for sale in the *pi-azza* at 100 lire per *chilo*"—are carried by a town crier wearing an official cap. ... Twenty-five upper-class men constitute a "circle" and maintain a clubroom where members play cards and chat. [But] none of the members has ever suggested that it concern itself with community affairs or that it undertake a "project." ... Most people ... find the idea of public-spiritedness unintelligible. When an interviewer explained to a young teacher that a "public-spirited" person is one who acts for the welfare of the whole community rather than for himself alone, the teacher said: "No one in town is animated by a desire to do good for all of the population. Even if sometimes there is someone apparently animated by this desire, in reality he is interested in his own welfare and he does his own business." (Banfield 1958: 17–20)

## Personal Rule in Traditional Societies

The further back we go in human history, the more frequently we encounter societies composed of such small, isolated, and self-referential groups. But the political element of society is, in fact, rarely entirely absent. As Aristotle remarked in his *Politics* more than 2,000 years ago, "man is by nature a political animal"—and, we would now add, woman too. For better and for worse, the search for power and the elements of its organization and application are ever-present elements of social life. Inherent in human nature is undoubtedly an existential drive to exercise control and authority over other people, though of course it is unequally present among different individuals. But there is a more objective, social consideration as well. Every collectivity, no matter how loosely organized, has the need, and indeed the potential, to be organized and administered. In this sense, politics and organizations are functional necessities, despite the gigantic differences in their historical shape. To be effective, organizations demand leadership; in order to exercise power, leaders must establish organization.

So it is not surprising that, even in simple and segmented societies composed of largely separated and self-referential associations, one group and its associated family members will eventually emerge as a dominant power. If social resources are sufficient, this kinship group will become a dominant clan and rule in a personalistic, self-absorbed manner.

It was such loosely ruled territories that characterized the vast stretch of what is called **traditional society**. The earliest human societies were merely "bands," extended kinship groups of sixty to eighty persons that did not, in fact, have any specifically political form. In some areas of the world, such simple, prepolitical societies extended well into the twentieth century. In most places, however, whether in South America, Asia, Africa, or Europe, social development extended beyond these early forms, pushed by the growing complexity of societies that extended over greater territorial expanse. These societies were loosely ruled by authorities who inherited their positions and exercised their power according to tradition. Such power was simultaneously personal and arbitrary.

To carry out their wishes and enforce their decrees, such rulers relied on their extended families (aristocracies) as well as on staffs of quasi-officials who were loyal to them personally. The territory they controlled was not a modern **state**, a clearly defined and impersonal political area, but rather a personal fiefdom, defined in much the same terms as a prince's massively extended household. Following Max Weber, Reinhard Bendix (1977: 33) described such extended, traditional, nonstate governance as a kind of personal patrimony: "Patrimonialism refers, first of all, to the management of the royal household and the royal domains. This management is in the hands of the king's personal servants, who are maintained as part of the royal household and rewarded for their services at the king's discretion. On this basis, patrimonial-

**Traditional society** A loosely organized territory in which power is concentrated in a kinship group or family. In traditional societies, authorities earn their position not through formal mechanisms (e.g., voting) but by inheritance, and power is exercised according to tradition rather than formal rules.

**State** A clearly defined and impersonal political area. The sociological concept of state refers to the formal organization of social power—namely, political power—in society. While the term *state* is often assumed to be interchangeable with *government* or employed to indicate a particular geographical area, these usages are not always synonymous.

ism develops as a structure of authority with the expansion of royal jurisdiction over territories outside the royal domains."

## The Origins of Impersonal Authority in Modernity

Such territorial rule was personal and group-based, not impersonal and public-spirited. It was every family, occupation, military cadre, and religious association for itself, including most of the ruling families that comprised the aristocracy. This personal and particularistic manner of ordering a territory could not sustain itself in the face of modernization. As societies became more developed and complex, as commerce and transportation connected faraway places, as cities developed, as economies became more productive, as the groups occupying a territory become more interdependent and intertwined, the combination of atomism and personal rule that characterized traditional societies became less viable. It was in this changing historical context that "states" first began to develop in the modern sense of the term.

Max Weber told the story of the origins of the modern state in a manner that has become emblematic for contemporary social science. According to Weber, it was as if the spread-out, personal, and private powers of the individual princes were expropriated by a centralized, impersonal, and public power:

> Everywhere the development of the modern state is initiated through the action of the prince. He paves the way for the expropriation of the autonomous and "private" bearers of executive power who stand beside him, of those who in their own right possess the means of administration, warfare, and financial organization, as well as politically usable goods of all sorts. The whole process is a complete parallel to the development of the capitalist enterprise through gradual expropriation of the independent producers. In the end, the modern state controls the total means of political organization, which actually come together under a single head. (Weber 1958a: 82)

Because it concentrated all power into one central place and institution, this emerging form of state rule was enormously strong. Its power also derived from the fact that such "state" administration was highly impersonal. As Max Weber put it: "No single official personally owns the money he pays out, or the buildings, stores, tools, and war machines he controls. In the contemporary 'state'—and this is essential for the concept of state—the 'separation' of the administrative staff, of the administrative officials, and of the workers from the material means of administrative organization is completed" (Weber 1958a: 82).

## The Rise of Absolutist States

In many large-scale traditional societies, patrimonial forms of personal rule developed into vast quasi-bureaucratic kingdoms, most famously in the imperial courts organized by the family dynasties that ruled China for more than two millennia. However, the modern bureaucratic state emerged only in Western societies. It first crystallized in the absolutist states of seventeenth-century Europe. Because this early state construction was carried out under the initiative of kings, it initially resulted in an increase in absolute personal power as well.

Under Louis XIV, the "Sun King," France experienced the most dramatic example of this bureaucratizing development. Political theorists Carl Friedrich and Charles Blitzer described the process this way: "In place of the great noble personages of the past, the chief ministers of state were becoming professional, one might almost say 'scientific,' civil servants" (1957: 113). Yet, Friedrich and Blitzer also record how, during this same period, "the entire governmental machine remained utterly subservient to the royal will." In this manner, the scientific, abstract, and rational qualities that characterize modernity were combined with the personal domination of traditional life:

> In the name of rationality and impersonal rule, Jean Baptiste Colbert, the controller general of France under Louis XIV, organized the vast resources of the nation's economic and military life. Under his tireless attention the entire economic life of France was organized to serve the interests of the state. Detailed standards for all branches of manufacture were issued and rigidly enforced; "infant industries" were established, freed from guild restrictions, and protected by tariffs; enterprises which were considered important to the state were granted special privileges, such as monopolies, and were financed at public expense …; internal communications by land and water were vastly improved; a great navy was created to protect French commerce abroad; finally, the entire administrative and fiscal apparatus … was ruthlessly reorganized and rationalized. (1957: 114–115)

This historic transformation of patrimonial rule into state power served the interests not only of "France" but also of its king, Louis XIV. Weber wrote that every bureaucracy is nonbureaucratic at its top. For the Sun King, the vast increase of impersonal power that he and his staff engineered represented not just a newfound ability to achieve collective goals but, indeed, a vast enhancement of resources for the king's personal rule. When King Louis XIV was confronted with criticisms of his government by the French parliament, he reaffirmed not only a bureaucratic but a personal and absolutist conception of government: "It is none of your business to meddle in the affairs of *my* state," he declared, admonishing further, "I forbid you to assume to be my tutors in so meddling with the affairs of state" (quoted in Friedrich and Blitzer 1957: 98). Such personalism and arrogance are well captured in the famous royal proclamation attributed to Louis XIV: *"L'état,"* he declared, *"c'est moi!"* Translated literally, this statement means "The state, it is me!" In more colloquial terms, it means quite simply "I am the state!"

## States as Bureaucracies

The first phase of modern state-building no doubt depended upon such megalomania as its fuel. This personalistic addition to bureaucratic power began to be challenged, however, by the revolutions against absolutism carried out in England (1642), America (1776), and France (1789). Of course, personal dictatorships have continued to be a recurring, often tragic form of political rule even in modern and postmodern societies. What has changed compared to patrimonial times, nonetheless, is striking: Personal authority can now be exercised only at the top of vastly powerful, impersonal, administrative organizations. It is now professional bureaucrats and experts who organize the territory of nation or empire. Whether ideologically inspired demagogues or constitutionally elected democrats, those who are in charge of such states are less personal rulers than leaders directing the course of enormous public organizations. As Quentin Skinner (1978), another noted political theorist, has put it: "One effect of this transformation was that the power of the State, not that of the ruler, came to be envisaged as the basis of government. And this in turn enabled the state to be conceptualized in distinctively modern terms—as the sole source of law and legitimate force within its own territory, and as the sole appropriate object of its citizens' allegiances" (quoted in Alford and Friedland 1985: 1).

Modern states are the very embodiment of **bureaucracy.** "The more complicated and specialized modern culture becomes," Weber observed, "the more its external supporting apparatus demands the personally detached and strictly 'objective' expert, in lieu of the master of older social structures, who was moved by personal sympathy and favor, by grace and gratitude" (Weber 1958b: 216). States represent bureaucratic organization of the national territory, and bureaucracy is the quintessence of power in its modern form. Eventually, according to Weber, every form of modern power becomes bureaucratic, for the simple reason that such impersonal organizations are the most technically efficient ways for collectivities to accomplish their goals:

The decisive reason for the advance of bureaucratic organization has always been its purely technical superiority over any other form of organization. The fully developed bureaucratic mechanism compares with other organizations exactly as does the machine with nonmechanical modes

**Bureaucracy** A system of formal organization in which power is allocated through a hierarchy of offices and social statuses. In a bureaucracy, people engage in specialized tasks and abide by rules and expectations that are clearly defined. For example, the Department of Motor Vehicles is a contemporary bureaucratic office with specifically allocated power and particular rules dictating the tasks to be performed (such as renewing drivers' licenses). Max Weber argued that bureaucracy was a fundamental characteristic of modern society.

of production. Precision, speed, unambiguousness, knowledge of the files, continuity, discretion, unity, strict subordination, reduction of friction and of material and personal costs—these are raised to the optimum point in the strictly bureaucratic administration. ... Bureaucratization offers above all the optimum possibility for carrying through the principle of specializing administrative functions according to purely objective considerations. Individual performances are allocated to functionaries who have specialized training and who by constant practice learn more and more. (1958b: 214–215)

## States as Servants of the Collectivity

This paean to the efficiency of state bureaucracy, no matter how accurate in historical terms, can certainly be questioned. When you stand in line for hours at the Department of Motor Vehicles waiting for some nameless clerk to figure out the "right" way to renew a lost automobile license, it hardly feels like you are being served by an official of an expert state! Indeed, you might long for the kind of personal interaction that the impersonal bureaucratic form was designed to overcome. Yet, if you stop to think about it, it would be hard to think of modern life without a government—staffs of officials in numerous organizations doing the kinds of habitual, everyday things that every one of us thinks we have a right to demand and expect.

If there were not a bureaucratic, impersonal government, who would organize traffic in a rational and safe manner, make sure there are stop signs and traffic lights, keep traffic moving at a reasonable speed, and sort matters out after traffic accidents? Who would build the schools and pay for teachers? Who would make sure the teachers are qualified and that the right mix of courses is being taught? Who would run the fire department and train the police? Who would organize armies and defend the nation's borders? Who would regulate

Town meetings have long been a form of collective political decisionmaking, as this illustration to John Trumbull's M'Fingall *Town Meeting* shows. (Bettmann/Corbis)

the flow of immigration? How would the promises of politicians, and the goals of the citizens who elect them, ever be put into effect? Who, in short, would make collective decisions, and how would they be carried out?

To think of the state in this manner is to see it as a form of government that serves the collectivity. This is what political scientist David Easton had in mind when he wrote, in *The Political System*, that "a minimum condition for the existence of any society is the establishment of some mechanisms, however crude or inchoate, for arriving at authoritative social decisions about how goods, both spiritual and material, are to be distributed, when custom fails to create other patterns" (1971: 135). From this point of view, power is a capacity: one that works to the benefit of every social system. It need not be feared; to the contrary, it should be supported, protected, and even enhanced. Without state power, we would not be able to accomplish anything. Talcott Parsons conceptualized this understanding in his "functionalist" theory:

> Power is a generalized facility or resource in the society. It has to be divided or allocated, but it also has to be produced and it has collective as well as distributive functions. It is the capacity to mobilize the resources of the society for the attainment of goals for which a general "public" commitment has been made, or may be made. It is mobilization, above all, of the action of persons and groups, which is binding on them by virtue of their position in the society… [and it is] communal rather than sectoral interests [that] are served. (1960: 220–221)

## States and Domination

It is undeniable that every complex society needs such power and, hence, a state and bureaucracy. But to see power and states exclusively in this manner is to wear rose-colored glasses. Differentiation from the interests of particular social groups allows the state to serve collective goals. At the same time, however, this distance and separateness permit the state to dominate society in turn. The modern state is Janus-faced. Because it is impersonal, rational, and efficient, it can be a finely tuned means for achieving goals. But such efficiency and impersonality also mean that the state has an existence apart from society—apart from the people whom, from a purely functionalist perspective, it is designed to serve. Bureaucracies, in

> **Power** The ability to mobilize the resources of society in order to attain a particular goal. Power is concentrated in and monopolized by the state, but individuals can "have power" as well. In this sense, it is not a thing, an object, but rather an elusive idea that shapes social relationships.

other words, have independent interests. In times of conflict or crisis, state officials may be more concerned with protecting the institutions of the state than with protecting popular interests. The very fact that the state is such a "perfect machine" means, moreover, that it can serve any power efficiently, not just those that are associated with democratic rights.

Indeed, there is a long and influential line of political thinking that has concentrated on just this fact—that the state has an interest in power as such. Theorists have explored how state officials might choose to serve not broader social needs but themselves, or even to use the independent power of the state to serve some particular economic, ethnic, or religious group. As compared with advocates of functionalist thinking, these theorists are more suspicious and critical of modern forms of power, and they have worried about trying to limit or even undermine it.

Weber himself played both sides of the fence. While he recognized the functional necessity for bureaucracy, he also emphasized the dangerous, but equally necessary, connection of state power to coercion and control. Indeed, Weber defined state organization, as compared with bureaucratic organization per se, by its ability to monopolize the exercise of violence over an extended territory. Rather than a means for attaining collective goals, the state, according to Weber's definition, is a "system of order" that "claims binding authority, not only over the members of the state, the citizens, most of whom have obtained membership by birth, but also to a very large extent over all action taking place in the area of its jurisdiction." The state, in other words, "is a compulsory organization with a territorial basis." Insofar as such a territorially based compulsory organization exists, "the use of force is regarded as legitimate only so far as it is either permitted by the state or prescribed by it," for "the claim of the modern state to monopolize the use of force is as essential to it as its character of compulsory jurisdiction and of continuous operation" (Weber 1978: 56).

This is not just a theoretical point. Weber had undoubtedly recognized a fundamental dimension of modern social life. The state is not only about capabilities; it is also about control, compulsion, domination, and force. It is not just any bureaucracy but, in fact, the only impersonal organization in modern society that can legally exercise force. In order to do so effectively, it must take the means of violence away from every other social group. States are bureaucracies that exercise a monopoly over the means of violence. This is why terrorism is both so anomalous and so frightening. Its existence points to politically ambitious, often radical groups capable of employing violence outside the offices of the state.

State domination can play the role of a referee, utilizing its monopoly of force to regulate conflict and to prevent groups in society from destroying one another. In 1651, Thomas Hobbes wrote *The Leviathan* to warn that, in the absence of a dominating and coercive state, such destruction would surely come about. Ever since, Hobbes's caustic and pessimistic remarks have been invoked to justify politically enforced order, often in a nondemocratic form: "If any two men desire the same thing, which neverthelesse they cannot both enjoy, they become enemies; and in the way to their end, which is principally their owne conservation, and sometimes their delectation only, endeavour to destroy, or subdue one another" (Hobbes 1651: 87).

In the face of such destruction, the independent, impersonal, and coercive state—the "Leviathan"—emerges. Hobbes believed that "there is no way for any man to secure himself" except by a

"power great enough to endanger him." The new bureaucratic and rational state, according to Hobbes, was a "power able to over-awe them all."

## The Autonomy of the State

This aspect of modern bureaucratic power inspired the "state-centered" approach to politics. It was initiated by a series of thinkers who followed Weber, including Robert Michels, Otto Hintz, and Samuel Huntington. For contemporary sociologists, it was an understanding of politics first articulated by Theda Skocpol: "States conceived as organizations claiming control over territories and people may formulate and pursue goals that are not simply *reflective* of the demands or interests of social groups, classes, or society. This is what is usually meant by state autonomy. Unless such independent goal formulation occurs, there is little need to talk about states as important actors" (1985: 9, italics added).

Skocpol emphasizes **state autonomy** because she disagrees with the functionalist insistence that power is necessarily a collective capability. She criticizes this view as overly optimistic and often conservative. She also views her state autonomy theory as an alternative to the radical theory of Marxism. In particular, she believes that the Marxian emphasis on economics over politics eliminates the autonomy of the political. Marx insisted that the state is not independent. In *The Communist Manifesto* (1848), he and Engels famously declared that the state is only the "executive committee of the bourgeoisie." The function of the state is to direct the nation's political affairs in such a manner that the economic interests of the capitalist class are maximized, to the detriment of every other economic group. Economic elites do influence even the most modern and independent bureaucratic state. But economic groups other than the upper class influence the state as well. Middle classes often develop political influence, as do working classes, especially when they are represented by a powerful, labor-oriented political party. In cases where lower-class groups are able to affect the state, then the state will take action against the upper class, demanding reforms in the conduct of capitalism, and not only the other way around. We explore this possibility later in the chapter.

Skocpol made the case for state autonomy theory as an alternative to the Marxian perspective on politics in *States and Social Revolutions* (1979), her landmark study of the radical transformation of traditional regimes in France, China, and Russia. In her view, revolutions are defined by the overthrow of one state and the creation of another, whereas Marxism insists that revolutions must be explained as the reflection of class struggles. This tenet is set forth in the very opening words of Marx and Engels's *Communist Manifesto:* "The history of all hitherto existing society is the history of class struggles. Freeman and slave, patrician and plebeian, lord and serf, guild master and journeyman, in a word, oppressor and oppressed, stood in constant opposition to one another, carried on an uninterrupted, now hidden, now open fight, a fight that each time ended, either in a revolutionary reconstitution of society at large, or in the common ruin of the contending classes" (Marx and Engels 1848: 219).

Against this view, Skocpol argues that the state must be taken seriously as a "macrostructure" in and of itself: "The state properly conceived is no mere arena in which socioeconomic struggles are fought out. It is, rather, a set of administrative, policing, and military organizations headed, and more or less well coordinated by, an executive authority. Any state first and fundamentally extracts resources from society and deploys these to create and support coercive and administrative organizations" (1979: 29).

The great social revolutions in France, China, and Russia, Skocpol explains, succeeded not only because economic conditions were poor but because the class rebellions triggered by these poor

**State autonomy** The ability of the state to define goals that are independent of social groups, classes, and societies.

conditions faced weakened, personalistic, and inefficient bureaucracies. In those still-traditional societies, social upheavals threw the political administrations into such chaos that they could no longer carry out their basic organizing functions, which normally would have included the task of repressing illegal and violent behavior. These traditional autocratic regimes were incapable of resisting violent challenges—whether internally, from civil wars, or externally, from ambitious foreign powers that wished to take advantage of their instability. The ability to defend national territory, and to secure internal peace, is central to the state's monopoly over the means of violence, which is the very essence of what it means to *be* a state:

Some theorists of world capitalism … attempt to explain in economically reductionist terms the structure and dynamics of … nation-states [as] instruments used by economically dominant groups to pursue … economic advantages. … But a different perspective is adopted here, one which holds that nation-states are, more fundamentally, organizations geared to maintain control of home territories and populations and to undertake actual or potential military competition with other states. … [Therefore,] such factors as state administrative efficiency, political capacities for mass mobilization, and international geographical position are also relevant. (Skocpol 1979: 22)

Faced with revolutionary upheavals at home and foreign invasions from abroad, the French, Chinese, and Russian states could neither control the boundaries of their territories nor administer them effectively. They could neither collect taxes nor conscript soldiers. Because they could not maintain armies, they could not defend their regimes. Revolutions became possible, in other words, for political rather than economic reasons. In none of these societies were the governments able to function as efficient, independent states:

> Modern social revolutions have happened only in countries situated in disadvantaged positions within international arenas. In particular, the realities of military backwardness or political dependency have crucially affected the occurrence and course of social revolutions. Although uneven economic development always lies in the background, developments within the international states system as such—especially defeats in wars or threats of invasion and struggles over colonial controls—have directly contributed to virtually all outbreaks of revolutionary crises ... [and] have helped to undermine existing political authorities and state controls. (Skocpol 1979: 23)

## POLITICS AND PERSONAL POWER

The state is the source of power in modern societies, but it is not the be-all and end-all of politics. States are central to any understanding of politics and power, but politics and power in modern and postmodern societies are about much more than states. The state provides an umbrella for modern politics. And politics aims at controlling the state. Pushing state power in a certain direction, making it work on behalf of this end rather than another—that is the aim and reward of modern politics. In this connection, see the graphs in Figures 17.1–17.4, each of which represents a well-known form of contemporary political action.

### What Is Politics?

Before an overflow audience of Munich students in 1918, in the highly unstable and polarized at-

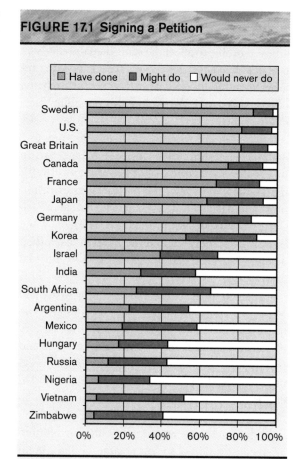

**FIGURE 17.1 Signing a Petition**

*Source:* Adapted from World Values Survey Association (2001).

mosphere of the just-defeated German nation, Max Weber spoke about the meaning of modern politics. In the years since, this lecture—titled "Politics as a Vocation"—has become famous.

Weber stressed the dignity of politics and its distinctive nature. He also wanted to remind his radically inclined students—who represented both rightist and leftist extremes—that politics can be effectively conducted within the framework of the state:

> What do we understand by politics? The concept is extremely broad and comprises any kind of *in-*

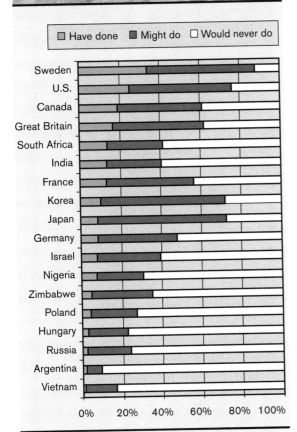

**FIGURE 17.2 Joining in Boycotts**

Source: Adapted from World Values Survey Association (2001).

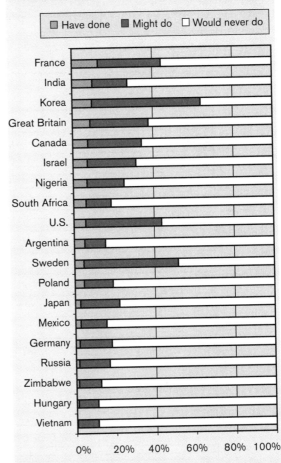

**FIGURE 17.3 Joining Unofficial Strikes**

Source: Adapted from World Values Survey Association (2001).

*dependent* leadership in action. One speaks of the currency policy of the banks [or] of the strike policy of a trade union; one may speak of the educational policy of a municipality or a township, of the policy of the president of a voluntary association, and, finally, even of the policy of a prudent wife who seeks to guide her husband. Tonight, our reflections are, of course, not based upon such a broad concept. We wish to understand by politics only the leadership, or the influencing of the leadership, of a *political* association, hence today, of a *state*. (1958a: 77, italics in original)

In the context of a state, then, **politics** is about gaining or losing power. Weber defined *power* in a realistic rather than idealistic manner: It is "the probability that one actor within a social relationship will be in a position to carry out his own will despite resistance, regardless of the basis on which this probability rests" (1978: 53). He clarified the connection between the two concepts as follows: "'Politics' for us means striving to share power or

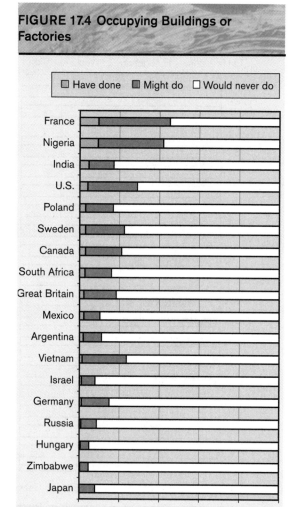

**FIGURE 17.4 Occupying Buildings or Factories**

*Source:* Adapted from World Values Survey Association (2001).

striving to influence the distribution of power, either among states or among groups within a state. … He who is active in politics strives for power either as a means in serving other aims, ideal or egoistic, or as 'power for power's sake,' that is, in order to enjoy the prestige-feeling that power gives" (1958a: 78).

Politics pulls us away from the impersonality of bureaucracy, from the modern emphasis on rationality and efficiency. It brings us back to personal interests and private resources. It moves political analysis from the impersonal to the personal, from state to party, from commands to persuasion, from rules to votes, from organizations to individuals. It allows us to think, in postmodern terms, about the cultural images and about symbolic manipulation.

## Authority and Legitimation

While *power* may be defined as the ability to carry out your will regardless of any resistance, it is much easier and more effective to exercise power if you take the will of the other into account. Insofar as another person obeys you, not from fear but from respect, you have exercised not only power but **authority**. Authoritative power possesses **legitimation**. According to Weber's classic definition, now accepted by virtually all political thinkers, there are three different types of legitimate authority, or "inner justifications," for the exercise of power. The first is based on *tradition:* "The authority of the 'eternal yesterday,' i.e. of the mores sanctified through the unimaginably ancient recognition and habitual orientation to conform. This is the 'traditional' domination exercised by the patriarch and the patrimonial prince of yore" (Weber 1958a: 78–79).

Quite the opposite of this traditional, patrimonial form of authority, which characterized power in premodern times, is the *rational-legal* mode of legitimation that defines the modern state: "There

**Politics** The process by which power is generated, organized, distributed, and used in societies. In the context of the state, politics can take the form of elections or legislative activity. In the context of the individual, it can mean participating in a protest or signing a petition.

is domination by virtue of 'legality,' by virtue of the belief in the validity of legal statute and functional 'competence' based on rationally created *rules*. In this case, obedience is expected in discharging statutory obligations. This is domination as exercised by the modern 'servant of the state' and by all those bearers of power who in this respect resemble him" (Weber 1958a: 79, italics in original).

Finally, power can be legitimated in much more personal terms, by reference to a leader's *charisma*: "There is the authority of the extraordinary and personal *gift of grace* (charisma), the absolutely personal devotion and personal confidence in revelation, heroism or other qualities of individual leadership. This is 'charismatic' domination, as exercised by the prophet or—in the field of politics—by the elected war lord, the plebiscitarian [i.e., popularly elected] ruler, the great demagogue, or the political party leader" (Weber 1958a: 79, italics in original).

## Postmodern Authority: Charisma and Culture

Weber thought that charisma would wither away in the face of modern rationalization—that its inspiring, volatile, innovative, and sometimes dangerous subjectivity would be no match for the rational-legal power of the bureaucratic machine. It has not turned out this way.

Nowadays, *charisma* is a term tossed around by every political commentator. Contemporary power reflects the shift from modern to postmodern society—a shift whose hows and whys we have explored throughout this book. In postmodern societies, the personal has taken on more public importance; subjectivity has become a vital concern. The postmodern self is protean and shifting, and emotions are openly and publicly displayed. Another reason is technological. The mass media, especially television, have allowed political images access into the most private realms of personal life.

**Authority** The ability to carry out one's will while maintaining the respect of others. (Those with authority are not necessarily liked or supported for carrying out their will; rather, they are merely respected for their ability to act in such a manner.)

**Legitimation** The way in which authority comes to be accepted and generally supported by those whom it affects. According to Max Weber, there are three types of legitimate authority in society: traditional, rational-legal, and charismatic.

The image of political actors is now critical. The aspiring political leader must inspire. It is not only a matter of intelligence, of appeals to abstract party platforms, of a lengthy expert résumé. Through the mass media, politics has become a part of everyday life for ordinary citizens. People follow politics in the news on television, on the radio, and in daily papers every day (see Figure 17.5).

Not only has postmodern society allowed charismatic power to fill up much more of the social stage, but the "cultural turn" that informs postmodern social theory allows charismatic authority to be much more clearly understood. Weber stressed that charisma refers to "the *extraordinary* quality of a person," regardless of "whether this quality is actual, alleged, or presumed" (1958c: 295). After the cultural turn, we know that even when an audience believes that a leader "really is" extraordinary, this belief is informed by a symbolic framework that precedes the action of charismatic actors themselves. Gaining charisma has less to do with actual activity than with the way an action achieves symbolic crystallization.

In an article that brought the cultural turn to Weber's political sociology, Philip Smith suggests that "charismatic authority is underpinned by binary cultural codes which elaborate and oppose sacred and evil grammars of motivations, along with narratives which employ events within a salvation framework." It is these "cultural structures," Smith maintains, that "mark out charisma

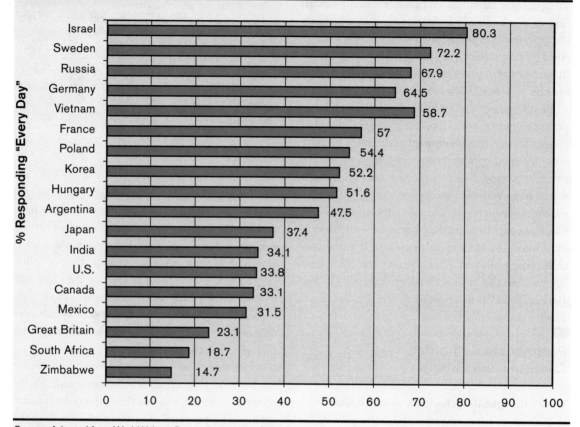

**FIGURE 17.5 How Often Do You Follow Politics in the News? (selected countries)**

*Source:* Adapted from World Values Survey Association (2001).

from routine deviance, suggesting that the charismatic is the bearer of a transcendent, positive essence" (2000: 103).

Smith finds that charisma is constructed not so much by representing the leader's own sacred qualities as by the leader's ability to convince those in his audience that they are threatened, and to vividly represent this evil in symbolic terms:

> Because the symbolic logic of charisma hangs upon binary codings and salvation narratives, images of "evil" must be present in the forest of symbols surrounding each charismatic leader. There

must be something for them to fight against, something from which their followers can be saved. In many cases this evil is an abstraction such as poverty, capitalism, heresy or injustice. In yet other cases, this evil finds its embodiment in another individual actor, a threatening person who can be taken as embodying a powerful "negative charisma." Love of the charismatic leader often seems to be predicated on hatred of the evil against which they fight. (2000: 103)

Smith illustrates his approach with case studies of some of the twentieth century's most powerful charismatic political leaders. Hitler's reputation as a charismatic leader, for example, developed only after 1920, in the latter part of the dictator's life. In the aftermath of Germany's defeat—at about the same time as Weber was giving his Munich speech—this fanatical ex-soldier and failed painter reconfigured the anxious sentiments generated by the economic and ideological crises facing post-war Germany. "Using superlatives and hyperbole," Smith writes, Hitler "elevated routine troubles into world historical struggles":

> Hitler's discourses spoke of the need for national salvation from disgrace and offered a "spiritual haven in a hostile world." For the mass populace this salvation was from poverty and unemployment, from national ignominy, from perceived foreign domination, from chaos, anomie and conspiracy. Symbolic enemies figured strongly. ... [For example,] Bolsheviks, Slavs, intellectuals, dithering and decadent parliamentary systems and nebulous conspiracies provided the foils against which Hitler could promote himself as a salvation figure. It was the Jew, however, who took center stage in the moral drama Hitler began to spin. Described as base, licentious, secretive, deformed and corrupt, the Jew provided a pervasive image of evil which only strong leadership could overcome. (2000: 105)

This symbolic focus on threatening evil is not confined to immoral and antidemocratic charismatic figures. Democratic leaders, too—if they are to succeed in exercising charismatic authority—must crystallize evil and represent their cause as the only viable alternative. Martin Luther King, Jr., is a case in point. Though not considered particularly charismatic in his earlier life, in the context of the crisis in Montgomery, Alabama, in 1955 he demonstrated extraordinary personal qualities on both the local and the national stage.

The crisis began when a young African-American woman, Rosa Parks, refused to move to the

Martin Luther King, Jr.'s extraordinary charisma drew hundreds of thousands of people to Washington, D.C., to hear his "I Have a Dream" speech on August 28, 1963. (AP Photo)

back of the bus to make room for white passengers. The bus driver called the police, who arrested Parks and threw her in jail. Throughout this ordeal, Parks displayed exceptional character, and her courageous action triggered the bus boycott that marked the beginning of the decade-long struggle for civil rights. But it was King, not Parks, who became the movement's charismatic leader—first in Montgomery and later on the broader national stage.

It was a surprise when the 26-year-old King, who had only just arrived in town, was asked by his fellow African-American ministers to lead the Montgomery Improvement Association (MIA), which had formed to protest Parks's arrest and the segregationist policies behind it. King's power as a charismatic leader first became evident the following evening, during the MIA's first mass meeting, in Holt Street Baptist Church. His soaring rhetoric drew from the salvation narratives of the Old and New Testaments, particularly from the Jewish exodus from Egyptian bondage and the Christian message of nonviolent redemption preached by Jesus.

The great political confrontations that brought the civil rights movement to national power were dramas produced by King's extraordinary charisma, and they followed these early symbolic scripts. In fact, it was through nationally televised symbolic confrontations that King built his charisma and exercised it:

> A series of evil and polluted opponents facilitated King's rise to charismatic status. Whilst the abstract "system" of inequality provided one source of evil, King's charismatic appeal was maximized when he confronted personal rivals who could be portrayed as violent, irrational and selfish. The "moral dramas" which King … attempted to create depended on strong narrative polarization. Thus the key mytho-poetic moments of the civil rights struggle are located in precisely those places where brutal and stupid establishment officials confronted King and his followers—Sheriff Clark and Colonel A. Lingo in Selma, Commissioner "Bull" Connor in Birmingham, Police Chief "Bubba" Pritchet in Albany and Connie Lynch in St. Augustine. Confrontations with these figures assisted King to exert his maximum influence in the period between the Birmingham demonstrations of 1963 and the Selma March of 1965. (Smith 2000: 108)

By the mid-1960s, the civil rights movement led by King had succeeded in abolishing legal segregation throughout the South. King then tried to bring the freedom movement into Northern cities. What followed was a series of political and symbolic fiascos, and King's charismatic power faded:

> King's later campaigns seemed to flounder when he could not locate an opponent. The Chicago housing initiative, for example, was consistently thwarted by Mayor Daley's compliant "façade of affability." In the case of Chicago, King's charisma was damaged once he was forced into compromise by city authorities, rival African American organizations and ghetto apathy. The accompanying shift towards realist narrative frames led to a deflation of salvation rhetoric. With this move-

ment came a widespread feeling that King was no longer a prophetic figure, but rather had become just another politician. (Smith 2000: 108)

Because postmodern politicians depend upon the mass media to construct their charismatic power, political strategists have become increasingly self-conscious about the image they present. Indeed, public political action has inextricably merged with "performance" (Alexander, Giesen, and Mast 2006). Those who struggle for power, whether conservative, liberal, or radical, must strive to project powerful symbolic images on the public stage. As we will see below, critics decry this emphasis on symbolic politics as manipulative and propagandistic, as a turning away from reality toward pretense and simulation. They urge politicians to speak simply about getting their message out.

In postmodern society, public relations (PR) has become fundamental to public life. Back in 1968, after Richard Nixon triumphed over Hubert Humphrey in a critical presidential election, the new rules of the political game were exposed in a book written by Joe McGinniss, *The Selling of the President, 1968*. McGinniss himself had worked for Nixon's campaign, and his tell-all book became a controversial, runaway best seller. At one point in his account, McGinniss revealed the contents of a secret strategy memo that had been prepared for Nixon before Robert Kennedy's assassination, when the telegenic "Bobby" looked to be Nixon's future democratic opponent (see the box titled "The Bobby Phenomenon"). The aim of the Republican staff memo was to convince Nixon to recast his public image. Its self-serving but still revealing subtext was that mass-mediated charisma had triumphed over reasoned political debate.

## Social Power and Politics

As this insider's account of the Bobby phenomenon suggests, the struggle for political power is

## The Bobby Phenomenon

The Bobby phenomenon; his screaming appeal to the TV generation. This certainly has nothing to do with logical persuasion; it's a total *experience,* a tactile sense. ... Thousands of little girls [*sic*] who want him to be president so they can have him on the TV screen and run their fingers through the image of his hair. ...

We [too must] leave spaces for them to fill in, in their own minds, like filling in the cartoon; low-definition, like Bobby's rhetoric, which conveys an emotional posture without bothering with a reasoned analysis. It's the emotion that gets across, the posture, the sense of involvement and concern. ...

To the TV-oriented, it's doubly important that we make them *like* the candidate. They're emotional, unstructured, uncompartmentalized, direct; there's got to be a straight communication that doesn't get wound through the linear translations of logic. ...

Saturation with a [campaign] film, in which [the] candidate can be shown better than he can be shown in person because it can be edited, so only the best moments are shown; then a quick parading of the candidate in the flesh so that the guy they've gotten intimately acquainted with on the screen takes on a living presence—not saying anything, just being seen, so there's the physical presence, the eye-contact. ...

Reason pushes the viewer back, it assaults him, it demands that he agree or disagree; [by contrast,] impression can envelop him, invite him in, without making an intellectual demand, or a demand on his intellectual energies. ...

When we argue with him we demand that he make the effort of replying. We seek to engage his intellect, and for most people this is the most difficult work of all. The emotions are more easily roused, closer to the surface, more malleable. Get the voters to like the guy, and the battle's two thirds won.

*Source:* Excerpt from Republican staff memo, quoted in McGinniss (1968: 187–189).

---

fueled, sometimes invisibly, by other forms of social power (Mann 1986, 1993). Indeed, the very idea of "selling" a president implies that the struggle for charismatic power is enabled, yet also constrained, by economic and intellectual power. It is both expensive (economic) and strategically demanding (intellectual) to mount a convincing presidential campaign (see Figures 17.6–17.8 as well as Tables 17.3 and 17.4). Effective politicians are, of course, usually talented strategic thinkers themselves. But professional strategists must also be hired, and the salaries of speechwriters must be paid. The politician who strives for charismatic power must purchase television time, and she will hire, if she can, professional spin doctors and other experts in public relations. Those who possess economic power can, in this way, exercise great influence over who gets power, and how much.

This layered complexity of power, its visible and its invisible parts, is explored in the three-dimensional model developed by Steven Lukes. The one-dimensional view of power, Lukes writes, "involves a focus on *behavior* in the making of *decisions* on issues over which there is an observable *conflict of interest*" (1974: 15, italics in original). While he criticizes this approach, Lukes acknowledges that it does capture one level of modern pol-

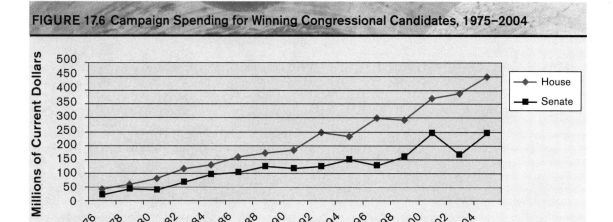

FIGURE 17.6 Campaign Spending for Winning Congressional Candidates, 1975–2004

*Source:* Stanley and Niemi (2006: 97).

itics—the level that is directly observable and that involves "policy preferences" and political "participation." The two-dimensional view goes deeper into the less visible aspects of social power, into "the question of the control over the agenda of politics and of the ways in which potential issues are kept out of the political process" (Lukes 1974: 21). The three-dimensional approach carries the search deeper still, exploring how power can be exercised in the absence of any overt participation in political institutions and without engendering any open political conflict. In this third dimension, hidden social powers ensure that a particular political agenda will be pursued, even while the forms of political legitimacy remain intact and the autonomy of the state seems to be maintained.

It is with respect to the second and third dimensions of power that Lukes points to the influence of social as compared to political elites. Social elites operate outside the political domain that is framed by the state and the political institutions of party and government. These elites use their social power to control political power, largely in private

ways. In short, they try to "wire" politics and politicians, as the political cartoon at the beginning of the chapter graphically implies.

## The Power Behind the Throne: The Power Elite?

Suspicions about social elites controlling political life are nothing new. They are the cynical outgrowth of idealism about the possibility for equality and democracy. As mentioned earlier, Marx articulated a particularly strident and powerful vision of hidden social control in his class theory, which held that the state is really nothing more than the executive committee of the bourgeoisie, the wealthiest economic class. Writing a century after Marx, American radical sociologist C. Wright Mills developed this class model into the more subtle form employed for critical, neo-Marxian analysis ever since. Mills published *The Power Elite* (1956) at the midpoint of the conservative political administration of President Dwight

Eisenhower and in the shadow of the most virulent phase of the Cold War. He gave voice to the frustrations of those who had been excluded from political decision-making and to those who were becoming increasingly pessimistic about the ability of average people to effect any substantial political change:

> The powers of ordinary men are circumscribed by the everyday worlds in which they live, yet even in these rounds of job, family, and neighborhood they often seem driven by forces they can neither understand nor govern. "Great changes" are beyond their control, but affect their conduct and outlook none the less. The very framework of modern society confines them to projects not their own. ... The men and women of the mass society ... accordingly feel they are without purpose in an epoch in which they are without power.
>
> But not all men are in this sense ordinary. As the means of information and of power are centralized, some men come to occupy positions in American society from which they can look down upon, so to speak, and by their decisions mightily affect, the everyday worlds of ordinary men and women. They are not made by their jobs; they set up and break down jobs for thousands of others; they are not confined by simple family responsibilities; they can escape. They may live in many hotels and houses, but they are bound by no one community. They need not merely "meet the demands of the day and hour"; in some part, they create these demands, and cause others to meet them. Whether or not they profess their power, their technical and political experience of it far transcends that of the underlying population. (1956: 3)

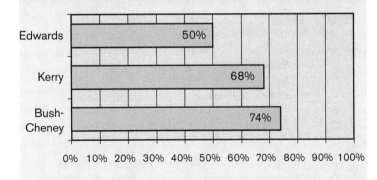

**FIGURE 17.7 Percentage of Expenditures on Media and Consulting in 2004 Primaries**

*Source:* Crotty (2005: 95).

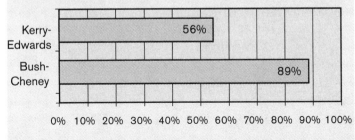

**FIGURE 17.8 Percentage of Expenditures on Media and Consulting in the 2004 General Election**

*Source:* Crotty (2005: 95).

In opposition to the traditional Marxian view, Mills sought to develop a more pluralistic model. He discussed elite power slightly as it pertained not only to the economic sphere but also to the political and military spheres, insisting that it is control of institutions, not wealth per se, that defines elite position: "The elite are not simply those who have the most, for they could not 'have the most' were it

## TABLE 17.3  The Professionalization of Election Campaigning

|  | Premodern | Television Revolution | Telecommunications Revolution |
|---|---|---|---|
| Campaign organization | Decentralized Local party organization Little standardization Staffing: party/candidate based, voluntary | Nationalization, centralization Staffing: party based, salaried professional | Decentralization of operation with central scrutiny Staffing: party/candidate based, professional, contract work |
| Campaign preparations | Short-term; ad hoc | Long-term; specialist committee established 1–2 years in advance of election | "Permanent campaign": the establishment of specialist campaign departments |
| Agencies, consultants | Minimal use "Generalist" role Politicians in charge | Greater use Growing prominence of "specialist" Politicians still in charge | Even greater use of consultants Consultants as campaign personalities International links ("Saatchi-ization") "Who is in charge?" |
| Sources of feedback | Impressionistic, "feel" Important role of canvassers, group leaders, and intuition | Large-scale opinion polls More scientific | Greater range of polling techniques Computer-aided telepolling Interactive capabilities of cable |
| Use of media | Direct and indirect Direct = party press, newspaper ads, billboards Indirect = newspaper coverage | Emphasis on indirect Direct = ad campaigns Indirect = public relations, media training, press conferences | Emphasis on direct Direct = targeted ads, direct mail, videomail, cable TV Indirect = as before |
| Campaign events | Public meetings Whistle-stop tours | TV debates Press conferences "Pseudo-events" | As before; events targeted more locally |
| Targeting of voters | Social class support base Object of maintaining vote of specific social categories | Catchall Trying to mobilize voters across all categories | Market segmentation Targeting of specific categories of voters |

Note: Premodern refers to pretelevision—that is, the period from the mid-nineteenth century to the 1950s.
Source: Farrell (1996: 170).

not for their positions in the great institutions. ... Higher politicians and key officials of government command such institutional power; so do admirals and generals, and so do the major owners and executives of the larger corporations" (1956: 9).

Domination by a **power elite,** which goes beyond pure economic control, is defined by three different forms of social power: "We do not accept as adequate the simple view that high economic men unilaterally make all decisions of national

**TABLE 17.4  Top Five Campaign Expenditures in Candidates' Primary Campaigns, 2004**

| Bush/Cheney | |
|---|---|
| Media | $119,137,683 |
| Credit card payments | $16,000,446 |
| Postage | $10,772,402 |
| Payroll | $8,918,775 |
| Printing | $7,277,684 |
| John Kerry for President, Inc. | |
| Media | $91,457,872 |
| Travel expenses | $19,336,130 |
| Salary | $9,905,349 |
| Other itemized expenses | $7,931,487 |
| Fundraising expenses | $5,838,368 |
| Edwards for President | |
| Consulting/Media | $10,113,105 |
| Salary | $3,916,190 |
| Airfare/Travel | $2,409,090 |
| Payroll taxes | $1,957,363 |
| Direct mail expense | $1,439,882 |

Source: Political Money Line, available at http://www.fecinfo.com/cgiwin/pml1_sql_PRESIDENTIAL.exe?DoFn=2004.

**Power elite**  As used by C. Wright Mills, a term referring to the thesis that American society is dominated by its elites. The power elite is made up of elites from three spheres: the economy, politics, and the military.

structural trends are seen at their point of coincidence: the military capitalism of private corporations exists in a weakened and formal democratic system containing a military order already quite political in outlook and demeanor. Accordingly, at the top of this structure, the power elite has been shaped by the coincidence of interest between those who control the major means of production and those who control the newly enlarged means of violence[:]... the corporate chieftains and the professional warlords. (1956: 276)

The glue that binds these elites together, according to Mills, is the capitalist interests of economic corporations: "The structural clue to the power elite today lies in the economic order ... [in] the fact that the economy is at once a permanent war economy and a private-corporation economy. American capitalism is now in considerable part a military capitalism, and the most important relation of the big corporation to the state rests on the coincidence of interests between military and corporate needs" (1956: 275–276).

The power elite thesis seems to resemble the Marxian theory Mills rejected. It differs in its understanding of the cultural and social elements that create an elite's sense of itself: "The power elite ... rests upon the similarity of its personnel, and their personal and official relations with one another, upon their social and psychological affinities. In order to grasp the personal and social basis of the power elite's unity, we have first to remind ourselves of the facts of origin, career, and style of life" (Mills 1956: 278).

The sociologists who have followed up on

consequence. We hold that such a simple view of 'economic determinism' must be elaborated by 'political determinism' and 'military determinism' [and] that the higher agents of each of these three domains now often have a noticeable degree of autonomy. ... Those are the major reasons why we prefer 'power elite' to 'ruling class'" (Mills 1956: 277).

Despite these theoretical reservations, Mills claimed he had discovered in his empirical analysis that, in practice, the three different elites closely coordinate their actions:

The shape and meaning of the power elite today can be understood only when these three sets of

Mills's pioneering, if one-sided, investigations have confirmed that there is, indeed, an economic elite in the United States. Wealth is vastly concentrated in the top 1 percent of the American population, and a large part of this wealth is inherited at birth. Many large-stockholding families, in fact, remain actively involved in controlling the direction of major corporations through family offices, investment partnerships, and holding companies.

Researchers such as William Domhoff (1967) have also followed up on Mills's claim that elite domination involves not only shared economic interest but shared collective identity. The product of private cultural institutions, this shared elite socialization generates a sense of trust. The super-rich go to school, socialize, and recreate in institutions to which ordinary people have little access. So they are linked to one another not only economically, through business transactions and corporate interests, but also socially, through shared culture and marriage. They attend the same exclusive private schools, are members of the same elite clubs, engage in the same leisure activities, and frequent the same vacation spots. Philip Bonacich studied membership in the exclusive social clubs of major American cities and their relation to corporate governing boards. He found a great deal of overlap and concentration: "There is sufficient overlap among eighteen of the twenty clubs to form three regional groupings and a fourth that provided a bridge between the two largest regional groups. The several dozen men who were in three or more of the clubs—most of them very wealthy people who sat on several corporate boards—were especially important in creating the overall pattern" (cited in Domhoff 1967: 88).

Middle-class people who rise to become members of the power elite gain not only great wealth but access to these social institutions, which define the lifestyles of America's largely invisible privileged class—a process that can be described as cultural assimilation into the American upper class.

## Does the Economic Elite Control Politics?

Mills and his followers have demonstrated that social power is distributed unevenly and that the economic elite is particularly powerful. But they have never succeeded in making a good case for their most ambitious claim—that the economic elite actually controls the state. To the contrary, it has been relatively easy to demonstrate that the state retains a very real autonomy from social power. In the often fiercely fought political struggles to influence state power, social elites fail time after time to exercise compelling control over either discourse or goals.

One way to clarify this point is to set side by side the biographies of those who wield great political power. Consider, for example, Richard Cheney's career, which at first glance would seem to prove the power elite thesis. Cheney went from being a Wyoming congressman to being defense secretary in the first Bush administration, then chief executive of the multibillion-dollar Halliburton (oil) company, and finally vice president in the administration of President George W. Bush. Yet, right alongside Vice President Cheney sat Secretary of State Colin Powell, one of the most powerful cabinet members in the same administration. Born into the African-American working class, Powell achieved military power as a four-star general and, later, as chairman of the Joint Chiefs of Staff. In short, for every scion of inherited wealth and Ivy League provenance who becomes president—whether a Bush, Roosevelt, or Kennedy—there is a brilliant political strategist from humble origins—a Lincoln, Johnson, or Clinton—who achieves the presidency through charisma and hard work. And for every giant corporation that exercises backroom influence on government policies—such as Enron—there is the counterinfluence of a charismatic outsider who—like Martin Luther King—brings an exploited minority to significant political power or—like Ralph Nader—

forces safety and environmental concerns onto the national political agenda.

Power elite theorists try to explain away such obvious examples of state autonomy and political pluralism. Mills (1956: 231), for example, makes the following claims:

- ✓ "The simple, old-fashioned sense of being elected up the political hierarchy" simply no longer exists.
- ✓ Politics has become "more of an appointed than an elected career."
- ✓ An "inner circle of political outsiders" representing the corporate rich "[has] taken over the key executive posts of administrative command," excluding figures from electoral politics and political parties.

If such assertions were true, then the open contestations for power that seem to characterize contemporary societies would be entirely without effect. Public opinion would be powerless, and social movements initiated by those outside the power elite would be doomed to fail.

Mills was aware that the power elite theory would have to respond to these challenges. The central empirical question for understanding modern politics, he agreed, has to do with "the degree to which the public has genuine autonomy from instituted authority" (1956: 303). If there does exist "the free ebb and flow of discussion," then there are "possibilities of answering back, or organizing autonomous organs of public opinion, [and] of realizing opinion in action" (1956: 298). Whether a concentration of institutional power ends up occurring is *not* critically important. If "the power elite ... is *truly* responsible to, or *even exists in connection with*, a community of publics, it carries a very different meaning than if such a public is being transformed into a society of masses" (1956: 302, italics added).

Mills asserts that the public has, in fact, been transformed in just this way. The same social forces that have created the new power elite, he claims, have turned the once-critical and independent public into a manipulated, dependent mass. Elites, he suggests, are "centers of *manipulation* as well as of authority." The public is "rather passively exposed to the mass media and rather helplessly opened up to the suggestions and manipulations that flow from these media" (Mills 1956: 305, italics added). "Alongside or just below the elite there is the propagandist, the publicity expert, the public relations man, who would control the very formation of public opinion in order to be able to include it as one more pacified item in calculations of effective power, increased prestige, more secure wealth" (Mills 1956: 315). Because the mass media have committed "psychical rape" (Mills 1956: 309), Mills believes, public opinion has been eliminated as a challenge to the power of the elite.

Such assertions about the transformation of the modern public into a pliant mass are central to arguments for the domination of political by social power. They define the questions for researchers who are interested in whether or not democracy continues to be a viable possibility in modern and postmodern societies. Is the public in democratic societies really manipulated in this way? Are the media fundamentally controlled by corporate wealth, or do they also provide a space for oppositional groups to broadcast alternative ideas? Can charismatic power serve anti-elite movements? Is the culture of political life merely the replication of class culture? Does political culture, both modern and postmodern, contain ethical aspirations that draw from noneconomic sources?

## CITIZENSHIP, PUBLICS, AND THE CIVIL SPHERE

Less than a decade after C. Wright Mills articulated his sociological pessimism about democratic publics, President Lyndon B. Johnson, a politician who had risen from the provincial poverty of south-central Texas, signed into law the Civil Rights Act of 1964. He did so in response to a social movement of working-class African-Americans whose grandparents had been slaves in the American South. Their charismatic leader, Martin Luther King, had created vast waves of sympathy among privileged Northern whites by challenging the power of the white racist Southern state. He did so by organizing a series of profoundly affecting performances on the stage of American public life. These black social dramas projected radical, antiracist challenges to established power. They were transmitted by a sympathetic mass media dominated by white journalists and controlled by vast corporate wealth. This supportive public opinion was transformed into political power through the votes of American citizens, both black and white.

Political struggles in contemporary societies are thus not solely determined by the power of social elites and state bureaucracies. Indeed, they are also deeply affected by moral ideas about citizenship and human rights. Between social power, on the one side, and state power, on the other, there sits a cultural and institutional space that can be called the "civil sphere" (Alexander 2006).

## Civil Solidarity and Public Life

The civil sphere is defined by legal norms that guarantee rights to individuals. It is also defined by feelings and values that stress solidarity among members of society, no matter what their status or power. Being a citizen doesn't only mean being part of a state. It also means being a member of the civil sphere, part of the imagined solidarity of the civil community that defines a democracy.

You are not born a full citizen; rather you become one if those who are already citizens feel that you have the capacity for civil behavior. This considered evaluation is reflected, for example, in the fact that children and convicted felons are not allowed to vote. Differential access to full **citizenship** is also reflected in the struggles of subjugated and excluded groups for political power. Such political struggles are not only about power; they also concern the recognition of civil qualities. Social movements demand power, but they also work to present themselves in a civil way, as groups of potentially good citizens. To be seen as a potentially good citizen, one must present oneself as rational and honest, trusting but critical, open rather than secretive, and cooperative but also independent. Those who strive to achieve political power must also strive to represent themselves in terms of these civil qualities. To do so, they need the mass media. Their audience is the public of citizens. Their goal is to influence the public's opinion.

The civil sphere is highly idealized. It reflects the aspirations and hopes crystallized by charismatic democrats like Thomas Jefferson, Abraham Lincoln, and Martin Luther King. It rests upon philosophical foundations that stretch from Socrates, who died for political and intellectual freedom in ancient Greece, to thinkers like John Locke and Jean-Jacques Rousseau, who resisted the divine rights of British and French kings, to the American founding fathers who created the Constitution and Bill of Rights. These ideals can sometimes have real teeth. **Civil society** comprises not only beliefs but institutions as well. These institutions create real rewards for civil behavior and punishments for uncivil action.

The members of civil society possess a wide range of highly material rights. Contract law punishes failure to disclose pertinent information—failure to be honest. Criminal law provides much more severe sanctions for violence—indeed, for coercion of any kind, which is the prototype of anticivil behavior between two people. The material powers that accrue to membership in civil society extend to voting, the process of selecting and discarding those who control state power. If you are a member of the civil sphere, you also have the right to meet with other people in public, to keep your private life invisible to state authorities, to form organizations, and to mount political campaigns and demonstrations.

Citizens have the right, in other words, to trigger and to alter the great tides of public opinion. One of the most important political theorists of democracy, Hannah Arendt, wrote that "everything that appears in public can be seen and heard by everybody and has the widest possible publicity" (1958: 50). Citizens have the right to publish newspapers and books and to make movies and write songs. They can start their own radio and television stations. They can raise money to fund pet projects. They can start social movements to raise issues, to redirect political and social power, to be critical of any and all the powers that be.

To the degree that there is democracy, the civil sphere ensures that these activities will have some independence from social power and state bureaucracy alike. When citizens mobilize themselves, when they become concerned and demanding citizens, the state governs *for* them and bureaucratic power is distributed in *their* interests. When opinion is fervent, elites offer compromises to co-opt aroused publics and reforms to calm them down. In such times, those who control political power offer to share it with charismatic civil leaders, and those who control social power offer to spend it on their behalf. Arendt emphasized this potential conflict between private social power and public political power. She wrote, "[T]he term 'public' signifies the world itself, in so far as it is common to all of us and distinguished from our privately owned place in it" (1958: 52).

The civil sphere defines an open space of public contention. Jürgen Habermas brought this element to light in *The Structural Transformation of the Public Sphere* (1962). Habermas describes how this new institution of democratic life first emerged in the eighteenth century. He believes that it emerged when the "bourgeoisie" struggled for political power against the aristocracy that ex-

ercised traditional authority: "The bourgeois public sphere may be conceived above all as the sphere of private people come together as a public; they soon claimed the public sphere regulated from above against the public authorities themselves, to engage them in a debate over the general rules governing [social] relations. ... The medium for this political confrontation was peculiar and without historical precedent: people's public use of their reason" (1962: 27).

Within the public space of the civil sphere, Habermas likes to say, the simple force of the better argument sometimes wins. This is a nonbureaucratic, more democratic version of Weber's "rational-legal" authority, which defines political legitimacy in the modern epoch. After the cultural turn, however, we understand "better argument" in a more symbolic way. Those who aspire to exercise public power in democratic societies rely less on reason and intellectual argument than on symbolic representation. Postmodern society is a mass-mediated society. Civil qualities are constructed through images, codes, and narratives

**Citizenship** According to T. H. Marshall, a social position with three characteristics: first, that a citizen is entitled to civil rights, such as the right to free speech or the right to own property; second, that a citizen is entitled to political rights guaranteeing the right to exercise political power, through either voting or holding office; and third, that a citizen is entitled to social rights affirming the right to an acceptable standard of living.

**Civil society** The sphere of social life that is separate from the state, governed by legal norms, and supported by institutions. Civil society is an idealized, imagined community resting on civil solidarity and based on a common belief in the possibilities of democracy. It is supported by institutions (e.g., courts) that enforce legal norms, punish anticivil behavior, and protect members' rights. Membership in such institutions is granted not by the state but by citizens of the state.

that can be effectively broadcast to the public audience of citizens.

But it is not only outsiders who must navigate the shoals of public opinion and mass media. The same applies to the powers of social elites and even to the highest powers of the state.

Corporations do not exercise some kind of automatic control over public life. No matter how much they would like to, at important moments they cannot control the political agenda. Particularly in times of crisis, the publics of democratic societies—composed of lower, middle, and upper classes—can turn against corporate power and force it to be regulated in a more responsive way.

Just listen to the civil indignation that flowed from U.S. senators during the Enron crisis; as recorded in the box titled "Congressmembers Being Aggressive in Enron Hearings," they fired off withering salvos to the corporation's former top executive, who appeared before the congressional panel. Here is the silver lining to the scandals that regularly rock our public spheres. It is this public and democratic face of government that *Newsweek* highlights in its blazing and indignant coverage of the conviction of Enron's chief executive officers:

Instead of making the world safe for capitalism, the Enron Era set off a corporate scandal wave that leapt the species barrier, morphing from a business-pages-only story into a national psychodrama. We saw crying Enron employees whose jobs and life savings both vaporized when Enron melted down [and exposed] Enron's close ties to George W. Bush, our first M.B.A. president, which lent a decidedly political aspect to the scandal. Enron became grist for the 24-hour news cycle, and was seared into the national consciousness like no other business story since the Great Depression. … The Enron epic, already the subject of a TV movie, got a made-for-TV ending last week when former chief executive Ken Lay was convicted on all 10 conspiracy and fraud charges the government brought against

him, and Jeff Skilling, a second former Enron CEO, was convicted on 19 of 28 counts. … The FBI's Enron task force examined the astounding total of more than four terabytes of data—equal to about 20 percent of all the information stored in the Library of Congress. … Enron seems like a fever dream, an illusion from the past that business unfettered could solve all problems, that all we needed to do was get out of the way of corporate titans … and let them work their magic on behalf of all of us. The convictions of Lay and Skilling write *finis* to that delusional era. (Sloan 2006)

Those who possess great wealth and social power must win the battle of public opinion if they are to exert power in the civil sphere. Toward that end, they create vast public relations machinery. They justify their environmental records in the civil sphere, apologize for chemical spills, and portray themselves as deeply respectful of nature. When well-known products (e.g., Ford Explorer) are exposed as dangerously unstable, the manufacturers rush publicly to pledge themselves to expensive structural reforms, buying advertising space in newspapers and on television to burnish rough spots in their corporate image. They do not always succeed.

## Presidents and Publics

Nor does success always come to the highest and most powerful politicians who, in purely bureaucratic terms, control the state. In *Presidential Power* (1960), political scientist Richard Neustadt described just how difficult it is for presidents to get their way. Neustadt himself had been a personal advisor to Presidents Truman and Kennedy. He knew from direct experience, not just from scholarly research, that even a president's direct orders—to military officers, to Cabinet secretaries, to their own staffs—are often not followed, or are

## media moments

### Congressmembers Being Aggressive in Enron Hearings

MR. FITZGERALD: Mr. Lay, I've concluded that you're perhaps the most accomplished confidence man since Charles Ponzi. I'd say you were a carnival barker, except that wouldn't be fair to carnival barkers. A carnie will at least tell you up front that he's running a shell game. You, Mr. Lay, were running what purported to be the seventh largest corporation in America.

MR. KERRY: ... As we fight a war on terrorism, and as we talk about holding other systems accountable, so we can follow the flow of money, we have—all of us—in this Congress allowed to stand for too long a system that undermines our capacity to do that, and that's offshore subsidiaries and tax havens.

MR. HOLLINGS: Well, much has been said about the development of a culture of corporate corruption, but there's also the culture of political corruption. And maybe we can get some good out of this whole situation, in that there's no better example than "Kenny Boy" [of] cash-and-carry government. I mean, I hope that this shames us into acting over on the House side and then on the Senate side, and sends a campaign reform bill to the president. We've got to clean up our own act, and maybe that's the good we'll get out of this situation.

*Source:* "Enron's Many Strands" (2002: C8).

SENATOR DURBIN: After all of the sound and fury of these investigations, the bottom-line questions are: Is Congress willing to amend the law to rein in the greed of the next Enron? Are we willing to concede that the genius of capitalism can result in ruthless behavior without our oversight and the protection of law? Can we save pensioners and investors—who were outsiders believing in the fairness of the market—from the corporate insiders who walk away from these colossal business train wrecks with their pockets full and without a scratch?

Over 100 million Americans who own stock and 42 million who own 401(k)'s will be watching to see if these hearings and many others on Capitol Hill are about more than face time on the nightly news.

To me, this national debate is about more than a failed corporate giant. It is about the values of our nation. Enron is a big story not just because of its bankruptcy. Sadly, bankruptcies occur every day. Enron is a big story because it reminds us of our vulnerability. It reminds us that without the enforcement of fair and just laws, the average American doesn't have a fighting chance.

*Source:* "Enron's Collapse" (2002: C9).

creatively misinterpreted in ways that amount to disobedience.

It is not command but persuasion that allows an American president to exercise power. Whether he has his way is determined by neither his formal powers of office nor his ability to generate social or military control. Rather it is a matter of his political prestige. Prestige defines a president's ability to persuade. It is determined by a president's public standing.

What and who are the president's publics? According to Neustadt, they are "as diverse and overlapping as the claims Americans and allied peoples press on Washington" (1960: 86–87). In short, they comprise the diverse members of the D.C. community—the "Washingtonians" who are lobbyists and citizens, governmental bureaucrats and members of Congress, journalists and congressional staff, think-tank members, social hostesses, and gossip columnists. But the opinions of these "inside-the-beltway" publics are deeply affected by their estimates of the opinions of publics outside themselves:

> The Washingtonians who watch a President … have to think about his standing with the public outside Washington. They have to gauge his popular prestige. Because *they* think about it, public standing is a source of influence for *him*, another factor bearing on their willingness to give him what he wants. … They anticipate reactions from the public. Most members of the Washington community depend upon outsiders to support them or their interests. The dependence may be as direct as votes, or it may be as indirect as passive toleration. Dependent men must take account of popular reaction to their actions. What their publics may think of them becomes a factor, therefore, in deciding how to deal with the desires of a President. (Neustadt 1960: 86, italics added)

In assessing the wider public's opinions, Washingtonians are looking beyond the desires of elites. They need to know the opinions of the proverbial "man in the street," the "average everyday citizen." To the degree that power is democratic, the ability of a president to sustain and deploy his prestige ultimately depends upon whether he makes his case in the civil sphere: "How do members of the Washington community assess a President's prestige with the American public? They talk to one

another and to taxi drivers. They read the columnists and polls and news reports. They sample the opinions of their visitors and friends. They travel in the country and they listen as they go [and] they watch Congress" (Neustadt 1960: 89).

## The Struggle for Full Citizenship

When the modern state first emerged, despite its commitments to bureaucratic formality and its aspirations to rationality and legality, most people were actually excluded from political power. Men without significant property could neither vote nor form associations, such as trade unions, to improve their economic position. Women were not allowed to vote, hold property, or exercise public office. And because Jews were not considered citizens, they could not own land, or vote, or use public services such as hospitals or schools. Nonwhite persons were also sharply segregated from public life. Subject to high levels of poverty, they could neither vote nor exercise civil liberties.

The story of political life over the last 200 years is less about the continued exercise of elite power than about how the space of the civil sphere has allowed such domination gradually to be overcome. It is a political story about how these subordinated groups have struggled to make good on the promises of citizenship. To understand this story, we must see that these groups view themselves not just as unequal and subordinated but as excluded from the civil sphere. Indeed, as Judith Shklar emphasizes in *American Citizenship* (1991: 14), they see themselves as "members of a professedly democratic society that was actively and purposefully false to its own vaunted principles." Accordingly, the excluded have demanded not only power but **civil repair.** Along the way, they have suffered humiliation and repression, but they have often succeeded in gaining control over state power. This process—the gradual expansion of civic membership—illustrates how the civil sphere opens up a space between state control and social power.

Voting is typically the most taken-for-granted dimension of citizenship. Yet it expresses membership in civil society in a particularly vivid and important way, for it transforms civil recognition into state power. As Shklar puts it, "the ballot has always been a certificate of full membership in society, and its value depends primarily on its capacity to confer a minimum of social dignity: People who are not granted these marks of civic dignity feel dishonored, not just powerless and poor. They are

American women fought for 72 years to gain "suffrage," or the right to vote, and many more years after that to win public office. (Library of Congress)

also scorned by their fellow citizens. The struggle for citizenship in America has, therefore, been overwhelmingly a demand for inclusion [and] an effort to break down excluding barriers to recognition" (Shklar 1991: 2–3). (See Table 17.5.)

The working-class struggle for voting rights during the industrial revolution in nineteenth-century Britain demonstrates how closely the recognition of civil capacity and the granting of political citizenship are intertwined. "The civic position of the common people," Reinhard Bendix noted in his extensive study, "became a subject of national debate." Such people were "[f]aced with the inequity of their legal position and a public debate over their civic reliability. [Social reformers] comment[ed] on the feeling of injustice among the workers, on their loss of self-respect, on the personal abuse which the rulers of society heap[ed] upon them ... and on the workers' feeling of being an 'outcast order' in their own country" (1977: 65–66).

Against such denial of their civic capabilities, working-class organizations loudly and publicly proclaimed their civic virtue. In 1818, in Manchester, England, a leaflet protested that labor was "the Cornerstone upon which civilized society is built," objecting that labor is "offered less ... than will support the family of a sober and orderly man in decency and comfort" (quoted in Bendix 1977: 66). Protests such as these eventually won workers not only the right to organize but the right to vote. (See Table 17.6 and Figure 17.9 for data regarding voter-turnout patterns.)

Once the right to vote was granted to the laboring classes, a process that extended from the early

**Civil repair** The process by which the civil qualities of previously excluded groups (e.g., women and African-Americans) are recognized and civil membership is expanded to include the members of such groups.

## TABLE 17.5  Landmarks in the Expansion of Suffrage in the United States

| Date | Event |
| --- | --- |
| 1776 | White men with property have the right to vote, but Catholics, Jews, Quakers, and others are barred from voting. |
| April 9, 1866 | The Civil Rights Act of 1866 grants citizenship, but not the right to vote, to all native-born Americans. |
| February 3, 1870 | The Fifteenth Amendment is ratified by the states, giving freed slaves and other African-Americans the equal right to vote. |
| 1890 | The Indian Naturalization Act grants citizenship to Native Americans by an application process. |
| August 26, 1920 | The Nineteenth Amendment, adopted by Congress on June 4, 1919, is finally ratified by the states and becomes national law, giving women the right to vote. |
| June 2, 1924 | The Indian Citizenship Act of 1924 declares all noncitizen Indians born within the United States to be citizens, giving them the right to vote. |
| December 17, 1943 | In a major civil rights victory, the Chinese Exclusion Act is repealed, giving Chinese immigrants the right to citizenship and the right to vote. |
| 1946 | Filipinos are granted the right to become U.S. citizens. |
| 1952 | The McCarran-Walter Act gives first-generation Japanese-Americans the right to become citizens. |
| August 29, 1957 | Congress passes the Civil Rights Act of 1957, giving the U.S. Attorney General the authority to bring lawsuits on behalf of African-Americans denied the right to vote. |
| May 6, 1960 | Congress passes the Civil Rights Act of 1960, which requires election officials to have all records relating to voter registration and permits the Department of Justice to inspect them. |
| July 2, 1964 | Congress passes the Civil Rights Act of 1964, making it illegal to discriminate on the basis of race, national origin, religion, or gender in voting, public places, the workplace, and schools. |
| August 6, 1965 | President Lyndon B. Johnson signs the Voting Rights Act into law, permanently barring direct barriers to political participation by racial and ethnic minorities, prohibiting any election practice that denies the right to vote on account of race, and requiring jurisdictions with a history of discrimination in voting to get federal approval of changes in their election laws before they can take effect. |
| July 5, 1971 | The Twenty-sixth Amendment gives 18-year-olds the right to vote. |
| 1975 | President Gerald Ford signs legislation reauthorizing the temporary provisions of the Voting Rights Act and making the permanent ban on literacy tests apply nationwide. The bill also mandates assistance for language-minority voters. |
| July 26, 1990 | Congress passes the Americans with Disabilities Act, which, among other things, requires that election workers and polling sites provide a range of services to ensure that people with disabilities can vote. |
| May 20, 1993 | The National Voter Registration Act, also known as the "Motor Voter" Bill, makes registration more uniform and accessible, especially for minority and low-income voters. |

*Sources:* Adapted from data available at http://www.aclu.org/votingrights/gen/12999res20050304.html and http://www.votingrights.org/timeline/?1971.

nineteenth to the early twentieth centuries, **political parties** formed to represent them. Since the 1920s, politicians representing trade unions have, in fact, exercised extensive state power in Europe and North America. It is through this political struggle that the social dimension of citizenship has become an increasing reality. The elite view of politics—that it is a simple reflex of economic power—fails to capture this critical feature of democratic societies. In his discussion of the debate over capitalism and citizenship, Bryan Turner highlights this failure:

> Why does modern capitalism depart from the economic model of capitalism which we find in Marx's economic sociology? Part of the answer is to be found in the extension of social citizenship over the last hundred years as a consequence of working-class struggles, trade-union organizations and the effects of social democracy. In other words, the full force of the marketplace is not felt by the working classes because the institutions of social welfare to some extent regulate the market and compensate for income inequality, poverty and unemployment. (1986: 5)

Despite the long struggle to achieve them, political rights are not consistently exercised, and social citizenship remains partial as well. In his important work *Class, Citizenship, and Social Development* (1964), T. H. Marshall outlined the stages of this struggle for inclusion. He defined citizenship as consisting of three related but separable dimensions: *Civil rights* refer to the "liberty of person, freedom of speech, thought and faith, the right to own property and to conclude valid contracts, and the right to justice" (Marshall 1964: 78). *Political rights* refer to people's ability to cast their votes, thereby allowing their citizenship to directly enter into control of the state. And *social citizenship* refers to the economic and cultural benefits that the exercise of such political rights might bring, ranging from "the right to a modicum of economic wel-

**TABLE 17.6  Voter Turnout Since 1945 (selected countries)**

| Country | Number of Elections | Average Voter Turnout |
|---|---|---|
| South Africa | 1 | 85.5 |
| Sweden | 17 | 83.3 |
| Germany | 13 | 80.6 |
| Israel | 14 | 80 |
| United Kingdom | 15 | 74.9 |
| Republic of Korea | 9 | 74.8 |
| Argentina | 16 | 70.6 |
| Japan | 21 | 69 |
| Canada | 17 | 68.4 |
| France | 15 | 67.3 |
| Hungary | 3 | 64.1 |
| India | 12 | 60.7 |
| Russia | 2 | 55 |
| Poland | 4 | 52.3 |
| United States | 26 | 48.3 |
| Mexico | 18 | 48.1 |
| Nigeria | 3 | 47.6 |

*Note:* Turnout is calculated as the percentage who voted from the total voting-age population.

*Source:* Reproduced by permission of International IDEA, available at http://www.idea.int/vt/survey/voter_turnout_pop2.cfm. Copyright © International Institute for Democracy and Electoral Assistance.

fare and security to the right to share to the full in the social heritage and to live the life of a civilized being according to the standards prevailing in the society" (Marshall 1964: 78).

To what extent do governments assume respon-

**Political parties** Ideological organizations that are responsible for articulating and forming political interests, developing slogans and candidates, and organizing and funding successful political campaigns in the interest of promoting a particular social order.

FIGURE 17.9 Voter Turnout by Age Group and Gender, Presidential Elections, 1972–2004

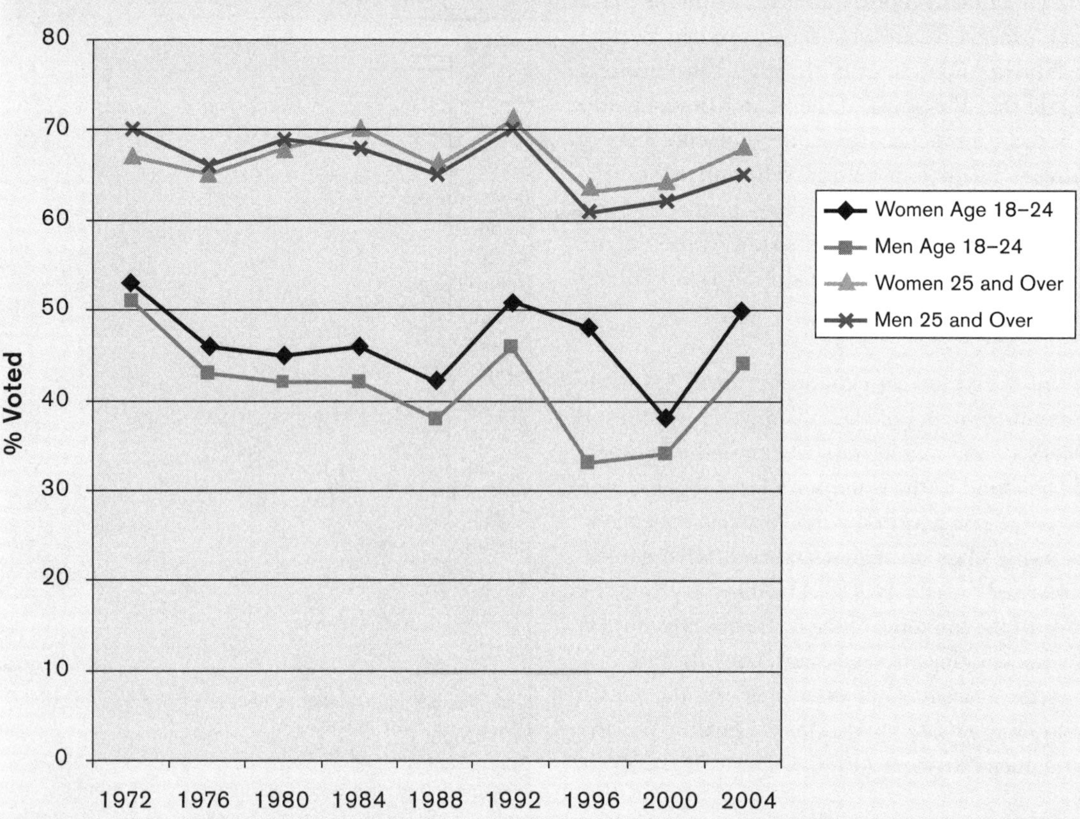
% Voted
80
70
60
50
40
30
20
10
0
1972
1976
1980
1984
1988
1992
1996
2000
2004
Women Age 18–24
Men Age 18–24
Women 25 and Over
Men 25 and Over

*Source:* Adapted from Lopez, Kirby, and Sagoff (2005).

sibility for supporting the standard of living of vulnerable citizens? One way to find out is to see how much of a country's gross domestic product (GDP) is spent on social programs for disadvantaged groups, such as the elderly, the disabled, the unemployed, low-income people, and youth. Social expenditure can take the form of cash benefits, tax breaks, or services (see Figure 17.10).

## Political Parties

As part of the struggle for political and social citizenship, a new organizational form emerged—the political party. Seymour Martin Lipset once referred to elections as "the democratic class struggle" (1960: 230). He described the class struggle as democratic because the framework of citizenship allows economic cleavages to be debated in the public sphere. This debate informs voting. But citizens do not vote directly on particular economic policies. They cast their votes for members of political parties that have promised to represent their divergent interests.

Parties are ideological organizations. They specialize in transforming public debate into votes, and votes into state power. They develop slogans and candidates, organize and fund political campaigns, and provide the strategic expertise to make them successful. Weber wrote that "parties live in a house of power" (1958d: 194). Typically, it is parties—not individuals per se—that vie for political power, control legislative majorities, and place their political-ideological representative into the top position in the state.

Parties form because the civil sphere of democratic societies gives interest groups the opportunity to get together and to make a public, political stand. When parties representing out-groups are successful, they extend social solidarity. Yet parties themselves are partisan and one-sided organizations. They specialize in developing a particular ideology, one that effectively represents the interests of their own groups. "The rationale of the party system," wrote Robert MacIver in *The Web of Government*, "depends on the alignment of opinion from right to left" (1947: 215). During modern industrial society, this ideological split was primarily understood as a division that was determined by economic class:

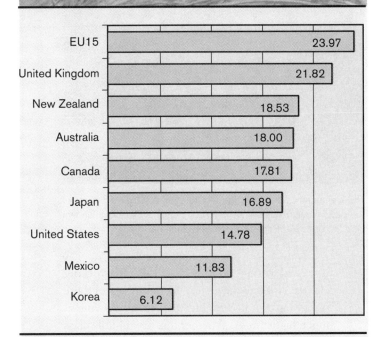

FIGURE 17.10 Social Expenditure as a Percentage of Gross Domestic Product (selected countries)

| | |
|---|---|
| EU15 | 23.97 |
| United Kingdom | 21.82 |
| New Zealand | 18.53 |
| Australia | 18.00 |
| Canada | 17.81 |
| Japan | 16.89 |
| United States | 14.78 |
| Mexico | 11.83 |
| Korea | 6.12 |

*Note:* "EU15" is the average of the fifteen countries in the European Union.
*Source:* OECD (2005: 167).

The right is always the party sector associated with the interests of the upper or dominant classes, the left the sector expressive of the lower economic or social classes, and the center that of the middle classes. ... The conservative right has defended entrenched prerogatives, privileges and powers; the left has attacked them. ... Defense and attack have met, under democratic conditions, not in the name of class but in the name of principle; but the opposing principles have broadly corresponded to the interests of the classes. (MacIver 1947: 215)

Later studies of party ideology and voting, such as Lipset's *Political Man: The Social Bases of Politics* (1960), demonstrated that this left/right cleavage is actually more complicated. The issue goes beyond just higher and lower classes, inasmuch as groups do not define their interests in economic terms only. As Lipset notes: "The poorer strata everywhere are more liberal or leftist on economic issues; they favor more welfare state measures, higher wages, graduated income taxes, support of trade unions, and so forth. But when liberalism is defined in noneconomic terms—as support of civil liberties, internationalism, etc.—the correlation is reversed. The more well-to-do are more liberal, the poorer are more intolerant" (1960: 92).

This contrast between the social and economic dimensions of political ideology explains a great deal of contemporary voting and party politics. As economies have moved from industrial to post-industrial forms, the professional and managerial segments of the middle class have become more

The Democratic Party was the first to elect a female Speaker of the U.S. House, Representative Nancy Pelosi of California, shown here in 2006. (AP Photo/J. Scott Applewhite)

powerful voting publics than the old working classes. Not only have the sheer numbers of these publics grown in size, but their members vote at much higher rates. Whether this new middle class is predominantly conservative and committed to the status quo, or predominantly liberal and oriented to expanding rights and supporting change, is an increasingly critical question, both practically and intellectually. But in any case, as Clem Brooks and Jeff Manza (1997) have discovered, it is hardly homogeneous. Managers have remained solidly Republican, but professionals have increasingly moved into the ranks of the Democratic Party. This division is not the result of income differences between the two groups; rather it reflects their orientation to social issues. Throughout most of the twentieth century, the Democratic Party was voted into power by the overwhelming nature of its working-class support. But as the old working class withered in size (see Chapter 12, on work and the economy), the Democrats increasingly relied not on the economic liberalism of the workers but on the social liberalism of highly educated professionals. Brooks and Manza describe this development as follows:

Our analyses demonstrate that socially liberal attitudes have critical explanatory value in understanding important trends in middle-class political behavior. Not only does social issue liberalism explain the recent trends and differences in the voting behavior of professionals and managers, it has increased among professionals in both magnitude and to a more limited extent in political salience. We can think of no firmer demonstration of the specifically *political* importance of socially liberal attitudes than a strong association with vote choice in presidential elections. Moreover, liberal views on social issues such as abortion, women's roles, and civil rights are the principal reasons behind professionals' realignment with Democratic candidates and their widening differences vis-à-vis managers. Without this specific ideological base of support, our analyses show that Democratic presidential candidates would have lost considerable ground. ... The long-term shift in voting behavior among professionals [is] a shift which is particularly remarkable when viewed from the perspective of their solidly Republican voting patterns in the 1950s. ... Increased liberalism on social issues has been sufficient to drive a wedge through the middle class and move professionals out of their earlier Republican alignment. (1997: 204–206, italics in original)

## The Discourse of Decline

Compared with "realist" arguments for state autonomy and pessimistic arguments about power elites, the focus on public sphere and civil society sets a high standard for democratic societies to meet. Civil society is, by definition, an unfinished project. Its very existence reflects idealism about the possibilities of democratic life.

For many of those who participate in civil life, whether as political activists or as secular or religious intellectuals, the quality of contemporary democracy seems insufficiently high: There is never enough "true" publicness, never enough "real" civility in the civil sphere, never enough solidarity in the democratic community's political and cultural life. But these pessimistic evaluations are not persuasive. Despite the vast difficulties and setbacks that have marked modern political life, the civil sphere has actually deepened and expanded, even if, at every step along the way, it has been subject to the persistent criticism that civil society and public life are diminishing—a criticism known as the **discourse of decline.**

In the mid-eighteenth century, Rousseau was already lamenting that "we no longer have citizens" (1750: 17). In 1840, in the second volume of *Democracy in America*, Alexis de Tocqueville claimed that American democracy produced not liberty and political equality but merely the tyranny of the majority and mass conformity. In 1925, in *The Phantom Public*, Walter Lippmann lamented the victory of political propaganda and public relations over reason and public-spiritedness. In the early postwar period, Hannah Arendt (1958) and Jürgen Habermas (1962)—along with C. Wright Mills (1959)—warned that mass society, fueled by the rise of advertising and the media of mass communications, had eroded the democratic capacities of the public sphere. In 1979, President Jimmy Carter proclaimed in a famous speech that American society was suffering from a "malaise" that heralded political and moral decline. And in the mid-1980s, Robert Bellah and his colleagues articulated this pessimism in their best-selling *Habits of the Heart* (1985), arguing that American culture had drifted from civil solidarity into individualistic self-absorption.

The decline argument has recently been refurbished by Robert Putnam's influential claim that Americans are, for the first time, "bowling alone." Putnam (1995a, 2000) asserts that the famous American propensity to start up and join voluntary organizations is withering away. He points to the decline of hands-on groups such as the Boy

Scouts and the Parent-Teacher Association (PTA) and to the rise of giant "checkbook" organizations such as Greenpeace and the American Civil Liberties Union. Americans, he says, have even stopped bowling in teams—hence his reference to "bowling alone." Putnam suggests that developments such as these, along with the increasing time that Americans spend watching television, explain the lower voting rates that characterized late twentieth-century American society and, more generally, its moral and political decline.

Although many would say that the discourse of decline falls short of accurately describing American political and cultural life, it is a vital moral component of American democracy. In persistently proclaiming the high ground of moral principle, its advocates add energy to the moral obligations of civil society. Indeed, in lamenting democratic decline, they are actually helping to make sure that it will not come about.

## The Deepening of the Civil Sphere

In the latter decades of the twentieth century, there has been, if anything, a marked intensification of the democratic current in American life. This is so despite the periods of conservatism and backlash that have followed hard upon the periods of social opening and political reform. Underneath these inevitable "shifting involvements" (Hirschman 1982), civic culture and its institutions have strengthened. The quiet and conservatism of the postwar era were shattered by the immensely powerful movement for civil rights. In *The Good Citizen: A History of American Civic Life*, Michael

Schudson places the civil rights movement at the center of what he calls the "profound revolution in rights" (1998: 242) that marked the last decades of the twentieth century:

> The civil rights movement provided a model and inspiration for a wide array of new social movements and political organizations. This bold example, even for those who did not participate in it, galvanized a new egalitarianism in American culture at large. Its radiating influence made litigation a tool of social change, it secured direct action and nonviolent demonstrations as weapons of protest, and it fixed a rights-centered citizenship at the center of American civic aspiration. (Schudson 1998: 255–256)

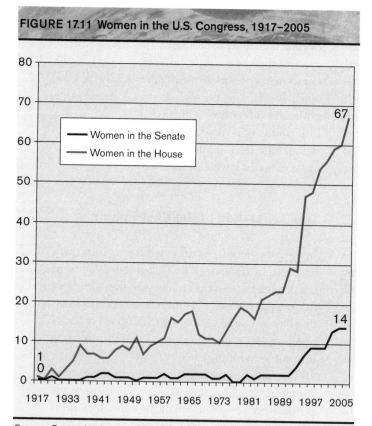

**FIGURE 17.11 Women in the U.S. Congress, 1917–2005**

Legend:
— Women in the Senate
— Women in the House

*Source:* Center for American Women and Politics (2006).

One way of measuring the scope of this rights revolution is to consider the rising numbers of women in Congress and of black elected officials (see Figures 17.11 and 17.12, respectively). Another is to look at the shifting nature of U.S. Supreme Court decisions. In 1935, only 2 of the Court's 160 opinions cited questions of civil liberties or civil rights. In 1989, by contrast, 66 out of 132 decisions were justified in this way (Schudson 1998: 249). But this silent revolution was not a top-down movement initiated from within one part of the state. Rather it started when the civil rights movement broadened the cultural understanding of civil rights—a bottom-up expansion that has quickened in the years since. As Schudson points out, "Lawyers not only initiated suits against hospitals that sought to reduce medical services to the poor, against landlords using evictions in ways prohibited by law, and against private companies seeking to defraud the poor, but also against government agencies, especially those responsible for providing welfare benefits. This work led to landmark cases that expanded citizens' rights to welfare and to fair hearings and due process inside the welfare bureaucracy" (1998: 257).

The last decades of the twentieth century witnessed the emergence of one social movement after another, each insisting on a fuller recognition of civil status (Schudson 1998: 265–274). Demands for civil repair have come not just from racial minorities such as Hispanics and Asian-Americans but also from students protesting against administrations and faculty, Native Americans demanding respect for long-neglected treaties, employees organizing for social rights in the workplace, women demanding fundamental reform at work and at home, and handicapped persons calling for the restructuring of legal, social, and material environments that have been constructed by "abled" people.

These challenges to social power show no indication of dying down anytime soon. Indeed, as Schudson (1998: 290) remarks, "scarcely a day passes without the media bringing news of another individual who crafts a social issue from a personal grievance and builds a community from a sense of a right denied."

## CONCLUSION

In this chapter, we have highlighted the importance of governments and states, paying particular attention to the distinctive roles they play as compared with other institutions of modern and postmodern society. We began by noting that political institutions did not exist in traditional societies—or at least were much more closely tied in to religious, familial, and economic groups than was the case in more modern times. Early agricultural communities were prepolitical, but with growing size and cultural and economic development there arose the need for more formal and centralized control. The emergence of "states" was linked to the interests of a dominant aristocratic class. These first states were military and administrative dictatorships, which gradually became more impersonal and bureaucratic in order to achieve more efficient control. The possibility for a new kind of "public" realm emerged as large cities formed, cultural life became more vibrant, and secular intellectuals came to the fore. Ancient Greece possessed the first such "polis," but it was submerged by the Roman Empire and disappeared during the Middle Ages.

The public sphere rose again during the Renaissance. In self-governing city-

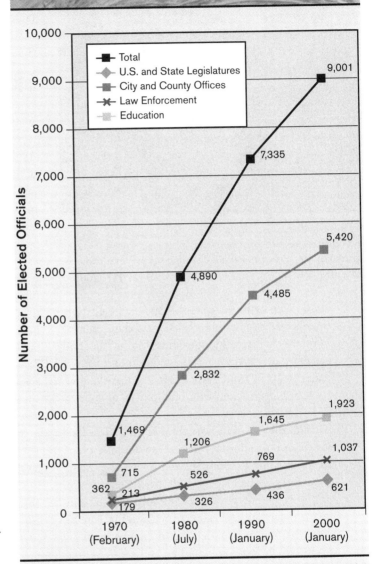

**FIGURE 17.12 Black Elected Officials in the United States by Office (selected years)**

*Source:* Adapted from Joint Center for Political and Economic Studies (2003).

Nelson Mandela of South Africa led one of the most important civil rights revolutions in world history when blacks overturned the apartheid system in 1994; here he votes for the first time. (AP Photo/John Parkin)

states such as Florence and Venice, elite citizens openly discussed public policy, rotated the control of offices, and voted for government officials. The secular democratic revolutions that took place in America (1776) and France (1789) sought to give such publics the constitutional power to control states.

With the rise of industrial capitalism, these historical opportunities for democracy, and the theories that sought to explain and legitimate them, were sharply challenged—both by the concentration of economic power in large corporations and by the polarization of economic classes that threatened the tenuous solidarity and "fellow feeling" upon which the public sphere relies. Whether dominant classes and power elites make democracy simply an empty promise remains a matter of intense debate today. Pessimistic predictions ring out from every corner of postmodern public life. Scandals also abound, exposing the corruption not only of business leaders but of government officials. Is it possible to understand these criticisms

and scandals, no matter how lamentable, as indications of the continuing vitality of the public sphere? That is the proposition we have entertained here.

## EXERCISES

### Exercise 1

As noted in this chapter, charisma and the image of the politician have become increasingly important in contemporary politics. Think back on the media coverage of the most recent American federal election and consider the ways in which the political parties used public relations to promote their presidential candidate as a charismatic leader. How did each party portray the personality of its candidate? What symbolic equipment was used to depict this personality? How did each party define sacred motives and the evil threatening the American public? Were some groups more convinced than others by a candidate's image? (In answering these questions, you might want to pay special attention to "photo opportunities" and how they are criticized.)

### Exercise 2

Take another look at the voter-turnout and political-action data charted in Table 17.6 and Figures 17.1–17.4. Which country do you consider the most politically active, and which do you consider the least? Can these forms of political action be understood in terms of the components of citizenship and the process of civil repair? Consider the findings concerning the United States. Do you think that political participation rates among Americans support the *discourse of decline*, or do they prove it wrong?

# STUDY QUESTIONS

1. Contrast political rule in traditional and modern societies. Describe the dominant form of power, the position of the ruler, the object of allegiance, and the kind of administration used to control territory in each case.

2. Explain why state power can be considered both a capacity and a threat. How did Max Weber capture this contradiction in his definition of the state?

3. What is *state autonomy*? In what way does Skocpol's theory of state autonomy challenge the Marxist explanation of revolution? How does Skocpol explain the success of the great revolutions in France, China, and Russia?

4. Briefly explain Weber's three types of legitimate authority. Which did he think would wither away in modern society?

5. Which characteristics of postmodern society have contributed to the increasing importance of charisma in contemporary politics? According to Philip Smith, what are the symbolic components that underpin the charismatic authority?

6. Describe Lukes's three-dimensional model of power. How does this model distinguish between political and social power?

7. Describe C. Wright Mills's power elite thesis. How does it differ from the traditional Marxian view? What two factors bind the power elite together?

8. What is *civil society*, and how does one become a member of it? What is *civil repair*?

9. What are the three dimensions of T. H. Marshall's definition of citizenship?

10. Why did Seymour Martin Lipset describe elections as "the democratic class struggle"? How has the shift to a postindustrial economy affected party ideology and voting?

11. What is the *discourse of decline*, and how has its main consequence been described? Is it a recent development? What evidence would suggest a deepening of the civil sphere in the American context?

# FURTHER READING

Delanty, Gerard. 2000. *Citizenship in a Global Age: Society, Culture, and Politics*. Buckingham/Philadelphia: Open University Press.

Kunovich, Sheri, and Pamela Paxton. 2005. "Pathways to Power: The Role of Political Parties in Women's National Political Representation." *American Journal of Sociology* 111, no. 2: 505–552.

Pierson, Christopher. 1996. *The Modern State*. London/New York: Routledge.

Schudson, Michael. 1998. *The Good Citizen: A History of American Civil Life*. Reprint ed. Cambridge, MA: Harvard University Press.

# chapter 18

# Social Change, Collective Action, and Social Movements

There are two main ways of looking at social change: We can focus either on major shifts of a *revolutionary* kind or on steady *evolutionary* development. A phenomenon related to the former perspective was the media hype surrounding the so-called digital revolution, illustrated by stories about get-rich-quick, dot-com millionaires in Silicon Valley. These enterprising individuals, it was said, had faith in themselves and their ability to succeed, and thereby brought about a revolution. Bill Gates's success story is the most famous example. It was only after the crash in technology shares in 2000 that commentators began to ask whether the reality of social change might be more complex. Before that, in 1999, a typical bullish story about Silicon Valley would have had the same breathless quality as the opening lines of the box titled "Generation Equity." Yet only a short time later this sunny vista was clouded over.

Taken together, the two items in this box raise questions about the nature of social change, especially change referred to as revolutionary. The first is an excerpt from a story that originally appeared in *Wired*—a glamorous story about the digital revolution. Pictured on the cover are five young entrepreneurs dressed in fashionable black, with glowing faces and a "deal with it" pose, framed against a clear blue sky—with no clouds on the horizon. They resemble the crew of *Star Trek*. They believe their mission has "historical implications." This, it is said, is no gold rush or mass mania, unlike many earlier episodes of irrational collective behavior. The media assure them that they are part of something bigger and historic—a revolution.

By 2001, less than two years after the *Wired* magazine story appeared, their dream lay in tatters. As detailed in the box's second item, they were now being informed that they had been victims of a "naïve delusion," a "classic bubble," or an "elaborate con job."

## AN INDIVIDUAL OR A SOCIAL STORY?

One possible lesson to be learned from this 2001 follow-up is that we should be wary of media stories of dramatic change brought about by individuals who, at the same time that they are transforming society, are themselves being transformed from "rags to riches." The belief in individual enterprise—the optimistic conviction that the individual is capable of making a difference—is part of the **American dream** (sometimes also referred to as the *American ideology*). But it is counterbalanced for many people by an awareness that, in their own lives, things may not be so simple. Meanwhile, on the larger stage of society and history, bringing about major social change is usually a complex process involving gradual institutional transformations—some the result of technological inventions and individual innovations, others the result of social movements or collective efforts over a long period of time. The question is especially pertinent today: Are we living through a **social revolution,** a transformation of the social order from one type of society to another?

## Analyzing Social Change

The **evolutionary view of social change** is the one favored by most sociologists. However, sociologists have also recognized that the accumulation

**American dream** The ideology that an individual of low social status and opportunity in the United States can, through hard work and perseverance, climb to the top of the social hierarchy.

**Social revolution** A revolution that involves a fundamental change in social practices (as distinct from a political revolution, which involves the overthrow of one type of political regime by another).

**theory**

## Generation Equity

By car, by plane, they come. They're just showing up. They're giving up their lives elsewhere to come here. They come for the tremendous opportunity, believing that in no other place in the world right now can one person accomplish so much with talent, initiative, and a good idea. It's a region where who-you-know and how-much-money-you-have have never been less relevant to success. They come because it doesn't matter that they're young, or left college without a degree, or have dark skin, or speak with an accent. They come even if it's illegal to come. They come because they feel they'll regret it the rest of their lives if they don't at least give it a try. They come to be part of history, to build the technology that will reshape how people live 5 or 10 years from now. They come for the excitement, just to be part of it. They come to make money, to score big. They come to make enough money so they will never have to think about money again.

*Source:* Bronson (1999: 113).

In July 1999—before the pink-slip parties, before bulls became bears and Yahoo pulled the plug here on its flashing freeway sign—five faces from the Digital Revolution appeared on a now-famous *Wired* magazine cover. The oldest was a scant 35.

Two were tech CEOs, one was in dot-com advertising, one claimed his work had "historical implications," one had become a minor celebrity chronicling the culture of the Internet. Four wore black. All struck that "deal with it" pose that then was obligatory in reports on Silicon Valley. This was no ordinary gold rush, the cover implied, no mere act of mass mania. This was bigger. This was historic. The quintet, in the months to come, would become poster children for all the best hopes of this moment. "Generation Equity," the cover story trumpeted.

Less than two years later, history is revising its take on the revolution. To the extent that "Generation Equity" comes up, it's in gleeful reports that it has crawled back to school or back to "real" jobs or back home. The new economy its members fueled, the one that was supposed to have boomed forever, is dismissed on good days as a naïve delusion; on bad days it's a "classic bubble" or an elaborate con job.

What became of those five poster children, though, conveys a more complex picture and helps illustrate why so many here at ground zero of the tech wreckage insist that, for all the diminished expectations, the new economy mustn't be written off yet. Though some on that old *Wired* cover got far less than they'd hoped for, and some failed to get rich despite almost comically close encounters with easy money, none has retreated to some chastened, old-economy version of his or her old dreams. Four remain in or near Silicon Valley, and the fifth has bet his career, fortune and best hopes on tech.

*Source:* Hubler (2001: 1).

**Evolutionary view of social change** A perspective on social change that implies a gradual transformation through a series of stages of increasing complexity (as distinct from the revolutionary view of social change, which assumes that a revolution is necessary for social change to occur).

of changes may eventually result in a transformation that amounts to a *revolution*—that is, a change from one type of social order to another type. For example, the great theorist of revolutionary change, Karl Marx, believed there would eventually be a revolutionary change of the capitalist social order to a socialist society (albeit one that would occur only after capitalism had developed through all its possible stages). He even suggested that in some countries, such as America and England, there would be a peaceful revolution, owing to their particular cultures and institutions (cited in Tucker 1978: 523). But in most countries, Marx argued, revolution could be expected to occur as the result of a final violent struggle by workers to overcome the resistance of the capitalist class, which, in turn, would fight to defend its wealth and power.

Usually, when sociologists talk about a social revolution, they are referring to a phenomenon different from the one that political commentators mean when they describe the overthrow of one type of political regime by another. A *social revolution* involves a fundamental change in social practices. So, when a revolution is described as a change in society as a whole, the word *society* is often included in the identifying phrase—such as *information society*. Some contemporary writers on the theme of social revolution, especially the digital revolution (also known as the *information revolution*), echo their nineteenth-century predecessors in presenting a picture that is a mix of long-term developments and revolutionary change. A typical example is the work of the famous "futurologist" Alvin Toffler, who has written over a dozen best-

sellers, starting back in 1970 with *Future Shock*. Toffler presents, in a popular form, ideas about stages of social development that can be traced back to the founders of sociology (e.g., Auguste Comte and Herbert Spencer) and have been elaborated by their successors to take account of the complexity of contemporary changes. The central premise is that human history, though complex and contradictory, can be seen to fit a pattern. According to Toffler, this pattern has manifested as three great advances or waves:

✓ The first wave of transformation began about 10,000 years ago when someone, probably a woman, planted a seed and nurtured its growth. That was the beginning of the *agricultural age*, and its social significance was that people moved away from nomadic wandering and hunting and began to cluster into villages and develop an elaborate culture. Wealth was land.
✓ The second wave, the *industrial age* or machine age, was based on machine power; commencing in the eighteenth century, it gathered momentum after America's Civil War. People began to leave the peasant culture of farming to work in city factories. This wave culminated in World War II, during which machine-age juggernauts clashed and atomic bombs exploded over Japan. Wealth diversified into three factors of production: land, labor, and capital.
✓ The third wave, the *information age* or knowledge age, is said to characterize our current era. Based on mind rather than muscle, it is powerfully driven by information technology. Wealth is increasingly contingent on the possession of knowledge/information.

This three-stage model of historical development has a long history. Sociologists in the nineteenth century (including Comte) could not have anticipated the development of the computer, but they did have a futuristic view that encompassed a vision of the increasing importance of scientific knowledge and associated social changes. Contemporary analysts such as Toffler have the advantage of being able to contrast some of the emerging characteristics of the computer age with aspects of the earlier industrial age.

A central characteristic of the industrial age was centralization and **standardization.** At its height, everything was "mass," from mass production to mass destruction. The task of factory workers was to turn out the longest possible line of identical products. This was one point on which there was agreement between the assembly-line capitalist Henry Ford and the leader of communist Russia (then called the U.S.S.R.) Joseph Stalin. The bureaucracy and pyramid power structure of the industrial age had many faults, but at its best it was efficient at turning out large quantities of standardized goods. One drawback was the sameness of the goods. As Henry Ford explained, "They can have a car any color they like, so long as it's black."

The pressures of competition led the giant producers of standardized goods to seek to *differentiate* their products and to satisfy (or create) different tastes. The arrival of computer technology brought about a period of transition in which the massive corporations were able to begin to provide more differentiated products for "niche markets." The large manufacturers of automobiles increased their range of vehicles to satisfy different market segments—sports utility vehicles (SUVs) for families with small children to ferry around, sports cars for affluent young singles, and saloon cars with varying engine sizes and accessories to suit different income levels. Even the humdrum cup of coffee underwent this series of changes. In the 1920s, towns still varied in terms of the kind of coffee they had available, but by the 1970s it was the likes of Maxwell House and McDonald's that made sure you had the same limited choice of coffee everywhere you went. In the 1990s many small coffeehouses sprang up, offering a rich variety of choices to satisfy consumer preferences, with ingredients and combinations that would have

McDonald's is ubiquitous as an example of standardization with choice. However, critics such as Morgan Spurlock in *Super Size Me* have pointed out that too much choice can be a problem. (AP Photo)

seemed exotic only a decade or two previously. Today, you can have industrial-age McDonald's-style standardization combined with information-age product choice simply by walking into one of the thousands of Starbucks coffee shops nationwide (soon to be worldwide). If anything, people are beginning to complain about too much choice—choice overload!

**Standardization** A characteristic of the industrial age whereby everything was produced en masse, following the same guidelines and design protocol and resulting in identical products.

As the coffee example makes clear, it wasn't just cars, furniture, and other household goods that were standardized in the industrial age. Many forms of culture and entertainment were also standardized for sale to mass markets. The Marxist sociologists in the famous Frankfurt Institute, founded before World War II in Germany, were fierce critics of the capitalist "culture industry"—especially that of Hollywood, which they accused of providing standardized culture for the masses. Whether mass culture had the kind of degrading ideological effects on working people that the Frankfurt critics imagined has been disputed. However, mass culture did not vanish with the arrival of the information society. Hollywood blockbusters, million-selling popular music recordings, and TV soap opera series are still very much around. But alongside these are many demassified niches. The Internet, for example, boasts thousands of special-interest newsgroups. This is the "plus side" of the current era. On the "negative side," however, it should be noted that the Internet has promoted a surge in hate groups. In March 1998, the *Los Angeles Times* ran an article reporting an all-time high of 474 hate groups in the United States; in just three years, 163 new websites had appeared on the Internet to preach hatred (Serrano 1998).

Inequalities of opportunity are also being reported. Access to the Internet is still markedly unequal among ethnic and income groups in the United States; in 2000, for example, 77 percent of white non-Hispanic children were living in homes with computers, compared with only 43 percent of African-American children and 37 percent of Hispanic children (U.S. Department of Education 2003). Indeed, determining the presence of a computer and the Internet among households is an effective way of measuring the digital divide in the United States. Table 18.1 illustrates this divide as a function of race/Hispanic origin, education, and family income.

The digital divide at the global level can be cal-culated using measures such as access to information and communications technology (ICT). Table 18.2 lists Digital Access Index values for the twenty highest-ranked and twenty lowest-ranked countries based on five variables: "availability of infrastructure, affordability of access, educational level, quality of ICT services, and Internet usage" (International Telecommunication Union 2003). The original study analyzed a total of 178 economies.

Returning to the "plus side" we find that the information age has witnessed a welcome increase in the number and variety of radio stations, offering music to suit all tastes, from classical to zydeco, and catering to different ethnic groups. In 1980 there were only 67 Spanish-language stations in the United States, but by 2000, according to the Arbitron ratings service, at least 559 of the nation's 12,800 stations were broadcasting in Spanish. Chronicling the long march of Spanish-language radio from Miami and Los Angeles to the rural towns of the Rocky Mountains, the Southeast, and the Great Plains, the *Los Angeles Times* reported: "Every month, it seems, another station gives up its English format—oldies or talk—in favor of what's known in the business as 'regional Mexican.' From one night to the next, the airwaves switch from farm reports and Howard Stern to the oom-pah-pah beat of the *norteña* and the wailing ballads of the *ranchera* and the *corrido*" (Tobar 2000).

Also on the rise, however, are "shock talk" radio programs, in which aggression and intolerance are worrying features. Some media sociologists even argue that the trend toward increasing diversity of radio content has begun to reverse direction. The evidence they cite is the massive consolidation that occurred following deregulation of ownership in 1996, with just a few giant media companies owning hundreds of radio stations. This "huge wave of consolidation," the trade publication *Variety* observed in 1999, "has turned music stations into cash cows that focus on narrow

TABLE 18.1 Presence of a Computer and the Internet Among U.S. Households, by Race/Hispanic Origin, Education, and Income, 2001

| Characteristics | Total Households* | Presence of a Computer | | Presence of the Internet | |
|---|---|---|---|---|---|
| | | Yes Percentage | No Percentage | Yes Percentage | No Percentage |
| Total Households | 109,106 | 56.3 | 43.7 | 50.4 | 49.6 |
| **RACE/HISPANIC ORIGIN** | | | | | |
| White | 90,680 | 58.6 | 41.4 | 52.7 | 47.3 |
| White not Hispanic | 80,734 | 60.9 | 39.1 | 55.2 | 44.8 |
| Black | 13,304 | 37.3 | 62.7 | 31.1 | 68.9 |
| Asian/Pacific Islander | 4,081 | 72.3 | 27.7 | 67.5 | 32.5 |
| Hispanic (of any race) | 10,476 | 40.0 | 60.0 | 32.2 | 67.8 |
| **EDUCATION** | | | | | |
| Less than high school graduate | 17,463 | 23.2 | 76.8 | 18.0 | 82.0 |
| High school graduate or GED | 33,469 | 46.4 | 53.6 | 39.7 | 60.3 |
| Some college or associate's degree | 29,410 | 64.5 | 35.5 | 57.7 | 42.3 |
| Bachelor's degree | 18,457 | 78.4 | 21.6 | 73.8 | 26.2 |
| Advanced degree | 10,308 | 82.2 | 17.8 | 77.7 | 22.3 |
| **FAMILY INCOME** | | | | | |
| Total Families | 74,044 | 64.6 | 35.4 | 57.9 | 42.1 |
| Less than $5,000 | 1,322 | 27.9 | 72.1 | 20.5 | 79.5 |
| $5,000–$9,999 | 2,287 | 24.6 | 75.4 | 18.0 | 82.0 |
| $10,000–$14,999 | 3,656 | 31.6 | 68.4 | 23.5 | 76.5 |
| $15,000–$19,999 | 3,034 | 36.0 | 64.0 | 24.9 | 75.1 |
| $20,000–$29,999 | 8,274 | 46.2 | 53.8 | 36.7 | 63.3 |
| $30,000–$39,999 | 7,891 | 59.3 | 40.7 | 50.9 | 49.1 |
| $40,000–$49,999 | 6,307 | 71.5 | 28.5 | 63.1 | 36.9 |
| $50,000–$59,999 | 6,334 | 76.3 | 23.7 | 68.7 | 31.3 |
| $60,000–$74,999 | 6,727 | 82.7 | 17.3 | 76.8 | 23.2 |
| $75,000 or more | 16,472 | 90.8 | 9.2 | 87.0 | 13.0 |
| Not reported | 11,740 | 53.6 | 46.4 | 48.2 | 51.8 |

*Note:* Numbers in thousands.

*Source:* U.S. Bureau of the Census (2001b: Table 1A).

play lists aimed at squeezing the most revenue from the richest demographics" (Stern 1999: 8).

According to the media watchdogs at the Project for Excellence in Journalism, the degree of consolidation in radio is not only greater than that in other media, such as television, but also more insinuating—in particular, because "technology has made it ever easier to seamlessly splice pieces of local information into a generic broadcast to give the appearance that the programming is local." Accordingly, "radio listeners may not give a second thought to what company might stand

**TABLE 18.2  Access to Information and Communications Technology (ICT), by Country, 2002**

| Highest Access | DAI* | Lowest Access | DAI* |
|---|---|---|---|
| Sweden | 0.85 | Gambia | 0.13 |
| Denmark | 0.83 | Bhutan | 0.13 |
| Iceland | 0.82 | Sudan | 0.13 |
| Korea (Rep.) | 0.82 | Comoros | 0.13 |
| Norway | 0.79 | Côte d'Ivoire | 0.13 |
| Netherlands | 0.79 | Eritrea | 0.1 |
| Hong Kong, China | 0.79 | D.R. Congo | 0.12 |
| Finland | 0.79 | Benin | 0.12 |
| Taiwan, China | 0.79 | Mozambique | 0.12 |
| Canada | 0.78 | Angola | 0.11 |
| United States | 0.78 | Burundi | 0.10 |
| United Kingdom | 0.77 | Guinea | 0.10 |
| Switzerland | 0.76 | Sierra Leone | 0.10 |
| Singapore | 0.75 | Central African Rep. | 0.10 |
| Japan | 0.75 | Ethiopia | 0.10 |
| Luxembourg | 0.75 | Guinea-Bissau | 0.10 |
| Austria | 0.75 | Chad | 0.10 |
| Germany | 0.74 | Mali | 0.09 |
| Australia | 0.74 | Burkina Faso | 0.08 |
| Belgium | 0.74 | Niger | 0.04 |

*On a scale of 0 to 1, where 1 = highest access. Digital Access Index (DAI) values are shown to hundreds of a decimal point. Countries with the same DAI value are ranked by thousands of a decimal point.

Source: International Telecommunication Union (2003).

behind their local radio station. They may be aware of the presence of corporations like Clear Channel or Infinity Broadcasting, but they might not understand how large their presence is. More than that, they might not know what impact the ownership question has on what they listen to" (Project for Excellence in Journalism 2004: 8). In fact, Clear Channel has the largest ownership of radio stations by a wide margin (see Figure 18.1).

The changes that have occurred in the economy and culture of the United States—from the massification and standardization of industrial society to the diversity said to be characteristic of the information society—have certainly not been clear-cut. Some features of the old order exist alongside those of the new, suggesting that the present period may be one of transition. In some areas there may even be reversals of trends, as in the context of radio-content diversity, which we discussed earlier, or in the economic sphere where corporations seek to maintain profits by taking over competitors or reducing the variety of products. Toffler regards such reversals as merely temporary setbacks in the inevitable development of the information society. He is less optimistic, however, about certain other social changes associated with the information society, such as the proliferation of family types that are replacing the standard industrial-age nuclear family, which had a working father and a stay-at-home mother. These new family types include the remarrieds, the adopteds, the blended family, the single-parent family, the same-sex family, the zero-parent family, the family of convenience, and the virtual family. (See also Chapter 7, on marriage and the family.) Toffler expresses concern about the effects of this fracturing of the American family that has occurred in the past thirty years, but it is, after all, in keeping with other recent social changes, especially the demands for greater individual freedom and choice.

Toffler's sweeping view of history, divided into three waves, is reminiscent of the work of nineteenth-century theorists such as Comte, Spencer, and Durkheim, as we will see. Other contemporary sociologists have not been quite so ambitious. When they do talk about *postindustrial society* or the *information age*, they are likely to specify contradictory developments and a limited range of changes. This point is well illustrated by Daniel Bell's theory of postindustrial society and Manuel Castells's theory of the information society (or *net-*

*work society*, as he now calls it), both of which we consider later in the chapter.

How have sociologists attempted to develop precise accounts of social change?

## Defining Social Change

Admittedly, it may not be very profitable to attempt a precise definition of **social change,** because the term refers to so many different phenomena that such a definition would likely end up being too broad or omitting something important. Nevertheless, we can recommend the usage offered by Wilbert Moore, who defines *social change* as the "significant alteration of social structures" and by *social structures* means "patterns of social action and interaction" (Moore 1967: 3). Moore's definition has the advantage of focusing on observable patterns of social action, such as changes in family and work patterns; however, it gives little specific attention to various cultural elements, such as values, norms, and beliefs, which may not be so easily observable. This is not to say that culture is less relevant to social change than are structures. But it is important to stress that culture should not be seen as a static set of norms, values, and beliefs, contrasted with the more dynamic social structures. Culture is a dynamic dimension of social practices or social actions. Being a member of a culture involves being engaged in a variety of practices that are distinguishable from those of other cultures and other times, ranging from ways of eating to religion and family life (Calhoun 1992: 280). It is true that elements of culture may sometimes lag behind changes in structure, as when religious beliefs and rituals change more slowly than scientific or technological innovations—a phenomenon that sociologist William Ogburn (1964) termed **cultural lag.** But sometimes the opposite is the case, such that

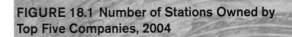

**FIGURE 18.1 Number of Stations Owned by Top Five Companies, 2004**

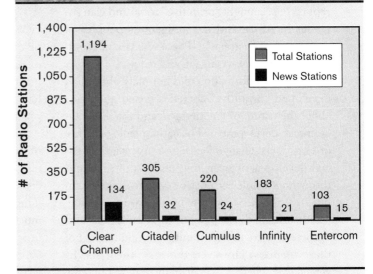

*Source:* PEJ (2005).

cultural changes lead to changes in economic, political, or technological structures. For example, in *The Protestant Ethic and the Spirit of Capitalism* (1904), Max Weber illustrated how changes in religion—specifically, the rise of Calvinism in the sixteenth century—influenced the development of capitalism.

Questions about social change have always been central to sociology. The social thinkers who laid the foundations of sociology in the nineteenth century were concerned about the impact of

**Social change** The alteration of social structures with respect not only to institutions and actions but also to changes in cultural elements, such as norms, beliefs, and values.

**Cultural lag** The phenomenon whereby cultural elements, such as religious beliefs, change more slowly than structural elements, such as technological innovations. The term *cultural lag* was coined by William Ogburn.

industrialization and urbanization on social life. They not only faced upheaval in their own societies in Europe and America but also were hearing reports of seemingly "primitive" tribal and clan societies in Africa and the indigenous peoples of America and Australasia. There was talk of cannibalism, polygamy, totemism, and magic.

Increased information and curiosity about less developed "primitive" societies raised questions about the nature of "modernity" and the direction of human development. The early sociological theories of social change focused on the stages of social development over long periods of time and throughout whole societies or even civilizations. In other words, they tended to be macrosocial, historical theories of development. "Modernization" and "progress" were the key motifs common to most of these theories. However, the early theorists diverged over whether to explain these developments in terms of social evolution or social revolution.

*Social evolutionary theories* viewed social change as advancing gradually through certain basic stages of development, such as from "military society" to "industrial society," and from simple agrarian forms to more complex industrial-urban ones. They were developed in the nineteenth century by some of the first thinkers to refer to themselves as sociologists—Auguste Comte, Herbert Spencer, and Émile Durkheim. In the mid-twentieth century, aspects of this evolutionary view were still to be found in *functionalism*, which regarded social change as the adaptation of a social system to its environment through **differentiation** (specialization of the parts) and increasing structural complexity (Parsons 1951b). For example, the institution of the family became more limited in its functions, and some of its former functions were taken over by institutions in other spheres such as education and the economy. By contrast, *theories of revolutionary change*, such as those deriving from Karl Marx, emphasized increasing *conflict* among different parts of society—particularly different economic groups (classes)—as the funda-

mental source of social change. The distinction between these two sets of theories can be illustrated in terms of the different images they favored: A typical functionalist image was that of society evolving gradually like the human organism from infancy to maturity, whereas Marx's conflict theory of revolutionary social change led him to prefer metaphors such as the sudden and sometimes violent emergence of the new baby from the womb, preceded by a period of painful labor.

These all-encompassing, macrosocial theories of development—sometimes referred to as **metanarratives**—began to come under sustained criticism in the second half of the twentieth century. They seemed to be attempting to explain too much—to be claiming to have discovered a kind of universal pattern of development. For example, Comte's social evolutionary theory of human development maintained that all humankind passed through three stages of intellectual development—theological reasoning, metaphysical thought, and positive (scientific) reasoning—and that these corresponded to three stages of social development—primitive military society, an intermediate stage of defensive military organization and a gradual switch of emphasis to production, and finally, modern industrial society.

One early twentieth-century theorist who warned against generalizations of this sort was Max Weber. Although he talked about long-term changes similar to those described by the other theorists, he emphasized the limited and specific historical character of social forms, such as Western capitalism and the modern form of bureaucratic organization. This approach proved attractive to professional sociologists in the second half of the twentieth century, who preferred "bite-sized" or "middle-range" theories (Merton 1949) over the sweeping generalizations that had suited the theorizing appetites of their predecessors.

It was only toward the end of the twentieth century that theories of macrosocial, historical change began to come back into prominence, with references to shifts from industrial to postindustrial society or information society, and from modernity to postmodernity. In contrast to the reception given to the earlier theories, these new theories have been challenged to specify the criteria and empirical evidence against which they can be judged. For example, some sociologists argue that it is misleading to talk about a change from industrial to postindustrial society because many service jobs are devoted to assisting manufacturing, as in the case of administrative staff in a factory. Furthermore, service jobs vary in type, some of which are still basically manual jobs, as is true of many cleaning and catering operations. Other sociologists, such as Manuel Castells (1996), prefer to use *information age* to emphasize the growing importance of information technology in the economy; this term, they say, is not only more specific than *service* but also allows for the fact that manufacturing may still constitute a major part of the economy. *Postmodern*, however, is even less clear-cut, as it is used to refer to a variety of social and cultural changes, not just to postindustrialism. Nevertheless, the theorist remains obligated to try to specify the criteria as clearly as possible. And, indeed, it might be easier to be specific if one links the term *postmodern* to certain changes in culture before going on to speak more generally of postmodern society—especially as *postmodernism* was originally the name of the cultural style that succeeded *modernism*.

## INDUSTRIAL SOCIETY

Both Karl Marx and Max Weber viewed modern industrial society as a socioeconomic system in which the *manufacturing firm* was central. For Marx, the factory was important as a prime example of the methods used by capitalists to make a profit out of combining machinery and workers to produce goods for sale; it was a means of concentrating and organizing labor. For Weber, the manu-

**Differentiation** In the context of development of the modern social system, this process involves the separation of major social functions so that each is the specialized responsibility of an appropriate social institution.

**Metanarratives** All-encompassing, macrosocial theories of development.

facturing firm typified the modern form of organization, which was highly rational and bureaucratic. The question to consider is: Have the changes implied by such terms as *postindustrial society* or *information society* been so revolutionary that they constitute a break with the modern society analyzed by Marx and Weber?

In addressing this question, let us consider Marx's theory of capitalism, which has been summarized as follows:

✓ Capitalism is a historically transient form of society—it emerged out of the constraints of a previous form of society (feudalism) and was destined to eventually give way to socialism once it had exhausted all its possibilities.

✓ It contains a distinctive way of producing goods, a *mode of production* that is (1) built around the production of commodities, (2) where human labor itself is commodified, and (3) where profit is created by the extraction or "exploitation" of surplus value from the workers.

✓ It is based on a division of ownership of the *means of production*, so that those who own the means of production (factories, machine tools, land, etc.)—the *capitalists*—are separated from those who work in or with them—the *working class*.

✓ It is a dynamic process, involving (1) technological progress—the incorporation of science [into] the production process in order to constantly develop methods of production through the use of increasingly complex and efficient machinery and (2) increasing the scale of production—to pay for more complex and expensive machinery, more commodities must be produced and sold to generate the profits that the enterprise requires. (Hamilton, 2002: 101, adapted from Bottomore 1985)

It is clear that, for Marx, what defines capitalism is neither the factory nor technology but rather the **social relations of production.** These are the relationships between the main groups engaged in the production of goods for sale—workers and those who supervise them on behalf of the capitalist owners. The factory, on the other hand, simply represented a way of concentrating workers within one space, working for a given period of clock time at a specific rate sufficient to yield a profit for the owner. Profit, in turn, represented the *surplus value* available to the owner once he or she had met all the costs of labor and machinery. From this point of view, the use of computerized information technology does not fundamentally alter the relations between workers and capitalist owners. And thus the introduction of such technology would not in itself indicate the emergence of an information society that could be regarded as a revolutionary change in the socioeconomic structure of capitalist industrial society.

Weber's approach to capitalism differed from Marx's in that he saw the emergence of the capitalist economic system in the West as one element of a wider socioeconomic phenomenon that he called **rationalization.** The process of rationalization entailed the replacement of traditional institutions and values by those based on principles of rational calculation regarding the most efficient means to achieve empirical ends. The process was exemplified in two main areas of modern social life: the *market economy* and the *modern bureaucracy*. The "free" market—unfettered by traditional customs and sentiments—represented an arena in which the formal, technical, calculative rationality of supply and demand operated. And the modern bureaucracy—whose performance could be checked and rechecked against quantifiable criteria—functioned on the basis of explicit, standardized, and calculable rules.

In the light of these two major components of modernity—rationalization and bureaucratization—we can see that Weber would have had no difficulty in regarding information and communications technology (ICT) as simply a continuation of such processes. Indeed, computerized financial data systems are an asset to the kind of accountancy practices that Weber regarded as typical of rationalization; for example, the personal computer (PC) achieved preeminence in the mid-1980s because of its ability to deliver standardized accounting techniques and word processing. ICT has also been a means of extending the technical rationality of bureaucracy by manipulating stored data and distributing them via **networks.** Bureaucrats no longer need to refer to written rules or to interpret them; rather, computers store the rules in application programs and apply them in standardized ways to all cases.

Weber regarded the bureaucratic administration of the state as the epitome of the rationalizing process at the heart of modernity, and computers have become its tools. The early form of the computer, the punch card machine, was invented in 1890 for the specific purpose of making the processing of U.S. Census information more rapid and efficient. Similarly, the Internet had its origins in linking federally funded defense researchers. It appears that ICT will continue to have close links

**Social relations of production** The relationships between the main groups engaged in the production of goods for sale—workers and those who supervise them on behalf of capitalist owners. According to Marx, it is neither the factory nor technology that defines capitalism but rather the emergence of new, problematic social relations of production.

with the formal and technical rationality of both the modern state and commercial organization. Thus, even though the PC offers individuals the promise of expanding human possibilities, computers continue to be used by government and corporations to exercise greater control over individuals. It is this kind of bureaucratic control that Weber described as the "iron cage" of modern society. From a Weberian perspective, then, the emergence of contemporary forms of ICT represents not a revolutionary change in society but simply an extension of rationalization and bureaucratization.

This pessimistic view of the capacity of ICT to transform society—to give individuals greater freedom and control over their lives—contrasts with the more optimistic view of those contemporary "futurologists" who, like Alvin Toffler, believe we are witnessing the dawn of a new, postindustrial society. A more mixed message is presented by the sociologist Daniel Bell.

## POSTINDUSTRIAL SOCIETY

For Bell, who popularized the concept of *postindustrial society* in the early 1970s, the term signifies an intermediate stage between industrial society and a future form of society, the precise nature of which was still to be established. In his book *The Coming of Post-Industrial Society* (1973), Bell divided society into three spheres: social (or techno-economic) structure, polity (the state and political institutions), and culture. The coming of postindustrial society, he argued, primarily involves changes in social structure, especially in the economy and in areas such as work, science, and technology. Although his focus in the book was directed to these structural changes, he was aware that they had implications for the polity and culture as well.

The main changes involved in the transition to postindustrial society are as follows:

**Rationalization** The process by which traditional institutions and values are replaced by those based on rational calculation regarding the most efficient means to achieve empirical ends. The market economy and modern bureaucracy are examples of this process. According to Max Weber, rationalization is the defining characteristic of modernity.

**Networks** The components of an interconnected system through which social actors are organized toward the attainment of goals. Networks arguably represent the new social structure and organization replacing the hierarchical form exemplified by the welfare state.

✓ A shift occurs from the predominance of goods production to that of services. Among the various types of services (including banking and retail, for example), health, education, research, and government service are the ones most important to postindustrial society.

✓ In the occupational realm, knowledge workers such as those in professional and technical work, especially scientists and technologists, rise to prominence. Assembly-line workers and other manual occupations become less central.

✓ The type of knowledge central to postindustrial society is theoretical knowledge, in contrast to the empirical knowledge valued in industrial society. In the transition to postindustrial society, science as well as research and development (R&D) work grows exponentially, catalyzed by the codification of theoretical knowledge.

✓ Given postindustrial society's orientation toward the assessment and control of technology and its impact, there is reason to hope that new forecasting and mapping techniques can be developed, making possible the planned advance of technological change and reduced economic uncertainties.

✓ Decisionmaking involves the creation of a new intellectual technology to handle the large-scale complexity of postindustrial society, the components of which include information theory, cybernetics, decision theory, game theory, utility theory, and stochastic processes. (Adapted from Bell 1973: 29)

Bell's account resembles some of the earlier grand theories (metanarratives) of social development, inasmuch as it comprises a narrative of change from preindustrial to industrial and finally postindustrial society. At the time he was writing, only the United States had reached the postindustrial stage; Western Europe, the (former) Soviet Union, and Japan had reached the industrial stage; and Asia, Africa, and South America were largely still stuck at the preindustrial stage. Bell drew out a number of distinctions among these three types of society or stages of development. In particular, he claimed that they differed with respect to dominant occupations: In preindustrial society, the central figures were farmers, miners, fishermen, and unskilled workers; in industrial society, they were semiskilled workers and engineers; and in postindustrial society, they are professionals and technical scientists. (One outcome relating to the transition under discussion has been the decline in U.S. manufacturing jobs, which is mapped in Figure 18.2.) The key power groups changed correspondingly: They comprised landowners and members of the military in preindustrial society, industrialists and politicians in industrial society, and scientists and researchers in postindustrial society.

Many criticisms can be made of this grand narrative of development. The most obvious one is that there is little sign that power has shifted from business to scientists. Similarly, although service jobs have increased in number and variety, many of them are routine and relatively unskilled, rather than technically and scientifically advanced. Furthermore, many service jobs are still devoted to servicing manufacturing and production processes—design, marketing, finance, and administration. However, when considering the validity of arguments about the coming of postindustrial so-

ciety, we should note that the thesis was developed on the basis of research carried out in the 1960s. The emergence of new information technologies from the 1980s onward, including the World Wide Web, was still some way off when Bell's *The Coming of Post-Industrial Society* was published and French sociologist Alain Touraine was writing *The Post-Industrial Society* (1971). Nevertheless, Bell can be given credit for forecasting some of the developments, especially in ICT, that led later sociologists to refer to the emergence of an information society. We also need to recognize that Bell did not claim that society had already undergone a revolutionary change; rather, he said it was in transition. Indeed, elements of preindustrial and industrial society were coexisting with emerging postindustrial elements. It could even be argued that some of these elements or stages remain in contradiction or conflict with one another.

The theme of contradiction became more prominent in Bell's later publication, *The Cultural Contradictions of Capitalism* (1976), when he turned his focus from social structural changes to cultural changes. The book is premised on the idea that the three focal realms are governed by contrary axial principles: for the economy, it is efficiency; for the polity, equality; and for culture, self-realization (or self-gratification) (Bell 1976: xi–xii). Bell's main concern here is with the conflict between the techno-economic and cultural realms: As he put it, the *techno-economic realm* still seemed to be ruled by the old character traits of self-discipline, restraint, and delayed gratification, which were in conflict with the hedonism that seemed to characterize the *cultural realm*. Bell discerned the emergence of a postmodern culture based on consumerism, "concerned with play, fun, display and pleasure" (Bell 1976: 70). He was ahead of his contemporaries in identifying some of the characteristics of the emerging postmodern culture. Among the issues that he mentioned in this connection were the dominance of visual culture, the presence of nonrationality and irrationality, the breakdown

**FIGURE 18.2  Map of Decline in U.S. Manufacturing Jobs, 1998–2005**

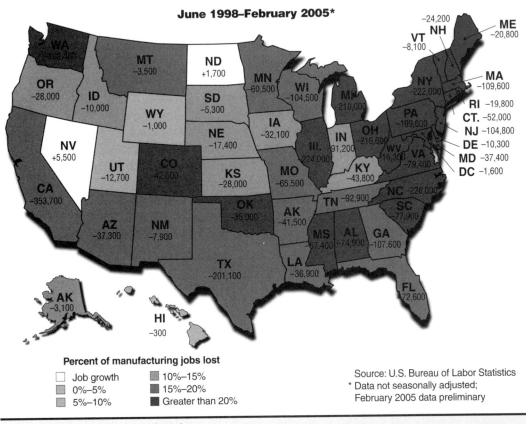

# THE STATE CRISIS: MANUFACTURING JOBS LOST

### June 1998–February 2005*

Percent of manufacturing jobs lost

☐ Job growth   ■ 10%–15%
■ 0%–5%   ■ 15%–20%
■ 5%–10%   ■ Greater than 20%

Source: U.S. Bureau of Labor Statistics
* Data not seasonally adjusted;
February 2005 data preliminary

*Source:* U.S. Department of Labor (2005).

of the distinction between high and low culture, and loss of the sense of a unified self.

Among the many scenarios or visions of the future that exist today, some paint a bleak picture while others are enthusiastically optimistic. Most of the people who have encountered the postmodern debate have done so through the cultural dimension, which encompasses the arts, architecture, and film. Consider, for instance, *Blade Runner* (1982), deemed the acme of postmodern

movies. A summary is provided in the box titled "Postmodern Futures."

What makes *Blade Runner* postmodern? According to sociologist David Lyon (1999), it contains several postmodern themes:

✓ "Reality" itself is in question within this movie. The replicants want to be real people, but the proof of "reality" is a photographic image, a constructed identity. One of the debates about

## media moments

### Postmodern Futures

Los Angeles, AD 2019, provides the setting for *Blade Runner*. A group of "replicants," bio-engineered near-people who normally reside "off-world," have returned to confront their makers, the high-tech Tyrell corporation. Their complaint is simple; understandably, they object to their four-year lifespan and seek an extension to full human status. Deckard, the "blade runner," has the unenviable task of tracking these escaped replicants and eliminating or "retiring" them.

The replicants are not robots, but skin jobs, simulacra. They live fast and furious, if not full, lives. Throughout, they keep appearing in different locations, apparently without having traveled. And they are subjected to testing by humans to determine whether or not they are replicants. One of them, Rachel, produces a photo of her mother, which at last gives a sense that she has a "real" past, a history, like humans. Deckard finds this enough, evidently, to form an emotional attachment with her, although in the 1992 "Director's Cut" version, this does not culminate in their joint flight to forests and mountains that figured in the earlier version.

The scene of *Blade Runner* is one of urban decay, once grand buildings lying damaged, crowded cosmopolitan streets, endless shopping malls, uncollected garbage and constant gray drizzle. Perhaps the nuclear holocaust has happened already? Undoubtedly, progress is in ruins. Nothing is recognizable as LA; it could be anywhere. Roman and Greek columns, Chinese dragons and Egyptian pyramids are mixed with giant neon ads for Coca-Cola and Pan-Am. Although well-lit transporters flit above the streets, and there are momentary scenes of slick-clean corporate suites, the dominant image is decrepitude, disintegration and a chaotic mish-mash of style.

*Source:* Lyon (1999: 1–2).

postmodernity is whether it's possible to have verifiable knowledge about society and people (including our own identities). Or are we faced with a mélange of artificial images from television and other media? A more optimistic view is that postmodernity liberates us from definitions of "reality" imposed by authorities, leaving us free to shop around.

✓ Another theme is that, in the postmodern or postindustrial economy, information/knowledge has replaced industry and labor as the axial organizing principle. According to Tyrell, the corporation featured in the movie, developing knowledge has produced commerce "more human than human," with genetic engineering producing human simulacra (imitations). The replicants exist in a world that has overcome the limitations of time and space, thanks to the information and communications technology (ICT) of the "global village." The traditional and modern structures of space and time have been supplemented or supplanted by "virtual" spaces. The solidity and coherence of once-separate societies, whether nation-states or other territorially bounded communities, are undermined as global communications and relations erode the older sense of time and space. Production is internationalized: An automobile may be designed in one country and manufactured in another, with the company headquarters located in a third. Sociology itself is forced to become more global in its analyses as it seeks some sense of the new patterns formed by flows of people, data, images, and capital.

✓ A less prominent but still discernible postmodern theme is that of "consumer society," where everything is a spectacle and images are what matter. Some of the most memorable scenes in the movie feature decadent entertainment spectacles with bizarre characters and costumes. For example, Zhora, a female replicant, dies crashing through storefront windows in a seemingly endless arcade. Everything is on offer to be consumed, no matter how strange, and boredom threatens to loom unless new excitements can be presented. One of the few things distinguishing replicants from humans is what they consume—echoing the postmodern theme that "we are what we eat." Otherwise, the difference between reality and simulacra is not obvious in the postmodern world of *Blade Runner*. It is as if America has become Disneyland for real, which is the conclusion of Frenchman Jean Baudrillard (1988), one of the foremost sociologists of postmodernity. According to Baudrillard, the postmodern cultural life of America is now so permeated with media images that it is impossible to distinguish a "real" America from that of Disneyland.

Social and cultural diversity is evident in the streets of the postmodern L.A. of *Blade Runner*, where all ethnic groups are represented. It a truly global city. We get an impression of social fragmentation and cultural pastiche—key themes of postmodernism. These tendencies were already evident in early-modern industrial society. As Karl Marx demonstrated, the meaning behind the constant revolutionizing of production was that "all that is solid melts into air." This process is accentuated in postindustrial, postmodern society, where everything has become a commodity for sale, including images and identities, and there is a

constant pressure to change. In the words of one *Blade Runner* replicant, experience is "washed away in time like tears in rain."

Of course, *Blade Runner* was set in a future time, and sociologists who prefer the term *late modernity* over *postmodernity* (Anthony Giddens is one of them) argue that many of the characteristics of modernity still exist—even in the most advanced global cities of the information age, such as Los Angeles. Alongside the gleaming dream factories of Hollywood and Disneyland, we find Third World people scraping a living and forming what Marx might call an exploited postindustrial proletariat. The Hispanic service workers who clean supermarket floors and tend the homes and gardens of the middle class may even be a vestige of a preindustrial servant class that is now on the increase again after having declined during the industrial phase of modernity. But one could also argue that the term *postmodernity* is useful precisely because it does point to the contradictory tendencies that are appearing, including new localisms and fundamentalisms in response to globalization and rationalization. The Taliban Islamic fundamentalism that dominated Afghanistan until it was overthrown after September 11, 2001, is a

The Taliban regime in Afghanistan continues to resist modernization of that country. (AP Photo/Amir Shah)

recent example of resistance to globalization and rationalization. The Taliban sought to reestablish traditional cultural practices, such as the confinement of women in the home and family, denying them education and employment. It is not alone in reacting in this way. Christian fundamentalists in America, too, are highly suspicious of globalization, opposing bodies such as the United Nations, championing biblical creationist beliefs against the scientific theory of evolution, and attempting to promote traditional family values.

## INFORMATION SOCIETY, GLOBALIZATION, AND SOCIAL MOVEMENTS

Some observers of the information society go so far as to insist that it is profoundly changing the very contours of social structure and organization. They claim that, in place of the hierarchical form of social structure and organization typified by the centralized **welfare state** and the bureaucratic corporation, an older form of organization—that of the *network*—has risen to a new global prominence thanks to the computerization of information, knowledge, and communication (Castells 1996–1998, 2000, 2002).

The danger posed by this new form of organization is that, once programmed to achieve certain goals, it may impose its own logic on its members (human actors). All computer-based systems work on a binary logic: inclusion/exclusion. And "[w]hat is not in the network does not exist from the network's perspective, and thus must be either

ignored (if it is not relevant to the network's task) or is eliminated (if it is competing in goals or in performance)" (Castells 2002: 127). Many sociologists would dispute Castells's pessimistic picture of the impossibility of bringing about internal change in the interpretation of organizations' goals. That is precisely how reforms occur in many organizations in society as groups and parties battle over the meanings that define the goals and the means to attain them. However, we can see that there is some truth in Castells's analysis wherever computer-based systems are in operation, as in global banking and financial systems, or in economic production systems that are programmed to switch production or sourcing of materials to the cheapest provider. In such cases, there may be a social struggle to assign goals to the network but afterward, members (actors) find themselves having to ply their strategies within the rules of the network. In order to bring about the assignment of different goals to the network, actors may have to challenge the network from the outside and, in fact, destroy it by building an alternative network around alternative values. Another option is to attempt to withdraw from the network and build a defensive, non-network structure (e.g., a "commune") that does not allow connections outside its own set of values. It is because global networks tend to exclude the possibility of changing their goals that there has been a growth of social movements opposing them (e.g., antiglobalization movements) and of "fundamentalist" communal movements seeking to separate themselves from them.

Castells discusses three types of social movements and identities that can be generated in response to the globalization of information flows and networks: *legitimizing*, *resistance*, and *project*. The first type—**legitimizing movements and identities**—is manifest in the mainstream institutions of society. They are generated by or in churches, labor unions, political parties, cooperatives, and civic associations. Such bodies constitute civil society—the part of political activity and

**Welfare state** A state in which the government takes responsibility for its citizens' well-being. A welfare state typically devotes a significant portion of its expenditures to programs that provide access to resources such as housing, health care, education, and/or employment for its citizens.

influence that lies outside the state but has legitimate access to state power. Once again, Castells is more pessimistic than many other sociologists—in this case, about the possibility that such legitimizing movements and identities will bring about substantial transformations in the information society by way of state action. The reason for this pessimism, according to Castells, is that the state itself is weakened by globalization (e.g., global corporations, global capital flows, and global information flows elude state control). Its power is also eroded by the decline of the bureaucratic *welfare state* that grew up in industrial society but is no longer so firmly rooted in the information society. For example, Castells concludes that the nationally based *labor movement* now has little prospect of wielding influence to bring about the rebuilding of a welfare state that would provide all its citizens with standardized forms of social security. In America, the labor movement is weaker than ever before and the growth of a strong welfare state has been opposed by the ideology of individualism, which favors private provision of security benefits (e.g., private health care and pensions). Even in Europe, where the welfare state is more highly valued, the influence of the labor movement has weakened and a shift has occurred toward more private provision of benefits.

In early 2005, the U.S. Department of Labor's Bureau of Labor Statistics issued a press release reporting the most recent data on the decline in labor union membership. These data revealed a reduction in the number of wage and salary workers who were union members from 12.9 percent in 2003 to 12.5 percent in 2004. This proportion had steadily declined from a high of 20.1 percent in 1983, the first year for which comparable union membership-rate data were available.

Highlights from this 2005 press release include the following:

✓ About 36 percent of government workers were union members in 2004, compared with about 8 percent of workers in private-sector industries.

✓ Two occupational groups—education, training, and library occupations, on the one hand, and protective-service occupations, on the other—exhibited the highest unionization rates in 2004 (about 37 percent each). Protective-service occupations include firefighters and police officers. Farming, fishing, and forestry occupations (3.1 percent) and sales and related occupations (3.6 percent) had the lowest unionization rates.

✓ Men were more likely to be union members (13.8 percent) than women (11.1 percent).

✓ Black workers were more likely to be union members (15.1 percent) than white workers (12.2 percent), Asian workers (11.4 percent), and Hispanic or Latino workers (10.1 percent).

✓ About 1.6 million wage and salary workers were represented by a union on their main job in 2004, while not being union members themselves.

✓ In 2004, full-time wage and salary workers who were union members had median usual weekly earnings of $781, compared with a median of $612 for wage and salary workers who were not represented by unions. (U.S. Department of Labor 2005b)

The second type described by Castells comprises **resistance movements and identities**. Familiar among the resistance identities are those

**Legitimizing movements and identities**  As described by Manuel Castells, social movements that are generated through institutions of civil society that are outside of the state, yet have legitimate access to state power.

**Resistance movements and identities**  As described by Manuel Castells, social movements that are based on the identity of excluded groups (i.e., racial and ethnic minorities) and are the product of resentment toward dominant institutions and alienation from mainstream ideologies.

Labor union participation declined in the last part of the twentieth century; however, one of the most powerful unions, the teachers' union, still mobilizes many members in support of state funding for schools, as this Pennsylvania rally shows. (AP Photo)

grounded in religious fundamentalism, race and ethnicity, queer culture, and other excluded groups. Castells describes resistance movements and the identities they produce as "defensive sociocultural formations"—that is, as products of alienation and resentment in relation to the dominant institutions and ideologies of society. He is

**Project movements and identities** As described by Manuel Castells, social movements that use available cultural resources to create new identities that redefine one's position in society and try to change the overall social structure. The women's movement and environmental movement are examples of project movements and identities.

pessimistic about the prospect that these movements will be able to bring about institutional changes, as he thinks they have little influence over the centers of state power. Other sociologists, however, have pointed to the successes of some of these groups in securing recognition for themselves and their demands.

The third type is **project movements and identities.** A project identity is formed "when social actors, on the basis of whichever cultural materials are available to them, build a new identity that redefines their position in society and, by so doing, seek the transformation of the overall social structure" (Castells 1997: 8). Castells cites the environmental movement and the women's movement as examples. In contrast to resistance movements, project movements move beyond issues of exclusion by seeking to transform existing institutions or by constructing new ones. For instance, the women's movement projects itself into society at large by undermining male dominance (patriarchy) and reconstructing the family on a new basis of equality, as well as by seeking to abolish gender distinctions in other major institutions such as work and politics. Castells notes that not all religious fundamentalisms can be ruled out as project identities; some religious communities, he argues, can be said to have transformative potential through their efforts aimed at "remoralizing society, reestablishing godly, eternal values, and embracing the whole world, or at least the whole neighborhood, in a community of believers, thus founding a new society" (Castells 1997: 357).

**Social movements** have attracted increasing attention from sociologists, especially those who believe we are entering a new stage of social development, such as the information society or network society described by Castells. But what are social movements, and why are they becoming so important?

Mario Diani has defined a social movement as "a network of informal interactions between a plurality of individuals, groups and/or organizations,

The U.S. feminist movement is the longest peaceful project movement in world history, spanning nearly 160 years; this photo captures the landmark protest of the Miss America Pageant in 1968. (Bettmann/Corbis)

engaged in a political or cultural conflict, on the basis of a shared collective identity" (1992: 13). Based on this definition, the key characteristics of a social movement can be summarized as follows:

✓ It is an *informal network* of interactions among activist groups, individuals, or organizations.

> **Social movements** Movements whose key characteristics are (1) an informal network of interactions among activist groups, individuals, and organizations; (2) a sense of collective identity; and (3) engagement in political or cultural conflict over social change.

✓ It is defined by a sense of *collective identity* among participants.

✓ It is engaged in *political or cultural conflict* over social change.

Diani's definition is useful because it makes a clear distinction between social movements and other temporary episodes of collective behavior, on the one hand, and established political organizations, on the other. Consider, for example, an episode of collective behavior such as a panic caused by a leak of radioactive material from a nuclear reactor. As a temporary phenomenon it does not in itself bestow an identity, but it may evolve into an environmentalist social movement devoted to closing nuclear power stations or halting their spread. Bear in mind, however, that while a social movement may become organized and even bring together a number of organizations to pursue its objectives, it is broader and more loosely structured through an informal network than the more rigidly structured single organization.

Analysis of social movements was originally included in the study of the broad range of phenomena referred to as **collective behavior**. Sociologist Neil Smelser defined collective behavior as "mobilization on the basis of a belief which redefines social action" (1962: 8). Following is a list, based on his analysis, of the stages through which an episode of collective behavior typically develops:

✓ *Structural conduciveness*. Conditions exist that permit or encourage collective behavior to occur, as when a money market creates conditions conducive to a panic about a financial crash.

✓ *Structural strain*. Uncertainty, conflict, or some other anxiety-producing circumstance is present.

✓ *Growth and spread of a generalized belief*. A shared belief identifies the source of strain, gives it meaning, and specifies certain appropriate responses.

✓ *Precipitating factors*. An event triggers an episode of collective behavior, as when a rapid drop in the price of tech stocks leads to a panic selling.

✓ *Mobilization of participants for action*. Information from or actions by influential figures summon people to act, as when a respected stockbroker's advice is quoted.

✓ *The operation of social control*. Collective behavior occurs as a result of lack of action by those otherwise capable of controlling the situation and thereby heading off the behavior.

According to Smelser, collective behavior occurs as a result of the passage through these stages in a cumulative progression—what amounts to a *value-added process*.

This approach has been found useful for understanding the emergence of certain forms of collective behavior, such as panics. But because the overall category of collective behavior is very broad, ranging from single events to long-lasting social movements, the study of social movements has given rise to other theories as well. These include resource mobilization theory and new social movements (NSM) theory (Storr 2002).

*Resource mobilization theory*, as developed by John D. McCarthy and Mayer N. Zald, starts with the question Why do people get involved in social movements? The seemingly obvious answer is that they get involved because they want to bring about social change as a result of their own experiences of disadvantage or oppression. Accordingly, we might expect gay men and lesbians to join a movement for social change because they suffer homophobia or blacks to join an antiracist movement because they suffer racism. McCarthy and Zald (1987) suggest that this is an oversimplification. On the one hand, some people experience oppres-

**Collective behavior** As defined by Neil Smelser, mobilization on the basis of a belief that redefines social action.

sion but do not join a social movement—and this may be a rational choice on their part. For example, homosexual individuals who do not actively participate in the lesbian and gay movement may have decided that it is not worth "coming out" in public if they risk losing their jobs, and perhaps they hope that homophobia will end at some indefinite point in the future. On the other hand, some people who do join social movements may not have experienced discrimination or disadvantage themselves. Indeed, there are heterosexuals who have been involved in the gay and lesbian movement, just as there are white people who participate in antiracist movements. Why do some people join a social movement and others do not? Or to put the question another way: How do social movements mobilize people to participate?

The key insight of resource mobilization theory is that social movements need resources—money, volunteers, know-how, and so on. The more resources they can mobilize, the more success they will achieve. In short, the main task of a social movement, according to resource mobilization theory, is to increase its pool of available resources. It can do this by persuading individuals to become involved as active members and to place some of their own resources at the disposal of the organization. In its search for resources, a social movement will not necessarily limit itself to those who stand to benefit directly from social change; for instance, a lesbian and gay movement may try to secure participation and resources from sympathetic heterosexuals as well as from gays and lesbians. And since there may be perfectly rational reasons for individual gays and lesbians not to join, it is no less rational for heterosexuals to join. In fact, resource mobilization theory assumes that social movements and individuals always operate on a rational basis and make rational choices. It is thus a form of *rational choice theory*, which signifies "that in acting rationally, an actor is engaging in some kind of optimization. This is sometimes expressed as maximizing utility, sometimes as minimizing cost,

sometimes in other ways" (Coleman and Fararo 1992: xi). Resource mobilization theory also tends to treat social movements as if they were companies in search of investors. For instance, McCarthy and Zald (1987) explicitly compare social movements with industries and use terminology from economics to analyze them.

The major problem with resource mobilization theory, however, is that it tends to reduce all sociological analysis to a form of economic analysis. It is not really interested in the aims of social movements—the social changes these movements want to achieve or the protest actions they employ. Consequently, it has little to tell us about the *culture* of specific movements—the kinds of symbols or styles they use and the meanings attached to them. For example, an interesting feature of the gay liberation movement is that its public demonstrations often feature members dressed up in "drag" costumes. This approach might not seem the best way to attract resources, but as a form of political action directed against heterosexual gender norms it is symbolically very expressive.

The other theory introduced above—*new social movements theory*—is more interested in the analysis of culture and meaning in social movements. What is new about NSM theory is not the theory itself but the social movements that have come to the fore—and those social movements are new because, according to many sociologists, the form of society in which they are occurring is new. Indeed, new social movements have emerged in the information society, and they are engaged in struggles over information—they are attempting to bring about social change by influencing the public to see things their way. These are struggles over meanings and identities: The new social movements are more concerned with nonmaterial issues—identity and lifestyle and the inequalities they are subject to—than with economic inequality, as was the case with the older social movements of the industrial age, such as the labor movement (Inglehart 1990).

One of the leading thinkers behind new social movement theory is the Italian sociologist Alberto Melucci. His outline of the key characteristics of the new social movements in the information society includes the following:

✓ The centrality of *information*. Activists in the information society are centrally concerned with the production and circulation of information and meaning.

✓ The *self-reflexive form of action*. Because new social movements are struggles about meanings, activists must take account of the meanings generated by their own actions. Actions are primarily viewed as acts of communication; the protest action is a form of message and so is the activist himself or herself.

✓ The *global dimension*. New social movements are able to make links with global events and issues by using global networks of communication, especially the Internet.

✓ *Latency and visibility*. There are times when social movement activity is very visible and other times when it seems almost to disappear. Hence sociologists sometimes talk about different "waves" of a social movement—for example, "first-wave feminism" followed by second-wave and even third-wave feminism (editorial, *Feminist Review* 64 [2000]: 1–2). Alberto Melucci maintains, however, that a wave of activism should not be understood as a new arrival of energy, which subsequently disappears; rather, sociologists should focus on the networks of individuals and communities that periodically become visible as "waves" of activism. (Melucci 1995; Storr 2002)

A final point made by Melucci is that the success or failure of a social movement should be judged not solely by its "political" achievements but also in terms of its more subtle cultural results. Since new social movements are concerned with conveying and changing meanings, the very fact that a protest action takes place could be responsible for changing old meanings or creating new ones. The protest can make people aware of power structures and imbalances of power.

Many sociologists who subscribe to the idea that the contemporary societies with the most developed economies have become postindustrial societies or information societies would also accept that the new social movements are expressions of a postmodern culture and lifestyle. Many members of such movements seem to be engaged in constructing a lifestyle from a pastiche of elements, picking and choosing among a number of choices on offer—from dress codes and food consumption codes to sexual identity. This point is borne out if we look at some of the main examples that are given of new social movements: the gay and lesbian movement, the environmental or ecology movement, the women's movement, and so on. It has been said that people do not so much "join" such movements as "live" them. This "picking and mixing" has led to the criticism that involvement in a new social movement is often itself an expression of a postmodern lifestyle.

It's easy to draw too sharp a contrast between old and new social movements. Some of the new social movements are still engaged in a struggle over perceived inequalities, even if they are inequalities of recognition and respect (as in the gay and lesbian movement) or of power and status (as with many movements in behalf of ethnic groups and the women's movement). However, the new social movements are also concerned with lifestyle and identity—that is, with influencing public perceptions of lifestyle options and identities that seem to deviate from established mainstream opinion. But in order to wield this influence, they have to grapple with images in the mass media and the ways in which these "frame" or socially construct the issues. This phenomenon has led sociologists to develop a **frame analysis** of social movements, drawing on the earlier work of Erving Goffman (1974). Frame analysis reveals forms of interpretation that allow individuals or groups "to locate, perceive, identify, and label" events, thereby rendering meaning, organizing experiences, and guiding actions (Goffman 1974: 21). It is an approach that has been used in media studies to analyze the process by which news organizations define and construct a political issue or public controversy. Sociologists who have employed this method suggest that social movements are more likely to succeed in getting their message across if they frame it so as to be aligned with the frames of those receiving the message ("frame alignment") (Snow et al. 1986); if they ensure that the message resonates in a way that transforms the receivers' existing frame (Snow et al. 1986); or if their performance in the dramas surrounding public controversy attracts sympathetic attention to their values and beliefs, drawing on symbolic aspects of the movements' own subculture and that of the wider culture (Alexander 2006).

One of the newest social movements to attract wide support from young activists in many parts of the more economically developed world is the antiglobalization movement (sometimes referred to as the anticapitalism movement), which combines some of the characteristics of the old social movement struggle on behalf of the disadvantaged against the powerful, on the one hand, with new social movement issues of lifestyle, such as excessive consumerism and protecting the environment, on the other. It also uses many of the symbolically expressive tactics of new social movements in order to catch public attention and encourage people to think differently. As suggested earlier, demonstrators who dress in unusual outfits or stage eye-catching stunts may gain media attention, but they also run the risk of being met with derision or even of being reduced to objects of ironical discussion in the newspaper style section. A review in *Extra!* of the media coverage of the Washington, D.C., demonstrations against the International Monetary Fund and the World Bank in April 2000 illustrates the problem, as detailed in

Globalization increases the flow of cultural products that shape the frames through which other cultures may view themselves, such as this *Star Wars* poster in Korea. (Reuters/Claro Cortes IV)

the box titled "For Press, Magenta Hair and Nose Rings Defined Protests."

Whatever success is attributable to the styles and symbols of the antiglobalization movement, it has drawn attention to a subject that many people in the poorer parts of the world believe is not sufficiently publicized in more economically devel-

**Frame analysis** A method of determining the ways in which social movements are socially constructed, interpreted, and represented both by actors in the movement itself and by outside influences, such as the mass media.

## theory

### For Press, Magenta Hair and Nose Rings Defined Protests

The success of the Washington, D.C. demonstrations against the IMF and World Bank can be measured in part by how well activists communicated their message to the general public. Without a doubt, the Mobilization for Global Justice succeeded in intensifying the national debate on globalization. This April, mainstream media featured a more sustained and substantive discussion of World Bank/IMF structural adjustment policies than ever before.

That said, serious investigations of World Bank/IMF policies were still the exception rather than the rule. What's more, this small broadening of coverage was accompanied by a formidable backlash on op-ed pages, and by a rash of reports more interested in tittering at activists' fashion sense than in examining their policies. ...

This refusal to take World Bank/IMF critics seriously was also evident in articles not explicitly labeled opinion pieces. Strangest was the *Washington Post* "Style" section profile of Ruckus Society program director Han Shan (4/15/00), in which reporter Ann Gerhart admonished: "Please do not call Han Shan a hunka hunk of burning radical love. That would be trivializing him." It is difficult, however, not to come away with the impression that Gerhart delighted in trivializing Shan—she pointed out that his shirt "cleverly matches his eyes," suggested that his "great looks" were a "recruiting tool" for his cause, and noted with evident surprise that "he neither sounds nor acts like a lunatic."

Unsurprisingly, a Nexis search of major media for the month of April found no articles in which IMF or World Bank officials were referred to as "hunka hunk" of burning anything.

*Source:* Coen (2000).

oped societies. Within the latter, especially the United States, emphasis tends to be placed on the advantages of worldwide communication through new information technologies, increased international trade, and the free flow of cultural products. The policies of international agencies like the International Monetary Fund (IMF) and the World Bank are intended to assist such developments; the antiglobalization movement seeks to publicize what it regards as their ill effects.

### GLOBALIZATION

Exactly what is *globalization*? The term has many definitions, but one of the simplest has been offered by David Held: "Globalization may be thought of initially as the widening, deepening and speeding up of worldwide interconnectedness in all aspects of contemporary social life, from the cultural to the criminal, the financial to the spiritual" (Held et al. 1999: 2). This seems a fairly straightforward and uncontroversial proposition. However, it is disputed on a number of grounds.

First, whereas the phrase *worldwide interconnectedness* implies a single world system, the interconnectedness may actually exist only among certain nations and regions. Indeed, evidence indicates that the majority of international trade and communication occurs between neighboring countries (e.g., the United States and Canada) and within regional groups of nations or "trading blocs" (e.g., the European Union, Asia Pacific, and North America) (Hirst and Thompson 1996).

Second, the common assumption that globalization involves a neutral process of increasing "interconnectedness" may disguise the possibility that the flows between connected points are mainly in one direction, or consist of one side dominating the other (i.e., the more economically developed societies dominating the less developed ones). In fact, research demonstrates that use of the Internet is overwhelmingly situated in North America and Europe, and that America exports more television programs than any other country and imports only a tiny amount from other countries (Held et al. 1999: 356–360).

Third, as opponents of globalization in the environmental and anticapitalist movements have argued, the pursuit of profits leads to overexploitation of global resources by the more economically developed societies. This observation does not invalidate the term *globalization*, but it does seem a valid criticism of the effects of certain aspects of globalization, particularly the overexploitation of natural resources such as fossil fuels (oil, coal, and natural gas) and some of the antiregulation policies of international institutions such as the World Trade Organization, the World Bank, and the IMF. On the other hand, the term *globalization* has also been used in the context of increasing environmental degradation. The Western predilections for the motor car and profligate energy use entail a very large release of greenhouse gases into the atmosphere that has significantly contributed to global warming. Some national governments have been reluctant to reach an international agreement to limit the growth in these and other pollutants if doing so jeopardizes their national commercial interests. The U.S. government, for example, withdrew from such an agreement—the Kyoto agreement—in 2002, on the grounds that it might adversely affect profits and jobs in America.

On balance, it is probably safe to say that there is evidence of increasing globalization in the sense of worldwide interconnections on various dimensions—communications, financial transactions, trade, cultural flows, environmental problems, and so on. But these connections are uneven and unequal in their effects. And, in any case, there have been reactions against globalization. On the one hand, national governments and regional blocs have taken action to protect their interests, and on the other, social movements, including not just the antiglobalization movement but also local and religious movements, have arisen to protest globalization.

## CONCLUSION

It is time to return to the question posed at the beginning of this chapter: Are we living through a social revolution, a transformation of the social order from one type of society to another? *Wired* magazine's famous five "poster children" were led to believe that they could "make a difference" and play a part in bringing about the digital revolution. Their hopes were dashed, but they still had faith that long-term changes were under way. As one of them said: "Tech is going to be around forever. It was overhyped a couple of years ago when magazines like *Fortune* said the Internet was going to change the world, and it's overhyped now when people say the whole economy is crashing. Who's to say things aren't going to get better next year?" (quoted in Hubler 2001: 2).

We live in a media-saturated culture that is described as postmodern because it has become increasingly difficult to avoid the hype and to judge what is really happening. It is an information society in the sense that we have access to vast quantities of information. The problem, however, is that we may be suffering from information overload. Futurologists have exploited this scenario by joining with the media to provide exciting stories of revolutionary social change, heralding a new type of society or a "new wave"—for example, Toffler's

*Third Wave* (1980). And sociologists have the task of carefully weighing the evidence and explaining where and to what extent long-term social changes are occurring. Sometimes the use of terms like *information society* can be helpful, by directing attention to significant changes; but they need to be qualified, in the sense of taking account of evidence of inequalities and reversals in these changes. Indeed, social sources of resistance to change as well as social movements influencing the course of change in a different direction can also be subjected to sociological analysis.

## EXERCISES

### Exercise 1

As noted in this chapter, a central question in research on social movements has to do with why people get involved in social movements. Have you ever participated in a social movement? Why did you decide to join? How did you convince others to get involved? Describe the goals or desired outcome of this social movement. Which of the theories discussed in this chapter best explains its success or failure?

### Exercise 2

Another important concept discussed in this chapter is *cultural lag*. This term refers to the gap that often exists between cultural practices and technological innovations. The failure of culture to keep up with science is often used to explain social conflict. Do you think that American society suffered cultural lag with the introduction of the Internet? Did the introduction of this technology raise new moral and legal questions?

## STUDY QUESTIONS

1. What is the difference between evolutionary and revolutionary social change? Are they mutually exclusive? How is social revolution different from political revolution?

2. What are Alvin Toffler's three "waves" of social development? Briefly describe each of these stages by identifying its dominant form of economic production, its basis of wealth, and its social significance. Which stage are we in now?

3. What is Wilbert Moore's definition of *social change*? What are the advantages and disadvantages of this definition? Why is *social change* so difficult to define?

4. What two types of theories of social change emerged during the nineteenth century? Who are the major theorists associated with each theory? Which one describes development in terms of evolution, and which one in terms of revolution?

5. What events prompted the first attempts to explain social change in the nineteenth century? How were the first theories of social change criticized by sociologists of the twentieth century?

6. How did Karl Marx understand the role of the factory in modern capitalism? How did Max Weber understand the role of the manufacturing firm? Does the information society constitute a radical break from the modern society that these two theorists describe?

7. Name the three social spheres described by Daniel Bell. What is the axial principle of each sphere? According to Bell, what conflict characterized the transition to postmodernism?

8. Briefly describe Manuel Castells's three types of social movements and the corresponding identities generated in response to the globalization of information flows. Which one is he most optimistic about in terms of its ability to bring about substantial changes in the information society?

9. What are the key characteristics of a social movement? What is the difference between social movements and collective behavior?

10. What is the central insight of resource mobilization theory? Why is it considered a form of rational choice theory? What is the major problem with resource mobilization theory?

11. What is David Held's definition of *globalization*? What are the main criticisms of this definition and of globalization in general?

## FURTHER READING

Eyerman, Ron, and Andrew Jamison. 1998. *Music and Social Movements: Mobilizing Traditions in the Twentieth Century*. New York: Cambridge University Press.

Langman, Lauren. 2005. "From Virtual Public Spheres to Global Justice: A Critical Theory of Internetworked Social Movements." *Sociological Theory* 23, no. 1: 42–74.

McAdam, Doug. 1996. *Comparative Perspectives on Social Movements: Political Opportunities, Mobilizing Structures, and Cultural Framings*. New York: Cambridge University Press.

Project for Excellence in Journalism Report. 2004. "State of the News Media 2004: An Annual Report on American Journalism." Available online at http://www.stateofthenewsmedia.org/chartland.asp?id=323&ct=col&dir=&sort=&col1_box=1 (accessed July 31, 2005).

———. 2005. "State of the News Media 2005: An Annual Report on American Journalism." Table based on unpublished data from BIAfn MediaAccess Pro, available online at http://www.biafn.com. Available online at http://www.stateofthenewsmedia.org/2005/chartland.asp?id=360&ct=col&dir=&sort=&col1_box=1&col2_box=1# (accessed January 16, 2006).

Ritzer, George. 2003. *The Globalization of Nothing*. Thousand Oaks, CA: Pine Forge Press.

Snow, David A., and Robert D. Benford. 1988. "Ideology, Frame Resonance, and Participant Mobilization." *International Social Movement Research* 1: 197–217.

Tilly, Charles. 1978. *From Mobilization to Revolution*. New York: McGraw-Hill.

U.S. Department of Labor. 2005. "Union Members Summary." USDL 05-112. Washington, DC: U.S. Bureau of Labor Statistics, Division of Labor Force Statistics. Available online at http://www.bls.gov/news.release/union2.nr0.htm (accessed July 31, 2005).

Webster, Frank. 2002. *Theories of the Information Society*. 2nd ed. Routledge.

# bibliography

Adam, Barbara, Ulrich Beck, and Joost van Loon, eds. 1992. *Risk Society and Beyond: Critical Issues for Social Theory*. Thousand Oaks, CA: Sage.

Adorno, Theodor, Else Frenkel-Brunswick, Daniel Levinson, and R. Nevitt Sanford. 1950. *The Authoritarian Personality*. New York: Norton.

Ahlburg, Dennis A., and Carol J. De Vita. "New Realities of the American Family." 1992. *Population Bulletin* 47: 1–44.

Alba, Richard, and Victor Nee. 2003. *Remaking the American Mainstream: Assimilation and Contemporary Immigration*. Cambridge, MA: Harvard University Press.

Alberts, Bruce, et al. 2003. "Essential Cell Biology." *Los Angeles Times*, February 28, 20.

Alexander, Charles N., Ellen J. Langer, Ronnie I. Newman, Howard M. Chandler, and J. L. Davies. 1989. "Transcendental Meditation, Mindfulness, and Longevity: An Experimental Study with the Elderly." *Journal of Personality and Social Psychology* 57, no. 6: 950–964.

Alexander, Charles N., John L. Davis, Carol A. Dixon, Michael C. Dillbeck, Steven M. Druker, Roberta M. Oetzel, John M. Muehlman, and David W. Orme-Johnson. 1990. "Growth of Higher Stages of Consciousness: Maharishi's Verdic Psychology of Human Development." In *Higher Stages of Human Development*, edited by Ellen J. Langer and Charles N. Alexander, 286–341. New York: Oxford University Press.

Alexander, Jeffrey C. 2003. *The Meanings of Social Life: A Cultural Sociology*. New York: Oxford University Press.

———. 2006. *The Civil Sphere*. New York: Oxford University Press.

Alexander, Jeffrey C., and Philip Smith. 1993. "The Discourse of American Civil Society: A New Proposal for Cultural Studies." *Theory and Society* 22, no. 2: 151–207.

Alexander, Jeffrey C., Bernhard Giesen, and Jason Mast, eds. 2006. *Social Performance: Symbolic Action, Cultural Pragmatics, and Ritual*. Cambridge, UK: Cambridge University Press.

Alford, Robert R., and Roger Friedland. 1985. *Powers of Theory: Capitalism, the State, and Democracy*. Cambridge, UK: Cambridge University Press.

Allen, R. E, ed. 1990. *The Concise Oxford Dictionary of Current English*. New York: Oxford University Press.

Allport, Gordon W. 1958. *The Nature of Prejudice*. Reading, MA: Addison-Wesley.

American Red Cross. 2002. "September 11, 2001: Unprecedented Events, Unprecedented Response: A Review of the American Red Cross' Response in the Past Year." Available online at http://www.redcross.org/press/disaster/ds_pr/pdfs/arcwhitepaper.pdf (accessed September 3, 2005).

American Society of Plastic Surgeons. 2005. Available online at www.plasticsurgery.org (accessed April 15, 2006).

Amin, Ash, and Stephen Graham. 1999. "Cities of Connection and Disconnection." In *Unsettling Cities: Movement/Settlement*, edited by Doreen Massey, Michael Pryke, and John Allen, 7–38. New York: Routledge/Open University Press.

Andersen, Margaret. 2005. "Socialization and the Formation of Gender Identity." In *Sociology: Understanding a Diverse Society*, edited by Margaret Anderson and Howard Taylor. Belmont, CA: Wadsworth.

Andersen, Nels. 1923. *The Hobo: The Sociology of the Homeless Man*. Chicago: University of Chicago Press.

Anderson, Sarah, John Cavanagh, Scott Klinger, and Liz Stanton. 2005. "Executive Excess 2005: Defense Contractors Get More Bucks for the Bang." Washington, DC/Boston: Institute for Policy Studies (IPS)/United for a Fair Economy (UFE).

Ang, Ien. 1985. *Watching Dallas: Soap Opera and the Melodramatic Imagination*. London: Methuen.

Angel, Ronald. 1985. "The Health of the Mexican Origin Population." In *The Mexican American Experience: An Interdisciplinary Anthology*, edited by Frank Bean, Rodolfo Alvarez, Charles M. Bonjean, Rodolfo de la Garza, and Ricardo Romo, 410–426. Austin: University of Texas Press.

Applebaum, Herbert A. 1981. *Royal Blue: The Culture of Construction Workers*. New York: Holt.

Arendt, Hannah. 1958. *The Human Condition*. Chicago: University of Chicago Press.

Arias, Elizabeth. 2004. "U.S. Life Tables, 2002." *National Vital Statistics Reports* 53, no. 6: 1–39.

Aries, Philip. 1962. *Centuries of Childhood: A Social History of Family Life*. New York: Vintage.

Aristotle. 1998. *Politics*. Indianapolis: Hackett. Originally written in 350 B.C.E.

Armato, Michael, Thurston Domina, Martine Hackett, Erin Jacobs, Hilary Levey, Christine Percheski, Dan Vos, Owen Whooley, Elizabeth Williamson, and Jonathan R. Wynn. 2006. "Discoveries: New and Noteworthy Research— Employer Hypocrisy." *Contexts* 5, no. 2 (Spring): 7–8.

Armstrong, David. 1983. *Political Anatomy of the Body: Medical Knowledge in Britain in the Twentieth Century*. New York: Cambridge University Press.

Arnett, Jeffrey Jensen. 2004. *Emerging Adulthood: The Winding Road from the Late Teens Through the Twenties*. New York: Oxford University Press.

Babbitt, Charles E., and Harold J. Burbach. 1990. "A Comparison of Self-Orientation Among College Students Across the 1960s, 1970s and 1980s." *Youth and Society* 2, no. 4: 472–482.

Bai, Matt. 1999. "Anatomy of a Massacre." *Newsweek* (May 3): 25–31.

Bailey, Beth L. 1988. *From Front Porch to Back Seat: Courtship in Twentieth-Century America*. Baltimore: Johns Hopkins University Press.

Bailey, Eric. 2000. "Defense Probing Brain to Explain Yosemite Killings." *Los Angeles Times*, June 15, 3.

Ballantine, Jeanne H. 1997. *The Sociology of Education: A Systematic Analysis*. Englewood Cliffs, NJ: Prentice-Hall.

Bandura, A. 1978. "Social Learning Theory of Aggression." *Journal of Communication* 28, no. 3: 12–29.

Banfield, Edward C. 1958. *The Moral Basis of a Backward Society*. New York: Free Press.

"Barbie Liberation." 1997. Available online at http://www.sniggle.net/barbie.php.

Barclay, Gordon C., and Cynthia Tavares. 2003. "International Comparisons of Criminal Justice Statistics, 2000." *Home Office Statistical Bulletin*.

Barnard, Chester I. 1968. *The Functions of the Executive*. Cambridge, MA: Harvard University Press.

Barnes, Patricia M., Eve Powell-Griner, Kim McFann, and Richard L. Nahin. 2004. "Complementary and Alternative Medicine Use Among Adults: United States, 2002." Hyattsville, MD: National Center for Health Statistics.

Barrett, David B., George T. Kurian, and Todd M. Johnson. 2001. *World Christian Encyclopedia: A Comparative Survey of Churches and Religions in the Modern World*, Vol. 1. New York: Oxford University Press.

Bartky, Sandra Lee. 1990. *Femininity and Domination: Studies in the Phenomenology of Oppression*. New York: Routledge.

Barton, Len, and Stephen Walker, eds. 1983. *Gender, Class, and Education*. Sussex, UK: Falmer.

Basch, Linda, Nina Glick Schiller, and Cristina Szanton Blanc. 1994. *Nations Unbound: Transnational Projects, Postcolonial Predicaments, and Deterritorialized Nation-States*. Langhorne, PA: Gordon and Breach.

Baudrillard, Jean. 1988. *America*. London: Verso.

———. 1995. *The Gulf War Did Not Take Place*. Bloomington: Indiana University Press.

Bauman, Zygmunt. 1987. *Legislators and Interpreters: On Modernity, Post-Modernity, and Intellectuals*. Ithaca, NY: Cornell University Press.

———. 1989. *Modernity and the Holocaust*. Ithaca, NY: Cornell University Press.

———. 1998. "On the Postmodern Uses of Sex." *Theory, Culture, and Society* 15, nos. 3–4: 19–33.

———. 1990. *Thinking Sociologically*. Cambridge, UK: Blackwell.

Beck, Allen J., and Paige M. Harrison. 2001. "Prisoners in 2000." Washington, DC: U.S. Department of Justice, Office of Justice Programs, Bureau of Justice Statistics.

Beck, Ulrich. 1992. *Risk Society: Towards a New Modernity*. London: Sage.

Becker, Gary. *The Economics of Life*. New York: McGraw Hill.

Becker, Howard Saul. 1963. *Outsiders: Studies in the Sociology of Deviance*. New York: Free Press.

Becker, Lovell E., W. J. H. Butterfield, A. McGehee Harvey, Robert H. Heptinstall, and Lewis Thomas, eds. 1986. *The International Dictionary of Medicine and Biology*, Vol. 2. New York: Wiley.

Beckett, Katherine. 1994. "Setting the Public Agenda: 'Street Crime' and Drug Use in American Politics." *Social Problems* 41, no. 3: 425–447.

Bell, Daniel. 1973. *The Coming of Post-Industrial Society: A Venture in Social Forecasting*. New York: Basic Books.

———. 1976. *The Cultural Contradictions of Capitalism*. New York: Basic.

Bellah, Robert N. 1967. "Civil Religion in America." *Daedalus* 96: 1–21.

———. 1970. "Civil Religion in America." In *Beyond Belief: Essays on Religion in a Post-Traditional World*, edited by Harper and Row, 168–189. New York: Harper and Row.

Bellah, Robert N., Richard Madsen, William M. Sullivan, Ann Swidler, and Steven M. Tipton, eds. 1985. *Habits of the Heart: Individualism and Commitment in American Life*. Berkeley: University of California Press.

Bendix, Reinhard. 1977. *Nation-Building and Citizenship: Studies of Our Changing Social Order*. New York: Wiley.

Bennett, William J. 1997. "School Reform: What Remains to Be Done." *Wall Street Journal*, September 2, 18.

Bennett de Marrais, Kathleen, and Margaret D. LeCompte. 1995. *The Way Schools Work: A Sociological Analysis of Education*. New York: Longman.

Berg, Christian D. 2000. "BASD Superintendent Links Academic, Societal Decline." *Morning Call*, May 18, 3.

Berger, Leslie. 2000. "A Racial Gap in Infant Deaths, and a Search for Reasons." *New York Times*, June 25, 13.

Berger, Peter L. 1963. *Invitation to Sociology: A Humanistic*

*Perspective.* Garden City, NY: Doubleday. Reprinted in 1966.

———. 1967. *The Sacred Canopy: Elements of a Sociological Theory of Religion.* Garden City, NY: Doubleday.

Berger, Peter L., and Thomas Luckmann. 1967. *The Social Construction of Reality: A Treatise in the Sociology of Knowledge.* New York: Irvington.

Bernstein, Basil. 1971. "On the Classification and Framing of Educational Knowledge." In *Knowledge and Control: New Directions for the Sociology of Education,* edited by Michael F. D. Young, 47–69. London: Collier-Macmillan.

Bertrand, Marianne, and Sendhil Mullainathan. 2004. "Are Emily and Greg More Employable Than Lakisha and Jamal? A Field Experiment on Labor Market Discrimination." *American Economic Review* 94, no. 4: 991–1013.

Best, Joel. 1991. "'Road Warriors' on 'Hair-Trigger Highways': Cultural Resources and the Media's Construction of the 1987 Freeway Shooting Problem." *Sociological Inquiry* 61: 327–345.

———. 2002. "Monster Hype: How a Few Isolated Tragedies—and Their Supposed Causes—Were Turned into a National 'Epidemic.'" *Education Next* 2: 51–55.

"Beyond the Nanohype." 2003. *Economist* (March 13): 28–29.

Bianchi, Suzanne M., Melissa A. Milkie, Liana C. Sayer, and John P. Robinson. 2000. "Is Anyone Doing the Housework? Trends in the Gender Division of Household Labor." *Social Forces* 79, no. 1: 191–228.

Bielby, William T., and Denise D. Bielby. 1988. "She Works Hard for the Money: Household Responsibilities and the Allocation of Work Effort." *American Journal of Sociology* 93, no. 5: 1031–1059.

Biggart, Nicole Woolsey. 1988. *Charismatic Capitalism: Direct Selling Organizations in America.* Chicago: University of Chicago Press.

BIGresearch. 2004. Simultaneous Media Usage Study. Available online at http://www.mediacenter.org/content/3673.cfm.

Blackely, Edward James, and Mary Gail Snyder. 1997. *Fortress America: Gated Communities in the United States.* Cambridge, MA: Lincoln Institute of Land Policy.

Blank, Rolf K., and Douglas A. Archbald. 1992. "Magnet Schools and Issues of Education Quality." *Clearing House* 66, no. 2: 81–86.

Blau, Peter M., and Otis Dudley Duncan. 1967. *The American Occupational Structure.* New York: Wiley.

Blaxter, Mildred, and Elizabeth Peterson. 1982. *Mothers and Daughters: A Three-Generational Study of Health Attitudes and Behavior.* London: Heinemann.

Bluestone, Barry, and Bennett Harrison. 1982. *Deindustrialization of America: Plant Closing, Community Abandonment, and the Dismantling of Basic Industry.* New York: Basic Books.

Bly, Robert. 1991. *Iron John: A Book About Men.* Reading, MA: Addison-Wesley.

Bollens, Scott. A. 1998. "Urban Policy in Ethnically Polarized Societies." *International Political Science Review* 19, no. 2: 187–215.

———. 2000. *On Narrow Ground: Urban Policy and Ethnic Conflict in Jerusalem and Belfast.* Albany: State University of New York Press.

Bonacich, Edna, and John Modell. 1980. *The Economic Basis of Ethnic Solidarity: Small Business in the Japanese American Community.* Berkeley: University of California Press.

Bonczar, Thomas P., and Tracy L. Snell. 2004. "Capital Punishment, 2003." U.S. Department of Justice, Office of Justice Programs.

Bordo, Susan. 1993. *Unbearable Weight: Feminism, Western Culture, and the Body.* Berkeley: University of California Press.

Bottomore, Tom B. 1985. *Theories of Modern Capitalism.* London: Allen and Unwin.

Bouchard, Thomas J. 1994. *Science* 264, no. 5166: 1700–1701.

Bourdieu, Pierre. 1977. "Cultural Reproduction and Social Reproduction." In *Power and Ideology in Education,* edited by A. H. Halsey and Jerome Karabel, 487–511. New York: Oxford University Press.

———. 1984. *Distinction: A Social Critique of the Judgment of Taste.* Cambridge, MA: Harvard University Press.

Bourdieu, Pierre, and Jean-Claude Passeron. 1977. *Reproduction in Education, Society, and Culture.* London: Sage.

Bowles, Samuel, and Herbert Gintis. 1976. *Schooling in Capitalist America: Educational Reform and the Contradictions of Economic Life.* New York: Basic Books.

Bragg, Rick. 2002. "Enron's Collapse: Workers Feel Pain of Layoffs and Added Sting of Betrayal." *New York Times,* January 20, 1.

Braverman, Henry. 1974. *Labor and Monopoly Capital: The Degradation of Work in the Twentieth Century.* New York: Monthly Review Press.

"The Bridget Jones Economy: Singles and the City." 2001. *Economist* 361: 32–34.

Brint, Steven. 1998. *Schools and Societies.* Thousand Oaks, CA: Pine Forge.

Bronfenbrenner, Urie. 1970. *Two Worlds of Childhood: U.S. and U.S.S.R.* New York: Russell Sage Foundation.

Bronson, Po. 1999. "Generation Equity," *Wired* 7, no. 7 (July): 113–123, 168–180.

Brooke, James. 1998. "Homophobia Often Found in Schools, Data Show." *New York Times,* October 14, 19.

Brooks, Clem, and Jeff Manza. 1997. "The Social and Ideological Bases of Middle-Class Political Realignment in the United States, 1972–1992." *American Sociological Review* 62, no. 2: 191–208.

Brooks, Peter. 2007. "The Morality Line." *New York Times,* April 19, A27.

Brough-Williams, Ian. 1996. "War Without End? The Bloody Bosnia Season on Channel Four." In *Bosnia by Television,* edited by Richard Paterson, James Gow, and Alison Preston, 19–33. London: British Film Institute.

Brown, David K. 1995. *Degrees of Control: A Sociology of Educational Expansion and Occupational Credentialism.* New York: Teachers College Press.

Brown, Helen Gurley. 1962. *Sex and the Single Girl.* New York: Bernard Geis Associates.

Brown, Mary Ellen. 1994. *Soap Opera and Women's Talk: The Pleasure of Resistance.* Thousand Oaks, CA: Sage.

Brown, Michael S., and Katherine A. Lyon. 1992. "Holes in the Ozone Layer: A Global Environmental Controversy." In *Controversy: Politics of Technical Decisions*, edited by Dorothy Nelkin, 59–79. Newbury Park, CA: Sage.

Brown, Phil, and Edwin J. Mikkelski. 1990. *No Safe Place: Toxic Waste, Leukemia, and Community Action.* Berkeley: University of California Press.

Bruhn, John G., and Stewart Wolf. 1979. *The Roseto Story: An Anatomy of Health.* Norman: University of Oklahoma Press.

Buhler, Charlotte. 1935. "The Curve of Life as Studied in Biographies." *Journal of Applied Psychology* 19: 405–409.

Bullock, Heather E. "Attributes for Poverty: A Comparison of Middle Class and Welfare Recipients' Attitudes." *Journal of Applied Social Psychology* 29, no. 10: 2059–2082.

Bumiller, Elisabeth. 2004. "Bush Backs Ban in Constitution on Gay Marriage." *New York Times*, February 25, 1.

Bunyavanich, Supinda, Christopher P. Landrigan, Anthony J. McMichael, and Paul R. Epstein. 2003. "The Impact of Climate Change on Child Health." *Ambulatory Pediatrics* 3: 44–52.

Burawoy, Michael. 1979. *Manufacturing Consent: Changes in the Labor Process Under Monopoly Capitalism.* Chicago: University of Chicago Press.

Burns, Arthur F. 1951. "Looking Forward: Thirty-First Annual Report." New York: National Bureau of Economic Research.

Burrell, Gibson. 1984. "Sex and Organizational Analysis." *Organization Studies* 5, no. 2: 97–118.

Burris, Beverly H. 1983. *No Room at the Top: Underemployment and Alienation in the Corporation.* New York: Praeger, 1983.

Burrows, Robert J. L. 1986. "Americans Get Religion in the New Age." *Christianity Today* 30, no. 8: 17–23.

Butler, Judith. 1990. *Gender Trouble: Feminism and the Subversion of Identity.* New York: Routledge.

Butsch, R. 1995. "Ralph, Fred, Archie, and Homer: Why Television Keeps Recreating the White Male Working-Class Buffoon." In *Gender, Race, and Class in Media*, edited by G. Dines and J. M. Hamez, 575–585. Thousand Oaks, CA: Sage.

CACI Ltd. Acorn Map. 2006. Available online at http://www.caci.co.uk/acorn/acornmap.asp (accessed April 15, 2006).

Calhoun, Craig, Paul Price, and Ashley Timmer, eds. 1992. *Habermas and the Public Sphere.* Cambridge: Massachusetts Institute of Technology Press.

——. 2002. *Understanding September 11.* New York: New Press.

Campbell, Colin. 2007. *The Easternization of the West.* Boulder, CO: Paradigm Publishers.

Campbell, Duncan. 2002. "Three Strikes and You're Out: Human Rights, U.S. Style." *Guardian*, January 26, 3.

"Canada's Ethnocultural Portrait: The Changing Mosaic." 2003. *2001 Canada Census: Analysis Series.*

Caradec, V. 1996. "Les Formes de la Vie Comjugale des 'Jeunes' Couple 'Âgés.'" *Population* 51: 897–928.

Carey, James W. 1986. "Why and How? The Dark Continent of American Journalism." In *Reading the News*, edited by Robert Karl Manoff and Michael Schudson. New York: Pantheon.

Carroll, Ginny. 1990. "Who Foots the Bill?" *Newsweek*: 81–85.

Cassanova, Jose. 1996. "Global Catholicism and the Politics of Civil Society." *Sociological Inquiry* 66, no. 3: 356–373.

Castells, Manuel. 1996. *The Information Age, Vol. 1: The Rise of the Network Society.* Malden, MA: Blackwell.

——. 1997. *The Information Age, Vol. 2.* Malden, MA: Blackwell.

——. 1998. *The Information Age, Vol. 3: End of Millennium.* Malden, MA: Blackwell.

——. 2000. "Materials for an Exploratory Theory of the Network Society." *British Journal of Sociology* 51, no. 3: 5–24.

——. 2002. "Materials for an Exploratory Theory of the Network Society." In Tim Jordan and Steve Pile, eds., *Social Change*, pp. 123–128. Oxford, UK: Blackwell.

Center for American Women and Politics. National Information Bank on Women in Public Office, Eagleton Institute of Politics, Rutgers University. Available online at http://www.cawp.rutgers.edu/Facts/Officeholders/cong.pdf#page=2. Accessed June 26, 2006.

Center for Information and Research on Civic Learning and Engagement. School of Public Policy, University of Maryland. Available online at http://www.civicyouth.org/research/areas/polpartic.htm.

Centers for Medicare and Medicaid Services. 2002. Office of the Actuary, National Health Statistics Group, National Health Expenditures. Available online at cms.hhs.gov/statistics/nhe.

Central Intelligence Agency. 2005. *The World Factbook.* Washington, DC: U.S. Government Printing Office.

Chambliss, William J. 1975. "Toward a Political Economy of Crime." *Theory and Society* 2, no. 3: 149–170.

——. 1994. "Policing the Ghetto Underclass: The Politics of Law and Law Enforcement." *Social Problems* 41, no. 3: 177–194.

Chaves, Mark. 2004. *Congregations in America.* Cambridge, MA: Harvard University Press.

Chen, David W. 2002. "With 9/11 Flag, a Mystery Unfurls." *New York Times*, September 4, B3.

Cherlin, Andrew J. 1981. *Marriage, Divorce, Remarriage.* Cambridge, MA: Harvard University Press.

Chodorow, Nancy. 1978. *The Reproduction of Mothering: Psychoanalysis and the Sociology of Gender.* Berkeley: University of California Press.

Chua-Eoan, Howard. 1998. "That's Not a Scarecrow: A Brutal Assault in Wyoming and a Rise in Gay Bashing Fuel the Debate over Sexual Orientation" *Time* (October 19): 72.

Clark, Burton R. 1998. *Creating Entrepreneurial Universities: Organizational Pathways of Transformation.* New York: Pergamon.

Clarke, Lee. 1992. "The Wreck of the Exxon *Valdez.*" In *Controversy: Politics of Technical Decisions,* edited by Dorothy Nelkin, 80–79. Newbury Park, CA: Sage.

Cleland, Nancy. 2000. "Heartache on Aisle 3: Sweatshops for Janitors." *Los Angeles Times,* July 2, 1.

Cloward, Richard A., and Lloyd E. Ohlin. 1960. *Delinquency and Opportunity: A Theory of Delinquent Gangs.* New York: Free Press.

Cockburn, Cynthia. 1983. *Brothers: Male Dominance and Technological Change.* London: Pluto.

Coen, Rachel. 2000. "For Press, Magenta Hair and Nose Rings Defined Protests." *Extra!* (July–August). Available online at http://www.fair.org/extra/0007/imf-magenta.html.

Cohen, Albert Kircidel. 1955. *Delinquent Boys: The Culture of the Gang.* Glencoe, IL: Free Press.

Cohen, Stanley. 1972. *Folk Devils and Moral Panics: The Creation of the Mods and Rockers.* London: MacGibbon and Kee.

Coleman, James S., and Thomas B. Hoffer. 1987. *Public and Private Schools: The Impact of Communities.* New York: Basic Books.

Coleman, James S., and Thomas J. Fararo. 1992. *Rational Choice Theory: Advocacy and Critique.* Newbury Park, CA: Sage.

Coleman, James S., Ernest Q. Campbell, Carol J. Hobson, James McPartland, Alexander M. Mood, Frederic D. Weinfeld, and Robert L. York. 1966. "Equality of Educational Opportunity." Washington, DC: U.S. Department of Health, Education, and Welfare, Office of Education.

Coleman, James S., Sara D. Kelly, and John A. Moore. 1975. "Trends in School Segregation, 1968–1973." Washington, DC: Urban Institute.

College Board Office of Academic Initiatives. 2006. "National Task Force on Minority High Achievement Report."

Collins, Harry M. 1985. *Changing Order: Replication and Induction in Scientific Practice.* Beverly Hills, CA: Sage.

Collins, Patricia Hill. 1990. *Black Feminist Thought: Knowledge, Consciousness, and the Politics of Empowerment.* Boston: Unwin Hyman.

Collins, Randall. 1971. "Functional and Conflict Theories of Educational Stratification." *American Sociological Review* 36, no. 6: 1002–1019.

——. 1979. *The Credential Society.* New York: Wiley.

Comfort, Alex, ed. 1972. *The Joy of Sex: A Cordon Bleu Guide to Lovemaking.* New York: Simon and Schuster.

Connell, Robert W. 1995. *Masculinities.* Berkeley: University of California Press.

——. 2000. "Sociology and World Market Sociology." *Contemporary Sociology* 29, no. 2: 291–296.

Coontz, Stephanie. 1992. *The Way We Never Were: American Families and the Nostalgia Trap.* New York: Basic Books.

Corea, Gena, Renate Duelli Klein, Jalna Hammer, Helen B. Holmes, Madhu Kishwar, Janice Raymond, Robyn Rowland, and Roberta Steinbacher. 1985. *Man-Made Women: How New Reproductive Technologies Affect Women.* London: Hutchinson.

Corsaro, W. A., and T. A. Rizzo. 1988. "*Discussione* and Friendship: Socialization Processes in the Peer Culture of Italian Nursery School Children." *American Sociological Review* 53: 879–894.

Cottle, Simon. 1997. "Society as Text: Documents, Artifacts, and Social Practices." In *The Student's Companion to Sociology,* edited by Jon Gubbay, Chris Middleton, and Chet Ballard. Malden, MA: Blackwell.

Cowan, Paul. 1982. *Orphan in History: Retrieving a Jewish Legacy.* Garden City, NY: Doubleday.

Cozzarelli, C., A. V. Wilkinson, and M. J. Tagler. 2001. "Attitudes Toward the Poor and Attributions of Poverty." *Journal of Social Issues* 57, no. 2: 207–227.

Cressey, Paul G. 1932. *The Taxi-Dance Hall: A Sociological Study in Commercialized Recreation and City Life.* Chicago: University of Chicago Press.

Crossette, Barbara. 1998. "Mutilation Seen as Risk for the Girls of Immigrants." *New York Times,* March 23, 3.

Crotty, William, ed. 2005. *A Defining Moment: The Presidential Election of 2004.* Amonk, NY: M.E. Sharpe.

Curran, Daniel J., and Claire M. Renzetti. 1996. *Social Problems: Society in Crisis.* Boston: Allyn and Bacon.

Currie, Dawn H. 1997. "Decoding Femininity: Advertisements and Their Teenage Readers." *Gender and Society* 11: 453–457.

Currie, Elliott. 1985. *Confronting Crime: An American Challenge.* New York: Pantheon.

Dahrendorf, Ralf. 1985. *Law and Order.* Boulder, CO: Westview.

Daley, Suzanne. 2000. "French Couples Take Plunge That Falls Short of Marriage." *New York Times,* April 18, 1.

D'Antonio, William V., James D. Davidson, Dean R. Hoge, and Katherine Meyer. 2001. *American Catholics: Gender, Generation, and Commitment.* Walnut Creek, CA: AltaMira.

DasGupta, Sayantani, and Shamita DasGupta. 1996. "Women in Exile: Gender Relations in the Asian Indian Community in the U.S." In *Contours of the Heart: South Asians Map North America,* edited by Sunaina Maira and Rajini Srikanth, 381–400. New York: Asian American Writers Workshop.

Davie, Grace. 2000. *Religion in Modern Europe: A Memory Mutates.* Oxford, UK: Oxford University Press.

Davis, James A., Tom W. Smith, and Peter V. Marsden. 2005. "General Social Surveys, 1972–2004." Berkeley, CA: Computer-Assisted Survey Methods Program.

Davis, Kathy. 1995. *Reshaping the Female Body: The Dilemma of Cosmetic Surgery.* New York: Routledge.

Davis, Kingsley. 2001. "Extreme Isolation." In *Down to Earth Sociology,* edited by James M. Henslin, 129–137. New York: Free Press.

Davis, Kingsley, and Wilbert E. Moore. 1945. "Some Principles of Stratification." *American Sociological Review* 10, no. 2: 242–249.

de Beauvoir, Simone. 1952. *The Second Sex.* New York: Knopf. Reprinted in 1953.

Debord, Guy. 1994. *The Society of the Spectacle.* New York: Zone.

De Certeau, Michel. 1984. *The Practice of Everyday Life.* Berkeley: University of California Press.

de Crevecoeur, Hector St. John. 1783. *Letters from an American Farmer.* New York: Dutton. Reprinted in 1912.

Deem, Rosemary, ed. 1980. *Schooling for Women's Work.* Boston: Routledge and Kegan Paul.

Dellinger, Kirsten, and Christine L. Williams. 1997. "Makeup at Work: Negotiating Appearance Rules in the Workplace." *Gender and Society* 11, no. 2: 151–177.

D'Emilio, John, and Estelle B. Freedman. 1988. *Intimate Matters: A History of Sexuality in America.* New York: Harper and Row.

DeNavas-Walt, Carmen, Bernadette D. Proctor, and Cheryl Hill Lee. 2005. "Income, Poverty, and Health Insurance Coverage in the United States: 2004." Washington, DC: U.S. Department of Commerce, U.S. Census Bureau.

Descartes, René. 1641. *Meditations and Other Metaphysical Writings.* New York: Penguin. Reprinted in 1999.

de Tocqueville, Alexis. 1840. *Democracy in America.* New York: New American Library. Reprinted in 1956.

Diani, Mario. 1992. "The Concept of Social Movement." *Sociological Review* 40: 1–25.

Dillon, David. 1994. "Fortress America: More and More of Us Are Living Behind Locked Gates." *Planning* 60, no. 6: 8–12.

Dimaggio, Paul J., and Walter W. Powell. "The Iron Cage Revisited: Institutional Isomorphism and Collective Rationality." *American Sociological Review* 48, no. 2: 147–160.

Domhoff, William G. 1967. *Who Rules America?* Englewood Cliffs, NJ: Prentice-Hall.

———. 1998. *Who Rules America? Power and Politics in the Year 2000.* Mountain View, CA: Mayfield.

Donaton, Scott. 1999. "CBS, TV's New Bauble Seller; Boasts When It Should Blush." *Advertising Age* 70, no. 27: 32.

Douglas, Jack D., and Paul K. Rasmussen. 1977. *Nude Beach.* Beverly Hills, CA: Sage.

Doyal, Lesley. 1995. *What Makes Women Sick: Gender and the Political Economy of Health.* New Brunswick, NJ: Rutgers University Press.

Doyle, James A. 1983. *The Male Experience.* Dubuque, IA: Brown.

D'Silva, Beverley. 1996. "Women: A Case of Mistaken Identity—Biologically, They Are Male; in Every Other Way, They Are Female." *Guardian,* August 29, 5.

D'Souza, Dinesh. 1991. "Travels with Rigoberta: Multiculturalism at Stanford." In *Illiberal Education: The Politics of Race and Sex on Campus,* edited by Dinesh D'Souza, 59–93. New York: Free Press.

DuBois, William Edward Burghardt. 1896. *The Suppression of the Slave-Trade to the United States of America.* New York: Longmans Green.

———. 1899. *The Philadelphia Negro: A Social Study—Published for the University.* Philadelphia: University of Pennsylvania Press.

Duncan, Margaret Carlisle, and Michael A. Messner. 2000. "Gender in Televised Sport: 1989, 1993, 1999." Review of Reviewed Item. *Amateur Athletic Foundation of Los Angeles.* Available online at http://www.aafla.org/9arr/ResearchReports/tv2000.pdf.

Durkheim, Emile. 1893. *The Division of Labor in Society.* Glencoe, IL: Free Press. Reprinted in 1964.

———. 1895. *The Rules of Sociological Method.* Glencoe, IL: Free Press. Reprinted in 1938.

———. 1897. *Suicide, a Study in Sociology.* Glencoe, IL: Free Press. Reprinted in 1951.

———. 1915. *The Elementary Forms of the Religious Life.* Glencoe, IL: Free Press. Reprinted in 1965.

———. 1925. *Moral Education: A Study in the Theory and Application of the Sociology of Education.* Glencoe, IL: Free Press. Reprinted in 1961.

———. 1938. *The Evolution of Educational Thought: Lectures on the Formation and Development of Secondary Education in France.* Boston: Routledge and Kegan Paul. Reprinted in 1977.

———. 1956. *Education and Sociology.* Glencoe, IL: Free Press.

Easton, David. 1971. *The Political System: An Inquiry into the State of Political Science.* New York: Knopf.

Edles, Laura. 2002. *Cultural Sociology in Practice.* Malden, MA: Blackwell.

Edgecliffe-Johnson, Andrew. 1999. "Girl Power, Spending Power." *Financial Times,* August 26, 16.

Ehrenreich, Barbara, and Deirdre English. 1978. *For Her Own Good: 150 Years of the Experts' Advice to Women.* Garden City, NY: Anchor.

Ehrenreich, Barbara, and John Ehrenreich. 1970. *The American Health Empire: Power, Profits, and Politics.* New York: Random House.

Eisenberg, D. M., R. B. Davis, S. L Ettner, S. Appel, S. Wilkey, M. Van Rompay, and R. C. Kessler. 1998. "Trends in Alternative Medicine Use in the United States, 1990–

1997: Results of a Follow-Up National Survey." *Journal of the American Medical Association* 280, no. 18: 1569–1575.

Eitzen, Stanley D., and Maxine Baca Zinn. 1991. "Introduction." In *Conflict and Order: Understanding Society,* edited by Stanley D. Eitzen and Maxine Baca Zinn. Boston: Allyn and Bacon.

Elias, Norbert. 1932. *The Civilizing Process: The History of Manners and State Formation.* Cambridge, UK: Blackwell. Reprinted in 1994.

Ellul, Jacques. 1954. *Technological Society.* New York: Vintage. Reprinted in 1964.

Ellway, Peter. 1966. "Shopping for Faith, or Dropping Your Faith?" Available online at www.csa.com/discovery guides/religion/overview.php (accessed December 28, 2006).

Emmison, Michael, and Mark Western. 1990. "Social Class and Social Identity: A Comment on Marshall et al." *Sociology* 24, no. 2: 241–253.

Engelhardt, Hugo Tristram, and Arthur L. Caplan, eds. 1987. *Scientific Controversies: Case Studies in the Resolution and Closure of Disputes in Science and Technology.* New York: Cambridge University Press.

England, Paula. 1992. *Comparable Worth: Theories and Evidence.* New York: de Gruyter.

"Enron's Collapse: Statements by Senator and Ex-S.E.C. Head at Senate Hearing on Enron." 2002. *New York Times,* January 25, C9.

"Enron's Many Strands: Excerpts from the Senate Committee Hearing on the Collapse of Enron." 2002. *New York Times,* February 13, C8.

Erikson, Erik. 1950. *Childhood and Society.* New York: Norton.

———. 1968. *Identity: Youth and Crisis.* New York: Norton.

Erikson, Kai. 1966. *Wayward Puritans: A Study in the Sociology of Deviance.* New York: Wiley.

Erikson, R., and J. H. Goldthorpe. 1994. *The Constant Flux: A Study of Class Mobility in Industrial Societies.* Oxford, UK: Clarendon Press.

Ernst, E., and A. White. 2000. "The BBC Survey of Complementary Medicine Use in the UK." *Complementary Therapies in Medicine* 8, no. 1: 32–36.

European Values Study Group and World Values Survey Association. 2005. European and World Values Surveys Integrated Data File, 1999–2002, Release, 2nd ICPSR Version. Inter-university Consortium for Political and Social Research.

Evans, Ellis D., Edith Rutberg, Carmela Sather, and Charli Turner. 1991. "Content Analysis of Contemporary Teen Magazines for Adolescent Females." *Youth and Society* 23, no. 1: 99–120.

Evans-Pritchard, Edward. 1937. *Witchcraft, Oracles, and Magic Among the Azande.* Oxford, UK: Clarendon.

Fagot, Beverly I., Richard Hagan, Mary Driver Leinbach, and Sandra Kronsberg. 1985. "Differential Reactions to As-

sertive and Communicative Acts of Toddler Boys and Girls." *Child Development* 56, no. 6: 1499–505.

Fainstein, Susan, Ian Gordon, and Michael Harloe. 1992. *Divided Cities: New York and London in the Contemporary World.* Cambridge, UK: Blackwell.

Fairchild, Henry Pratt. 1913. *Immigration: A World Movement and Its American Significance.* New York: Macmillan.

Faludi, Susan. 1992. *Backlash: The Undeclared War Against American Women.* New York: Anchor.

Farrell, David M. 1996. "Campaign Strategies and Tactics." In *Comparing Democracies: Elections and Voting in Global Perspective,* edited by Richard G. Niemi, Lawrence LeDuc, and Pippa Norris, 60–183. Thousand Oaks, CA: Sage.

Feagin, Joe R. 1978. *Racial and Ethnic Relations.* Englewood Cliffs, NJ: Prentice-Hall.

Feher, Shoshanah. 1997. "Managing Strain, Contradictions, and Fluidity: Messianic Judaism and the Negotiation of a Religio-Ethnic Identity." In *Contemporary American Religion: An Ethnographic Reader,* edited by Nancy L. Eiesland and Penny Edgell Becker, 25–49. London: AltaMira.

Fennel, Mary L., and Jeffrey C. Alexander. 1993. "Perspectives on Organizational Change in the U.S. Medical Care Sector." *Annual Review of Sociology* 19, no. 1: 89–112.

Fenton, John Y. 1988. *Transplanting Religious Traditions: Asian Indians in America.* New York: Praeger.

Ferree, Myra Marx. 2003. "Resonance and Radicalism: Feminist Framing in the Abortion Debates of the United States and Germany." *American Journal of Sociology* 109: 304–344.

Ferrell, Jeff, and Mark S. Hamm. 1998. *Ethnography at the Edge: Crime, Deviance, and Field Research.* Boston: Northeastern University Press.

Feyerabend, Paul. 1975. *Against Method: Outline of an Anarchistic Theory of Knowledge.* Atlantic Highlands, NJ: Humanities Press.

Fields, Jason, and Lynne M. Casper. 2001. "America's Families and Living Arrangements: Population Characteristics." In *Current Population Reports,* 20–537. Washington, DC: U.S. Department of Commerce, U.S. Census Bureau.

Fine, Gary Alan. 1987. *With the Boys: Little League Baseball and Preadolescent Culture.* Chicago: University of Chicago Press.

———. 1997. "Naturework and the Taming of the Wild: The Problem of 'Overpick' in the Culture of Mushroomers." *Social Problems* 44, no. 1: 68–88.

Finke, Roger, and Rodney Stark. 1992. *The Churching of America, 1776–1990: Winners and Losers in Our Religious Economy.* New Brunswick, NJ: Rutgers University Press.

Fishman, Mark. 1980. *Manufacturing the News.* Austin: University of Texas Press.

Fiske, John. 1989. *Understanding Popular Culture.* Boston: Unwin Hyman.

Flax, Jane. 1990. *Thinking Fragments: Psychoanalysis, Femi-*

*nism, and Postmodernism in the Contemporary West.* Berkeley: University of California Press.

Foner, Nancy. 1997. "What's New About Transnationalism? New York Today and at the Turn of the Century." *Diaspora* 6, no. 3: 355–375.

Form, William H. 1987. "On the Degradation of Skills." *Annual Review of Sociology* 13: 29–47.

Foucault, Michel. 1973. *The Birth of the Clinic: An Archaeology of Medical Perception.* New York: Pantheon.

———. 1977. *Discipline and Punish: The Birth of the Prison.* New York: Pantheon.

———. 1978. "Introduction." In *The History of Sexuality,* by Michel Foucault. New York: Pantheon.

———. 1979. *The History of Sexuality.* Vol. 1. London: Allen Lane.

———. 1985. "The Use of Pleasure." In *The History of Sexuality,* by Michel Foucault. New York: Pantheon.

———. 2005a. "Care of the Self." In Michel Foucault, *The History of Sexuality,* 2nd ed. New York: Pantheon.

———. 2005b. *The Hermeneutics of the Subject: Lectures at the College de France, 1981–1982.* New York: Palgrave Macmillan.

Fox, Mary Frank. 1995. "Women and Scientific Careers." In *Handbook of Science and Technology Studies,* edited by Gerald E. Markle, Sheila Jasnoff, James C. Petersen, and Trevor Pinch, 205–223. Thousand Oaks, CA: Sage.

Frank, Lawrence, and Mary Frank. 1954. *How to Be a Woman.* New York: Bobbs-Merrill.

Fraser, Nancy. 1994. "Foucault on Modern Power." In *Social Control: Aspects of Non-State Justice,* 3–20. Aldershot, UK: Dartmouth.

Freedle, Roy O. 2003. "Correcting the SAT's Ethnic and Social-Class Bias: A Method for Reestimating SAT Scores." *Harvard Educational Review* 73: 1–43.

A Free Loveyer. 1859. *Directory to the Seraglios in New York, Philadelphia, Boston and All the Principal Cities in the Union.* New York: Printed and published for the trade. Beinecke Rare Book and Manuscript Library, Yale University.

Freidson, Eliot. 1970. *Profession of Medicine: A Study of the Sociology of Applied Knowledge.* New York: Harper and Row.

Freud, Sigmund. 1900. *The Interpretation of Dreams.* New York: Macmillan. Reprinted in 1913.

———. 1930. *Three Contributions to the Theory of Sex.* New York: Nervous and Mental Disease Publishing.

Freudenburg, Nicholas. 1984. *Not in Our Backyards! Community Action for Health and the Environment.* New York: Monthly Review Press.

Freund, Peter E. S., and Meredith B. McGuire. 1999. *Health, Illness, and the Social Body: A Critical Sociology.* Upper Saddle River, NJ: Prentice-Hall.

Frey, William H., Bill Abresch, and Jonathan Yeasting, eds. 2001. *America by the Numbers: A Field Guide to the U.S. Population.* New York: New Press.

———. 2004. *The New Great Migration: Black Americans' Return to the South, 1965–2000.* Washington, DC: Brookings Institution.

Friedan, Betty. 1963. *The Feminine Mystique.* New York: Norton.

Friedland, Roger, and Richard Hecht. 1996. *To Rule in Jerusalem.* Cambridge, UK: Cambridge University Press.

Friedman, Sara Ann. 1986. *Celebrating the Wild Mushroom: A Passionate Quest.* New York: Dodd, Mead.

Friedrich, Carl J., and Charles Blitzer. 1957. *The Age of Power.* Ithaca, NY: Cornell University Press.

Fronczek, Peter, and Patricia Johnson. 2003. "Occupations 2000: Census 2000 Brief." Washington, DC: U.S. Department of Commerce, U.S. Census Bureau.

Fuller, Steve. 1997. *Science.* Minneapolis: University of Minnesota Press.

Furstenberg Jr., Frank F., Sheela Kennedy, Vonnie C. McLoyd, Rubén G. Rumbaut, and Richard A Settersten, Jr. 2004. "Growing Up Is Harder to Do." *Contexts:* 33–41.

Fussell, Paul. 1975. *The Great War and Modern Memory.* New York: Oxford University Press.

Gallup, George, Jr. 1977. "U.S. in Early Stage of Religious Revival." *Journal of Current Social Issues* 14: 50–55.

———. 1978. "Religion in America 1977–1978—Gallup Opinion Index, Report No. 145." Princeton, NJ: American Institute of Public Opinion.

———. 1997. *Emerging Trends.* Princeton, NJ: Princeton Religion Research Center.

———. 1999. "Hopes and Fears Happiness Survey." University of Connecticut Roper Center.

Gamson, Joshua. 1998. *Freaks Talk Back: Tabloid Talk Shows and Sexual Nonconformity.* Chicago: University of Chicago Press.

Gans, Herbert. 1962. "Urbanism and Suburbanism as Ways of Life: A Re-Evaluation of Definitions." In *Human Behavior and Social Processes,* edited by Arnold Marshall Rose, 625–648. Boston: Houghton Mifflin.

———. 1967. *The Levittowners.* New York: Pantheon.

———. 1988. *Middle American Individualism: The Future of Liberal Democracy.* New York: Free Press.

Garbarino, James. 1999. "Some Kids Are Orchids." *Time* (December 20): 51.

Garber, Marjorie B. 1992. *Vested Interests: Cross-Dressing and Cultural Anxiety.* New York: Routledge.

Gardner, Carol Brooks. 1994. "Out of Place: Gender, Public Places, and Situational Disadvantage." In *Nowhere: Space, Time, and Modernity,* edited by Roger Friedland and Deirdre Boden, 335–352. Berkeley: University of California Press.

Garfinkel, Harold. 1967. *Studies in Ethnomethodology.* Englewood Cliffs, NJ: Prentice-Hall.

Garland, David. 2001. *Culture of Control: Crime and Social Order in Contemporary Society.* Chicago: University of Chicago Press.

Garreau, Joel. 1991. *Edge City: Life in the New Frontier*. New York: Doubleday.

Gates, Henry Louis. 2004. "Breaking the Silence." *New York Times*, August 1.

Geertz, Clifford. 1973. "Religion as a Cultural System." In *The Interpretation of Cultures*, edited by Clifford Geertz, 88–125. New York: Basic Books. Originally written in 1966.

———. 1983. "'From the Native's Point of View': On the Nature of Anthropological Understanding." In *Local Knowledge: Further Essays in Interpretive Anthropology*, edited by Clifford Geertz, 55–70. New York: Basic Books.

George, L. K. 1993. "Sociological Perspectives on Life Transitions." *Annual Review of Sociology* 19: 353–373.

Gerbner, George, and Larry Gross. 1976. "Living with Television: The Violence Profile." *Journal for Communication* 26, no. 2: 172–199.

Gerbner, George, Larry Gross, Nancy Signorielli, and Michael Morgan. 1980. "Growing Older: Perceptions and Representations; Aging with Television: Images on Television Drama and Conceptions of Social Reality." *Journal for Communication* 30, no. 1: 37–48.

Gergen, Kenneth J. 1991. *The Saturated Self: Dilemmas of Identity in Contemporary Life*. New York: Basic Books.

Gewertz, Deborah. 1981. "A Historical Reconsideration of Female Dominance Among the Chambri of Papua New Guinea." *American Ethnologist* 8, no. 1: 94–106.

Gibson, Campbell J., and Emily Lennon. 1999. "Historical Census Statistics on the Foreign-Born Population of the United States: 1850–1990." Population Division Working Paper No. 29. Washington, DC: U.S. Bureau of the Census Population Division.

Giddens, Anthony. 1991. *Modernity and Self-Identity: Self and Society in the Late Modern Age*. Cambridge, UK: Polity.

Gieber, Walter. 1964. "News Is What Newspapermen Make It." In *People, Society, and Mass Communications*, edited by Lewis Anthony Dexter and David Manning White. New York: Free Press.

Gill, Richard T. 1997. *Posterity Lost: Progress, Ideology, and the Decline of the American Family*. Lanham, MD: Rowman and Littlefield.

Gilligan, Carol. 1982. *In a Different Voice: Psychological Theory and Women's Development*. Cambridge, MA: Harvard University Press.

Gilroy, Paul. 1993. *The Black Atlantic: Modernity and Double-Consciousness*. Cambridge, MA: Harvard University Press.

Gitlin, Todd. 1983. *Inside Prime Time*. New York: Pantheon.

Glaser, Barney G., and Anseln L. Strauss. 1965. *Awareness of Dying*. Chicago: Aldine.

———. 1968. *Time for Dying*. Chicago: Aldine.

Glazer, Nathan, and Daniel Patrick Moynihan. 1963. *Beyond the Melting Pot: The Negroes, Puerto Ricans, Jews, Italians, and Irish of New York City*. Cambridge: Massachusetts Institute of Technology Press.

"Global Aids Epidemic a Picture of Devastation." 2000. *Los Angeles Times*, June 28, 20.

Goffman, Erving. 1959. *The Presentation of Self in Everyday Life*. Garden City, NY: Doubleday.

———. 1961. *Asylums: Essays on the Social Situation of Mental Patients and Other Inmates*. Garden City, NY: Anchor.

———. 1963. *Stigma: Notes on the Management of Spoiled Identity*. Englewood Cliffs, NJ: Prentice-Hall.

———. 1974. *Frame Analysis*. Cambridge, MA: Harvard University Press.

Goldin, Claudia. 1994. "Labor Markets in the Twentieth Century." In NBER Working Paper Series, Historical Paper No. 58. Cambridge, MA: National Bureau of Economic Research.

Goldscheider, Frances K., and Linda J. Waite. 1991. *New Families, No Families? The Transformation of the American Home*. Berkeley: University of California Press.

Goleman, Daniel, and Joel Gurin. 1993. *Mind, Body Medicine: How to Use Your Mind for Better Health*. New York: Consumer Reports Books.

Goode, William Josiah. 1963. *World Revolution and Family Patterns*. New York: Free Press.

———. 1993. *World Changes in Divorce Patterns*. New Haven, CT: Yale University Press.

Gordon, Diana R. 1990. *The Justice Juggernaut: Fighting Street Crime, Controlling Citizens*. New Brunswick, NJ: Rutgers University Press.

Gordon, Milton Myron. 1964. *Assimilation in American Life*. New York: Oxford University Press.

Gould, Madelyn S., Ted Greenberg, Drew M. Veltin, and David Shaffer. 2003. "Youth Suicide Risk and Preventive Interventions: A Review of the Past 10 Years." *Journal of the American Academy of Child and Adolescent Psychiatry* 42, no. 4: 386–405.

Gould-Martin, Katherine, and Chorswang Ngin. 1981. "Chinese Americans." In *Ethnicity and Medical Care*, edited by Alan Harwood, 131–171. Cambridge, MA: Harvard University Press.

Gouldner, Alvin Ward. 1954. *Patterns of Industrial Bureaucracy*. Glencoe, IL: Free Press.

Grace, Sherry L., and Kenneth L. Cramer. 2002. "Sense of Self in the New Millennium: Male and Female Student Responses to the TST." *Social Behavior and Personality* 30, no. 3: 271–280.

Gracey, Harry L. 1991. "Learning the Student Role: Kindergarten as Academic Boot Camp." In *Down to Earth Sociology*, edited by James M. Henslin, 377–390. New York: Free Press.

Graham, Loren R. 1979. "Concerns About Science and Attempts to Regulate Inquiry." In *Limits of Scientific Inquiry*, edited by Robert S. Morison and Gerald Holton, 1–21. New York: Norton.

Gramsci, Antonio. 1971. *Selections from the Prison Notebooks of Antonio Gramsci.* London: Lawrence and Wishart.

Gray, Edward R., and Scott L. Thumma. 1997. "The Gospel Hour: Liminality, Identity, and Religion in a Gay Bar." In *Contemporary American Religion: An Ethnographic Reader*, edited by Nancy L. Eiesland and Penny Edgell Becker, 79–98. Walnut Creek, CA: AltaMira.

Greeley, Andrew M. 1974. *Ethnicity in the United States: A Preliminary Reconnaissance.* New York: Wiley.

Greenberg, David F. 1988. *The Construction of Homosexuality.* Chicago: University of Chicago Press.

Gross, Jane. 1993. "Combating Rape on Campus in a Class on Sexual Consent." *New York Times*, September 25, 1.

Gross, Paul R., and Norman Levitt. 1994. *Higher Superstition: The Academic Left and Its Quarrels with Science.* Baltimore: Johns Hopkins University Press.

Groves, Martha. 2000. "Rivalry for Top Colleges Equals Stress for Students; Education: Teenagers Face Tougher Competition, Crushing Workloads, and High Expectations." *Los Angeles Times*, June 22, 1.

Grusky, David. 1998. "Can Class Analysis Be Salvaged?" *American Journal of Sociology* 103: 1187–1234.

GSS. 2006. "General Social Surveys, 1972–2004 [Cumulative File]." Computer-Assisted Survey Methods Program.

Gusfield, Joseph R. 1963. *Symbolic Crusade: Status Politics and the American Temperance Movement.* Urbana: University of Illinois Press.

———. 1981. *The Culture of Public Problems: Drinking-Driving and the Symbolic Order.* Chicago: University of Chicago Press.

Gutek, Barbara A. 1985. *Sex and the Workplace.* San Francisco: Jossey-Bass.

Habermas, Jürgen. 1962. *The Structural Transformation of the Public Sphere: An Inquiry into a Category of Bourgeois Society.* Cambridge: Massachusetts Institute of Technology Press. Reprinted in 1991.

———. 1989. *The Structural Transformation of the Public Sphere.* Cambridge: Massachusetts Institute of Technology Press.

Hacker, Sally L. 1981. "The Culture of Engineering: Woman, Workplace, and Machine." *Women's Studies International Quarterly* 4, no. 3: 341–353.

Hall, Stuart. 1980. "Encoding/Decoding." In *Culture, Media, Language: Working Papers in Cultural Studies, 1972–79*, edited by Dorothy Hobson, Stuart Hall, Andrew Lowe, and Paul Willis. London: Hutchinson.

———. 1996. "The Centrality of Culture." In *Media and Cultural Regulation*, edited by Kenneth Thompson, 207–238. London: Sage.

Hall, Stuart, Chas Critcher, Tony Jefferson, John Clarke, and Brian Roberts. 1978. *Policing the Crisis: Mugging, the State, and Law and Order.* New York: Holmes and Meier.

Hamilton, Peter. 2002. "From Industrial to Information Society." In *Social Change*, edited by Tim Jordan and Steve Pile, 96–120. Oxford: Blackwell.

Hamm, Mark S. 1993. *American Skinheads: The Criminology and Control of Hate Crime.* Westport, CT: Praeger.

Handlin, Oscar. 1951. *Uprooted: The Epic Story of the Great Migrations That Made the American People.* Boston: Little, Brown. Reprinted in 1973.

Hanmer, Jalna. 1985. "Transforming Consciousness: Women and the New Reproductive Technologies." In *Man-Made Women: How New Reproductive Technologies Affect Women*, edited by Gena Corea, Renate Duelli Klein, Jalna Hammer, Helen B. Holmes, Madhu Kishwar, Janice Raymond, Robyn Rowland, and Roberta Steinbacher, 88–109. London: Hutchinson.

Hanna, Kathi E., ed. 1991. *Biomedical Politics.* Washington, DC: National Academy Press.

Haraway, Donna Jeanne. 1989. *Primate Visions: Gender, Race, and Nature in the World of Modern Science.* New York: Routledge.

———. 1991. *Simians, Cyborgs, and Women: The Reinvention of Nature.* London: Free Association.

Harding, Sandra. 1986. *The Science Question in Feminism.* Ithaca, NY: Cornell University Press.

Harrison, Paige M., and Allen J. Beck. 2004. "Prisoners in 2003." U.S. Department of Justice, Office of Justice Programs, Bureau of Justice Statistics.

Hartley, W. 1968. "Self-Conception and Organizational Adaptation." Mideast Sociological Association.

Hartstock, Nancy. 1983. "The Feminist Standpoint: Developing the Ground for a Specifically Feminist Historical Materialism." In *Discovering Reality: Feminist Perspectives on Epistemology, Metaphysics, Methodology, and Philosophy of Science*, edited by Merrill B. Hintikka and Sandra Harding, 283–310. Dordrecht, Holland: Reidel.

Hawton, Keith, Karen Rodham, Emma Evans, and Rosamund Weatherall. 2002. "Deliberate Self-Harm in Adolescents: Self-Report Survey in Schools in England." *British Medical Journal* 325: 1207–1211.

Hearn, Jeff, and Wendy Parkin. 1987. *Sex at Work: The Power and Paradox of Organization Sexuality.* New York: St. Martin's.

Heelas, Paul. 1996. *New Age Movement: The Celebration of the Self and the Sacralization of Modernity.* Cambridge, UK: Blackwell.

Heimdal, Kristen R., and Sharon K. Houseknecht. 2003. "Cohabiting and Married Couples' Income Organization: Approaches in Sweden and the United States." *Journal of Marriage and Family* 65, no. 3: 525–538.

Heise, Lori, Mary Ellsberg, and Megan Gottemoeller. 1999. "Ending Violence Against Women." *Population Reports, Series L*, no. 11. Baltimore, MD: Johns Hopkins School of Public Health, Poplation Information Program.

Held, David, Anthony G. McGrew, David Goldblatt, and

Jonathan Perraton, eds. 1999. *Global Transformations: Politics, Economics, and Culture.* Palo Alto, CA: Stanford University Press.

Helmore, Edward. 2000. "College Football Hero Corey Johnson Came Out and No One Was Outraged: In a Tolerant America, Gay Is the New Straight." *Observer*, April 30, 26.

Henslin, James M. 1991. "On Becoming Male: Reflections of a Sociologist on Childhood and Early Socialization." In *Down to Earth Sociology*, edited by James M. Henslin, 122–132. New York: Free Press.

Herberg, Will. 1955. *Protestant, Catholic, Jew: An Essay in American Religious Sociology.* Garden City, NY: Doubleday.

Herbert, Bob. 2007. "A Volatile Young Man, Humiliation, and a Gun." *New York Times*, April 19.

Hersch, Patricia. 1993. "Sex and the Boomers' Babies." *Family Therapy Networker* 17 no. 2: 25–31.

Herzberg, Frederick. 1966. *Work and the Nature of Man.* New York: World Press.

Hess, David J. 1995. *Science and Technology in a Multicultural World: The Cultural Politics of Facts and Artifacts.* New York: Columbia University Press.

Hesse-Biber, Sharlene, Margaret Marino, and Diane Watts-Roy. 1999. "A Longitudinal Study of Eating Disorders Among College Women—Factors That Influence Recovery." *Gender and Society* 13, no. 3: 385–408.

Higham, John. 1963. *Strangers in the Land: Patterns of American Nativism, 1860–1925.* New York: Atheneum.

Hind, John. 2002. "The Digital Prophet: Vernor Vinge." *Observer*, December 29, 34.

Hirschman, Albert O. 1982. *Shifting Involvements: Private Interest and Public Action.* Princeton, NJ: Princeton University Press.

Hirst, Paul Q., and Grahame Thompson. 1996. *Globalization in Question: The International Economy and the Possibilities of Governance.* Cambridge, UK: Blackwell.

Hitt, Jack. 2000. "The Second Sexual Revolution." *New York Times Magazine* (February 20).

Hobbes, Thomas. *The Leviathan.* 1651. Cambridge, UK: Cambridge University Press. Reprinted in 2002.

Hobbs, Frank, and Nicole Stoops. 2002. *Demographic Trends in the 20th Century.* U.S. Census Bureau. Available online at http://www.census.gov/prod/2002pubs/censr-4.pdf.

Hochschild, Arlie Russell. 1983. *The Managed Heart: Commercialization of Human Feeling.* Berkeley: University of California Press.

———. 1989. *The Second Shift: Working Parents and the Revolution at Home.* New York: Viking.

———. 1997. *The Time Bind: When Work Becomes Home and Home Becomes Work.* New York: Holt.

Hochschild, Jennifer R. 1995. *Facing Up to the American Dream: Race, Class, and the Soul of the Nation.* Princeton, NJ: Princeton University Press.

Hodson, Randy. *Dignity at Work.* 2001. Cambridge, UK: Cambridge University Press.

Hodson, Randy, and Teresa A. Sullivan. 1995. *The Social Organization of Work.* Belmont, CA: Wadsworth.

Hoff, David J. 1999. "ETS Creating Demographic Index for SAT." *Education Week* 19, no. 1: 1–2.

"Hollywood's Gay Power Surge." 2000. *Entertainment Weekly* (October 6).

Holmes, Amy M. 2000. "From Material to Maternal Girls." *USA Today*, March 31, 17.

hooks, bell. 1981. *Ain't I a Woman: Black Women and Feminism.* Boston: South End Press.

———. 1984. *Feminist Theory: From Margin to Center.* Boston: South End Press.

Horkheimer, Max, and Theodor W. Adorno. 1947. *Dialectic of Enlightenment.* New York: Herder and Herder. Reprinted in 1972.

Horrigan, John. 2004. "Content Creation Online." PEW Internet and American Life Project.

Hubbard, Ruth. 1990. *The Politics of Women's Biology.* New Brunswick, NJ: Rutgers University Press.

Hubler, Shawn. 2001. "How Green Was the Valley: Five 'Poster Children' for Silicon Valley's Heady Glory Days Reflect on Money, Reality, and Changing the World." *Los Angeles Times*, March 25, 1.

Huffstutter, P. J., and Robin Fields. 2000. "A Virtual Revolution in Teaching." *Los Angeles Times*, March 3, 1.

Hughes, Thomas P. 1999. "Edison and Electric Light." In *The Social Shaping of Technology*, edited by Judith Wajcman and Donald MacKenzie, 50–64. Philadelphia: Open University Press.

Hulse, Carl. 2004. "Senators Block Initiative to Ban Same-Sex Unions." July 15, 1.

Hunter, James. 1991. *Culture Wars: The Struggle to Define America.* New York: Basic Books.

Huntington, Samuel P. 2004a. "The Hispanic Challenge." *Foreign Policy* 141: 30–45.

———. 2004b. *Who Are We? The Challenges to America's National Identity.* New York: Simon and Schuster.

Huntington, Samuel P., and Allen Wolfe. 2004. "Credal Passions." *Foreign Affairs* (September–October): 155–159.

Hutter, Mark. 1991. *The Family Experience: A Reader in Cultural Diversity.* New York: Macmillan.

Illich, Ivan. 1976. *Limits to Medicine: Medical Nemesis—The Expropriation of Health.* London: Boyars.

Illouz, Eva. 1998. "The Lost Innocence of Love: Romance as a Postmodern Condition." *Theory, Culture, and Society* 15, nos. 3–4: 161–186.

ILO (International Labour Organisation). 2000. Available online at http://www.ilo.org/public/english/standards/ipec/simpoc/others/globalest.pdf.

———. 2002. "Women and Men in the Informal Economy: A Statistical Picture." Geneva, Switzerland: ILO Employment Sector.

———. 2005. "Report of the Director General: A Global Alliance Against Forced Labour—Global Report Under the

Follow-up to the ILO Declaration on Fundamental Principles and Rights at Work 2005." Available at http://www.ilo.org/dyn/declaris/declarationweb.download_blob?Var_DocumentID=5059.

Information Please Database. 2005. "Educational Attainment by Race and Hispanic Origin, 1940–2005."

Inglehart, Ronald. 1990. *Culture Shift in Advanced Industrial Society*. Princeton, NJ: Princeton University Press.

Inglis, Christine. 1996. "Multiculturalism: New Policy Responses to Diversity." In *Management of Social Transformations (MOST)*. Paris: UNESCO.

International Institute for Democracy and Electoral Assistance. 2005. "Turnout in the World—Country by Country." Stockholm, Sweden: IDEA.

International Telecommunication Union. 2003. Digital Access Index: World's First Global ICT Ranking. New York: ITU (a UN agency). Available online at http://www.itu.int/newsarchive/press_releases/2003/30.html (accessed April 10, 2006).

Inter-Parliamentary Union. 2005. "Women in National Parliaments, Table: World Classification Access." Geneva, Switzerland: Inter-Parliamentary Union.

Irvine, Janice M. 1995. *Sexuality Education Across Cultures; Working with Differences*. San Francisco: Jossey-Bass.

"Is God Dead?" 1966. *Time* (April 8): cover.

"Is Your TV Set Gay? They're Here, They're Queer ... and They'll Be Back After This Commercial Message. From 'Will and Grace' to Richard on 'Survivor,' Gay TV Is Staking Its Claim." 2000. *Entertainment Weekly* (October 6).

Jackson, Linda A. 1992. *Physical Appearance and Gender: Sociobiological and Sociocultural Perspectives*. Albany: State University of New York Press.

Jacobson, Paul H. and Pauline F. Jacobson. 1959. *American Marriage and Divorce*. New York: Rinehart.

Jasper, James M., and Dorothy Nelkin. 1992. *Animal Rights Crusade: The Growth of a Moral Protest*. New York: Free Press.

Jaynes, Gregory. 1982. "Suit on Race Recalls Lines Drawn Under Slavery." *New York Times*, September 23, 16.

Jaynes, Julian. 1976. *The Origin of Consciousness in the Breakdown of the Bicameral Mind*. Boston: Houghton Mifflin.

Jefferson, Thomas. 1950. *Papers of Thomas Jefferson*. Edited by Julian P. Boyd. Princeton, NJ: University Press.

Jencks, Charles. 1977. *The Language of Post-Modern Architecture*. New York: Rizzoli.

Jencks, Christopher, Lauri Perman, and Lee Rainwater. 1988. "What Is a Good Job? A New Measure of Labor-Market Success." *American Journal of Sociology* 93, no. 6: 1322–1357.

Jenkins, Philip. 1994. *Using Murder: The Social Construction of Serial Homicide*. New York: de Gruyter.

Joint Center for Political and Economic Studies. 2003. Black Elected Officials: A Statistical Summary, 2003. Available at http://www.jointcenter.org/publications1/Publications Detail.php?recordID=118. Accessed June 26, 2003.

Jong, Erica. 1973. *Fear of Flying: A Novel*. New York: Rinehart and Winston.

Jonsen, Albert R. 1991. "American Moralism and the Origin of Bioethics in the United States." *Journal of Medicine and Philosophy* 16: 113–130.

Jordan, Winthrop. 1968. *White over Black: American Attitudes Toward the Negro*. Chapel Hill: University of North Carolina Press.

Judd, Dennis R., and Susan S. Fainstein. 1999. *The Tourist City*. New Haven, CT: Yale University Press.

Judith, Stacey. 1996. *In the Name of the Family: Rethinking Family Values in the Postmodern Age*. Boston: Beacon.

Kahn, Faith. 2002. "Enron, Financial Fraud, and September 11, 2001." *Tulane Law Review* 76: 1579.

Kaiser Family Foundation and the Children's Digital Media Centers. 2003. "Zero to Six: Electronic Media in the Lives of Infants, Toddlers, and Preschoolers." Review of Reviewed Item. Available online at www.kff.org.

Kamp Dush, Claire M., Catherine L. Cohan, and Paul R. Amato. 2003. "The Relationship Between Cohabitation and Marital Quality and Stability: Change Across Cohorts?" *Journal of Marriage and Family* 65, no. 3: 539–549.

Kandiyoti, Deniz. 1991. "Introduction." In *Women, Islam, and the State*, edited by Deniz Kandiyoti, 1–21. Philadelphia, PA: Temple University Press.

Kant, Immanuel. 1764a. *Observations on the Feeling of the Beautiful and the Sublime*. Berkeley: University of California Press. Reprinted in 1960.

———. 1764b. *Anthropology from a Pragmatic Point of View*. Berkeley: University of California Press. Reprinted in 1960.

Kanter, Rosabeth Moss. 1977. *Men and Women of the Corporation*. New York: Basic Books.

Kasindorf, Martin. 2002. "$1.5b of 9/11 Donations Distributed; More Than Half of Charity Funds Have Gone Out." *USA Today*, August 19, 3.

Katakis, Michael, ed. 1988. *The Vietnam Veterans Memorial*. New York: Crown.

Katz, Daniel, and Kenneth W. Braly. 1935. "Racial Prejudice and Racial Stereotypes." *Journal of Abnormal and Social Psychology* 30: 175–193.

Katz, Elihu, and Paul F. Lazarsfeld. 1955. *Personal Influence: The Part Played by People in the Flow of Mass Communications*. Glencoe, IL: Free Press. Reprinted in 1966.

Katz, Jack. 1988. "Seductions of Crime: Moral and Sensual Attractions in Doing Evil." New York: Basic Books.

Kelley, Dean M. 1972. *Why Conservative Churches Are Growing: A Study in Sociology of Religion*. New York: Harper and Row.

Kellogg, John Harvey. 1886. *Plain Facts for Young and Old: Embracing the Natural History and Hygiene of Organic Life*. Burlington, IA: Segner.

Kelly, Liz. 1988. "The U.S. Ordinances: Censorship or Radical Law Reform?" In *Feminism and Censorship*, edited by Gail Chester and Julienne Dickey, 52–61. Bridgeport, CT: Prism.

Keniston, Kenneth. 1965. *The Uncommitted: Alienated Youth in American Society*. New York: Harcourt, Brace.

———. 1968. *Young Radicals: Notes on Uncommitted Youth*. New York: Harcourt, Brace.

Kennedy, Dennis James. 1995. "Residential Associations as State Actors: Regulating the Impact of Gated Communities on Non-Members." *Yale Law Journal* 105: 761–793.

Kim, Sujeong. 1999. "Beyond Active Audience Theory: Rethinking Interpretation and Pleasure in Audience Studies. San Diego: University of California Press.

Kimani, Mary. 2002. "'Hate Radio' Urged Hutus to Break 'Small Noses,' Expert Witness Testifies." Review of Reviewed Item. *Internews* (Arusha), March 20. Available online at http://www.internews.org/activities/ICTR_reports /ICTRnewsMar02.html#0320a.

Kinder, Donald R., and Donald O. Sears. 1981. "Prejudice and Politics: Symbolic Racism Versus Racial Threats to the Good Life." *Journal of Personality and Social Psychology* 40: 414–431.

King, L. S. *Medical Thinking: A Historical Preface*. Princeton, NJ: Princeton University Press.

Kinsey, Alfred C., Wardell B. Pomeroy, and Clyde E. Martin. 1948. *Sexual Behavior in the Human Male*. Philadelphia, PA: Saunders.

Kinsey, Alfred C., Wardell B. Pomeroy, Clyde E. Martin, and Paul H. Gebhard. 1953. *Sexual Behavior in the Human Female*. Philadelphia, PA: Saunders.

Kivisto, Peter, ed., 2005. *Incorporating Diversity: Rethinking Assimilation in a Multicultural Age*. Boulder, CO: Paradigm Publishers.

Klein, Renate Duelli. 1985. "What's 'New' About the 'New' Reproductive Technologies?" In *Man-Made Women: How New Reproductive Technologies Affect Women*. edited by Gena Corea, Renate Duelli Klein, Jalna Hammer, Helen B. Holmes, Madhu Kishwar, Janice Raymond, Robyn Rowland, and Roberta Steinbacher, 64–73. London: Hutchinson.

Kleinman, Arthur. 1980. *Patients and Healers in the Context of Culture: An Exploration of the Borderland Between Anthropology, Medicine, and Psychiatry*. Berkeley: University of California Press.

Kluegel, James R., and Eliot. R. Smith. 1986. *Beliefs About Inequality: Americans' View of What Is and What Ought to Be*. New York: de Gruyter.

Kochar, Rakesh. 2005. "Latino Labor Report, 2004." Washington, DC: PEW Hispanic Center.

Koenig, Harold George, Harvey J. Cohen, L. K George, J. C Hays, D. B. Larson, and D. G. Blazer. 1997. "Attendance at Religious Services, Interleukin-6, and Other Biological Parameters of Immune Function in Older Adults." *International Journal of Psychiatry in Medicine* 27, no. 3: 233–250.

Kohn, Melvin L., and Carmi Schooler. 1983. *Work and Personality: An Inquiry into the Impact of Social Stratification*. Norwood, NJ: Ablex.

Kolada, Gina. 1994. "America Keeps Onan in the Closet." *New York Times*, December 18, 5.

Korda, Michael. 1972. *Male Chauvinism! How It Works*. New York: Random House.

Korman, Sheila K., and Gerald R. Leslie. 1982. "The Relationship of Feminist Ideology and Date Expense Sharing to Perceptions of Sexual Aggression in Dating." *Journal of Sex Research* 18, no. 2: 114–129.

Krakauer, Jon. 1998. *Into Thin Air: A Personal Account of Mount Everest*. Garden City, NY: Anchor.

Krimsky, Sheldon. 1991. *Biotechnics and Society: The Rise of Industrial Genetics*. New York: Praeger.

Kuhn, Manford H. 1964. "Major Trends in Symbolic Interaction Theory in the Past Twenty-Five Years." *Sociological Quarterly* 5: 61–84.

Kuhn, Thomas. 1962. *The Structure of Scientific Revolutions*. Chicago: Chicago University Press. Reprinted in 1970.

Kurien, Prema. 1999. "Gendered Ethnicity: Creating a Hindu Indian Identity in the United States." *American Behavioral Scientist* 42, no. 4: 648–670.

———. 2001. "Religion, Ethnicity, and Politics: Hindu and Muslim Indian Immigrants in the United States." *Ethnic and Racial Studies* 24, no. 2: 263–293.

Labaree, David F. 1988. *The Making of an American High School: The Credentials Market and the Central High School of Philadelphia, 1838–1939*. New Haven, CT: Yale University Press.

———. 1997. "Public Goods, Private Goods: The American Struggle over Educational Goals." *American Educational Research Journal* 34, no. 1: 39–81.

Laguerre, Michael. 1999. *The Global Ethnopolis: Chinatown, Japantown, and Manilatown in American Society*. New York: St. Martin's.

Laline, Suzette, and Lori Leibovich. 1997. "The Skinny on Barbie: Essential Facts About Her Checkered Past." Review of Reviewed Item. *Salon* (November 26). Available online at http://archive.salon.com/mwt/feature/1997/11/26facts.html.

Laming, S. 1985. "Sex in the Suburbs." *News of the World* (December 22).

Lamont, Michele. 2000. *The Dignity of Working Men: Morality and the Boundaries of Race, Class, and Immigration*. Cambridge, MA: Harvard University Press.

Landesco, John. 1929. *Organized Crime in Chicago*. Chicago: University of Chicago Press.

Langan, Patrick A., and David P. Farrington. 1998. "Crime and Justice in the United States and in England and Wales, 1981–1996." U.S. Department of Justice, Office of Justice Programs, Bureau of Justice Statistics.

Lasch, Christopher. 1977. *Haven in a Heartless World: The Family Besieged*. New York: Basic Books.

Laska, Shirley Bradway, and Daphne Spain. 1980. *Back to the City: Issues in Neighborhood Renovation*. New York: Pergamon.

Latour, Bruno, and Steve Woolgar. 1979. *Laboratory Life: The Construction of Scientific Facts*. Princeton, NJ: Princeton University Press.

Laumann, Edward O., John H. Gagnon, Robert T. Michael, and Stuart Michaels. 1994. *The Social Organization of Sexuality: Sexual Practices in the United States*. Chicago: University of Chicago Press.

Lawlor, Julia. 1998. "Earning It: For Many Blue-Collar Fathers, Child Care Is Shift Work, Too." *New York Times*, April 26, 11.

Lawrence, Paul R., and Jay W. Lorsch. 1967. *Organization and Environment; Managing Differentiation and Integration*. Cambridge, MA: Harvard University Press.

Lee, Jennifer. 1999. "Retail Niche Domination Among African American, Jewish, and Korean Entrepreneurs." *American Behavioral Scientist* 42, no. 9: 1398–1416.

Lee, Sharon M., and Barry Edmonston. 2005. "New Marriages, New Families: U.S. Racial and Hispanic Intermarriage, Population Bulletin 60: 2." Washington, DC: Population Reference Bureau.

Leites, Edmund. 1986. *The Puritan Conscience and Modern Sexuality*. New Haven, CT: Yale University Press.

Leland, John. 2000. "O.K., You're Gay. So? Where's My Grandchild?" *New York Times*, December 21, 1.

Leland, John, Debra Rosenberg, Nadine Joseph, Victoria Scanlan Stefanakos, and Michael Cronin. 2000. "Shades of Gay." *Newsweek* (March 20): 46.

Lembo, Ron. 1997. "Situating Television in Everyday Life: Reformulating a Cultural Studies Approach to the Study of Television Use." In *From Sociology to Cultural Studies: New Perspectives*, edited by Elizabeth Long. Malden, MA: Blackwell.

Lemert, Edwin McCarthy. 1967. *Human Deviance, Social Problems, and Social Control*. Englewood Cliffs, NJ: Prentice-Hall.

Lester, David. 2003. "Adolescent Suicide from an International Perspective." *American Behavioral Scientist* 46, no. 9: 1157–1170.

Lever, W. F. 1997. "Delinking Urban Economies." *Urban Studies* 19, no. 2: 227–238.

Levin, Irene. 2004. "Living Apart Together: A New Family Form." *Current Sociology* 52, no. 2: 223–240.

Levine, Arthur, and Jeanette Cureton. 1992. "The Quiet Revolution: Eleven Facts About Multiculturalism and the Curriculum." *Change* 24, no. 1: 24–29.

Levine, James A., and Todd L. Pittinsky. 1997. *Working Fathers: New Strategies for Balancing Work and Family*. Reading, MA: Addison-Wesley.

Levine, Lawrence W. 1988. *Highbrow/Lowbrow: The Emergence of Cultural Hierarchy in America*. Cambridge, MA: Harvard University Press.

Levinson, Daniel, C. N. Darrow, C. N. Klein, M. H. Levinson, and B. McKee. 1978. *Seasons of a Man's Life*. New York: Knopf.

———. 1990. "A Theory of Life Structure Development in Adulthood." In *Higher Stages of Development: Perspectives on Adult Growth*, edited by Ellen J. Langer and Charles N. Alexander, 35–53. New York: Oxford University Press.

Lewis, James R. 1996. "Introduction." In *Magical Religion and Modern Witchcraft*, edited by James R. Lewis, 1–5. Albany: State University of New York Press.

Lewis, Michael. 2000. *The New New Thing: A Silicon Valley Story*. New York: Norton.

———. 2005. "The Artist in the Gray Flannel Pajamas." *New York Times*, March 5, 45.

Lewis, Oscar. 1961. *The Children of Sanchez: Autobiography of a Mexican Family*. New York: Modern Library.

"The Liberated, Exploited, Pampered, Frazzled, Uneasy New American Worker." 2000. *New York Times Magazine* (March 5).

Lifton, Robert J. 1993. *The Protean Self: Human Resilience in an Age of Fragmentation*. New York: Basic Books.

Lincoln, James R., and Arne L. Kalleberg. 1990. *Culture, Control, and Commitment: A Study of Work Organization and Work Attitudes in the United States and Japan*. New York: Cambridge University Press.

Lindner, Eileen W. 2005. *Yearbook of American and Canadian Churches, 2005*. Nashville, TN: Abingdon Press.

Lippmann, Walter. 1922. *Public Opinion*. New York: Harcourt, Brace.

———. 1925. *The Phantom Public*. New York: Harcourt, Brace.

Lipset, Seymour Martin. 1960. *Political Man: The Social Bases of Politics*. Garden City, NY: Doubleday.

Lipset, Seymour Martin, and William Schneider. 1978. "The *Bakke* Case: How Would It Be Decided at the Bar of Public Opinion?" *Public Opinion* (March–April): 38–44.

Liptak, Adam. 2005a. "To More Inmates, Life Term Means Dying Behind Bars." *New York Times*, 1.

———. 2005b. "Locked Away Forever After Crimes as Teenagers." *New York Times*, October 3, 1.

"A Little Local Color." 1982. *New York Times*, September 19.

Lofland, John. 1966. *Doomsday Cult: A Study of Conversion, Proselytization, and Maintenance of Faith*. Englewood Cliffs, NJ: Prentice-Hall.

Long, Marilee, Greg Boiarsky, and Greg Thayer. 2001. "Gender and Racial Counter-Stereotypes in Science Education Television: A Content Analysis." *Public Understanding of Science* 10: 255?269.

Lopes, Sal. 1987. *The Wall: Images and Offerings from the Vietnam Veterans Memorial*. New York: HarperCollins.

Lopez, Mark Hugo, Emily Kirby, and Jared Sagoff. 2005. "Voter Turnout Among Young Women and Men." Washington, DC: Center for Information and Research on Civic Learning and Engagement.

Lorber, Judith. 1994. *Paradoxes of Gender*. New Haven, CT: Yale University Press.

Lord, M. J. 1994. *Forever Barbie: The Unauthorized Biography of a Real Doll*. New York: Morrow.

*Los Angeles Almanac*. 2006. Available online at http://www.laalmanac.com.

Los Angeles 2000 Committee. 1998. "LA 2000: The City for the Future." Los Angeles: Los Angeles 2000 Committee.

Loy, Pamela, and Lea Stewart. 1984. "The Extent and Effects of the Sexual Harassment of Working Women." *Sociological Focus* 17, no. 1: 31–43.

Lukes, Steven. 1974. *Power: A Radical View*. New York: Macmillan.

Luo, Michael. 2006. "Big Tent Religion: Evangelicals Debate the Meaning of 'Evangelical.'" *New York Times*, April 16, section 4, p. 5.

Luttrell, Wendy. 1997. *Schoolsmart and Motherwise: Working-Class Women's Identity and Schooling*. New York: Routledge.

Lynd, Robert Staughton, and Helen Merrell Lynd. 1929. *Middletown in Transition: A Study in Cultural Conflicts*. New York: Harcourt, Brace. Reprinted in 1937.

Lyon, David. 1999. *Postmodernity*. Minneapolis: University of Minnesota Press.

MacDonald, J. Fred. 1979. *Don't Touch That Dial! Radio Programming in American Life, 1920–1960*. Chicago: Nelson-Hall.

MacDonald, Kevin B., and R. D. Parke. 1986. "Parent-Child Physical Play: The Effects of Sex and Age of Children and Parents." *Sex Roles* 15: 367–378.

Macionis, John J. 2000. *Society: The Basics*. Englewood Cliffs, NJ: Prentice-Hall.

MacIver, Robert Morrison. 1947. *The Web of Government*. New York: Macmillan.

MacKinnon, Catharine A. 1987. *Feminism Unmodified: Discourses on Life and Law*. Cambridge, MA: Harvard University Press.

Maffesoli, Michel. 1996. *The Time of the Tribes: The Decline of Individualism in Mass Society*. London: Sage.

Males, Mike. 1999. "Drive-by Journalism: *Rolling Stone*'s Glam-Crime Reports Misrepresent Young People—and America's Violence Problem." *Extra!* (January–February).

Malinowski, Bronislaw. 1948. *Magic, Science, and Religion*. London: Souvenir.

Mann, Michael. 1986a. *The Sources of Social Power: A History of Power from the Beginning to A.D. 1760*, Vol. 1. New York: Cambridge University Press.

———. 1986b. *The Sources of Social Power: The Rise of Classes and Nation-States, 1760–1914*, Vol. 2. New York: Cambridge University Press.

Manne, Anne. 2005. *Motherhood: How Should We Care for Our Children?* Crows Nest, Australia: Allen and Unwin.

Manski, Charles F. 1992. "Educational Choice (Vouchers) and Social Mobility." *Economics of Education Review* 11, no. 4: 351–369.

Mantsios, Gregory. 1995. "Media Magic: Making Class Invisible." In *Race, Class, and Gender in the United States: An Integrated Study*, edited by Paula S. Rothenberg, 409–417. New York: St. Martin's.

Marcus, Steven. 1966. *The Other Victorians: A Study of Sexuality and Pornography in Mid-Nineteenth-Century England*. New York: Basic.

Markle, Gerald E., and James C. Petersen. 1980. *Politics, Science, and Cancer: The Laetrile Phenomenon*. Boulder, CO: Westview.

Markus, Hazel Rose, Patricia K. Mullaly, and Shinobu Kitayama. 1997. "Selfways: Diversity in Modes of Cultural Participation." In *The Conceptual Self in Context: Culture, Experience, Self-Understanding*, edited by David A. Jopling and Ulrich Neisser, 13–61. New York: Cambridge University Press.

Marshall, T. H. (Thomas Humphrey). 1964. *Class, Citizenship, and Social Development*. Garden City, NY: Doubleday.

Martin, E. 1989. *The Woman in the Body*. Milton Keynes, UK: Open University Books.

Martin, Emily. 1991. "The Egg and the Sperm: How Science Has Constructed a Romance Based on Stereotypical Male-Female Roles." *Signs: Journal of Women in Culture and Society* 16, no. 3: 485–501.

Martin, Philip, and Elizabeth Midgley. 1994. "Immigration to the Unites States: Journey to an Uncertain Destination," *Population Bulletin* 49, no. 2. Washington, DC: Population Reference Bureau.

Marwick, Charles. 1995. "Should Physicians Prescribe Prayer for Health? Spiritual Aspects of Well-Being Considered." *Journal of the American Medical Association* 273, no. 20: 1561–1562.

Marx, Karl. 1867. *Capital*. New York: International. Reprinted in 1975.

———. 1978. "The Possibility of Non-Violent Revolution." In *The Marx-Engels Reader*, edited by Robert C. Tucker, 522–524. New York: Norton.

Marx, Karl, and Friedrich Engels. 1844–1846. *The German Ideology*. New York: International. Reprinted in 1974.

———. 1848. *The Communist Manifesto*. New York: Monthly Review Press. Reprinted in 1964.

Maslow, Abraham Harold. 1965. *Eupsychian Management: A Journal*. Homewood, IL: Irwin.

Massey, Dorren, John Allen, and Steve Pile, eds. 1999. *City Worlds*. London: Routledge.

Massey, Douglas S. 2004. "The Revenge of the Chicago School." *Contemporary Sociology* 4: 408–410.

Matthews, Warren. 2007. *World Religions*, 5th ed. Belmont, CA: Wadsworth.

Maynard-Moody, Steven. 1992. "The Fetal Research Dispute." In *Controversy: Politics of Technical Decisions*, edited by Dorothy Nelkin, 3–25. Newbury Park, CA: Sage.

Mayo, Elton. 1933. *Human Problems of an Industrial Civilization*. New York: Macmillan.

Mazur, Allan. 1981. *Dynamics of Technical Controversy*. Washington, DC: Communications.

McCaffrey, Shannon. 2002. "9/11 Red Cross Donations Reach $1b." Review of Reviewed Item. Associated Press Online, September 5.

McCarthy, John D., and Mayer N. Zald, eds. *Social Movements in an Organizational Society: Collected Essays*. New Brunswick, NJ: Transaction.

McCormick, Naomi B., and Clinton J. Jesser. 1983. "The Courtship Game: Power in the Sexual Encounter." In *Changing Boundaries: Gender Roles and Sexual Behavior*, edited by Naomi. B. McCormick and Elizabeth Rice Allgeier, 64–86. Palo Alto, CA: Mayfield.

McCracken, Ellen Marie. 1993. *Decoding Women's Magazines from* Mademoiselle *to* Ms. London: Macmillan.

McDevitt, Thomas M., and Patricia M. Rowe. 2002. "The United States in International Context: 2000." Washington, DC: U.S. Department of Commerce, U.S. Census Bureau.

McDonald, Lynn. 1993. *The Early Origins of the Social Sciences*. Montréal: McGill-Queen's University Press.

McGinniss, Joe. 1968. *The Selling of the President, 1968*. New York: Trident.

McGregor, Douglas. 1960. *The Human Side of Enterprise*. New York: McGraw-Hill.

McGrew, Anthony. 1990. "The Political Dynamics of the New Environmentalism." *Industrial Crisis Quarterly* 4: 291–305.

McKinney, John C. 1966. *Constructive Typology and Social Theory*. New York: Appleton-Century-Crofts.

McPartland, T. S., John H. Cummings, and Wynona S. Garretson. 1961. "Self-Conception and Ward Behavior in Two Psychiatric Hospitals." *Sociometry* 24: 111–124.

McRobbie, Angela. 1978. "Working-Class Girls and the Culture of Femininity." In *Women Take Issue: Aspects of Women's Subordination*, edited by Centre for Contemporary Cultural Studies Women's Studies Group, University of Birmingham, 96–108. London: Hutchinson.

Mead, George Herbert. 1934. *Mind, Self, and Society from the Standpoint of a Social Behaviorist*. Chicago: University of Chicago Press.

Mead, Margaret. 1935. *Sex and Temperament in Three Primitive Societies*. New York: Morrow.

Meltzoff, Andrew N., and M. Keith Moore. 1977. "Imitation of Facial and Manual Gestures in Human Neonates." *Science* 198, no. 4312: 75–78.

———. 1990. "Foundations for Developing a Concept of Self: The Role of Imitation in Relating Self to Other, and the Value of Social Mirroring, Social Modeling, and Self-Practice in Infancy." In *The Self in Transition: Infancy to Childhood*, edited by Marjorie Beegly and Cicchetti Dante, 139–164. Chicago: University of Chicago Press.

Melucci, Alberto. 1995. "The New Social Movement Revisited: Reflections on a Sociological Mis-Understanding." In *Social Movements and Social Classes: The Future of Collective Action*, edited by Lewis Maheu, 107–119. London: Sage.

———. 1996. *The Playing Self: Person and Meaning in a Planetary System*. New York: Cambridge University Press.

Merton, Robert K. 1949. *Social Theory and Social Structure: Toward the Codification of Theory and Research*. Glencoe, IL: Free Press.

———. 1957. *Social Theory and Social Structure*. Glencoe, IL: Free Press.

———. 1968. *Social Theory and Social Structure*. New York: Free Press.

Merton, Robert K., George G. Reader, and Patricia L. Kendall. 1957. *Student-Physician: Introductory Studies in the Sociology of Medical Education*. Cambridge, MA: Harvard University Press.

Messner, Michael A. 2002. *Taking the Field: Women, Men, and Sports*. Minneapolis: University of Minnesota Press.

Mestel, Rosie. 2000. "Despite Big Spending, U.S. Ranks 37th in Study of Global Health Care, Survey." *Los Angeles Times*, June 21, A20.

———. 2003. "The Day DNA Met Its Match." *Los Angeles Times*, February 28.

Michael, Robert T., John H. Gagnon, Edward O. Laumann, and Gina Kolata. 1994. *Sex in America: A Definitive Survey*. Boston: Little, Brown.

Miles, Maria. 1987. "Why Do We Need All This? A Call Against Genetic Engineering and Reproductive Technology." In *Made to Order: The Myth of Reproductive and Genetic Progress*, edited by Patricia Spallone and Deborah Lynn Steinberg, 34–47. New York: Pergamon.

Miles, R. 1985. "Sex on the Job." *Cosmopolitan* (July).

Milkman, Ruth. 1987. *Women, Work, and Protest: A Century of U.S. Women's Labor History*. Boston: Routledge and Kegan Paul.

Miller, Perry. 1953. *The New England Mind*. Cambridge, MA: Harvard University Press.

Miller, Walter. 1958. "Lower-Class Culture as a Generating Milieu of Gang Delinquency." *Journal of Social Issues* 14: 5–19.

Mills, C. Wright. 1940. "Situated Actions and Vocabularies of Motive." *American Sociological Review* 5, no. 6: 904–913.

———. 1953. *White Collar: The American Middle Classes*. New York: Oxford University Press.

———. 1956. *The Power Elite*. New York: Oxford University Press.

———. 1959. *The Sociological Imagination*. New York: Grove.

Mitra, Ananda. 1997. "Virtual Commonality: Looking for India on the Internet." In *Virtual Culture: Identity and Communication in Cybersociety*, edited by Steven G. Jones, 55–79. London: Sage.

Mitroff, Ian I. 1974. *Subjective Side of Science: A Philosophical*

*Inquiry into the Psychology of the Apollo Moon Scientists.* New York: Elsevier.

Mollenkopf, John H., and Manuel Castells, eds. 1991. *Dual City: Restructuring New York.* New York: Russell Sage Foundation.

Moore, Wilbert Ellis. 1967. *Order and Change: Essays in Comparative Sociology.* New York: Wiley.

Morgall, Janine Marie. 1992. *Technology Assessment: A Feminist Perspective.* Philadelphia, PA: Temple University Press.

Morgan, Robin. 1980. "Theory and Practice: Pornography and Rape." In *Take Back the Night: Women on Pornography,* edited by Laura Lederer, 134–140. New York: Morrow.

Morley, David. 1980. *The Nationwide Audience: Structure and Decoding.* London: British Film Institute.

Morris, Philip. 1955. "Finster Goes Everywhere and Shares Expenses Fifty-Fifty with Mary Alice Hematoma, a Lovely Three-Legged Girl with Sideburns." *Massachusetts Collegian* (March 18): 3.

Morse, Nancy C., and Robert S. Weiss. 1955. "The Function and Meaning of Work and the Job." *American Sociological Review* 20, no. 2: 191–198.

Mosher, William D., Gladys M. Martinez, Anjani Chandra, Joyce C. Abma, and Stephanie J. Willson. 2004. "Use of Contraception and Use of Family Planning Services in the United States: 1982–2002." In *Advanced Data from Vital and Health Statistics,* 350.

Mukherji, Chandra, and Michael Schudson, eds. 1991. *Rethinking Popular Culture: Contemporary Perspectives in Cultural Studies.* Berkeley: University of California Press.

Mulkay, Michael Joseph. 1979. *Science and the Sociology of Knowledge.* Boston: Allen and Unwin.

Munson, Wayne. 1993. *All Talk: The Talkshow in Media Culture.* Philadelphia, PA: Temple University Press.

Murdock, George Peter. 1937. "Comparative Data on the Division of Labor by Sex." *Social Forces* 15, no. 4: 551–553.

———. 1949. *Social Structure.* New York: Macmillan.

MyBestSegments.com. 2006. PRIZM NE, a segmentation system from Claritas Inc. "Table: Prizm Lifestyle Types, United States."

Nash, Dennison J., and Alvin W. Wolfe. 1957. "The Stranger in Laboratory Culture." *American Sociological Review* 22, no. 4.

National Academy of Sciences. 1991. *Biomedical Politics.* Washington, DC: National Academy Press.

———. 1999. *The Changing Nature of Work: Implications for Occupational Analysis.* Washington, DC: National Academy Press.

National Commission on Excellence in Education. 1983. "A Nation at Risk: The Imperative for Educational Reform." Washington, DC: U.S. Department of Education.

National Opinion Research Center. 1999. "NORC 1999," edited by University of Chicago.

———. 2004. "NORC 2004," edited by University of Chicago.

National Science Foundation. 1990. "Women and Minorities in Science and Engineering." Washington, DC: NSF.

———. 2001. "Survey of Doctorate Recipients." Arlington, VA: NSF.

Navarro, Mireya. 2004. "When Gender Isn't a Given." *New York Times,* September 9, 1.

Navarro, Vicente. 1976. *Medicine Under Capitalism.* New York: Prodist.

———. 1992. "The Middle Class: A Useful Myth." *Nation* (March 23): 1.

NCHS. 2004. *Health, United States, 2004, with Chartbook on Trends in the Health of Americans.* Hyattsville, MD: NCHS. Available online at http://www.cdc.gov/nchs/data/hus/hus04trend.pdf#hi (accessed April 16, 2006).

———. 2006. "Death Rates for Suicide, According to Sex, Race, Hispanic Origin, and Age: United States, Selected Years 1950–2003," Table 46. Available online at http://www.cdc.gov/nchs/fastats/suicide.htm.

———. 2007. News Release, June 25. Available at http://www.cdc.gov/nchs/pressroom/07newsreleases/insurance.htm.

Negroponte, Nicholas. 1995. *Being Digital.* New York: Knopf.

Nelkin, Dorothy, ed. 1982. *Creation Controversy: Science or Scripture in the Schools?* New York: Norton.

———. 1985. *The Language of Risk: Conflicting Perspectives on Occupational Health.* Beverly Hills, CA: Sage.

———. 1992. *Controversy: Politics of Technical Decisions.* Newbury Park, CA: Sage.

———. 1995a. "Science Controversies: The Dynamics of Public Disputes in the United States." In *Handbook of Science and Technology Studies,* edited by Gerald E. Markle, Sheila Jasanoff, James C. Petersen, and Trevor Pinch, 444–456. Thousand Oaks, CA: Sage.

———. 1995b. *Selling Science: How the Press Covers Science and Technology.* New York: W. H. Freeman.

Neustadt, Richard E. 1960. *Presidential Power: The Politics of Leadership.* New York: Wiley.

Newman, David M. 2000. *Sociology: Exploring the Architecture of Everyday Life,* 3rd ed. Thousand Oaks, CA: Pine Forge.

Nichols, John, and Robert W. McChesney. 2000. *It's the Media, Stupid.* New York: Seven Stories.

Nisbet, Robert A. 1962. "Sociology as an Art Form." In *Tradition and Revolt.* New York: Random House. Reprinted in 1968.

Novak, Michael. 1972. *The Rise of the Unmeltable Ethnics: Politics and Culture in the Seventies.* New York: Macmillan.

Oakley, Ann. 1974. *The Sociology of Housework.* New York: Pantheon, 1974.

———. 1987. "From Walking Wombs to Test-Tube Babies." In *Reproductive Technologies: Gender, Motherhood, and Medicine,* edited by Michelle Stanworth, 36–57. Cambridge, UK: Polity.

———. 1998. "Gender, Methodology, and People's Ways of Knowing: Some Problems with Feminism and the Paradigm Debate in Social Science." *Sociology* 32, no. 4 (1998): 707–731.

O'Connor, Carla. 1997. "Dispositions Toward (Collective) Struggle and Educational Resilience in the Inner City: A Case Analysis of Six African-American High School Students." *American Educational Research Journal* 34, no. 3 (1997): 593–629.

O'Dea, Thomas F. 1993. *The Sociology of Religion.* New York: Free Press

OECD (Organization for Economic Cooperation and Development). 2002. "Society at a Glance: OECD Social Indicators, Underlying Data." Washington, DC: OECD. Available online at www.oecd.org/els/social/indicators.

———. 2003. Health Data File. Available online at www.oecd.org/els/health.

———. 2005a. "Database on Labor Force Statistics." Washington, DC: OECD.

———. 2005b. "OECD Factbook 2005." Washington, DC: OECD.

———. 2006. "OECD Factbook 2006: Economic, Environmental, and Social Statistics." Washington, DC: OECD.

O'Farrell, Brigid, and Joyce L. Kornbluh. 1996. *Rocking the Boat: Union Women's Voices, 1915–1975.* New Brunswick, NJ: Rutgers University Press.

Ogburn, William Fielding. 1964. *On Culture and Social Change.* Chicago: University of Chicago Press.

O'Hara, Mary. 2005. "Walking the Happy Talk." *Guardian,* 2005.

Omi, Michael, and Howard Winant. 1994. *Racial Formation in the United States: From the 1960s to the 1990s.* New York: Routledge.

Orzechowski, Shawna, and Peter Sepielli. 2003. "Current Population Reports: Net Worth and Asset Ownership of Households: 1998 and 2000." In *Demographic Programs, Household Economic Studies,* No. P70-88. Washington, DC: U.S. Department of Commerce, U.S. Census Bureau, Economics and Statistics Administration.

Osherson, Samuel, and Lorna Amara Singham. 1981. "The Machine Metaphor in Medicine." In *Social Contexts of Health, Illness, and Patient Care,* edited by Lorna R. Amara Singham, Elliot G. Mishler, Stuart T. Hauser, Ramsay Liem, Samuel D. Osherson, and Nancy E. Walker, 218–249. Cambridge, UK: Cambridge University Press.

Osterman, Paul. 1999. *Securing Prosperity: The American Labor Market—How It Hanged and What to Do About It.* Princeton, NJ: Princeton University Press.

Pager, Devah. 2003. "The Price of a Criminal Record." *American Journal of Sociology* 108, no. 5: 937–975.

Pager, Devah, and Bruce Western. 2005. "Discrimination in Low-Trust Labor Markets." Paper presented at the American Sociological Association Annual Meeting, Philadelphia.

Pager, Devah, and Lincoln Quillian. 2005. "Walking the Talk? What Employers Say Versus What They Do." *American Sociological Review* 70, no. 3: 355–380.

Palmer, Laura. 1987. *Shrapnel in the Heart: Letters and Remembrances from the Vietnam Veterans Memorial.* New York: Random House.

Palmer, Robert Roswelland, and Joel Colton. 1971. *A History of the Modern World.* New York: Knopf.

Parenti, Michael. 1986. *Inventing Reality.* New York: St. Martin's.

Park, Robert Ezra. 1904. *Masse Und Publikum.* Bern: Buchdruckerei, Lack, and Grunau.

———. 1928. "Human Migration and the Marginal Man." *American Journal of Sociology* 33, no. 6: 881–893.

———. 1950a. *Race and Culture.* New York: Free Press.

———. 1950b. "Racial Assimilation in Secondary Groups with Particular Reference to the Negro." In *Race and Culture: Essays in the Sociology of Contemporary Man,* 204–220. New York: Free Press.

Park, Robert Ezra, and Ernest W. Burgess. 1921. *Introduction to the Science of Sociology.* Chicago: University of Chicago Press.

Parkin, Frank. 1979. *The Marxist Theory of Class: A Bourgeois Critique.* London: Tavistock.

Parlee, Mary Brown. 1994. "The Social Construction of Premenstrual Syndrome: A Case Study of Scientific Discourse as Cultural Contestation." In *The Good Body: Asceticism in Contemporary Culture,* edited by Letha B. Cole and Mary G. Winkler, 91–107. New Haven, CT: Yale University Press.

Parsons, Talcott. 1949. "Social Classes and Class Conflict in the Light of Recent Sociological Theory." In *Essays in Sociological Theory,* 323–347. Glencoe, IL: Free Press. Reprinted in 1963.

———. 1951a. "Illness and the Role of the Physician: A Sociological Perspective." *American Journal of Orthopsychiatry* 21: 452–460.

———. 1951b. *The Social System.* Glencoe, IL: Free Press.

———. 1959. "The School Class as a Social System: Some of Its Functions in American Society." *Harvard Educational Review* 29: 297–318.

———. 1960. *Structure and Process in Modern Societies.* Glencoe, IL: Free Press.

———. 1967. *Sociological Theory and Modern Society.* New York: Free Press.

———. 1972. "Definitions of Healthcare and Illness in Light of American Values and Social Culture." In *Patients, Physicians, and Illness: A Sourcebook in Behavioral Science and Health,* edited by Jaco E. Gartly, 97–117. New York: Free Press.

Pastore, Ann L., and Kathleen Maguire, eds. 1994. *Sourcebook of Criminal Justice Statistics.* Washington, DC: U.S. Government Printing Office.

Pateman, Carole. 1992. "Equality, Difference, Subordination:

The Politics of Motherhood and Women's Citizenship." In *Beyond Equality and Difference: Citizenship, Feminist Politics, and Female Subjectivity*, edited by Gisela Bock and Susan James, 17–31. New York: Routledge.

Patton, Clarence. 2007. "Anti-Lesbian, Gay, Bisexual, and Transgender Violence in 2006." New York: National Coalition of Anti-Violence Programs.

Paul, Pamela. 2002. *The Starter Marriage and the Future of Matrimony*. New York: Random House.

Payer, Lynn, ed. 1988. *Medicine and Culture: Varieties of Treatment in the United States, England, West Germany, and France*. New York: Holt.

Peirce, Kate. 1990. "A Feminist Theoretical Perspective on the Socialization of Teenage Girls Through Seventeen Magazines." *Sex Roles* 23: 491–500.

PEJ (Project for Excellence in Journalism). 2004. "State of the News Media 2004: An Annual Report on American Journalism."

———. 2005. "State of the News Media 2005: An Annual Report on American Journalism."

Perlmann, Joel, and Roger Waldinger. 2000. "Are the Children of Today's Immigrants Making It?" In *Race and Ethnicity in the United States: Issues and Debates*, edited by Stephen Steinberg, 223–233. Malden, MA: Blackwell.

Perrucci, Carolyn C., Robert Perrucci, Dena B. Targ, and Harry R. Targ. 1993. *Plant Closings: International Context and Social Costs*. New York: de Gruyter.

Perry, Barbara. 2001. *In the Name of Hate: Understanding Hate Crimes*. New York: Routledge.

Persons, Stow. 1987. *Ethnic Studies at Chicago, 1905–1945*. Urbana: University of Illinois Press.

Peters, Thomas J., and Robert H. Waterman. 1982. *In Search of Excellence: Lessons from America's Best-Run Companies*. New York: Harper and Row.

Petersen, James R., and Hugh M. Hefner. 1999. *The Century of Sex: Playboy's History of the Sexual Revolution, 1900–1999*. New York: Grove.

Peterson, Gary W., and Boyd C. Rollins. 1987. "Parent-Child Socialization." In *Handbook of Marriage and the Family*, edited by Suzanne K. Steinmetz and Marvin B. Sussman, 471–508. New York: Plenum.

Pew Internet and American Life Project. 2004. *Pew Internet and American Life Project, May–June 2004 Tracking Survey*. Washington, DC: Author.

Pew Research Center for the People and Press. 2004. *Pew Research Center for the People and Press Media Consumption and Believability Study*. Washington, DC: Author. Available online at http://people-press.org.

Phillips, Kevin. 2000. "The Wealth Effect: With Inequality of Income and Tax Burden Growing, Expect the Widening Rich/Poor Divide to Focus the Political Debate." *Los Angeles Times*, April 16, 1.

———. 2002. *Wealth and Democracy: A Political History of the American Rich*. New York: Broadway.

Phillips, Tim, and Philip Smith. 2003. "Everyday Incivility: Towards a Benchmark," *Sociological Review* 51, no. 1: 85–108.

Pierard, Richard V., and Robert D. Lindar. 1988. *Civil Religion and the Presidency*. Grand Rapids, MI: Academie Books.

Piore, Michael J., and Charles F. Sabel. 1984. *Second Industrial Divide: Possibilities for Prosperity*. New York: Basic Books.

Plummer, Kenneth. 1984. "Sexual Diversity: A Sociological Perspective." In *The Psychology of Sexual Diversity*, edited by Kevin Howells, 219–253. Malden, MA: Blackwell.

Polsky, Ned. 1967. *Hustlers, Beats, and Others*. Chicago: Aldine.

Poniewozik, James. 1999. "TV's Coming-Out Party." *Time* (October 25): 116–118.

Popenoe, David. 1988. *Disturbing the Nest: Family Change and Decline in Modern Societies*. New York: Gruyter.

Portes, Alejandro, and Min Zhou. 1993. "The New Second Generation: Segmented Assimilation and Its Variants Among Post-1965 Immigrant Youth." *Annals of the American Academy of Political and Social Science* 530, no. 74: 98.

Portes, Alejandro, and Rubén Rumbaut. 1996. *Immigrant America: A Portrait*. Berkeley: University of California Press.

Postman, Neil. 1985. *Amusing Ourselves to Death: Public Discourse in the Age of Show Business*. London: Heinemann.

Powell, Larry. 1995. *Hunger of the Heart: Communion at the Wall*. Dubuque, IA: Islewest.

Pratt, John. 2000. "How Will Our Soul Be Saved?" *New York Times*, September 29, 9.

Public Agenda Foundation. 1993. *Criminal Violence: What Direction Now for the War on Crime?* New York: McGraw-Hill.

———. 2000. "Clarifying Issues 2000." Available online at http://www.publicagenda.org.

———. 2005. "Crime Overview." Review of reviewed item. Available online at http://www.publicagenda.org.

Public Broadcasting Service. 2001. "People Like Us: Statistics." Available online at http://www.pbs.org/peoplelikeus/resources/stats.html.

Putnam, Robert D. 1995a. "Bowling Alone: America's Declining Social Capital." *Journal of Democracy* 6, no. 1: 65–78.

———. 1995b. "Tuning in, Tuning Out: The Strange Disappearance of Social Capital in America." *Political Science and Politics* 28, no. 4: 664–683.

———. 2000. *Bowling Alone: The Collapse and Revival of American Community*. New York: Simon and Schuster.

Quinney, Richard. 1970. *Social Reality of Crime*. Boston: Little, Brown.

———. 1974. *Critique of Legal Order: Crime Control in Capitalist Society*. Boston: Little, Brown.

———. 1977. *Class, State, and Crime: On the Theory and Practice of Criminal Justice*. New York: Longman.

Radway, Janice. 1984. *Reading the Romance: Women, Patriarchy, and Popular Literature*. Chapel Hill: University of North Carolina Press.

Rainie, Lee. 2005. "The State of Blogging." PEW Internet and American Life Project.

Rasmusson, Erika. 2000. "Strong Signals." *Sports Illustrated for Women* (January 27): 12–15.

Raven, Charlotte. 2001. "A Bully with a Bloody Nose Is Still a Bully." *Guardian*, September 18.

Rayaprol, Aparna. 1997. *Negotiating Identities: Women in the Indian Diaspora*. New York: Oxford University Press.

Rees, Martin J. 2003. *Our Final Hour: A Scientist's Warning: How Terror, Error, and Environmental Disaster Threaten Humankind's Future in This Century—on Earth and Beyond*. New York: Basic Books.

Rehn, Elisabeth, and Ellen Johnson Sirleaf. 2002. "Women, War, and Peace: The Independent Experts' Assessment on the Impact of Armed Conflict on Women and Women's Role in Peace Building." New York: UN Development Fund for Women.

Reich, Robert B. 1991. "The Secession of the Successful." *New York Times*, January 20, 16–21.

Reiman, Jeffrey H. 1979. *The Rich Get Richer and the Poor Get Prison: Ideology, Class, and Criminal Justice*. New York: Wiley. Reprinted by Macmillan 1998.

———. 1990. *Justice and Modern Moral Philosophy*. New Haven, CT: Yale University Press.

Reinharz, Shulamit. 1992. *Feminist Methods in Social Research*. New York: Oxford University Press.

Reisman, David. 1950. *The Lonely Crowd: A Study of the Changing American Character*. New Haven, CT: Yale University Press.

Rennison, Callie Marie. 2001. "Criminal Victimization, 2000: Changes 1999–2000 with Trends 1993–2000." Washington, DC: U.S. Department of Justice.

*Research Today*. 1999. Available online at http://www.ed.gov/pubs/ResearchToday/98-3038.html.

Reskin, Barbara F., and Patricia A. Roos. 1990. *Job Queues, Gender Queues: Explaining Women's Inroads into Male Occupations*. Philadelphia, PA: Temple University Press.

Rheingold, Harriet L., and Kaye V. Cook. 1975. "The Contents of Boys' and Girls' Rooms as an Index of Parents' Behavior." *Child Development* 46, no. 2: 459–463.

Rich, Adrienne. 1994. "Compulsory Heterosexuality and Lesbian Existence." In *Living with Contradictions: Controversies in Feminist Social Ethics*, edited by Alison M. Jaggar, 487–490. Boulder, CO: Westview.

Riding, Alan. 1999. "Arts Abroad: French Comic Book Heroes Battle Hollywood's Hordes." *New York Times*, February 10, 32.

Rifkin, Jeremy. 2003. "Comment and Analysis: Dazzled by the Science—Biologists Who Dress Up Hi-Tech Eugenics as a New Art Form Are Dangerously Deluded." *Guardian*, January 14, 17.

Rincon, Paul. 2006. "U.S. Troops Taught Iraqi Gestures." Review of Reviewed Item. *BBC News*. Available online at bbc.co.uk./1/hi/technology/4729262.stm.

Rindfuss, Ronald R., C. Gray Swicegood, and Rachel A. Rosenfeld. 1987. "Disorder in the Life Course: How Common and Does It Matter?" *American Sociological Review* 52: 785–801.

Rist, Marilee C. 1990. "Angling for Influence." *American School Board Journal*.

Roberts, Donald F., and Ulla G. Foehr. 2004. *Kids and Media in America*. Cambridge, UK: Cambridge University Press.

Roberts, Donald F., Ulla G. Foehr, and Victoria Rideout. 2005. "Generation M: Media in the Lives of 8–18-Year-Olds," Kaiser Family Foundation Study. Available at http://www.kff.org/entmedia/7251.cfm (accessed July 27, 2006).

Robson, Colin. 1993. *Real World Research: A Resource for Social Scientists and Practitioner-Researchers*. Cambridge, UK: Blackwell.

Rodham, Karen, Keith Hawton, and Emma Evans. 2005. "Deliberate Self-Harm in Adolescents: The Importance of Gender." *Psychiatric Times* 22, no. 1 (January). Available online at http:www.psychiatrictimes.com/article/showArticle.jhtml?articleId=60400121.

Roethlisberger, Fritz Jules, and William J. Dickson. 1939. *Management and the Worker*. Cambridge, MA: Harvard University Press.

Roof, Wade Clark, and William McKinney. 1987. *American Mainline Religion: Its Changing Shape and Future*. New Brunswick, NJ: Rutgers University Press.

Roozen, David A., and C. Kirk Hadaway. 1993. *Church and Denominational Growth*. Nashville, TN: Abingdon.

Roscoe, Bruce, and Karen L. Paterson. 1983. "The TST for Assessing the Self-Concepts of College Students: Comparisons with Earlier Years." *College Students Journal* 17, no. 2: 134–136.

Rose, Suzanna, and Irene Hanson Frieze. 1989. "Young Singles' Scripts for a First Date." *Gender and Society* 3, no. 3: 258–268.

Rosenblatt, Roger. 1999. "Welcome to the Works of the Trench Coat." *Time* (May 3): 88.

Rosenfelt, Deborah Silverton. 1994. "'Definitive' Issues: Women's Studies, Multicultural Education, and Curriculum Transformation in Policy and Practice in the United States." *Women's Studies Quarterly* 22, nos. 3–4: 26–41.

Rosenthal, Andrew. 1992. "After the Riots: Quayle Says Riots Sprang from a Lack of Family Values." *New York Times*, May 20, 1.

Rosenthal, Robert, and Lenore Jacobson. 1968. *Pygmalion in the Classroom: Teacher Expectation and Pupils' Intellectual Development*. New York: Holt, Rinehart, and Winston.

Rosner, David, and Gerald Markowitz. 1991. *Deadly Dust:*

*Silicosis and the Politics of Occupational Disease in Twentieth-Century America.* Princeton, NJ: Princeton University Press.

Ross, Chuck. 1999. "NBC's *Passions* to Join TV Merchandizing Parade." *Advertising Age* (June 28): 64.

Ross, Edward Alsworth. 1914. *The Old World in the New: The Significance of Past and Present Immigration to the American People.* New York: Century.

Roszak, Theodore. 1970. "The Monster and the Titan." *Daedalus* 103, no. 3: 17–32.

Roudometof, Victor. 2005. *Collective Memory, National Identity, and Ethnic Conflict.* Westport, CT: Praeger.

Rouse, Roger. 1992. "Making Sense of Settlement: Class Transformation, Cultural Struggle, and Transnationalism Among Mexican Migrants in the United States." In *Towards a Transnational Perspective on Migration*, edited by Linda Basch, Nina Glick Schiller, and Cristina Blanc-Szanton, 25–52. New York: New York Academy of Sciences.

Rousseau, Jean-Jacques. 1750. "Discourse on the Sciences and the Arts." In *Basic Political Writings of Jean-Jacques Rousseau*, edited by Donald A. Cress, 1–21. Indianapolis: Hackett. Reprinted in 1964 and 1987.

Rowland, Robyn. 1985. "Motherhood, Patriarchal Power, Alienation, and the Issue of 'Choice' in Sex Preselection." In *Man-Made Women: How New Reproductive Technologies Affect Women*, edited by Gena Corea, Renate Duelli Klein, Jalna Hammer, Helen B. Holmes, Madhu Kishwar, Janice Raymond, Robyn Rowland, and Roberta Steinbacher, 74–87. London: Hutchinson.

Roy, Donald. 1952. "Quota Restriction and Goldbricking in a Machine Shop." *American Journal of Sociology* 57, no. 427–442.

Rubin, J. Z., F. Provenzono, and Z. Luria. 1974. "The Eye of the Beholder: Parents' Views on Sex of Newborns." *American Journal of Orthopsychiatry* 44, no. 4: 512–519.

Rúmbaut, Ruben G. 1991. "Passages to America: Perspectives on the New Immigration." In *America at Century's End*, edited by Alan Wolfe, 208–244. Berkeley: University of California Press.

Ryan, Chris. 2001. *Sex Tourism: Marginal People and Liminalities.* New York: Routledge.

Salamon, Julie. 2002. "For Richer, for Poorer, and for a Documentary." *New York Times*, June 17, 5.

Samenow, Samuel, and Stanton E. Yochelson. 1976. *The Criminal.* New York: Aronson.

Samuelson, Paul A. 1947. *The Foundations of Economic Analysis.* Cambridge, MA: Harvard University Press.

Sanchez, Rene. 2002. "John Walker's Restless Quest Is Strange Odyssey." *Washington Post*, January 14, 1.

Santino, Jack. 1989. *Years of Smiles, Years of Struggle: Stories of Black Pullman Porters.* Urbana: University of Illinois Press.

Sarantakos, S. 1993. *Social Research.* Melbourne, Australia: Macmillan.

Sasson, Theodore. 1995. *Crime Talk: How Citizens Construct a Social Problem.* New York: de Gruyter.

Savitch, H. V., and Grigoriy Ardashev. 2001. "Does Terror Have an Urban Future?" *Urban Studies* 38, no. 13: 2515–2533.

Saxenian, AnnaLee. 1994. *Regional Advantage: Culture and Competition in Silicon Valley and Route 128.* Cambridge, MA: Harvard University Press.

Schatten, Gerald, and Helen Schatten. 1984. "The Energetic Egg." *Medical World News* (January 23): 52–53.

Scheder, Jo. 1988. "A Sickly-Sweet Harvest: Farmworker Diabetes and Social Equality." *Medical Anthropology Quarterly* 2, no. 3: 251–277.

Scheingold, Stuart. 1991. *The Politics of Street Crime: Criminal Process and Cultural Obsession.* Philadelphia, PA: Temple University Press.

Schiller, Herbert I. 1969. *Mass Communications and American Empire.* New York: Kelley.

Schlegel, Alice, and Herbert Barry III. 1991. *Adolescence: An Anthropological Inquiry.* New York: Free Press.

Schlesinger, Jacob M. 1987. "Costly Friendship: Auto Firms and UAW Find That Cooperation Can Get Complicated" *Wall Street Journal*, August 25, 1.

Schneider, Joseph W., and Peter Conrad. 1980. "In the Closet with Illness: Epilepsy, Stigma Potential, and Information Control." *Social Problems* 28, no. 32–44.

Schneider, Norbert F. 1996. "Partnerschaften mit Getrennten Haushalten in den Neuen und Alten Bundesländern." In *Familie an der Schwelle zum Neuen Jahrtausend*, edited by Walter Bien, 88–97. Opladen, Germany: Leske and Budrich.

Schoeni, Robert, F., and Karen E. Ross. 2005. "Material Assistance from Families." In *On the Frontier of Adulthood: Theory, Research, and Public Policy*, edited by Richard A. Settersten Jr., Frank F. Furstenberg Jr., and Rubén G. Rumbaut. Chicago: University of Chicago Press.

Schor, Juliet B. 1991. *The Overworked American: The Unexpected Decline of Leisure.* New York: Basic Books.

Schudson, Michael. 1995. *The Power of News.* Cambridge, MA: Harvard University Press.

———. 1998. *The Good Citizen: A History of American Civic Life.* Reprint ed. Cambridge, MA: Harvard University Press.

Schumacher, Ernst Friedrich. 1973. *Small Is Beautiful: A Study of Economics as if People Mattered.* London: Blond and Briggs.

Schuman, Howard, and Charlotte Steeh. 1996. "The Complexity of Racial Attitudes in America." In *Origins and Destinies: Immigration, Race, and Ethnicity in America*, edited by Sylvia Pedraza and Ruben G. Rumbaut. Belmont, CA: Wadsworth.

Schwartz Cowan, Ruth. 1983. *More Work for Mother: The Ironies of Household Technology from the Open Hearth to the Microwave.* New York: Basic Books.

Scott, Malvin B. 1968. *Racing Game*. Chicago: Aldine.

Scott, W. Richard. 1981. *Organizations: Rational, National, and Open-System*. Englewood Cliffs, NJ: Prentice-Hall.

Scruggs, Jan C., and Joel L. Swerdlow. 1985. *To Heal a Nation: The Vietnam Veterans Memorial*. New York: Harper and Row.

Seidler, Victor J. 1989. *Rediscovering Masculinity: Reason, Language, and Sexuality*. New York: Routledge.

Seidman, Steven. 1991. *Romantic Longings: Love in America, 1830–1980*. New York: Routledge.

Select Committee Appointed to Consider Science and Technology, House of Lords: United Kingdom House of Parliament. 2000. "Sixth Report: Complementary and Alternative Medicine."

"Self and Circuitry." 2003. *Scientific American* (January 8).

Serrano, Richard A. 1998. "Internet Promotes a Surge in Hate Groups, Study Finds; Racism: Organizations Showed 20% Increase Nationwide from 1996 to 1997, Report Says. Computer Network, Doomsday Rhetoric Are Blamed." *Los Angeles Times*, March 28, 10.

Shachar, Orly. 2000. "Spotlighting Women Scientists in the Press: Tokenism in Science Journalism." *Public Understanding of Science* 9, no. 4: 347–358.

Shanahan, Michael J., and Ross Macmillan. 2008. *Biography and the Sociological Imagination: Contexts and Contingencies*. New York: Norton.

Shaw, Clifford Robe. 1930. *The Jack Roller: A Delinquent Boy's Own Story*. Chicago: University of Chicago Press.

Shelley, Kristina J. 1992. "The Future Jobs of College Graduates." *Monthly Labor Review* 115, no. 7: 13–21.

Shelley, Mary Wollstonecraft. 1922. *Frankenstein*. New York: Dutton.

Sherif, Muzar, and Carolyn Sherif. 1953. *Groups in Harmony and Tension: An Integration of Studies on Intergroup Relations*. New York: Harper.

Shi, David E. 1995. *Facing Facts: Realism in American Thought and Culture, 1850–1920*. New York: Oxford University Press.

Shinagawa, Larry Hajime. 1996. "The Impact of Immigration on the Demography of Asian Pacific Americans." In *The State of Asian-Pacific America: Reframing the Immigration Debate—A Public Policy Report*, edited by Bill Ong Hing and Ronald Lee, 59–126. Los Angeles: LEAP Asian Pacific American Public Policy Institute/UCLA Asian American Studies Center.

Shklar, Judith N. 1991. *American Citizenship: The Quest for Inclusion*. Cambridge, MA: Harvard University Press.

Shweder, Richard A. 2000. "What About "Female Genital Mutilation"? And Why Understanding Culture Matters in the First Place." *Daedalus* 129, no. 4: 209–232.

Signorielli, N., and A. Bacue. "Recognition and Respect: A Content Analysis of Prime Time Television Characters across Three Decades." *Sex Roles* 40, no. 7–8: 527–544.

Silverstein, Brett, Lauren Perdue, Barbara Peterson, and Eileen Kelly. 1986. "The Role of the Mass Media in Promoting a Thin Standard of Bodily Attractiveness for Women." *Sex Roles* 14: 519–532.

Simmel, Georg. 1903. "The Metropolis and Mental Life." In *The Sociology of Georg Simmel*, edited by Kurt H. Wolf, 409–424. New York: Free Press. Reprinted in 1950.

Sismondo, Sergio. 1995. "The Scientific Domains of Feminist Standpoints." *Perspectives on Science* 3, no. 1: 49–65.

Skinner, Quentin. 1978. "The Foundations of Modern Political Thought." Cambridge, UK: Cambridge University Press.

Skocpol, Theda. 1979. *States and Social Revolutions: A Comparative Analysis of France, Russia, and China*. Cambridge, UK: Cambridge University Press.

———. 1985. "Bringing the State Back In: Strategies of Analysis in Current Research." In *Bringing the State Back In*, edited by Dietrich Rueschemeyer, Peter B. Evans, and Theda Skocpol, 3–37. Cambridge, UK: Cambridge University Press.

Skrentny, John David. 1996. *The Ironies of Affirmative Action: Politics, Culture, and Justice in America*. Chicago: University of Chicago Press.

Sloan, Allan. 2006. "Laying Enron to Rest." *Newsweek* (June 5).

Smeeding, Timothy M. 1997. "The International Evidence on Income Distribution in Modern Economics." In *Poverty and Inequality: The Political Economy of Redistribution*, edited by Jon Neill, 79–103. Kalamazoo, MI: W. E. Upjohn Institute for Employment Research.

Smelser, Neil. 1962. *Theory of Collective Behavior*. New York: Free Press.

Smelser, Neil, and Jeffrey Alexander. 1999. *Diversity and Its Discontents: Cultural Conflict and Common Ground in Contemporary American Society*. Princeton, NJ: Princeton University Press.

Smith, Dorothy E. 1987. *The Everyday World as Problematic: A Feminist Sociology*. Boston: Northeastern University Press.

Smith, Neil, and Peter Williams. 1986. *Gentrification of the City*. Boston: Allen and Unwin.

Smith, Philip. 2000. "Culture and Charisma: Outline of a Theory." *Acta Sociologica* 43, no. 2: 101–111.

Smith, Thomas M., Marianne Perie, Nebeel Alsalam, Rebecca Pratt Mahoney, Yupin Bae, and Beth Aronstamm Young. 1995. "The Condition of Education." Washington, DC: National Center for Education Statistics.

Smith, Vicki. 2001. *Crossing the Great Divide: Worker Risk and Opportunity in the New Economy*. Ithaca, NY: ILR.

Sniggle.net. 1997. "Barbie Liberation." Available online at http://www.sniggle.net/barbie.php.

Snow, D. A., and C. Phillips. 1982. "The Changing Self-Orientation of College Students: From Institution to Impulse." *Social Science Quarterly* 63: 462–476.

Snow, D. A., et al. 1986. "Frame Alignment Processes, Micromobilisation, and Movement Participation." *American Sociological Review* 51: 464–481.

Soja, Edward W. 1989. *Postmodern Geographies: The Reassertion of Space in Critical Social Theory*. New York: Verso.

———. 1997. "Six Discourses on the Postmetropolis." In *Imagining Cities: Scripts, Signs, Memory*, edited by Sallie Westwood and John Williams, 19–30. New York: Routledge.

Sokal, Alan, and Jean Bricmont. 1998. *Fashionable Nonsense: Postmodern Intellectuals' Abuse of Science*. New York: Picador.

Spenner, Kenneth L. 1983. "Deciphering Prometheus: Temporal Change in the Skill Level of Work." *American Sociological Review* 48, no. 6: 824–837.

Sprigge, Elizabeth. 1957. *Gertrude Stein: Her Life and Work*. New York: Harper.

Stanley, Harold W., and Richard G. Niemi. 2006. *Vital Statistics on American Politics, 2005–2006*. Washington, DC: Congressional Quarterly Press.

Stark, Rodney, and William Sims Bainbridge. 1987. *A Theory of Religion*. New Brunswick, NJ: Rutgers University Press.

Steinberg, Stephen. 1995. *Turning Back: The Retreat from Racial Justice in American Thought and Policy*. Boston: Beacon.

Steinhauer, Jennifer. 2007. "Korean-Americans Brace for Problems in Wake of Killings." *New York Times*, April 19, A19.

Stephens, William N. 1963. *The Family in Cross-Cultural Perspective*. New York: Holt, Rinehart, and Winston.

Stern, B. J. 1938. "Restraints upon the Utilization of Inventors." *Annals of the American Academy of Political and Social Science* 200: 13–32.

Stern, Christopher. 1999a. "D.C. Spin." *Variety* (June 28–July 11): 8.

———. 1999b. "Radio Receives Rivals by Satellite." *Variety* (June 28–July 11).

Stevenson, Richard W. 1992. "Maker Is Accused of Faulty Tests on Parts for Missiles and Aircrafts." *New York Times*, April 23.

Stevenson, Richard W., and Jeff Gerth. 2002. "Enron's Collapse: The System; Web of Safeguards Failed as Enron Fell." *New York Times*, January 20, 1.

Stocks, Janet. 1997. "To Stay or to Leave? Organizational Legitimacy in the Struggle for Change Among Evangelical Feminists." In *Contemporary American Religion: An Ethnographic Reader*, edited by Nancy L. Eiesland and Penny Edgell Becker, 99–119. Walnut Creek, CA: Alta-Mira.

Storr, Merl. 2002. "Sociology and Social Movements: Theories, Analysis, and Ethical Dilemmas." In *The Uses of Sociology*, edited by Kenneth Thompson and Peter Hamilton, 175–220. Cambridge, UK: Blackwell.

"Study Finds That Women Pressure Many Fraternity Pledges into Sex." 1999. *Chronicle of Higher Education* (August 6).

Sullivan, Oriel. 2000. "The Division of Domestic Labor: Twenty Years of Change?" *Sociology* 34, no. 3: 437–456.

Sullivan, Randall. 1998. "A Boy's Life." *Rolling Stone*: 46–53.

Sulloway, Frank J. 1996. *Born to Rebel: Birth Order, Family Dynamics, and Creative Lives*. New York: Pantheon.

Surette, Ray. 1998. *Media, Crime, and Criminal Justice: Images and Realities*. Belmont, CA: Wadsworth.

Takahashi, Dean. 1998. "Ethnic Networks Help Immigrants Rise in Silicon Valley." *Wall Street Journal*, March 18, 1.

Talbot, Margaret. 1997. "Love, American Style." *New Republic* (April 14): 30–38.

Talese, Gay. 1980. *Thy Neighbor's Wife*. Garden City, NY: Doubleday.

Tang Nain, Gemma. 1991. "Black Women, Sexism, and Racism: Black or Anti-Racist Feminism?" *Feminist Review* 37: 1–22.

Tarnas, Richard. 1991. *The Passion of the Western Mind: Understanding the Ideas That Have Shaped Our World View*. New York: Harmony.

Taylor, Frederick Winslow. 1911. *The Principles of Scientific Management*. New York: Harper.

Teather, David. 2003. "U.S. Wages Divide Is Wider Than Ever." *Guardian*, April 1, 19.

Teinowitz, Ira. 1999. "Study: Net Prime-Time Clutter Worsens." *Advertising Age* 70, no. 16: 36.

Thomas, William Isaac. 1931. *On Social Organization and Social Personality; Selected Papers*. Chicago: University of Chicago Press. Reprinted in 1966.

Thomas, William Isaac, and Florian Znaniecki. 1927. *The Polish Peasant in Europe and America*. New York: Knopf.

Thompson, Kenneth. 1976. *Auguste Comte: The Foundation of Sociology*. New York: Halsted.

———. 1994. "Identity and Belief." In *The United States in the Twentieth Century: Culture*, edited by Richard Maidment and Jeremy Mitchell, 13–38. London: Hodder and Stoughton.

———. 1997. *Media and Cultural Regulation*. Thousand Oaks, CA: Sage.

———. 1998. *Moral Panics*. New York: Routledge.

———. 2002. "Border Crossings and Diasporic Identities: Media Use and Leisure Practices of an Ethnic Minority." *Qualitative Sociology* 25, no. 3: 409–418.

———. 2005. *The Early Sociology of Race and Ethnicity in the United States*. London: Routledge.

Thorne, Barrie, and Zella Luria. 1986. "Sexuality and Gender in Children's Daily Worlds." *Social Problems* 33, no. 3: 176–190.

Thrasher, Frederic. 1927. *The Gang: A Study of 1,313 Gangs in Chicago*. Chicago: University of Chicago Press. Reprinted in 1936.

Tibaijuka, Anna. 2005. *The State of the World's Cities 2004–2005: Globalization and Urban Culture.* New York: UN Human Settlements Programme.

Tipton, Steven M. 1982. *Getting Saved from the Sixties: Moral Meaning in Conversion and Cultural Change.* Berkeley: University of California Press.

Tobar, Hector. 2000. "Column One; Heartland Tuning in to Spanish; Even in Remote Parts of the Plains and Rockies, Oldies and Talk Radio Stations Are Giving Way to Mexican Ballads and the Norteña." *Los Angeles Times,* June 23, 1.

Toffler, Alvin. 1970. *Future Shock.* New York: Random House.
——. 1980. *The Third Wave.* New York: Morrow.

Tonnies, Ferdinand. 1887. *Community and Society.* New Brunswick, NJ: Transaction. Reprinted in 1963.

"Totally Wired: Who Should Rescue?" 2002. *TomPaine.common sense: A Public Interest Journal.* Available online at http://www.tompaine.com/Archive/scontent/5031.html.

Touraine, Alain. 1971. *The Post-Industrial Society: Tomorrow's Social History—Classes, Conflicts, and Culture in the Programmed Society.* New York: Random House.
——. 1980. *Prophe?tie Anti-Nucle?aire.* Paris: Seuil.

"A Tragedy at Columbine." 1999. *Denver Rocky Mountain News* (editorial), April 21, 4.

Treaster, Joseph B., and Melody Peterson. 2000. "Florida Study Claims That Prudential Cheated Customers." *New York Times,* December 22, 20.

Troeltsch, Ernst. 1931. *The Social Teaching of the Christian Churches.* New York: Macmillan.

Trost, Jan. 1979. *Unmarried Cohabitation.* Vasteras: International Library.

Tucker, Ken. 2001. "On the Air: TV Shifts Back to Entertainment Coverage." *Entertainment Weekly* (September 17): 8–10.

Tucker, Robert C., ed. 1978. *The Marx-Engels Reader.* New York: Norton.

Tumin, Melvin M. 1953. "Some Principles of Stratification: A Critical Analysis." *American Sociological Review* 18, no. 4: 387–394.

Tunnell, Kenneth D. 1992. *Choosing Crime: The Criminal Calculus of Property Offenders.* Chicago: Nelson-Hall.

Turner, Bryan S. 1986. *Citizenship and Capitalism: The Debate over Reformism.* London: Allen and Unwin.

Uchitelle, Louis. 1997. "The Nation; More Work, Less Play Make Jack Look Better Off." *New York Times,* October 5, 4.

Uhlenberg, Peter. 1980. "Death and the Family." *Journal of Family History* 5 (Fall): 313–320.

UNAIDS/WHO (UN Programme on HIV/AIDS and World Health Organization). 2004. "Aids Epidemic Update: December 2004." Geneva, Switzerland: UNAIDS/WHO.
——. 2005a. "Aids Epidemic Update: December 2005." Geneva, Switzerland: UNAIDS/WHO.

——. 2005b. "AIDS Epidemic Update 2005: Sub-Saharan Africa Fact Sheet." Geneva, Switzerland: UNAIDS/WHO.

UN Department of Economic and Social Affairs. 2004. "World Urbanization Prospects: The 2003 Revision." New York: UN Department of Economic and Social Affairs Population Division.

UN Development Program. 1992. *Human Development Report 1992.* New York: Oxford University Press.
——. 1999. *Human Development Report 1999.* New York: Oxford University Press.
——. 2001. *Human Development Report 2001.* New York: Oxford University Press.
——. 2005. *Human Development Report 2005.* Oxford: Oxford University Press.

UNESCO (United Nations Educational, Cultural, and Scientific Organization). 2004. "The Literacy Decade: Getting Started, 2003–2004." In *The UN Literacy Decade (2003–2012) Report.* Paris: UNESCO.
——. 2005a. "Literacy Assessment and Monitoring Programme (Lamp)." Montreal, Canada: UNESCO Institute for Statistics.
——. 2005b. "Women Still Left Behind in Efforts to Achieve Global Literacy (Fact Sheet 6)." Montreal, Canada: UNESCO Institute for Statistics.

United Kingdom House of Parliament. 2000. Sixth Report: "Complementary and Alternative Medicine." House of Lords, Select Committee Appointed to Consider Science and Technology, November 21. Available online at http://www.parliament.the-stationery-office.co.uk/pa/ld199900/Idselect/Idsctech/123/12301.htm (accessed April,16, 2006).

United Nations. 2000. *The World's Women, 2000: Trends and Statistics.* New York: United Nations.

UN Population Fund. 2000. "The State of World Population 2000: Lives Together, Worlds Apart—Men and Women in a Time of Change." New York: UN Population Fund.

UN Statistics Division. UN Common Database (UNCDB). Available online at http://unstats.un.org/unsd/cdb/cdb_help/cdb_quick_start.asp.

Updike, John. 1968. *Couples.* New York: Knopf.

U.S. Census Bureau. 1993. "Education: The Ticket to Higher Earnings." Washington, DC: U.S. Department of Commerce, U.S. Census Bureau.
——. 1996. "Current Population Reports: P25-1130, 13, Table J—Population Projections of the United States by Age, Sex, Race, and Hispanic Origin, 1995–2050." Washington, DC: U.S. Department of Commerce.
——. 1999. "Income Inequality (Middle Class)." Washington, DC: U.S. Department of Commerce.
——. 2000. Sample Edited Detail File. Washington, DC: U.S. Department of Commerce.
——. 2001a. "Current Population Survey, March 2000. De-

rived from Table 3.6—Year of Entry of the Foreign-Born Population by Sex and World Region of Birth: March 2000." Washington, DC: U.S. Department of Commerce.

———. 2001b. "Current Population Survey: Computer and Internet Use in the United States—September 2001 Detailed Tables," 1–175. Washington, DC: U.S. Department of Commerce.

———. 2002. Available online at www.census.gov/prod/2002 pubs/p23-210.pdf.

———. 2002. Statistical Abstract of the United States. "Death Rates from Suicide by Sex and Race: 1990 to 2002," Table 114. Available online at http://www.census.gov/compendia/statb/vital_statistics/deaths.

———. 2003. Available online at http://www.census.gov/acsd/www/history.html.

———. 2004a. "Historical Income Tables: People, Table P-36—Full-Time, Year-Round Workers (All Races) by Median Income and Sex, 1955–2001." Washington, DC: U.S. Department of Commerce.

———. 2004b. "Educational Attainment: Table PINC-03—People 25 Years Old and Over, by Total Money Earnings in 2003, Work Experience in 2003, Age, Race, Hispanic Origin, and Sex." Washington, DC: U.S. Department of Commerce.

———. 2005a. "Historical Income Tables: People; Table P-2—Race and Hispanic Origin of People by Median Income and Sex, 1947–2003." Washington, DC: U.S. Department of Commerce.

———. 2005b. Current Population Survey. March and Annual Social and Economic Supplements, 2004 and Earlier. Table MS-2. Washington, DC: U.S. Department of Commerce.

U.S. Department of Commerce. 1975. Historical Statistics of the United States: Colonial Times to 1970. Washington, DC: U.S. Government Printing Office.

———. 1998. "'Rust Belt' Rebounds." Washington, DC: U.S. Government Printing Office.

U.S. Department of Education, National Center for Education Statistics. 1987. "The Condition of Education." Washington, DC: NCES.

———. 2003a. "The Condition of Education 2003 (NCES 2003–067)," Table 15-2. Washington, DC: NCES.

———. 2003b. "Young Children's Access to Computers in the Home and at School in 1999 and 2000." Washington, DC: NCES.

———. 2004. "The Condition of Education 2004 (NCES 2004–077)," Indicator 14 and Table 14-1. Washington, DC: NCES.

U.S. Department of Justice, Bureau of Justice Statistics. 2001a. "Criminal Offenders Statistics, 2001." Washington, DC: Bureau of Justice Statistics.

———. 2001b. "Property Crime Rates Continue to Decline." Bureau of Justice Statistics.

U.S. Department of Labor. 2003. Current Population Survey.

Washington, DC: U.S. Bureau of Labor Statistics, Division of Current Employment Statistics.

———. 2005a. Current Population Survey. Washington, DC: U.S. Bureau of Labor Statistics, Division of Current Employment Statistics.

———. 2005b. Current Employment Statistics. Washington, DC: U.S. Bureau of Labor Statistics, Division of Current Employment Statistics.

———. 2005c. "The State Crises: Manufacturing Jobs Lost." U.S. Department of Labor, Bureau of Labor Statistics.

———. 2005d. Press Release, Union Members Summary. USDL 05-112. U.S. Department of Labor, Bureau of Labor Statistics. Available online at http://www.bls.gov/news.release/union2.nr0.htm (accessed July 31, 2005).

Van den Berghe, Pierre L. 1978. Race and Racism: A Comparative Perspective. New York: Wiley.

Van Natta, Don, and Jane Fritsch. 1997. "$250,000 Buys Donors Best Access to Congress." New York Times, January 27, 1.

Venturi, Robert, Denise Scott Brown, and Steven Izenour. 1977. Learning from Las Vegas. Cambridge: Massachusetts Institute of Technology Press.

Verbrugge, Lois M. 1985. "Gender and Health: An Update on Hypotheses and Evidence." Journal of Health and Social Behavior 26, no. 3: 156–182.

Vigil, James Diego. 1988. Barrio Gangs: Street Life and Identity in Southern California. Austin: University of Texas Press.

Vinge, Vernor. 1993. "The Singularity." Review of Reviewed Item. Available online at http://hem.passagen.se/replikant/vernor_vinge_singularity.htm.

Wajcman, Judy. 1995. "Feminist Theories of Technology." In Handbook of Science and Technology Studies, edited by Gerald E. Markle, Sheila Jasnoff, James C. Petersen, and Trevor Pinch, 189–204. Thousand Oaks, CA: Sage.

Walby, Sylvia. 1990. Theorizing Patriarchy. Cambridge, UK: Blackwell.

Waldron, Ingrid. 1981. "Why Do Women Live Longer Than Men?" In Sociology of Health and Illness: Critical Perspectives, edited by Peter Conrad and Rochelle Kern, 45–66. New York: St. Martin's.

Walsh, Mary Williams. 2000a. "Latinos' Net Worth Shrinking Despite Boom Times." Los Angeles Times, March 25, 16.

———. 2000b. "'New Economy' Deepens the Wealth Divide." Los Angeles Times, April 19, 1.

Waltzer, Michael. 1990. "What Does It Mean to Be an 'American'?" Social Research 1, no. 3: 633–654.

Warner, R. Stephen. 1993. "Work in Progress Toward a New Paradigm for the Sociological Study of Religion in the United States." American Journal of Sociology 98, no. 5: 1044–1193.

Warner, W. Lloyd, and Leo Srole. 1945. Social Systems of American Ethnic Groups. New Haven, CT: Yale University Press.

Wartik, Nancy. 2000. "Depression Comes Out of Hiding." *New York Times*, June 25, 1.

Waters, Mary C., and Karl Eschbach. 1999. "Immigration and Ethnic and Racial Inequality in the United States." In *Majority and Minority: The Dynamics of Race and Ethnicity in American Life*, edited by Norman R. Yetman, 312–327. Boston: Allyn and Bacon.

Watters, Ethan. 2001. "The Way We Live Now." *New York Times*, October 14, 25.

Weber, Max. 1904. *The Protestant Ethic and the Spirit of Capitalism*. New York: Scribner. Reprinted in 1930.

———. 1947. *The Theory of Social and Economic Organization*. Glencoe, IL: Free Press.

———. 1958a. *From Max Weber: Essays in Sociology*, edited by C. Wright Mills and H. H. Gerth. New York: Oxford University Press.

———. 1958b. "Bureaucracy." In *From Max Weber: Essays in Sociology*, edited by C. Wright Mills and H. H. Gerth, 196–244. New York: Oxford University Press.

———. 1958c. "Class, Status, Party." In *From Max Weber: Essays in Sociology*, edited by C. Wright Mills and H. H. Gerth, 180–195. New York: Oxford University Press.

———. 1958d. "Politics as a Vocation." In *From Max Weber: Essays in Sociology*, edited by C. Wright Mills and H. H. Gerth, 77–128. New York: Oxford University Press.

———. 1958e. "Religious Rejections of the World and Their Directions." In *From Max Weber: Essays in Sociology*, edited by C. Wright Mills and H. H. Gerth, 323–359. New York: Oxford University Press.

———. 1958f. "The Social Psychology of World Religions." In *From Max Weber: Essays in Sociology*, edited by C. Wright Mills and H. H. Gerth, 267–301. New York: Oxford University Press.

———. 1968. *Economy and Society*. New York: Bedminster. Reprinted 1978 by University of California Press.

Weedon, Chris. 1987. *Feminist Practice and Poststructuralist Theory*. Cambridge, UK: Blackwell.

Weeks, Jeffrey. 1986. *Sexuality*. New York: Tavistock.

———. 1998. "The Sexual Citizen." *Theory, Culture, and Society* 15, nos. 3–4: 35–52.

Weisman, Jonathan. 1990. "$25,000 Bonuses for Exemplary Teachers Include One String—Their Donor, Milken." *Education Week* 10, no. 11: 1–18.

Wells, Matt. 2001. "Repeat Showings of Towers 'Pornographic.'" *Guardian*, November 15, 13.

West, Candace, and Don H. Zimmerman. 1987. "Doing Gender." *Gender and Society* 1, no. 2: 125–151.

White, David Manning. 1950. "The 'Gate Keeper': A Case Study in the Selection of News." *Journalism Quarterly* 27, no. 4: 383–390.

Whitehead, Barbara Dafoe. 1997. *The Divorce Culture*. New York: Knopf.

Whitehead, Harriet. 1981. "The Bow and the Burden Strap: A New Look at Institutionalized Homosexuality in Native North America." In *Sexual Meanings: The Cultural Construction of Gender and Sexuality*, edited by Sherry B. Ortner and Harriet Whitehead, 80–115. Cambridge, UK: Cambridge University Press.

Whitney, Craig R. 1999. "France Begins Trial of Ex-Officials over H.I.V.-Tainted Blood." *New York Times*, February 9, 32.

WHO (World Health Organization). 2000a. *The World Health Organization Report 2000: Health Systems—Improving Performance*. Geneva, Switzerland: WHO.

———. 2000b. *WHO Issues New Healthy Life Expectancy Rankings*. Washington, DC/Geneva, Switzerland, June 4.

Whyte, William Foote. 1943. *Street Corner Society*. Chicago: University of Chicago Press.

Whyte, William H. 1956. *Organization Man*. New York: Simon and Schuster.

Wilkinson, Richard. 1996. *Unhealthy Societies: The Afflictions of Inequality*. New York: Routledge.

Williams, Daniel. 2003. "In France, Students Observe Scarf Ban. Hostage Takers in Iraq Had Called for Repeal." *Washington Post*, September 3, 11.

Williams, Robin Murphy. 1951. *American Society: A Sociological Interpretation*. New York: Knopf.

Wilson, Bryan R. 1966. *Religion in Secular Society*. London: Watts.

Wilson, James Q., and Richard J. Herrnstein. 1985. *Crime and Human Nature*. New York: Simon and Schuster.

Wilson, Sloan. 2002. *Man in a Gray Flannel Suit*. New York: Thunder's Mouth Press. Originally written in 1955.

Wilson, William Julius. 1979. *The Declining Significance of Race: Blacks and Changing American Institutions*. Chicago: University of Chicago Press.

———. 1987. *The Truly Disadvantaged: The Inner City, the Underclass, and Public Policy*. Chicago: University of Chicago Press.

———. 1996. *When Work Disappears*. New York: Knopf.

———. 2003. "Race, Class, and Urban Poverty: A Rejoinder." *Ethnic and Racial Studies* 26, no. 6: 1096–1114.

Winant, Howard. 1994. *Racial Conditions: Politics, Theory, Comparisons*. Minneapolis: University of Minnesota Press.

Wirth, Louis. 1938. "Urbanism as a Way of Life." *American Journal of Sociology* 43, no. 6: 1–24.

———. 1945. "The Problem of Minority Group." In *The Science of Man in the World Crisis*, edited by Ralph Linton, 347–372. New York: Columbia University Press.

Wise, Tim. 2002. "Failing the Test of Fairness: Institutional Racism and the SAT." *Z Magazine* (August 12).

Wiseman, Jacqueline P. 1970. *Stations of the Lost: The Treatment of Skid Row Alcoholics*. Englewood Cliffs, NJ: Prentice-Hall.

Wolf, Stewart, and John G. Bruhn. 1993. *The Power of the Clan: The Influence of Human Relationships on Heart Disease*. London: Transaction.

Wolfe, Alan. 2004. "Native Son: Samuel Huntington Defends the Homeland." *Foreign Affairs* (May–June): 120–125.

Wonders, Nancy A., and Raymond Michalowski. 2001. "Bodies, Borders, and Sex Tourism in a Globalized World: A Tale of Two Cities—Amsterdam and Havana." *Social Problems* 48, no. 4: 545–571.

Woodward, Kath. 2000. *Questioning Identity: Gender, Class, Ethnicity*. London: Routledge.

World Values Survey Association. 1994. "World Values Survey, 1990–1993." Ann Arbor, MI: Inter-University Consortium for Political and Social Research.

———. 2001. "World Values Survey, 1999–2000." Ann Arbor, MI: Inter-University Consortium for Political and Social Research.

———. 2003. "World Values Survey, 1999–2002." Ann Arbor, MI: Inter-University Consortium for Political and Social Research.

Worldwatch Institute. 2004. *The State of the World 2004: Progress Towards a Sustainable Society*. London: Earthscan.

Wouters, Cas. 1998. "Balancing Sex and Love since the 1960s Sexual Revolution." *Theory, Culture, and Society* 15, nos. 3–4: 187–214.

Wright, Erik Olin. 1985. *Classes*. London: Verso.

Wright, Richard T., and Scott H. Decker. 1994. *Burglars on the Job: Streetlife and Residential Break-Ins*. Boston: Northeastern University Press.

Wuthnow, Robert. 1988. *The Restructuring of American Religion: Society and Faith Since World War II*. Princeton, NJ: Princeton University Press.

———. 1997. "The Cultural Turn." In *Contemporary American Religion: An Ethnographic Reader*, edited by Nancy L. Eiesland and Penny Edgell Becker, 245–266. Walnut Creek, CA: AltaMira.

Zeller, Richard A., and Edward G. Carmines, eds. 1980. *Measurement in the Social Sciences: The Link Between Theory and Data*. Cambridge, UK: Cambridge University Press.

Zimmerman, Jan, ed. 1983. *Technological Woman: Interfacing with Tomorrow*. New York: Praeger.

Zlolniski, Christian. 1994. "The Informal Economy in an Advanced Industrialized Society: Mexican Immigrant Labor in Silicon Valley." *Yale Law Journal* 103, no. 8: 2305–2335.

Zurcher, Louis A. 1977. *The Mutable Self: A Self Concept for Social Change*. Beverly Hills, CA: Sage.

# index

Lerner, Max, 192
Lesbians: feminists and, 293; movement, 198, 577; religion and, 474; sexuality of, 195
Less developed countries (LDCs): cities in, 486; gender bias in, 508; immigration from, 506, 507; megacities of, 491; population of, 507, 507 (fig.), 508; sex ratio in, 507
*Leviathan, The* (Hobbes), 522
Lewis, Michael, 366, 367, 377, 383, 385, 388; on cultural changes, 368; on new economy, 392
Liberalism, 170, 458, 459, 472, 482, 547
"Liberated, Exploited, Pampered, Frazzled, Uneasy New American Worker, The" (*New York Times Magazine*), 385
Libertinism, 185
Libido, 190; definition of, 189
Life: chances, 249 (definition of, 242); choices, 317; course, 154, 164 (definition of, 150); histories, 51–53; -long learning, 399, 417, 420, 423; stories, 52, 240
Life cycles, 151–153, 163, 194, 273; anxiety of, 18–19; culture and, 495; expansion of, 18; lifestyle and, 495; open-ended sequencing of, 212; socialization and, 289; transitions in, 148, 158
Life expectancy: African-Americans and, 446; definition of, 444; ethnicity and, 446; gender and, 447; genetic factors and, 446; highest, 445 (fig.); HIV/AIDS and, 428; lengthening of, 230–231; lifestyle and, 446; lowest, 446 (fig.); marriage and, 488; stress and, 446; stretching/elongating, 147; violence and, 445. *See also* Disability adjusted life expectancy
Life stages: definition of, 153; emotional challenges of, 150–158; life cycle and, 147–148, 150–161
Lifestyles, 76, 155, 241, 242, 308, 335, 356, 502; changes in, 18; cities and, 488; communities, 499; comparing over generations, 235–236; consumer, 355; deviant, 416; gay, 490; Gothic, 335–336; groupings based on, 265, 266; health care and, 251; identity and, 578; life cycle and, 495; life expectancy and, 446;

middle-class, 258, 396; postmodern, 578; singles and, 489; social class and, 495; social movements and, 578; subcultural, 83; tolerance of, 498; types in United States, 262–263 (table); youth, 482
Literacy, 399, 419; rates, adult by gender, 420 (fig.)
Locke, John, 416, 538
London, 486; city life in, 489; gays in, 490; as IMC, 499; singles in, 504; trade in, 491
*Lonely Crowd, The* (Reisman), 130
Los Angeles, 486, 488; edge cities of, 496; African-Americans in, 319–320; development of, 497 (fig.); megacity of, 496; population of, 496; postmodern, 504; urban sprawl and, 493, 498
Loss of family values, definition of, 233
Louis XIV ("Sun King"), 518, 519
Love: marriage and, 209, 218; romance and, 112, 228; sex and, 202; sexuality and, 225
Low culture, 86, 87, 569
Luther, Martin, 177
Lynchings, 336

Macrosocial, definition of, 410
Magnet schools, 418; definition of, 417
Making out, 381; definition of, 380
Male domination, 289, 290; heterosexuality and, 198; protests of, 176
Male infants, support for, 139
Malnutrition, 251, 444
*Managed Heart: Commercialization of Human Feeling, The* (Hochschild), 162, 387
Manners, manuals on, 128
Manufacturing, 373, 565; crisis in, 387; decline of, 392, 568, 569 (map); employment in, 392; postindustrial, 374
Marginalization, 55, 199
Marital status, 212; female population in selected years, 215 (fig.); male population in selected years, 214 (fig.)
Market economy. *See* Capitalist economic system
Marriage, 130, 150, 155, 202; adulthood and, 156, 157; alternatives to, 218–219, 220; arranged, 223;

baby boomers and, 211; children outside, 18; Christianity and, 176; comparing over generations, 235–236; contracts, 211, 219; counseling, 158; crunch, older women and, 212–213; cultural concept of, 506; decline of, 234; delaying, 212, 213–214, 218, 488; denaturalization of, 219; divorce ratio with, 215–216; economic benefits of, 218; eroticism and, 182, 183; family and, 208–211; feminist criticism of, 226, 228; first, 212, 213, 216; heterosexuality and, 211; instability of, 18; life expectancy and, 488; lifelong, 186; love and, 209, 218; median age of, 212, 212 (fig.), 213 (fig.); models of, 209; modernism and, 209, 211–216, 218–219; moralization of, 176; natural status of, 210–211, 226; parenthood and, 154; postmodernism and, 210, 211–216, 218–219; practice, 216; preserving, 219; prospects, undermining, 213; rate of, 211; second, 216; sex and, 176, 180, 182, 186, 192, 194; sexuality and, 230; shifts in, 18, 226; social benefits of, 218; socialization and, 150, 177; sociological study of, 32; strains in, 225; transformation of, 212, 219. *See also* Same-sex marriage
Marx, Karl, 30, 162, 244, 253, 350, 366, 374, 379, 491, 522, 523, 558, 571; capitalism and, 565, 566; class and, 245, 252, 255, 261, 532; on conflict, 353, 564; determinism and, 21; dominant ideology and, 265; economic production/class relations and, 261; economic sociology of, 545; on exploitation, 245; property/class relations and, 252; radical sociologists and, 95; religion and, 463, 477, 481; revolutionary social change and, 564
Marxism, 93, 113, 410, 522, 523
Masculinity, 271; changing ideas of, 294; definition of, 296; New Man, 294; sense of, 140, 274, 382; stereotypes of, 272; Victorian notions of, 187
Mass culture, 101, 112, 113, 115, 116, 264, 560; working class and, 95
Mass media. *See* Media

# credits

Table 1.1 (p. 13) Lisa McCormick

Box 1.1 (p. 24) Jeffrey Alexander

Box 2.1 (p. 31) Simon Cottle, in *The Student's Companion to Sociology*, ed. Jon Gubbay, Chris Middleton, and Chet Ballard (Malden, MA: Blackwell, 1997). Reprinted by permission.

Box 2.2 (p. 32) Copyright © 2002 by the New York Times Co. Reprinted by permission.

Box 2.3 (p. 35) Ron Lembo, "Situating Television in Everyday Life," in Elizabeth Long, ed., *From Sociology to Cultural Studies* (Malden, MA: Blackwell, 1997). Reprinted by permission.

Table 2.1 (p. 40) Adapted from Emile Durkheim, *Suicide: A Study in Sociology*, trans. J. A. Spaulding and G. Simpson (New York: Free Press).

Box 2.4 (p. 45) U.S. Census Bureau.

Box 2.5 (p. 49) Ned Polsky, *Hustlers, Beats, and Others* (Chicago: Aldine, 1967), 119–120, 128. Reprinted by permission.

Box 2.6 (p. 57) Joel Best, *Education Next* (Summer 2002). Reprinted by permission.

Figure 3.1 (p. 65) American Society of Plastic Surgeons.

Figure 3.2 (p. 65) American Society of Plastic Surgeons.

Fig. 3.3 (p. 65) American Society of Plastic Surgeons.

Table 3.1 (p. 68) Lisa McCormick.

Table 3.2 (p. 72) Tim Phillips and Philip Smith, "Everyday Incivility: Towards a Benchmark," *Sociological Review* 51, no. 1 (2003): 85–108. Reprinted by permission.

Table 3.3 (p. 73) Ibid.

Figure 3.4 (p. 76) William H. Frey, Bill Abresch, and Jonathan Yeasting, eds., *America by the Numbers* (New York: New Press, 2001). Reprinted by permission.

Figure 3.5 (p. 82) Myra Marx Ferree,

"Resonance and Radicalism," *American Journal of Sociology* 109, no. 2 (2003): 304–344. Reprinted by permission of the University of Chicago Press.

Fig 3.6 (p. 82) Ibid.

Box 3.1 (p. 84) Armato, et al., "Discoveries: New and Noteworthy," *Contexts* 5, no. 2 (2006): 7–8. Reprinted by permission of the University of California Press.

Table 4.1 (p. 99) "New Audiences Increasingly Politicized: Online News Audience Large, More Diverse," Pew Research Center for the People and Press, 2004. Reprinted by permission.

Table 4.2 (p. 99) Ibid.

Table 4.3 (p. 103) Kenneth Thompson.

Table 4.4 (p. 105) Pew Internet and American Life Project (2004). Reprinted by permission.

Figure 4.1 (p. 106) UNDP, *Human Development Report* (2001).

Box 4.1 (p. 110) Lisa McCormick.

Box 5.1 (p. 123) Davis Kingsley, "Extreme Isolation," in James M. Henslin, ed., *Down to Earth Sociology* (New York: Free Press, 2001), 129–137. Reprinted by permission.

Figure 5.1 (p. 125) Reprinted by permission from Thomas J. Bouchard, "Genes, Environment, and Personality," *Science* 264 (1994): 1700–1701. Copyright AAAS.

Table 5.1 (p. 126) Ibid.

Table 5.2 (p. 130) Sherry L. Grace and Kenneth L. Cramer, "Sense of Self in the New Millennium," *Social Behavior and Personality* 30, no. 3 (2002): 276. Reprinted by permission.

Figure 5.2 (p. 131) Lisa McCormick.

Figure 5.3 (p. 134) H. R. Markus, P. Mullaly, and S. Kitayama, "Selfways: Diversity in Modes of Cultural Participation," in U. Neisser and D. Jopling, eds., *The Conceptual Self in*

*Context* (Cambridge, UK: Cambridge University Press, 1997). Reprinted by permission of Cambridge University Press.

Figure 5.4 (p. 136) Gary W. Peterson and Boyd C. Rollins, "Parent-Child Socialization," in Suzanne K. Steinmetz and Marvin B. Sussman, eds., *Handbook of Marriage and the Family* (New York: Plenum, 1987), 475. Reprinted by kind permission from Springer Science and Business Media.

Box 5.2 (p. 140) James Henslin, "On Becoming Male," in James M. Henslin, ed., *Down to Earth Sociology* (New York: Free Press, 1991), 124–127. Reprinted by permission.

Box 5.3 (p. 141) http://www.sniggle.net/barbie.php.

Figure 5.5 (p. 145) Donald F. Roberts, Ulla G. Foehr, Victoria Rideout, and M. Brodie, "Generation M: Media in the Lives of 8–18-Year-Olds" (no. 7251), March 2005. Reprinted by permission of the Henry J. Kaiser Family Foundation.

Table 5.3 (p. 146) Ibid.

Figure 5.6 (p. 146) Donald F. Roberts and Ulla G. Foehr, *Kids and Media in*

*America* (Cambridge, UK: Cambridge University Press). Reprinted by permission of Cambridge University Press.

Table 5.4 (p. 149) "Every Child Counts: New Global Estimates on Child Labour." Copyright © 2000 International Labour Organisation.

Figure 5.7 (p. 151) U.S. Census Bureau.

Figure 5.8 (p. 152) NCHS.

Figure 5.9 (p. 152) Ibid.

Figure 5.10 (p. 153) Keith Hawton et al., "Deliberate Self-Harm in Adolescents," *BMJ* 325 (2002): 1207–1211. Reprinted by permission.

Figure 5.11 (p. 156) GSS (2002).

Figure 5.12 (p. 157) Frank F. Furstenberg, Jr., et al., "Growing Up Is Harder to Do," *Contexts* 3, no. 3 (August 2004): 37. Reprinted by permission of the University of California Press.

Figure 5.13 (p. 157) Ibid.

Figure 5.14 (p. 158) Ibid and Robert Schoeni and Karen Ross, "Material Assistance from Families," in Richard A. Settersten Jr., Frank F. Furstenberg Jr., and Ruben G. Rumbaut, eds., *On the Frontier of Adulthood* (Chicago: University of Chicago Press, 2005). Reprinted by permission of University of Chicago Press.

Box 6.1 (p. 168) Edward Hellmore, "College Football Hero Corey Johnson Came Out and No One Was Outraged: In a Tolerant America, Gay Is the New Straight," *Observer*, April 30, 2000. Reprinted by permission.

Box 6.2 (p 169) Howard Chua-Eoan, "That's Not a Scarecrow: A Brutal Assault in Wyoming and a Rise in Gay Bashing Fuel the Debate over Sexual Orientation," *Time* (October 19, 1998): 72. Reprinted by permission.

Figure 6.1 (p. 173) Edward O. Laumann, John H. Gagnon, Robert T. Michael, and Stuart Michaels, *The Social Organization of Sexuality* (Chicago: University of Chicago Press, 1994), 300–301. Reprinted by permission of University of Chicago Press.

Figure 6.2 (p. 173) Ibid.

Box 6.3 (p. 178) Copyright © 1994 by the New York Times Co. Reprinted by permission.

Box 6.4 (p. 181) Beinecke Rare Book and Manuscript Library, Yale University.

Figure 6.3 (p. 184) Lisa McCormick.

Table 6.1 (p. 185) Laumann et al. 1994, 135. Reprinted by permission of University of Chicago Press.

Figure 6.4 (p. 187) Chris Ryan, *Sex Tourism: Marginal People and Liminalities* (New York: Routledge, 2001), 62. Reprinted by permission.

Table 6.2 (p. 188) "A Global Alliance Against Forced Labour: Global Report Under the Follow-up to the ILO Declaration on Fundamental Principles and Rights at Work," Table 1.2. Copyright © 2005 International Labour Organisation.

Figure 6.5 (p. 189) Ibid., Figure 1.4.

Figure 6.6 (p. 189) Ibid., Figure 1.6.

Table 6.3 (p. 195) Lisa McCormick.

Table 6.4 (p. 199) Lisa McCormick.

Table 6.5 (p. 201) National Coalition of Anti-Violence Programs, http://www.avp.org.

Figure 7.1 (p. 210) U.S. Census Bureau.

Figure 7.2 (p. 212) Ibid.

Figure 7.3 (p. 213) Ibid.

Figure 7.4 (p. 214) Ibid.

Figure 7.5 (p. 215) Ibid.

Box 7.1 (p. 216) Pamela Paul, *The Starter Marriage and the Future of Matrimony* (New York: Random House, 2002), 29–30. Reprinted by permission.

Table 7.1 (p. 217) Based on "Society at a Glance: OECD Social Indicators, Underlying Data." Copyright © 2002 OECD.

Box 7.2 (p. 220) Copyright © 2000 by the New York Times Co. Reprinted by permission.

Box 7.3 (p. 227) Irene Levin, "Living Apart Together: A New Family Form," *Current Sociology* 52, no. 2 (2004), 223–228. Reprinted by permission.

Table 7.2 (p. 230) Based on "Society at a Glance: OECD Social Indicators, Underlying Data." Copyright © 2002 OECD.

Table 7.3 (p. 231) Ibid.

Box 7.4 (p. 232) Copyright © 1998 by the New York Times Co. Reprinted by permission.

Box 8.1 (p. 240) Wendy Luttrell, *School-smart and Motherwise: Working-Class Women's Identity and Schooling* (New York: Routledge 1997), 46–47. Reprinted by permission.

Table 8.1 Center for New American Media, PBS.

Figure 8.1 (p. 248) Anderson et al., *Executive Excess 2005: Defense Contractors Get More Bucks for the Bang* (Washington, DC: Institute for Policy Studies/United for a Fair Economy). Reprinted by permission.

Figure 8.2 (p. 255) U.S. Census Bureau.

Figure 8.3 (p. 256) Ibid.

Table 8.2 (p. 257) UNDP, *Human Development Report* (1992).

Table 8.3 (p. 260) CACI Ltd. Reprinted by permission.

Table 8.4 (p. 262) Claritas Inc. Reprinted by permission.

Box 9.1 (p. 271) Copyright © 2004 by the New York Times Co. Reprinted by permission.

Table 9.1 (p. 275) Amateur Athletic Foundation of Los Angeles, http://aafla.org/9arr/ResearchReports/tv2004.pdf.

Table 9.2 (p. 275) Ibid.

Box 9.2 (p. 277) Erika Rasmusson, "Strong Signals," *Sports Illustrated for Women*, January 27, 2000, 12–15.

Table 9.3 (p. 279) U.S. Census Bureau.

Table 9.4 (p. 279) Ibid.

Table 9.5 (p. 280) Ibid.

Table 9.6 (p. 281) Ibid.

Table 9.7 (p. 283) "Women and Men in the Informal Economy: A Statistical Picture." Copyright © 2002 International Labour Organisation.

Table 9.8 (p. 284) Ibid.

Table 9.9 (p. 285) Suzanne M. Bianchi, Melissa A. Milkie, Liana C. Sayer, and John P. Robinson, "Is Anyone Doing the Housework?" *Social Forces* 79, no. 1 (2000): 191–228. Reprinted by permission.

Table 9.10 (p. 285) Ibid.

Table 9.11 (p. 286) Oriel Sullivan, "The Division of Domestic Labour," *Sociology* 34, no. 3 (2000): 433. Reprinted by permission of Cambridge University Press.

Table 9.12 (p. 286) Ibid.

Figure 9.1 (p. 287) Lori Heise, Mary Ellsberg, and Megan Gottemoeller,